SHIFRA STEIN'S **DAY TRIPS**®
FROM **PHOENIX,**
TUCSON, AND FLAGSTAFF

PRAISE FOR EARLIER EDITIONS:

"The introduction is practically worth the price of the book with its vital information on when to travel where in Arizona. Thirty-five day trips follow and special directories of 'festivals and celebrations' and the 'great outdoors' complete the picture."

—*Family Travel Times*

"A calendar of seasonal festivals and celebrations is appended along with lists of national parks, Indian reservations, and tour associations. A valuable adjunct to more general books on the Southwest."

—*ALA Booklist*

"The trips are planned within a convenient drive from the cities, though there are 'worth more time' sections for not-to-be-missed attractions."

—*The* (Chicago) *Star*

"Presents a diversity of explorations including Indian ruins, ghost towns, lost mines, and artist colonies."

—*The Los Angeles Times*

Help Us Keep This Guide Up-to-Date

Every effort has been made by the author and editors to make this guide as accurate and useful as possible. Many things, however, can change after a guide is published—establishments close, phone numbers change, facilities come under new management, and so on.

We would love to hear from you concerning your experiences with this guide and how you feel it could be improved and kept up-to-date. While we may not be able to respond to all comments and suggestions, we'll take them to heart and we'll make certain to share them with the author. Please send your comments and suggestions to the following address:

The Globe Pequot Press
Reader Response/Editorial Department
P.O. Box 480
Guilford, CT 06437

Or you may e-mail us at:
editorial@globe-pequot.com

Thanks for your input, and happy travels!

Day Trips® Series

GETAWAYS LESS THAN TWO HOURS AWAY

SHIFRA STEIN'S # DAY TRIPS®

FROM # PHOENIX, TUCSON, AND FLAGSTAFF

Seventh Edition

Pam Hait

The Globe Pequot Press

GUILFORD, CONNECTICUT

ISBN 0-7627-2279-7

Manufactured in the United States of America
Seventh Edition/Third Printing

CONTENTS

NORTH

NORTHEAST

EAST

PREFACE

Arizona. The name sings with romance. This is the landscape celebrated in western films where rugged cowboys still ride a vast, rolling range. This is a countryside blessed with sunsets that burst upon the horizon spilling apricot and purple hues as far as you can see. This is a land of immense physical size and unparalleled variety. Mountains and desert, cities and wilderness—Arizona has all of them.

While directions are as clear and exact as possible, you should refer to an Arizona road map as you travel. Write to the Arizona Office of Tourism, 2702 North Third Street, Suite 4015, Phoenix, AZ 85007, or call (602) 230-7733 to request a map. You may also write or call the communities or regional tourism information offices of the specific areas you plan to visit and ask for city maps. Read these and refer to them as you travel. Always note the scale of the map. If you are accustomed to eastern maps, you're in for a shock. With 113,956 square miles of land, Arizona is the sixth largest state in the nation. Only 17 percent of the state is private land. In these wide open spaces, one inch on the state road map equals approximately 16 miles!

In addition to its sheer physical size, Arizona is dazzling in its infinite sights, sounds, and moods. In a short two-hour trip from the urban centers of Phoenix, Tucson, or Flagstaff, you can drive from the floor of the desert to a rocky red precipice and travel in time from prehistorical to frontier days.

There's variety in the climate, too. Travelers should consider both the season and their destinations when they plan day trips in and around the three metropolitan areas. Plan summer trips in the Phoenix area with special caution. Because of its low elevation and irrigated Sonoran desert location, the capital city can sizzle under extremely hot daytime temperatures from late May through mid-September. Getting in and out of a hot car saps the enthusiasm of even the most dedicated tourist. In contrast, the fall, winter, and early months of spring offer warm days and cool evenings that guarantee almost ideal conditions for driving and sightseeing.

Although Tucson and Phoenix have similar desert climates, because Tucson is about 1,200 feet higher than Phoenix, Tucson's summer temperatures generally are about ten degrees cooler than those in Phoenix. Tucson is less humid as well, making summer sightseeing more comfortable there than in Phoenix. Winter temperatures in both cities, however, are comparable.

On the other hand, the Flagstaff area offers travelers a radically different experience. Perched at an elevation of over a mile high, Flagstaff's climate is similar to that of Michigan or Wisconsin. The cold winters can come complete with deep snows, making winter day trips around Flagstaff risky. However, a delightful climate with warm, sunny days and cool evenings makes northern Arizona a perfect vacationland during spring, summer, and fall.

Be prepared for some local idiosyncrasies. For instance, if you ask a direction, you'll generally hear, "It's just twenty minutes down the road," or "That's only a couple hours away." Arizonans measure distance in time more frequently than in miles. And they think nothing of driving two hours to a destination—that's hardly even a jaunt—which is why many of the day trips included in this book stretch the two-hour getaway time to three hours and sometimes more.

Once you venture even a few miles outside of the three major cities, you'll often encounter open, empty country. This is a treat for people who love the wild, untamed outdoors, but it can pose challenges for those who prefer urban conveniences. One delightful way to handle the great distances when planning day trips is to carry a picnic lunch. Frequently you will find good restaurants few and far between, so you can eat at any of the scenic roadside rest stops. You bring the food; the state provides the ambience, with shaded *ramadas* and sweeping vistas.

Heed the road signs at *all* times of the year. If you see a warning: "Not recommended for sedan travel," believe it! Arizona roads can be rugged and extremely rough on automobiles. When driving through country marked "open range," be alert. Although a rare occurrence, you could encounter loose cows, sheep, or other livestock wandering across the road. Obey both flash flood warnings and dust storm warnings. That dry wash may appear harmless, but a wash can quickly turn into a deadly torrent. Specific directions for dealing with flash floods are included in the back of this book.

Safe driving in the desert demands that travelers take certain precautions. Arid lands can be unforgiving, especially during the hot summer months. Always carry water in your car for emergencies. You may need it for drinking during the early morning hours or after the sun sets. Always tell someone where you are going and when you expect to return. If you are overdue, somebody will know when to start worrying and can alert the authorities. If you have car problems, stay with your vehicle. Don't wander off for help; let help find you. Refer to the back of the book for desert survival tips.

Finally, don't hike into the wilderness alone. Even experienced hikers get lost.

You can take every day trip and hike described in this book without running into any of the aforementioned emergency situations. Arizona is not hazardous to your health. If you treat this unique and often untamed landscape with the respect it deserves, however, you can have safe and exhilarating experiences. What's more, you will be free to appreciate its magnificence and learn to love it as I do.

—Pam Hait

The prices and rates listed in this guidebook were confirmed at press time. We recommend, however, that you call establishments before traveling to obtain current information.

Maps provided are for reference only and should be used in conjunction with a road map. Distances suggested are approximate.

HOW TO USE THIS BOOK

Restaurant prices are designated as $$$ (Expensive, $25 and over); $$ (Moderate to $15 to $25); $ (Inexpensive, $15 and under).

Lodging rates are designated as $$$ (Expensive, $200 and over, per night); $$ (Moderate, $100 to $200, per night); $ (Inexpensive, $100 and under, per night). Rates often change seasonally, so be sure to call first for prices.

Credit cards: The symbol ☐ denotes that at least one credit card is accepted.

Highway designations: Federal highways are designated US. State roads use A. County roads are identified as such.

Hours: In most cases, hours are omitted in the listings because they are subject to frequent changes. Instead, phone numbers are provided for up-to-date information.

PHOENIX

Welcome to Phoenix, capital city of the state of Arizona and hub of "The Valley of the Sun." The valley is surrounded by mountain ranges, clear cool lakes, and more five-star resorts than any metropolitan area in the country—a veritable paradise for tourists. Because visitors have such a choice of accommodations, it is suggested that you write to the Arizona Hotel & Lodging Association, 1240 East Missouri Avenue, Phoenix 85014-2912, and request a brochure describing the hotels, motels, dude ranches, and cabins in the state. Or you may call (602) 604-0729 for information.

Because of the way this book is organized, some of the best Phoenix attractions are listed in the section Day Trip 1 Northwest from Tucson. You'll want to check out this day trip if you are planning on staying in Phoenix.

With Phoenix as your starting point, you'll be amazed to discover how much variety awaits you even in a two-hour drive. Some easy day trips can take you to urban areas, such as Scottsdale, Mesa, Tempe, or even Tucson. On other trips, you can climb quickly from the desert floor to mountainous pine forests, or you can enter a time warp that takes you back to pioneer and ancient Native American eras.

Ideally, visitors to Arizona should plan to spend some vacation time in Phoenix, Tucson, and Flagstaff, taking day trips from each. In this way, you'll get a true flavor of the state. A second plan could include Phoenix as your hub, because it is centrally located and is the largest metropolitan area in the state. As you journey around the Phoenix environs, you'll soon discover that many of the Phoenix-based trips easily fall within the two-hour limitation. In some cases, you'll need to drive longer than two hours; however, each trip is worth it.

If you use Flagstaff as your starting point for several of the Phoenix-based day trips, you can cut your travel time by an hour or

1

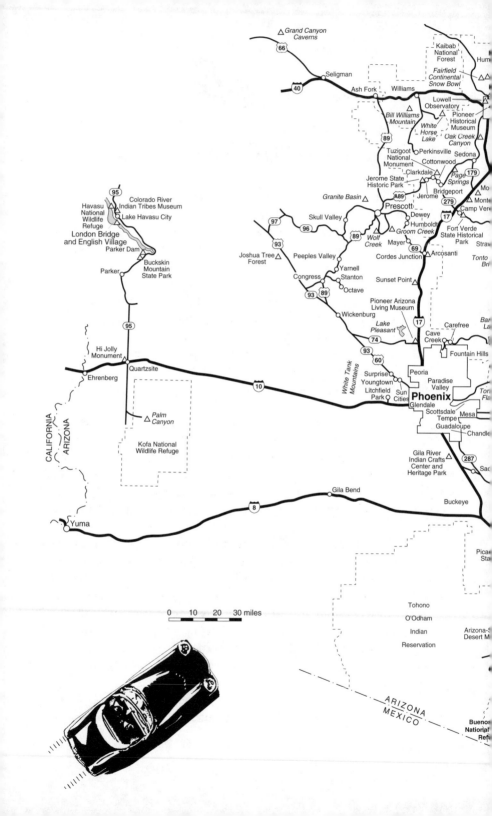

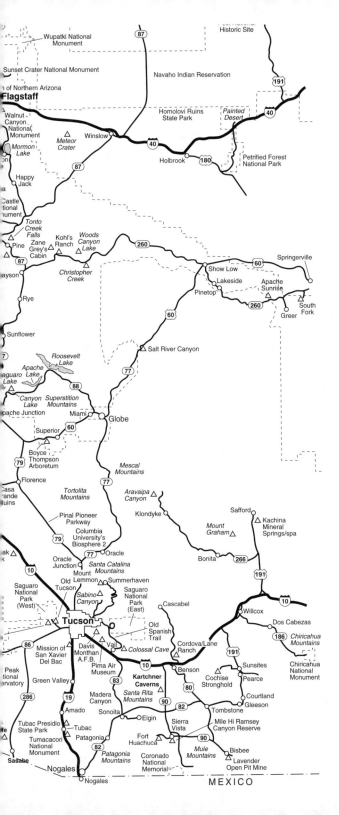

even more. The vast majority of tourists, however, start their day trips from the Phoenix metropolitan area rather than from the smaller, northern Arizona community of Flagstaff.

As you read along, you'll note that many of the itineraries described can be done as an overnight instead of a single day's journey. If you have the time, it's always nice to stay over in a destination town. That way you can spend more hours seeing the sights and exploring the area, and proportionately less time on the road.

One last piece of advice: As you peruse the Phoenix section of this book, you'll read about sights to see, canyons to explore, side roads to wander along, shops not to miss, and special trips to take. In your enthusiasm to do it all, don't overload yourself. This is especially true when traveling during the summer, because the high desert temperatures can be extremely tiring. If you decide to visit a museum or Native American ruin, allow enough time to study the exhibits or soak up the atmosphere of a few selected attractions rather than rushing from point to point. The essential Arizona experience is a casual, laid-back lifestyle. Whether sitting at a sidewalk cafe in Scottsdale or standing silently before Montezuma Castle, don't push yourself to cover too much too fast.

For brochures, maps, and specific information on the fascinating Phoenix metropolitan area, contact the Phoenix & Valley of the Sun Convention & Visitors Bureau, 1 Arizona Center, 400 East Van Buren Street, Suite 600, Phoenix 85004; call (602) 254–6500; or for general tourism information, call (800) 842–8257.

PRESCOTT

This trip covers some of the same territory found in Day Trip 2 North from Phoenix. However, in this itinerary, Prescott is the primary destination. A pine-studded jewel of a town two hours north of Phoenix and once the capital of the Territory of Arizona, it is the seat of Yavapai County. It's famous for its Victorian-style homes, Fourth of July celebrations, and temperate climate. Since there are so many scenic drives in the Prescott area, you may want to spend the entire day there.

The town of Prescott was founded not too long after gold was discovered in nearby hills in 1863—the same year that Abraham Lincoln signed an act to create the Arizona Territory. Prescott has approximately 525 buildings on the National Register of Historic Places and is a favorite destination for Phoenix residents who enjoy the cool summer days, when Prescott's high temperatures average in the eighties. Visitors will especially enjoy the Fourth of July weekend, when Prescott's rodeo is held. This is billed as the "World's Oldest Rodeo" parade and festivities.

Prescott offers cool summer days and moderate winter days, so it's always safe to take a sweater or lightweight jacket with you. If possible, visit during any of the festivals and celebrations that occur during every month of the year. Obtain details from the Prescott Chamber of Commerce at 117 West Goodwin Street, Prescott 86301, or call (928) 445-2000.

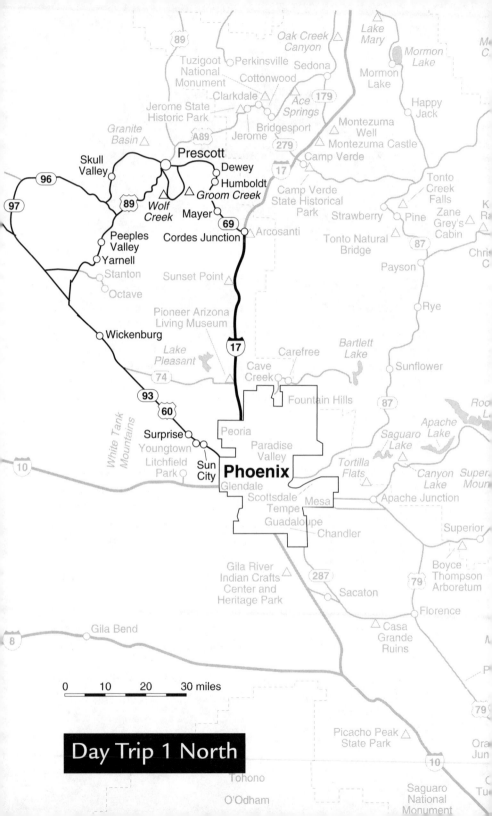

Day Trip 1 North

To reach Prescott, follow I-17 north to Cordes Junction. Take A-69 northwest and meander past the small towns of Mayer, Humboldt, Dewey, and the fast-growing community of Prescott Valley. Mayer is located in the foothills of the Bradshaw Mountains. Founded in 1881 by Joseph Mayer, it began as a store, saloon, and Wells Fargo Stage station. Mayer was a stop along the stage line between Phoenix and Prescott. Today, it continues the tradition as a stop along A-69 for motorists.

In Dewey, stop at Young's Farm, a wonderful place to enjoy rural Arizona, especially during the month of October.

Enter Prescott on A-69 west until it meets Gurley Street. Travel left on Gurley past Marina Street, and you're in the heart of town. Park anywhere between Cortez and Montezuma Streets for your tour of this historic area.

As you gaze at the gingerbread homes and tall brick buildings, you may think that Prescott is an unlikely Arizona town. Remember that the desert, with its low-slung adobe structures, is only one Arizona image. In the more northern parts of the state, two-story brick and wood buildings are just as appropriately an "Arizona" style.

Here, territorial Arizona springs to life. Prescott flourished when the area was a wild and untamed place. As military personnel and miners moved in, no doubt they were anxious to make it seem like home, so they built what they knew: "back-East" buildings, proper brick and two-story structures reminiscent of Ohio or Pennsylvania.

The first capital of the Arizona Territory, Prescott ultimately lost its bid to become the permanent state capital. The honor went to Phoenix instead. Still, much Arizona history was made here and, fortunately for visitors, remains well preserved.

WHERE TO GO

Courthouse Plaza. This is the area bounded by Cortez and Montezuma, Gurley and Goodwin Streets. It's a real town square that functions much as it did during territorial times. During festivals, the grassy square is lined with booths, and people sprawl on the lawns. In more quiet times, you can soak up the serenity that the solid courthouse building exudes. The statue is of Bucky O'Neil, a newspaper publisher who became mayor and led the volunteer cavalry up San Juan Hill in 1898. Wander through the streets to explore the galleries and stores. Although Prescott is a tourist mecca, it has resisted ticky-tacky tourist shops. You'll find a real community here, not cardboard storefront images.

Sharlot Hall Museum. 415 West Gurley Street. This museum is actually a number of separate buildings grouped together to give visitors a living panorama of Southwestern history. Spanning the years from the founding of Prescott in 1864 to the present, the buildings appear to be in architectural sequence. You can tour the Governor's Mansion, which was built on this site in 1864 from local ponderosa pine. Several territorial officials, including Governor John Goodwin, lived in this mansion.

The John C. Fremont House. Built in 1875, it is constructed of wood and reflects the rapid growth Prescott experienced during its first ten years. Fremont, known as "the Pathfinder," served as the fifth territorial governor of Arizona from 1878 to 1881.

Arizona became a state on February 14, 1912. The **William C. Bashford House** represents the type of architecture common to the area during the two decades before statehood. Complete with a solarium, this house was built in another location and moved to the museum grounds in 1974.

The **Sharlot Hall** building, completed in 1934, is the primary exhibit hall and includes the Museum Shop and display rooms for pre-Columbian artifacts, historic Southwestern items, and old photographs. These pictures capture the essence of what it was like for white and red men to live in this territory more than one hundred years ago. This exhibit is all the more remarkable when you realize that Native Americans feared—and some still do fear—the camera, believing that it takes away a person's soul.

Who was Sharlot Hall that an entire enclave of a museum is devoted to her? She was an outstanding woman—a writer, poet, collector of Arizona artifacts, and territorial historian—who moved to Arizona from Kansas in 1882. She remained fascinated with Arizona until her death in 1943.

As you stroll along the sidewalks, which circle and connect the museum's major buildings, you can visit other memorials and exhibits, including the Blacksmith Shop; one of the town's first boardinghouses, which the frontiersmen called "Fort Misery"; a replica of Prescott's first public school; and the Pioneer Herb and Memorial Rose garden. The museum is closed Monday, but the grounds are open. Donation requested. (928) 445-3122.

Smoki Museum. 147 North Arizona Street. Designed to resemble a Native American pueblo, this museum opened to the public in 1935. Thousands of pine logs were used for the columns, *vigas* and *latillas* of the ceiling, and for the *slav* doors and window enclosures. A Hopi-style kiva is in the center of the building, and a Zuni-style fireplace extends along the north wall. The museum houses collections of pre-Columbian and contemporary pottery; pre-Columbian jewelry of shell, stone, and turquoise; and an outstanding collection of basketry, kachinas, stone artifacts, and textiles all from the Southwest. A collection of war bonnets, costumes, and beadwork are from the Plains Indians. Open daily in the summer; closed in winter from November 1 through April 15. However, special arrangements can be made for groups and school tours. Call ahead to arrange a tour of the museum in winter. Visitors can also arrange tours by appointment. Donations accepted. (928) 445-1230; fax (928) 777-0573. www.smoki.com.

Phippen Museum of Western Art. 4701 A-89 North. George Phippen was one of the founders of Cowboy Artists of America. Western art buffs will enjoy the collection of works by Phippen and other Cowboy Artists including Joe Beeler and Frank Polk. Bronzes, paintings, and Native American arts and crafts are on display, and special exhibitions are mounted. A major art show and sale on Courthouse Plaza is held every Memorial Day. Open 10:00 A.M. to 4:00 P.M., Monday through Saturday, 1:00 P.M. to 4:00 P.M. Sunday. Call ahead for summer hours. Fee. (928) 778-1385. www.phippenmuseum.org.

Whiskey Row. Montezuma Street between Goodwin and Aubrey Streets. This is Prescott's famous "wicked" street. The name says it all. Everyone needs to walk up Whiskey Row, even if he or she isn't thirsty. Today it is more sedate, except during festivals and celebrations. Then the Old West springs to life again as cowboys belly up to the crowded bars.

Prescott Historical Tours. Prescott and the Bradshaw Mountains. Several years ago, Melissa Ruffner, dressed in authentic period costumes, began giving tours of Prescott's Victorian homes. Since then, she and her husband have offered walking tours of the 4-block historical district.

Call ahead to find out more about this trip. You'll need good walking shoes and a sack lunch. Ms. Ruffner also puts together specialty tours of Prescott, which can cover anything from how the frontier settlers used solar energy to the area's early religious or ethnic populations. Fee. Contact Melissa Ruffner, (928) 445-4567.

WHERE TO STAY

Forest Villas. 3645 Lee Circle. Take I-17 North and exit at Cortez Junction (A-69), going toward Prescott. After you pass the town of Prescott Valley, you will see the mauve-colored Forest Villas on your right. Prescott's newest hotel brings European ambience to this small western town. Guests can enjoy rooms with great views, fireplaces, and whirlpools. The hotel offers a mountainside heated pool and spa, and complimentary continental breakfast. (800) 223-3449, ext. AZR. www.forestvillas.com.

Hassayampa Inn. 122 East Gurley Street. Established in 1927 and recently renovated, this is Prescott's historic grand hotel. It is centrally located in the heart of town and offers a step back in time to the West of 1927. Rooms are spacious and accented with lace curtains, comforters, and period furniture. Charming and comfortable, the inn provides complimentary breakfast in the graceful Peacock dining room. $$-$$$; ☐. (928) 778-9434; or in Arizona, (800) 322-1927. www. hassayampainn. com.

The Prescott Resort. 1500 A-69. As you head into town, look up at the intersection of Highways 89 and 69, and you'll see this resort nestled high on a hill. The Prescott Resort offers rooms with views of Prescott, large suites, a full health club, dining room, and two lounges. $$$; ☐. (928) 776-1666. www.prescottresort.com.

SpringHill Suites by Marriott. 200 East Sheldon Street. From US-89 North, follow Gurley Street to Marina, then turn right. Go 2 blocks to SpringHill Suites. This hotel is centrally located in historic downtown Prescott. SpringHill Suites offers complimentary continental breakfast. Spacious suites include an in-room refrigerator, microwave, coffeemaker, and wet bar. Each suite is also equipped with a large well-lit desk; adjustable ergonomic chair; two phone lines with data port and voice mail; and a pull-out sofa. Other amenities include a pool, whirlpool spa, and exercise room. For reservations call (928) 776-0998; toll free (888) 446-8440. www.springhillsuites.com.

WHERE TO SHOP

Downtown Prescott. Prescott is a great place to hunt for antiques. The town is filled with converted homes that offer "treasures." In addition to antiques, Prescott has two stores you shouldn't miss and a mini-mall that is fun to browse through.

The Llama House. 108 South Montezuma. This is a fun shop filled with beautiful women's clothes and accessories at very reasonable prices. Proprietor Marsha Rishar has assembled a varied collection. The earrings and jewelry are great. (928) 445–9689.

SCENIC DRIVES

Granite Dells. Drive east on Gurley Street and north on US–89 for about 4 miles. Just north of Prescott, nature has carved a sculpture garden of ancient rock formations. As you approach, you'll notice that the rocks appear to have human or animal forms. That's Mother Nature, the artist, at work. Centuries of wind, rain, snow, and sun worked on these granite cliffs to form eerie figures. Formerly known as the "Point of Rocks," the Granite Dells is set off by Watson Lake, a clear blue pool that contrasts vividly with the subtle colors of the smooth, round boulders.

Granite Mountain and Granite Basin. This trip will take about twenty minutes each way. Drive west on Gurley Street to Grove Avenue. Turn right on Grove and continue out Miller Valley Road. Bear left at the junction of Iron Springs and Willow Creek Roads onto Iron Springs and continue to the Prescott National Forest sign on the right side of the road. Turn right and continue to Granite Basin Recreation site, a unique geological and historical wilderness area. Long before Congress declared the Granite Mountain Trail a National Recreation Area in 1979, hikers and rock climbers were well acquainted with its spectacular scenery. If you are in good shape and dressed for outdoor action, you can hike to the overlook. Otherwise, walk along the trails and marvel at the sheer, smooth cliffs.

Lynx Lake. Fifty-five acres of lake just fifteen minutes away! Follow A–69 east for 4 miles to Walker Road. Turn right for approximately 3 miles. Lynx Lake, which is fed by nearby Lynx Creek, has a rich history. Gold was discovered at the creek during territorial days, giving frontiersmen and -women even more reason to make the trip to Prescott. Fishing is good year-round, and during the summer, you can rent a boat from the lakefront concession. Take your sweetheart on a moonlight cruise across the smooth, clear waters.

Senator Highway Drive. This is an hour's round-trip that's well worth it, especially if you like to relive history. Drive east on Gurley Street to South Mount Vernon/Senator Highway. Along the way, you'll pass by Groom Creek, which was a Mormon settlement. Turn right on South Mount Vernon/Senator Highway and head south to Wolf Creek picnic grounds. If you are so inclined, head for either Wolf Creek or Lower Wolf Creek campgrounds, where you can hike, picnic, or do some four-wheeling on all-terrain vehicles (ATVs) if you trailer them in with you. Continue following this road to the right as it goes down the pine-studded mountain to the Indian Creek picnic grounds. Join US-89 6 miles from Prescott. Turn right and continue back to town. This used to be an old stage route that connected Prescott with Crown Point. As you make this drive, you can imagine how the pioneers felt as they bounced along on rutted roads shaded by these tall ponderosas.

Skyline Drive (also called Thumb Butte Loop). Plan on forty-five minutes to cover this truly spectacular drive. Head south on Montezuma Street (US-89) to Copper Basin Road. Turn right on Copper Basin Road, make a circle, and return to Thumb Butte Road. Along the way, you will see the Sierra Prieta Mountain range, which overlooks Skull Valley. As you approach Thumb Butte, you'll have a panoramic view of the San Francisco Peaks. These mountains are sacred to the Hopis, who believe that these peaks are home to their kachina gods. During this drive, you'll ascend some 1,500 to 1,700 vertical feet. If you think this is a steep drive, imagine what it's like to *run* up this road. The Whiskey Row Marathon Society uses it as its course.

Along the way, you'll see a number of places to pull off to drink in the views. Be sure to do so when you see a viewpoint for Skull Valley. The name, Skull Valley, came from a group of cavalrymen who discovered mounds of sun-bleached skulls there in 1884. Later it was decided that these were the skulls of Apache and Maricopa Indians who clashed over stolen horses.

If you're dressed properly and not bothered by the altitude, take advantage of the hiking trails. These are well marked. A 2⅓-mile trail leads to Thumb Butte. It begins easily. For almost a mile you can stroll along shaded ponderosa pines and three kinds of oak trees. Gradually, the vegetation changes . . . the pines recede, and junipers, prickly pears, piñons, and other scrub vegetation gain on you as the trail approaches the exposed ridge. You'll come to a junction at 1¹⁄₁₀ miles. To the left, the trail rises to the base of the butte. This climb involves 200 feet of steep cliff and is not recommended for non-climbers. Instead, hikers should follow the right fork and continue about 150 yards to a vista point. When you reach it, you'll understand why you've made this trip.

Short trails also lead to Mount St. Francis and West Spruce Mountain. When you're tired and hiked out, head back to your car and continue into Prescott on West Gurley Street.

The city of Prescott is virtually surrounded by the Prescott National Forest. Just a few minutes outside of town are campgrounds, picnic sites, lakes, and areas for nearly every kind of outdoor activity, including exploring, prospecting, rockhounding, backpacking, horseback riding, and fishing. If you do any of these drives, wear comfortable shoes so you can get out of the car and walk around. The views are breathtaking.

WHERE TO EAT

Murphy's. 201 North Cortez Street. In this general store setting, you can munch on mesquite-broiled seafood or chow down on a variety of entrees, including excellent prime rib. $$; ☐. (928) 445-4044.

The Porter House Prescott Mining Company. 155 Plaza Drive. Great for fresh fish, prime rib, and steaks. The outdoor patio is a standout. Eat amidst a sylvan setting of flowers and trees (and ignore the condos in the distance). $$; ☐. (928) 445-1991.

Note: Both the Hassayampa Inn and The Prescott Resort have beautiful dining rooms. See "Where to Stay."

YARNELL–PEEPLES VALLEY

For the most direct route back to Phoenix, head south on US-89 through Yarnell and Peeples Valley. The road bisects the densely wooded Prescott National Forest and is exceptionally scenic. You'll be looking at the Sierra Prieta Mountains or the Black Mountains named by the Spaniards who explored this part of the state. The Black Mountains owe their dark color to their volcanic origin.

Peeples Valley is named for Abraham Peeples, who supposedly gathered between $4,000 and $7,000 worth of gold nuggets before breakfast one morning when he was walking on Weaver Mountain. Not surprisingly, the area commemorating Peeples's find is called "Rich Hill."

For more scenic beauty, follow A–96 (a back road) west from Prescott as it meanders past Iron Springs and into Skull Valley. The views are as great as the names. Where A–96 intersects with A–97, follow A–97 toward Phoenix for 16 miles to where it joins US–93/US–89. Follow US–93/US–89 to Wickenburg, Surprise, and Sun City; about 60 miles northwest of Phoenix the route becomes US–60.

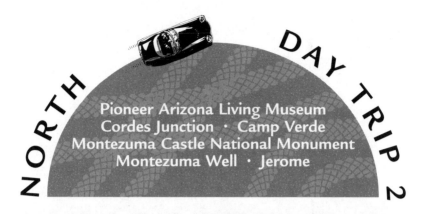
PIONEER ARIZONA LIVING MUSEUM

Prepare to move through time from a prehistoric era to the future. The drive begins in rolling desert but climbs into steep mountain terrain in Jerome. You'll begin with endless vistas, and, as the mountains close in around you, saguaros give way to scrub and ultimately to sycamores. This landscape is filled with silent memories of the Sinaguas, an ancient Native American tribe who lived here hundreds of years ago. During the late 1800s, this countryside was alive with the ring of picks and shovels and the shouts of prospectors who worked in Rawhide Jimmy Douglas's silver mines.

Although the driving time from Phoenix to Jerome is three hours, this is considered a full-day trip in this land of wide open spaces. Should you choose to hike and sightsee, you'll arrive home in the evening tired but happy.

Start off early and take I–17 north toward Camp Verde to the Pioneer Arizona Living Museum. Plan to arrive around 9:00 A.M. to do this trip easily in a day.

WHERE TO GO

Pioneer Arizona Living Museum. 3901 Pioneer Road, Black Canyon Freeway and Pioneer Road. On I–17, 12 miles north of Bell Road, take exit 225 and follow signs to the museum. You'll spend a good hour touring the many authentic and replicated buildings on the grounds of this privately supported museum. Although a restaurant exists here, it's closed Monday and Tuesday. A shaded picnic

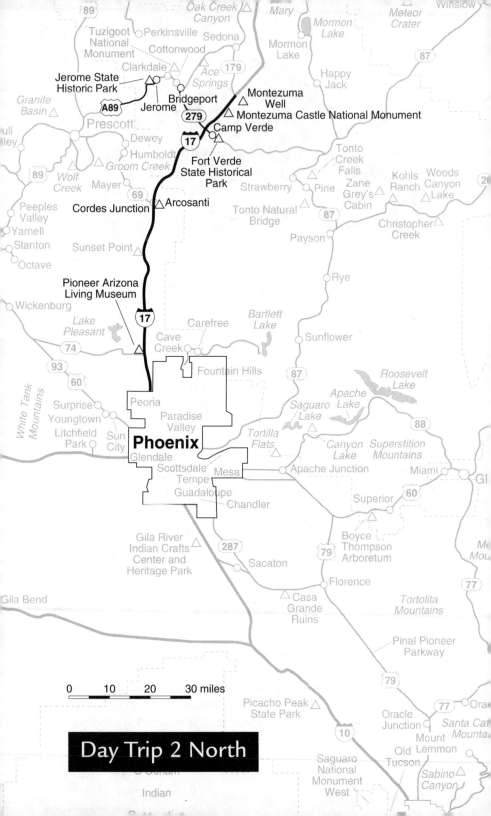

Day Trip 2 North

area is always open, 187 Wedding Chapel Road. Call ahead for museum hours. Fee. (623) 465–1052.

Sunset Point. Follow the signs back to I–17 north. You may want to stop for a breathtaking view at this unique roadside rest stop, winner of an architectural award for excellence. Along with a sweeping panorama, you'll find a map, clean rest rooms, and picnic tables.

CORDES JUNCTION

Back on I–17 north, continue to the Cordes Junction exit and Arcosanti, where you can visit a unique construction site.

WHERE TO GO

Arcosanti. I–17 at Cordes Junction, Mayer. Turn right at Cordes Junction Road and left at the stop sign. Follow a dirt road about 3 miles to Arcosanti—architect Paolo Soleri's vision of an alternative future. Called the boldest experiment in urban living in the country, this energy-efficient town, which integrates architecture and ecology, has been under construction since 1970.

Soleri coined the word *arcology* to express his vision of a community in which people can live and work in harmony with the environment. In designing this prototype "city" under a single roof, Soleri combines an urban environment with a natural setting all within one structure. Ultimately, Soleri's plan utilizes both above- and underground space to concentrate human activity into an energy-efficient environment while carefully leaving the vast surrounding acreage natural and undisturbed.

Arcosanti is being built by students and professionals who work and attend seminars on the site. Workshops are open to the general public. Festivals and performances by visiting artists are scheduled during the year. Daily tours are available with a minimum of four people. Stop at the bakery and buy some of the excellent homemade breads and baked goods. Fee for guided tours only. (928) 632–7135. www.arcosanti.org.

WHERE TO EAT

The Cafe. The cafe at Arcosanti serves breakfast and lunch and features homemade foods prepared without preservatives or additives. A kids' menu is available. The cafe is not fancy, but the food is hearty and healthful. $-$$; ☐. (928) 632-7135.

CAMP VERDE

As you follow I-17 north, it plunges into a long downgrade that reveals the Verde Valley in all its splendor. Camp Verde is located near the geographical center of the state. Settled in 1864, it is the oldest town in the Verde Valley, literally growing up around what is now Fort Verde State Historical Park. If you've not been this way before, pull off at the marked scenic viewpoints and enjoy grand vistas along the way to this historic area. www.pr.state.az.us.

WHERE TO GO

Fort Verde State Historical Park. Lane Street. Take the first Camp Verde exit, 285; follow that road into Camp Verde; and turn right onto Lane Street. Visit the ten-acre Fort Verde Historical Park and see where Gen. George Crook accepted the surrender of Apache Chief Chalipun and 300 of his warriors in 1873. Crook left a distinctive mark on Arizona. In addition to his meeting with the Apache chief, the general had a rough wagon road cut up along the Mogollon rim in 1884 to shorten the distance between Fort Apache and Fort Verde. Even today, that area is referred to as Crook's Trail.

Fort Verde was a major base for General Crook's scouts, soldiers, and pack mules during the Native American campaigns of the 1870s. As you walk along the dusty street of Officers' Row, you'll return to territorial days and better understand what it was like for the officers and their families who lived at Fort Verde during this period in history.

Self-guided tours of the officers' quarters overlooking the parade ground, which are furnished in authentic 1880s military style are available. As you continue walking through the park, you may wonder at the Post Surgeon's spacious accommodations. In those days, patients were treated and surgery performed in the doctor's residence, while the post hospital was used only for quarantine and convalescence. Fee. (928) 567-3275.

MONTEZUMA CASTLE NATIONAL MONUMENT

To travel farther back in time, follow Montezuma Castle Road 5 miles north from Camp Verde to Montezuma Castle National Monument. The ancient, five-story Native American dwelling is carved out of a great limestone cliff. Although Native Americans lived in the valley as early as A.D. 600, it's believed that Sinagua farmers began building this dwelling sometime during the twelfth century A.D. When it was completed about three centuries later, the dwelling contained nineteen rooms, many of them suitable for living space.

The name *Montezuma Castle* is a misnomer. Montezuma, the Aztec king, never slept here. In fact, he was never here at all. When pioneers discovered the cliff dwelling, they mistook it for an ancient Aztec settlement and named it Montezuma Castle. Although the historical inaccuracy was determined later, the name stuck.

Stop at the visitors center first before taking the self-guided tour. Take time to view the hand-fitted stone walls and foot-thick sycamore ceiling beams; let your imagination fly.

The picnic grounds offer lots of shady spots for lunch. (928) 567–3322.

MONTEZUMA WELL

Back on I-17 north, continue a few miles to the McGuireville exit. Follow the side road to Montezuma Well, but be ready for a bumpy, rough ride. This limestone sink was formed centuries ago by a collapsed cavern. Springs feed it continuously, and both the Hohokam Indians (who settled the Phoenix area in pre-Columbian times) and the Sinagua used the well for crop irrigation.

Just below the well are cliff dwellings built by the Sinagua Indians who were the northern neighbors of the Hohokam Indians, who once inhabited the Salt River Valley. The Sinaguans left no written records, so their culture is interpreted only from archaeological evidence and the study of the Hopi, who are believed to be their descendants. A hiking trail follows the rim of the sinkhole and then descends to the water's edge, where more Sinaguan ruins can be seen. The rim trail is well marked with informational markers that describe native plants. The trail ultimately leads to the creek, where the water from the well emerges through an underground passageway. The water, which maintains a constant temperature of seventy-six degrees, flows through irrigation ditches built by the Sinaguan hundreds of years ago. These canals are still in use today.

This area contains a Hohokam pit house, built around A.D. 1100, and Sinaguan dwellings. It's estimated that around 150 to 200 Sinaguans lived here between A.D. 1125 and A.D. 1400, when apparently they were forced out by a drought. Montezuma Well is free; the Montezuma Castle is $2.00 per person. (928) 567-3322.

JEROME

This area is as rich in lore as it was in ore. Although the steep ascent into Jerome is not for the faint of heart, the climb is replete with expansive views of the broad Verde Valley. In the distance you can see the Red Rocks of Sedona and even the far-off San Francisco Peaks in Flagstaff.

This is an unforgettable "living" ghost town that is perched atop Mingus Mountain (7,743 feet). Underneath the town, more than 100 miles of subterranean tunnels and shafts honeycomb the mountain where miners tore out a billion dollars in copper and other ore during the wild heyday of 1876. Back then Jerome lured men in search of luck and women in search of men. Gold and silver flowed, and people poured in, building glorious residences fit for an eastern city.

Today all that remains of its former glory teeters on the precipitous slopes of Cleopatra Hill. The twisted, narrow streets, reminiscent of Europe, inspire even the most unimaginative photographer, so bring your camera and lots of film.

To get to Jerome from Montezuma Well, backtrack to I-77 South and A-279. From Montezuma Castle, pick up A-279 at I-17 and head northwest for 12 to 15 miles toward Jerome. Just north of Bridgeport, A-279 joins US-89A; follow US-89A into Jerome.

WHERE TO GO

Gold King Mine and Museum. Located 1 mile northwest of Jerome on Perkinsville Road. Mining enthusiasts will enjoy seeing miners' cages and artifacts displayed as well as an outdoor exhibit of a turn-of-the-twentieth-century mining camp. Open daily. Fee. (928) 634-0053.

    Jerome State Park. UVX Road. Originally the home of mining pioneer James S. Douglas, the state park features an extensive display of mining equipment. Museum lovers should follow UVX Road to the park, where exhibits recounting the story of this once-flourishing copper-mining community are displayed. As you browse through the mansion of "Rawhide" Jimmy, as he was known, you'll gain a sense of the personalities, places, and technology that forged this period of Arizona history. You'll need to retrace your steps to US-89A when you leave here. Open daily. Fee. (928) 634-5381. www.pr.state.az.us.

    Main Street. US-89A becomes Main Street as it continues into Jerome. Park anywhere and walk around to get a sense of this special community. Now a popular tourist stop, Jerome almost became a ghost town; however, it's safe to assume that the ghosts now have left for quieter spots. Revived during the 1960s when hippies discovered it was both cheap and charming, Jerome today is a haven for people who eschew the urban scene.

    As you walk around, you may want to stop in the shops, galleries, and restaurants that flourish in this area. Don't expect any uptown flash. Jerome is long on quaintness and short on commercial appeal. It's worth your time to spend a few minutes in the Jerome Historical Society on the corner of Main and Jerome Streets to learn more about the town. You may contact the Jerome Historical Society at P.O. Box 156, Jerome 86331, or call (928) 634-5477 in advance to request a town map and more information. Additional information is available at www.jeromehistoricalsociety.org. If you're a history buff, pick up a Jerome tour guide, which outlines a complete historic walking tour. While you are at the historical society, visit the Mine Museum in the building to see artifacts and exhibits illustrating Jerome's past glory.

    Jerome attracts an eclectic mix of people, everyone from bikers to retirees. But up here everyone is mellow.

    In the past ten years this town has become a center for arts and crafts, especially pottery. Items are fairly priced, and help is routinely friendly. You can discover some good bargains—especially during the annual arts and crafts show, which is held over the Fourth of July weekend.

Don't miss the Mining Museum Gift Shop as well as Made in Jerome, which specializes in pottery, and Nellie Bly's, a jewelry shop that features a wonderful variety of kaleidoscopes.

Stop in at the Chamber of Commerce and ask for a copy of the art registry, which describes the many art galleries in town. Pick up a directory to lodging and eating and the self-guided walking tour brochure. www.chamberofcommerce.org

WHERE TO EAT

The Palace-Haunted Hamburger. 414 Clark Street. Gourmet burgers to prime rib are featured along with salads and "seductive" desserts. Inside, the atmosphere is casual. Seating is also available on the outdoor deck. The Palace Bar serves cocktails. $$. (928) 634–0554.

Flatiron Cafe. 416 Main Street. Light meals like black bean hummus and lavosh, smoked salmon quesadillas, fresh juices, and espresso drinks are on the menu here. This is Jerome's most urban outpost. $$. (928) 634–2733.

WHERE TO STAY

Like many other small Arizona towns, Jerome is experiencing a growth of bed-and-breakfast establishments. Recommended are:

The Cottage Inn. 747 East Avenue. Turn right after the state park, third house on the right. This B&B can accommodate four guests in two antiques-decorated rooms with a sitting room. The owners serve a full breakfast. For reservations write P.O. Box 823, Jerome 86331. $$; ☐. (928) 634–0701 or cottageinn@azjerome.com.

Ghost City Inn. 541 Main Street. Originally built in 1898, the Ghost City Inn bed and breakfast offers five theme rooms with shared bath, and the Cleopatra Hill Room, with a private bath. Gourmet breakfast and afternoon tea and cookies, a spacious veranda with never-ending views, and turn-down service complete with chocolate await visitors. $$; ☐. (928)-63GHOST. E-mail: reservations@ghostcityinn.com.

Jerome Grand Hotel. 200 Hill Street. This twenty-two-room hotel was once a hospital and today welcomes guests. Every room is different whether standard, deluxe, or the hotel's fine two-room suite. Furnishings are contemporary southwest. The fine dining restaurant is called **The Asylum** because it is, they say, "a restaurant on the fringe." The chef prepared original dishes that are intriguing and delicious. Reservations are recommended, especially on the weekends. Ask about senior and AAA discounts at the hotel. $$–$$$. (928) 634-8200.

The Rosegarden Bed & Breakfast. 3 Juarez Street. Call or write for directions. Juarez Street is directly opposite the Old Haven Methodist Church. This charming B&B accommodates a group of four, traveling together. Guests have the entire first floor of the home. There's a gorgeous view, an outer sitting room, and two rock walls as the house is built right into the corner of a mountain. An elaborate and elegant breakfast is served at a table complete with cut glass and sterling silver. No check-in time, and breakfast is served at the guests' convenience. For reservations write P.O. Box 313, Jerome 86331. $$. (928) 634-3270.

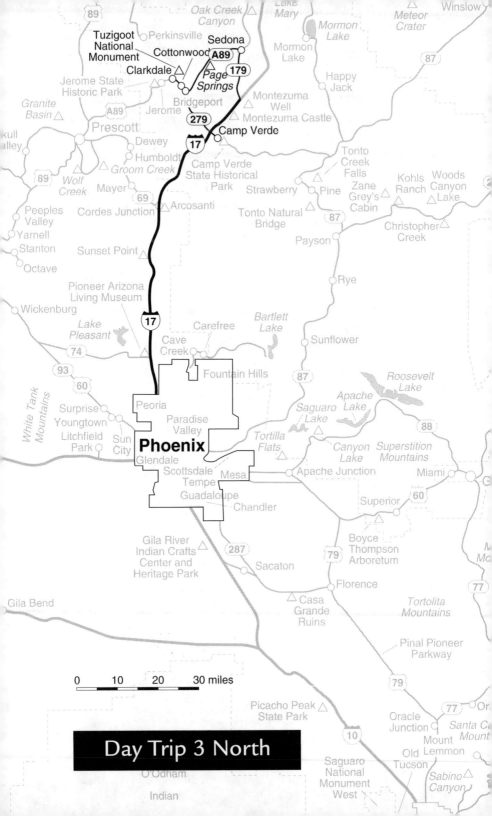

Day Trip 3 North

Begin the day with a visit to a prehistoric Native American ruin and complete it with a breathtakingly scenic ride through the Verde Valley. Arizona is proud to have several excursion trains running in the state. What's special about the Verde Valley train is that it traverses an area that is not accessible to vehicular traffic. The cars are modern, but the scenery is ageless. For maximum beauty, take this trip during the spring or autumn, when the verdant valley is dressed in its seasonal finest.

COTTONWOOD

From Phoenix, head north on I–17 to the Camp Verde junction. Follow A–279 northwest to Cottonwood.

According to legend, Cottonwood is named for the cottonwood trees that grew in a circle near what is now the center of town. Arizona historian Marshall Trimble disagrees. He attributes the name to the large stands of cottonwood trees that grew along the Verde River.

Regardless, visitors to the historic old town of Cottonwood will find that cottonwoods are still as plentiful as the western flavor. Here you can walk on high sidewalks and see false-front buildings. But don't let those "old tyme" places fool you. This town is growing as a retirement center and is home base for Alfredo's Wife, a popular clothing and gift manufacturer.

WHERE TO GO

Alfredo's Wife. 417 Willard Street. As you approach Cottonwood, this factory and outlet store is on the corner where US-89A and Willard Street meet. If you love whimsical, hand-appliquéd clothing, this outlet is a must. Everything is designed by one designer, and yes, there really is an Alfredo. Alfredo's Wife's signature is a small mouse. All clothing and gift items are handmade by a cadre of women who stitch the designs in the Cottonwood workshop. (928) 634–5808 or (800) 200–6805, ext. 13. E-mail: info@alfredoswife.com.

WHERE TO EAT

Blazin' M Ranch, adjacent to Dead Horse Ranch State Park on the Verde River. This family owned ranch is still farmed. But four days a week (Wednesday through Saturday) Blazin' M Ranch, which is owned by the Maebery family, offers Chuckwagon Suppers with entertainment by local cowboy singers. This down-home cowboy experience includes wagon rides, specialty shops, a western village, and farm animals to see. Children under three eat free. $$. Call (928) 634–0334 or (800) WEST643 for reservations. Closed the months of January and August.

CLARKDALE

Continue on A–279 to Clarkdale, which was once the smelting town for the mines in Jerome. Today Clarkdale is the departure point for Tuzigoot National Monument, the wilderness of Sycamore Canyon, and the Verde River Canyon Railroad.

WHERE TO GO

Tuzigoot National Monument. If you are up for more Native American ruins, don't veer west onto US-89A, but continue north on A–279 to see another Sinaguan village. This ancient ruin is located between Cottonwood and Clarkdale and was forgotten until the 1930s, when a team of archaeologists from the University of Arizona began excavating and exploring it. Their work was amply rewarded. They deduced that the original pueblo was two stories high and had seventy-seven ground-floor rooms. Built between A.D. 1125 and A.D. 1400, this ruin offers yet another intimate view of the ancient people who hunted and farmed here. The pueblo is situated on a 120-foot-high ridge that presents a panoramic view of the Jerome-Clarkdale area. No doubt the Sinaguas stood there, centuries ago, and marveled at the undisturbed view.

Take some time to walk along the trail at Tuzigoot. If you are fascinated by these people, don't leave without visiting the museum. Open daily. Fee. (928) 634–5564. www.pr.state.az.us.

The museum displays rare turquoise mosaics, beads and bracelets made of shells, painted pottery, and a variety of grave offerings, items the native people left in graves to carry into the afterlife.

The Verde Canyon Railroad and Railroad Inn. The Verde Canyon Train travels through the Verde River Canyon, one of the richest riparian habitats in the Southwest. The train started service in November 1990. The modern diesel winds through extraordinary scenery. Sharp-eyed travelers, at appropriate times of the year, can spot eagles soaring, and everyone can enjoy white-water rapids and the majesty of the Promethean cliffs.

Trains have been running in this area since well before World War I. This particular train was called the "Verde Mix" because it carried people and coal and was bankrolled originally by Senator William Clark. Clarkdale was named for his family. Clark ran his own 73-foot Pullman Palace luxury car on the tracks.

Today, it's possible to duplicate Senator Clark's extravagance as railroad cars can be rented for private parties. The cost for a first-class, private railroad trip is $54.95 per person. Wildflowers may be viewed from mid-March through May, and there are open-air gondola cars for outdoor viewing and photography.

The train leaves from 300 North Broadway, which is about 16 miles west of I–17, via exit 287. The 20-mile trip is scheduled every day but Tuesday, departing at 1:00 P.M. and returning at 5:00 P.M., except on days when double trains are scheduled. On those days, trains depart at 9:00 A.M. and 2:30 P.M. Summer starlight rides are also offered. The train winds through Verde Canyon adjacent to the Sycamore Wilderness Area and passes a continuously changing landscape—from prickly pear in the desert to hardwood trees. A naturalist on board provides narration. The 40-mile round trip follows the river past red sandstone formations reminiscent of those seen in nearby Sedona. As

Sinagua Indians once lived in this area, the thousand-year-old Sinagua ruins can be seen in the cliffs high above the water. At one point the train slows to go over S.O.B. Trestle, named for the foreman who ordered his crew to build this edifice. First-class passengers receive hors d'oeuvres and cocktail service; coach passengers can purchase drinks and snacks. Overnight packages are available. Along the way, it passes a bald eagle nest, Native American ruins, and sandstone cliffs and goes through a 680-foot manufactured tunnel. For information on schedules, fares, and tour packages, call Sedona SuperRate at (928) 639-0010 or (800) 293-7245 (reservation line). E-mail: info@verdecanyonrr.com.

PAGE SPRINGS

From the Cottonwood and Clarkdale area, saddle up for a true western adventure by following US-89A to the Page Springs–McGuireville exit.

WHERE TO EAT

Page Springs Bar & Restaurant. 1975 Page Springs Road. A twenty-minute drive from Jerome on 89A, heading toward Sedona. Take the Page Springs–McGuireville exit and proceed for about 21 miles until you see the restaurant on your left. Page Springs is situated along Oak Creek and is shaded by big sycamore trees. If you are lucky to get a window seat, you can watch the ducks paddling in the creek. Food is down-home American cooking with all-you-can-eat specials of barbecue ribs and prime beef. $–$$. For information write HC 66, Box 2204, Cornville 86325; call (928) 634-9954 for hours of operation.

Sedona
Oak Creek Canyon

SEDONA

This is one of the most popular day trips for visitors and residents alike. Desert dwellers love the lush green of Oak Creek Canyon, and one never tires of the Red Rocks or the startling view as the highway plunges into the heart of this magnificent country. Dedicated shoppers enjoy poking around the intriguing boutiques and art galleries in Sedona and in the village of Oak Creek. Outdoor buffs have a veritable banquet to choose from—everything from water sports and Native American ruins and hiking to running or jogging up Schnebley Hill for the more hardy.

Although you can approach Sedona in a couple of ways, I–17 north to A–179 is a popular route. At the junction of A–179 and US–89A, head north on A–179 and continue toward Sedona. The trip is an easy, nonstop, two-hour drive from Phoenix. Along the way, you get a full dose of Sedona's famous Red Rocks, one of the reasons for the town's popularity. Although recently humans have made their mark here with condominiums, shopping centers, and elegant homes, the Red Rocks still dominate the landscape. At an elevation of 4,300 feet, Sedona's weather is usually delightful. Although snow occasionally falls in winter and summer temperatures can peak from warm to hot, the climate generally is ideal. You can easily spend a day (not to mention money) exploring indoors as Sedona offers a full complement of culture and recreation. Outdoor enthusiasts will find plenty to do as well. The area is rich with campgrounds and Native American ruins. Hatcheries keep the fishing good. Between the

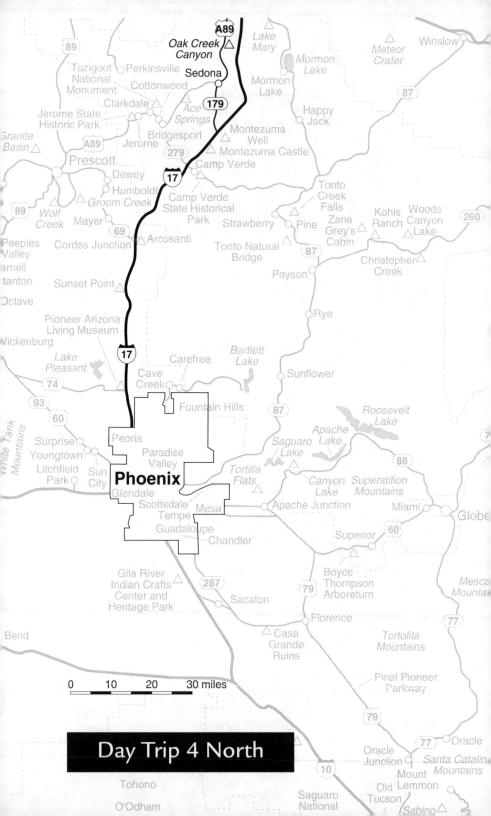

Day Trip 4 North

glorious apricot-to-peach-to-purple sunsets and the burnished Red Rocks, Sedona is awash with color.

In 2000, Sedona initiated a new policy designed to help pay for the cost of wear and tear on its natural area. Many popular hiking areas now require a $5.00 parking (or hiking) fee. Be prepared to pay the fee, and enjoy the huge scenery knowing you are also helping to assure that future generations will enjoy the beauty.

WHERE TO GO

Chapel of the Holy Cross. Heading toward Sedona on A-179, you pass the Village of Oak Creek. Continue on A-179 for approximately 5 miles. In the distance, on your right, you will see the Chapel of the Holy Cross against the Red Rocks. Turn right on Chapel Road, which leads to the church. The road is well marked with three signs announcing the turnoff. This is an inspirational and architectural treat. Be sure to read the plaque on the exterior of the building that describes the history of this unusual place of worship. Although often busy with tourists, the chapel nevertheless remains a very sacred and inspiring place that should not be missed. It is open daily to the public free of charge. (928) 282-4069.

Tlaquepaque. Continue north on A-179. As it bends right before crossing Oak Creek, make a sharp left turn. The entrances are immediately on your left. The cobblestone driveways are marked by rustic-looking stone gates that are almost hidden beneath the tall trees.

Tlaquepaque (Ta-la-kee-pah-kee) is a shopping center worth your time. Named for a suburb of Guadalajara, Mexico, this is a favorite gathering place for locals and tourists. Indulge yourself in the boutiques that feature everything from superb pottery, elegant glass, clothing, and gifts to art and sculpture. You can also feed your body, as well as your soul, at a number of excellent dining establishments.

As you walk through Tlaquepaque, notice the bell tower, which is a Sedona landmark. Peek inside the tiny chapel near the central plaza. Just as each Spanish and Mexican village has a church, Tlaquepaque has its chapel, which holds approximately twenty people and is used for private weddings and other ceremonies. For more information contact Tlaquepaque, P.O. Box 1868, Sedona 86336. (928) 282-4838.

The Red Rocks. There's no better way to see the Red Rocks of Sedona than by going off-road. There are about a half-dozen companies in Sedona that provide escorted tours. Here are recommended favorites:

Sedona's famous **Pink Jeep Tours** and **Sedona Adventures** offer adventure for everyone who is daring enough to ride off the road in a pink Jeep or open Land Cruiser and up the hills and over the creeks to gain this special view of the majestic Sedona landscape. Pink Jeep Tours takes you through the Broken Arrow off-road areas, and Sedona Adventures explores the more remote Diamondback Gulch and includes some easy to moderate scenic hikes. You may call ahead to reserve space on one of the seven jeeps. Take anywhere from a one-and-a-half to a three-hour tour, or sign up for a rollicking all-day trip. Sunrise or sunset tours are particularly spectacular, and custom tours or barbecues can be arranged. This excursion is recommended for all ages, but be prepared for some wild driving and even wilder views. For more information about times and prices, write Pink Jeep Tours, P.O. Box 1447, Sedona 86336. Fee. (928) 282-5000. Or call Pink Jeep Tours's Sedona Adventures at (800) 873-3662. www.pinkjeep.com.

Honancki Ruins Tours. Run by the Pink Jeep Tours operation, this tour gives you a chance to be escorted on an archaeological expedition of Native American ruins. Travel by jeep to backcountry, unexcavated, unreconstructed cliff dwellings, which you'll explore room by room. For more information on these tours, write to Pink Jeep Tours's Ancient Expeditions, P.O. Box 1447, Sedona 86339, or phone (928) 282-2137.

Sedona Red Rock Jeep Tours. Another great way to see the Red Rocks is through this excellent jeep-tour company. The guides are informative, and the jeeps provide exciting transportation over the backcountry. This company also offers horseback rides through backcountry trails. All horseback rides are walking rides, and age and weight restrictions do apply to protect riders and horses. Experienced wranglers and gentle horses make this an unforgettable way to experience Sedona for those who like the view on horseback. Sedona Red Rock Jeep Tours also offers archaeological tours. Prices quoted include transportation to and from guests' hotels. For reservations call (928) 282-6826 or (800) 848-1851.

Red Rock State Park. Follow US-89A 3 miles. Turn off onto Lower Red Rock Loop Road. Nestled on lower Oak Creek near Sedona, this 286-acre park was planned as an environmental center. A naturalist program offers tours that introduce you to the plants and animals in this special riparian setting. Approximately 11¾₀ miles of Oak Creek wind through the park, and more than 135 species of birds and 450 species of plants and grasses have been identified here. First stop should be the visitors center. Then head off on any of the several trails. If you visit in winter, take a jacket or sweater. Fee. (928) 282-6907.

Sedona Arts Center. US-89A at Barn Road. This center offers theater productions, visual arts exhibitions, and other art exhibits as well as concerts and festivals. Free entrance to the Exhibition Hall; art themes change monthly. (928) 282-3809. www.sedonacenter.com.

Slide Rock State Park. On US-89A about 4 or 5 miles past uptown Sedona. Developed around a natural water slide that has been smoothed over by centuries of water (not to mention blue-jeaned derrieres), this park is a favorite spot for kids of all ages. Years ago, this was a casual experience. Today, the park is well maintained and organized. There's a fee for parking, but sliding in Oak Creek is still free. The less adventurous will enjoy the verdant scene and the grassy picnic grounds.

Red Rock Crossing. Touted as the best all-around hiking trail in the Sedona–Oak Creek area, this trail is good for adults of all ages and fitness levels, kids, and pets. To reach this hiking area, take A-89A west from Sedona to Upper Red Rock Loop Road. Go south on Red Rock Loop and look for signs to direct you to Red Rock Crossing. Parking costs $3.00. The hike begins by walking on a sidewalk that goes through a meadow surrounded by cottonwood trees. The sidewalk ends at Oak Creek. From there the hike continues along a gravel trail for approximately twenty minutes to the base of Cathedral Rock. The tricky part of this hike involves walking across some logs at the deeper parts of the creek.

Schnebley Hill. One of the most well-known hiking and mountain biking routes in Sedona, this is a 23-mile round-trip through mind-boggling Sedona scenery. The road begins ½ mile south of the intersection of highways 89-A and SR-179 in town. The dirt road leads west from SR-179. Hikers and cyclists will see the ruins of the old Foxboro Lake Resort about halfway through the trip. The old carriage house stands on the left side of the road with the main building and swimming pool at the meadow's edge to the right. This is not a good ride after rain or snow, so it's a good idea to check with the Coconino National Forest Office for road conditions.

WHERE TO EAT

Enchantment Resort. Boyton Canyon. 525 Boyton Canyon Road, Sedona. Serves breakfast, lunch, and dinner and a champagne brunch on Sunday from 11:30 A.M. to 2:30 P.M. Pants and collared shirts are required for men for dinner. $$-$$$; ☐. Reservations are recommended for dinner and Sunday brunch. (928) 282-2900.

Garland's Oak Creek Lodge. P.O. Box 152, Sedona 86336. Coming north from Sedona, go 8 miles on US-89A, and the sign for Garland is on your left. Cross the creek, and you're at one of Oak Creek Canyon's most charming settings. Call ahead for reservations for breakfast or dinner and sample some super home-cooked meals. Closed for the winter from November 15 through March 31. $$$; ☐. (928) 282-3343.

Heartline Cafe. 1610 West US-89A. At the Y in the road, turn left and continue approximately a mile. It's on the right-hand side as you go toward West Sedona. The menu varies, but the food is always fresh and delicious. For health-conscious eaters, there is a spa menu. Pastas and pizzas are excellent. Request to eat on the patio. Lunch is served Monday through Friday only; dinner is served seven days a week. $$-$$$; ☐. (928) 282-0785.

L'Auberge de Sedona. 301 L'Auberge Lane. On US-89A, 1 block north of A-179. L'Auberge is gourmet without being stuffy. It offers an impressive menu from hors d'oeuvres to a six-course dinner. An outstanding selection of entrees and superb preparation and presentation have garnered raves, including being honored by the Chefs in America organization as one of "America's Finest Restaurants." Call for reservations. $$-$$$ (breakfast less); ☐. (928) 282-1661; www.lauberge.com.

René at Tlaquepaque. This authentic French restaurant features great French bread and superb cuisine. The house specialty is an excellent rack of lamb. Don't be turned away by the French exterior. Inside, you'll find elegantly casual surroundings. You can come as you are, dressed for sightseeing. $$-$$$; ☐. (928) 282-9225.

WHERE TO STAY

Enchantment Resort. Boyton Canyon. 525 Boyton Canyon Road, Sedona. Heading west on US–89A, turn right on Dry Creek Road and continue approximately 3 miles. Here you'll come to a T in the road. Turn left where you see the sign for Boyton Canyon. Go 2 miles farther. You'll come to a second T in the road. Turn right and follow the signs toward Boyton Canyon. This spectacular resort is carved into the most gorgeous setting in all of Sedona and is definitely worth the trip. The guard will direct you to the clubhouse, set high into Boyton Canyon. Indulge in tennis, swimming, golf, and hiking. $$$; ☐. For reservations call (928) 282-2900 or (800) 826-4180. www.enchantmentresort.com.

Garland's Oak Creek Lodge. P.O. Box 152, Sedona 86336. Coming north from Sedona, go 8 miles on US–89A, and the sign for Garland's is on your left. Cross the creek, and you're at one of Oak Creek Canyon and Arizona's best-kept treasures. This is a homey nine-acre resort set just across Oak Creek. Rooms are individual; freestanding log cabins have no locks. Twelve of fifteen units have fireplaces, and all are charming. Although Garland's traditionally fills up on weekends—up to a year in advance—you are encouraged to call at the last minute, because cancellations do occur. A two-night stay is required, and breakfast and dinner are included. Open April 1 through November 15. $$$; ☐. (928) 282-3343.

L'Auberge de Sedona. 301 L'Auberge Lane. On US–89A, 1 block north of A–179. This informal yet elegant French-style country inn is fast becoming well known throughout the country. The grounds alone are worth a visit. Its rosemary-scented pathways, shade trees, picnic tables, and stepping stones create a magical ambience for the various pine cottages nestled among the cottonwood trees. Beds are handcrafted and canopied. Love seats are overstuffed. Televisions and telephones are nowhere to be seen. $$$; ☐. Reservations: (800) 272-6777. www.lauberge.com.

BED & BREAKFASTS

In recent years, Sedona has become a mecca for upscale bed and breakfasts and charming inns that provide the perfect "home" for travelers who want to discover this fascinating country. Day trippers who decide to stay overnight (or longer) in Sedona now have many properties from which to choose, from romantic lodges to western-style inns and rustic cabins. The Chamber of Commerce has a complete list of bed-and-breakfast establishments to please every taste. Here are just two:

Graham Bed & Breakfast Inn. 150 Canyon Circle Drive. This elegant bed and breakfast is owned by Carol and Roger Redenbaugh. In addition to home-cooked breakfasts prepared by the hosts, guests enjoy designer touches in the individual suites and special amenities like a double Jacuzzi. This award-winning Mobil four-star inn also boasts a lushly landscaped pool area. $$$; ☐. (928) 284-1425.

Territorial House Bed & Breakfast. 65 Piki Drive. Hosts John and Linda Steele offer a choice of four rooms, which include full breakfast and afternoon refreshments. The Red Rock Crossing room features a romantic, king-size, four-poster canopy bed; oval marble whirlpool tub, with separate glass shower; and private deck. Grasshopper Flats features a queen-size barnwood bed as well as Old West movies made in Sedona. Indian Garden is a pueblo-style room with a second-floor balcony that comes equipped with a telescope for viewing the stars. Schnebley Station is a western two-bedroom suite that is perfect for families or couples traveling together. $$; ☐. (928) 204-2737 or (800) 801-2737. www.oldwestbb.com.

OAK CREEK CANYON

Oak Creek Canyon is just north of Sedona on US-89A. Don't see one without seeing the other. Oak Creek glimmers in autumn, sparkles cool and clear in summer, and occasionally is tinged with winter snow. The drive through Oak Creek Canyon is steep enough to satisfy a roller-coaster lover, but once on the canyon floor, you may park your car and walk around the area. Plan to take this drive north to south for the most breathtaking views.

For many sightseers, the drive through Oak Creek Canyon is experience enough. More ambitious types should take a casual stroll through the wooded area along the creek. Serious hikers may prefer more rugged challenges, so if you don't mind getting wet (you'll need to wade across the creek), there are more rigorous routes described in several books on outdoor Arizona available at local bookstores.

West Fork of Oak Creek Canyon. Continue on US–89A about 10 miles north of Sedona between milepost 384 and 385. Watch for two large posts with a heavy chain on the west side of the road about 100 feet north of a Dos Pinos sign. The trail begins as an asphalt path. You'll pass the ruins of the old Mayhew Lodge and then emerge into a riparian wonderland of red cliffs and pungent leaves. The trail crosses Oak Creek several times, so be prepared to balance on slippery rocks or wade across. Although this is a very popular hike, the trail offers a special slice of Arizona: peaceful, green, and wet! The deeper you go into the canyon, the more verdant the scene and, during autumn, more brilliantly colored. Free.

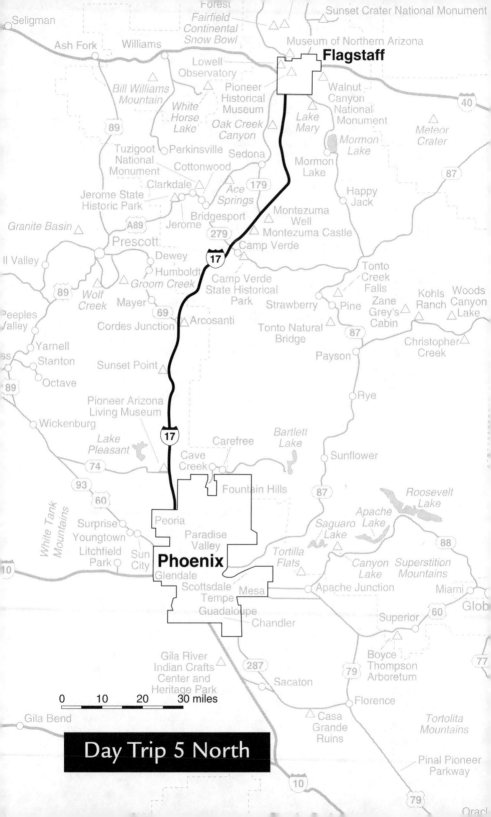

Day Trip 5 North

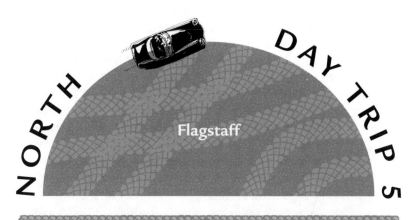

NORTH

DAY TRIP 5

Flagstaff

FLAGSTAFF

Often called "The City of Seven Wonders," Flagstaff is approximately two-and-a-half hours north of Phoenix, an easy day trip by Arizona standards. The scenic highway dips through the Verde Valley, climbs over the Mogollon Rim, or "the Rim," as it's better known, and ultimately reaches this 7,000-foot-high city. This is a trip of strong natural contrast: You travel from prickly pears to pines. If you take this drive in winter, you can swim in your heated Phoenix pool in the morning, ski all afternoon in Flagstaff, and return home to Phoenix that night!

Trivia lovers may enjoy knowing that most stories concerning the origin of the name *Flagstaff* involved some person lopping off branches of a lone pine and running a flag up the pole. Fortunately, someone thought "Flag-staff" had a better ring to it than "Flag-pole." In any event, it is documented that to celebrate the naming, a centennial flag was flown from a tall pine tree on July 4, 1876.

Today, this city is the seat of Coconino County, second-largest county in the country and home to Northern Arizona University. The northern hub of the state, Flagstaff is a bustling little city, bisected by railroad tracks, surrounded by pines, and dominated by the 12,670-foot Mount Humphreys Peak, the tallest mountain in the state. The downtown has recently undergone a wonderful restoration. You'll find outdoor cafes and some fun shops here, everything from a terrific bookstore to outdoor stores. Surrounded by verdant splendor, the town is ringed with appealing new sections that feature reddish wood tones and rustic, ski-lodge motifs. During ski season, Flagstaff's Snow Bowl hums with the whoosh of downhill skiers coursing down Mount Humphreys. Throughout the year, the city is home to a hardy breed of students and outdoor types. If you love plaid flannel shirts, this may be your place. With Flagstaff as your jumping-off point, the whole of northern Arizona opens up, and a wonderland of day trips opens to you. (Read about these in the section titled Day Trips from Flagstaff.) In the meantime, here's a sampling of the sights to see when you visit this hub of northern Arizona.

WHERE TO GO

Arboretum at Flagstaff. On Woody Mountain Road off US-66, about 4 miles west of town. The center is located in a beautiful wooded area. At an elevation of 7,150 feet, it is the highest botanic garden in the United States that does horticultural research. The display gardens offer landscaping ideas for the arid West, but even nongardeners will enjoy this quiet respite. Here are Arizona plants and flowers, many of which are rare and specially bred for this climate. For information write P.O. Box 670, Flagstaff 86002-0670. (928) 774-1442.

Coconino Center for the Arts. 2300 North Fort Valley Road. On A-180 (Fort Valley Road). This regional art center offers a variety of arts programming including exhibits, musical performances, workshops, and demonstrations as well as a folk art program. Gallery shows of national importance are mounted. The center offers "Trappings of the American West" every May and June, which brings together fine art and crafts that reflect the life of the American cowboy. Closed Monday during the winter months. Free. (928) 779-6921.

Lava River Cave. Nine miles north of Flagstaff on US-180. Turn west (left) on FR-245 and continue 3 miles to FR-171. Turn south 1 mile to where FR-171A turns left. Continue a short distance to the mile-long lava tube cave. This primitive cave was formed 700,000 years ago by molten rock that erupted from a volcanic vent in nearby Hart Prairie. If you look at the floor, you can see wavelike undulations that are the remains of frozen ripples in the last trickle of molten rock that flowed from this cave. Inside, the temperature is forty-two degrees—even in summer—so dress warm. This is a rugged adventure. The entry is steep and can be slick with ice. Inside, the left route is easy; the right-hand side has very low ceilings and forces you to crawl a short distance. In winter, the cave can only be accessed by skiing to it. Bring flashlights because the interior is dark, slippery, and rugged. Free. For information call the Public Affairs office at (928) 527-3600. You can also contact the Ranger Station at (928) 526-0866 or get more information at www.nps.gov/waca.

Lowell Observatory. 1400 West Mars Hill Road. Travel west on Santa Fe Avenue and follow it to the end, then climb Mars Hill. Dr. Percival Lowell built the wooden, world-famous observatory in 1894. The planet Pluto was discovered here in 1930, and today the observatory continues to be a center of important scientific work. Interesting and informative guided tours are available daily. If you visit during the summer, plan on spending Friday night here, when the observatory is open to the public. Fee. (928) 774-3358. www.lowell.edu.

Meteor Crater Museum of Astrogeology. (See Day Trip 1 East from Flagstaff.)

The Museum of Northern Arizona. 3101 North Fort Valley Road. Three miles north of Flagstaff on US-180 at Fort Valley Road. From downtown Flagstaff, follow the signs to the Grand Canyon via US-180. A small jewel for those interested in knowing about northern Arizona—especially the Navajo and Hopi cultures—the museum offers an outstanding rug display and gift shop. This museum is a "must" for visitors who are unfamiliar with northern Arizona, as it provides a superb introduction to the Kaibab Plateau, the area that is home to the Grand Canyon. The museum has excellent interpretive exhibits for children as well as adults, as well as one of the best bookstores in the state. During the summer, several tribes showcase traditional arts and activities on the beautiful museum grounds. For more information write Route 4, Box 720, Flagstaff 86001. Open daily. Fee. (928) 774-5211. www.musnaz.org.

Pioneer Historical Museum. 2340 North Fort Valley Road. From downtown Flagstaff, follow the signs to the Grand Canyon via US-180. The museum is 2 miles north of town (just a mile before you get to the Museum of Northern Arizona). Operated by the Pioneer Historical Society, the facility is devoted to preserving Arizona's pioneer heritage. All kinds of artifacts depicting pioneer life are on display here to help you understand what it was like for those who settled the area. Donation suggested. Closed Sunday. Mailing address: Box 1968, Flagstaff 86001. For information call the Arizona Historical Society at (928) 774–6272.

Sunset Crater Volcano National Monument. (See Day Trip 1 North from Flagstaff.)

Walnut Canyon National Monument. Off I–40 east, 7½ miles east of Flagstaff at the Walnut Canyon turnoff. A beautifully preserved Sinaguan cliff dwelling, Walnut Canyon whispers of bygone centuries. This is one of the most beautiful spots in Flagstaff and is a great destination for people of all ages. Almost always peaceful and sylvan, Walnut Canyon offers well-marked trails as well as more rugged adventures. Stop first at the visitors center and decide whether to travel into this time warp by strolling on Rim Walk Trail or hiking down Island Trail, a 185-foot descent. Both provide a splendid view of the 300 small cliff dwellings that are found within this 400-foot-deep canyon. If you choose the more strenuous path, prepare to take your time: It takes twice the effort to ascend as it does to descend. Fee. (928) 526–3367. www.nps.gov/waca.

Flagstaff Snow Bowl. (Twenty-eight-mile round-trip.) Take A–180 (Humphreys Street) north 7 miles. Turn right at Snow Bowl Road and continue climbing up that dirt road another 7 miles to the end of the path, where you'll see the lodge. Indoor types can eat at the Snow Bowl snack shop and imbibe at the bar. Weather permitting, the top of the Snow Bowl is great for a panoramic view or picnic. A ski lift runs up Mount Humphreys, Arizona's highest peak, which towers over the San Francisco Mountain range. It's open in summer until mid-July and on weekends and holidays.

The view is dazzling. You go almost to the top of Mount Agassiz to an elevation of 11,500 feet in thirty minutes. If you do this in the summer, take a jacket, as it's cool. As you ride you can see the Grand Canyon's North Rim more than 80 miles away as well as the dormant volcano field that surrounds the city. Kendrick Peak, Wild Bill, and Wing Mountain are prominent landmarks. You'll enjoy views of Mount Humphreys, Hart Prairie, and ponderosa pines. The skyride is usually open only on the weekend.

Once at the top, you can hike on any of a variety of interpretive trails, which have good descriptions of the vegetation and historical significance of the area. (928) 779-1951.

Riordan Mansion. 1300 Riordan State Historic Park. The mansion was built in 1904 for Timothy and Michael Riordan, who established the logging industry in Flagstaff. The interior has more than 13,000 square feet with forty rooms, stained-glass windows, and unique window transparencies created by the renowned turn-of-the-twentieth-century photographer Jack Hillers.

Don't miss the visitors center, which maintains an exhibit area and informative slide program. You can also bring a picnic and eat in the park. Guided tours are available. Call for hours. Fee. (928) 779-4395. www.pr.state.az.us/parkhtml/riordan.html.

Historic walking tour. From the Riordan Mansion, continue north on Milton. From the arrival of the first railroad in 1882 throughout the postwar expansion after 1945, this was the business center for most of northern Arizona. The downtown has been restored and features many shops and galleries that offer a fine array of Southwestern arts and crafts, specialty items, and clothing.

SCENIC DRIVE

Around the Peaks Loop. This loop takes you all the way around Arizona's highest mountain, winding through pine forest, aspen groves, open prairies, and rustic homesteads. You can do this drive any time when snow doesn't close the road. In spring you'll enjoy a carpet of wildflowers; in autumn the trees blaze gold. Along the way you can get out of the car and hike or camp.

To enjoy this loop, drive northeast on US-89 from Flagstaff for 14 miles. Turn west 12 miles to FR-151. Then go south 8 miles to US-180. It's 9½ miles back to Flagstaff.

The entire loop is 44 miles, and roads are suitable for cars. Plan on spending about two hours enjoying the magnificent scenery.

WHERE TO EAT

You can't tell this from the highway, but Flagstaff is a full-service restaurant town. Everything is here from Asian to Thai, barbecue to coffee shops, natural to elegant continental dining. Here are some favorites. Ask the Flagstaff Convention and Visitor Bureau for a brochure with a complete listing. Stop in at or write to 101 Route 66, Flagstaff 86001, or call (928) 774-4505.

Black Bart's Steak House. 2760 East Butler Avenue. This is a good family place that features steaks and chicken, cowboy beans and biscuits. See the old-time review put on by the waiters and waitresses. You'll pay extra for the show, but it's worth it. $$; □. (928) 779-3142.

Cafe Espress. 16 North San Francisco Street. Indulge in lots of good natural food, homemade baked pastries, and a variety of coffees. $-$$; □. (928) 774-0541.

Charly's Restaurant and Pub. 23 North Leroux Street, in the old Weatherford Hotel in downtown Flagstaff. Built in 1898 by John Weatherford, a Flagstaff merchant, the Victorian-style structure is one of the best examples of red-sandstone architecture in Flagstaff. Fun and funky, it is great for lunch or dinner, and Sunday brunch is special. Enjoy outstanding soups; there's lovely music while you dine. Open daily. $$; □. (928) 779-1919.

Chez Marc Bistro. 503 North Humphreys Street. Dine inside in a restored house or outside on the patio. Nouvelle French. $$-$$$; □. (928) 774-1343.

Cottage Place. 126 West Cottage Street, in the old town area south of the railroad tracks. This famous landmark restaurant is in an old Flagstaff house. Service is gracious. The food is worth the wait. $$-$$$; □. (928) 774-8431.

El Charro Cafe. 409 South San Francisco Street. This family-owned restaurant offers authentic Mexican food. On Saturday night, the family mariachi band performs. $; □. (928) 779-0552.

Horsemen Lodge and Restaurant. 8500 North 89. Old West atmosphere is set against a background of the San Francisco peaks. Steaks and other western casual fare are served in a rustic atmosphere. $$; □. (928) 526-2655.

Macy's. 14 South Beaver (on the south side of the Santa Fe Railroad tracks). This funky coffeehouse is a local favorite. In addition to serving breakfasts (they have great teas, coffees, baked goods, etc.), Macy's also serves excellent lunches and dinners. $-$$; no □. (928) 774-2243.

Main Street Bar & Grill. 16E Route 66. This is a neat little place with great food. Barbecue is a specialty. Homemade soups and desserts are served up along with live entertainment. $; ☐. (928) 774-1519.

Mama Luisa Italian Restaurant. 2710 North Steves Boulevard. Tiny but terrific. Italian food here is excellent. $-$$$; ☐. (928) 526-6809.

Pasto. 19 East Aspen Avenue. Excellent Italian food. Flagstaff has a small but charming historic downtown that makes this special. $$; ☐. (928) 779-1937.

WHERE TO STAY

All kinds of accommodations await tourists. Choose from bed and breakfasts and rustic cabins to modern motels and resorts. Check with the Flagstaff Convention and Visitor Bureau, 323 West Aspen Avenue, Flagstaff 86001, or call (928) 779-7611 for a complete listing of hotels, motels, and other accommodations. Here are three to start you off:

Best Western Woodlands Plaza. 1560 East Santa Fe Avenue. This is an elegant resort hotel that offers luxury at surprisingly reasonable prices. It won a Three Diamond Award and has a heated swimming pool. Nonsmoking rooms are available, and fine dining is nearby. $$; ☐. (928) 774-7168, or Best Western reservations at (800) 528-1234.

Little America. Butler Avenue and I-40. This is a large (248-room) facility. The rooms are big and well appointed, and the bathrooms are luxurious and equipped with telephones. You have several dining rooms to choose from. $$-$$$; ☐. (928) 779-2741 or (800) 352-4386.

Quality Suites. 2000 South Milton Road. You will find very comfortable rooms with VCRs. The owner started the "no smoking" room concept. Breakfast is included. $$; ☐. (928) 774-4333 or (800) 326-2779.

BED & BREAKFASTS

These are all in beautiful old homes and are privately owned and run. Each one serves outstanding breakfasts.

Birch Tree Inn. 824 West Birch Avenue. This is a lovely place with amenities including a pool table. Nonsmoking only. $$; ☐. (928) 774-1042 or (888) 779-1042.

Colton House. Located across the street from the Museum of

Northern Arizona, this historic home is owned by the museum and was built by its founders, Dr. Harold S. Colton and his wife, Mary-Russell Ferrell Colton. Construction on this home began in June 1929. Recently opened as a guest house for the museum, the Colton House is a magical place with original tile floors, a massive fireplace, and comfortable period furniture that seems right at home in these elegantly casual surroundings. Almost hidden in a pine forest, this enchanted get-away features four spacious, very special bedrooms. The Colton House alone is reason enough to make the trip to Flagstaff. Stay includes a continental breakfast; other meals can be arranged for an additional fee. Nonsmoking only, $$$; □. (928) 774-5211, ext. 202.

Dierker House. 423 West Cherry. Just three rooms are available in this wonderful old house, but each room is furnished with lovely antiques. The owner cooks a fabulous breakfast and keeps fresh cookies out for munchy attacks. $$. (928) 774-3249.

Inn at 410. 410 North Leroux. Nine suites are decorated to perfection. Some are singles; some are suites. Each has its own bathroom, and the breakfast is superb. $$$; □. (928) 774-0088. www.inn410.com.

Jeanette's Bed & Breakfast. 3380 East Lockett Road. This comfortable, Victorian-style home is outfitted with antiques that have been collected by the owners, who are happy to share their antiquing stories with you. All rooms are named for their grandparents. Grandma Amelia's Room boasts a clawfoot bathtub, brass-trimmed fireplace, and queen-size oak bed. Stella's Room is done in maple furnishings. Mamie's Room, on the first floor, has rich walnut furnishings, while Icie Vean's Room includes unique collectibles like a dental cabinet masquerading as an armoire and the 6-foot-long china bathtub the owners rescued from the Broadmoor Hotel in Denver. $$; □. (928) 527-1912 or (800) 752-1912.

CAVE CREEK

This day trip begins at Cave Creek and offers a peek into the not-so-distant past. Along the way, you see the Phoenix urban area at its most posh. Comfortable distances and good shopping make this a relaxing, easy trip. Although the desert northeast of Phoenix is rapidly being developed, the vast Tonto National Forest is just an arrowhead's throw away. If you are concerned that this close-in desert is fast disappearing, remember that only 18 percent of Arizona is privately owned. Since most of the land belongs to the state and federal governments, hopefully much of it will be saved for posterity.

Cave Creek is a funky little old town that has resisted urban flash, unlike its sister city, Carefree, which was built to attract the well-heeled. A mining camp in the 1880s and a ranching community after the mines gave out, Cave Creek offers modern city dwellers an alternative to urban life. Don't miss the Town Dump, a rambling "shop" on the main road (Cave Creek Road). It's filled with curiosities and some old and new bargains.

When Tonto National Forest was established here in 1903, the first tourists started to arrive. Bartlett Dam, built in 1935, brought more people. The terrain adjacent to Tonto National Forest is dotted with lakes, punctuated by mountains, and provides an array of outdoor recreation opportunities. There is an abundance of wild game in the area, including deer, wild pig, mountain lion, duck, quail, and dove, and opportunities abound for hiking, fishing, horseback riding, and rockhounding.

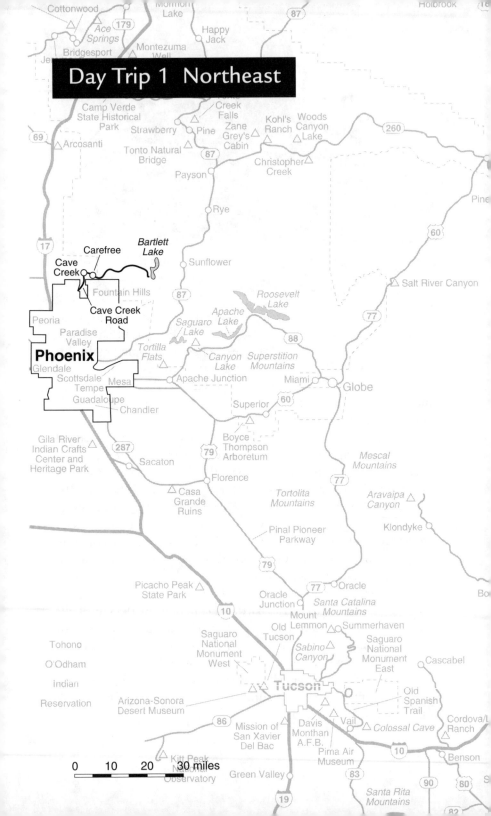

Day Trip 1 Northeast

Cottonwood

Ace Springs

Bridgesport

Mormon Lake

Happy Jack

Montezuma Well

Holbrook

Creek Falls

Camp Verde State Historical Park

Strawberry

Pine

Zane Grey's Cabin

Kohl's Ranch

Woods Canyon Lake

Arcosanti

Tonto Natural Bridge

Payson

Christopher Creek

Rye

Bartlett Lake

Carefree

Cave Creek

Sunflower

Fountain Hills

Roosevelt Lake

Salt River Canyon

Cave Creek Road

Peoria

Paradise Valley

Apache Lake

Saguaro Lake

Phoenix

Glendale

Tortilla Flats

Canyon Lake

Superstition Mountains

Scottsdale

Mesa

Tempe

Apache Junction

Miami

Globe

Guadaloupe

Chandler

Superior

Gila River Indian Crafts Center and Heritage Park

Sacaton

Boyce Thompson Arboretum

Mescal Mountains

Florence

Casa Grande Ruins

Tortolita Mountains

Aravaipa Canyon

Klondyke

Pinal Pioneer Parkway

Picacho Peak State Park

Oracle Junction

Oracle

Santa Catalina Mountains

Tohono O'Odham Indian Reservation

Saguaro National Monument West

Old Tucson

Mount Lemmon

Sabino Canyon

Summerhaven

Saguaro National Monument East

Cascabel

Arizona-Sonora Desert Museum

Tucson

Old Spanish Trail

Cordova/L Ranch

Mission of San Xavier Del Bac

Davis Monthan A.F.B.

Vail

Colossal Cave

Benson

Kitt Peak National Observatory

Pima Air Museum

Green Valley

Santa Rita Mountains

0   10   20   30 miles

Keep your eye out for antiques shops. There are some intriguing places to browse. To get to Cave Creek, follow I-17 to the Carefree Highway eastbound. Turn east. It becomes Desert Foothills Drive. Individuals who cared about the desert made the 101 signs identifying the desert plants along the road. As you maneuver along the dips, take time to notice these identifying markers and learn about the unusual environment.

WHERE TO GO

Cave Creek Museum. 6140 Skyline Drive. Open October to May. The living history of the desert foothills area is presented in this small museum through displays of pioneer living, ranching, mining, and old guns. Exhibits also describe the cultures of the Hohokam, Yavapai, and Apache. Donations are welcome. Closed Mondays, Tuesdays, and holidays. (480) 488-2764.

WHERE TO EAT

El Encanto Mexican Cafe. 6248 East Cave Creek Road. Right across the street from the Satisfied Frog, this comfortable hacienda-style restaurant satisfies that urge to binge on burritos. Request a table on the outside patio and overlook a lagoon where you can watch the ducks and sip a frosty margarita. Great respite after a busy day of sightseeing in the desert. $-$$; □. (480) 488-1752.

    The Horny Toad. 6738 East Cave Creek Road. This is a *gen-u-ine* western joint. Fried chicken (lots of it) is a specialty, and the hamburgers are great. Lunch and dinner served daily. $$; □. (480) 997-9622.

    Satisfied Frog. 6245 East Cave Creek Road. Just up the street from the Horny Toad, this restaurant serves equally delicious food. Lunch and dinner, featuring western fare, are served daily. Plan to kick up your heels Friday and Saturday when the "Frog" rocks with country music. Don't miss the honky-tonk piano and the popcorn wagon. Cool off by strolling through the western "town," filled with western souvenir shops. $$; □. (480) 488-3317.

CAREFREE

Another 1950s Arizona phenomenon, Carefree was a real estate developer's dream that was planned to lure those who have the means and the time to enjoy their leisure. Continue east on Cave Creek Road a mile or so, and you're there. The street names say it all—Easy Street, Nonchalant Avenue, Ho and Hum Streets, Rocking Chair Road. Carefree is an elegant little community of large homes, green golf courses, and busy boutiques set like jewels into rocky bezels.

WHERE TO GO

El Pedregal. Heading north on Scottsdale Road from Scottsdale, continue north toward Carefree. You'll see the bright colors of this Moroccan-inspired, fiesta-style center in the distance on the east side of the road. Park and have fun! Wander through the various boutiques, stop at the yogurt shop for outstanding frozen yogurt, and spend time at the numerous art galleries. This area is becoming a second destination (besides downtown Scottsdale) for viewing art. You'll find fine restaurants and, on Thursday evenings during the summer, free concerts held on center stage. Open daily.

The Sundial. Go east on Cave Creek Road to Sunshine Way and turn right. You'll see the sundial right ahead of you. This is the largest sundial in the western hemisphere and a Carefree landmark.

The Spanish Village. Carefree. Follow Tom Darlington Drive (Scottsdale Road) south to the signs for shopping. Here you'll find narrow streets trimmed with wrought iron and lined with gift shops and restaurants.

The Boulders Resort & Club. In Carefree. Head south on Tom Darlington Drive (Scottsdale Road) and turn left just prior to the pile of boulders. Follow the signs to The Boulders Resort & Club. This top-class resort is consistently rated as one of the best resorts in the country in terms of service, amenities, and natural beauty. The free-form architecture and desert setting are amazing and offer one of the most elegant experiences during almost any time of year.

WHERE TO STAY

The Boulders Resort & Club. 34631 North Tom Darlington Drive. Head south on Tom Darlington Drive (Scottsdale Road) and turn left just prior to the pile of boulders. Follow the signs to The Boulders Resort & Club. Breakfast, lunch, and dinner are available at the resort and club, which is one of Arizona's finest and most posh resorts. If service and superb amenities appeal to you, if you love golf and want to see the desert in its most pristine state of elegance, The Boulders is for you. Reservations are recommended at both restaurants. Room prices include all meals. Golf is extra. $$$; □. (480) 488-9009.

BARTLETT LAKE

To get to Bartlett Lake, continue east on Cave Creek Road about 6 miles. You'll see a fork in the road and a sign to Bartlett Dam Road. Follow the road to the right. It's unimproved, which means dirt, but if you want an adventurous drive, it's for you. The last miles are the roughest. As your teeth jounce inside your mouth, you may wonder why this section of the road isn't paved. You'll understand when you reach this relatively quiet and undisturbed body of water. Boaters and anglers love keeping Bartlett Lake somewhat inaccessible. It gives them acres of water virtually untouched. If you decide to make this trip, know at the outset that the lake is the attraction. Except for a ranger station, there are no facilities here. That's the allure—rustic beauty unmarred by concession stands.

To return to Phoenix, retrace your steps. Follow Bartlett Lake Road to Cave Creek Road and turn south on Scottsdale Road to Scottsdale. From there, it's an easy trip back to Phoenix via Lincoln Drive and Camelback, Indian School, or Thomas Roads.

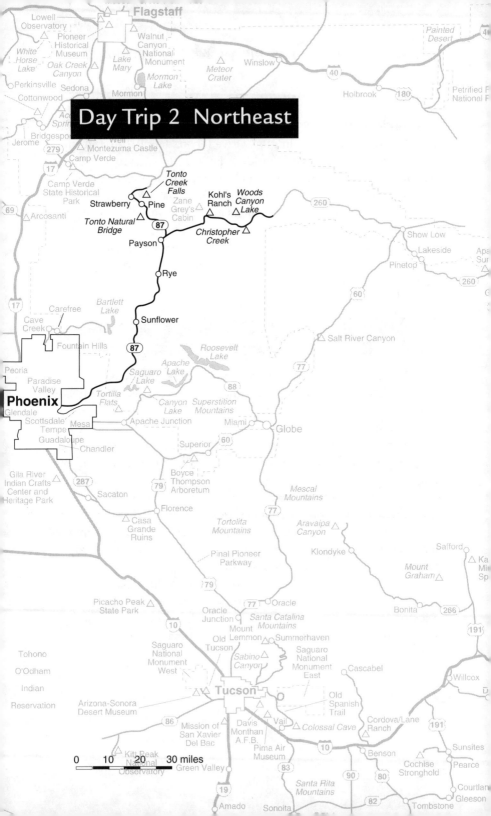

Day Trip 2 Northeast

NORTHEAST

DAY TRIP 2

Payson
Tonto Natural Bridge
Kohl's Ranch

Worth More Time:
Christopher Creek and
Woods Canyon Lake

PAYSON

Beginning with Payson, this excursion features a scenic Arizona highway, elegant in every season. You'll cross the Fort McDowell Indian Reservation, enter the Tonto National Forest, climb through the Mazatal Mountains, and ultimately experience the carved cliffs and dramatic landscape of the Mogollon Rim country. This is an excellent summer getaway and a "must-see" in the autumn. In winter, you'll see cars loaded with ski equipment as families head for the Sunrise ski area. Your main destination is Payson, considered the "Festival Capital" of Arizona. Payson can thank Zane Grey and Grizzly Adams for some of its fame, but nobody can beat Mother Nature for good press.

To reach Payson, head northeast on the Beeline Highway (A-87)—it's right near the border of Scottsdale and Mesa on your map. After crossing the Native American reservation, you'll enter the Tonto National Forest. The road will begin to twist and turn, and you'll pass Sunflower and Rye. Thirteen miles later, you'll reach Payson. Located in the exact center of the state in the world's largest stand of ponderosa pine, Payson sits at 5,000 feet and is a sportsman's paradise.

Founded in 1881 as a gold mining camp, Payson counts tourism as its number-one industry. Payson hosts myriad festivals. Stop in at the Chamber of Commerce, at Beeline Highway and Main Street, to pick up maps and information on what's doing.

53

WHERE TO GO

The Swiss Village. A-87 on the north side of Payson. Friendly people, gingerbread architecture, a good doughnut shop, and lots of gift shops make this a good shopping and refreshment stop.

Rim Country Museum. 700 Green Valley Parkway. This three-building complex, operated by the Northern County Historical Society, offers a reception area, gift shop, archaeology library, two-story exhibit building (handicapped accessible), meeting room, and outdoor picnic area. Exhibits depict northern Gila County history, pioneer families, and archaeology. Open Wednesday through Sunday, 12:00 P.M. to 4:00 P.M. Free. (928) 474-3483.

Zane Grey Museum and Counseller Art. 503 West Main Street. The original Zane Grey cabin was destroyed by fire. This museum contains photos, books, memorabilia, letters, and free video viewings of Zane Grey's life and times. Open Monday through Friday, 10:00 A.M. to 3:00 P.M. Free. Closed on weekends. (928) 474-6243.

TONTO NATURAL BRIDGE

About 12 miles north of Payson on A-87, the world's largest travertine natural bridge arches 183 feet above the streambed. Measuring 150 to 400 feet in width, it is composed of travertine, white limestone, and red coral deposits. The area is laced with ancient Native American caves. The walk down (and back up) to Tonto Natural Bridge is steep and rocky; if you aren't in good shape, you may want to reconsider. Do wear rubber-soled shoes. *Be forewarned,* but also know that the view is well worth the trek. Once you are down at the bridge, obey *all* signs and watch your step.

This is a small place by Arizona standards but is one that rewards the visitor with amazing views. At the bottom of this deep ravine filled with pine and sycamore trees is a cathedral-size chamber, 183 feet high, which has been carved out by a flowing creek. The natural area contains a small waterfall that cascades from the roof of the chamber and creates rainbows across the face of the rock. Natural Bridge is the newest of Arizona's twenty-six state parks and is quite undiscovered by state- and national-park standards. The 160-acre park has recently undergone a $5 million renovation that has paved the road, built parking lots, and renovated the lodge that was built in 1927.

The access road inclines sharply down and ends at the lodge, which is nestled in the wooded valley. To reach the trailhead, park your vehicle ($5.00 charge) and continue to the top of the broad bridge. From here you can look down to the deep gorge below. Turn left and navigate an incredibly steep trail with carved-in-stone steps and metal-cable railings. It is a fun but challenging trek. The Parks Department has created an alternate route down with a gentler incline and easier footing. (Pets are not allowed on trails.)

Both trails go down 180 feet to the bed of Pine Creek. The trails end at the wooden platform built over the creek. Wooden steps down from the platform lead to the chamber. While the footing is slippery in some places, once past the falling water, the shaded chamber is dry and peaceful. This is a good place to sit and enjoy the mystery of this special place. Hikers can continue on, following a set of arrows designed by the Parks Department to keep hikers on the trail. The hike leads upstream past a variety of fantastic sculptures carved by erosion and tumbling rocks. Numerous caves are hidden within the walls. The trail leads to the other side of the bridge along a wooded streambed for about ½ mile. At one point, it leads across the top of another waterfall.

Tonto Natural Bridge was discovered by a prospector, David Gowan, who found the hidden gorge in 1877 while being chased by Apaches. He hid in one of the caves for two nights. Later, he convinced his nephew in Scotland to bring his family to Arizona and live on the property. The nephew, David Gowan Goodfellow, built the lodge and the bridge and opened it to tourists in 1908. The lodge houses a visitor center and a small but excellent museum filled with Gowan Goodfellow family heirlooms. It is available for rental to groups only through advance registration. Open daily except Christmas, weather permitting. Fee. (928) 476–4202.

WHERE TO GO

Tonto Creek Falls. A half mile above the junction of Tonto and Horton Creeks, 10 miles north of Payson, is the site of this natural waterfall. The area around Payson is studded with sylvan splendor, so stop for a cool respite in a busy day of sightseeing.

KOHL'S RANCH

East Highway 260, Payson. Known for its rustic elegance, Kohl's Ranch is a favorite with locals and visitors. Turn right onto A-260 at the junction of A-87 and A-260 and continue 17 miles to the ranch. Be sure to call ahead for breakfast, lunch, or dinner at this longtime Payson landmark. While you're there, enjoy Tonto Creek, which runs through the property. If you have time for a quiet retreat at this rustic lodge, burrow in for a weekend in one of the cabins that dot the property. $$$; ☐. (928) 478-4211.

WORTH MORE TIME: CHRISTOPHER CREEK AND WOODS CANYON LAKE

Hikers and outdoor types will want to continue east another hour on A-260 to see Christopher Creek and Woods Canyon Lake. Both destinations offer excellent opportunities for camping, fishing, boating, and hiking.

Or you may prefer to head north on A-87 another 15 to 20 miles to see the town of Strawberry and, just 3 miles away, its neighbor, Pine. Both communities are nestled in spectacular woodsy settings and offer travelers a taste of rural, rustic Arizona at its best. Although Strawberry has the oldest standing schoolhouse in the state, most tourists come for the views rather than specific sights. If you decide to visit the area, Strawberry and Pine are geared to handle visitors.

From Payson, take A-87 south for a direct return to Phoenix.

Or branch off on A–188 toward Punkin Center and Roosevelt Lake and return on the Apache Trail (A–88), past Tortilla Flat and on into Mesa, Tempe, and Phoenix. This is a secondary road, and part of it is unpaved. The Apache Trail is renowned for its gorgeous scenery. However, if you come back this way, you're in for some steep climbing and curvy driving on a gravel road. (Refer to Day Trip 1 East from Phoenix for more information about the area.)

Salt River Recreation Center
and Saguaro Lake

SALT RIVER RECREATION CENTER AND SAGUARO LAKE

For a real change of pace, take a short drive and a long float down the river. Drive north on A–87 to the Saguaro (Sa-wa-ro) Lake cutoff (Bush Highway). Follow the signs past the entrance to Saguaro Lake and the Salt River Recreation Center.

Saguaro Lake was formed by Stewart Mountain Dam and is one of the several lakes built for water reclamation purposes. You can find out all about tubing at the central office, including where to get in and out on the Salt River. Tubing is fast becoming Arizona's state sport, as a visit to the Blue Point area of the Salt River will attest on any hot day.

Follow the signs to the recreation area's parking lot. Here you'll find a place to rent inner tubes and a bus that takes you to the "put in" spot. Getting into the river involves a slippery descent. While you're tubing, pay attention to signs so you know when to get off the Salt River. At the designated spot, there will be a bus to take you back to the parking lot where you left your car. If you miss the "get off," you'll have to hike back to the bus stop.

Wear shorts or a bathing suit and tennies; pack beverages and an inner tube (or rent one there). Bring sunscreen, friends, rope, a Styrofoam cooler you can lash to an extra tube, and a hat or visor if the day is extremely warm. Be prepared for some gentle, but exciting, rapids. While the water is rarely deep, tubers can get into trouble if they don't

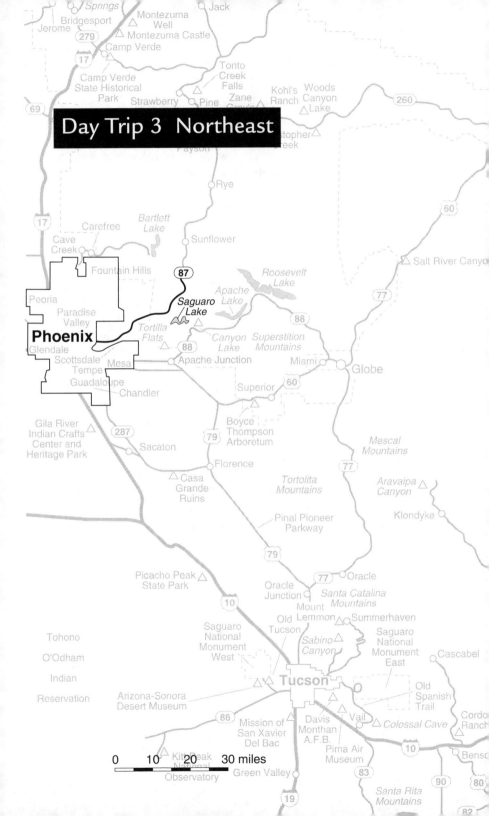

Day Trip 3 Northeast

Jerome
Bridgesport
Springs
Jack
Montezuma Well
Montezuma Castle
Camp Verde
Camp Verde State Historical Park
Strawberry
Pine
Zane Grey's
Tonto Creek Falls
Kohl's Ranch
Woods Canyon Lake
Christopher Creek
Payson
Rye
Carefree
Bartlett Lake
Sunflower
Roosevelt Lake
Salt River Canyon
Cave Creek
Fountain Hills
87
Saguaro Lake
Apache Lake
Peoria
Paradise Valley
Phoenix
Tortilla Flats
Canyon Lake
Superstition Mountains
Glendale
Scottsdale
Mesa
Apache Junction
Miami
Globe
Tempe
Guadaloupe
88
60
Chandler
Superior
Gila River Indian Crafts Center and Heritage Park
287
Sacaton
79
Boyce Thompson Arboretum
Mescal Mountains
Florence
Casa Grande Ruins
Tortolita Mountains
Aravaipa Canyon
77
Klondyke
Pinal Pioneer Parkway
79
Picacho Peak State Park
10
Oracle Junction
77
Oracle
Santa Catalina Mountains
Summerhaven
Tohono
O'Odham
Saguaro National Monument West
Old Tucson
Mount Lemmon
Saguaro National Monument East
Cascabel
Indian
Sabino Canyon
Reservation
Arizona-Sonora Desert Museum
Tucson
Old Spanish Trail
86
Mission of San Xavier Del Bac
Davis Monthan A.F.B.
Vail
Colossal Cave
Cordo Ranch
Pima Air Museum
10
Benso
0 10 20 30 miles
Kitt Peak National Observatory
Green Valley
83
90
80
19
Santa Rita Mountains
82

17
279
69
17
69
260
60
77
88
60

pay attention to the rocks and snags. Tubing is a great way to spend a day from May through September. Life vests are recommended for children. To check on river conditions, call (480) 984-3305.

If getting wet and wild doesn't appeal to you, follow the signs to Saguaro Lake for a more peaceful view of water life.

WHERE TO GO

Fort McDowell Casino. On the Fort McDowell Apache Indian Reservation. On A-87 (known as the Beeline Highway). Going northeast from Fountain Hills, northeast of Scottsdale, you'll see signs announcing the casino before you approach the Saguaro Lake cut-off (Bush Highway). Like other reservations, the Fort McDowell tribe has discovered a steady source of income. Games run every day and night, and the crowds pour in. Although this is no competition for Las Vegas or even Laughlin, Nevada (just across the Colorado River from Arizona), this casino is very popular. (480) 837-1424.

Fort McDowell Adventures. On the Fort McDowell Apache Indian Reservation. Fort McDowell Adventures offers trail rides, cattle drives, hayrides, river rafting, jeep tours, overnight pack trips, desert cookouts, and trailrides. Enjoy the beauty of unspoiled open desert near the Verde River and have great outdoor fun. Open all year. (480) 816-6465. www.fortmcdowelladventures.com.

Saguaro Lake. Eight miles north of Shea Boulevard on SR-88 at the Saguaro Lake Marina. Saguaro Lake is a popular summer destination for all water sports. For a less rugged experience, take a ride on the *Desert Belle,* an 86-foot stern-wheeler. Day tours are offered for one-hour narrated cruises. Fee. (480) 671-0000.

Precision Boating. Rent a boat to fully enjoy a day on the lake. Call the Arizona Marine Office, (480) 986-0969.

Saguaro Lake Excursion. Cruise the lake on a paddle boat. Fee. For schedule information call (480) 984-5311. E-mail: saguaro lake@aol.com

Usery Mountain Park. At Bush Highway and Usery Pass Road. Continue on Bush Highway to Usery Pass Road. Turn left onto Usery Pass Road and follow it for 2 or 3 miles to this elegant mountain park. Spend time hiking the well-marked nature trails, or riding (if you trailer in your own horses). This is one of the nicest mountain parks "out in the tules." For useful information call (602) 506-2930.

WHERE TO EAT

Lake Shore Inn Restaurant. At the Saguaro Lake Marina. 14011 North Bush Highway, Mesa. A full-service menu features down-home fare. Come for biscuits and gravy at breakfast, barbecued chicken and sandwiches at lunch, and steaks and seafood at dinner. Call for hours. $$; ☐. (480) 984-5311.

WHERE TO STAY

Saguaro Lake Guest Ranch. 13020 Bush Highway, Mesa. Follow Shea Boulevard to A-88. Continue to the Saguaro Lake turnoff and follow signs. Privately owned and operated since the 1930s, this rustic ranch is nestled beneath towering red cliffs that border the Salt River. The drive to the ranch is worth the time just for the view. If you take a raft trip with the Cimarron River Company, which floats the river here, guides will point out the eagles' nests high on the cliffs. Float trips offer all the fun of white-water rafting without the fear of rapids. This section of the Salt is scenic and serene, and wildlife abounds. Cardinals and Baltimore orioles can be seen flitting through the trees in the spring.

The twenty-five cabins are comfortable, clean, and air-conditioned. Many hold four people comfortably. The lodge includes a large room dominated by a huge river-rock fireplace, piano, and bookshelves stuffed with books. The dining room is equally spacious. There's even a small swimming pool to cool you off on a hot spring day.

Call ahead to reserve a cottage for an overnight or make reservations for lunch or dinner as part of a day's outing.

From the ranch you can also take two- and three-hour trail rides that offer gorgeous views of Four Peaks, Saguaro Lake, and the desert. $$; ☐. Closed from late May to September except for special groups. (480) 984-2194.

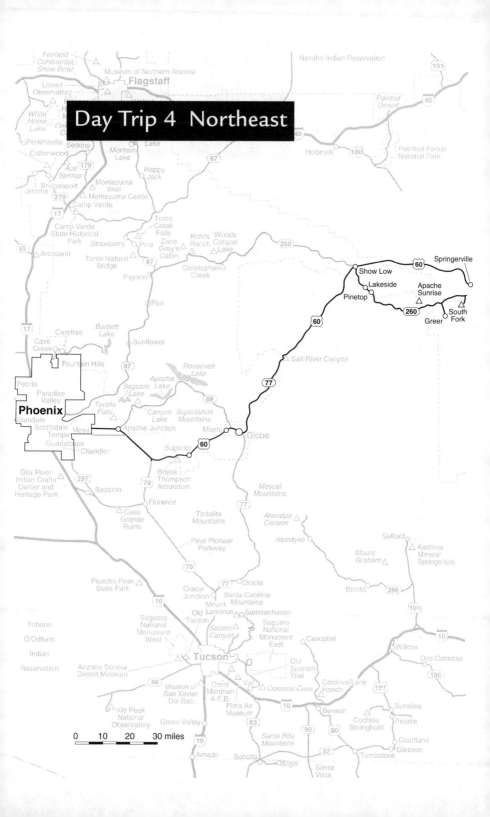

Day Trip 4 Northeast

Springerville and Casa
Malpais Pueblo

Day Trips 4 and 5 are "Arizona style," which means long hauls for a single-day adventure. If, though, you have the stamina—or better yet, a night to stay over—these places have much to offer, including activities not found anywhere else in the state.

SPRINGERVILLE AND CASA MALPAIS PUEBLO

Head northeast from Phoenix on US-60, 220 miles to Springerville, home of Casa Malpais Pueblo. Springerville is a small town (approximately 2,000 people) set amid great beauty.

Casa Malpais. 318 East Main Street. On US-60. A National Historic Landmark, this was once the site of a thriving city that was occupied for about 200 years and then mysteriously abandoned in about A.D. 1400.

The museum opened in 1991, although the first professional anthropologist, Frank Cushing, visited the area in 1883. While the area is miles away from the Colorado or New Mexico border, the pottery found here is similar to that found in the Four Corners region.

The "House of the Badlands," or Casa Malpais, overlooks the Little Colorado River's Round Valley. From the site, there is a breathtaking view of the White Mountains, which lie to the south.

What makes this archaeological site so special is that the museum and field laboratories are open to the public. Guided tours are available for a fee, and participatory workshops are given in both education and excavation. Call for tour information. Museum entrance is free. (928) 333–5375.

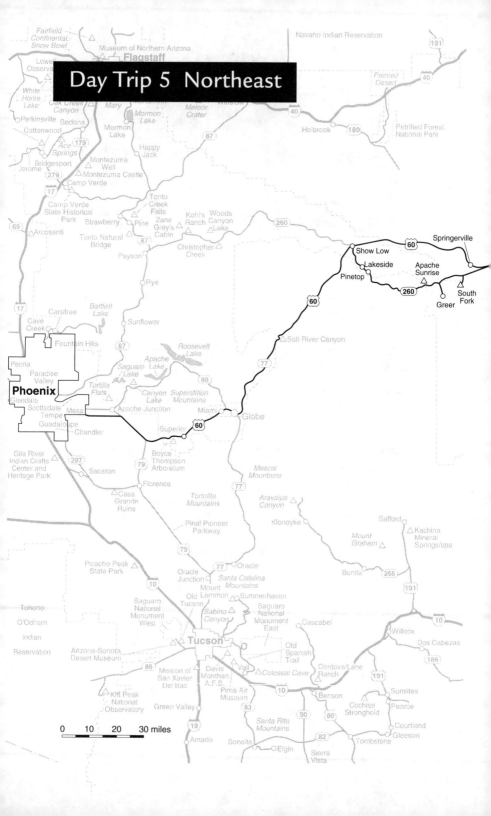

Day Trip 5 Northeast

Greer · South Fork
Sunrise

GREER

From Springerville, head southwest for 13 miles to Greer. You'll pass by South Fork Canyon before finding this small mountain village 5 miles south of A-260. Greer is perched at 8,525 feet, which makes it an ideal destination year-round. The area is a sportsman's paradise that offers fishing, backpacking, ice skating, sleigh rides, and downhill and cross-country skiing. In cooperation with the U.S. Forestry Service, Greer has developed 35 miles of cross-country ski trails.

WHAT TO DO

Butterfly Lodge Museum. Southeast corner of the intersection of SR-373 and CR-1126. Open Memorial Day through Labor Day, this historic lodge was the mountain residence and hunting lodge of author James Willard Schultz and his son, the artist Hart Merriam Schultz, known as Lone Wolf. The Butterfly Lodge Museum is listed on the National Register of Historic Places and was built in 1913-14. Schultz was an advocate for Native American rights and was influential in obtaining citizenship and voting rights for Native Americans. The authentic furnishings and artifacts illustrate the colorful careers of both father and son. Fee; children free. (928) 735-7514. www.wmonline.com/butterflylodge.htm; e-mail: bfylodge@aol.com.

WHERE TO STAY

Red Setter Inn. 8 CR-1120 or P.O. Box 133, Greer 85927. From Phoenix, take US-60 to Globe. Continue on 60 to Show Low. Then take A-260 east to Greer Junction, A-373. The inn is at the end of A-373. This no-smoking and no-kids upscale bed and breakfast can accommodate eighteen to twenty guests who enjoy seeing the great outdoors from relaxing Adirondack chairs. Formal landscaping is kept to a minimum. Each room opens onto a small private deck or large common deck. Common rooms provide guests with more places to read and relax, and the innkeepers offer guests plenty of books and magazines. The Red Setter Inn was voted Arizona's Best Bed and Breakfast by the *Arizona Republic* in 1996. The inn does not have a liquor license, and a minimum of two nights is required during the weekend. Included in all room rates is a full cooked breakfast and a sack picnic lunch for guests who stay two nights or longer. $$; ☐. (928) 735-7441. www.redsetterinn.com.

SOUTH FORK

WHERE TO STAY

Sierra Springs Ranch. 101 Sky High Road, Pinetop. Located in Arizona's White Mountains, Sierra Springs Ranch was once a high-country working cattle ranch. With five unique, luxurious cottages located on seventy-six acres, the ranch can accommodate up to fourteen people. Each cottage boasts its own individual decor, and the lodge offers a full exercise and fitness center as well as a game room. To reach the property, turn on Bucksprings Road (1 mile from Pinetop), drive %10 mile, and turn left on SkyHi Road. Drive 2 miles to Sierra Springs Ranch. $$-$$$; ☐. For information write: P.O. Box 32100, Pinetop 85935. For reservations call (928) 369-3900. www.sierra springsranch.com.

South Fork Guest Ranch. Located between Springerville and Sunrise, right off A-260, 5 miles east of the Greer Junction, this family-owned guest ranch sits on the banks of the Little Colorado River and South Fork Creek. You may roam through thirty-eight wooded acres as you picnic or participate in lots of recreation opportunities. There are seventeen units, many featuring multiple bedrooms. All cottages are equipped with dishes, silverware, pots, pans, linens, coffeepot, and toaster. During the winter, there's a minimum stay of two nights; in summer, four nights. $$–$$$; ☐. For information write Box 627, Springerville 85938. For reservations call (928) 333-4455.

SUNRISE

Sunrise Park Resort. P.O. Box 217, McNary 85930. This is a fully developed downhill ski area with a lodge, restaurant, and ski school located on the White Mountain Apache Indian Reservation. The mountains offer a variety of challenges, and the snow is often excellent. Open all year long, in the summer the area is a center for hiking and mountain biking as well as fishing and sailing on Sunrise Lake. Horseback riding, in-line skating, archery tournaments, and volleyball are also scheduled. In the winter, call for snow conditions and reservations. (800) 772-SNOW. E-mail: sunrise@cybertrails.com. Sunrise Sport Center, or (928) 735-7669.

To return to Phoenix, continue east on A-260 to Show Low and the junction of US-60. Follow US-60 east to Phoenix.

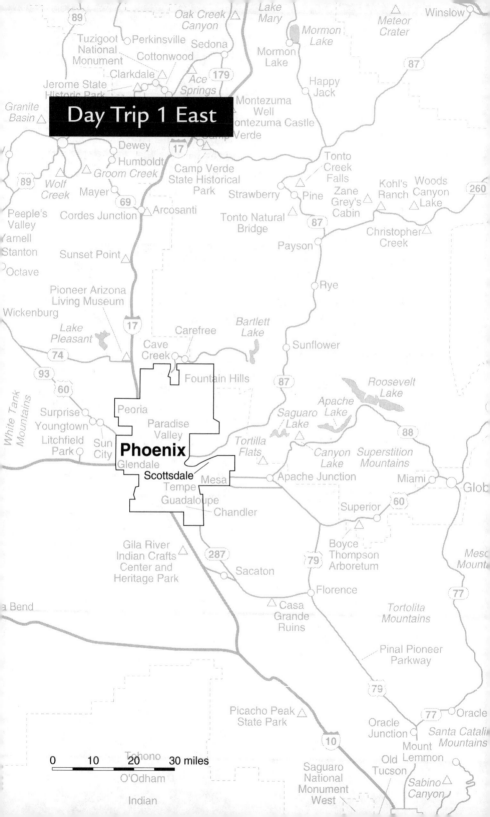

Day Trip 1 East

89 · Oak Creek Canyon · Lake Mary · Mormon Lake · Meteor Crater · Winslow

Tuzigoot National Monument · Perkinsville · Sedona · Cottonwood · Mormon Lake · 87

Clarkdale · 179 · Happy Jack

Jerome State Historic Park · Ace Springs

Granite Basin · Montezuma Well · Montezuma Castle · Tonto Creek Falls · Kohl's Ranch · Woods Canyon Lake · 260

Dewey · Camp Verde · Camp Verde State Historical Park · Strawberry · Pine · Zane Grey's Cabin

89 · Humboldt · *Groom Creek* · Wolf Creek · Mayer · 69 · Arcosanti · Tonto Natural Bridge · 87 · Christopher Creek

Peeple's Valley · Cordes Junction · Payson

Yarnell · Stanton · Sunset Point · Rye

Octave

Pioneer Arizona Living Museum · Sunflower

Wickenburg · 17 · Carefree · *Bartlett Lake*

Lake Pleasant · Cave Creek · *Roosevelt Lake*

74 · Fountain Hills · 87

93 · 60 · Peoria · *Apache Lake* · 88

White Tank Mountains · Surprise · Youngtown · Paradise Valley · *Saguaro Lake* · Superstition Mountains

Litchfield Park · Sun City · **Phoenix** · *Tortilla Flats* · *Canyon Lake* · Miami · Glob

Glendale · Scottsdale · Mesa · Apache Junction · 60

Tempe · Superior · *Meso Mount*

Guadaloupe · Chandler · Boyce Thompson Arboretum

Gila River Indian Crafts Center and Heritage Park · 287 · 79

Sacaton · Florence · *Tortolita Mountains* · 77

a Bend · *Casa Grande Ruins* · Pinal Pioneer Parkway

Picacho Peak State Park · 79

Tohono · O'Odham · 77 · Oracle

Oracle Junction · *Santa Catali Mountains*

Mount Lemmon · Old Tucson

10 · Saguaro National Monument West · *Sabino Canyon*

Indian

0 · 10 · 20 · 30 miles

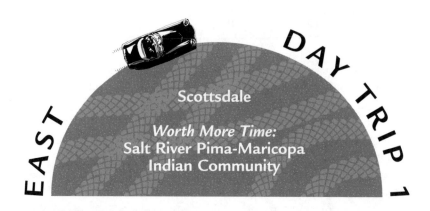

EAST

DAY TRIP 1

Scottsdale

Worth More Time:
Salt River Pima-Maricopa
Indian Community

SCOTTSDALE

No trip around Phoenix is complete without a day in Scottsdale. Famous as "The West's Most Western Town," Scottsdale is the shopping and art hub of the Valley of the Sun. It's difficult to believe that only a few decades ago Scottsdale Road was unpaved and cowboys rode into town on Saturday night to whoop it up. Today it's a gathering spot for art aficionados, dedicated shoppers, and gourmets.

Follow Glendale Avenue east to Scottsdale. East of Sixteenth Street, Glendale becomes Lincoln Drive. Continue east on Lincoln Drive and, as you near Twenty-fourth Street and Lincoln, look to your left. There's Squaw Peak, one of Phoenix's in-town mountain parks. Fit Phoenicians routinely climb Squaw Peak—some do this daily. If you have time and good walking shoes, turn toward the mountain at the sign to the park and explore a bit.

Continue on Lincoln Drive to Scottsdale Road. You'll pass through the town of Paradise Valley (not to be confused with the Paradise Valley area of Phoenix). This is a wealthy residential community of one-acre-plus home sites and a few well-manicured resorts. Paradise Valley is nestled between Mummy Mountain to the north and Camelback Mountain to the south.

Turn south onto Scottsdale Road and head into town for shopping and browsing. Later, you'll drive north to see other attractions. Scottsdale prides itself on its thriving downtown, outstanding art galleries, and variety of fine restaurants. During the tourist season (October through April), be prepared for traffic.

Scottsdale is named for Gen. Winfield Scott, and, although it has only come of age as a city, the town has long been a favorite vacation spot. Turn-of-the-twentieth-century residents rented out rooms and screened sleeping porches to visitors. Scottsdale's civic history is punctuated with innovation and creativity. City fathers got on the urban redevelopment bandwagon early and turned a run-down section of downtown into a showcase for business and government. They were also instrumental in developing the flood-prone Indian Bend Wash into a series of green city parks and lakes. Today this beautiful, nationally acclaimed park runs the entire length of town along Hayden Boulevard. Every day of the year you can find activity there—from roller skating, fishing, and soccer to volleyball, baseball, and jogging.

WHERE TO GO

Fifth Avenue. As you head south on Scottsdale Road, turn west onto Fifth Avenue (there's a light). Drive slowly and look for a free parking space anywhere along the street. The city also maintains several free lots. This shopping area is replete with boutiques and gift shops. Fifth Avenue ultimately meets Indian School Road, a main east–west thoroughfare. Bring plenty of cash and be ready to browse.

Craftsman's Court. Running south from Fifth Avenue, 1 block west of Scottsdale Road. If you don't know it's there, you can miss this charming section. Walk down this narrow, short street to discover specialty shops and a quaint patio setting.

Marshall Way. Intersects with Fifth Avenue, 1 block west of Craftsman's Court. Marshall Way is also a unique street. Some places to visit here include:

Art One. 4120 North Marshall Way. Emerging artists are featured in two galleries that always are fun to explore. Some featured artists are students at Arizona State University. (480) 946–5076.

Bentley Gallery. 4161 North Marshall Way. Bentley carries provocative, fine contemporary art and sculpture in an elegant gallery setting. A "must" for contemporary art-lovers. (480) 946–6060.

Gallery Materia. 4222 North Marshall Way. More a mini-museum than a crafts gallery, Gallery Materia features nationally recognized craftspeople. Shows are held for artists. If you enjoy seeing the best in sophisticated contemporary crafts, this is the place for you. (480) 949-1262.

Lisa Sette Gallery. 4142 North Marshall Way. The most "New York" space in Scottsdale, this gallery features very fine and very contemporary art and photographs. Museum quality shows are mounted. Owner Lisa Sette is knowledgeable and approachable. (480) 990-7342.

Occasions!. 4223 North Marshall Way. This shop elevates tablewear to an art, combining innovative design with elegant accessories. Also shown is contemporary and abstract artwork. (480) 423-0506 or (800) 482-2532.

Waddell Gallery. 4251 North Marshall Way. The gallery features the finest Native American artists, jewelers, and sculpters. A good stop if you are gallery browsing. (480) 949-1596.

MAIN STREET

During your stroll through the Fifth Avenue area, be sure to wander along Stetson Drive, Seventieth Street (recently renamed Goldwater Boulevard), and Sixth Avenue as well. Once you have covered Fifth Avenue, you're ready to move on to Main Street. Main Street is lined with western and traditional art galleries, and this area, more than any other in Scottsdale, reflects the city's emphasis on the arts. More than ninety galleries serve a town of 130,000, and you quickly realize that painting, sculpture, and crafts are big business here.

To reach Main Street, drive east on Fifth Avenue to Scottsdale Road. Turn south on Scottsdale Road and turn west at Main Street. Later you'll turn east to visit Old Town Scottsdale and its shops.

WHERE TO GO

You'll notice immediately that east of Scottsdale Road, Scottsdale's Old Town area projects an "Old West" image. The pedestrian crossing areas are set off in simulated brick, and the sidewalks along Main Street are shaded by wooden-shingled porticos extending from the buildings. These serve a practical as well as an aesthetic purpose. During the hot summer months, when temperatures climb upward to 110 degrees, the roofs afford essential shade.

Park free anywhere on Main Street. If you arrive in Scottsdale during the tourist season (October through April), do attend one of the Thursday evening art walks, when galleries host open houses and openings.

Art enthusiasts will discover that Main Street represents a mix of styles and schools. Many collectors visit Scottsdale because of its fine western, contemporary, Native American, and graphic art galleries for artifacts, home accessories, and antiques.

One to check out is **Bill Faust Gallery,** 7103 East Main Street. Bill is the nephew of the legendary Lovena Ohl and he continues her tradition of showcasing the finest contemporary Native American artists. Among the "name" artists who show here are Larry Golsh and Harvey Begay, both acclaimed as masters of contemporary Native American jewelry. Faust's gallery includes a superb collection of collector Native American textiles, intriguing sculpture and sculptural furniture, paintings, and kachina dolls. Extraordinarily knowledgeable, Faust is a gentle man who knows his art and his artists and only displays the highest quality work. Even collectors not interested in Native American art should make this shop a "must" on any Scottsdale tour. (480) 946–6345.

A sampling of other fine galleries on Main Street:

Joan Cawley Gallery. 7135 East Main Street. Showcases American contemporary and southwest imagery. A long-time favorite. (480) 947-3548; www.jcgltd.com.

Husberg Fine Arts. 7137 East Main Street. The finest western and representational fine art is showcased in this inviting gallery. (480) 947-7489.

Vanier Galleries. 7106 East Main Street. A wonderful, large space filled with eclectic sculpture and art, from representational to ultra-contemporary. (480) 946-7507.

Victoria Boyce Galleries. 7130 East Main Street. The owner selects uniformly superb contemporary art and photographic art for her distinctive shows. (480) 941-2494.

As you cross Scottsdale Road, heading east on Main Street, another world opens—one dedicated to the Old West. Park on Main Street east of Scottsdale Road, walk east to Brown Street, and then turn north. This area is a mecca for tourists; shops range from junk to funk—with some fine jewelry and clothing shops that feature western wear tossed in for good measure.

Stroll north on Brown Street toward Indian School Road for more browsing at Pima Plaza. Located on First Avenue between Scottsdale

Road and Brown, Pima Plaza has restaurants, art galleries, and unusual shops, including one devoted to music boxes.

CIVIC CENTER MALL

The Civic Center Mall area backs up to Old Town. Once a run-down section of Scottsdale, it is now a source of pride. The government complex includes the Scottsdale City Hall, City Court, Library, and Center for the Arts, all designed by local architect Bennie Gonzales. The rolling lawns of the mall also act as an outdoor art museum for an impressive collection of contemporary sculpture.

WHERE TO GO

Historic Old Town Walking Tour. At the Little Red Schoolhouse on Civic Center Mall, pick up a self-guided walking tour guide to fourteen destinations including the Center for the Arts and the Scottsdale Library. The Little Red Schoolhouse is almost in the center of the original Scottsdale town site. It was built in 1909 at a cost of $4,500 and had two classrooms for grades one through eight.

From the 1920s until the 1960s, the area around the schoolhouse contained a barrio, or neighborhood, that began when Mexican laborers and their families arrived to work in the cotton fields that surrounded Scottsdale.

Walking west to Brown Street, you can see the next points of interest at the corner of Brown and Main Streets. **Bischoff's Shades of the West** is a western collectibles store today, but in 1897 it was the site of the first general store. By the 1940s it was an arts and crafts center called Arizona Craftsmen. **Affordable Elegance/Cactus Cones** still has a portion of the original adobe wall visible. Walking south on Brown Avenue, you see **Our Lady of Perpetual Help Catholic Church,** which today is the home of the Scottsdale Symphony. Built in 1933 by volunteer labor and donated materials, it consists of 14,000 adobe blocks, each weighing fifty pounds.

Continuing south on Brown to **Cavaliers's Blacksmith Shop** brings you to what was the edge of town. The original building was tin. The Cavaliers still own and operate it and, along with conventional smithing, produce ornamental wrought-iron items.

Heading east on Second Street brings you to **Los Olivos** restaurant, established by the Corral family more than fifty years ago. It was named for the olive trees that lined the street, which were planted in 1895 by Gen. Winfield Scott, the founder of the town. From here the tour continues to the **Scottsdale Center for the Arts, Scottsdale Library,** and **Scottsdale Historical Museum.**

Scottsdale Historical Museum. 7333 Scottsdale Mall. In the area of Brown and Main Streets, this museum includes photographs, furniture, and other items that depict Scottsdale's early days. Free. www.scottsdalemuseum.com.

The Scottsdale Library. 3839 Civic Center Plaza. Stop in to enjoy the architecture and ambience. Visit the Arizona room as well. Here you'll see displays featuring items from Arizona history—from rare books to silver saddles.

This is worth a trip just to enjoy the architecture of the new wing. Note the dove of peace that "floats" high above the entrance; the image is naturally projected by sunlight. Also marvel at the magnificent quill pen that hovers above the inkwell. The children's section is fun and offers enticing places to get turned on to books and reading.

The Scottsdale Center for the Arts. 7380 East Second Street. This facility boasts a theater for the performing arts and a visual arts gallery. Both the theater and gallery feature outstanding, nationally known artists. In addition, the Scottsdale Arts Center Association sponsors special events during the year, including an outdoor crafts show. There's also a unique gallery shop for browsing. Admission to the center is free, but performances and exhibits often have fees. The gift shop is one of the best secrets of the city. Shop for unusual objets d'art, jewelry, books, and other unique items—all very well priced. Check with the box office for schedules. (480) 994–ARTS. www.scottsdalecvb.com.

Scottsdale Museum of Contemporary Art. 7374 East Second Street. Located next to the Scottsdale Center for the Arts, the museum building is the work of well-known Phoenix architect Will Bruder and is worth a visit just to see Bruder's vision. Inside is a sometimes controversial but always interesting collection of fine contemporary art, architecture, and design. The museum is billed as a "laboratory" for exploration and inquiry. Fee. (480) 994–2787. www.scottsdalearts.org.

Trailside Galleries. 7330 Scottsdale Mall. Western art lovers will find much to enjoy at this gallery, where a variety of works by important artists is featured. (480) 945-7751.

FASHION SQUARE AREA

For more shop-'til-you-drop, head for Fashion Square at Scottsdale Road and Camelback. What used to be two malls is now a mega-mall that ranks as the largest in the valley. Wander through several department stores and browse through row upon row of boutiques. Dine at fine and casual restaurants.

This mall stretches across Camelback Road with a "bridge" of new shops that connects Nordstrom's to the main mall. Parking is ample and available near Nordstrom's, Neiman Marcus, and Robinson's. The mall looks massive, and it is. Inside are all the best chains, from Tiffany to Banana Republic, plus some unique Arizona shops.

THE BORGATA

For a taste of Rodeo Drive Arizona-style, continue north on Scottsdale Road to one traffic light north of McDonald Drive. You'll see what looks like a fortress on the left. This is the Borgata. (When it was new, locals called it "Fort Ostentatious," but since then it has won the hearts and minds of all.) It was designed to resemble an ancient Italian village. Why Italy in the midst of Arizona? Who knows? As you stroll through the interior brick courtyard, you'll find a clutch of Arizona's—and the world's—most chic shops. Friday afternoons through May there's a fun farmer's market with live music.

Complete the day with a visit to The Cosanti Foundation and Taliesin West, north on Scottsdale Road. Finish up with some Arizona mountain scenery on your way to Fountain Hills, a scenic planned community, where you'll see the world's tallest fountain.

NORTH SCOTTSDALE

These destinations are north of Shea Boulevard and east of Scottsdale Road.

The Desert Center at Pinnacle Peak. 8711 Pinnacle Peak Road. Travel north on Pima Road to Pinnacle Peak Road. Turn west (left) to the Desert Center at Pinnacle Peak, which is located in a quaint Mexican-style village center. The center specializes in bringing the essence of the Sonoran Desert to life through hands-on scientific experiences. Ethnobotany, archaeology, and ancient Native American skills are featured for groups. Desert aficionados will want to do a morning or afternoon at The Desert Center. Tours are available by reservation. The scenery in North Scottsdale, under the nose of Pinnacle Peak, is straight out of a western film. Call for information about hours. Free (but donations preferred). (480) 473-0338.

The Fleischer Museum. 17207 North Perimeter Drive. Take Pima Road north, crossing Frank Lloyd Wright Boulevard (Bell Road). Take the first left past Frank Lloyd Wright. Continue ½ mile to Perimeter Drive. Turn right to this impressive museum. More than 200 paintings by more than eighty artists create a comprehensive study of the California School of American Impressionism, which flourished from the late 1800s to 1940. Free. (480) 585-3108.

Out of Africa. Fountain Hills. Follow Shea Boulevard east to Beeline Highway. Turn left on Bee Line and follow it for 2 miles. Watch carefully for the turnoff to the Fort McDowell Indian Reservation and follow the OUT OF AFRICA sign, which you'll see on your right. Here you'll find a rustic but unique demonstration of the relationship that can exist between big cats and people. The cats—lions, tigers, leopards, etc.—are in habitats; the people are walking all around them. The owners of Out of Africa put on "shows," which are really lectures about the cats' behavior. While both adults and young children will enjoy this outing, be prepared to sit and watch for an hour and a half at least. Snacks and drinks are available. This "bare bones" operation, although not a park in any of the usual senses, nevertheless offers a fascinating insight into these magnificent creatures. Often visitors can pet lion cubs and get to know the cats personally. The idea for Out of Africa began with psychological research on big cats. Call ahead for show times and tours. Open all year. Fee. (480) 837-7779 or (480) 837-6683.

The Cosanti Foundation. 6433 Doubletree Ranch Road. As you leave the Borgata, go north on Scottsdale Road to Doubletree Ranch Road at the fourth stoplight. Turn west and watch for the sign to The Cosanti Foundation on the south side of the street. Wander through Paolo Soleri's enchanted studio. You'll be fascinated by the Soleri wind chimes; made and sold on the premises, they make wonderful Arizona keepsakes. You also can ask to see the scale model for Arcosanti, the prototype community that Soleri is building in the desert north of Phoenix. Donation suggested. (480) 948-6145.

Taliesin West. Scottsdale Road to Shea Boulevard. Turn east on Shea for about 4 miles and make a left at Via Linda. Go approximately ⁹⁄₁₀ mile and turn left at North 108th Street. Follow that to Taliesin West.

Taliesin West is the headquarters for Taliesin Associated Architects and an architectural school that teaches the design principles and philosophy of Frank Lloyd Wright, one of America's most respected architects. Wright died in 1959, but his belief that environment and structure should blend into a total harmony continues to influence architects throughout the world. Call for information on night nature-walk tours.

"Under construction" since the 1930s, Taliesin West has been built and maintained by professionals and students who live and work there. (The original Taliesin was built in Wisconsin in the early 1900s.) The structures serve as a living testimony to Wright's enduring genius.

The compound is constructed of native Arizona materials, and the main building is positioned and designed to take full advantage of the warm winter sun. Hour-long tours given by Taliesin staff and students are available daily. These talks are exceptionally informative. Ask about the new tours that are available, such as tours of apprentice homes and studios. Be sure to save plenty of time to browse through the bookstore—it is a treasure trove of memorabilia about Mr. Wright as well as a great resource center for architecture. Closed during the summer. Call for information. Fee. (480) 860-8810.

Rawhide. 23023 North Scottsdale Road. On Scottsdale Road, 4 miles north of Bell Road. Privately owned, this authentic 1880s town is a great stop for families. It has shops, a museum, an ice cream parlor, a stagecoach ride, and more. If you visit during July and August, wear a hat, because the "town" is hot and dusty. You'll get a real appreciation for the Arizona pioneers. See the Conestoga wagon and hear the story of what it was like to come west. Authentic Native American dances are performed daily, and the more than twenty shops sell handmade jewelry and crafts. Admission is free, but fees are charged for various rides and activities. Hours change according to season, so call ahead. (480) 502-1880.

Arizona Cowboy College. 30208 North 152nd Street. If the Cowboy life entices, Arizona Cowboy College offers the real thing in workshops that run as one-week camps. No frills—just thrills—it operates on a ranch in North Scottsdale and on a working cattle ranch in northern Arizona. Great for cowboys and cowgals who want a taste of real cowboy life and have had a hankerin' to learn to ride and rope. Classes often are scheduled to coincide with fall and spring roundups. Fee. (480) 471-3151 or (888) 330-8070. www.cowboy college.com.

WHERE TO EAT

While Scottsdale is renowned for restaurants, these special places serve up unique Arizona atmosphere.

El Chorro Lodge. 5550 East Lincoln Drive, across from Marriott's Mountain Shadows Resort. A "must" for visitors and a longtime favorite of locals, El Chorro offers a large patio for outside dining. During the cooler months, this patio is perfumed with mesquite smoke that drifts from the big outdoor fireplace. Inside El Chorro, diners have their choice of rooms that meander through the old lodge. Owners Evie and Joe Miller pride themselves on the fine, home-cooked menu. El Chorro "sticky buns," made with pure butter, grace each table. $$$; □. (480) 948-5170.

Handlebar-J. 7116 East Becker Lane. One block northwest of Shea Boulevard off Scottsdale Road. Good for steaks and ribs and live country music, this is a place locals frequent to eat and dance country-western. Tourists should try the house special drink. $$; □. (480) 948-0110.

Medizona. 7217 East Fourth Avenue. Medizona is located 2 blocks north of Indian School Road in Old Town Scottsdale. This restaurant is a creation of chef Lenard Rubin, who has shown the world his innovative Southwestern specialties as a guest chef at hotels and restaurants around the world. In his intimate and colorful new restaurant, Rubin creatively brings together the savory flavors of the Southwest and Mediterranean cuisine. $$–$$$. The restaurant is open for dinner only, Tuesday through Saturday. For reservations call (480) 947-9500. E-mail: Medizona@prodigy.net.

Pinnacle Peak Patio. 10426 East Jomax Road, Scottsdale. To get there, take Scottsdale Road north toward East Shea Boulevard. Turn right onto North Greenway Hayden loop, then turn right onto East Bell Road. Turn left onto North Perimeter Drive. Next, turn right onto East Princess Drive, then turn left onto North Pima Road. Turn right onto East Happy Valley Road and turn left onto North Alma School Road. Finally, turn left onto Pinnacle Peak Parkway, and then turn right onto East Jomax Road. You can't miss this huge rambling complex, which is famous for mesquite broiled steaks, as well as for cutting off the neckties of unsuspecting "dudes" who come into a cowboy place too dressed up. There is indoor seating for 2,400 and outdoor accommodations for nearly 6,000. If you take an unsuspecting friend, make sure he wears an old tie, because Pinnacle Peak Patio is merciless. (After the tie is cut, it is displayed along with the owner's business card.) Stay for dancing to live cowboy music, or walk off your dinner by strolling around the grounds or browsing in the shops. $$; ☐. Open daily. (480) 585-1599. www.arizona-restaurants.com/scotts.htm.

Rancho Pinot Grill. 6208 North Scottsdale Road, located on the west side of Scottsdale Road in a corner shopping mall just south of Lincoln Drive and immediately north of the Borgata shopping center. This is an informal gourmet dining experience that features dishes prepared with fresh, local ingredients. The sophisticated dining area is decorated with cowboy memorabilia. A long wooden bar is a great place to wait for your table, sipping a glass of wine from their outstanding collection of wines. This is a local favorite, so call for reservations. The restaurant is open for dinner only and is closed Sunday and Monday. $$$; ☐. (480) 468-9463.

Rawhide. 23023 North Scottsdale Road. Head north on Scottsdale Road, 4 miles north of Bell Road. Steaks, chicken, and ribs are served in a western dance-hall atmosphere. This is especially recommended for families since young children are welcome. *Hint:* You can also enjoy the ambience by visiting the saloon, where you'll find live country-western music served by waitresses in full Gay 1890s regalia. $$; ☐. (480) 502-5600.

WHERE TO STAY

Scottsdale is a mecca of resorts. Here are a few favorites.

Four Seasons Resort at Troon North. 10600 East Crescent Moon Drive. The newest luxury resort to open in Scottsdale, Four Seasons appears like a contemporary pueblo village terraced against the mountainscape of North Scottsdale. With golf privileges at nearby Troon North golf course, this ultra-posh but super-comfortable resort features an intimate and excellent fine-dining restaurant, a full-service and elegant spa, four tennis courts, and a multilevel swimming pool. A special feature is the children's pool, where pint-size teak lounge chairs are positioned next to Mom and Dad's. $$$; ☐. (480) 515–5700.

Hyatt Regency Scottsdale at Gainey Ranch. 7500 East Double Tree Ranch Road. Contemporary architecture, great golf, tennis, and a pool featuring a sand beach are part of the charm here. You can ride a gondola on the lake and have dinner at one of the hotel restaurants.

Another reason to stay at this beautiful hotel is to see the Hopi Cultural Center. The Hyatt Regency Scottsdale has made a strong commitment to the Hopi. A small exhibition is run by Hopi "hosts" who share some of their culture with hotel guests. A visit to the Hopi Cultural Center is the next best thing to making a trip to the Hopi reservation. The hotel's fine-dining restaurant, The Golden Swan, continues this commitment by including native foods as ingredients in some of the cuisine. $$$; ☐. (480) 991–3388.

Hermosa Inn. 5532 North Palo Cristi Road. Take Fortieth Street to Stanford Drive and turn west, following Stanford to Palo Cristi (Thirty-sixth Street). You'll see the sign on the northwest corner of the intersection. This is an old, small resort that was recently "saved" by a local developer with an eye for history. The low-slung buildings are surrounded by green lawns. The rooms are spacious and well designed, and the dining room is cozy and delightful with a great bar area for relaxing. Homey but chic, this hotel has been a local favorite since it was reopened. $$$; ☐. (602) 955–8614.

Marriott's Camelback Inn Resort Spa and Golf Club. 5402 East Lincoln Drive. The Camelback Inn has maintained its four-star, five-diamond rating since the awards were introduced. It features sprawling grounds, elegant pools, and one of the most complete and beautiful spas in the valley. Casitas are private and tucked away under the shadow of Mummy Mountain. $$$; ☐. (480) 948–1700. www.camelbackinn.com.

Marriott's Mountain Shadows Resort. 5641 East Lincoln Drive. One of the old grand resorts in the area, it boasts fabulous gardens and a lovely pool. There's a challenging eighteen-hole, par-3 course on the grounds. Tennis and health club facilities are also available. Restaurants are excellent. $$$; ☐. (480) 948–7111. www.marriott.com.

The Phoenician. 6000 East Camelback Road. The newest and most lavish resort in the valley, it features rolling golf courses, a jungle swimming pool setting, and a nature trail with more than one hundred kinds of cactus along the way. Rooms are oversized; suites are vast. Sunday brunch is the best in the valley. $$$; ☐. (480) 941–8200. www.thephoenician.com.

Sanctuary Camelback Mountain. 5700 East MacDonald. This renovated, upscale boutique resort is a luxurious hideaway high on the north face of Camelback Mountain. New hillside casitas have recently been added to the compound along with an intimate spa, new pool area, and fine dining restaurant, **Elements**. $$$. ☐. (480) 948–2100.

The Scottsdale Princess. 7575 East Princess Drive. Grand and impressive, this ultra-large, Moorish-style resort features world-class golf and tennis, patios that go on forever, and sumptuous dining. $$$; ☐. (480) 585–4848. www.fairmont.com.

WORTH MORE TIME: SALT RIVER PIMA-MARICOPA INDIAN COMMUNITY

The Salt River Pima-Maricopa Indian Community is surrounded by Scottsdale, Tempe, Mesa, and Fountain Hills. Established in 1879, it is home to two tribes, the Pima and the Maricopa Indians. About 6,000 people live at this community, which covers a little more than 52,000 acres.

Visitors are welcome to visit the Hoo-hoogam Ki Museum, located at 10,000 East Osborn Road, to learn about the heritage and culture of these two tribes. The word *Hoo-hoogam Ki* means "house of those who have gone" and refers to the Pima's ancestors, the Hohokam Indians, who were the original residents of the Salt River Valley.

The small museum is constructed of adobe and desert plants and contains interpretive exhibits that describe these tribes' heritage. Baskets, pottery, photographs, and other historic articles are on display, and community members are often at the museum demonstrating their skills as potters and basket weavers.

An added treat is the outside dining room located at the back of the museum. There is a walk-up order window and some picnic tables grouped under a thatched *ramada*. The ladies of the community cook authentic Native American fry bread, burritos, and other favorites. The dining cafe serves breakfast and lunch and is open to the public.

This urban tribe owns several business enterprises, including Casino Arizona (with two locations, one at Loop 101 and McKellips and the other at Loop 101 and Indian Bend Road) and the Pavilions Shopping Mall at Indian Bend and Pima Roads, which is the largest retail outlet built on Native American land.

Both locations of Casino Arizona are open twenty-four hours a day and feature dining rooms, gift shops, shuttle service, and other amenities. Originally opened in temporary tentlike facilities, Casino Arizona at Loop 101 and McKellips opened a permanent gaming complex in spring 2000. In addition to slot machines, poker, and other games of chance, this large facility includes a fine-dining room and lounge entertainment theater that showcases outstanding performers. All of these facilities are open to the public with or without a visit to the gaming rooms. Tribal officials point out that revenues generated from both casinos fund government, social, health, and educational services for the tribe. For information on Casino Arizona, call (480) 850-7777. www.casinoaz.com.

Visitors are always welcome at powwows, which are held in April and November. For information call the Hoo-hoogam Ki Museum at (480) 850-8190. For general information about the community, contact Tribal Administration at (480) 850-8000.

Tempe · Mesa
Apache Junction
Tortilla Flat · The Lakes

TEMPE

The East Valley is booming. Just twenty years ago, most of eastern metropolitan Phoenix was open space. Snowbirds, or winter visitors, as they are more politely called, flocked to the East Valley in cold weather. Farms flourished, and although small towns hinted that one day they would become urban centers, such amazing growth seemed light-years away. Cotton was king, but much of that is history now. As you drive out of Mesa toward Tortilla Flat you'll pass through an unrelenting wave of development for the first few miles.

New homes and businesses sprout faster than any crop here. Consequently, as you leave the urban area behind and continue along the famous Apache Trail, you'll marvel at the wild natural beauty so near the city. When your day is done, you'll even know the answer to those ubiquitous bumper stickers that ask: WHERE THE HELL IS TORTILLA FLAT?

Tempe once was a sleepy little college town. No more. Today it is the home of one of the nation's largest universities—Arizona State. Originally called "Hayden's Ferry," Tempe has a history that's liberally sprinkled with famous Arizona names. The town owes its past, present, and future to Judge Trumbell Hayden, a miller, educator, and all-around promoter who established a ferry across the Salt River in 1872. The community, which quickly followed, became known as Tempe by 1877. Almost immediately, Judge Hayden began lobbying the territorial government to establish a teacher's college in Tempe. That tiny college grew up to be Arizona State University (ASU).

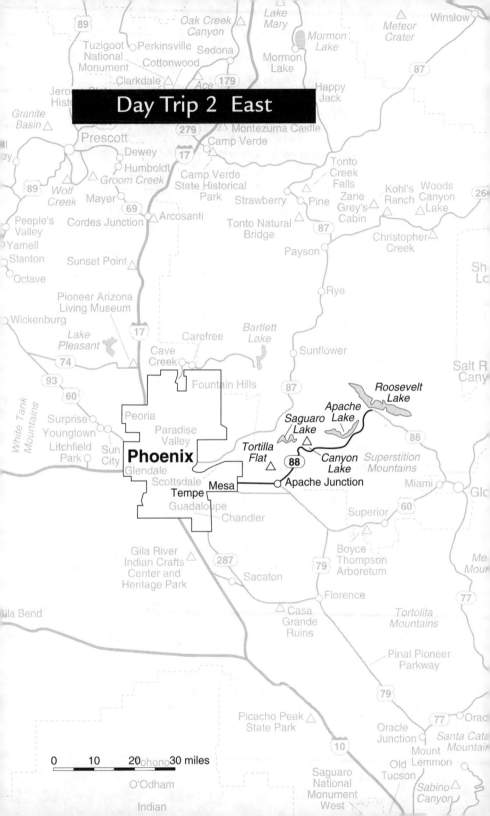

Day Trip 2 East

Today Tempe continues to be a pioneer community. The city is building one of the initial demonstration projects for a redeveloped Salt River, the Rio Salado project. Twice a year the town hosts a superb crafts festival along Mill Avenue. And, of course, it continues to be proud of its hometown school, ASU.

If you want to see the campus, park in one of the visitors' lots and walk around the palm-lined malls. When school's in session, parking is tight—you'll understand why parking is the bane of a college student's existence.

To get a sense of Tempe's past and future, drive through the quaint downtown. Follow Mill Avenue south past Gammage Center for the Performing Arts. You may wish to make a quick jog east to see Tempe City Hall at 31 East Fifth Street. Turn east off Mill Avenue onto East Fifth for a short half block to get a glimpse of this unusual contemporary structure. Designed in the shape of an inverted pyramid, the glass-and-steel building shades itself from the glaring Arizona sun.

WHERE TO GO

Arizona State University Gammage Center for the Performing Arts. On the corner of Mill Avenue and Apache Boulevard. This was the last public building Frank Lloyd Wright designed. Although he did not live to see it completed, it's a hallmark of Wright's vision. Follow Scottsdale Road south into Tempe, where it becomes Rural Road. Turn west onto University Drive and south on Mill. You'll see the center's distinctive pink color and scalloped roofline just beyond the curve on Mill between University and Apache. The public may purchase tickets to events at Gammage—there's a full season of music, dance, theater, and lectures. To inquire about scheduled events, write to the Gammage Box Office, Arizona State University, Tempe 85287. Half-hour tours of the building are available on a limited basis. Call for times and days. Free. (602) 965–5062.

If you want to spend more time on campus, pick up a map from an attendant at any of the visitors' parking lots. The map will direct you to other points of interest such as:

The J. Russell Nelson and Bonita Nelson Fine Arts Center. Tenth Street and Mill Avenue on campus. ASU boasts a magnificent visual-and-performing-arts complex by noted architect Antoine

Predock. This Egyptian-inspired group of buildings is definitely worth a visit. Within the complex you'll find the University Art Museum, which has one of the finest American ceramics collections in the country. The various traveling shows as well as the permanent collection are all outstanding. The complex also includes the Paul V. Galvin Playhouse, the University Dance Laboratory, and other interior and exterior exhibition and performing space.

The Red River Opry. 730 North Mill Avenue. Situated in the environmental and historic tourism area called The Papago Trail, the 1,000-seat Opry stages live variety shows that feature country music. Concerts held year-round. Fee. Call for show information. (480) 829–OPRY.

MESA

To get to Mesa from Tempe, follow Apache Boulevard east. As it enters Mesa, Apache becomes Main Street. Once known primarily for its wide streets—wide enough for an ox team to turn around—Mesa is a fast-growing city that is proud of its excellent schools and churches. The Chamber of Commerce, 120 North Center, has information on the community center, the historical and archaeological museum, little theaters, and the youth museum. (480) 969–1307.

WHERE TO GO

The Arizona Museum for Youth. 35 North Robson Street. One of only two children's museums in the country that focuses on the fine arts, this is a special family place. The museum is owned by the city of Mesa and the Arizona Museum for Youth Friends Inc. It opened in 1981 in a temporary facility, moved to its permanent facility in 1986, and has been nationally honored in a *USA Today Weekend* magazine article as the "Most Outrageously Artful" children's museum in America.

The exterior of the brick building gives no hint of the exciting interior environment designed to titillate the imagination, stimulate the mind, and captivate the eye. Three exhibits are mounted annually, one for each of the fall, spring, and summer school semesters. Artwork is installed at a child's eye level, and traditional museum displays are interspersed with participatory activities to enhance and reinforce the visual experience.

School and community groups are led by trained museum staff in the morning. The public can enjoy the museum at its leisure or take escorted tours. In addition to the exhibits, the museum holds workshops and classes and puts on special events. Group tours are available Wednesday morning and afternoon. Closed Monday. The museum is also closed for two weeks every spring, summer, fall, and winter. Fee. (480) 644-2468.

Champlin Fighter Museum. 4636 East Fighter Aces Drive. Located at Falcon Field on McKellips Road just east of Greenfield Road. If you want to see vintage aircraft, this is the place to go. The collection contains fighter aircraft from World War I through Vietnam. The collection is stored in two hangars that were part of a secret British Royal Air Force training ground built in the early stages of World War II before the United States entered the war. The World War I aircraft date almost to the beginning of aviation history and are works of remarkable craftsmanship. Since 1983 the Champlin Fighter Museum has been the home of the American Fighter Aces Association, which is an exclusive association of top pilots. An "Ace" must be credited with downing five or more enemy aircraft in aerial combat. Fee. (480) 830-4541. www.champlinfighter.com.

Mesa Southwest Museum. 53 North MacDonald. Located in the heart of downtown Mesa, the museum recently underwent a $4.5 million face-lift. With its grand opening in May 2000, the museum nearly doubled the number of displays. The mission of the museum is to interpret the natural history of the Southwest, from dinosaurs and ancient Native American civilizations to the settlement of the West. Visitors are ushered through a chronologically correct journey that includes a flashing "time tunnel." The exhibits include the creation of the universe (Big Bang) and the emergence of life, the formation of the Grand Canyon, and the building of Roosevelt Dam. Children will love the brand-new Dino-mation exhibit, which brings these prehistoric giant creatures to life complete with Disney-esque movement and roars. The dinosaur exhibit is one of the largest such exhibits west of the Mississippi. Another new addition is the 1,000-plus-gallon aquarium, which is ringed with mirrors to make the fish appear larger. The new expansion allows the museum to feature its own collection of regional artifacts and related art as well as traveling exhibits and art shows. Special children's activities and workshops are scheduled. There are accessible, hands-on exhibits as well as outdoor displays, which include a one-room schoolhouse and gold-panning stream. Fee. (480) 644-2230.

The Mormon Temple. 525 East Main Street. This imposing structure serves as Arizona headquarters for the Church of Jesus Christ of Latter-Day Saints. Although the sanctuary is open only to Mormons, the visitors center welcomes guests. There you may learn something about the Mormon faith and hear about the Mormon men and women who came west to establish homes, farms, and communities. Tours of the temple's visitors center are conducted every half hour. Call for more information. (480) 964-7164.

Usery Mountain Recreation Area. Follow Usery Pass Road 12 miles northeast of Mesa to the main entrance. This 3,324-acre recreation area provides trails for hiking and horseback riding, camping and picnic areas, and an archery range. Eleven hiking trails are lush with desert vegetation and are of varied difficulty. The most popular are Wind Cave Trail and Pass Mountain Trail. Open daily. Fee. (480) 984-0032.

WHERE TO EAT

Rockin' R Ranch. 6136 East Baseline Road. Mosey on over to Arizona's Wild West town. The specialty is chuck wagon suppers, and the Cowboy Steakhouse serves huge steaks as well as fish, ribs, and chicken. Kids enjoy the western town complete with petting zoo. Enjoy horse-drawn wagon rides, pan for gold, and see mountain men, gunfights, and entertainment by the Rockin' R Wranglers. Good family entertainment. Reservations are requested, and private steak fries can be arranged. Open Saturday only in the summer. Call for information and reservations. $$-$$$; ☐. (480) 832-1539. www.rockinr.net.

APACHE JUNCTION

Continue east on US-60/US-89 to Apache Junction, which calls itself "The Gateway to the Superstition Mountains." This range has fascinated people for almost a century, ever since German immigrant Jacob Waltz arrived in Arizona in 1863 to prospect for gold. According to legend, Waltz found, or possibly stole, one of the very rich Peralta gold mines deep in the Superstitions. Try as he did, however, he never again was able to find the mine and prove his claim.

Because people mistakenly thought that the immigrant was from Holland, as Waltz continued his search, the story grew about the "Dutchman's Lost Mine." In time, the unproven claim became known as "The Lost Dutchman's Lost Mine," a misstatement that no one has bothered to correct.

Apache Junction itself is a sprawling conglomeration of commercial property and mobile homes set against the spectacular Superstition range. Drive through Apache Junction and continue on A–88 to begin the Apache Trail, a section of Arizona that quite impressed President Theodore Roosevelt. Observing that it combined the grandeur of the Alps, the glory of the Rockies, and the magnificence of the Grand Canyon, he called it "the most awe-inspiring and most sublimely beautiful panorama Nature has ever created." Teddy Roosevelt predicted in 1911 that the Salt River Valley would boom and attract people from throughout the country.

WHERE TO EAT

The Mining Camp Restaurant and Trading Post. 6100 East Mining Camp Road. Turn left onto A–88 at Apache Junction and continue north for 4 miles.

This landmark restaurant is built of rough-sawn ponderosa pine that was hauled from Payson. A replica of the old mining camp cook shanty sits at the base of the Superstition Mountains. The interior has also been copied with amazing authenticity. A trading post sells authentic Native American relics, legendary maps, and photos of early mining days. Food is served family-style and is all you can eat. If you like never-ending amounts of hearty western food amidst a rustic gold-mining atmosphere, this place is for you. Dinner only. $$; ☐. (480) 982–3181.

TORTILLA FLAT

Travel 18 miles northeast on A–88 to reach Tortilla Flat, one of the last true outposts of the West. Here visitors will find a rustic dining room that features hamburgers and chili, a weatherbeaten-looking small hotel, and a public rest room. This is a fun place to stop.

Although tiny by anyone's standards, Tortilla Flat is the last town between Apache Junction and Roosevelt Dam. A few miles east of Tortilla Flat, the Apache Trail turns into a rough gravel road. If you decide to continue east to Roosevelt Lake, prepare yourself for a rugged and even hair-raising trip.

A–88 is one of the most crooked roads in the nation. It was named for the Apache Indians who helped build it, and it was constructed to haul materials for Theodore Roosevelt Dam. The route snakes through some of the prettiest mountains and desert in the Phoenix area. Along the way is Tortilla Flat, the only surviving stagecoach stop on the route. The buildings were destroyed by fire some years ago but have since been rebuilt. Today you can stop at the general store, cafe, and post office. The prickly pear cactus ice cream and the chili are specialties.

WHERE TO GO

Goldfield Ghost Town. 4650 North Mammoth Mine Road. Four miles northeast of Apache Junction on A–88, just past mile marker 200. This is an authentic ghost town where you can go on a mine tour and pan for gold. There are specialty shops and antiques, a museum, a unique steak house with spectacular views of the Superstition Mountains, and you can ride the state's only narrow-gauge railroad. (480) 983-0333. www.goldfieldghosttown.com; www.ghosttownsaz.com.

THE LAKES

If you're ready for more scenery, follow the Apache Trail on A–88 east 28 miles through the chain of manufactured lakes on the Salt River that includes Canyon Lake, Apache Lake, and Roosevelt Lake, which is much larger than the other two. Roosevelt Lake is located on the gravel road after the pavement ends. The unpaved stretch is notable, not only for its rough surface, but also for its steep descent into Fish Creek Canyon. Adventurous tourists are advised to make this trip by traveling east, not west, in order to easily see approaching automobiles.

The Apache Trail is a trip of unforgettable beauty in all seasons. The trip winds through scenic desert mountain vistas, climbs in hairpin turns, and finally plunges into Fish Creek Canyon. Because of the condition of the road, it is slow going in places. But that only gives travelers more time to enjoy the breathtaking views of desert lakes, saguaros, and mountain landscapes.

Fish, water-ski, relax, swim, or just enjoy the desert lake views. Each lake offers services for travelers.

WHERE TO GO

Canyon Lake. Follow A–87 for 16 miles north of Apache Junction to the Canyon Lake Marina. Like all Arizona lakes, Canyon Lake is a hotbed of summertime activity from power boating to waterskiing to Jet Skiing. Those who prefer to have a less strenuous experience will enjoy *The Dolly,* a 103-foot stern-wheeler. The day cruise takes 1½ hours and is narrated. Lunch is available, and box lunches may also be purchased. Romantics may prefer the dinner cruises, which are priced according to the changing menu. Call ahead for reservations and menu information. Canyon Lake also caters to visitors with the Lakeside Restaurant and Cantina, a family restaurant at 9593 East Anasazi Place (480–288–8290). $$; fee for the cruises. (480) 827–9144.

Apache Lake. You'll find a full-service resort and marina with boats for fishing and tackle. Check with the Apache Lake Resort for more information. (520) 467–2511. E-mail: apachelake@kachina.com.

Roosevelt Lake. Roosevelt Lake is your ultimate destination and is well worth the trip, which traverses paved and unpaved roads that snake through some of the best desert scenery in central Arizona. Although the road through Fish Canyon is not paved, it is graded. The Apache Trail is a magnificent drive at all times of the year but especially beautiful in the spring and fall. A year-round haven for unwinding, Roosevelt Lake is popular among skiers, bass anglers, and campers. There's a full-service marina. The visitors center is definitely worth a visit as it tells the story of how Roosevelt Dam was constructed through models, exhibits, and outstanding photographs. It also affords a magnificent view of the panorama of Roosevelt Dam, one of the major masonry dams in the world. (520) 467–2245.

Roosevelt Dam. Roosevelt Dam remains one of the most important reclamation projects in the United States. Without the dam's ability to stop flooding and provide a well-managed source of water, the Phoenix metropolitan area would not have developed as it has. The dam is also a sight of amazing beauty.

Tonto Basin Ranger Station and Visitor Center. Located at Roosevelt Lake, this new visitor's center tells the story of Roosevelt Dam through models and exhibits. A good bookstore provides you with additional information about the dam and this riparian area. If you are interested in camping, the center has current information on Roosevelt Lake's modern campgrounds. Some even have solar-heated showers. Open daily. Fee. (520) 467-3200.

Apache Lake Ranch. At milepost 227.5, north of Tortilla Flat on the Apache Trail in the Tonto National Forest. Adventurous travelers can find plenty of outdoor fun here. One-hour to overnight horseback trips are available, and the ranch also organizes hiking trips to nearby 200-foot Reavis Falls as well as more exotic tours of this rugged country, including horseback pack trips to Salado Indian cliff dwellings, Hummer tours, and helicopter rides. Call for information and reservations. (520) 467-2822.

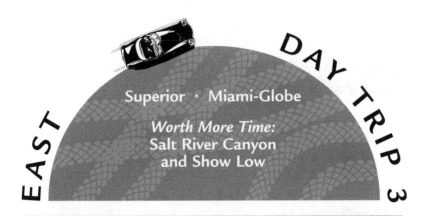

EAST

DAY TRIP 3

Superior · Miami-Globe

Worth More Time:
Salt River Canyon
and Show Low

SUPERIOR

Pick up this trip in Apache Junction and travel southeast on US-60/US-89 toward Superior. The approximately 50-mile drive from Mesa to Superior takes you deep into copper-mining country. Arizona owes its history to the mines and the railroads, for the presence of precious minerals—gold, silver, and copper—lured people west. The railroads opened the land so that men could carry those treasures out and, in the process, made the territory accessible to settlers.

The main street of this small town follows Queen Creek, which is nestled among the copper-stained mountains. In 1875 this was a bustling silver- and gold-mining center. Today its future hangs on a precarious copper thread.

WHERE TO GO

Boyce Thompson Southwestern Arboretum. US-60/US-89 just a few miles west of Superior. As you drive toward Superior on US-60/US-89, turn right at the sign and follow the driveway into the arboretum. This vast (1,076-acre) living museum was the dream of William Boyce Thompson, a mining magnate and philanthropist. He endowed not only this site, but also a sister institution, The Boyce Thompson Institute for Plant Research. The Arizona arboretum is all the more intriguing because of its Sonoran desert location.

This is one of the most special spots in Arizona. The grounds are well marked and, in most places, are wheelchair accessible. The long

93

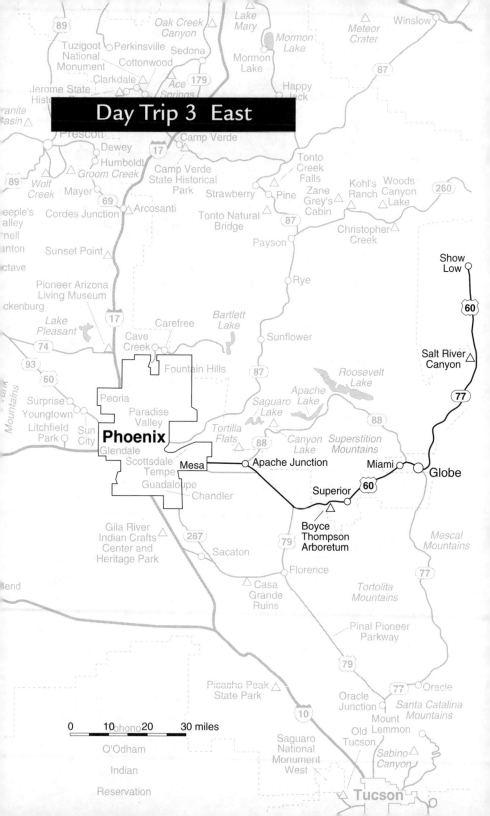

Day Trip 3 East

loop trail will take you an hour to two hours depending upon how long you stay at each designated stop along the way. There are myriad side loops to follow depending upon your interest and the season.

If you have never meandered through a shady and fragrant eucalyptus grove, stared at the myriad twisted arms of a 200-year-old giant saguaro cactus, or tried to figure out how the bizarre Boojum tree grows, you've missed some of the desert's best pleasures. Begin your tour at the visitors center and get acquainted with this living garden before heading out on the well-marked trails. They begin with some "easy-does-it" walks and graduate to more challenging terrain.

One fascinating section is devoted to old-world trees, including the pomegranate, Chinese pistachio, and olive, that are of major economic importance in various parts of the world. You will be amazed to learn how many different trees can grow in the Arizona desert. Open daily except Christmas. Fee. (928) 689-2811. www. arboretum@AG.arizona.edu.

MIAMI-GLOBE

Continue on US-60/US-89 east to Miami and Globe. As you enter Miami, look for the sign noting the site of the Bloody Tanks Massacre of Apaches. Proceed east to Globe, the seat of Gila County and a center for cattle and mining. Globe began as a mining town in 1886, but now it is the trading center for the San Carlos Apache Indian Reservation and a favorite headquarters for wild pig *(javelina)* hunting. Apart from the natural setting, the main attraction here is mining, although in recent years the town has become a focus for historical renovation. A historic home tour is held each February in which the whole town participates. Pick up a self-guided walking and driving tour map at the Chamber of Commerce. Stop in at the Globe-Miami Chamber of Commerce, 1360 North Broad Street, Highway 60, Globe 85501, or call (928) 425-4495 for information on the area.

As in many Arizona small towns, public buildings often do not have street addresses. However, Arizonans are a friendly bunch, so you can always ask directions. You should include the **Gila County**

Historical Museum on US-60/US-89 in your tour. This small museum holds a treasure trove of pioneer and mining artifacts collected throughout the region. It's open daily and is free. (928) 425-7385.

You can see local and regional artists represented at the restored old courthouse, now the **Cobre Valley Center for the Arts,** at Broad and Oak Streets. This museum is open daily and is free. Then, too, the area is laced with fascinating Pueblo Indian ruins. Ask about them at the Chamber of Commerce 101 Broad Street, Globe 85501. (928) 425-0884.

Group tours of the open pit mine and smelter operations are available. If you want to learn more about mining on your own, however, pick up A-77 at Globe and head south to Winkleman and Hayden, two small copper-mining communities that are 1 mile apart. Here you can hook into Day Trip 1 Southeast from Phoenix by circling through San Manuel to Oracle Junction. At Oracle Junction follow US-89 for a 42-mile drive north to Florence. You can also continue on A-287 from Horace to A-87 back through Chandler to Mesa. This is a 246-mile drive, and much of it traverses old stagecoach routes that are surrounded by massive copper-stained mountains.

WHERE TO GO

Besh-Ba-Gowah Archaeological Park. Jess Hayes Road. Take Broad Street through historic downtown Globe for approximately 1½ miles. You'll see the turnoff for the park. Besh-Ba-Gowah is the remains of a prehistoric village that overlooks Pinal Creek in the shadow of the Pinal Mountains. The walls and structure are made of rounded river cobble and mud, and the careful reconstruction lets you experience the plazas and living quarters as they must have been centuries ago. Artifacts, including a weaving loom, grinding stones, and even a large squash, are carefully positioned in some of the reconstructed rooms.

Besh-Ba-Gowah means "a place of metal" or "metal camp." This pueblo consists of more than 300 rooms and once housed 400 people. It was built and occupied from about A.D. 1225 to A.D. 1400 by the Salado Indians. These people were accomplished farmers and grew crops including corn, beans, and squash along the banks of Pinal Creek.

The community also functioned as a trading center. The Salado made pottery and traded widely. They also wove baskets of sotol and yucca fibers as well as fine cotton cloth, and they adorned themselves with bracelets and necklaces made of shells they acquired by trading their pottery and baskets.

Like many pueblos, it is suspected that drought drove the people out. Besh-Ba-Gowah lay abandoned for years but underwent excavation and stabilization in the 1980s. The park opened in 1988. There is an excellent, small museum on the grounds that displays artifacts relating to this site. Group tours by arrangement. Open daily. Fee. (928) 425-0320.

Gila Pueblo. Gila Pueblo College, 6 Shooter Canyon. Gila Pueblo is just a five-minute drive south of Globe past Besh-Ba-Gowah park. Owned and operated by Eastern Arizona College, it was originally excavated in the early 1920s by an amateur archaeologist who owned the property where the dig is located. At the height of its occupation, it contained more than 400 rooms, and approximately 1,500 people once lived here.

The inhabitants were skilled potters and weavers. Unlike other pueblos, Gila Pueblo was never abandoned. Instead, sometime around A.D. 1450, the entire community was destroyed by an act of war. Most of the people were murdered, and the village burned to the ground. Researchers suspect that the violence was perpetrated by the nearby Salado populations. Free. (928) 425-3151. www.eac.cc.az.us.

WHERE TO SHOP

Antiques and collectibles. The Globe/Miami area is becoming a treasure trove for antiques lovers. Johnny's Country Corner, 383 South Hill, has an outstanding array of quilts and quilting supplies. Pick up a brochure from the Chamber of Commerce that details the antiques trail.

The Cobre Valley Center for the Arts. 101 North Broad Street. This cooperative is housed in the historic Gila County Courthouse, which has been renovated to its original splendor. The arts and crafts exhibited are by local artists. Free. (928) 425-0884.

WHERE TO STAY

Noftsger Hill Inn. 425 North Street. Call for directions. This is a bed and breakfast housed in an old elementary school that sits on a hilltop overlooking Globe. Built in 1907, it was originally known as the North Globe Schoolhouse. Generations of successful Arizonans were educated here, including Rose Mofford, former governor of Arizona. The owners, Rosalie and Dom Ayala care for it with love, dedication, and great attention to detail. When completed, there will be 10 rooms, some large enough to house a family comfortably. Breakfast is gourmet Southwest, and the company is delightful. $$. (928) 425-2260 or (877) 780-2479. www.noftsgerhillinn.com.

WORTH MORE TIME: SALT RIVER CANYON AND SHOW LOW

From the Miami-Globe area, continue northeast on A-77/US-60 another 87 miles for a magnificent plunge through the wild beauty of the Salt River Canyon and a visit to the community of Show Low. You should plan to spend the night in Show Low or head southeast for approximately 5 miles on A-160 to Lakeside or Pinetop and stay there.

The Salt River Canyon begins about 30 miles northeast of Globe on A-77/US-60 and is often called "The Mini Grand Canyon." Take this drive during the daytime so you can appreciate the spectacular sights. The highway twists and turns for 5 miles from the top of the canyon to its floor.

This is one of the most scenic stretches in all of Arizona. Along the way, you can pull off at several lookout points to admire the artistry wrought by millions of years of erosion. If you have packed a light lunch, picnic at one of the several shady spots provided at the bottom of the canyon. This area is well marked. Pull off, park, and walk down a flight of steps to the riverbank. Adventurous adults and children will want to explore the river, swim, or fish. If you travel 7 miles downstream on a dirt road, you'll see the amazing **Salt Banks.** The formations tower 1,000 feet above the river, looking like giant ocean waves frozen in time and about to crest.

When you're ready for the long climb out of the canyon, continue approximately 60 miles northeast on A-77/US-60 to Show Low.

This small community is a hub of activity with the four million acres of the White Mountain Recreation Area, which include 500 miles of trout streams and fifty lakes. It is also home to **Sunrise Park,** the state's most complete ski center and resort.

Show Low enjoys a high, cool climate and a backdrop of exceptional forest land. Its name reputedly came from an incident involving C. E. Cooley, who had been a government scout with Gen. George Crook. Cooley married the daughter of Chief Pedro of the White Mountain Apaches and, in 1875, established a home on what is now called Show Low Creek. His place became a favorite spot for travelers. Marion Clark was Cooley's partner, but at some point in the relationship, Clark decided to end their hotel venture. To settle on who should stay and who should leave, the two agreed to play a card game of Seven-Up. When the hand was dealt, Cooley lacked a single point to win. As they prepared to draw cards, Clark is reputed to have said, "If you can show low, you can win." Cooley tossed his hand down and said, "Show low it is." Clark moved up the creek to what is now Pinetop, and thanks to the deuce of clubs, Cooley stayed. More importantly, the name stuck.

Today Show Low is the trade and service center for southern Navajo County and portions of southern Apache County. Tourists use it as a jumping-off point for recreation in the White Mountains. You'll find modest facilities here, including motels, cabins, and campgrounds. For more information contact the Show Low Chamber of Commerce, 951 West Deuce of Clubs 85901, Show Low 85902, or call (928) 537-2326. www.showlow.com; www.wmonline.com.

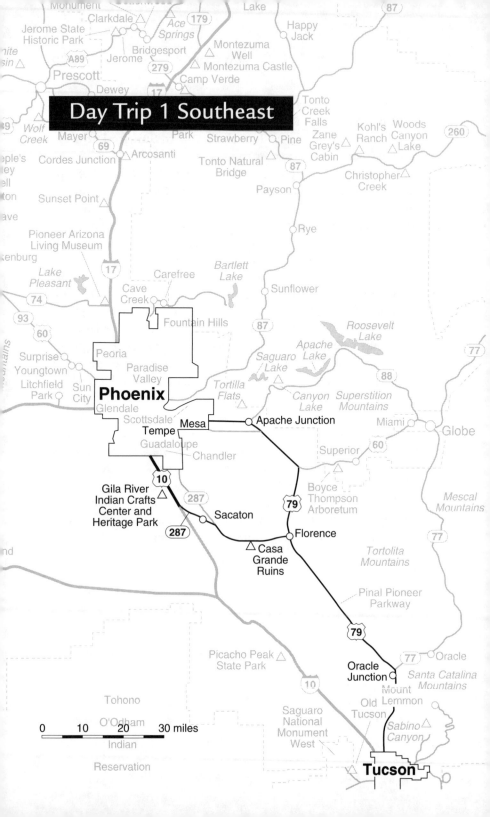

Day Trip 1 Southeast

Monument
Clarkdale
179
Lake
87
Happy
Jack
Jerome State
Historic Park
Ace
Springs
Montezuma
Well
A89
Bridgesport
Jerome
279
Montezuma Castle
hite
sin
Camp Verde
Tonto
Creek
Falls
Kohl's
Ranch
Woods
Canyon
Lake
260
Prescott
Dewey
17
Strawberry
Pine
Zane
Grey's
Cabin
9
Wolf
Creek
Mayer
Park
Tonto Natural
Bridge
87
Christopher
Creek
69
Cordes Junction
Arcosanti
Payson
eple's
ey
ell
ton
Sunset Point
Rye
ave
Pioneer Arizona
Living Museum
kenburg
Lake
Pleasant
Carefree
Bartlett
Lake
Sunflower
Roosevelt
Lake
74
Cave
Creek
Fountain Hills
77
93
17
87
Apache
Lake
60
Peoria
Paradise
Valley
Saguaro
Lake
Canyon
Lake
Superstition
Mountains
88
Surprise
Youngtown
Litchfield
Park
Sun
City
Phoenix
Tortilla
Flats
Roosevelt
Mescal
Mountains
Glendale
Scottsdale
Tempe
Mesa
Apache Junction
Miami
Globe
Guadaloupe
Chandler
Superior
60
10
Gila River
Indian Crafts
Center and
Heritage Park
287
Sacaton
79
Boyce
Thompson
Arboretum
287
Casa
Grande
Ruins
Florence
77
Tortolita
Mountains
Pinal Pioneer
Parkway
79
Picacho Peak
State Park
77
Oracle
10
Oracle
Junction
Santa Catalina
Mountains
Tohono
O'Odham
Indian
Reservation
Saguaro
National
Monument
West
Old
Tucson
Mount
Lemmon
Sabino
Canyon
Tucson

0   10   20   30 miles

SACATON

Gila River Indian Crafts and Heritage Park. Follow I-10 east to exit 175, which leads to the center. If you have never visited a Native American reservation, this may appear a stark landscape. The word *sacaton* means "tall, rank herbage unfit for forage." Historian Marshall Trimble notes that the grass is good for forage, so maybe the meaning is that of another definition for *sacaton,* which is "broad, flat land." The old Butterfield Stage Line ran through here in 1858 on its way from Tucson to Yuma. The **Gila River Indian Crafts Center** does a brisk business in authentic Native American jewelry of turquoise, silver, and beadwork; pottery from many different tribes; Seri wood carvings; Navajo rugs; and other gift items. In addition, there is a Native American art gallery, historical museum, park, and a coffee shop featuring piping-hot Native American fry bread. The center is open daily. (520) 562-3334.

CASA GRANDE

Casa Grande was traditionally an agricultural and manufacturing town that has now expanded into the retail industry with two major shopping outlet centers located conveniently along I-10. The community is located midway between Phoenix and Tucson. It was founded in 1879 and named for the famous Hohokam Indian Ruins,

101

which are located 20 miles to the northeast. This is the largest community in Pinal County.

WHERE TO GO

Casa Grande Valley Historical Society. 110 West Florence Boulevard. Located in downtown Casa Grande, this museum presents many historical facts about the area. Exhibits focus on the history of the region from the arrival of the railroad in 1879 to the present. Agriculture, mining, and transportation are all represented. There is a landmark 1920s stone church and a one-room schoolhouse on the grounds. Fee. Call for hours. (520) 836-2223. www.spma.org.

FLORENCE

Continue east on A-287 to Florence, approximately 9 miles from Coolidge. Florence has two main claims to fame: its courthouse and the prison. The fifth oldest city in the state, it was established in 1866 by a local Native American agent, Levi Ruggles. The community grew rapidly and became the county seat when Pinal County was chartered in 1875. In spite of its desert setting, Florence is an agricultural community. Local crops include cotton, cattle, sugar beets, grain, and grapes.

Poston Butte, named for Charles Poston, the "Father of Arizona," is a nearby landmark. A monument at the summit of the butte marks his grave. The town is also known as the "Cowboy Cradle of the Southwest." During the depression, when jobs and money were scarce and the bottom fell out of the milk market, ranchers were planning to dump their milk rather than sell it at a loss. A local rancher, Charlie Whittlow, declared that he would give his milk free to the schoolchildren rather than waste it. Other communities soon picked up Whittlow's idea, and as a result, the national milk and free lunch program for schoolchildren was started in this country. An odd sidelight to this story is that while Whittlow was a rancher and *not* a cowboy, as a result of his actions his home became known as "The Cowboy Cradle of the Southwest."

If you want to continue to Tucson (See Day Trip 2 Southeast from Phoenix), you may take US-79 south (Pinal Pioneer Parkway) for a

42-mile scenic stretch between Florence and Oracle Junction and then continue south to Tucson. This drive takes you through a unique natural garden where virtually every type of Arizona desert flora is displayed. Depending upon your time and botanical interest, you can explore easily accessible side roads along the way.

To return to Phoenix from Florence, take US-79 north for 16 miles to its junction with US-60. Turn west and follow US-60/US-89, 47 miles to Phoenix through Apache Junction, Mesa, and Tempe (Day Trip 2 East from Phoenix).

WHERE TO GO

McFarland Historical State Park. Corner of Main and Ruggles. This park features the first Pinal County Courthouse, an 1878 adobe structure. Inside are exhibits that describe how the building was used as a courthouse and later as a hospital. There is also a historical exhibit featuring Arizona notables Charles Poston, Levi Ruggles, and Pearl Hart. The career of Ernest West McFarland, who was a senator, governor, and justice, is also highlighted, and his personal and public collections are displayed in the archives. The first Saturday in March is Florence Founders' Day. Fee. (520) 868-5216.

Pinal County Visitor Center. 330 East Butte, P.O. Box 967, Florence 85232-0967. Located in the heart of the historic district, visitors are asked to sign the official guest book here. This is the place to get maps and brochures about special events that take place during the year as well as inquire about the local businesses and restaurants. Open weekdays 9:00 A.M. to 4:00 P.M. (520) 868-4331 or (888) 469-0175. www.co.pinal.az.us/visitorcenter.

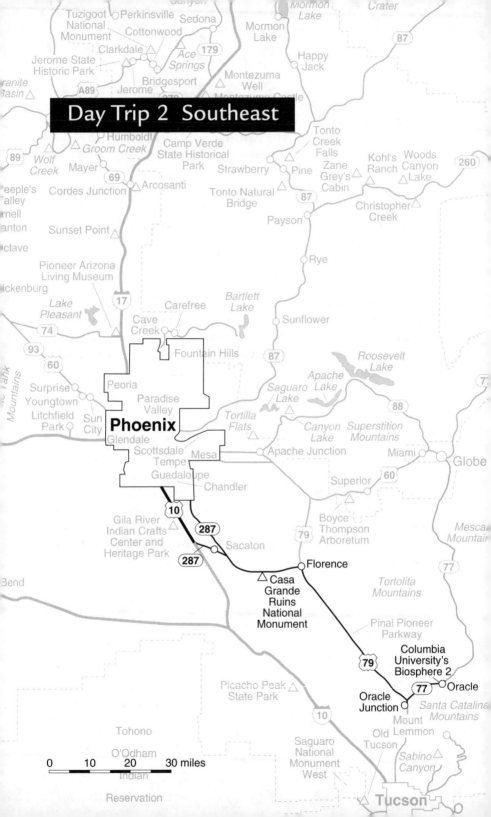

Day Trip 2 Southeast

CASA GRANDE RUINS
NATIONAL MONUMENT

This day trip takes you "back to the future" with a full day of touring an ancient Native American ruin and then a space-age environment. From Phoenix, take I-10 east to exit 175 through Sacaton. From Sacaton take A-287 southwest for approximately 14 miles to Coolidge. As you approach Coolidge you will come to the Casa Grande Ruins National Monument, an eleven-room, eleven-family, 600-apartment building built by the ancient Hohokam and Pueblo Indian farmers. This structure was constructed of hardened mud blocks that are 5 feet long, 2 feet high, and 4 feet thick. Today it is protected by a giant steel "umbrella." While its original use is still debated, this is the only four-story Native American ruin structure found in the United States, and the only example in Arizona of a structure from the Classic Period (A.D. 1300–A.D. 1400).

Discovered in 1694 by Father Kino, the structure had already been burned when he came upon it. The Pima Indians had a custom of burning the inside of their buildings when they abandoned them. The ruins were explored in 1882 by Dr. J. Walter Fewks of the Smithsonian Institution. Dr. Fewks returned to do more exploration in 1906 and 1908.

As you wander through these imposing ruins, pay special attention to the calendar holes. Two small openings in the east and center rooms are placed so the sun's rays come through. The streak of light passing through both holes and lining up on a target occurs near the spring and fall equinoxes.

If you visit with smaller children, ask for the special trail guides that are available for youngsters. The guides are free, but a donation is always appreciated. Fee. (520) 723-3172.

COLUMBIA UNIVERSITY'S BIOSPHERE 2

From Casa Grande Ruins National Monument, continue on A-287 west to Florence. Then travel south on US-79 to Oracle Junction and join A-77. Follow A-77 to mile marker 96.5 at Oracle and follow the signs to Biosphere 2 and SunSpace Ranch.

Columbia University has taken over Biosphere 2 and added a new educational and research dimension to this project. The university offers degree study programs and conferences on the site. The Earth Exploration Program joins Biosphere 2 Center scientists and Columbia University faculty and other leading educators and researchers meet with visitors to provide stimulating educational experiences at this self-contained, simulated "world."

This two-and-a-half-acre enclosure is a microcosm of Earth, or Biosphere 1. The project has been under way since 1984 and is a human experiment in which four men and four women have periodically lived inside a sealed and re-created "earth environment" for extended periods of time.

Stocked with nearly 4,000 species of plants and animals, the project replicates seven life zones, or biomes, including a tropical rain forest, marshland, desert, savanna, mountains, and ocean.

Although it was controversial, Columbia University has "legitimized" Biosphere 2 in the eyes of educational and research interests. The original purpose of the project was to see if humans could live in a sealed environment and whether that environment could sustain itself. Columbia University's Biosphere 2 continues the research but emphasizes education. Exhibits demonstrate how the actions of humans and natural forces are changing the planet and its environment.

Columbia has also opened a portion of Biosphere 2 to visitors—Mission Crew living quarters and the Command and Control "Nerve Room." In addition, study courses are offered both on and off campus that focus on a variety of "earth friendly" topics. Courses are held throughout the year.

The Biosphere sits nestled on a ridge between two rocky outcroppings. It is a dramatic structure, almost like a futuristic ship from another galaxy, surrounded by several domelike structures, which are the "lungs" of the project.

The informative tour takes visitors around the Biosphere and inside the newly opened area. The tour begins in the theater, where visitors learn about the philosophy behind this experiment, in which virtually everything is recyclable and nothing is disposable. It then continues around the grounds of the project to give visitors an understanding of this massive experiment. Fee. Ask for the monthly event calendar and tour times. (520) 896-6200 or (800) 828-2462.

WHERE TO EAT

The Cañada del Oro Restaurant. On the grounds of Biosphere 2, the restaurant features unique cuisine and panoramic views of the mountain and city. Indoor and outdoor seating are available all year round. The cafe serves Biospherean recipes as well as other fare. Visitors can buy a cookbook that contains recipes the Biosphereans used, *Eating In.* $$; ☐. (520) 896-6222.

WHERE TO STAY

Columbia University's Biosphere Hotel and Conference Center. Highway 77, mile marker 96.5, P.O. Box 689, Oracle 85623. Oversized rooms with views of the Catalina Mountains and Biosphere 2 await you. The atmosphere is serene, and the rooms are immaculate. Some have minibars. Overnight tour package includes tour, dinner, and breakfast. Call for rates. $$-$$$; ☐. (520) 896-6222. www.bio2.edu.

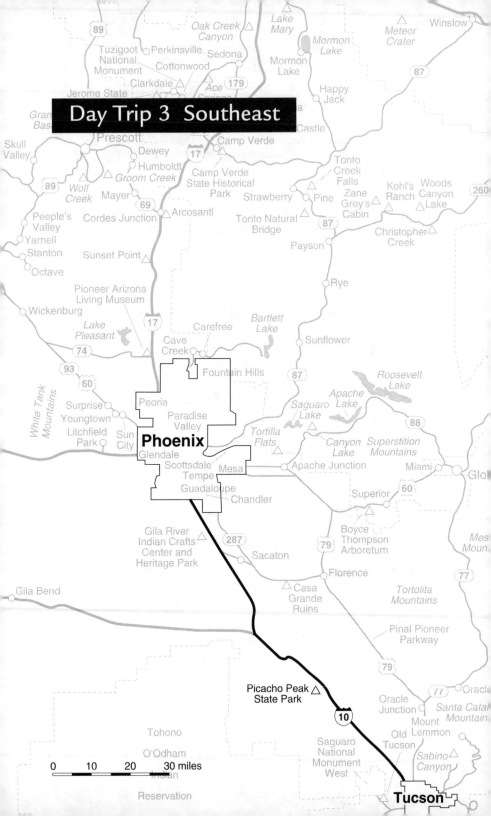

Day Trip 3 Southeast

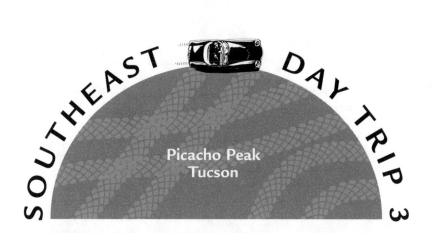

PICACHO PEAK

Tucson is an easy two-hour trip from Phoenix on I-10. Along the way, you can stop at Picacho Peak State Park, or you may wish to drive straight through and spend the entire day in Tucson.

Picacho Peak State Park. Picacho Peak State Park is located 60 miles southeast of Phoenix, just off I-10. From the ranger station, follow the Barrett Loop to the trailhead of Hunter Trail.

Located halfway between Tucson and Phoenix, this landmark soars to 3,400 feet. Calloway Trail (7/10 mile) and a short nature loop (½ mile) offer pleasant excursions, but hotshot hikers should head for Hunter Trail and a steep 2 1/10-mile trek to the summit.

The ascent begins immediately on a clearly marked, difficult path. In forty-five minutes, even the semi-fit can reach the saddle where a panoramic view of the Sonoran desert extends beyond the Picacho Mountains to the Catalinas near Tucson. In spring the desert floor may be carpeted with bright orange Mexican poppies, adding vibrant color to the stands of sun-bleached ocotillo and saguaro.

From the saddle the trail gets rough, plunging down 300 feet before climbing to the summit. Twelve sets of cable, anchored into bare rock, provide handholds. Hardy hikers will discover that the view from the top is glorious. Carry water, wear boots and gloves, and expect a rugged, three- to five-hour round-trip. Hikers should avoid the summit trail during June, July, and August.

Long a beacon for wayfarers, Pichacho Peak was known to prehistoric Hohokam Indians who traveled here on trade routes. Later Pima Papago Indians and Spanish missionaries camped on this site.

On April 15, 1862, two advance Union and Confederate units clashed near Picacho in the westernmost battle of the Civil War. Reports of casualties vary, but it's known that three Union soldiers were killed. A monument commemorates the skirmish, and the battle is reenacted every March.

A second memorial within the park honors the Mormon Battalion, which built the first wagon road across the Southwest in 1846. Fee. (520) 466–3183. www.pr.state.az.us.

TUCSON

When you think of Tucson, think mountains. The oldest continuously inhabited city in the country, Tucson is surrounded by the Santa Catalinas to the north, the Rincons to the east, the Santa Rita Mountains to the south, the Tucson Mountains to the west, and the Tortolita Mountains to the northwest. With an elevation of 2,410 feet above sea level (about 1,000 feet higher than Phoenix), the "Old Pueblo," as Tucson is called, has a drier and slightly cooler climate than its big sister 100 miles to the north.

Tucson wears its Hispanic heritage like an elegant mantilla. Mexico lies just 60 miles to the south, but the Mexican influence is only one force that helped shape this city. Four cultures coexist here: Spanish, Mexican, Native American, and, of course, contemporary American.

This cultural blend adds an intellectual vitality to Tucson. Where Phoenix shines with glass and chrome, Tucson glows with pink adobe and wrought iron. Where Phoenix can be wide-open western, Tucson can slip back in time and roll its "Rs." Whether you stroll through the Barrio, the old, mostly Mexican-American neighborhood, or walk along the "movie-set" campus of the University of Arizona (U. of A.), you'll be acutely aware of how this half-old, half-new city pursues its blended destiny.

WHERE TO GO

Metropolitan Tucson Convention and Visitors Bureau. 110 South Church. (520) 624–1817. Pick up additional information about the Old Pueblo to learn how the original walled Presidio of

San Agustin del Tucson was built by the Spaniards in 1776. You can see a piece of that wall preserved under glass on the second floor of the old **Pima County Courthouse** at the corner of Washington Street and Main Avenue. You'll also learn about the four flags that have flown over Tucson. In 1776, the Spanish claimed it. Later, it belonged to Mexico. In 1853, Arizona was included in the Gadsden Purchase, and Tucson became part of the United States. Then, during the Civil War, the city became part of the Confederate territory.

There is recent history to discover as well, for Tucsonians were determined to rescue their decaying downtown. As you walk around the revitalized central city and drive through the omnipresent foothills, you'll be introduced to contemporary Tucson, a city for tomorrow. *Megatrends* author John Naisbitt singled out Tucson as one of the ten cities of great opportunity in the United States.

As the Pima County seat, this city of about 600,000 people serves as the economic hub for both southern Arizona and northern Mexico. As you shop and dine here, you will notice that many of the restaurants and retail outlets serve both Phoenix and Tucson. But despite the desert climate, open skies, and familiar names, you'll soon feel the difference in spirit between urban Phoenix and more laid-back Tucson, a difference that the smaller community celebrates.

Arizona Historical Society/Tucson. 949 East Second Street. This museum features changing and permanent exhibits that tell Arizona's history from Spanish Colonial times through the territorial years. There's also a research library and gift shop, and docent-led tours are available by reservation. Free. (520) 628-5774. www.w3.arizona.edu/~azhist.

Center for Creative Photography. On the University of Arizona campus. During the week, park in the garage at Speedway and Park on the northeast corner and walk across the street to the center. A collection of more than 50,000 photographs are housed in this striking, contemporary building. The archives of Ansel Adams are housed and displayed here. A research library is open to the public. Donations suggested. Free. (520) 621-7968. www.creativephotography.org.

John C. Fremont House. 151 South Granada Avenue. The Arizona Historical Society operates this home, which is a restored 1880s adobe. It was once rented by territorial governor Fremont. It was also

the home of the pioneer Sosa and Carrillo families and contains
nineteenth-century furnishings as well as a collection of American
antiques. There is a unique "touch table" for children. Reservations
are suggested. Open Wednesday through Saturday only, 10:00 A.M.
to 4:00 P.M. Free. (520) 622–0956.

International Wildlife Museum. 4800 West Gates Pass Road.
Nearly 300 mammals and birds from six continents are realistically
displayed in natural habitats with many excellent interactive exhibits
that provide additional information. While the building looks like a
misplaced castle-fortress in the desert, the collection is complete and
well displayed. There are guided tours, wildlife films, videos, and
restaurants. Fee. (520) 617–1439.

Playmaxx, Inc. 2520 North Coyote Drive. This museum features
a unique collection of yo-yos from 1930 through the future. Exhibits
include a photo history, and factory tours are available. Free; donation requested. (520) 623–7085. www.proyo.com.

Tohono Chul Park. 7366 Paseo del Norte. This park is land-
scaped beautifully with natural vegetation and gardens that feature nature trails, demonstrations, and ethnobotanical gardens.
There's also a geological re-creation of the nearby Catalina Mountains, a recirculating stream, *ramadas,* an art gallery with good
quality arts and crafts displayed, and an exhibit hall. The gift shop
is worth browsing through, and a tearoom is available for refreshments. This is a great destination for a breakfast or lunch respite.
Fee. (520) 742–6455. www.phonochulpark.org.

Tucson Botanical Gardens. 2150 North Alvernon Way. Enjoy a
collection of gardens that includes a historical Tucson area, arid landscaping, herbs, irises, tropical greenhouses, wildflowers, Native American crops, and vegetables. Fee. (520) 326–9255. www.azstarnet.com.

University of Arizona Museum of Art. On the campus of the U.
of A. A permanent collection of art spans the Middle Ages through
the twentieth century. There are changing exhibitions that feature
student, faculty, and guest artists. Free. (520) 621–7567.

WHERE TO EAT

Tucson has wonderful restaurants that serve all varieties of ethnic
food. Mexican food is served Sonoran-style and is slightly spicier
than the Phoenix version. Continental cuisine is as elegant as that

found in any city three times its size. Here are some with special historic or cultural significance:

Arizona Inn. 2200 East Elm Street. Continental dining is graciously served at this landmark hotel. Located in the central city, the dining room is quiet and relaxing. Furnishings are all original and were made by the returning veterans of World War I. You can eat indoors or outdoors where you face the lovely gardens. The food is as terrific as the setting. $$-$$$; ☐. (520) 325-1541.

Janos. 3770 East Sunrise Drive. Janos is acknowledged as one of the best chefs in Tucson. Service at this restaurant is friendly and warm, and the menu, which changes seasonally, is uniformly superb. Presentation is special, and reservations are required at this four-star, award-winning dining favorite. $$$; ☐. (520) 615-6100.

Karichimaka Restaurant. 5252 South Mission Road. When it opened in 1949, this restaurant, on the way to San Xavier Del Bac, was out in the country. The city has grown up, but the location remains the same, as does the cuisine: Sonoran-style Mexican food. $-$$; ☐. (520) 883-0311.

Li'l Abners. 8501 North Silverbell Road. Li'l Abners claims it serves up "world famous" mesquite-broiled steaks and chicken. They are delicious. This location was a Butterfield Express stage stop during pioneer days. Today it offers dining, drinking, and dancing served up in a lush desert area. To get there, you'll head west on Ina Road to Silverbell. Turn north on Silverbell. $$-$$$; ☐. (520) 744-2800.

Pinnacle Peak. 6541 East Tanque Verde Road, in Trail Dust Town. Like the Phoenix edition, this is western living at its most casual—and dangerous, if you wear a tie. Anyone who wears a tie in Pinnacle Peak risks its being cut off by the waitress or waiter in a public ceremony. The cut tie is displayed in the restaurant along with the wearer's business card. Cowboy steaks, ribs, and western pit beef in a skillet are specialties. After dinner, walk around Trail Dust Town and enjoy the shops. Even if you don't buy anything, the walk will do you good after downing a gigantic steak. $$; ☐. (520) 296-0911.

The Tack Room. 7300 East Vacor Ranch Trail. Tucson's only five-star restaurant and a local favorite for years, this definitely is worth your time and money. The continental food is excellent, the atmosphere polished and genteel. The restaurant name refers to the fact that the property was once the site of the nation's first championship quarter-horse race track, Moltacqua. The white adobe hacienda that became the Tack Room was built overlooking that track. In 1946, the property was turned into Rancho Del Rio guest ranch, and in 1965 the Tack Room opened as Arizona's first gourmet dining room. The same family has owned and operated the restaurant since then. Some of the original recipes of Alma Vactor, who did all the cooking for the guest-ranch guests, are featured. Plan an entire evening enjoying the twinkling views of Tucson in the distance, impeccable service, and outstanding cuisine. $$$; ☐. (520) 722–2800.

WHERE TO STAY

Like Phoenix, Tucson is famous for its resorts. If you have a "hankerin'" for a dude ranch, Tucson is bursting with them. There are more guest and dude ranches in southern Arizona than anywhere else in the country. If you prefer a quick overnight in a basic motel, you can find that, too. But if you want to stay in out-of-the-ordinary accommodations, read on. For a more complete list of accommodations, contact the Arizona Hotel & Lodging Association, 1240 East Missouri Avenue, Phoenix 85014-2912, or call (602) 604-0729.

Arizona Inn. 2200 East Elm Street. If you like historical Tucson at its most serene, you'll enjoy this world-famous hotel. There is no flash or glitz here, just unhurried, unchanged hospitality served up at its best. In the heart of town, the Arizona Inn has served an illustrious clientele over the years. Ask the staff about the celebrity guests who like the paneled, hacienda mood of this homey inn.

The inn has eighty rooms, all individually decorated, and many have private patios. The atmosphere is 1930s with modern amenities. The library in the main sitting room is filled with books, the living room is stately but inviting, and the 60-foot heated pool is sheltered on all sides. The restaurant is one of the city's best and features continental cuisine. But while the main dining rooms are lovely, plan to have breakfast on the patio. Then be sure to stroll around the grounds to enjoy the gardens of this gracious hotel.

The history of the Arizona Inn is fascinating. Take time to read the small book placed in each room that tells its story. This is one of the best places to stay in the city if you enjoy a very civilized approach to vacationing. Even one evening here can do a lot to unwind a harried guest. Prices are reasonable in the winter and a downright bargain in the summer. $$-$$$; ☐. (520) 325-1541.

Loews Ventana Canyon. 7000 North Resort Drive. Tucson's most elegant addition to the total resort scene has it all. Choose from golf, tennis, swimming pools, horseback riding, nature trails, superb restaurants, and health club facilities in an incomparably beautiful desert setting.

Golfers rave about the desert courses. The Gold Room presents ultra-sophisticated dining. But man-made attractions pale beside following the nature trail on the property, a gentle, easy, twenty-minute walk you can do in the daytime or evening. A gorgeous waterfall greets you at the end of your brief journey. $$$; ☐. (520) 299-2020 or (800) 522-5455. www.loewshotel.com.

The Westin La Paloma. 3800 East Sunrise. The hotel offers tennis, racquetball, volleyball, swimming, a Jack Nicklaus-designed golf course, and more. Rooms have balconies or patios, and child care can be arranged. Five restaurants serve everything from fresh seafood to gourmet meals, and hungry swimmers can simply swim up to the poolside bar and grill to chow down. $$; ☐. (520) 742-6000. www.westin.com.

GUEST RANCHES

The Tucson area has a number of excellent guest ranches within an hour or two of the city. For a complete listing, contact the Metropolitan Tucson Convention and Visitor Bureau at (520) 624-1817. Most guest ranches are small and accommodate no more than sixty guests. Some offer opportunities for "dudes"; others are for more rugged riders. Names to know include the **Lazy K Bar Guest Ranch,** 16 miles northwest of Tucson; **White Stallion Ranch,** 17 miles northwest of Tucson; and **Wild Horse Ranch,** in Tucson. All are close to the city.

Tanque Verde Guest Ranch. 1431 East Speedway. This year-round ranch, a Tucson landmark, features comfortable, western accommodations; one hundred horses; tennis courts; an indoor health spa; and gourmet dining. You'll need to stay longer than overnight to get a flavor of all that this ranch has to offer. The ranch backs up to a national forest filled with saguaros. Riding trails wind through unspoiled desert. Tanque Verde runs an excellent riding school. Instruction is available, and all levels of riders can be accommodated. The breakfast trail ride is a special treat. Don't be surprised to hear many languages being spoken here, as this is a favorite with international guests.

The atmosphere is western casual. The patios and dining areas are spacious. It's great in the winter, spring, and fall. Summer packages make this an affordable destination for families and international guests. $$$; ☐. (520) 296-6275. www.tanqueverderanch.com.

BED & BREAKFASTS

El Presidio Inn. 297 North Main Avenue. This is an award-winning luxury B&B in a historic Victorian adobe mansion built in 1880. The garden is romantic and lush, and the appointments are superb. Located within walking distance of Tucson's historic downtown, guests enjoy a complete breakfast, evening treats, and elegant surroundings. $$-$$$. (520) 623-6151.

BUCKEYE

Eagle Mountain Ranch. 12100 South Dean Road, Rainbow Valley. Take I–10 West to exit 121, Jackrabbit Trail. Go south on Jackrabbit Trail to Narramore Road. Turn west onto Dean Road and follow the signs to Eagle Mountain Ranch. This rustic, western stables and miniature western town is located forty-five minutes west of Phoenix in the town of Rainbow Valley, just outside of Buckeye. Buckeye is an agricultural community that is testimony to what Phoenix looked like prior to the population boom following World War II.

Although now connected by a freeway to the big city, Buckeye clings to its rural roots. The drive to the ranch is lined with cotton and cornfields, with mountains rising in the distance, unimpeded by intruding tall buildings. The sense of wide open space is so great, utility lines seem almost nonexistent.

Eagle Mountain Ranch is surrounded by the Estrella and White Tanks Mountains. It offers guests the opportunity to see the wide open real west from horseback (or hayride wagon) any day of the week. The ranch is adjacent to 300 square miles of open desert range and is punctuated by the Buckeye Hills, which offer miles of varied riding trails.

Owners Dale and Pat Parker organize trail rides at the ranch, complete with steak cookouts, campfires, and traditional cowboy breakfasts. Rides are organized for groups or individuals. The Parkers ask that individuals (as opposed to groups that book further in advance) call for reservations at least twenty-four hours in

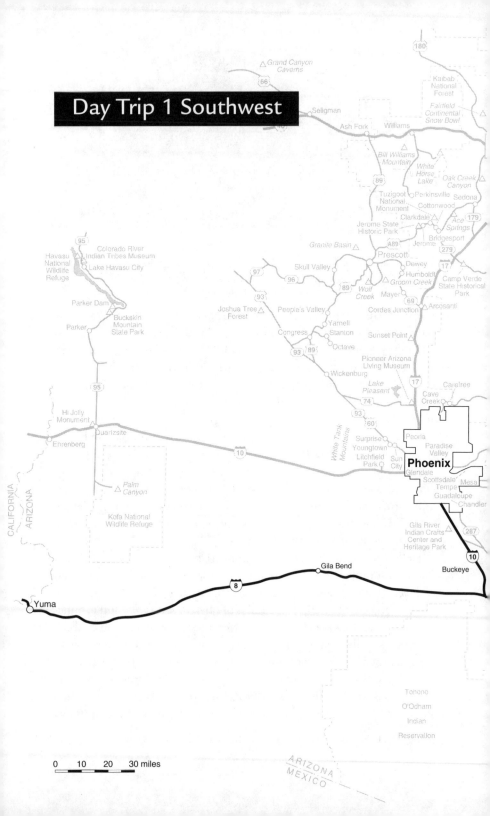

Day Trip 1 Southwest

180

Kaibab National Forest

Fairfield Continental Snow Bowl

△ Grand Canyon Caverns

66

Seligman

Ash Fork   Williams

Bill Williams Mountain   *White Horse Lake*   Oak Creek Canyon

89

Tuzigoot National Monument   Perkinsville   Sedona

Cottonwood

Clarkdale   Ace Springs   179

Jerome State Historic Park

Granite Basin △   A89   Jerome   279

95   Colorado River Indian Tribes Museum

Havasu National Wildlife Refuge   Lake Havasu City

Prescott   Dewey   17

Skull Valley   Humboldt

97   96   *Groom Creek*   Camp Verde State Historical Park

93   89   *Wolf Creek*   Mayer   69   Arcosanti

Parker Dam

Buckskin Mountain State Park

Joshua Tree Forest   People's Valley   Cordes Junction

Parker

Yarnell

Congress   Stanton   Sunset Point

93   89   Octave

Pioneer Arizona Living Museum

Wickenburg

95   *Lake Pleasant*   17   Carefree

Hi Jolly Monument   74   Cave Creek

93

Quartzsite   60   Peoria

Ehrenberg   Surprise   **Phoenix**   Paradise Valley

10   Youngtown

Litchfield Park   Sun City   Scottsdale   Mesa

Glendale   Tempe   Chandler

Guadalupe

Palm Canyon

Kofa National Wildlife Refuge

Gila River Indian Crafts Center and Heritage Park   287

10

Buckeye

Gila Bend

8

CALIFORNIA   ARIZONA

Yuma

White Tank Mountains

Tohono O'Odham Indian Reservation

0   10   20   30 miles

ARIZONA
MEXICO

advance. They request a minimum of two people to book a ride. Eagle Mountain Ranch is open every day of the year.

Eagle Mountain Ranch was desert—claimed at the turn of the twentieth century by two horsebreakers and bought from them by the Parker family. After more than thirty-five years living an urban life as an engineer, Dale Parker decided to come back to a simpler way of life and returned to the family farm, where he grew up raising cotton and cattle, to share this special lifestyle.

Recently the Parkers have begun constructing a small "western town" for their guests' enjoyment. The "town," designed and built by an ex–Hollywood stuntman friend, spreads under the shade of an enormous cottonwood tree. The area enables visitors to enjoy cookouts, breakfast, or relaxing while visiting with Dale Parker, who is a wealth of information about the geology and history of the area.

Two-hour trail rides are offered as well as sunset rides during the summer months. $$. (623) 386–2316.

WHERE TO EAT

La Placita. 424 East Monroe Avenue. This newly remodeled Mexican restaurant was designed by owner Joe Amabisco and serves authentic Mexican dishes made from recipes handed down through generations of Joe's family. Groups can ask about arranging a Mexican fiesta. Open daily for lunch and dinner except Sunday. $-$$. (623) 386–4632.

After a day of the Old West, "riding the range," and indulging in homemade Mexican fare, day trippers can head east on I–10 to return to Phoenix or stay the night in nearby Goodyear.

GILA BEND

Pick up this day trip by following I–10 southeast out of Phoenix to its junction with I–8. Then go 62 miles west on I–8 to Gila Bend.

This is a long (approximately four-hour) trip; however, there are enough historical attractions to make it worthwhile. If you make this trip during the hot summer months, drive during the early morning or evening hours. Along the way, you'll see the surrealistic California sand dunes near Yuma.

Gila Bend is often called the fan belt capital of the world, not because fan belts are made here, but because there are probably more belts *replaced* here than any other place in the world.

Originally, the town grew up where the Gila River took a deep bend toward the south before heading west. The community prospered when the Butterfield Overland Stage scheduled stops here in the 1870s. Miners en route to California gold fields, mail-order brides, and eastern businessmen who were sizing up the future made themselves at home in Gila Bend for a night or two.

Then, in 1880, the train came near town, and the town gradually moved away from the river toward the tracks. Ultimately the river changed its course and moved north of town. All that's left of the river's influence is the city's name.

YUMA

To get to Yuma from Gila Bend, travel I-10 for 117 miles. Situated in the southwestern corner of the state, Yuma has an interesting heritage. History confirms that the area was visited as early as 1540 by the Spaniards. By the 1870s this community was the key southwestern city in the territory. First called Colorado City (for the river), then Arizona City (for the territory), and eventually Yuma City, the name finally was shortened to Yuma.

Yuma won a permanent place in Arizona Territory by 1870. Today the residents of this city rely on the same river waters to support agriculture, commerce, recreation, and the military. Located close to San Diego and Mexico, this small city attracts thousands of winter visitors to its sunny environs.

Today some historic buildings commemorate what was once the busy **Yuma Crossing.** The Colorado and Gila Rivers once converged here before the Gila changed its course. Eighty years before the Pilgrims landed, beginning in 1540, Spanish explorers rode through this land in search of the Seven Cities of Gold.

As time passed, countless trails met at this junction. Kit Carson guided American troops. The Mormon Battalion trudged through, carving the first road from Santa Fe to San Diego, and during the gold rush days, more than 30,000 people seeking their fortunes trekked across the river here on their way to California.

In the 1850s, the shallow draft steamboat opened the Colorado River to shipping, and Yuma became a major port of entry for Arizona. The Fort Yuma Quartermaster Depot swarmed with the bustle of a military supply hub. During the 1860s, 1870s, and 1880s, during the height of the Apache Wars, the Yuma Quartermaster Depot supplied military posts throughout the region. Then the train arrived in 1877, and the depot was abandoned in 1883.

For more information, contact the Yuma Convention and Visitor Bureau. (928) 783-0071.

WHERE TO GO

U.S. Army Quartermasters Depot/Arizona State Park. Second Avenue behind City Hall. The depot was established in 1864 and served the entire Southwest as a matériel transfer and distribution point for troops stationed at the military outposts throughout the Arizona Territory. The depot saw much activity during the 1870s and 1880s during the height of the Apache Wars, but it was abandoned in 1883 after trains arrived here in 1877. Both the Quartermaster's office and the stone Water Reservoir have been restored to their original condition.

Yuma Old Territorial Prison. Giss Parkway and Prison Hill Road, right off I-8 near the Colorado River. Now a state park, the prison operated from 1876 to 1909 and had a miserable reputation. Western bad men (and women) used it as their address—folks such as Buckskin Frank Leslie and "Heartless" Pearl Hart. Museum exhibits document the story of the prison cells, which are authentically furnished and add a hands-on sense of reality. You can also take a ranger-guided tour of the facility. Fee. (928) 783-4771. www.pr.state.az.us.

Century House Museum. 240 South Madison Avenue. This was the home of pioneer merchant E. F. Sanguinetti and is one of Yuma's most historic buildings. Now a regional museum of the Arizona Historical Society, it holds historical documents, photographs, and artifacts. Walk through the gardens and aviaries on the grounds. Free. (928) 782-1841.

Quechan Indian Museum. Across the Colorado River from Yuma at Fort Yuma on Indian Hill Road, this museum is located near the territorial prison. Fort Yuma, one of the oldest military posts in Arizona, is now headquarters for the Quechan tribe. Inside you'll see exhibits of tribal artifacts. Fee. (760) 572-0664.

Yuma Art Center. 281 Gila Street. Located in a restored Southern Pacific Railroad depot, the center presents exhibitions of contemporary Arizona and Native American artists. Fee. (928) 783-2314. www.yumachamber.org.

Peanut Patch. 4322 East County Thirteenth Street. This store was opened in 1977 on the Didier Family Farm and sells some of the finest peanut products in the West. Nuts are grown on the farm and are sold at the store on the property. Tours of the plant are available. Free. (928) 726-6292.

Yuma County Live Steamers. Eighth Street and Levee. From October through June, train buffs can ride back through time on the historic Yuma Valley Railroad. The train travels along the banks of the Colorado River through the Cocopah Indian Reservation. Passengers ride aboard a 1922 Pullman pulled by a first-generation 1941 diesel locomotive. A local historian tells stories, which adds to the fun. Lunch and dinner rides are scheduled, but the train has been known to run sporadically. Fee. Call for more information and reservations. (928) 783-3456.

Yuma River Tours. 1920 Arizona Avenue. Don't see Yuma without taking a river tour. The boats travel past ruins and petroglyphs, ferry crossings, and homesteads. You'll see steamboat landings and mining camps and visit a wildlife refuge, one of the few untouched refuges in the entire country. This is a special experience that shouldn't be missed. Fee. (928) 783-4400.

Pick up a self-guided tour pamphlet from the Chamber of Commerce, 377 Main Street, for more to see in Yuma. (928) 782-2567.

WHERE TO EAT

Chretins. 485 South Fifteenth Avenue. This family-owned Mexican restaurant is huge, old, and funky. Expect to wait if you arrive on a weekend during the winter, but the Mexican menu is homemade and worth it. The atmosphere is old Yuma with a touch of Mexico. $$; □. (928) 782-1291.

La Fonda Tortilla Factory. 1095 South Third Avenue. This place serves excellent Mexican food. The service is slow, but the tortillas are delicious. $$; □. (520) 783-6902.

QUARTZSITE

To visit the main destination of this day trip, Lake Havasu City, you'll drive four and one-half to five hours—one way. Obviously this trip is best done as an overnight in Lake Havasu City. Head west out of Phoenix on I-10 past Litchfield Park. Eventually, after 112 miles, I-10 intersects with A-95 to Quartzsite.

Situated in the Mohave Desert, Quartzsite is best known for its great numbers of "snowbirds" (winter visitors, as they are called), who flock to this community each year in vast numbers, pulling mobile homes with them. Visitors appreciate the sunshine and inexpensive, quiet living Quartzsite affords. The town hosts an annual rock and mineral show in February that attracts more than 850,000 people.

WHERE TO GO

Hi Jolly Monument. Quartzsite, in the Quartzsite City Cemetery. Go west on the main street from the center of town about ¼ mile and follow the signs to the road leading to the city cemetery. Here you will see an unusual reminder of a pioneer experiment.

In the 1850s the U.S. War Department decided to introduce camels into the desert. The Hi Jolly Monument honors Hadji Ali, one of the Arab camel drivers who was brought here to drive the beasts. The experiment was successful, but the cavalry members disliked riding the disagreeable, smelly animals and wanted to disband the camel corps. The official report stated that the beasts got sore feet

123

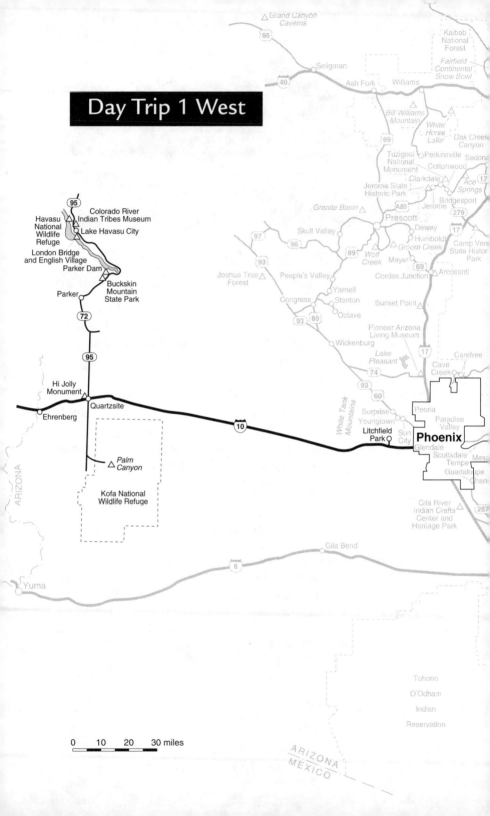

Day Trip 1 West

from walking over the desert, when in actuality the cavalry got sore from riding the camels!

When the camel experiment ended, most of the other drivers went home, but Hadji Ali, or Hi Jolly, as he was called, stayed to become a prospector. He is buried in the city cemetery.

Nineteen miles west of Quartzsite is Ehrenberg, a haven for rock hunters looking for agates, limonite cubes, and quartz—all abundant in the area.

PALM CANYON

Hikers will want to detour south for about 20 miles on A-95 to the Kofa National Wildlife Refuge. Watch for the sign 18⅞₀ miles south of Quartzsite that reads: PALM CANYON AND KOFA GAME RANGE (It's an old sign; it should say PALM CANYON AND KOFA NATIONAL WILDLIFE REFUGE.) Turn east and follow the gravel road leading to the canyon. You must drive slowly for about 9 miles. There's a parking area at the end of this road. You can hike ¼ mile through the towering narrow canyon on a trail to Palm Canyon. This secluded spot, nestled in the Kofa Mountains, is home to Arizona's only native stand of palm trees.

Don't attempt to visit Palm Canyon during the hot summer months. Temperatures soar, and you'll sizzle. Hiking is at its best during the spring and autumn. The best time to visit is from the end of October through April. Free. (928) 783-7861.

PARKER

Retrace your route by driving north on A-95 to its intersection with A-72. Follow A-72 northwest to Parker, which is 35 miles north of Quartzsite. If you have time to explore, stop at the Parker Chamber of Commerce, 1217 California Avenue (928-669-2174), to pick up information. There are a variety of events held during the year, including several boat races, so check to see what's going on.

Parker is a river town—part California beach, part Arizona river rat—and exists for power and water sports. Late summer can be brutal. August temperatures climb to 120 degrees, sometimes for a week at a time.

Each year the community hosts an international inner tube race in mid-June. It attracts hundreds of dedicated tubers, who travel along the 7 miles in a variety of outlandish outfits. www. coloradoriver info.com/parker.

WHERE TO GO

Buckskin Mountain State Park. Twenty miles north of Parker on A–95. Situated along a grassy, shady section of the riverbank, this park offers a quiet respite in often-raucous Parker. Enjoy the many campsites and hiking trails. There is a concession operation, but you might prefer to bring a picnic lunch. Fee. (928) 667–3231. www.pr.state.az.us.

Colorado River Indian Tribes Museum. Corner of Agency and Mohave Roads in Parker. This newly renovated museum displays the world's largest collection of Chemehuevi Indian basketry. In addition, visitors will enjoy seeing Mohave pottery and exhibits that interpret the four tribes in the area: Mohave, Chemehuevi, Hopi, and Navajo. The only museum in La Paz County, it stresses both historical and cultural exhibits. Inquire here about how to see the Blythe Intaglios, ancient Mohave figures that are etched in the nearby desert. For more information write to the Colorado River Indian Tribes Museum, Route 1, Box 23-B, Parker 85344. A donation is suggested. (928) 669–9211. www.critlibrary.com.

Parker Dam. On A–95 in Parker Dam, California, 17 miles north of Parker, Arizona. Continue on A–95 through Parker and turn right at Agency Road. There's a stoplight. Continue on that road to the dam. As you cross the river onto the dam, you'll enter California; the Colorado River is the state boundary.

Parker Dam was built on the Colorado in 1934 and is one of the deepest dams in the world. You'll see only about one-third of the structure; the rest is under the water's surface. With a height of 320 feet and base thickness of 100 feet, it's an imposing edifice. Behind it is Lake Havasu, which contains 648,000 acre-feet of water. (An acre-foot is the amount of water it takes to cover one acre at a depth of one foot.)

You can take a self-guided tour of the dam, which includes stops from the top of the dam to the generating station below the water. Taped speeches describe what you're seeing. If you've never visited a desert dam and you have a spare half hour, treat yourself to the experience and marvel at the technology. Free. For more information contact the Parker Chamber of Commerce in Arizona, (928) 669-2174. www.coloradoriverinfo.com/parker.

LAKE HAVASU CITY

From the dam, drive north for an hour on A-95, which winds along the riverbank to Lake Havasu City. This area, like neighboring Parker, is best known for water-based recreation. You can make the Phoenix–Lake Havasu City trip in a day, but then it's more of a marathon than a day trip. It is better to plan this trip as an overnight, or even two overnights, so you have time to enjoy the area.

Lake Havasu City, established in 1963, was designed as a self-sufficient, planned community for several thousand residents. Although somewhat isolated from the rest of the state, it continues to attract newcomers and is growing into an attractive community for people who love a quiet, water-recreation lifestyle. Don't expect to see any "big city" stuff here. Come to relax, not for fine dining. Lake Havasu City is strictly small-town.

Geologically, the area around Lake Havasu and Lake Havasu City is a gold mine. Within a 10-mile radius there are specimens of volcanic rock, geodes, jasper, obsidian, turquoise, and agate. Native American relics and abandoned mines also make this trip worthwhile for adventurous backpackers. If colored chips interest you more than pretty rocks, you're just 150 miles from Las Vegas and less than an hour from Laughlin, Nevada, across the Colorado River.

Make the Lake Havasu Tourism Bureau your first stop in town. As you enter Lake Havasu City, you'll come to a stoplight. Head away from the lake and drive to the top of the hill. Turn left and then take the first immediate left into the parking lot. The tourism bureau is located at 1930 Mesquite Avenue. Ask for a visitor's packet and dining guide. (928) 453-3444. www.azguide.com.

WHERE TO GO

Blue River Safari. Plan to take this guided boat trip while you're in Lake Havasu City to learn about the lake and the **Havasu National Wildlife Refuge,** which is located along the north shore of Lake Havasu, a few miles north of town. This wildlife preserve is home to a number of birds and small game. Fee. (928) 453–5848.

The *Dixie Bell.* Anchored at the dock near London Bridge. Lake Havasu is a dream come true for water-sports fans. Nearly every form of boating is available, from canoeing and waterskiing to Jet Skiing to riding paddle wheelers. The *Dixie Bell* is a replica of an Old South stern-wheeler. It's the largest boat of its nature on the Colorado River and maintains a regular cruise schedule. The tour is narrated and takes one hour and twenty minutes. Fee. For information call (928) 453–6776 or (928) 855–0888.

Lake Havasu and Lake Havasu State Park. This lake, which was formed when Parker Dam was built on the Colorado River, is 45 miles long and attracts anglers, boaters, water, and Jet Skiers, and nature lovers. From town, follow Lincoln Bridge Road, which sweeps along the western boundary of Lake Havasu City. As you drive, you'll see signs for many public beaches that are state owned and operated. All types of facilities are offered—from camping to resort living.

You can rent a houseboat, Jet Skis, or speedboat and cruise the blue lake expanse, or you can just drive to a beach, roll up your pant legs, and wade around to your heart's content. The beachfront is rocky, so those with tender toes should take tennis shoes.

The 13,000-acre park, which was developed along the 23 miles of shoreline surrounding Lake Havasu, contains beaches and campgrounds.

Three beaches are especially popular. **Pittsburg Point,** at Lake Havasu City, is across from the London Bridge and has a variety of concession facilities. Follow McCulloch Boulevard across the bridge and continue on McCulloch as it loops around and becomes Beachcomber Boulevard. **Windsor Beach,** north of the London Bridge on the mainland, is a good day facility and has boat-launching ramps. From McCulloch Boulevard, turn north onto London Bridge Road and go north to Windsor Beach. **Cattail Cove,** 15 miles south of Lake Havasu City on A-95, has concession campgrounds and is easily accessible to the lake. Fee. For more information call Lake Havasu State Park. (928) 855-7851.

London Bridge. At McCulloch Boulevard and A-95, spanning Thompson Bay. Gimmicky? Of course. But there is a thrill to walking, bicycling, or driving over the London Bridge, as incongruous as it seems suspended over the Colorado River in Arizona.

How did it get there? In 1967 the city of London decided that the London Bridge was too small for the current volume of traffic, so after 136 years of use, the bridge was offered for sale. Robert P. Mc-Culloch Sr., the founder of Lake Havasu City, purchased it, had it dismantled in England with every block numbered, and shipped it to the United States. Three years later, the reconstruction was finished at a total cost of $7.5 million. It was a publicity stunt of grand proportions that instantly put Lake Havasu City on the map. The London Bridge formally opened in Arizona in October 1971 to the delight of everyone who sees it.

The English Village. This is the area around the bridge that sports a full-size village featuring gift shops and restaurants. Somehow, under the shadow of the London Bridge, it doesn't seem incongruous in its Arizona desert setting. Wander around or stop to eat at one of the restaurants or cafes.

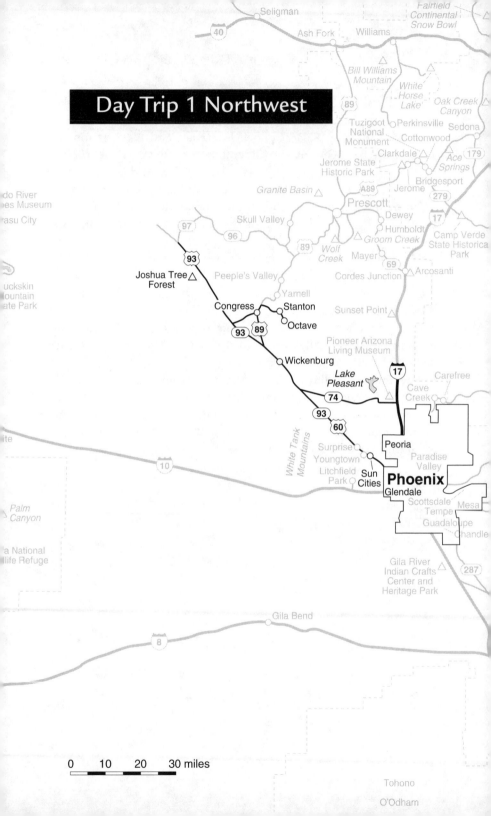

Day Trip 1 Northwest

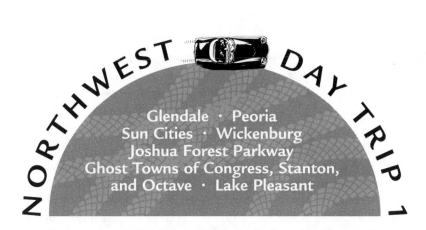

Glendale · Peoria
Sun Cities · Wickenburg
Joshua Forest Parkway
Ghost Towns of Congress, Stanton,
and Octave · Lake Pleasant

GLENDALE

Unlike most Arizona drives, this excursion is not scenic at first. But take heart—the gorgeous desert foothills await. Along the way you'll pass through urban Phoenix, visit the world's largest retirement community, and get a taste of the Old West. Be prepared for city driving and long, open stretches. You'll cross the Agua Fria River (which may or may not have water in it depending upon the season) and view the White Tank Mountains in the distance.

Drive northwest on Grand Avenue (US–60) from Phoenix through Glendale, once called "The City of Perpetual Harvest." Established in 1885 as a church community, Glendale soon became a farming town. Today it is one of the largest shipping points for fresh garden vegetables in the country.

Glendale in recent years has found its niche as a center for antiques and quaint shops. Although it is Arizona's fourth-largest city, it purposefully looks back to the days when life was simpler and people were friendlier. Tourists are discovering Glendale's historic downtown, which looks like a turn-of-the-twentieth-century village. Antiques buffs appreciate finding the state's greatest concentration of antiques shops as well as a fine assortment of craft galleries, restaurants, and tearooms. Of special interest is the candy factory, which is open to tours. Free trolley rides loop through downtown and Catlin Court. The third Thursday of every month in November and December, more than forty antiques stores and galleries host the Antique Walk until 9:00 P.M.

WHERE TO GO

Catlin Court Historical District. 5890 West Palmaire Avenue. Located near the heart of Glendale, Catlin Court is bordered by white picket fences and brick-trimmed sidewalks. There are gazebos and gaslights and gardens as well as historic craftsman bungalows, which have been beautifully restored. Catlin Court contains tearooms, where visitors can turn back the clock to more gracious times, and rows of antiques shops and craft boutiques. For information call (623) 435–2559.

Cerreta Candy Company. 5345 West Glendale Avenue. This family-owned business makes candy for Disneyland, Magic Mountain, and Knotts Berry Farms, among others. Free tours of the factory are offered. The wrapped candies are terrific. Free. For tours call (623) 930–1000. www.cerretas.com.

Sahuaro Ranch Park. Located on Fifty-ninth Avenue north of Olive. Sahuaro Ranch includes a sixteen-acre park and preserves one of the Phoenix area's finest and oldest homesteads. The ranch has seven original buildings, a lavish rose garden, and more than one-hundred peacocks that roam the grounds. When you enter the park you will see the main house and buildings. Continue on, and you will see the public park area, complete with *ramadas* and playgrounds. It is listed on the National Register of Historic Places. To reserve a special *ramada,* call the City Parks and Recreation department at (623) 930–2820. Tours of the main house begin in mid-October through May weekends from 1:00 to 4:00 P.M. Tours are held every thirty to forty-five minutes. For more information, or to book *ramadas* for large parties or weddings, call the Glendale Historical Society at (623) 435–0072.

The Bead Museum. 5754 West Glenn Drive. The museum is easily accessible from I–17 by exiting west on Glendale Avenue and traveling a few miles to Fifty-eighth Avenue. Turn north (right) on Fifty-eighth Avenue and travel 1 block, and the museum will be clearly visible on the northeast corner of Glenn Drive and Fifty-eighth Avenue. Beads from all over the world are on display, proof of the ingenuity and imagination that have gone into human adornment throughout history. Special exhibitions are mounted, and there is even a reference library. The Bead Museum Store sells a full range of beads, beading supplies, and books. Open seven days a week from 10:00 A.M. to 5:00 P.M. Free. For more information call (623) 931-2737. www.thebeadmuseum.com.

PEORIA

Peoria was founded in 1885 by four farming families who came from the Midwest and named the town for their hometown in Illinois. According to the city's history, these early settlers either built adobe homes or used large tents. Half the tent contained a floor and served as the living quarters while the other half housed grain, hay, spare furniture, and tools. Rattlesnakes, scorpions, and desert rats often sought refuge under the floor from the hot desert sun. Life became more difficult when floods washed out the canal diversion dam, forcing a 6-mile trek to the Grand Canal for water which they hauled in barrels back to town.

As production at the Vulture Mine in Wickenburg increased, traffic got busier along the route leading to the Grand Canal. In 1887, the road was named Grand Avenue. By 1888, Peoria had a U.S. Post Office and a population of 27. By 1970, Peoria sported only 2,500 people but in the last decade growth soared. Today, Peoria is a fast-growing city of more than 100,000 people, more in spring, when the Peoria Sports Complex hosts spring training for the Chicago Cubs.

Challenger Learning Center. One of more than forty learning centers in the United States, Canada, and Great Britain, the Challenger Learning Center of Arizona offers kids and grown-ups the thrill of space travel without ever leaving Earth. The Center is located within a striking architectural building that blends with the Sonoran desert. Inside, adults and children experience special flight simulations, viewings, and multimedia presentations. If you've never visited one of these centers, you are in for a treat. Tucson is also home to a Challenger Learning Center if you're touring that part of the state. Call ahead for information on special opportunities and camps. 21170 North Eighty-third Avenue. Fee. Open daily. (623) 322-2001. E-mail: clcaz@azchallenger.net.

The Wildlife World Zoo. Three miles west of Litchfield Road on Northern Avenue. Follow Grand Avenue (US-60) and turn right on

Litchfield Road. At Northern Avenue, turn right again. The zoo is 4 miles west on Northern. Walk through an aviary with more than thirty species of tropical birds and see the largest collection of marsupials (kangaroos and wallabies) in the country, all five types of the world's ostriches, and America's most complete pheasant display. There's always something new to see. The park also offers a safari train ride through exhibits, a giraffe feeding station, Arizona's first white tiger, and a carousel. It's a great place for children! Fee. (623) 935-WILD.

SUN CITIES

Back on Grand Avenue (US-60), continue northwest through Youngtown to Del Webb's Sun City, Sun City West, and Sun City Grand. These retirement cities are about 20 miles from downtown Phoenix. You'll know you're near when you see more electric golf carts than cars on the streets! Established in 1954, Youngtown was the first retirement community in the United States and continues to attract retirees. However, that town has been eclipsed in size by the Del Webb developments, which were begun in 1960. Today Sun City, Sun City West, and Sun City Grand compose the world's largest retirement communities. Even if you aren't thinking of giving up the office for golf, they are worth a visit.

At Sun City West, your driving tour includes Sundome Plaza, the Sundome Center for the Performing Arts, sports pavilion, Johnson Library, and other points of interest. For information call (623) 975-1900, or visit the development office at 13323 Meeker Boulevard.

WICKENBURG

Leaving the golf cart set behind, follow A-93 north to Wickenburg for a taste of the old and new West. As you proceed, you'll enter rolling foothills dotted with saguaros, ocotillos, and mesquite.

Wickenburg is located approximately 54 miles northwest of Phoenix and sits at the foot of the Bradshaw Mountains on the banks of the Hassayampa (Hah-sa-yampa) River. Legend has it that anyone who drinks from the Hassayampa never tells the truth again. As you approach the Hassayampa you may wonder how anyone ever drinks out of the river anyway, since usually it is a wide, dry, sandy riverbed. But look again. The green, lush area around it demonstrates the power of a desert river. Even a sporadic flow of water creates fertile soil out of dusty ground, and a stretch of the river flows underground.

Wickenburg was established by Henry Wickenburg, who searched for an elusive vein of gold for ten years. There are numerous stories about how he finally found that treasure. Some may be more truthful, but this legend is the best: When the failed prospector landed in what is now called Wickenburg, he was discouraged and alone. His partner had no faith in him, and to make matters worse, Wickenburg's balky burro refused to move. Looking up, the prospector saw a vulture circle, land, and eye the stubborn beast. In utter disgust, Wickenburg picked up a rock to throw at the bird. When the rock dropped, it split in half and revealed gold.

Regardless of the veracity of that tale, Wickenburg did stumble over the richest gold lode in Arizona and named it the Vulture Mine. Although his claim has long been exhausted and is no longer even open for tours, the town of Wickenburg retains its rustic gold rush image.

WHERE TO GO

Frontier Street. This area is preserved as it was in the 1800s, with a fine railway station, a former hotel, and other buildings. Follow US-60 west as it crosses the Hassayampa River. Frontier intersects with US-60. Wander at will.

Desert Caballeros Western Museum. 21 North Frontier Street. Turn left onto Frontier from US-60. Parking is next to the railroad tracks. Staffed and built by dedicated volunteers, this museum contains works by well-known western artists, including Frederic Remington and George Phippen. In addition to the art gallery, visit the Hall of History, period rooms, mineral room, and Mexican room. This museum is one of the state's lesser known gems, and the collection and the facility are both outstanding. The museum can be toured in an hour and is very much worth the trip. Free for children under six. (928) 684-2272.

Old 761. At Apache and Tegner Streets behind the Town Hall. From the museum, follow Frontier Street northwest to Apache Street.

Turn right on Apache to just north of Tegner Street. Here you will see the original steam engine and tender that chugged along the tracks from Chicago to the West.

Jail Tree. Tegner and Center Streets. From Old 761, follow Apache Street south. Turn left onto Tegner Street. You'll come upon a large, 200-year-old mesquite tree. Since Wickenburg didn't have a jail, the law used this tree to tether rowdies who caused trouble. You can see the leg irons, still attached to the tree, which accomplished the task. Law-abiding citizens can stop, clamp on the irons, and have their pictures taken.

Hassayampa River Preserve. On US-60, 3 miles southeast of Wickenburg. The preserve entrance is on the west side of the highway near mile marker 114. Although the Hassayampa River flows underground for most of its length, it comes to the surface near Wickenburg. Owned by the Nature Conservancy, the area has been restored to its natural state as a shady, life-filled riparian area. Today the Hassayampa Preserve consists of 4 miles of one of Arizona's last and finest Sonoran Desert streamside habitats. It supports 230 species of birds.

The preserve and headquarters were once parts of the Frederick Brill Ranch, now listed on Arizona's State Register of Historic Places. The four-room adobe core, which serves as the Visitor Center, was built in the 1860s by Brill, a Prussian immigrant who raised cattle and operated a stagecoach way station. An entrepreneur, Brill planted fruit orchards and operated the first carp farm in the state near Palm Lake.

When the Nature Conservancy purchased the property in December 1986, much of the land had been overgrazed and returned to desert. With care, it has become an invaluable biologic riparian resource.

Trails are easily accessible and not strenuous. A 1-mile nature trail leads through the leafy, gladed area next to the river. There's a less scenic but shorter loop trail around Palm Lake. On both trails it is important that all visitors respect the fragile ecosystem of the preserve. The revegetation has been one of the miracles of Mother Nature, and the conservancy wants to protect it for generations to come.

In addition to the self-guided walks, naturalists lead hikes on a seasonal schedule. These tours last about an hour and a half and are quite informative.

Save time to enjoy the Hassayampa Bookstore. It's located in a lovely adobe structure and has books and guides on plants and animals of the Southwest, including history, travel guides, and gift items. There's also a reference library the public can use.

There's no picnicking, and pets must be left at home. However, this peaceful, serene setting is comfortable even on a warm spring day. Free, but a donation is appreciated. Call for hours. (928) 684-2772.

WHERE TO EAT AND STAY

Chaparral Ice Cream & Bakery. 45 North Tegner. This ice cream parlor features homemade ice cream. The best flavor is Hassayampa Mud. You can have breakfast, lunch, or an early dinner here of pastries, soup, and sandwiches. The atmosphere is authentic 1950s with red-and-white-checked tablecloths, roomy wooden booths, and a friendly staff. $-$$. (928) 684-3252.

Kay El Bar Ranch. Box 2480, Wickenburg 85358. This is a charming historic guest ranch owned and managed by two sisters and their husbands. Listed on the National Register of Historic Places, this small, intimate guest ranch is beautifully maintained and offers visitors an authentic western experience from trail riding to family-style dining. The setting is uniquely territorial-style Arizona. A two-night minimum stay is required, but to get the full flavor of this special getaway guest ranch, visitors will want to spend a week. The Kay El Bar is open from October through April. $$$; ☐. (928) 684-7593. www.kayelbar.com.

Rancho de los Caballeros. Five miles west of Wickenburg and 2 miles south of US-60 on Vulture Mine Road. Located in an especially scenic high desert setting, this "Ranch of the Gentlemen on Horseback" combines a luxurious resort setting with the relaxing ambience that is the hallmark of Southwestern hospitality. A unique combination of golf and riding allows guests to ride through miles of magnificent desert trails and tee off on rolling, challenging fairways in the same day without leaving the grounds. An elegant resort, Rancho de los Caballeros boasts a superb golf shop on its premises. Fine dining is available along with hearty western favorites. Open late fall to early spring. Reservations suggested. $$$. (928) 684-5484. E-mail: home@sunc.com.

JOSHUA FOREST PARKWAY

Northwest on US-93, 20 miles beyond Wickenburg, you'll be greeted by one of nature's more unusual welcoming committees: a strange, dense forest of Joshua trees. Located on both sides of the highway, hordes of thick-trunked cacti crowd the landscape and mesmerize passing tourists.

Joshua trees, which are actually tall, bristly yucca plants, were named by Mormon pioneers who thought the upright branches pointed toward the promised land. These slow-growing trees provide homes for twenty-five species of birds. In addition, pack rats gnaw off spiny leaf blades, and night lizards find that the rotted-out bark of wind-toppled Joshua trees provides their entire world. Usually found in the Mohave Desert, Joshua trees are rarely found in the Sonoran Desert, which makes this dense stand all the more exciting.

GHOST TOWNS OF CONGRESS, STANTON, AND OCTAVE

You may return to Phoenix from Wickenburg by heading southeast on US-89/A-93. Or, if you are up for adventure and have adequate gas in the tank, follow US-89 north 16 miles on a paved road to Congress for a leisurely journey through some authentic ghost towns. In Arizona, "authentic" means that you won't find snack bars, concession stands, or gift shops. What you *will* find are the ghosts of buildings from Arizona's past—crumbling structures slowly dying in the desert. Consequently, before you turn off onto the back road leading to Congress, Stanton, and Octave, if you see facilities and need to stop, do so.

You may prefer to combine this excursion with your return trip on US-89 south from Yarnell and Peeples Valley (see Day Trip 2 North from Phoenix).

Started as a mining camp, Congress was established in 1887. By 1891 it was estimated that $600,000 in ore was shipped from that mine, although it's possible that more than $1 million actually was taken out. After 1919 mining activity slowed to a trickle, and the town faded away. As you drive on this paved road, known only as "the road to Congress," look around at the crumbling foundations and faded memories of a once-glorious past. Only the dump of the mine stands within sight of the present town of Congress Junction.

Continue through Congress Junction about 4 miles and then turn right onto a gravel road. Watch for the sign that says that this is the road to Stanton and follow it. It looks rough, but it is graded and passable for passenger cars. Stanton is about 7 miles from Congress. As you bump along the road to this ghost town, note that it was built by pioneer C. C. Genung in 1871 at a cost of $7,650. Genung paid white men $75 a month, Mexicans received $65 a month, and Native Americans got 50 cents a day plus beans, flour, sugar, coffee, and venison to build that road. Today Stanton is privately owned.

When you reach Stanton, you'll want to investigate what's left of this mining camp. Originally called Antelope Station, the town was located on an old stage route and renamed for Charles P. Stanton, who was deputy county recorder. Legend has it that Stanton was a defrocked priest. For sure, he was a man of doubtful character as he ran the town, and he and the "Stanton Gang" raked in gold at the expense of the community. It's rumored that his gang cost Arizona settlers "more than all the Apaches put together." Ultimately Charles Stanton met his demise when he was shot by a man who believed that Stanton had insulted his sister.

Travel a few more miles on this same road to reach Octave, which is located 13 miles from Wickenburg. Now a maze of stone foundations, cellar pits, and ruins, it was once a bustling town of 3,000 hardy souls who came here for gold in 1863. Eventually $8 million was taken out of the quartz veins of Octave Mine. The mine continued in operation until World War II. Today it belongs to the wind, sun, and sand and to those adventurous types who love the silent, brooding allure of ghost towns.

As is true of any of Arizona's back roads, don't attempt to navigate the road to Stanton during rainy weather. The slick mountains and the barren desert make flash floods a real hazard. (See the section on flash floods at the end of this book.)

LAKE PLEASANT

To complete your day, what better excursion than to get out of the dusty ghost towns and head for Lake Pleasant? To reach this recreation site, go southeast on US–89 and backtrack for about 11 miles. At the junction of US–89 and A–74, follow A–74 east to Lake Pleasant, one of the many manufactured lakes dotting the Arizona desert. Arizonans take water seriously and dam rivers for flood control, surface water, and recreation. You may be surprised to know that Arizona has one of the highest boats-per-capita ratios in the country.

Lake Pleasant was formed when the Waddell Dam was constructed on the Agua Fria River. Today 24,000 acres of lake await, featuring every outdoor and water sport from camping and fishing to scuba diving, parasailing, and ultralight gliding. Watercraft can be rented at the marina. Picnic, rent Jet Skis, or just enjoy the rocky landscape and cool views before returning to Phoenix. When you're ready to end your day, travel east on A–74 to I–17. Follow I–17 south to Phoenix. Or backtrack west on A–74 and pick up A–93 southeast to Phoenix.

WHERE TO GO

Lake Pleasant Dinner Cruise. Mail Address: 3828 North Twenty-eighth Avenue Phoenix, 85017. The newest way to see the lake is to cruise the Lake Pleasant *Desert Princess II*. Cruises run year-round with dinner, dancing, and live entertainment nightly and a champagne brunch on Sunday. The trip takes two and a half hours, and a paid reservation is required forty-eight hours in advance. Fee. (623) 815–2628. E-mail: desertprincessii@aol.com.

Tucson

Welcome to southern Arizona. With Tucson as your base, you can roam back roads, poke around ghost towns, or ascend Kitt Peak to view some of the world's most sophisticated optical instruments. You'll find everything here, from quaint historical settings to a gleaming, growing city. Because southern Arizona encompasses such a vast area, you may wonder how you're going to see it all if you're not familiar with the territory. Relax. As you read through the suggested trips, you'll quickly understand the logical progression described. Several of the day excursions link up easily with each other, creating pleasant opportunities for overnight vacations.

Because of the way this book is organized, some of the best Tucson attractions are listed in the section Day Trip 3 Southeast from Phoenix. You'll want to check out this day trip if you are planning on staying in Tucson.

Historically, agriculture and copper mining served as the basis for the economy in this part of the state. However, tourism quickly is becoming the most important industry. You'll discover, as you travel through this region, that even the smallest towns offer clean, comfortable facilities for visitors.

Before you set off, examine your road map. The land in southern Arizona is owned by a number of different entities. Most of the countryside belongs to Yuma, Pima, Cochise, Pinal, and Graham Counties, but the area also includes several national monuments, wildlife preserves, national forests, and Native American reservations, the largest of which is the Tohono O'odham west of Tucson. In Arizona, driving in and out of reservations is like crossing into different counties. You won't notice much difference except, possibly, a change in the surface of the road.

You'll also see, if you look closely, that two areas are labeled "Saguaro National Monument." This isn't a mistake. The larger

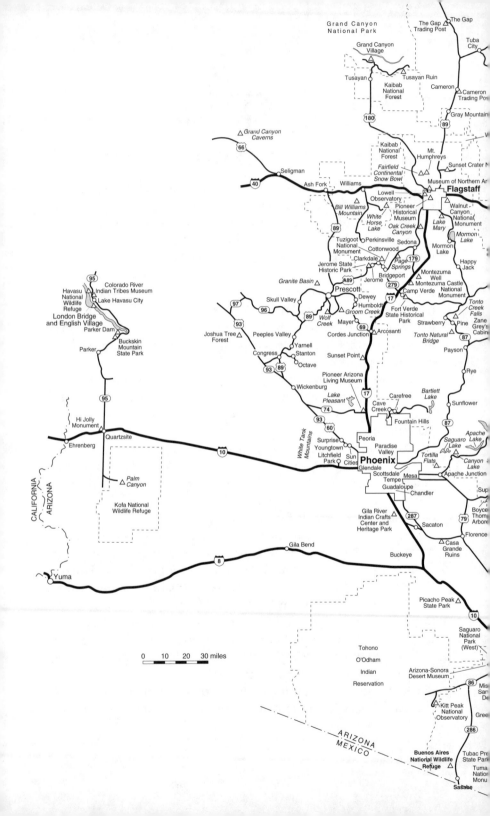

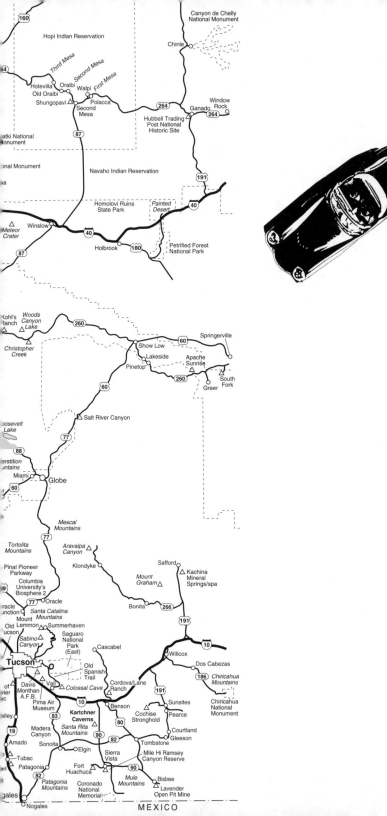

160

Canyon de Chelly
National Monument

Hopi Indian Reservation

Chinle

84

Third Mesa

Hotevilla
Old Oraibi
Oraibi △
Walpi *First Mesa*

Second Mesa

Shungopavi △
Second
Mesa

Polacca △

264

Window
Rock

Ganado

264

Hubbell Trading
Post National
Historic Site

tki National
Monument

87

nal Monument

Navaho Indian Reservation

191

ia

Homolovi Ruins
State Park

*Painted
Desert*

40

△
*Meteor
Crater*

Winslow

40

87

Holbrook

180

Petrified Forest
National Park

Kohl's
Ranch

*Woods
Canyon
Lake*

260

Springerville

60

*Christopher
Creek*

Show Low

Lakeside
Pinetop

Apache
Sunrise

△

South
Fork

260

Greer

60

△ Salt River Canyon

oosevelt
Lake

88

77

erstition
untains

60

Miami

Globe

*Mescal
Mountains*

77

*Tortolita
Mountains*

*Aravaipa
Canyon* △

Safford

Klondyke

△ Kachina
Mineral
Springs/spa

Pinal Pioneer
Parkway

Columbia
University's
Biosphere 2

*Mount
Graham* △

266

191

racle
unction

77

Oracle

Bonita

*Santa Catalina
Mountains*

Mount
Old Lemmon
ucson

Summerhaven

Saguaro
National
Park
(East)

Cascabel

10

*Sabino
Canyon*

Willcox

Tucson

Old
Spanish
Trail

Dos Cabezas

186

*Chiricahua
Mountains*

of
rier
ac

Davis
Monthan
A.F.B.

Vail

△ Colossal Cave

Cordova/Lane
Ranch

191

Sunsites

Chiricahua
National
Monument

Pima Air
Museum

10

Benson

Cochise
Stronghold

Pearce

alley

**Kartchner
Caverns**

83

Madera
Canyon

*Santa Rita
Mountains*

80

Courtland
Gleeson

19

Amado

Sonoita

90

82

Tombstone

Tubac

Elgin

Sierra
Vista

Mile Hi Ramsey
Canyon Reserve

Patagonia

82

*Patagonia
Mountains*

Fort
Huachuca

90

*Mule
Mountains*

Bisbee

ri

Coronado
National
Memorial

Lavender
Open Pit Mine

gales

Nogales

MEXICO

one lies due east of Tucson; the smaller portion of the park is located west of the city, and both are referred to as "Saguaro National Monument."

Although southern Arizona is located south of Phoenix, the elevation around Tucson is higher than that of the capital city. You drive "down" to Tucson, but you are actually driving "up." Be prepared for slightly cooler and drier temperatures in the immediate vicinity of the Old Pueblo.

You may want to refer to Day Trip 2 Southeast from Phoenix to brush up on what's available in Tucson before reading this portion of the book.

Sabino Canyon
Mount Lemmon

SABINO CANYON

Prepare for a day in the great outdoors. You'll begin your drive in Tucson, surrounded by the urban scene. But as you head out toward the Santa Catalina Mountains, you'll quickly leave the city behind. One of the beauties of this day trip is that you can enjoy some of the area's most magnificent wilderness so close to a city. To do both areas justice in one day, you'll need to leave early and not linger too long at either. This could be a problem because both Sabino Canyon and Mount Lemmon have endless trails to hike on and acres of serenity to enjoy.

Although this day trip stars Mother Nature at her finest, she is fickle. Take an extra wrap along. Depending upon the season, carry a windbreaker, heavy sweater, or even a ski jacket in the car. As you climb to the summit of Mount Lemmon, you'll experience a major change in climate. You also need comfortable walking shoes. Although primarily an unspoiled area, there are easy trails and nearby amenities.

If you plan to drive to the top of Mount Lemmon during the winter months, it's wise to call ahead to check on the weather. If it's cloudy or rainy in Tucson, it could be snowing at the summit. Although the road to Mount Lemmon is paved, snow can make it impassable. Even the most adventurous types wouldn't get caught without chains or a four-wheel-drive vehicle.

New York City has Central Park, but Tucson has Sabino Canyon, a woodsy respite close to town. Nestled in the foothills of the Santa Catalina Mountains, Sabino Canyon is a hiker's, picnicker's, and

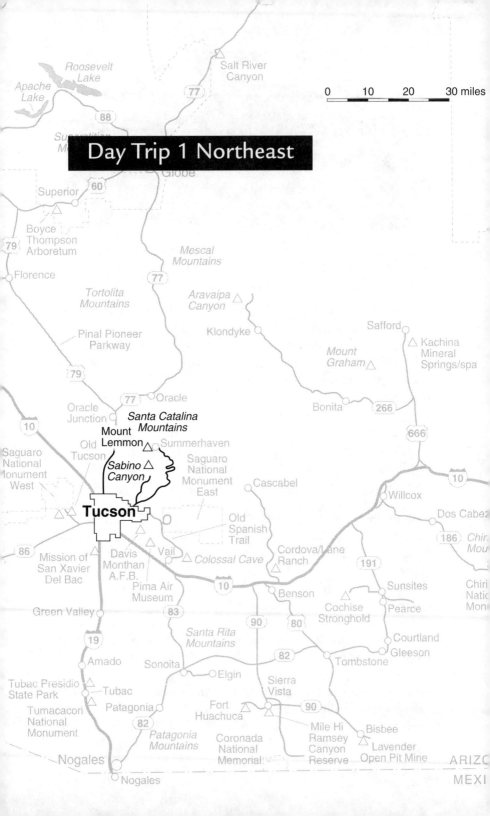

Day Trip 1 Northeast

Roosevelt Lake

Apache Lake

Salt River Canyon

0   10   20   30 miles

88

Superstition M

Globe

Superior   60

Boyce Thompson Arboretum

79

Florence

Mescal Mountains

77

Tortolita Mountains

Aravaipa Canyon

Klondyke

Safford

Kachina Mineral Springs/spa

Pinal Pioneer Parkway

Mount Graham

79

Bonita   266

77   Oracle

Oracle Junction

666

10

Santa Catalina Mountains

Mount Lemmon   Summerhaven

Old Tucson

Saguaro National Monument East

Saguaro National Monument West

Sabino Canyon

Cascabel

Willcox

10

Dos Cabez

Tucson

Old Spanish Trail

186   Chir Mou

86

Mission of San Xavier Del Bac

Davis Monthan A.F.B.

Vail   Colossal Cave

Cordova/Lane Ranch

191

Pima Air Museum

10

Benson

Sunsites

Chiri Natic Mon

Green Valley

83

Santa Rita Mountains

90

80

Cochise Stronghold

Pearce

19

Amado   Sonoita

Elgin

82

Courtland   Gleeson

Tombstone

Tubac Presidio State Park

Tubac

Sierra Vista

Tumacacori National Monument

Patagonia

82

Fort Huachuca

90

Nogales

Patagonia Mountains

Coronada National Memorial

Mile Hi Ramsey Canyon Reserve

Bisbee

Lavender Open Pit Mine

ARIZO

Nogales

MEXI

outdoors lover's dream. With its streams and waterfalls, hiking and biking trails, this natural area manages to absorb the hordes of visitors who turn to it every day for a needed dose of calm and quiet.

To get there, follow Wilmot Road north to where it joins with Tanque Verde Road. Head northeast on Tanque Verde and across the Pantano Wash to its intersection with Sabino Canyon Road, which takes you to the visitors center. You must park your car here and proceed either on foot or by tram for the 4-mile trip to the first of several recreation areas. The tram runs frequently, and there are regular moonlight rides offered from April through December. Fee. (520) 749-2861.

WHERE TO GO

Pick up a trail map at the visitors center. As you walk along, you may observe the different kinds of trees growing here. Pine and fir forest the slopes above the streambed. Deep within the canyon, you'll find other trees, including willow, box elder, and alder. In the lower elevations, Sabino Canyon is host to cactus, paloverde, and even saguaros, while along the streambed you'll find shady sycamore, cottonwood, ash, and walnut trees.

Why the name Sabino? No one is exactly sure. One school of thought insists that the name comes from a plant called sabino or savino. The more accepted story is that it was named for a Mexican rancher who lived in the area in the 1870s.

Formed about 200 million years ago, the canyon has established itself as an ideal getaway no matter what the season. The tram was installed to help preserve the air quality and environment. Along the way it stops at designated observation sites, and during the summer months, moonlight excursions offer a totally different experience. If you've never taken a guided tour in a national park at night or seen a wild area after sunset, you should do this. Tickets are available next to the visitors center parking area. For more information contact Sabino Canyon Shuttle, 5900 North Sabino Canyon Road, Tucson 85750 or call (520) 749-2861.

MOUNT LEMMON

To get to Mount Lemmon from Sabino Canyon, follow Sabino Canyon Road south to Tanque Verde Road. Turn east on Tanque

Verde to Catalina Highway. Follow Catalina Highway northeast to Mount Lemmon. This is an extremely popular area and is well marked. Watch for signs to Mount Lemmon.

As you drive along Tanque Verde toward Catalina Highway, you will see some elegant residential areas. Tucson is famous for its low-slung, hacienda-style homes and bright blue pools hidden among the saguaros and ocotillos.

Catalina Highway, also called the road to Mount Lemmon, climbs the mountain's southern slope. From this point, the 30-mile drive will take about an hour up the 9,157-foot mountain. Although the road is perfectly safe for automobile traffic, those who can't look down from a tall building may not enjoy this experience. Queasy passengers who still want a view should just look up.

As you head up this queen peak of the Santa Catalinas, you'll pass scenic viewpoints and see areas marked for camping and picnicking. You can even stop and fish; signs will lead you to a lake stocked with trout. Along the way you'll get a graphic lesson in physical geography. Even if you've never taken a course in this subject and know nothing about it, you cannot help but learn something on this trip. Your drive will take you through five distinct life zones—areas that support specific types of vegetation. You'll begin with the Sonoran Desert and climb through piñon and juniper. Soon you'll be into elevations that support fir trees and, eventually, aspen trees. This is the same vegetation change you would observe were you to drive from Arizona to the Canadian border. Not surprisingly, the drive is especially gorgeous in autumn and spring.

Along the way, you will have to pay a $5.00 toll for the privilege of driving this road. While few people enjoy handing over $5.00, the money goes to support the state's park system. At Summerhaven (see Where to Go) you will pass some commercial development—bars and restaurants. This area can be crowded during weekends and holidays.

Construction of this road began in 1933 and was not completed until 1950. Much of the road clings to a narrow ledge or skirts high ridges. During years when southern Arizona gets hit by storms, the road can get washed out in places, but it is quickly repaired. Three miles from the tollbooth is the overlook for Seven Cataracts, which, when it's running, is a cascading stream. One other word of warning: The temperature at the top is usually about 20 degrees cooler than the bottom of Mount Lemmon, so it's a good idea to bring sweaters or jackets if you plan to hike around.

Once at the top, hike around. If you've packed a picnic lunch, spread it out and relax. Enjoy the crisp, cool air and the views that stretch forever. Remember, while perched in this northern clime, that you are just one hour—and some 7,000 feet—away from the desert floor.

To return to Tucson, retrace your steps down the mountain and follow Tanque Verde Road back into town.

WHERE TO GO

Summerhaven. At the summit of Mount Lemmon. Spend time walking around this friendly mountaintop hamlet. There's an entire community up here, including a lodge that offers rustic accommodations, small cabins, campgrounds, and other amenities. You can eat and use the rest rooms. You will *not* find gas. Because you're at the top of a 9,100-plus-foot mountain, don't expect too much luxury, and you'll be pleasantly surprised by the charm. (520) 576-1400.

Mount Lemmon Ski Lift. In the winter, if the snow is right, Mount Lemmon becomes the southernmost ski area in the United States. In the summer, ride the lift for the breathtaking view. The thirty-minute round-trip covers approximately 1 mile. You'll depart near the base area and look over the San Pedro Valley, the Reef of Rocks, and the towns of Oracle and Mammoth. Fee. (520) 576-1400.

WHERE TO EAT

Iron Door Restaurant. In Ski Valley, at the base of the Mount Lemmon ski area. Come for salads, sandwiches, homemade soups, skiers, chili, and corn bread. The restaurant is named for a lost mine with an iron door that, legend has it, was operated by Jesuit padres in the Catalinas during the 1700s. According to the story, Apache raiders killed the Native American mine workers and the Jesuits. Lunch only. $$. 10300 East Ski Run Road. (520) 576-1321.

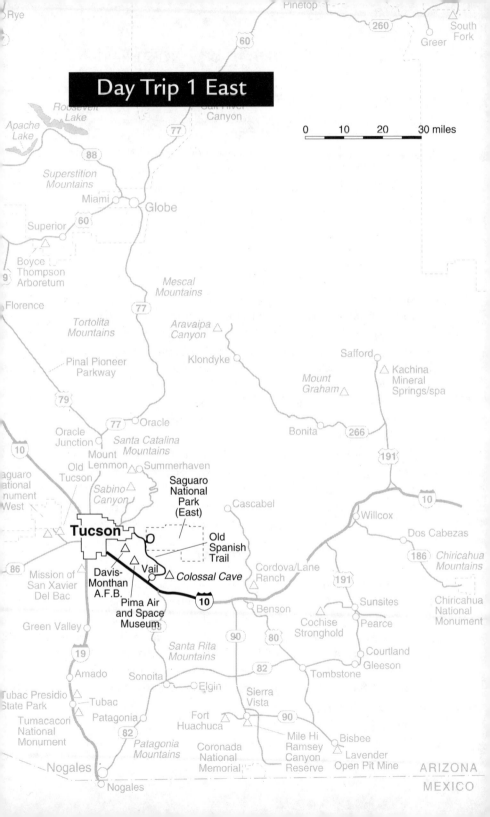

Day Trip 1 East

Rye

Pinetop

260

Greer

South Fork

60

Roosevelt Lake

Apache Lake

77

Salt River Canyon

88

0   10   20   30 miles

Superstition Mountains

Miami

Globe

Superior

60

Boyce Thompson Arboretum

9

Florence

Mescal Mountains

77

Tortolita Mountains

Aravaipa Canyon

Klondyke

Safford

Kachina Mineral Springs/spa

Pinal Pioneer Parkway

Mount Graham

79

77

Oracle

Oracle Junction

Santa Catalina Mountains

Bonita

266

191

10

Mount Lemmon

Summerhaven

Saguaro National Park (East)

Cascabel

Willcox

10

Old Tucson

Sabino Canyon

Dos Cabezas

Saguaro National Monument West

Tucson

Old Spanish Trail

Cordova/Lane Ranch

186

Chiricahua Mountains

86

Mission of San Xavier Del Bac

Davis-Monthan A.F.B.

Vail

Colossal Cave

191

Sunsites

Pearce

Chiricahua National Monument

Green Valley

Pima Air and Space Museum

10

Benson

90

80

Cochise Stronghold

Courtland

Gleeson

19

Santa Rita Mountains

Amado

Sonoita

Elgin

82

Tombstone

Tubac Presidio State Park

Tubac

Patagonia

Sierra Vista

Fort Huachuca

90

Mile Hi Ramsey Canyon Reserve

Bisbee

Lavender Open Pit Mine

Tumacacori National Monument

82

Patagonia Mountains

Coronada National Memorial

ARIZONA

Nogales

Nogales

MEXICO

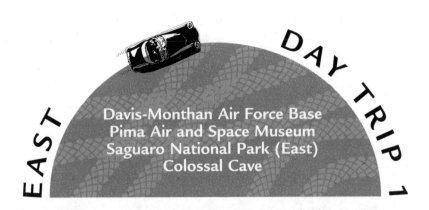

Davis-Monthan Air Force Base
Pima Air and Space Museum
Saguaro National Park (East)
Colossal Cave

DAVIS-MONTHAN AIR FORCE BASE OR PIMA AIR AND SPACE MUSEUM

It's difficult to imagine that this immense base started as a municipal airport established by civic-minded citizens in 1919. Located on Craycroft Road at Golf Links Road in Tucson, Davis-Monthan is named for Lts. Samuel H. Davis and Oscar Monthan, two early Air Corps officers from Tucson.

The Army Air Corps made its first investment in D-M in 1931, and modern paved roads and runways followed in the mid-1930s. Shortly before Pearl Harbor, $3 million was earmarked for expansion, and D-M soon became one of the best heavy-bombardment training stations in the nation.

After World War II, the base was nearly deserted until it was designated an Air Technical Service Command storage area. Because of the arid climate, hundreds of aircraft are stored here now.

Currently D-M is a diversified military installation. It is home to the largest outdoor aircraft storage facility in the world, and A-10 combat crew training and OA-37 Forward Air Control operations also are conducted. With all the fighter planes and helicopters constantly in the air, the skies over D-M are rarely quiet.

WHERE TO GO

Pima Air and Space Museum. 6000 East Valencia Road, just east of I-10, 1 mile from the interstate. It houses more than 5,000 military planes ranging from bombers to drone fighters on 2,600 acres. More than seventy different aircraft types may be seen.

Although not technically part of Davis-Monthan, the facility works closely with the base. The third-largest air museum in the country, it is exceeded in size only by the Smithsonian Institution's National Air and Space Museum in Washington, D.C., and the Wright-Patterson Air Museum in Dayton, Ohio. Ask if a special volunteer is available to take you through the presidential aircraft located on the grounds. Base tours are provided by the museum Monday through Friday, excluding major holidays.

Snacks and soft drinks may be purchased at the museum, which is open every day except Christmas and Thanksgiving. Fee. (520) 574-0646. www.pimaair.org; e-mail: azaeroof@azstarnet.com.

Challenger Learning Center of the Southwest. On the campus of the Pima Air and Space Museum, this center provides children and adults with invaluable experience in the fields of math, science, and technology by providing simulated space missions that kids "fly." The program is part of an international effort to bring the wonders of space within the reach of youngsters. Open daily. Call for operations of "mini missions." Fee (520) 618-4821.

SAGUARO NATIONAL PARK (EAST)

As you look at your map of this area, note that the Saguaro National Park is actually two parks. The larger one, the Rincon Mountain Section unit, is located due east of Tucson, while the smaller park, the Tucson Mountain District unit, lies to the west. Both parks were established March 1, 1933, for the protection of a remarkable stand of saguaro (pronounced sa-wa-ro) cactus found here. Thanks to excellent management, desert travelers are offered a treat for the eyes. Be apprised that there are no accommodations available other than picnic tables at either of these facilities.

Return to I-10 when you leave the Pima Air and Space Museum. Go east on I-10 to exit 275 and continue north on this road to Old Spanish Trail. Turn east on Old Spanish Trail for 2 miles to the entrance and visitors center of **Saguaro National Park East** or Rincon Mountain Section unit. The park is open from 7:00 A.M. to sunset. The visitors center is open from 8:00 A.M. to 5:00 P.M. daily.

Driving through a stand of saguaros is unlike driving through any other kind of forest. The profusion of angles will constantly delight you. Some saguaros signal with their arms in crazy directions; others stand almost perfectly symmetrical with arms reaching up in supplication. Although a stately plant, saguaros nevertheless strike some humorous poses.

As you walk or drive through the 62,499 acres of this section of Saguaro National Park, you'll be amazed at the endless variety and sheer numbers of the plants. The visitors center has information on the native vegetation, and you'll get an overview of the biology and geology found in this area of the state. Hopefully you'll come away with a better understanding of how plants and animals adapt to an arid existence. Above all, you'll gain a new appreciation for a wondrous plant, the saguaro.

The saguaro cactus is remarkable. A natural desert condominium, it provides homes for a variety of creatures. Several species of birds eat its seeds, live in its walls, and build nests in its arms. By the time a saguaro grows to 20 feet and has its first branch, the plant has lived through seventy-five years of strenuous desert sun, wind, and rain. With a root structure stretching for miles just barely beneath the surface, the plant is an unparalleled natural balancing act. Superbly adapted to make the most of an unpredictable desert water supply, the plant's accordion-style pleats allow it to shrink during droughts and plump up after rains. Given optimum conditions, secure from bulldozers and development, this queen of the desert can grow to 50 feet and survive to age 200.

Bird-watchers will have a field day at Saguaro National Park. More than fifty species of reptiles also roam around the park. If you've thought of the desert as an empty place, think again. As you wander through this rolling, saguaro-studded landscape with its endless shades of sun-bleached green, look for desert tortoises, gophers, coach-whip snakes, ground squirrels, peccaries, coyotes, and mule deer. Listen, too, for the whistle of the curve-bill thrasher, the churring of the cactus wren, and a yipping coyote chorus.

Take a self-guided stroll down one of the more gentle nature trails mentioned in a free pamphlet you can pick up at the visitors center. If you visit between February and May, you may be fortunate enough to witness an outstanding wildflower display. These fragile blooms are dependent upon winter rain, so a superb show is not guaranteed each year. If you're there when these blossoms peak, you're in for a special desert experience.

Outdoor types may prefer hiking in the forest of the Rincon Mountains. A backpacking permit is required in the backcountry. Contact the National Park Service, Saguaro National Park, 3693 South Old Spanish Trail, Tucson 85730 for more details. Fee. (520) 733-5100. www.nps.gov/sagu.

COLOSSAL CAVE

As you leave Saguaro National Park, continue south on Old Spanish Trail for 10 more miles. You'll see the signs for Colossal Cave, an underground wilderness experience.

Thanks to the work of the Civilian Conservation Corps, touring this cave is easy. Navigable pathways lead through the entire cave. Stairways are lighted. There are no difficult areas to traverse; no narrow spaces to squeeze through. Even the temperature is comfortable. It remains at 72 degrees Fahrenheit year-round.

Cave buffs who are used to wet caves may be disappointed by the interior. A dry cave means just that. There are no glistening, colorful stalactites and stalagmites to capture your imagination. The formations have dried to a sandy, dusty surface.

The story of the cave, however, is very colorful as it is pure western lore. It seems that three bandits robbed a train in 1887 and made off with $70,000 to $90,000 worth of gold and paper money. A posse from Tucson hit their trail the next day and went after them. The sheriff was Virgil Earp. Searchers discovered the entrance to the cave and evidence that the robbers were hiding there. The bandits were eventually caught in El Paso without their booty. So, the legend lives on that the gold and money may still be in the cave.

Frequent guided tours ferry visitors through the cavern. 16711 East Colossal Cave Road. (520) 647-7275. www.colossalcave.com; e-mail: info@colossalcave.com.

To return to Tucson, continue on Old Spanish Trail from Colossal Cave to Vail. At Vail, pick up I-10 (A-86) northwest and continue into Tucson. Or you can head east on I-10 to Day Trip 2 East from Tucson.

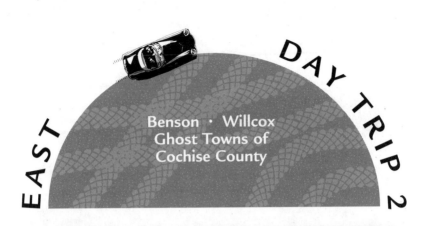

BENSON

Follow I–10 east to Benson about 45 miles from Tucson. This small community, like its neighbor Willcox, was founded along the main line of the Southern Pacific Railroad. During the late 1800s it served as a shipping point for the livestock- and mineral-producing areas to the south. It nestles in an intermountain valley created by the San Pedro River. Although the original streets were designed in a grid on a 160-acre plat, the town grew haphazardly.

Today Benson is emerging as a suburb of Tucson. Surrounded by natural beauty, the immediate area offers a wealth of things to see and do.

WHERE TO GO

Amerind Foundation. Exit 318, south of I–10 in Texas Canyon between Benson and Willcox. Take the Dragoon exit (318) on I–10 and continue east 1 mile to the Amerind Foundation turnoff, then turn left into the foundation.

This museum is a jewel. A privately funded center for archaeological field research, the center also houses a museum and art gallery dedicated to archaeological and ethnographical material on Indians from all the Americas. The gallery contains a superb collection of western, Native American, and American art.

Why a fine museum in the middle of the desert? The answer lies in the passions of one man, William Shirley Fulton, a Connecticut industrialist. Fulton purchased this property, 65 miles east of

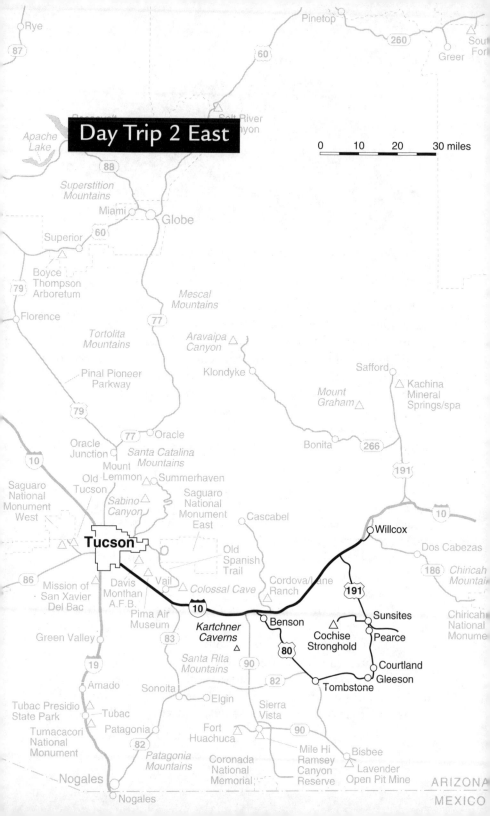

Day Trip 2 East

0   10   20   30 miles

Rye
87

Apache
Lake
88

Superstition
Mountains

Miami   Globe

Superior   60

Boyce
Thompson
Arboretum
79

Florence

Tortolita
Mountains

Pinal Pioneer
Parkway

79

Oracle
Junction   77   Oracle

Santa Catalina
Mountains

Old   Mount
Tucson   Lemmon   Summerhaven

Sabino   Saguaro
Canyon   National
Monument
East

Saguaro
National
Monument
West

10

Tucson

86   Mission of
San Xavier
Del Bac   Davis
Monthan
A.F.B.   Vail   Colossal Cave

Pima Air
Museum

Green Valley   83

19   Kartchner
Caverns

Santa Rita
Mountains   90

Amado

Tubac Presidio   Sonoita   Elgin
State Park   Tubac

Tumacacori   Patagonia
National   82
Monument

Nogales   Patagonia
Mountains

Nogales

Pinetop
260

Greer   Sou
For

Salt River
Canyon

Mescal
Mountains

77

Aravaipa
Canyon

Klondyke   Safford   Kachina
Mineral
Springs/spa

Mount
Graham

Bonita   266

191

Cascabel

Willcox   10

Dos Cabezas

186   Chiricah
Mountai

Cordova/Lane
Ranch

191

Benson   Cochise   Sunsites
Stronghold   Pearce

80   Chiricahua
National
Monume

Courtland
Tombstone   Gleeson

82

Sierra
Vista

Fort
Huachuca   90

Mile Hi   Bisbee
Ramsey
Canyon   Lavender
Coronada   Reserve   Open Pit Mine
National
Memorial   ARIZONA

MEXICO

Tucson, in the early 1930s and became intensely involved in Native American cultures. As he began to acquire a sizable collection of diverse artifacts, Fulton hired noted architect H. M. Starkweather to design and build a permanent home for his important collection. Starkweather visualized the Spanish Colonial Revival–style structure as an eloquent contrast to the massive natural boulders of this part of Arizona.

Until recently, the Amerind Foundation (the name refers to the prehistoric Native Americans who lived in the Americas) concentrated more on research than outreach. However, the Amerind has redirected its focus to make its impressive collection of artifacts, arts, and crafts more accessible to visitors. Fee. Call for hours of operation. (520) 586-3666. www.amerind.org; e-mail: amerind@amerind.org.

Cascabel Clayworks. Twenty-four miles north of Benson on Pomerene Road. Expect to travel on a dirt road for many miles to reach this community of artists. Handmade clay works are fashioned in a unique setting with shade trees, the San Pedro River, and a backdrop of gold cliffs. No phone.

Singing Wind Book Shop. 700 West Singing Wind Road. Two and ¼ mile north of Benson on Ocotillo Road. Turn right (east) on Singing Wind Road. Don't be put off by the closed ranch gate. Stop your car, get out, open the gate, and continue driving down the road. (Close the gate behind you!) You'll find a white ranch house nestled in a scene straight out of a western film. This renowned bookshop contains a complete collection of books about the Southwest and western Americana as well as an amazing assortment of books on nearly any subject. Plan to spend quality time browsing through the many rooms. (520) 586-2425.

San Pedro Valley Arts and Historical Society. 242 South San Pedro. In 1983, the San Pedro Valley Arts and Historical Society purchased a building that had been boarded up for nearly fifty years. After renovating it, the society opened a museum/gallery that features changing exhibits and a permanent display. There's also a gift shop that features handcrafted items, ceramics, and paintings by local artisans. Free, but donations are appreciated. (520) 586-3070.

Texas Canyon. Located 14 miles east of Benson on I-10. This is a lovely natural area with spectacular rock formations. You can picnic here, hike, or simply enjoy the views of nature as the master sculptor.

WILLCOX

From Benson, follow I-10 east 36 miles to Willcox. This small Arizona community was settled in 1880 as a construction camp for the Southern Pacific Railroad. When the track went down, Willcox sprang to life. It quickly became a focal point in Cochise County for cattle shipping and still holds that position. Some of the largest cattle ranches in the state are located in the broad, grassy valleys in this area.

Often called the "Gateway to the Chiricahua Wonderland," Willcox is rich with Native American lore. Here the U.S. Cavalry battled the Chiricahua Apaches. Many sites commemorate various skirmishes. This is the country of Cochise, the legendary Apache chief who stalked and struck deep in the valleys and then faded back into the shadowy mountains. This land was holy to all Apaches. The Apache chief Geronimo wrote: "There is no place equal to that of Arizona. I want to spend my last days there and be buried among those mountains."

Today Willcox is known as the home of television, movie, and radio personality Rex Allen. But if ghosts intrigue you more than cowboys, you'll want to see the wonderful old ghost towns and graveyards in this vicinity, which lie silently under the Arizona sun. If you pay a visit to the Old Willcox Cemetery, southeast of town, you'll see where Warren Earp, brother of the famous frontier marshal Wyatt Earp, is buried. For more information about the ghost towns in the area and other points of interest, drop by the Willcox Chamber of Commerce, 1500 North Circle I Road. (520) 384-2272. www.willcoxchamber.com; e-mail: willcoxchamber @vtc.net.

WHERE TO GO

Apple Orchards and Pistachio Groves. Follow Fort Grant Road northwest 20 miles from town to arrive at these private orchards and nut groves. Willcox is a major apple-producing area and, in season, hosts popular U-Pick-Em days. Call the Chamber of Commerce at (520) 384-2272 to find out when these days are scheduled.

The Cochise Information Center and Museum of the Southwest. 1500 North Circle I Road. Stop for information about this area and tour the museum. When you enter, you'll be greeted with an impressive bust of Cochise. Take the time to read some of his sayings, and you'll get an insight into the mind of this unusual man. You may also want to stroll around Heritage Park, on the grounds of the center, where you'll see a replica of a Native American village, a nature trail, and a mining display. (520) 384-2272.

Cochise Stronghold. Follow I-10 west about 8 miles from Willcox. Take US-666 south about 17 miles. About a mile before you get to the community of Sunsites, there is an unnamed graded road that heads west. Look for the sign indicating that this is the road to Cochise Stronghold. Take this road west for 10 miles until it ends at the parking lot and campgrounds.

Cochise Stronghold is the area of the Dragoon Mountains that served as home, headquarters, and safe haven for Apache chief Cochise. Cochise was a fierce leader, on par with Geronimo and Mangas Coloradas. As you drive into the mountains, more than one writer has noted a "presence" that seems to linger over the landscape. Somewhere in this tangle of rocks and canyons, towers and domes, and manzanita shrubs lie the bones of Cochise. Even in death, he remains a controversial character.

One legend says that when Cochise died in 1874, his braves buried him in full regalia. They lowered his body into a deep crevice along with his horse, dog, and rifle. According to another story, his men, fearing vandalism by white men, buried their chief on a grassy mesa and then ran their horses back and forth to mask the grave site. In any event, although the exact location of Cochise's body is unknown, his spirit is everywhere.

As you enter the area of the stronghold, you'll see a Forest Service campground. A good hiking trail into the Dragoon Mountains begins here. If you decide to explore this region, remember that the area is not commercially developed. You won't find any souvenir shops or cafes at the end of your journey, which takes about four hours. If you're prepared for a rugged walk, park at the campground and follow the well-marked 3-mile trail. Some of the climb is steep, but eventually you'll arrive at an open area where you can gaze over a 40-mile vista. This point on the trail is designated as the heart of the stronghold. As you stand there, surrounded by the cliffs and sculpted spires, it's easy to imagine Apache bands moving in and out of the shadows.

When you start down, you'll need to watch your footing because the path is steep. Around the 2-mile mark, turn to see towering above the walnut and sycamore trees an almost overpowering view of Cochise Stronghold. It's the same scene that greeted Gen. O. O. Howard as he marched into the stronghold in 1872 carrying a flag of truce. As a result of Howard's trek, Cochise agreed to end the hostilities at last.

No doubt General Howard had other things on his mind than the scenery, but, as you leave the stronghold, take one last, lingering look at this Apache sanctum. Don't be surprised if you have the distinct feeling that the great Chief Cochise is looking back at you.

A word of caution: This area has no amenities other than picnic tables—not even a telephone.

Stout Cider Mill. Located at I-10, exit 340. This is the only cider mill on I-10 from the East Coast to the West. The apple pies are stuffed to overflowing and are superb. The cider is delicious. Even if you're not hungry, the place is fun for browsing. (520) 384-3696. www.cidermill.com.

Walking tour. The Willcox Chamber of Commerce has published a historical walking tour of the area that gives you insight into this old western town. If you take the tour, be sure and stop in at the **Commercial Hotel/Brown's Ice Cream Parlor.** The hotel was built in the 1800s and has been restored. It's now operated as an old-fashioned ice cream parlor.

WHERE TO STAY

Mule Shoe Ranch. 298 East Seventh Street. From Bisbee Avenue (next to the shopping center), go to Airport Road. Turn right and continue for 30 miles on a washboard road. This ranch is owned and operated by the Nature Conservancy and sprawls over 55,000 acres of the Sonoran and Chihuahuan Deserts. There are seven permanently flowing streams that make this a wonderful riparian habitat. The four casitas and one small stone cabin are comfortable and newly rebuilt. Most have kitchenettes; some have clawfoot tubs, woodstoves, and even corrals and are available from September to May. $$. (520) 586-7072.

GHOST TOWNS OF COCHISE COUNTY

To do the ghost towns justice, plan a full day of touring. It's tough to rush ghosts. The entire area—bounded by Sierra Vista, Benson, and Willcox to the north and the Mexican border to the south—is a ghost-town hunter's dream. During the mining boom, this countryside was thick with camps and communities that sprang up with a shout and died out with a whimper when the ore disappeared.

Visitors may stand among the crumbling rubble and easily imagine wild-eyed young men and sassy women who lived here, drunk on the easy money. Even if you don't believe in spirits, ghost towns have a calming effect that infects the most skeptical tourist. As you stand looking at the wisps of streets, pieces of foundation, and crooked walls that defy gravity, you cannot help but hear the whispers of past action.

Each of these communities once burst with activity. They were crowded with saloons and stores and homes, and as long as the gold, silver, and copper came in, so did the men hunting quick fortunes and fast women. Now, although the music has stopped, the energy lingers.

If you visit during the summer months, bring a jug of water and wear a hat so that you don't fade too fast. As you visit the ghost towns, you'll find that at least two communities, Dos Cabezas (Day Trip 3 East of Tucson) and Pearce, have refused to give up the ghost completely. Real-live people reside in these communities, and you'll even find food and drink at Pearce.

WHERE TO GO

Pearce. From Cochise Stronghold, retrace your route and head east on the graded road to Arizona Sunsites, a new community that caters to the family and retirement crowd. One and a half miles south of Sunsites, on your right, is the road to Old Pearce. This is where Ghost Town Trail begins. Follow the signs directing you to the Old General Store.

The Commonwealth Mine put Pearce on the map around 1890 when Johnny Pearce struck gold. More gold came from this mine than from any other mine in the territory. At Pearce you can visit the old cemetery, which is still used today. Abraham Lincoln's bodyguard is buried here, as are some Union and Confederate soldiers and a few of Pearce's "tarnished belles" from its more lively era. The Old General Store and museum are full of Old West items that visitors enjoy poking through.

WHERE TO STAY

Grapevine Canyon Ranch. Call for directions, or write to P.O. Box 302, Pearce 85625. This is an authentic working guest ranch that backs up to a western view straight out of a John Wayne movie, secluded in the Dragoon Mountains 85 miles southeast of Tucson. This ranch offers guests the opportunity to work on spring roundups and all aspects of daily life. Horseback instruction is available; food is served family-style. And all "hands" are friendly and ready to help "dudes" learn how to cowboy. There are eight casitas and three cabins for thirty-four guests. This working ranch is open year-round. No children under twelve are allowed. The Grapevine is a favorite with international guests because of its remotely splendid setting and real West ambience. There is a three-night minimum stay year-round. $$$ (includes meals and riding); ☐. (520) 826–3185. www.grapevinecanyonranch.com.

WANDERING THE BACK ROADS

To visit more ghost towns, continue south on the road past Pearce. It winds through the old mining towns of Courtland and Gleeson, ending up at Tombstone, where you can connect to Day Trip 1 Southeast of Tucson.

Courtland. On Ghost Town Trail to Tombstone. There's one resident in Courtland, and he does not encourage visitors. As you drive by, you may want to take a passing glance at this once-thriving mining camp. If you decide to explore on foot, don't expect to be greeted by any famous Southwestern hospitality.

Gleeson. On Ghost Town Trail, 16 miles east of Tombstone. Turquoise put Gleeson on the map. Even before the Spaniards arrived, the Native Americans in the area mined this stone. Later residents found zinc, copper, and lead. Modern visitors will find picturesque ruins to wander through and a cemetery to explore.

To get a complete listing of Arizona ghost towns, contact the Arizona Office of Tourism, 2702 North Third Street, Suite 4015, Phoenix 85004; (602) 230-7733; www.arizonaguide.com. You can spend a day or two exploring the old towns in this region of the state. If you have time, pick up a book on Arizona history. The more you know, the more you'll appreciate what you're seeing.

After Gleeson, you have a choice. Continue to Tombstone (see Day Trip 1 Southeast of Tucson) and stay overnight there or go through Tombstone, heading north on US-80 to I-10, and follow I-10 west to Tucson.

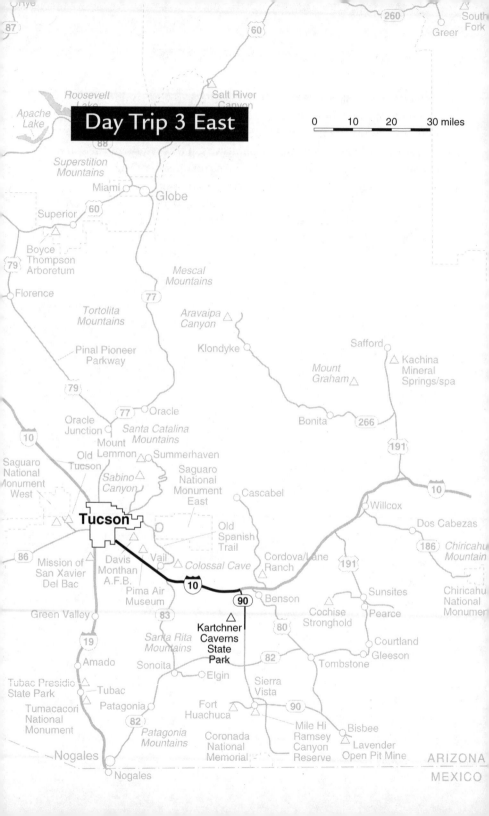

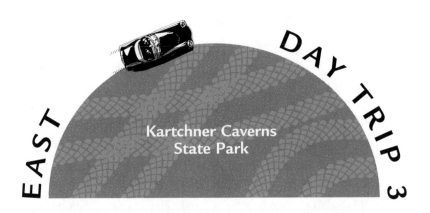

KARTCHNER CAVERNS STATE PARK

Kartchner Caverns State Park is the newest state park to open in Arizona and has one of the finest examples of caves found anywhere in the world. It is located 160 miles southeast of Phoenix and about 50 miles southeast of Tucson. From I–10, take exit 302 and travel south for 9 miles on A–90. It is 19 miles north of Sierra Vista.

This is definitely worth a special day trip, as there is much to see and do here. However, you *must* make a reservation to see the cave. Don't expect to show up on a whim and be able to get inside. What makes this day trip so special is that Kartchner Caverns is a wet, alive cave that is continuing to form. It is extremely unusual for nonspelunkers to have the opportunity to visit such a vast, living underground formation.

Kartchner Caverns, an absolutely magnificent limestone cave, was discovered in the Whetstone Mountains by accident. Amateur spelunkers, Randy Tufts and Gary Tenen, found a sinkhole into the cave while on a hike in 1974. Fortunately for all of us, these two young men swore themselves to secrecy about their amazing find until they could be sure that the cave would be protected.

Establishing protection for the cave took more than ten years. Not until 1988 was the director of the Arizona State Parks system, Ken Travous, able to crawl into the hole to see the cave firsthand. Then it took Arizona State Parks until November 1999 to open even a portion of this amazing, wet cave to the general public. Happily, everyone involved in this unique project pledged from the start to protect the cave so its "live" status would not be negatively impacted. The result is a project that, under the protection of the Arizona State Park system, does a spectacular job of protecting the cave while, at the same time, making it accessible to those who want to experience its wonders.

Technically, Kartchner Caverns was formed by underground water cutting through Escabrosa limestone over eons. Water, mixing with mineral deposits, formed the sculptural and colorful formations. Although the formations within the cave are breathtaking, the size and scope of the project deserves equal attention. The state of Arizona has poured $28 million into this project to develop it aesthetically and ecologically, and it is not done yet. Cave experts maintain that Kartchner Caverns established new standards for how caves should be developed.

The surveyed portion of the cavern is 2⁹⁄₁₀ miles long, but the park includes a 23,000-square-foot Discovery Center that explains the geography and natural history of this unique underground feature and the story of the caverns. Plan ample time to peruse the Discovery Center, because the exhibits are definitely worthwhile. Your entire park experience will take a minimum of three hours and includes the tour of the cave, walk through the visitors center's exhibits, perusal of the gift shop, and enjoyment of the outdoor scenery. The complete cave tour lasts about an hour and includes a tram trip to the cave entrance and a forty-five-minute underground tour.

Because this is a wet desert cave, be prepared for almost 100 percent humidity inside the underground chambers. The temperature is sixty-eight degrees just below the surface. An elaborate tunnel and door-lock system assures that the environment of the cave is not affected by visitors entering or leaving.

Once inside the air locks, visitors follow 1,800 feet of hand-poured concrete trails to see the wonders of this underground labyrinth, such as the longest "soda straw" formation in the United States (21 feet, 2 inches) and the most massive column in Arizona, Kubla Kahn, which measures 58 feet. The two main galleries are both the size of football fields and contain extraordinary formations. From May to mid-September, the cave is a maternity ward for about 1,000 female Myotis velifer bats that roost here.

After stepping through the second air lock, visitors are greeted by a chamber with walls climbing almost four stories to a ceiling that is dotted with stalagtites. All rooms in this cavern have stood untouched for thousands of years.

As you walk through the cave, pay attention to how visitors are accommodated in this unique environment. Construction inside the caverns was done almost totally by hand, by a devoted crew of local workers (many of whom had worked in mines previously) who care deeply about the success of this project.

Reservations are a must. All tours are guided by a park ranger, and tours run approximately every fifteen to twenty minutes. The rules of the cavern must be obeyed. These include no touching or breaking of formations; no coin tossing; and no flash photography, tripods, or video cameras. No food, drink, gum, or tobacco products allowed inside. No strollers, walkers, backpacks, or pets (except assist dogs), and, of course, no littering.

Reservations can be booked up to one year in advance and cancelled fifteen minutes prior to tour departure time. Cost of the underground trek (as of February 2000) is $12.00 for adults, $4.00 for ages seven through thirteen, and free for children six years and younger. Open daily except Christmas. Fee. For reservations or additional information, call (520) 586–2283.

WHERE TO STAY

The area around Sonoita and Sierra Vista offers some good and very convenient choices of accommodations, from motels to B&Bs. See Day Trip 1 Southeast from Tucson and Day Trip 1 South from Tucson for additional recommendations.

Skywatcher's Inn, The Arizona Astronomy and Nature Retreat. 5655 North Via Umbrosa. Located minutes away from Benson at the Vega-Bray Observatory, this unique inn features three bedrooms. Because the inn is devoted to astronomy, the decor is comfortable rather than charming. The observatory contains a sliding-roof observing room with a 14½-inch Newtonian telescope, a 6-inch refractor, two computerized 12-inch Schmidt-Cassegrains, and a 6-inch astrograph reflector. In addition, the complex includes two Dobsonian telescopes. Astronomy observing sessions or classes may be arranged with amateur astronomers or with professors. Astronomy equipment can be rented for a modest fee. Rates are for one or two and include full breakfast or continental breakfast, which may be served at any time to accommodate night sky watchers. In addition to the three larger rooms, a smaller studio is available for a lesser fee. $$; ☐. For reservations and information, call (520) 615–3886.

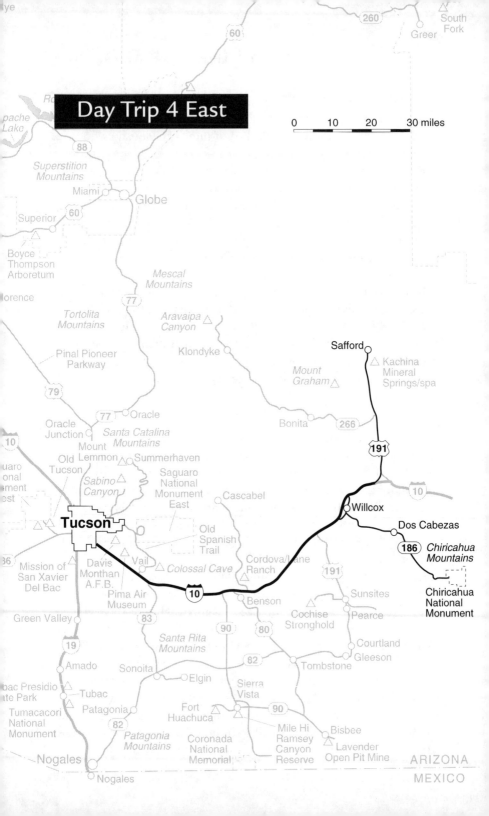

Day Trip 4 East

0 10 20 30 miles

South Fork
Greer
260

Rockie
Apache Lake
88
Superstition Mountains
Miami
Globe
Superior
60
Boyce Thompson Arboretum
Florence
Mescal Mountains
77
Tortolita Mountains
Aravaipa Canyon
Klondyke
Safford
Kachina Mineral Springs/spa
Mount Graham
Pinal Pioneer Parkway
Bonita
266
79
77 Oracle
Oracle Junction
Santa Catalina Mountains
191
10
Mount Lemmon
Summerhaven
Old Tucson
Sabino Canyon
Saguaro National Monument East
Cascabel
10
aquaro onal ment est
Tucson
Willcox
Dos Cabezas
Old Spanish Trail
186 Chiricahua Mountains
36
Mission of San Xavier Del Bac
Davis Monthan A.F.B.
Vail
Colossal Cave
Cordova/Lane Ranch
191
Chiricahua National Monument
Green Valley
Pima Air Museum
83
10
Benson
Sunsites
Cochise Stronghold
Pearce
Santa Rita Mountains
90
80
Courtland
Gleeson
19
Amado
Sonoita
82
Tombstone
Tubac Presidio ate Park
Tubac
Elgin
Sierra Vista
Tumacacori National Monument
Patagonia
82
Fort Huachuca
90
Patagonia Mountains
Coronada National Memorial
Mile Hi Ramsey Canyon Reserve
Bisbee
Lavender Open Pit Mine
ARIZONA
Nogales
Nogales
MEXICO

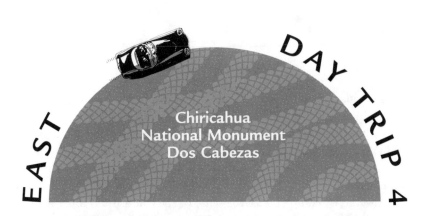

EAST

DAY TRIP 4

Chiricahua
National Monument
Dos Cabezas

CHIRICAHUA NATIONAL MONUMENT

From Tucson, follow I-10 east to Willcox. At the junction of A-186, turn south and follow this road about 20 miles to the Chiricahua National Monument. If you pick up this trip at Safford, take US-191 south to I-10, head west to A-186, and follow it to the park. After paying the entrance fee, proceed to the visitors center. The exhibits here graphically describe both the manufactured and natural history of this mountainous area. You may pick up pamphlets or buy guidebooks that describe the various trails. If you take the time to go through the visitors center first, you'll appreciate this region of the country much more.

Described as "a wonderland of balanced rocks, volcanic spires, and grotesquely eroded cliffs," Chiricahua National Monument was established in 1924. Endlessly mysterious, this is an ever-changing landscape. One moment shadows caress the spires that rise nearly 200 feet into the air; the next, light plays hide-and-seek with chiseled rocks that stand silently shoulder to shoulder.

Plan this day trip when you have lots of time and energy. If you want advance information, contact the Chiricahua National Monument, HCR 2, Box 6500, Willcox 85643. (520) 824-3560. www.nps.gov/chir.

169

WHAT TO DO

To see this sprawling park from the comfort of your car, follow Massai Point Drive, a 6½-mile paved road that leads up Bonita Canyon to Massai Point. From the top you'll get a good view of Sulphur Springs Valley to the west and San Simon Valley to the east. The Massai Point Exhibit Building is a worthwhile stop, for it offers more information on the natural history of the area.

However, you'll experience the sense of the Chiricahuas more if you travel on foot. There are more than 17 miles of trails to choose from. If you plan to hike for more than an hour, take water with you. Whether you decide on a twenty-minute stroll or a two-and-a-half-hour hike, you're sure to succumb to the strange beauty of this rocky place. Let your imagination fly—and you may even sense the spirit of Geronimo lurking in the shadows.

From here you can retrace your steps, heading north on A–186 to Willcox and then going west on I-10 back to Tucson, or you can go on to see the ghost towns of Cochise County. If you plan to visit the ghost towns, stay overnight in Benson or Willcox (see Day Trip 2 East from Tucson).

DOS CABEZAS

This is one of several ghost towns in Cochise County. The others can be found in Day Trip 2 East from Tucson. From Chiricahua National Monument, take A–186 north for 9 miles to Dos Cabezas. During its mining heyday, this community was a stage station. Not quite a ghost town, Dos Cabezas supports enough people to maintain a U.S. post office. As you walk around, you'll get a sense of what this place felt like when gold fever raged through the region.

SAFFORD

From Tucson, head east on I-10 to its junction with US-191. Go north on US-191 about 34 miles to Safford.

Dwarfed by towering Mount Graham, which rises 10,713 feet above it, Safford has grown as an agricultural and copper mining community. Like many small Arizona towns, this Graham County community offers the casual visitor more outdoor than indoor activities.

Graham County was organized in 1881, but its history dates back to the Anasazi Indians, an ancient people who inhabited the area around the time of Christ. The Anasazi were followed by the Hohokams, farmers who disappeared in the thirteenth century, and finally by the Apaches, who were nomadic, fierce fighters. Although Coronado visited this area in 1540, it wasn't until tiny Camp Goodwin was established in 1864 that Caucasians made their presence known in this area. Not surprisingly, the Apaches were not about to give up this land easily, and they battled to keep their territory. The last of the Apache chieftains, Geronimo, finally surrendered in 1888.

As you drive through the sculpted countryside, with its broad valleys and secluded canyons, you will be enthralled by the strange, twisted beauty and may understand why the Apaches believed this landscape was worth fighting for.

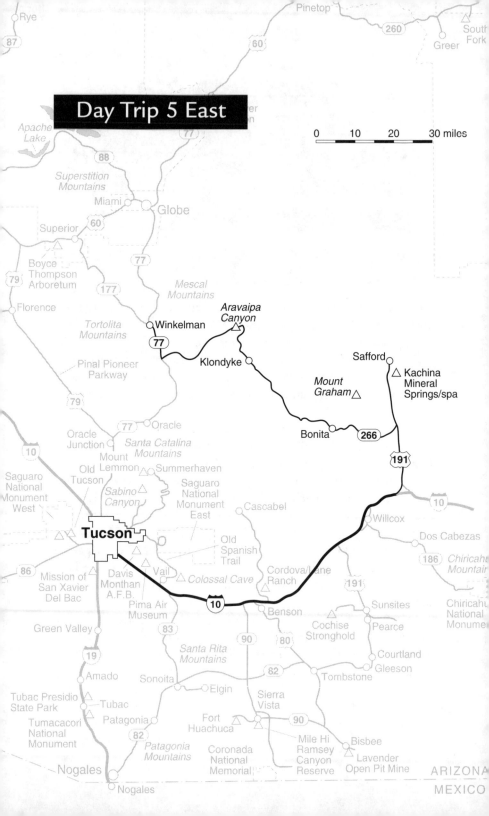

Day Trip 5 East

0   10   20   30 miles

Rye
87
Pinetop
260
South Fork
Greer
60

Apache Lake
77
Superstition Mountains
88
Miami
Globe
Superior
60
Boyce Thompson Arboretum
79
177
Florence
Mescal Mountains
Tortolita Mountains
Winkelman
77
Aravaipa Canyon
Klondyke
Safford
Kachina Mineral Springs/spa
Pinal Pioneer Parkway
79
Mount Graham
Oracle
77
Bonita
266
191
Oracle Junction
Santa Catalina Mountains
10
Mount Lemmon
Summerhaven
Old Tucson
Saguaro National Monument West
Sabino Canyon
Saguaro National Monument East
Cascabel
Willcox
Dos Cabezas
186
Chiricahua Mountains
Tucson
Old Spanish Trail
86
Mission of San Xavier Del Bac
Davis Monthan A.F.B.
Vail
Colossal Cave
Cordova/Lane Ranch
191
Chiricahua National Monument
Pima Air Museum
10
Benson
Sunsites
Pearce
Green Valley
83
Cochise Stronghold
19
Santa Rita Mountains
90
80
Courtland
Gleeson
Amado
Sonoita
82
Tombstone
Tubac Presidio State Park
Tubac
Elgin
Sierra Vista
Tumacacori National Monument
Patagonia
82
Fort Huachuca
90
Bisbee
Patagonia Mountains
Coronada National Memorial
Mile Hi Ramsey Canyon Reserve
Lavender Open Pit Mine
ARIZONA
Nogales
Nogales
MEXICO

WHERE TO GO

Mount Graham. About 9 miles south of Safford, off US-191, you will see A-366, or Swift Trail. Turn right and follow this road for a spectacular journey to the summit of Mount Graham. Like the drive to Mount Lemmon, this takes you through five of the seven ecological zones of western North America. You'll begin in desert cactus and end in mountainous aspen.

When you see a sharp right-hand turn leading to Marijilda Canyon, *don't* take it. This road is not recommended for passenger cars. (As you travel around Arizona, *always obey a sign that says:* NOT RECOMMENDED FOR PASSENGER CAR OR SEDAN TRAVEL. These roads can go from rough to impassable fast.) Instead, continue on Swift Trail. The first 22 miles are paved, but then the road becomes well-maintained gravel. With its many switchbacks, you'll need about two hours to make it to the top. As you traverse the 36 miles to the summit, you'll pass campgrounds—complete with showers—and picnic grounds. Pull off at the scenic turnouts to drink in the views.

Although the drive is worth the trip, Mount Graham has nine major trails to hike on, once you ascend. Dutch Henry Trail originates at Ladybug Saddle; Ash Creek Trail begins at the summer-home area of Columbine, at 9,500 feet. You can pick up Grant Goudy Ridge Trail at Soldier Creek Campground. Try the Round-the-Mountain Trail, which covers 14 miles and touches on some of the most popular features of the area, or High Peak Trail, which originates a short distance southeast of Columbine, at 9,600 feet. In addition, you can hike on Clark Peak Trail in the Taylor Pass and West Peak area, Bear Canyon Trail, Snake Trail, and Arcadia Trail. Pick up information and trail guides at the Safford–Graham County Chamber of Commerce, 1111 Thatcher Boulevard, Safford 85546. (928) 428-2511. www.chamber.safford.az.org.

Kachina Mineral Springs Spa. Six miles south of Safford, just off US-191, 1155 West Cactus Road. For a relaxing interlude, soak up the natural hot mineral springs that come out of the ground at 108 degrees Fahrenheit. Bathe in tiled Roman-style tubs. Enthusiasts believe that the stimulating combination of bathing, sweating, and massage cleanses both the body and the mind. Fee. (928) 428-7212. E-mail: kachina@zekes.com.

WORTH MORE TIME: ARAVAIPA CANYON

You *must* contact the Bureau of Land Management (BLM) before making a trek into this jewel of a wilderness area, and there is a fee. Write to the Bureau of Land Management, 1906 West Thatcher Boulevard, Safford 85546, or call (928) 348-4400. www.az.blm.gov.

To get to Aravaipa Canyon from Safford, take US-191 south to A-266. Follow A-266 west to Bonita and then pick up the secondary road to the village of Klondyke. Follow this road to the canyon entrance. Park your vehicle and proceed on foot.

Aravaipa is located in the Galiuro Mountains, and the creek supports an abundance of wildlife. More than 230 species of birds have been recorded here, including some rare black-and-zone tailed hawks and yellow warblers. To protect the wildlife, only fifty people per day are permitted to hike on the trail, and permits should be obtained in advance. It is always important to ask about the condition of the canyon in terms of weather.

This canyon is *not* for the casual hiker. Aravaipa is designated as a wilderness area; it is not a picnic ground. The area covers 4,044 acres and offers hikers and backpackers a relaxing-to-challenging experience. Bring water and a trail map (which you receive when you contact the BLM), even if you plan to spend only a few hours in this desert splendor.

Today Aravaipa is such a tranquil place that it's difficult to remember its violent history. The confluence of Aravaipa Creek and the San Pedro River, however, was the original site of Camp Grant (now Fort Grant). Although the U.S. Army swore that the Aravaipa Indians had not been responsible for raiding the white settlements, both the white men and the Papago (now Tohono O'odham) Indians were unconvinced. In 1872, a group of Tucson citizens and Papagos approached the Aravaipa Reservation and, before the sun rose, massacred eighty-five men, women, and children.

As you hike in the canyon, you'll be flanked by cliffs rising 700 feet or more on either side of you. In some areas you must squeeze through narrow stone hallways. If you choose to follow Aravaipa Creek, plan on having wet shoes at times. You'll be wise to move quietly and carry a good camera to catch much of the endangered wildlife on film. Bighorn sheep take refuge here, and the largest number of native fish in any stream in the state populate the water. Aravaipa is also a bird-watcher's paradise.

While hikers wax eloquent about an autumn backpacking trip into Aravaipa Canyon, enthusiasts insist it's ideal any time of year.

To return to Tucson after such a full day, follow US-191 south to I-10 and head west back to the "Old Pueblo." Or you can go on to Chiricahua National Monument (Day Trip 4 East from Tucson).

WHERE TO STAY

Aravaipa Farms. From Aravaipa Canyon, follow A-177 north to Winkelman and the turnoff to the B&B. It is two hours southeast of Phoenix and one hour north of Tucson, just outside Winkelman. Carol Steele, a well-known former Phoenix culinary star, is the hostess of this charming and gourmet B&B, which features just three cottages located on a fifty-five-acre fruit orchard. The unique furniture is made on the premises as are the birdhouses that hang everywhere. The daily rate includes three great meals prepared by your hostess. Two- and three-course dinners prepared by the hostess are memorable and are served at 7:00 P.M. On weekends, a two-night minimum stay is required, but during the week, guests may book a single night. During the fruit season, guests can pick apricots, peaches, and pears in the Aravaipa orchard. There's a nominal fee to pick fruit by the pound so you can carry it home with you. Dinner is served at a round table in the Steele's home. $$$. (520) 357-6901; www.aravaipafarms.com.

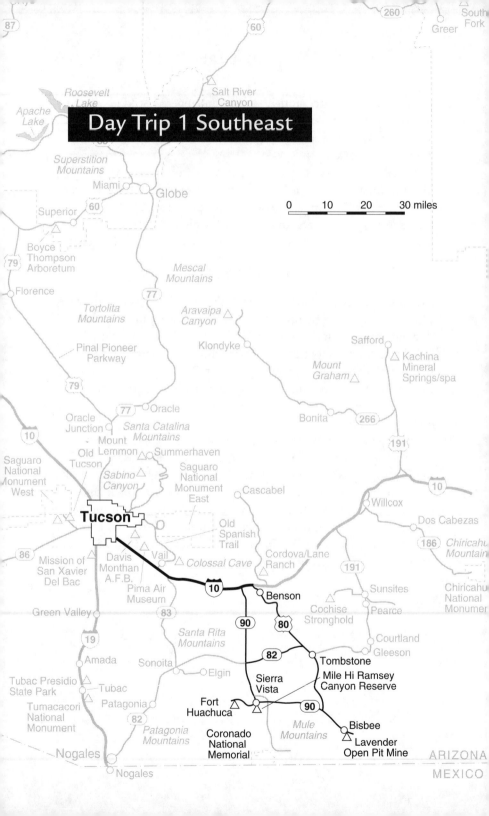
Day Trip 1 Southeast

87

260

60

South
Fork
Greer

Roosevelt
Lake

Salt River
Canyon

Apache
Lake

Superstition
Mountains

Miami
Globe

Superior
60

0   10   20   30 miles

79
Boyce
Thompson
Arboretum

Florence

Mescal
Mountains

77

Tortolita
Mountains

Aravaipa
Canyon

Klondyke

Safford

Kachina
Mineral
Springs/spa

Pinal Pioneer
Parkway

Mount
Graham

79

Oracle
Junction

77 Oracle

Santa Catalina
Mountains

Bonita

266

191

Mount
Old Lemmon
Tucson   Summerhaven

10

Saguaro
National
Monument
West

Mount
Old
Tucson

Sabino
Canyon

Saguaro
National
Monument
East

Cascabel

Willcox

Dos Cabezas

Tucson

Old
Spanish
Trail

10

186 Chiricahu
Mountain

86

Mission of
San Xavier
Del Bac

Davis
Monthan
A.F.B.

Vail

Colossal Cave

Cordova/Lane
Ranch

Pima Air
Museum

10

191

Benson

Chiricahu
National
Monumer

Green Valley

83

90

80

Sunsites

Cochise
Stronghold

Pearce

Chiricahu
National
Monumer

19

Santa Rita
Mountains

82

Courtland
Gleeson

Amada

Sonoita

Elgin

Sierra
Vista

Tombstone

Mile Hi Ramsey
Canyon Reserve

Tubac Presidio
State Park

Tubac

Patagonia

Fort
Huachuca

90

Bisbee

Tumacacori
National
Monument

82

Patagonia
Mountains

Coronado
National
Memorial

Mule
Mountains

Lavender
Open Pit Mine

ARIZONA

Nogales

Nogales

MEXICO

Although this day trip can be done in one day, you may prefer this as a more leisurely two-day excursion. Plan to arrive in Tombstone by midmorning and reach Bisbee by suppertime. Stay overnight in Bisbee and then drive on to Sierra Vista, Fort Huachuca, and back to Tucson the following day.

Should you decide to cover this portion of southern Arizona in one day, know at the outset that you can't see everything described here. Choose carefully among the attractions. There is so much to see that if you aren't careful, you'll arrive home in the wee hours of the morning, overtired and oversatiated.

TOMBSTONE

Begin in familiar territory by taking I-10 east to Benson. At US-80, head south to Tombstone. Here's where all your western fantasies will come true. This is "The Town Too Tough to Die." It's where Ed Schieffelin went prospecting in 1878 for silver, warned that all he would find in this Apache-infested land was his tombstone. Instead, he found one of the richest silver strikes in the country.

Tombstone, for all its touristy atmosphere, is no false-front, made-up western town. This is the *real* thing, and has emerged in recent years as a fun and fascinating destination. Once it boasted a population of about 10,000 wild and respectable souls. Today the community caters to tourists, but all the legends are alive and well here. As you walk along the dusty streets, you'll see the O.K. Corral, the Bird Cage Theater, the Crystal Palace, and other historic sites.

Tombstone is the Wild West preserved at its raunchiest and best. It personifies the frontier experience in those wild days before the turn of the twentieth century.

What was it like to live here? George Parsons, an early settler, noted in his diary in 1880 that "a man will go to the devil pretty fast in Tombstone. Faro, whiskey, and bad women will beat anyone." And Wyatt Earp once commented, "We had no YMCAs."

As you come into town on US–80, you'll hit Fremont Street. Park anywhere. Since the entire town is a living museum, you'll want to see this national historic site on foot. And save time to shop. The wooden sidewalks are faced by as fine an array of shops as one can find in urban settings. Tombstone has definitely discovered fine boutiques.

Begin with a liberal dose of history. Stop at the *Tombstone Epitaph,* 9 South Fifth Street, and pick up a map describing the points of interest.

Take a moment to familiarize yourself with the town. Most of what you'll want to tour lies within a few main streets. The sites are concentrated in a square framed by Fremont and Toughnut Streets to the north and south, and Third and Fifth Avenues on the west and east.

Since most of the attractions have an entrance fee, you may prefer to stop in at the O.K. Corral or Tombstone Historama and buy a combination ticket rather than pay separately for each. The combination ticket saves you a little money and a lot more time waiting to buy other tickets.

For more information before you go, write the Tombstone Tourism Association, 9 South Fifth Street, Tombstone 85638, for a map and a brochure. (520) 457–2211. www.tombstoneaz.com.

WHERE TO GO

Tombstone Courthouse. On the corner of Toughnut and Third Streets. This elegant structure was built in 1882 for the then amazing sum of $43,000. It served as the Cochise County Courthouse until 1929, when the county seat was moved to Bisbee. Two floors of exhibits await visitors. There's a ghoulish side trip out the side door to see the hangman's platform, a room devoted to cattlemen, another to lawyers, and rooms full of costumes, jewelry, and china. This is a good first stop to get you in the mood for the 1880s. (520) 457–3311. E-mail: courthouse@pr.state.az.us.

Tombstone Historama. Allen Street between Third and Fourth Streets, next to the O.K. Corral. Enter this bright, airy building and slide back into time thanks to this unique, informative electronic presentation of Tombstone's history. You'll be seated in a small theater to watch an excellent mini-sound-and-light production and will gain an understanding of the forces that shaped this tough little town. Fee. (520) 457-3456. E-mail: info@tombstonaz.com

O.K. Corral. Allen Street between Third and Fourth Streets. This is where it all happened, where history was made that bloody, dusty October day in 1881 when the Earp brothers and Doc Holliday faced off against the Clanton and McLaury brothers. You'll see the lifelike figures positioned as they stood in the dust that fateful day, and you'll marvel that a major gunfight was staged in such a small space. Even non-western history buffs will be strongly affected by this site. Live shows daily 9:00 A.M. to 5:00 P.M. Fee. (520) 457-3456.

Bird Cage Theatre. On the corner of Allen and Sixth Streets. Here tired miners bragged of strikes yet to come. Gamblers and gunmen cavorted. The law kept order, and pretty young girls charmed them all. Preserved as it was in the 1880s, this theater was the gathering place for Tombstone citizens looking for fun. There's less glamour than you might expect, but remember that in the 1880s, this place was "it." Open daily 8:00 A.M. to 6:00 P.M. Fee. (520) 457-3421. E-mail: oldbirdcage@juno.com.

Rose Tree Inn Museum. On the corner of Fourth and Toughnut Streets. The world's largest rose bush, which grew from one slip sent to a Scottish bride living in Tombstone, spreads for more than 7,000 square feet. Inside the museum, antique furnishings give visitors a glimpse of how people lived in Tombstone more than a century ago. Open daily 9:00 A.M. to 5:00 P.M. Fee. (520) 457-3326.

Crystal Palace Saloon. Allen and Fifth Streets. While the Bird Cage Theatre was bawdy, the Crystal Palace was more refined. Here the elite and not-so-elite gathered for food and drink. You can belly up to the bar and eat and drink (both soft drinks and alcohol) in the carefully preserved interior. Come for good food, atmosphere, and loud, vintage 1890s saloon music. $ at the bar. (520) 457-3611.

Tombstone Epitaph. Fifth Street near Fremont Street. Visit the original newspaper building where people continue to publish the famous *Tombstone Epitaph*. Purchase a subscription for $7.00 and keep up on Tombstone once you are home. Open daily 9:30 A.M. to 5:00 P.M. (520) 457-2211.

Boot Hill. You pass the sign to Boot Hill as you come into town on US-80. You can stop either on the way in or on your way out of town to discover the many infamous gunslingers who are buried at Boot Hill. Read the epitaphs, as they are wonderfully cryptic and humorous. Open daily. Donations suggested.

Tombstone has many other museums and points of interest. Depending upon your time and enthusiasm, spend a full day or just a few hours to get the flavor of this bawdy, rugged place.

WHERE TO EAT

Longhorn Restaurant. 501 East Allen Street. Come for breakfast, lunch, or dinner and feast on Italian, Mexican, and American food. Ask about the lunch special; it's always good. $$; ☐. Visa and Mastercard only. (520) 457-3405. www.bignosekates.com.

WHERE TO STAY

Tombstone has joined the twenty-first century (or maybe it's just returned to the 1880s) by sprouting a bouquet of bed and breakfasts. All are close to town and convenient.

Best Western Lookout Lodge. On US-80 about 1 mile northwest of town. This is the largest motel in the area, featuring forty units and a swimming pool. Although there is no restaurant, a continental breakfast is served. US-80 West, P.O. Box 787, Tombstone 85638. $$; ☐. (520) 457-2223. www.tombstone1880.com.

Buford House. Second and Safford Streets. This 1880 two-story adobe residence is registered as a National Historic Landmark. The house has two rooms and serves full breakfast. (520) 457-3969 or (800) 273-6762.

Marie's. Fourth and Safford Streets. A 1906 Victorian adobe home that is 2 blocks from the Historic District, it offers two rooms and serves full breakfast. (520) 457-3831. E-mail: maries@theriver.com.

Priscilla's. Third and Safford Streets. An historic country Victorian home 2 blocks from the O.K. Corral, it features three rooms and a full breakfast. www.tombstone1880.com/priscilla/index.htm.

Silver Nugget. Sixth and Allen Streets. The home offers four rooms with a balcony that overlooks historic Allen Street. Serves continental breakfast. (520) 457-9223 or (520) 457-3657. www.tombstone1880. com/silvernugget.

Tombstone Boarding House. Fourth between Safford and Bruce Streets. Two 1880 adobe houses combined offer eight rooms with private baths. Breakfast is provided. (520) 457-3716. E-mail: tomb stonebandb@theriver.com.

Tombstone Bordello. Allen and Haskell Streets. This original 1880 bordello is a two-story Victorian and offers two rooms. Full breakfast is served. (520) 457-2394.

Victoria's B&B and Wedding Chapel. Toughnut between Second and Third Streets. Three rooms are available at this 1880 adobe home with private baths. (520) 457-3766 or (800) 952-8216. www.tombstone1880.com/vsbb.

BISBEE

Continue south about 25 miles on US-80 to Bisbee. Just 6 miles north of the Mexican border, this charming community is famous for its mountainous setting; steep, winding streets; and a crazy patchwork of architectural building styles. You'll enter town on US-80 through Mule Pass Tunnel. A third of a mile long, it is Arizona's longest tunnel. As you get near town, watch for the Bisbee business loop, which will be on your right. Follow it to Old Bisbee, and you'll wind up on Main Street.

Bisbee has been described by Arizona writer Joseph Stocker as a "larger and newer version of Jerome." (See Day Trip 2 North from Phoenix.) Like Jerome, Bisbee began as a mining town. During its heyday, this was *the* place to stop between New Orleans and San Francisco. Millions of tons of copper, gold, and silver were pulled from the Mule Mountains, which surround the town. Until the late 1880s, Bisbee offered every cultural, culinary, and sporting diversion found in any major American city.

The Phelps Dodge Corporation closed its copper operations in Bisbee in the mid-1970s, but instead of dying, the community determined to survive as a tourism center of southeastern Arizona. During the late 1960s and 1970s, hippies heard about the community and flocked here in droves, attracted by the temperate climate and inexpensive housing. Today most of the hippie culture has vanished, but some artists, poets, and artisans remain in residence. Thanks to a strong dose of community spirit, Bisbee is succeeding as a tourist center, and visitors appreciate the blend of historical charm and modern-day convenience the town offers.

Bisbee is quite small, with a population of less than 10,000, but it supports a lively cultural scene. Classical concerts are presented at the Bisbee Women's Club. There are gallery openings by local artists, poetry readings, dinner theater, even melodramas. Most weekends the town hums with activities. Antiques shops are everywhere.

The unique blend of Victorian and 1930s art deco images have inspired many creative people who have come to work here. The late world-renowned Arizona artist Ted De Grazia once lived in Bisbee and managed the now-restored Lyric Theatre.

You'll want to wander around "Old Bisbee," as it's called. Don't be deceived by the sleepy facade. This isn't a living museum like Tombstone. Rather, this is a very much alive community populated with Bisbee boosters. You'll enjoy touring the old residential sections where turn-of-the-twentieth-century homes are squeezed onto narrow, steep streets wedged into equally narrow, scenic canyons. The result is an intriguing web of tangled mountain roads and architecturally interesting structures.

If possible, do take a complete walking tour of downtown. Stop in at the Chamber of Commerce, 31 Subway Street, and pick up a brochure (520-432-5421; www.bisbeearizona.com). Even if your time is limited, plan to walk around some of Bisbee's historical district to savor its past. If you aren't up to a strenuous stroll, take a bus tour of Old Bisbee and the hilly residential neighborhood known as the Warren area. Each tour lasts approximately one and one-half hours and allows you plenty of time to take pictures. Fee. For information regarding hours of departure, call (520) 432-2071.

WHERE TO GO

Queen Mine and Lavender Open Pit Tours. 478 Dart Avenue. To get to the Queen Mine building, drive or walk immediately south of Old Bisbee's business district off the US-80 interchange. Underground mine tours leave daily at scheduled hours. As you explore the mine with your guide, you'll hear about George Warren, who, having celebrated with a few too many on the Fourth of July, bragged that he could outrun a horse and rider. In a burst of inebriated pluck, he bet his mining claim, the Copper Queen Mine, on the race. He ran and lost. Eventually his claim panned out, ultimately worth more than $40 million. Today George Warren's biggest claim to fame is that he was the model for the man who stands with his shovel in the center of the Arizona State Seal.

During this educational tour, you'll learn how Bisbee miners coaxed minerals from the mountains. Much of the original mining equipment stands in place. Although you walk into the Copper Queen, you'll ride out on small train cars. Bring a sweater. The mine remains a chilly 47 degrees Fahrenheit. Fee. For information about tour times, call (520) 432-2071.

Lavender Open Pit. Drive to a viewpoint on US–80 that is ¾ mile beyond the Queen Mine building to see the open pit, or take a guided tour that leaves from the Queen Mine building every day at noon. As you gaze into this huge bowl scooped out of the landscape, you'll marvel at how humans ever carved such an immense niche in the earth. Although the Lavender Open Pit shimmers with color, the name comes from a mine manager, Harry Lavender. Fee. (520) 432-2071.

Brewery Gulch. 13–17 Brewery Avenue. Also known as the Muhlheim Block, this street shoots dramatically uphill or downhill (depending upon your vantage point) from Howell Avenue. Completed in 1905, Brewery Gulch was once home to the Bisbee Stock Exchange, brothels, restaurants, lodging facilities, and saloons. Now under restoration, it emits old echoes of wilder days when gamblers and miners traipsed up Brewery for excitement. Today visitors can poke through new shops and art galleries along this narrow street.

Bisbee Mining and Historical Museum. In front of the Copper Queen Hotel. The permanent exhibition opened in September 1991 and combines mural-size photography, artifacts, minerals, and hands-on displays. The mineral collection is small but select and features a variety of copper-related materials, such as azurite, that can be found in the area. A one-hour visit will explain the political, economic, and labor history of this mining camp turned cosmopolitan town. The Mexican Revolution lives in photographs and commentary; the World War I labor section describes how Arizona cleaned up prostitution and gambling so it could join the Union. A rare faro table illustrates gambling; prostitution is left largely to the imagination.

A poignant exhibit tackles discrimination. Through a mirror device, visitors' faces are superimposed on heads of an Asian man and a black woman. The question asked is: Does it make a difference?

The museum is located in a historic structure built in 1897. Fee. For information call (520) 432-7071. www.azstarnet.com/non profit/bisbeemuseum.

Old Phelps Dodge General Office Building. 5 Copper Queen Plaza. This structure was completed in 1895 and was designed as the general offices of the copper company. A National Historic Landmark, the Old Phelps Dodge building is located in Bisbee's "Grassy Park." It is now the town's Mining and Historical Museum. Here you can see early mining equipment and a diorama that depicts a mining operation. In another setting, such a display may not excite you, but it springs to life in Bisbee. Fee. (520) 432-7071.

Covenant Presbyterian Church. 19 Howell Avenue. Next to the Copper Queen Hotel, this imposing European-style church was built in 1903. At the time it was built, a 579-pipe organ was installed. Over the years the organ has been enlarged, and it remains in excellent condition. Free. (520) 432-4327.

WHERE TO STAY

Bisbee has experienced an explosion of good to terrific bed-and-breakfast inns, making this a great place to spend the night in southern Arizona. Here are some suggestions:

The Bisbee Inn. 45 OK Street. This old hotel has been renovated to bring back a feeling of Bisbee at its heyday. Not as luxurious as the Copper Queen, it is nevertheless a good choice for travelers who want to experience life in the Old West. Originally built in 1916 as a miner's hotel, the Bisbee Inn offers twenty guest rooms. *A special note:* The original name of the hotel was "La More," which leaves little of its history to the imagination. $$. (520) 432-5131. www.bisbeeinn.com.

Copper Queen Hotel. 11 Howell Avenue. This famous hotel was built by the Copper Queen Mining Company (later Phelps Dodge Corporation) shortly after the turn of the twentieth century, when Bisbee was the largest mining town in the world. It is

Arizona's oldest hotel—it has been run continuously as a hotel since that time. The present owners have restored most of the rooms to their former glory, making this a good choice for travelers. The rooms are large, and each one is different. Some bathtubs come with feet attached; wallpapers are period restoration. Although the lobby still feels dark and old, the renovated rooms are bright and cheery. The Copper Queen may not be quite as quaint as you may hope it to be, but it is authentic. When you sleep here, you are in good company. Theodore Roosevelt stayed at the Copper Queen, as did Gen. John J. Pershing when he was on his way to Mexico to catch up with Pancho Villa. Ask, too, about the special Murder Mystery Weekends.

The dining room at the Copper Queen is recommended. The fare is sophisticated and well prepared. Have breakfast, lunch, or dinner here. Dine outdoors at the patio cafe or sit inside in the historic, restored dining room. The varied menu features old-fashioned American food spiced with a liberal dash of Mexican dishes. P.O. Box CQ, Bisbee 85603. $$; ☐. (520) 432–2216.

High Desert Inn. 8 Naco Road. The best luxury inn to open in Bisbee, the High Desert Inn bills itself as "A Modern Hotel in a Timeless Town." It is an apt description. The inn features five rooms—each designed with a unique, historic-yet-contemporary feeling. With queen-size, wrought-iron beds from France; craftsman tables; and other fine appointments, the rooms are exceptionally inviting. The High Desert Inn offers full hotel services. A small, intimate bar and unique dining room are open Thursday, Friday, and Saturday evenings and certain holidays. The Cordon Bleu–trained chef offers seasonally changing menus that emphasize fresh, locally grown ingredients. A small but excellent wine list is available. $$; ☐. (520) 432–1442 or (800) 281–0510. www.highdesertinn.com.

The Inn at Castle Rock. 112 Tombstone Canyon Road. This B&B was once a miner's boardinghouse and was located on Main Street in Old Bisbee. The three-story, red Victorian structure, trimmed with cream-colored balconies, is on the National Register of Historic Places. Castle Rock features fifteen rooms and suites, each with private bathrooms. In addition, there are gardens and parlors that guests are invited to enjoy. The Inn at Castle Rock offers guests and Bisbee visitors the opportunity to dine at Eccentricity's Restaurant, which features French-Flemish cuisine. Fine wines and cocktails are available. $$; ☐. (520) 432-4449 or (800) 566-4449. www.theinn.org.

The Oliver House. 26 Soule. This B&B has fourteen units. The house, in the heart of town, was supposedly haunted. A full breakfast is served; king-size beds and suites are available. $$; ☐. (520) 432-4286.

School House Inn. 818 Tombstone Canyon. Nine units (nonsmoking) are available in a 1918 schoolhouse. A full breakfast is served, and private baths are provided. $-$$; ☐. (520) 432-2996 or (800) 537-4333.

SIERRA VISTA

From Bisbee, backtrack 9 miles north on US-80 and follow A-90 west 20 miles to Sierra Vista. Perched at an elevation of 4,623 feet, this fast-growing city is nestled on the slopes of the Huachuca Mountains. Surrounded on all sides by mountain ranges and never-ending views of the San Pedro Valley, the climate is as awesome as the scenery. Sierra Vista ranks as one of the three most temperate regions in the nation, and its cool summers and moderate winters make this city increasingly popular with newcomers and tourists.

With an abundance of outdoor pleasures nearby (everything from hiking trails to ghost towns and a mountain lake), Sierra Vista has become an important southern Arizona town. In the past, its biggest claim to fame was nearby Fort Huachuca. While the economy remains closely tied to the military installation, Sierra Vista is establishing itself as a manufacturing, wholesale, and retail center.

WHERE TO GO

The Mile Hi/Ramsey Canyon Preserve. Six miles south of Sierra Vista on A-92. Turn right onto Ramsey Canyon Road and drive 4 miles to The Mile Hi. This small and limited facility, owned by the Nature Conservancy, is sheltered in a deep gorge within 280 acres of the Huachuca Mountains and was closed to the public for a year in 1999 for habitat restoration. It's a favorite place for bird-watchers and others who are interested in learning more about this unique, fragile environment. Should you decide to spend time here, try to arrive on a weekday. It's much less crowded, and you'll have more opportunity to walk along the two nature trails and enjoy the serenity of this preserve.

Ramsey Canyon is located at an ecological crossroads where habitats and species from the Sierra Madres of Mexico, the Rocky Mountains, and the Sonoran and Chihuahuan Deserts all can be found. The preserve is a haven for one of the largest arrays of plant and animal species of any preserve in the United States, with 210 species of birds (including 14 species of hummingbirds), 420 species of plants, 45 species of mammals, and 20 species of reptiles and amphibians found in the canyon. Some, like the Ramsey Canyon leopard frog and the lemon lily, are found in few other places on Earth.

Ramsey Canyon was the first Nature Conservancy preserve to provide overnight accommodations as well as daytime visits. It continues to be the center of the conservancy's upper San Pedro River ecosystem program and is eloquent testimony to the work that the conservancy does.

Both nature trails open windows to a world populated by a great variety of birds, reptiles, and other animals. Guided hikes can be arranged by contacting the Ramsey Canyon Preserve manager in advance. A visitors center, bookstore, gift shop, and nature reference library are on the grounds.

When you plan a trip here, remember that not every type of bird can be seen at the canyon during all times of the year. Ramsey Canyon is known as a hummingbird sanctuary, but these delicate creatures are in residence only from April through August. During the winter, they migrate farther south.

Because of the comparatively small size and ecological fragility of the area, certain rules are strictly enforced. No picnicking is allowed within the confines of the preserve, and parking is extremely limited. *All parking reservations must be made in advance.* RVs and campers cannot be accommodated. Whenever possible, carpooling is encouraged. In addition, pets are not allowed on the property. Visitor hours are strictly enforced. For more information contact The Mile Hi, 27 Ramsey Canyon Road, Hereford 85615. Fee. (520) 378-3010. www.tnc. org/ramseycanyon/ramseycanyoninn.

San Pedro National Conservation Area. The visitors center, San Pedro House, is 8 miles east of Sierra Vista on A-90. This 46,000-acre area stretches 33 miles from the Mexican border near Palominos to about 3 miles south of St. David. It includes one of the most significant broadleaf riparian ecosystems in Arizona and perhaps the entire Southwest. More than 350 species of birds, 82 species of mammals, and 47 species of reptiles and amphibians may be seen here. This is a wonderland for hikers, bird-watchers, and nature lovers. For more information contact the Bureau of Land Management, 1763 Paseo San Luis, Sierra Vista 85635-4611. (520) 458-3559.

WHERE TO STAY

Casa de San Pedro. 8933 South Yell Lane, Hereford. From Sierra Vista, take A-90 Business Loop to the intersection of A-90 and A-92 in Sierra Vista. Travel south on A-92 for 18½ miles to Palominos Road. Turn north on Palominos Road for 2 miles to Waters Road. Turn east on Waters Road for 1 mile. This charming, new bed and breakfast is backed by the San Pedro riparian area and is situated on ten acres that border the San Pedro River. Cotton-wood and willow along the river provide a verdant habitat for a variety of wildlife—more than 330 species of birds, 82 species of mammals, and 47 species of reptiles and amphibians. A birders' paradise, this special B&B is an ideal getaway for any traveler seeking peace and relaxation. Built in territorial style around a courtyard and fountain, this property has ten guest rooms. All are well appointed and have private patios. A comfortable Great Room invites lounging and reading, and superb breakfasts are served in the sunny dining room. The hosts are personable; the facility is superb. A list of special events from lectures to hikes is available. $$; ☐. (520) 366-1300. www.naturesinn.com.

The Mile Hi. Ramsey Canyon Preserve. This is one of the few Nature Conservancy properties in the country with overnight accommodations on the grounds. The name, The Mile Hi, comes from a private ranch the conservancy bought in 1975. As a result of this purchase, six cabins are available for rent. Each comes equipped with outdoor barbecue grill, picnic table, fully equipped kitchens, and linens. You'll need to bring your own food. Although you may rent the cabins by the day or week, during the spring and summer months you must reserve cabins for a minimum of three nights. Call in advance, or write to The Mile Hi, 27 Ramsey Canyon Road, Hereford 85615. $$. (520) 378–3010.

Ramsey Canyon Inn. Next to Ramsey Canyon Preserve. Also known as the Bed and Breakfast, this delightful B&B is owned and operated by Shirleen Desantis and is a great alternative for couples or nature lovers who crave ambience. There are six rooms and a cabin, all lovingly decorated with antiques. Guests enjoy herb teas, fresh brewed coffee, and a variety of gourmet breakfasts. Order a fluffy omelet, German apple pancake, or the specialty, Dutch babies. Or sample fresh-fruit cobblers before heading out to hike. The B&B has a beautiful living area with large fireplace. All rooms have private baths. $$. (520) 378–3010.

GHOST TOWNS

Want more ghost towns? Cochise County is your place. From Sierra Vista, go north on A–90 and A–92 approximately 9 miles to the junction with A–82. Go east on A–82 for 10 miles to Fairbank. From Fairbank, take an unnumbered dirt road that goes south for approximately 6 or 7 miles to Charleston. To return to Sierra Vista, either continue 8 more miles on that road, which will take you to the junction of A–90 and A–92, or retrace your steps.

There are more than thirty ghost towns in Cochise County, all that remain of once-vital mining towns. Charleston, for instance, was once described as tougher and livelier than Tombstone but was abandoned in 1886 after the Tombstone mines closed. Fairbank was named for Nathaniel Kellogg Fairbank, who helped finance the building of the railroad and organize the Grand Central Mining Company in Tombstone in 1879.

While you're in the area, see the Brunckow cabin, which has one of the bloodiest histories in Arizona. It's considered by some to be haunted and is located on Charleston Road before the Charleston bridge on the way to Sierra Vista from Tombstone. Watch on the left side of the road for an adobe building. Just behind that building is Brunckow cabin, the site of at least twenty murders. The first victim to have been murdered there was Frederick Brunckow himself, who in 1860 met his demise along with two coworkers. His mine was sold to Maj. Milton B. Duffield, Arizona's first U.S. Marshal, who was appointed by Abraham Lincoln. Major Duffield was shot at the former Brunckow mine in 1874. A newspaper account of the shooting stated, "It is claimed by some good men that he [Major Duffield] had redeeming qualities. Such may be the case, but we could never find them."

These roads are rutted but passable for cars. Be careful if you travel after a rain or during rainy weather, for the roads can become impassable. For more information on the area, call the Bureau of Land Management at (520) 458-3559.

CORONADO NATIONAL MEMORIAL

Located 20 miles south of Sierra Vista off A-92, Coronado National Memorial salutes the Spanish explorer Francisco Vasquez de Coronado, who searched for the Seven Cities of Cibola looking for gold.

From Sierra Vista, head south on A-92. Turn west onto Montezuma Canyon Road and continue for 5 miles until you come to the visitors center and museum. The road is paved for just about a mile west of the visitors center, and then it becomes a mountainous gravel path that leads to Montezuma Pass, a narrow passageway over the Huachuca Mountains. Park and pick up the hiking trail of your choice. From the pass, you can gaze west over the San Rafael Valley and Patagonia Mountains toward Nogales (see Day Trip 3 South of Tucson).

The Coronado National Memorial is the name given to this entire area and includes both natural and manufactured historical features. There is no plaque or statue commemorating Coronado's adventures. Instead, hiking trails lace the 4,976 acres that are home to a variety of birds, animals, and plants.

Told that cities existed where streets were paved with gold, Coronado arrived in Mexico in 1535. On February 23, 1540, he headed north with 336 Spanish soldiers and four priests to search for treasure. Instead of finding golden cities, Coronado found mud houses—adobe pueblo—inhabited by Native Americans. Pushing on, he ultimately came upon Hopi Indian villages in northeastern Arizona. Driven by the promise of gold, he continued to search past Acoma and onward to the upper Pecos River. Finally, discredited and disheartened, Coronado admitted defeat and died in relative obscurity. Although he never found gold, Coronado did change the course of Southwestern history. The Spaniards left behind horses that helped the Native Americans dominate the plains and mountains, and they introduced the Caucasian religion to the region. Historians agree that the Coronado expedition formed the basis for contemporary Hispanic-American culture.

If you have a car that can go over miles of dirt road—and you have the time—the trip over Montezuma Pass is well worth the effort. It is perhaps the most outstanding physical feature in this memorial. The pass is located at an elevation of 6,575 feet, and once at the top, visitors are treated to sweeping views of the San Rafael Valley to the west and the San Pedro River Valley to the east. The road has steep grades and tight switchbacks, and the top of the pass serves as a parking area for hikers who are exploring the memorial's trails. Standing at the top of Montezuma Pass is a living lesson in the geography and history of this area. You can easily imagine how it must have been when Coronado discovered this place and determined to conquer it. A picnic area near the visitors center is open from dawn to dusk, but there is nothing at the top of the pass other than an excellent national park plaque that describes the sweeping vista. The road continues to Sonoita—the scenery is spectacular, but the going will be slow. Or you can turn around and return to the visitors center.

The Coronado National Memorial is well known for the variety of birds that live in the area. The Park Service reports that more than 140 species have been recorded, including fifty resident birds. Free. (520) 366-5515. www.nps.gov/coro.

FORT HUACHUCA

From the Coronado National Memorial, return to Sierra Vista on A-92, then drive west for 4 miles to Fort Huachuca. To get to the main gate, follow A-90 south to where it intersects with Squier Avenue. The main gate is on the corner of Squier Avenue and A-90.

This 73,000-acre installation lies within the boundaries of Cochise and Santa Cruz Counties and is closely tied to the history of Arizona. Now the largest employer in southern Arizona, Fort Huachuca was established in 1877 as a base for American soldiers during the Native American wars of the 1870s and 1880s. Fresh running water, high ground, and shade trees convinced the Army that this was a wise location for a fort. When Geronimo surrendered and the Native American hostilities ended, Fort Huachuca was kept active to guard against problems around the Mexican border.

Many well-known units were stationed here, but the most famous is the "Buffalo Soldiers," the Tenth Cavalry Division of Black fighters who accompanied General Pershing when he chased Pancho Villa into Mexico in 1916.

Closed down after World War II, Fort Huachuca was later reactivated, and in 1953, became the home of the U.S. Army Electronic Proving Ground. Again, its physical setting saved the fort, because the mild, dry climate and open spaces made it a natural for the electronics field. Today the base buzzes as a center for intelligence and worldwide communications. For information regarding the base, write: Headquarters, Fort Huachuca, Attn: ATZS-CDR, Fort Huachuca 85613. (520) 533-3638.

Fort Huachuca Historical Museum. Corner of Boyd and Grierson Streets, overlooking the Brown Parade Field. The museum is housed on the historic Old Post, where almost all of the original buildings are still in use. Opened in 1960, the museum tells the story of Fort Huachuca and of southwestern Arizona. It showcases military memorabilia from the 1800s to the present. Because Arizona history is closely tied to the military, the exhibits will help you understand events leading up to this young territory becoming the forty-eighth state. There's ample parking, and a gift shop features items and books related to the Southwest. Free. (520) 533-5736. www.huachuca-usaic.army.mil.

To return to Tucson from Fort Huachuca, drive north on A-90 to I-10, then west on I-10 to Tucson.

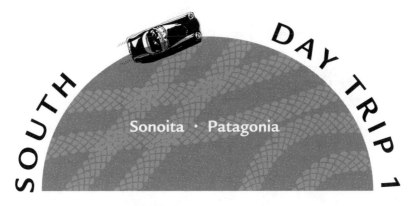

This day trip can also be done from Phoenix if you don't mind adding an extra two hours driving time each way. If you do it from Tucson, it's an easy hour or less to Sonoita and Patagonia.

From Tucson, take the scenic drive southeast on I-10 toward Nogales. Go south on A-83 for 27 miles to Sonoita. The route takes you through magnificent country studded with cactus, beveled with foothills, and ringed with wide, open valleys. As the road climbs toward Sonoita, the landscape grows more lush—the area is nurtured by Sonoita Creek. Even during the summer, when the rest of the Arizona desert is bleached to a coarse yellow, the high grasses here retain their green tint.

If you decide to stay overnight in Tombstone (see Day Trip 1 Southeast of Tucson), you can start this day trip by heading south the next morning. Follow US-80 north of Tombstone to A-82, continue west on A-82 to Sonoita, and then go south on A-82 to Patagonia and Nogales. You can return to Tucson by driving north on I-19, stopping at Tumacacori and Tubac on your way back. This makes a pleasantly packed two- or three-day mini-vacation. Spend the first night in Bisbee, the second in Tombstone, and arrive in Tucson the third evening.

If you make this trip in a single day from Tucson, plan on a long, full day to travel to the Mexican border and return to the Old Pueblo. Everybody likes to visit Mexico at least once while in Arizona. What makes this trip easier than most Mexican vacations is that you don't drive across the border. You'll park in Nogales, Arizona, and walk across the international line into Nogales, Mexico. Once you leave Arizona and enter the state of Sonora, Mexico, you'll feel worlds away from the United States. Border towns are usually

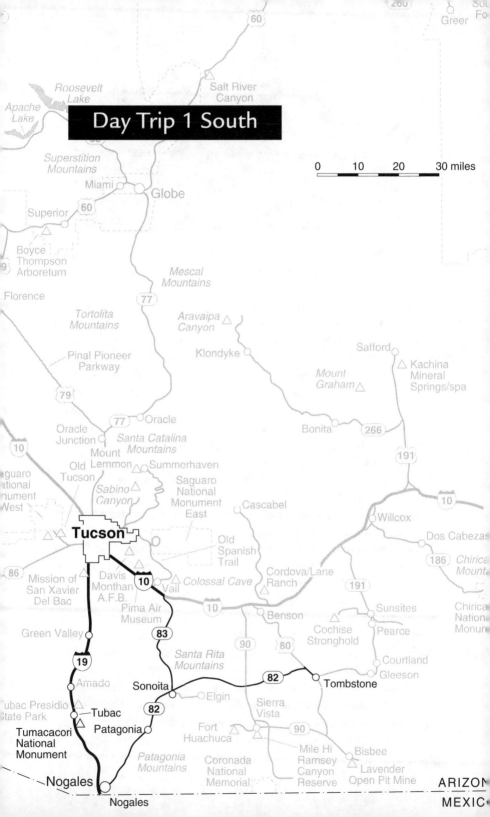

Day Trip 1 South

safe as long as you stay on the main streets. If you're a naturalized citizen or not an American citizen, you *must* bring your proof of citizenship or passport so that you can reenter the United States.

SONOITA

Sonoita is a very old community that dates to around 1699. Originally it was the site of a Vista, a mission that only occasionally received personal visits by Spanish padres.

According to Arizona historian Marshall Trimble, the modern-day town of Sonoita owes its existence to the Benson-to-Nogales railroad line, which was built in 1882. Today this community is still on the transportation "line" for visitors who take what locals call "the back way"—the scenic and more interesting non-interstate route—to Nogales.

More than a place along the way, Sonoita is coming into its own as the site of Arizona's flourishing wine industry. And now with the opening of Kartchner Caverns, visitors have even more reason to visit this tiny Arizona town.

WHERE TO GO

Callaghan Vineyards. I-10 east to A-83 south, to A-82 east and south to Elgin. The vineyard is located on Elgin Road, 5 miles south of town. Owned by Kent Callaghan, the wines produced are considered outstanding. Established in 1991, this is a family-owned winery that produces a variety of blends. Open on Sunday, the winery is quite rustic and not set up for tourist visits. However, if you call ahead for an appointment, the winery is usually happy to accommodate visitors who want to enjoy a wine tasting. Among the wines made here are barrel-fermented sauvignon blanc, zinfandel, cabernet sauvignon, and the buena suerta civee (a blend of merlot, cabernet franc, and cabernet sauvignon). Mourvedre, petit verdo, and viognier production began in 1998. (520) 455-5322.

Dos Cabeza Wineworks. Another very rustic family-owned winery, Dos Cabeza concentrates on making a variety of good wines rather than showcasing the winery to tourists. Those who call for an appointment or e-mail (grapeman@dakotacom.net) can set up an appointment to tour and taste. Its primary focus is on chardonnay, viognier, sauvignon blanc, pinot gris, and riesling, but it also has sangiovese and petite syrah "resting comfortably in oak barrels." The actual winery is located in Wilcox, about an hour and a half from Sonoita, in the Kansas Settlement area of that town. You need to call for directions, because the owners say that visitors cannot find them without a compass. (520) 803-0165.

Sonoita Vineyards. On Elgin Canelo Road, 12 miles southeast of town and 2 miles south of Elgin. Take the delightful tour through the winery, and sample some excellent wines being made in southern Arizona. In the past ten years, Arizona has experienced a growth of wineries, as its climate and soil are similar to that found in the Napa Valley area around San Francisco and the great wine country of France.

Sonoita Vineyards was selected for the 1989 Inaugural Food and Wine Gala for President George Bush. The winery is situated in rolling hills and is surrounded by grape arbors with the Huachuca Mountains clearly visible in the not-far-off distance.

Sonoita Vineyards makes private reserve cabernet sauvignon, pinot noir, fume blanc, Cuvee Sonoita, Sonora Blanca, Sonora Rossa, Arizona Sunset, and Cochise County Colombard. Wines are available for purchase and sampling. Tour requires a fee but includes wine tasting. (520) 455-5893. www.sonoitavineyards.com.

The Chapel of Santa Maria. Located in the village of Elgin. The chapel is overseen by the Monks of the Vine, a Wine Brotherhood of vintners. The Santa Fe–style chapel is a nondenominational shrine. Local legend is that vines planted around the shrine are thought to come from cuttings from the earliest conquistador cultivars. In April the "Blessing of the Vine Festival" is held, with music, processions, and food and wine tastings.

Village of Elgin Winery. Within walking distance from the Chapel of Santa Maria in Elgin. Located 4½ miles from upper Elgin Road. The winery is located in an old brown hay barn and is the only winery in Arizona to stomp its grapes. The winery accents small-lot red and white wines ranging from single varietals such as pinot noir, cabernet sauvignon, and colombard to blended varieties and clarets. The winery is open daily from 10:00 A.M. to 5:00 P.M. (520) 455-9309. www.earl-of-ellam.com.

WHERE TO EAT

The Steak Out Restaurant and Saloon. Next door to the Sonoita Inn, at the crossroads of A–82 and A–83. Opened in December 1999, the Steak Out serves mesquite-broiled steaks, seafood, ribs, and chicken, and the menu touts their "famous" margaritas. Built on the site of a famous western restaurant that burned to the ground, the new restaurant re-creates the fifty-year-old historic landmark building. The Steak Out is owned and operated by the owners of the Sonoita Inn, who also operate and own the country store, deli, and gas station on the property. $$; ☐. (520) 455–5205.

WHERE TO STAY

Sonoita Inn. At the crossroads of A–82 and A–83, 3243 Highway 82. This upscale country lodge was designed by local owner Margaret Charmichael, who owned the famous race horse Secretariat. The lodge is a tribute to that thoroughbred, who won the Kentucky Derby in 1973, the Preakness, and the Belmont. Photographs, press clippings, and other memorabilia are displayed in the lobby of the lodge.

The inn features eight rooms downstairs and ten rooms upstairs. Opened in 1998, each room is named for a ranch in the Sonoita area as a tribute to those families who have operated those ranches for centuries. Guests will find photos and bibliographical accounts of the ranches and the families in the hallways.

Your overnight lodging fee includes continental breakfast in the morning. Although the outside of the inn appears plain, inside you'll find a homey and comfortable atmosphere, with every well-appointed room decorated in a western theme Located just 30 miles from Mexico and close to Kartchner Caverns, the Sonoita Inn offers a welcome alternative to look-alike motel rooms. $$; ☐. (520) 455–5935. www.sonoitainn.com.

The Vineyard Bed & Breakfast. 92 Los Encinos Road, 2 miles from the intersection of A–82 and A–83. An intimate B&B run by Ron and Sue DeCosmo, this is the original B&B in the Sonoita area. It is located in a historic house, the original Hacienda Los Encinos, which sits on twenty-two high desert acres. With an elevation of 5,100 feet, this B&B enjoys a nearly ideal environment year-round.

Guests have their choice of any of three rooms with private bath, all located in the Hacienda, or the Casita, a separate house that includes a bedroom, private bath, and sitting room. Ron and Sue serve their guests a full, delicious breakfast. When making a reservation, the owners request one night's deposit.

Open year-round, the owners plan their own vacation during the months of July or September, so if you plan to visit the area in either of these months, be sure to call ahead to make sure they will be there. Children older than age twelve are welcome, but no pets are allowed. Smoking is not allowed within the Hacienda or the Casita. $$. (520) 455-4749.

PATAGONIA

Patagonia is a picturesque town that lies in a narrow valley bounded by the Santa Rita Mountains to the north and the Patagonias to the south. The mountains and the town were named after the now closed Patagonia Silver Mine, which operated there in 1858. Also known as the Mowry Mine after Sylvester Mowry purchased it in the 1850s, it produced more than $1.5 million worth of ore during its heyday. By the early 1900s the veins were too diminished to merit any more activity.

Today Patagonia has some of the finest quarter horse and cattle ranches in the Southwest. It is known throughout the state for its inviting location and, thanks to the higher elevation, slightly cooler temperatures.

In recent years, Patagonia has become its own tourist destination. There's an excellent arts-and-crafts gallery to peruse and two excellent restaurants in the vicinity. In addition, the Patagonia-Sonoita Creek Sanctuary has become a bird-watcher's paradise.

The town is also attracting film-industry people from Los Angeles who appreciate the serenity and majesty of the hillsides. Beautiful ranch homes are sprouting in the hills, most of which are hidden from passing motorists' eyes.

There are only two main streets in town, McKeown and A-82. You can't get lost in "downtown" Patagonia.

WHERE TO GO

Mesquite Grove Gallery. 373 McKeown Avenue. Owner Nancy Merwin and manager Regina Medley have assembled a special array of art, most by local artists. You'll find sculpture, needlework, jewelry, wood, and dozens of other kinds of artwork all crafted with high style and talent. The prices are excellent, and the work is uniformly fine. (520) 394-2358.

The Patagonia–Sonoita Creek Preserve. South of Patagonia on A-82 between Patagonia and Nogales. As you enter Patagonia on A-82, watch for the Stage Stop Inn and the Patagonia Market. Turn right onto Third Avenue. You may want to stop at the filling station in town to use the rest rooms since there are no facilities at the sanctuary. Continue south on Third Avenue to Pennsylvania Avenue and turn east onto Pennsylvania. Follow the road across a small creek and watch for signs that say NATURE CONSERVANCY. (The conservancy operates the sanctuary.) Look for Gate 2, which will be on your left. Turn in and drive to the Information Center. All visitors must register at an entrance gate.

Bird-watchers and naturalists flock to this 312-acre preserve. Located in a narrow floodplain, the sanctuary features a majestic stand of cottonwood trees interspersed with Arizona walnut and velvet ash. Avid bird-watchers from all over the world know that this is the place to see more than 200 species.

To protect the fragile character of the sanctuary, rules are strictly enforced. Pets are not allowed on the grounds. There is no picnicking, camping and fires are prohibited, and motorized vehicles are not allowed on trails within the conservancy. This is especially lovely to visit in the spring and fall. Free. For information contact the Nature Conservancy, P.O. Box 815, Patagonia 85624. (520) 394-2400. www.tnc.org/arizona.

WHAT TO DO

Senoita Stables. For experienced riders, Senoita Stables offers a rare opportunity to ride Peruvian Paso horses, "the Rolls Royce with four wheel drive." These are considered the smoothest riding horses in the world. This stable makes this opportunity available only to experienced riders who will appreciate the gait.

The ride is through a landscape that is part of a 45,000 acre Empire-Cienega Resource Conservation Area. The area has pronghorn antelope, mule deer, whitetail deer, javelina, mountain lion, badgers, ringtail cats, coati mundi, racoons and three species of native fish, along with 200 species of birds and four species of rattlesnakes.

Hosts Bob and Rusty Ness have opened their private stable to the public and expect guests to be able to use subtle controls to direct and ride the horse. Reservations are required. Children over age 9 are accepted based upon experience. Adults and children must wear long pants and closed-toe shoes. Adults must weigh less than 225 pounds. (520) 455-9266.

WHERE TO EAT

Karen's. 3266 A-82, Sonoita. Take the Sonoita exit from A-82. Turn left at the stop sign, and you will see the restaurant just down the road. Watch for signs! Karen's made its name in Elgin when it was in a charming, renovated home. It has now gone upscale in Sonoita. Salad dressings are still homemade, and the food is still good. $$-$$$; ☐. (520) 455-5282.

WHERE TO STAY

Circle Z Ranch. Write or call for directions. P.O. Box 194, Patagonia 85624. A working ranch, Circle Z is open November 1 through May 15. Requires a three-day stay in season. There are rooms, suites, and cottages for forty guests. The ranch is located in the rolling grasslands just north of the Mexican border. $$-$$$. (520) 394-2525. www.circlez.com.

The Duquesne House. 357 Duquesne Street. This B&B is almost directly across the street from Cady Hall and was once miners' apartments. The charming adobe building has been renovated with love and attention to detail by Regina Medley, who has furnished it with antiques. Medley is an artist and manages the Mesquite Grove Gallery. $$. Call for reservations. (520) 394-2732.

Amado
Green Valley · Madera Canyon

From Tucson, follow I-19 south toward Nogales, Arizona, and Nogales, Sonora, Mexico. This day trip is devoted to manufactured wonders of the high-tech world. Because of the time involved for the tours, if you want to cover both sights, I recommend going first to Amado and Whipple Observatory and then seeing the Titan Missile Museum on the way back to Tucson. This is not recommended for young children, but older children and teenagers will enjoy it.

AMADO

Follow I-56 to exit 56 (Canoa). Then follow directions to the observatory.

Fred Lawrence Whipple Observatory. From exit 56, turn left and drive under the freeway to the frontage road on the east. Turn right and drive south 3 miles to Elephant Head Road. Turn left and drive east. Follow the signs to Mount Hopkins Road for about 7 miles to reach the observatory office.

Operated by the Smithsonian Institution and the University of Arizona, Whipple Observatory sits atop Mount Hopkins, the second-highest peak in Arizona. It commands a heavenly panorama north beyond Tucson and south into Sonora, Mexico, over hundreds of miles of saguaro-studded Coronado National Forest, desert floor, and rolling mountain ranges.

Visitors take a daylong tour that describes a brief history of astronomical time and includes visits to the computer laboratories, massive telescopes, optical arrays, and celestial mirrors.

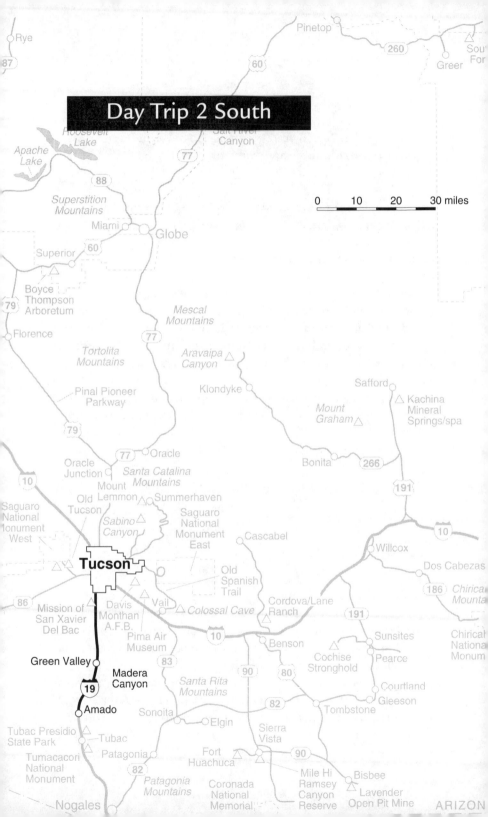

Day Trip 2 South

Rye
87
Pinetop
260
Sou
For
Greer
60

Roosevelt
Lake
Salt River
Canyon

Apache
Lake
77

88

0   10   20   30 miles

Superstition
Mountains
Miami
Globe

Superior
60

Boyce
Thompson
Arboretum
79

Florence
Mescal
Mountains

Tortolita
Mountains
77
Aravaipa
Canyon

Pinal Pioneer
Parkway
Klondyke
Safford
Kachina
Mineral
Springs/spa

79
Mount
Graham

77 Oracle
Bonita
266

Oracle
Junction
Santa Catalina
Mountains
191

10
Mount
Lemmon
Summerhaven

Old
Tucson
Saguaro
National
Monument
East
10

Saguaro
National
Monument
West
Sabino
Canyon

Cascabel
Willcox
Dos Cabezas

Tucson
186 Chirica
Mounta

86
Old
Spanish
Trail

Mission of
San Xavier
Del Bac
Davis
Monthan
A.F.B.
Vail
Colossal Cave
Cordova/Lane
Ranch
191
Sunsites
Chirical
Nationa
Monum

Pima Air
Museum
10
Benson
Cochise
Stronghold
Pearce

Green Valley
83
90
80
Courtland
Gleeson

19
Madera
Canyon
Santa Rita
Mountains
82
Tombstone

Amado
Sonoita
Elgin
Sierra
Vista

Tubac Presidio
State Park
Tubac
Fort
Huachuca
90

Tumacacori
National
Monument
Patagonia
82
Patagonia
Mountains
Coronada
National
Memorial
Mile Hi
Ramsey
Canyon
Reserve
Bisbee
Lavender
Open Pit Mine

Nogales
ARIZONA

From the visitors center, everyone boards a bus for the forty-five-minute climb to the top of the mountain and the observatories. The bus travels through various Arizona life zones, from desert to high chaparral to pine forest. The first stop is at 7,600 feet, for a tour of 48-inch and 60-inch telescopes and a gamma-ray collector. After lunch (you bring it; it's not provided), there's a short, steep ride to the 8,550-foot summit, where the Multiple Mirror Telescope (MMT) stands. You learn that the building rotates slowly so the "eyes" stay focused. Computers synchronize the entire operation. With its new 276-inch mirror, Whipple claims the world's largest telescope.

Whipple Observatory is open March through Thanksgiving. Fee. The tour departs at 9:00 A.M. and returns by 3:00 P.M. Reservations are required. (520) 670-5707. www.linmax.sao.arizona.edu/help/FLWO/whipple.html.

From Whipple Observatory, head back to Tucson via I-19 to Green Valley. This is less than a twenty-minute drive, and you can still make the last (4:00 P.M.) tour at the missile museum.

GREEN VALLEY

Pima Air Museum's Titan Missile Museum. From I-19 south, take exit 69. Go west ⅒ mile past La Cañada. Turn right. This is the only intercontinental ballistic missile complex in the world that is open to the public. This museum is dedicated as a memorial to all loyal Americans who served their country so valiantly in peace and in war. Guided, hour-long tours are available through the complex and the silo Wednesday through Sunday, May 1 through October 31. The museum is open daily November 1 through April 30. Closed Christmas. The last tour starts at 4:00 P.M. *Note:* High heels cannot be worn at this museum. Fee. (520) 625-4759 or 625-7736.

MADERA CANYON

From I-19 south, follow the signs to Madera Canyon. This wooded riparian island in the sky offers an excellent choice of well-marked hiking trails. Trails range from moderate to difficult, and the Nature

Trail and Amphitheater Trail are both good choices for beginners. Madera Canyon, with its abundance of trees and a running creek, is especially gorgeous in fall and spring. For information about trails and the park, call Santa Rita Lodge at (520) 625-8746. Free, but donation suggested. www.maderacanyon.net.

WHERE TO STAY

Rex Ranch. 131 Amado Montosa Road. Located thirty minutes south of Tucson, the ranch is also thirty minutes from Mexico. Some years ago this romantic ranch was a small B&B. Over time, it has expanded to include a fine dining room, Cantina Romantica, and a full service spa. The dining room serves European gourmet cuisine Thursday through Saturday from 5:30 P.M. to 9:00 P.M. $$-$$$; the spa, Cielo Health Spa, offers a full range of therapies to pamper the body and soul. What hasn't changed is the pink hacienda ambience of this historic property and the magnificent views of the high chaparral desert that surrounds it. Available to individuals and to groups, the property contains sixteen adobe casitas, each furnished with unusual antiques and collectibles from around the world. $$-$$$; ☐. (520) 398-2914. www.rexranch.com.

SOUTH

DAY TRIP 3

Tubac
Tumacacori National Monument
Nogales, Arizona, U.S., and
Nogales, Sonora, Mexico

Worth More Time:
Buenos Aires National Wildlife
Refuge · Sasabe

This day is filled with arts and crafts and great shopping. It's not recommended for nonshoppers, but anyone with even a passing interest in local art and native culture will find it very enjoyable. This trip can be combined with seeing the Titan Missile Museum (Day Trip 2 South from Tucson).

Don't be concerned about driving to Mexico. The drive to Nogales is an easy one, with a divided highway much of the way. Americans can conveniently park on the U.S. side and walk across the border.

TUBAC

From Tucson, follow I-19 south for 45 miles to Tubac. According to archaeologists and anthropologists, the Santa Cruz River area has been home to many different people for perhaps 10,000 years. It is likely that the prehistoric Hohokam tribe lived here between A.D. 300 and A.D. 1400 to 1500. The Ootam (Pima and Tohono O'odham) arrived here in the 1500s.

The Spaniards came in the 1600s, led by Father Kino, who explored Arizona beginning in 1691. In 1821 the area belonged to Mexico, which won it along with its independence. Since 1853, when the Gadsden Purchase was signed, Tubac has been part of the United States.

Tubac claims to be the first European settlement in Arizona, and it housed the state's first newspaper and state park. It also had the first schoolhouse. In 1751 the Pima Indians swept through Tubac, burning and murdering. They were defeated, and the Spanish established a garrison, the Tubac Presidio, to defend the missions and the Spanish settlers. The Presidio was moved to Tucson in 1776, leaving

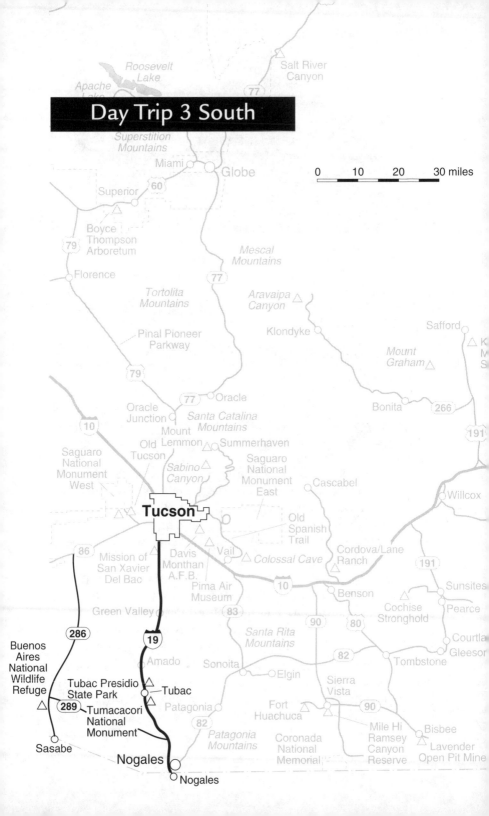

Day Trip 3 South

0   10   20   30 miles

Roosevelt Lake
Apache Lake
Salt River Canyon
77
Superstition Mountains
Miami
Globe
60
Superior
79
Boyce Thompson Arboretum
Florence
Mescal Mountains
77
Tortolita Mountains
Aravaipa Canyon
Safford
Pinal Pioneer Parkway
Klondyke
Mount Graham
K M S
79
77
Oracle
Oracle Junction
Santa Catalina Mountains
Bonita
266
10
Mount Lemmon
Summerhaven
191
Saguaro National Monument West
Old Tucson
Sabino Canyon
Saguaro National Monument East
Cascabel
Willcox
Tucson
Old Spanish Trail
Cordova/Lane Ranch
191
86
Mission of San Xavier Del Bac
Davis Monthan A.F.B.
Vail
Colossal Cave
Benson
Sunsites
Pima Air Museum
10
Cochise Stronghold
Pearce
Green Valley
83
90
80
Courtla
Gleesor
286
19
Santa Rita Mountains
82
Tombstone
Buenos Aires National Wildlife Refuge
Amado
Sonoita
Elgin
Sierra Vista
289
Tubac Presidio State Park
Tubac
Fort Huachuca
90
Tumacacori National Monument
Patagonia
82
Mile Hi Ramsey Canyon Reserve
Bisbee
Lavender Open Pit Mine
Sasabe
Patagonia Mountains
Coronada National Memorial
Nogales
Nogales

the town open to Apache attacks. The area quieted, and R. Toribio de Otero applied for and got a land grant in 1789.

When the United States took possession with the Gadsden Purchase of 1853, Tubac was a ghost town. But when ancient mines were discovered and minerals unearthed, it became a favorite spot for prospectors, miners, and journalists.

The Tubac Presidio State Historic Park, Arizona's first, was established in 1959, and the museum opened in 1964.

Today, Tubac is a center of arts and crafts for southern Arizona, touted as the place where "art and history meet." For once, hype is not far from the truth, for Tubac is a unique artistic community.

In 1948 Dale Nichols opened an art school, and over the years, potters, painters, and designers of batik, gold, silver, and wood have all "discovered" Tubac. Today more than eighty galleries, shops, and studios are located here. Tubac sponsors many festivals. Check with the Chamber of Commerce, (520) 398-2704, for dates. Two festivals are scheduled in December: the Fiesta—Annual Intercultural Fiesta— and Fiesta Navidad, when the village is lit by luminarias. The Tubac Art Festival is held in February, and the Artwalk is scheduled for early March. www.tubacaz.com.

WHERE TO GO

The Presidio Museum and Ruins. Tubac Presidio State Park. As you continue on Tubac Road past the business area, it becomes Wilson Road after it crosses Burruel Street. Then, as it curves toward the Presidio, it is called Presidio Drive.

The Presidio Museum offers a glimpse into life in a Spanish fort around 1750. An underground exhibit includes some of the original wall and floor. Open daily. Fee. (520) 398-2252. www.pr.state.az.us/ parkhtml/tubac.html.

WHERE TO EAT AND STAY

Amado Territory Inn Bed and Breakfast. Amado Territory Inn, East Frontage Road, north of the village in Amado. Off I-19, Amado exit. This charming nine-room ranch-style B&B is located on seventeen acres. The inn is new, not historic, and all rooms have private baths, patios, and balconies. Excellent home cooked breakfasts are served. (520) 398-8684. www.amado-territory-inn.com.

Burro Inn Restaurant and Suites. Off of the West Frontage Road just north of the village of Tubac. Deluxe two-room suites, T.V., phones, breakfast bar, microwave, and refrigerator. Surrounded by the State Forest overlooking beautiful Tubac Valley. Casual western dining, with real mesquite wood cooking, full bar, lunch, and dinner. One mile west of Tubac, exit 40. (520) 398-2281. www.tubacaz.com/burroinn.htm.

Mí Sueño Bed and Breakfast. "My dream" is described as a spacious hacienda bed and breakfast located in Tumacacori on twelve acres. The hosts say they invite guests who are traveling with horses to stable them in their "Mare Motel!" (520) 398-0775. www.misuenobandb.com

Rio Rico Resort and Country Club. Eight miles south of Tubac on Camino Caralampi in Rio Rico, this AAA four-diamond resort features a championship Robert Trent golf course, tennis, horseback riding, swimming, and fine dining. (520) 281-1901. www.rioricoresort.com.

The Tubac Golf Resort and Restaurant. P.O. Box 1297, Tubac 85646 (just north of the village). When you take the Tubac exit off I-19, continue north on Frontage Road for 1½ miles. The public is welcome at the club restaurant, which offers the most relaxing place to eat between Tucson and Nogales. The menu is mostly American, although some south-of-the-border dishes are included.

This picturesque, small resort sports a golf course and hotel accommodations surrounded by patio homes. Book a room by the day or week, or for the entire season. Reservations are suggested in the summer and necessary during the rest of the year. $$–$$$; ☐. (520) 398-2211 or (800) 848-7893. www.arizonaguide.com/tubac.

Tubac Secret Garden Inn. 13 Placita de Anza. This B&B is a Spanish colonial home located on three private acres in Tubac's historic zone. (520) 398-9371.

WHERE TO SHOP

Gift shops, arts and crafts galleries, and boutiques are clustered within an area bounded by Tubac Road and Camino Otero, Calle Baca, and Presidio Drive. Here you find many one-of-a-kind items created by local residents. Most shops are open Monday through Saturday, and many have Sunday hours as well. Ask for a free illustrated map of the area at any store.

Tubac Center of the Arts. Plaza Road (there are no street addresses in Tubac). As you head toward Tubac on Frontage Road, Plaza Road intersects with Frontage. You're welcome to browse during the season, October through May. This is the home of the Santa Cruz Valley Art Association, which showcases a variety of styles and types of art by local painters, sculptors, and craftspersons. The center is open Tuesday through Sunday from October through May. Donations are suggested. (520) 398-2371. www.az.art.asu.edu/tubac.

TUMACACORI NATIONAL MONUMENT

From Tubac, continue south on I-19 for 3 miles to Tumacacori National Monument.

The Tumacacori mission is a national monument that rises from the desert floor like a half-finished cathedral. Built by the Franciscans around 1800, this church was a functioning religious center for five years. Then the Franciscans were expelled, and the church was abandoned. Unattended, the mission was gutted repeatedly by Apaches and fortune hunters.

In 1929 the National Park Service restored it to its former, if unfinished, glory. Visitors can take a self-guided tour and see a scale model of how Tumacacori might have looked around 1820. If you call ahead, arrange a guided tour. For information write Tumacacori National Historical Park, P.O. Box 67, Tumacacori 85640. Fee. (520) 398-2341. www.nps.gov/tuma.

NOGALES, ARIZONA, U.S., AND NOGALES, SONORA, MEXICO

Back on I-19 continue to Nogales, Arizona, and Nogales, Sonora, Mexico. Notice the colors of the houses on the Mexican side and how different the two cities look, even from a distance. As you continue into town, you'll be in the heart of Nogales, Arizona, where A-89 and A-82 join I-19.

The community on this side is a bustling place complete with a good manufacturing and retail base.

WHAT TO DO

Crawford Street Historic District. It is possible to tour the historic homes that still stand on Crawford Street as reminders when Nogales was one of the most important cities in the state and the border was less of an impediment to traffic. There was even a saloon here that straddled the border, with one door in Mexico and one in the United States. Home tours may be scheduled through the Nogales Chamber of Commerce. www.nogaleschamber.com.

Jesse Hendrix Hummingbird Ranch. According to the National Audubon Society, the American Birding Association, and other sources, this ranch has the largest number of hummers that anyone has seen in one spot in the United States. Owner Jesse Hendrix puts about 150 feeders around his remote Nogales home to keep up with the thousands of birds that visit him each year between the peak period of April and October. The ranch has been featured in *People* magazine and on PBS and the BBC, and people come from all over the world to visit. To visit, call Jesse for directions and an appointment. (520) 287-8615.

WHERE TO STAY

Dos Marias Bed & Breakfast and Gallery. 455 West Crawford. Recommended by the Nogales Chamber of Commerce. (520) 287-2830.

Nogales, Sonora, is an equally active area. The Mexican city projects a south-of-the-border feeling. Even though you're only a few feet into Mexico, the mañana atmosphere prevails, and the more you compare the two cities, the more you'll realize how far away Arizona seems once you step across the international line. This is Old Mexico, with bullfights, fiestas, and streets lined with small shops.

The border is always teeming with cars and trucks that are jammed with people and packages. Some of the guards will check every package thoroughly, so allow enough time to get across the border on the return trip.

It's recommended that you park your car on the Arizona side and do not attempt to drive into Mexico. Obey signs, and don't park illegally. Parking is usually available by the railroad tracks on the Arizona side, and you can proceed across the border on foot. Should you decide to drive into Mexico, take out Mexican automobile insurance first, since U.S. insurance doesn't cover you in foreign countries. You can buy Mexican car insurance by the day in Tucson or in Nogales, Arizona, at several agencies.

WHERE TO GO

In Mexico, walk up any of the main streets in Nogales and browse. You'll find good shops on Elias Calles, Lopez Mateos, and Obregon Avenues and on Hidalgo Street. Think of the shopping area as a long rectangle bounded by Elias Calles Avenue and Hidalgo Street, stretching from the border to Andonegui Street. Look for good buys on pottery, baskets, leather, wrought iron, and Mexican silver. You can also find lovely embroidered clothing as well as linens and crystal. Remember, this is Mexico, and you are expected to bargain. Take your time and look around. You'll find the shop owners friendly and happy to make your trip worthwhile.

When you buy in Nogales, you'll deal in U.S. dollars. When you return to the United States, you must verbally declare your U.S. citizenship and purchases. You are allowed to bring back up to $400 of merchandise duty free, including one quart of liquor and one carton of cigarettes per adult.

La Roca. 91 Elias Street. After you cross the border, turn left and cross over the railroad tracks. Continue 2 blocks, turn right onto Elias Street, and walk 2 more blocks to La Roca, an elegant, enclosed shopping center that resembles a large, pinkish-red, adobe-style hotel. Inside you'll find more expensive items than on the main shopping streets. Most shopkeepers here accept credit cards. You'll encounter some rough sidewalks and high curbs en route to La Roca, so be careful where you walk.

Arizona Vineyards. 1830 Patagonia Highway. Two miles east of Nogales. Visit a rural, nineteenth-century, European-style winery. The owner has decorated the interior with oil paintings he has done, pottery, wooden gargoyles, folk art, sculpture, a hat collection, and winged horses. Everything is done by hand, and visitors can watch the entire process and taste the production. The wines are pretty basic, but the operation is fun. This winery is open daily from 10:00 A.M. to 5:00 P.M. (520) 287-7972.

WHERE TO EAT

La Roca. 91 Elias Street. Mexican food is an obvious specialty here. The upstairs dining room offers margaritas and nachos as well as complete lunches and dinners. $-$$; ☐. 2-0760 (in Mexico) or 011-52-631-20760 (from the United States).

WORTH MORE TIME: BUENOS AIRES NATIONAL WILDLIFE REFUGE

In the 1800s, the Altar Valley was open grassland that supported large herds of pronghorn, Mexican wolves, black bear, jaguar, and a variety of birds. By the 1860s, settlement had changed the landscape. When the government seeded the acreage with African grass, ecological problems intensified. Fortunately, in 1985 the U.S. Fish and Wildlife Service bought the Buenos Aires Ranch to preserve the habitat for masked bobwhite. Today, the ranch, which is part of the Altar Valley, is part of an intensive program designed to bring back the landscape to its original ecological state.

Happily, the Buenos Aires National Wildlife Refuge now represents one of the best examples of how to manage land using an ecosystem approach. More than 300 species of birds have been recorded here as well as a great variety of wildlife. If you want to see wildlife, the best times to view them are dawn and dusk.

The refuge office hosts dozens of programs and tours for casual and serious nature lovers. Visitors have a choice of driving the back roads or hiking or backpacking numerous nature trails. It's best to visit the headquarters of the refuge before setting off for maps and information. Open from 7:00 A.M. to 4:00 P.M. daily, Monday through Friday. The refuge is closed on holidays. (520) 823-4251.

SASABE

Rancho de la Osa. Write P.O. Box 1, Sasabe 85633, Attn: Veronica. From Tucson, follow I-19 south to A-86 or Ajo Way. Turn west (right) for 24 miles to Robles Junction, which is A-286. Turn south (left) for 44 miles. At the sign for Sasabe, turn right for 1½ miles to the ranch. *Note:* If you reach the Mexican border, you have gone 1 mile too far.

The only and best reason to go to Sasabe is to visit the historic Rancho de la Osa. The ranch dates back to 1730. The sixteen-room guest ranch has been refurbished with Mexican antiques and wonderfully eclectic art. The old adobe ranch has been reborn into a gourmet Southwest experience. Rooms have private entrances and wood-burning fireplaces.

This intimate ranch is set amid magnificent desert wilderness and offers lots of bird-watching opportunities. The ranch has always been a favorite with Tucsonians who wanted a true getaway destination. The new owners have replaced the old ultra-rustic experience with one that is much more guest-oriented.

The best option is to make the trip and plan to stay a few days or a week or more. The ambience is the best in all of southern Arizona, and the food is equally outstanding. While the horses are gentle, the riding is challenging because of the mountain landscape. However, the staff at the ranch provide enough instruction for guests to feel comfortable after a few days. $$; ☐. (520) 823-4257. www.guestranches.com/ranchodelaosa.

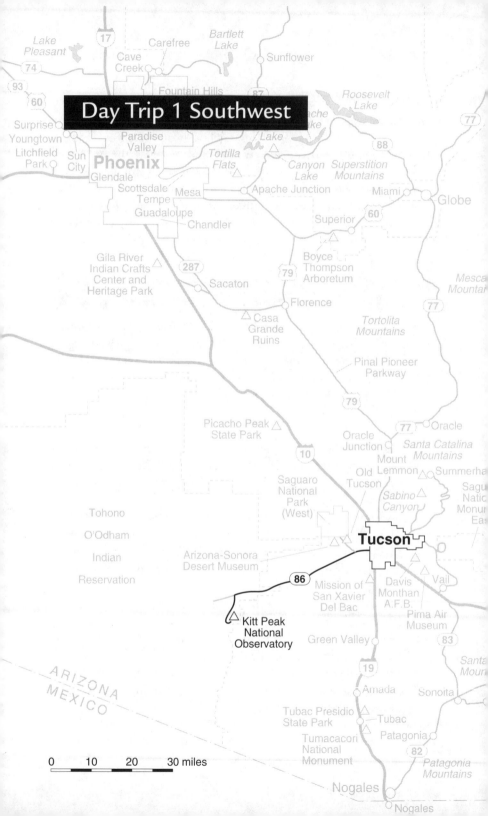

Day Trip 1 Southwest

Lake Pleasant

74

17

Carefree

Bartlett Lake

Sunflower

93

60

Cave Creek

Fountain Hills

87

Roosevelt Lake

77

Surprise

Youngtown

Litchfield Park

Sun City

Paradise Valley

Glendale

Phoenix

Scottsdale

Tempe

Guadaloupe

Mesa

Chandler

Lake

Tortilla Flats

Canyon Lake

Superstition Mountains

Apache Junction

88

Miami

Globe

60

Superior

Mesca Mountar

Gila River Indian Crafts Center and Heritage Park

287

Sacaton

79

Boyce Thompson Arboretum

Florence

77

Casa Grande Ruins

Tortolita Mountains

Pinal Pioneer Parkway

79

Picacho Peak State Park

10

Oracle Junction

77

Oracle

Santa Catalina Mountains

Tohono

O'Odham

Indian

Reservation

Saguaro National Park (West)

Old Tucson

Mount Lemmon

Summerha

Sabino Canyon

Sagu Natic Monur Eas

Tucson

Arizona-Sonora Desert Museum

86

Mission of San Xavier Del Bac

Davis Monthan A.F.B.

Vail

Kitt Peak National Observatory

Pima Air Museum

Green Valley

83

ARIZONA

MEXICO

19

Amada

Sonoita

Santa Mour

Tubac Presidio State Park

Tubac

Patagonia

Tumacacori National Monument

82

Patagonia Mountains

Nogales

Nogales

0   10   20   30 miles

KITT PEAK AND KITT PEAK NATIONAL OBSERVATORY

From Tucson, pick up A–86 (Ajo Highway) and follow it southwest for 37 miles. At the junction of A–386, turn left (the only way you can) and begin the 12 ⁷⁄₁₀-mile climb to Kitt Peak. Although this is an excellent road, it twists and winds around the mountain, giving passengers sometimes breathtaking views of sheer drop-offs and broad valleys.

The Kitt Peak National Observatory is located on top of Kitt Peak in the Quinlan Mountains and is on the Tohono O'odham Indian Reservation. At an elevation of 6,882 feet, this giant eye-in-the-sky houses the largest concentration of facilities for stellar and solar research in the world. The primary mission of Kitt Peak National Observatory is optical astronomical research. Solar astronomers work from sunrise to sunset; stellar and planetary astronomers work during the hours of darkness but also, thanks to special scientific equipment, during daylight.

Scientists from all over the world regularly visit Kitt Peak. Although the astronomy center employs more than fifty people, only the necessary support staff live on the mountaintop. The rest make the daily round-trip to the summit. There is plenty for the public to see here. You can spend an hour or a full day, depending upon your interest in astronomy.

Stop first at the visitors center. You can pick up an illustrated brochure for a self-guided walk, or you can join one of the regularly scheduled tours conducted twice daily, including weekends, that begin at the visitors center. You also will find exhibits and models to study, films to watch, and even a model of the large telescope that you can operate.

There is also an excellent exhibit about the Tohono O'odham people, whose ancestors were the Hohokam, and a fine display of baskets made by Tohono O'odham weavers. Baskets are for sale.

As you walk out of the visitors center, look out over Altar Valley. Some 18 miles to the southwest you will see Sells, headquarters of the Tohono O'odham tribe. Due south, there is a dome-shaped mountain peak called Baboquivari, the traditional home of the Tohono O'odham Indian god I-I'toy.

While at the Kitt Peak National Observatory, you'll want to see the McMath Solar Telescope, which is the largest solar telescope in the world. It is always aligned with the celestial North Pole at Tucson's latitude, and the entire structure that houses it is encased in copper. Coolants are piped through the scope's outer casing, or "skin," as it is called, to ensure that this sensitive instrument is maintained in a uniform temperature.

Another fascinating device to see is the Nicholas U. Mayall Four-Meter Telescope, the nation's second-largest optical instrument. It allows astronomers to study objects six million times fainter than the dimmest star visible with the naked eye.

Only candy and soft drinks are sold on Kitt Peak, so if you decide to make a day of it, pack a picnic lunch. Follow the signs to the picnic area, complete with tables and fire pits.

Since it's usually about 15 degrees cooler at the top of the mountain than in Tucson, take a jacket or sweater. Free, but donations are suggested. For more information including arrangements for group tours, write to National Optical Astronomy Observatories (Kitt Peak National Observatory), 950 North Cherry, Tucson 85726- 6732, or call (520) 318-8600.

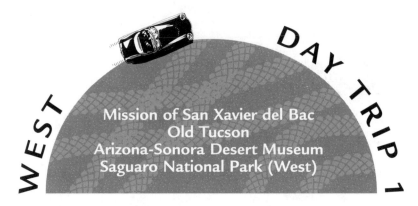

Mission of San Xavier del Bac
Old Tucson
Arizona-Sonora Desert Museum
Saguaro National Park (West)

Just 14 miles from Tucson is a cluster of worthwhile attractions. This day trip takes you through one of the most majestic forests of saguaro cacti you'll ever see. You can spend a full day of glitz and glamour combined with a liberal dose of science and education and unparalleled natural beauty. Visit each of these attractions in separate half-day trips and spend a few hours, or spend an entire day, seeing each one of them. If you decide to take in all four at once, be ready for a long, full day—not because the distances are great, but because there's so much to see at each destination.

MISSION OF SAN XAVIER DEL BAC

Pick up I–19 and head south for this 9-mile trip through Tucson and South Tucson to San Xavier (Ha-veer) del Bac. At Valencia Road, turn west and enter the district of San Xavier on the Tohono O'odham Indian Reservation. Small houses and broad, tilled fields stretch in all directions.

In the distance, you will see the White Dove (as it's called) rise dramatically from the desert floor. Dazzling white, San Xavier shimmers like a bird caught between the brown-beige land and indigo sky. With its imposing dome and lofty parapets and towers, the mission contrasts brilliantly against the violet of the nearby mountains. You'll quickly see why it has been called the finest example of mission architecture in the United States.

Turn south at Mission Road and follow it to the church. Constructed over a period of fourteen years, from 1783 to 1797, San Xavier

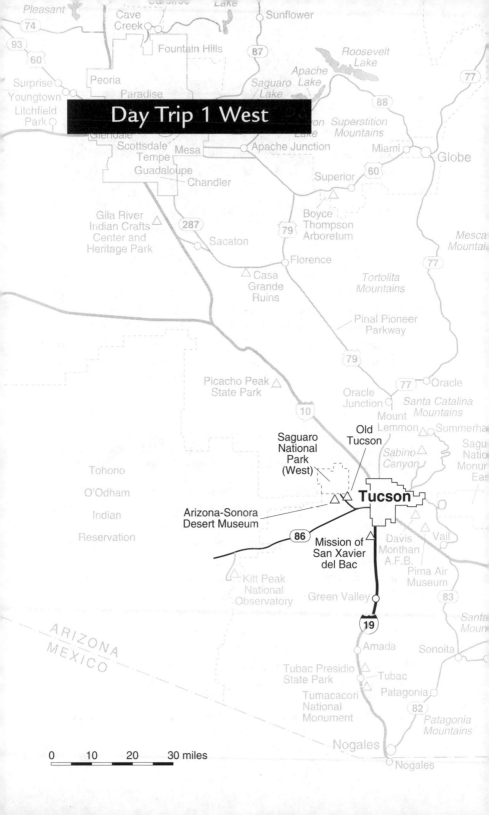

Day Trip 1 West

Pleasant
74
93
60
Surprise
Youngtown
Litchfield Park
Peoria
Paradise
Glendale
Scottsdale
Tempe
Guadaloupe
Chandler
Mesa

Cave Creek
Fountain Hills
87

Sunflower

Roosevelt Lake
77
Apache Lake
Saguaro Lake
88
Superstition Mountains
Apache Junction
Miami
Globe
Superior
60
79
Boyce Thompson Arboretum
Mesca Mountai
Florence
77
Tortolita Mountains
Pinal Pioneer Parkway
79
77
Oracle
Oracle Junction
Santa Catalina Mountains
Mount Lemmon
Summerha
Sabino Canyon
Sagu Natio Monur Eas

Gila River Indian Crafts Center and Heritage Park
287
Sacaton
Casa Grande Ruins
Picacho Peak State Park
10

Saguaro National Park (West)
Old Tucson

Tohono
O'Odham
Indian
Reservation

Arizona-Sonora Desert Museum
86
Mission of San Xavier del Bac
Kitt Peak National Observatory
Green Valley

Tucson
Davis Monthan A.F.B.
Vail
Pima Air Museum
83

ARIZONA
MEXICO
19
Amada
Sonoita
Tubac Presidio State Park
Tumacacori National Monument
Tubac
Patagonia
82
Santa Moun
Patagonia Mountains

Nogales
Nogales

0   10   20   30 miles

is a graceful blend of Moorish, Byzantine, and late Mexican Renaissance styles. Mass is celebrated daily every morning and in three services on Sunday. A vital, living mission, this church is used regularly by the nearby Tohono O'odham and San Xavier Indians. (The vast Tohono O'odham reservation is just west of the San Xavier land.)

Stand outside and contemplate the structure. The entire building is a series of domes and arches, and every surface is intricately adorned. Notice that wood was used only in the door and window frames. Look carefully to see a cat and a mouse carved into the facade of the building, one in each tower. Legend has it that if the cat ever catches the mouse, the world will end.

Walk inside. As your eyes become accustomed to the interior of the church, you'll see that, thanks to a cleaning project undertaken by Italian restorers and local residents, the mission is alive with vibrant color once again. A profusion of statues and paintings give this mission a warm, lived-in feeling.

Father Kino, a Jesuit padre widely revered in this area, visited this site in 1692. The padre laid the foundations for the first church, which was 2 miles north of the present mission, and named it San Xavier in honor of his chosen patron, St. Francis Xavier, who was the illustrious Jesuit "Apostle of the Indies." The reclining statue to your left, as you face the main altar, is St. Francis Xavier.

To many people in the Southwest, this image of St. Francis Xavier has become a place of pilgrimage. If possible, plan to sit a while inside the church and experience the special ambience. A taped narrative provides an educational commentary about the mission.

Outside once again, visit the mortuary chapel and then climb the hill east of the mission to see the replica of the grotto in Lourdes, France. Be sure to pick up a brochure as you enter the church for a more detailed explanation of the history of San Xavier del Bac. Free, although donations are accepted. (520) 294-2624.

OLD TUCSON

Old Tucson. 201 South Kinney Road. From San Xavier, travel north on Mission Road to Ajo Road (A–86). Take Ajo Road west to Kinney Road. Follow Kinney north to Old Tucson.

If you are coming from Tucson rather than from San Xavier, drive west on Speedway Boulevard to where it joins Anklam Road and becomes Gates Pass Road. As you continue west, you'll climb quickly into the foothills of the Tucson Mountains. Soon you'll be engulfed by the desert. As you get near Gates Pass, the road will twist and dip and climb until even the sky seems filled with mountains and saguaros. Once you are over the mountaintop, you'll gently descend into the valley. Watch for Kinney Road to your left. You'll turn south on Kinney and follow that a few miles to Old Tucson. If you are driving a large motor home or towing a trailer, take the Ajo Road–Kinney Road route and avoid Gates Pass.

Old Tucson is great fun for the entire family. This complete frontier town is peopled with characters who perform stunts, do trick riding, and have shootouts. Visitors like to get a part in a saloon musical or appear in a western film shoot. Youngsters and oldsters will get a kick out of the almost-real gunfights. There are movie sets to ogle and a narrow-gauge railroad that takes you around the grounds. Enjoy amusement park rides, climb aboard a stagecoach, or take a tour behind a sound stage. Naturally, it's a little bit fake, but after all, Old Tucson never pretended to be authentic.

Old Tucson serves up plenty of good western grub—mesquite-broiled steaks and barbecue and authentic Mexican dishes. There are lots of places to shop here, including stores filled with western wear, movie memorabilia, and gifts.

Built originally in 1939 as a set for the epic movie *Arizona,* this location continues to attract crowds. Cinematographers and tourists love the place. Since *Arizona,* more than one hundred other movies, television shows, and national commercials have used Old Tucson as a setting. Fee. (520) 883-0100. www.oldtucsonstudios.com.

ARIZONA-SONORA DESERT MUSEUM

The museum is on Kinney Road. From Old Tucson, head north on Kinney Road. Continue on Kinney as it bends northwest and follow the signs to the entrance of the Arizona-Sonora Desert Museum.

If you think of museums as stodgy places you visit when it rains, think again. This one has a well-defined mission: to tell the story of life in the Sonoran Desert and of all the creatures who call this region home. An exciting combination of a zoo, an aquarium, and a botanical garden, this one-of-a-kind place defies a simple definition.

Look carefully. You'll see samples of nearly everything that crawls, runs, climbs, flies, or slithers in the desert as well as a wondrous display of plants indigenous to this special environment. Some are gorgeous; others almost grotesque. If you've ever wondered what a Boojum tree looks like, this is the place to see one.

Stroll along manicured garden paths to see well-designed, educational exhibits. With the addition of the Earth Sciences Center, the Desert Museum has created an exhibit that mimics the underworld. Through an ingenious display, it opens this little-seen place to visitors. There's even an imitation limestone cave where stalactites and stalagmites "grow."

Another section of the Earth Sciences Center transports you back billions of years to the time when the desert began. Thanks to films, photographs, and maps, this exhibit enables you to understand how this part of the world was formed.

In the earth-science cave, you can follow a loop trail for 75 feet. There is also a mineral exhibit that covers almost every known mineral on Earth, from large crystals to ones so tiny they can only be seen through the microscopes provided.

Before you leave the museum grounds, be sure to browse through the gift shop, which is filled with various arts, crafts, and scientific displays.

If you have time to see only one museum in southern Arizona, this is the place to visit. To make your day more enjoyable, try to arrive during the morning so you can observe the creatures when they are most active. (Like all smart residents of the desert, they siesta in the afternoon.) Please leave your pets at home. Temperatures in unventilated vehicles, especially during the summer, can be fatal to animals. Fee. For more information, write to the museum at 2021 North Kinney Road, Tucson 85743-9989. (520) 883–1380. www.desertmuseum.org.

SAGUARO NATIONAL PARK (WEST)

This is the western (Tucson Mountain) park of Saguaro National Park (see Day Trip 1 East from Tucson for information on the eastern Rincon unit). There are two areas that make up Saguaro National Park: One lies to the east of Tucson, and the other to the west. Both are worth your time.

As you leave the Arizona-Sonora Desert Museum, continue northwest on Kinney Road to the Red Hills Information Center in the Tucson Mountain section of the Saguaro National Park. Pick up a map at the information center, or sightsee from your car by taking the Bajado Loop drive. To do this, continue on Kinney Road until it becomes Golden Gate Road. Follow this road until you see Hohokam Road to your right. Take Hohokam Road south back to where it meets Kinney.

In a recent poll of Arizona's most visited sites, Saguaro National Park (East and West) ranked just behind the Grand Canyon in popularity. While traffic can be slow over Gates Pass, the area is so vast that visitors who choose to get out of the car and hike can always be assured of plenty of "getaway" space.

If you aren't walked out from Old Tucson and the Desert Museum, there are several good hiking trails, some of which lead to the 1,429-foot-high **Wasson Peak.**

This section of Saguaro National Park is slightly smaller than the Rincon Mountain area. However, the 21,078 acres contain an unusually dense and vigorous saguaro forest. The cacti, coupled with dramatic foothills and mountain views, make this a favorite photographic and relaxation stop. Although firewood and water are not available in the park, you will find picnic areas, scenic overlooks, and rest rooms. At the end of a long day, you may be happy to just drive through and save the hiking for another time. Free. (520) 733-5100. www.nps.gov/sagu.

From Saguaro National Park, it's an easy trip south on Kinney to either Gates Pass Road or Ajo Road to Tucson.

Phoenix

PHOENIX

From Tucson, follow I-10 northwest to Phoenix. This is an easy freeway drive that takes two hours.

Contemporary Phoenix, which is the sixth-largest city in the nation, cherishes its desert, water supply, sunshine, and famous leisure lifestyle. A fine climate translates into the good life. With 3,177,016 acres of city, state, and county parks; federal lands; and freshwater lakes within one hour's drive, play's the thing in Phoenix. Outdoor sports are de rigueur here. People jog, climb, swim, and bike all year long. Everyone who stays comes to appreciate the natural setting. Those who didn't know a maple from an oak tree when they lived "back East" move to Phoenix and become connoisseurs of cactus.

In the old legend, the Phoenix bird spread her wings and rose from the ashes. Today's version stars its own legendary "bird"—the construction crane. The city is growing fast. Some look at the spread-out shape of Phoenix and call it "urban sprawl." Others smile and say that's what they moved west for—space.

Even with all the development, there's plenty of room here. The 13,000-acre South Mountain Park is the largest municipally owned facility in the world. Squaw Peak, the Phoenix Mountain Preserve, and North Mountain Parks each provide many more thousands of recreational acres.

Yet with all its emphasis on the big and the new, Phoenix is equally proud of its beginnings. A former mayor spearheaded the move to restore and dedicate a special section of downtown as

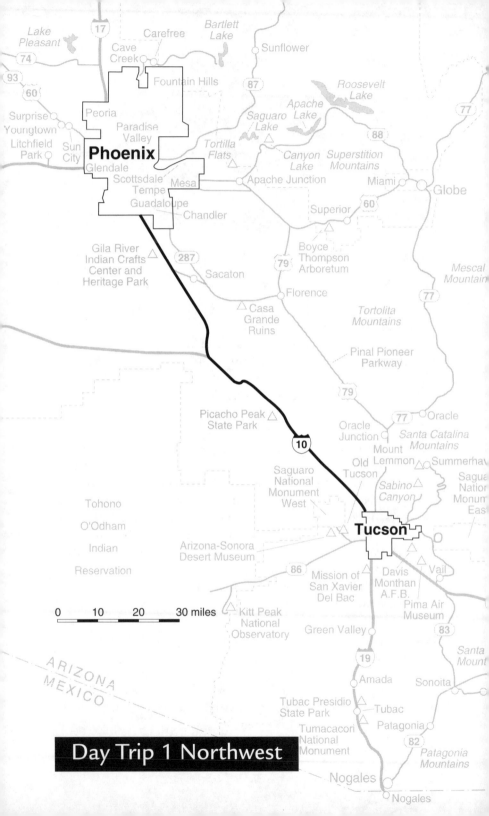

Day Trip 1 Northwest

Heritage Square. A stretch of freeway that leads to Sky Harbor Airport, called the Hohokam, is painted with designs derived from ancient Native American symbols.

As you approach Phoenix, don't be put off by its size. It's an easy town to get around. Washington Street runs east and west and is the zero ("0"), or starting point for all north and south addresses. Central Avenue runs north and south and is the starting point ("0") for east and west addresses. East of Central, the roads are labeled as streets, while west of Central they are called avenues. Keep this in mind, and you won't find yourself at Thirty-fifth Avenue looking for a number that is on Thirty-fifth Street.

Stop first at the Phoenix & Valley of the Sun Convention & Visitors Bureau, 1 Arizona Center, 400 East Van Buren, Suite 600, Phoenix 85004 or call (602) 254-6500. Here you can inquire about accommodations, attractions, special events, and dining and pick up brochures that describe these in more detail. www.phoenixcvb.com.

WHERE TO GO

The following is a sample of what Phoenix has in store for visitors. For a more complete listing, read the brochures from the Phoenix & Valley of the Sun Convention & Visitors Bureau.

The Old State Capitol. 1700 West Washington Street. Pick up Washington in downtown Phoenix and follow it directly west to the capitol building. There is ample free parking in two large lots on the east side of Seventeenth Avenue. When you park and turn toward the west, you'll be facing the old capitol building with its copper dome. Inside is a museum that features an exhibit of territorial and Arizona history and government. You can take either a self-guided or guided tour. This is a recommended trip for people who have a strong interest in the state. Free. Call for tour hours. (602) 542-4675. www.dlapr.lib.az.us.

Arizona Gem & Mineral Museum. 1502 West Washington. With the restoration of the old El Zaribah Shrine near the Arizona capitol at Fifteenth Avenue and Washington, the Arizona Mineral and Mining Museum acquired a shining new gem in a lustrous old/new setting. Outside, the blue and white structure has been restored to vintage 1922 elegance. Inside, more than 3,000 minerals collected from Arizona and the world are on display. (The collection includes more than 8,000 pieces.) Rock hounds of all ages will find much to marvel at here, and friendly lapidary club volunteers are on site to answer questions. Be sure to visit the separate Governor Rose Mofford room at the museum. The former governor has donated the collection of artifacts and gifts she acquired from her more than four decades of public service. Free. (602) 255-3791. www.admmr.state.az.us.

Heritage and Science Square. Sixth Street and Monroe Street. In this area, you'll find the best of the old, and, with hotels and the convention center looming nearby, the most dazzling of the new that symbolize contemporary Phoenix. The centerpiece of Heritage Square is the **Rosson House,** a restored home built in 1894. With its spires and turrets, it casts a benevolent shadow on downtown. Surrounded by other houses, including the **Silva House, Stevens House,** and **Stevens-Haugsten House,** and topped off with the airy **Lath House,** Heritage Square has become a favorite gathering place for residents and tourists.

As you walk through this charming block of homes, you'll be transported to a gracious time when people slept on open sleeping porches to survive the desert summer and ladies fanned themselves and sipped cool lemonade. A fee is charged to tour the Rosson House, but the others are free of charge. (602) 262-5071. www.accessarizona.com/community/groups/hhssquare.

Arizona Doll and Toy Museum. 602 East Adams. Children and adults will enjoy this constantly changing scenario of dolls and toys from the past and present. An authentic 1912 schoolroom features antique dolls as the "students." Free. Closed August. (602) 253-9337. www.az.hub.com.

Arizona Science Center. 600 East Washington Street. Located in Science and Heritage Square. The museum is the work of famous Albuquerque architect Antoine Predock and is one of the city's newest points of civic pride. Inside find an array of hands-on exhibits geared for preschool to junior high students to explain the natural and manufactured world—from health to astronomy, technology to weather. The museum is organized around thoughtful topics such as "Communication" or "All About Me" and contains colorful exhibits on all floors. In addition, there are classrooms in the adjoining building as well as a lunch cafe. This is a favorite destination for families, but it is also appealing to adults with or without kids. Another plus is the museum gift shop, Amazing Atom.

Visit the Dorrance Planetarium, the first public planetarium in Phoenix, and enjoy the full-size theater that shows IWERKS films. Visitors to the Arizona Science Center can select which programs they want to see and pay for those separately (e.g., museum exhibits, the planetarium, or IWERKS). Fee. (602) 716-2000. www.azscience.org.

The Civic Plaza. 225 East Adams Street. From the Rosson House, you can walk west to the Civic Plaza, which contains the **Phoenix Civic Plaza Convention Center and Symphony Hall.** Both are focal points for business and entertainment for the entire valley. The convention center can host the world's largest conventions, and top-name talent is booked into Symphony Hall throughout the year. Don't miss the elegant life-size sculptures of dancers on the plaza. These are the work of Arizona artist John Waddell, a nationally acclaimed sculptor. Parking is available under the Civic Plaza complex. For more information on the convention center, call (602) 262-6225. To inquire about events at Symphony Hall, call (602) 262-7272. www.ci.phoenix.az.us/civplaza.html.

Phoenix History Museum. 105 North Fifth Street, located in Heritage and Science Square at Sixth Street and Monroe. Visit this impressive contemporary-design museum to learn about the history not only of Phoenix but of the entire Salt River Valley. Well-designed exhibits bring history to life, enabling visitors of all ages to enjoy the collection and understand how the valley grew from its Hohokam beginnings into the modern metropolis it is today. Don't miss seeing the calendar stick carved by the last known Pima carver, Owl Ears. The Pimas carved these sticks to record their history. Fee. (602) 253-2734.

The Phoenix Art Museum. 1625 North Central Avenue, on the corner of Central Avenue and McDowell Road. Long known for its fine collections of both Asian and Mexican art, the remodeled and expanded museum also is home to an impressive collection of western American art. Each October the Cowboy Artists of America ride into Phoenix to hold their annual show and sale at this facility. The museum's permanent collection concentrates on eighteenth- and nineteenth-century American and European art and sculpture. There is a distinguished collection of exquisitely detailed Thorne Miniature Rooms, and the museum is home to the Arizona Costume Institute, which affords the facility an elegant display of period clothing.

This museum underwent extensive renovation in 1995. In addition to the museum's own collection, visitors can view fine traveling exhibitions scheduled throughout the year. Tours led by museum docents are available by special arrangement. The museum shop is a good place to find unusual gift items and art books. Open daily except Monday. Fee. (602) 257-1222. www.phxart.org.

The Heard Museum. 2301 North Central Avenue. Considered one of the finest anthropological museums in the world, the Heard has an impressive permanent collection, an inspiring audiovisual exhibit, and important traveling shows. All of this excitement is encased in a lovely new building that faces Central Avenue and preserves the hacienda building style that shows off old Phoenix at its best.

As you enter the museum from Central Avenue, you will find yourself in a spacious courtyard. If your time is limited, go directly to the audiovisual production that is shown in the original part of the museum.

Sit on a bench and lose yourself in this thirty-minute experience, *Our Voices, Our Land.* As you watch and listen, you'll begin to understand something of the deep relationship that exists between the Native American people and their lands.

After the show, continue through the gallery. There's a time line on the wall that graphically traces the development of the Southwest from the Paleo-Indian era (c. 1500 B.C.) through the present day. This is the Heard's major exhibit, "Native People of the Southwest, " and it lets you into a special world illustrated by life-size Hopi, Navajo, and Apache dwellings. The exhibit presents a scholarly and beautiful explanation of the relationship between the environment and Native American culture. For instance, rather than demonstrate how corn is ground, it explains why the Hopis believe that corn is life. This is done through a sensitive blending of art, natural history, and anthropological information.

Next visit the **Kachina Gallery,** which holds a dazzling display of nearly 1,000 kachina dolls. These hand-carved, hand-painted wooden figurines represent various Hopi religious spirits. You can trace the progression of this important art form from old, crudely carved figures to today's slick, sophisticated statues collectors vie for. Be sure to spend time in the museum's art galleries as well, where different artists are showcased. On your way out, browse through the spacious gift shop. Here you can find fine works by both established and undiscovered Native American artists. After visiting the Heard Museum, you'll know why this facility is the pride of the entire Southwest.

If you have more time, take a guided docent tour of the museum. The volunteer docents are extremely knowledgeable and will add to your enjoyment of the museum. The Heard also has opened a new cafe that serves excellent light meals. Call for hours. Fee. (602) 252–8848. www.heard.org.

Phoenix Mountains. The southern trailhead is at a small parking lot at the northeast corner of Thirty-second Street and Lincoln Drive in Phoenix. Or park at the north trailhead at Fortieth Street, just south of Shea Boulevard. The Quartz Ridge trail is a semistrenuous 2½-mile (one way) trail that leads to the top of this ridge. The climb ascends from 1,300 to 1,800 feet. By comparison with Squaw Park summit trail, the Quartz Ridge trail is practically deserted. It is easy to follow and can be completed in an hour, round-trip. The trailhead off of Shea Boulevard has rest room facilities, water, a covered *ramada* for a quick picnic, and room for parking about seventy cars. Leashed pets are allowed. Plastic "poop" bags are available at the trailhead, and hikers are expected to use them and clean up after their pets. Free. No phone.

Squaw Peak Mountain Park. 2701 East Squaw Peak Drive. Head east on Lincoln Drive to Squaw Peak Drive. Turn left at the light. For a quick desert experience in the heart of the urban scene, drive into Squaw Peak, park, and hike. If you have the inclination, join the crowds who religiously trek up and down the well-marked trail to the summit. The park has many *ramadas,* shelters that offer shady areas for picnicking. Water and rest rooms are available. You can call ahead to reserve one of these roofed areas for a large gathering. Since mountain parks are very popular with local residents during the fall, winter, and spring, reserved space is often at a premium.

The trail to the summit is 1⁷⁄₁₀ miles and is an excellent aerobic exercise as well as a fine social activity. It's a crowded trail. Know that parking spaces can be scarce. The hike up starts at 1,400 feet and climbs to 2,600 feet. There are also excellent trails that circle around Squaw Peak. While these don't offer the strenuous climb, they have the advantage of being more peaceful ways to experience Squaw Peak. Free. (602) 262–7901. www.ci.phoenix.az.us.

South Mountain Park. 10919 South Central Avenue. Take Central Avenue south to the far end of town, a fifteen- to twenty-minute drive beyond downtown Phoenix. Eventually Central Avenue will curve to the west, and you'll approach the park. This more than 13,000-acre mountain range was a gift to the city of Phoenix in the 1920s by a group of farsighted Phoenix boosters including Clare Boothe Luce and Elizabeth Arden. As you enter the park, the ranger at the stone gatehouse will ask you not to bring any glass containers or alcoholic beverages.

Take a scenic drive up to a mountaintop for a thrilling look down at Phoenix, or park your car and walk along the trails. There are many opportunities here for serious biking, walking, or hiking. Picnic facilities and rest rooms are plentiful. Free. (602) 495-0222.

The Papago Salado. This route takes you through the heart and soul of the Phoenix metropolitan area. Encompassing miles of picturesque natural desert and studded with outstanding manufactured attractions, the Papago Salado links the 1,496-acre Papago Park with the Rio Salado project, which is being developed across the Salt River in Tempe. When that project is complete, it will add 5 miles of linear park that parallels the Salt River.

WITHIN THE PAPAGO SALDO

Arizona Historical Society Museum. 1300 North College Avenue. This museum is located at the crossroads of Sixty-eighth Street and Curry. Sixty-eighth Street is called College after it crosses McKellips. Housed in an impressive structure, this contemporary history museum features exhibits on agriculture, tourism, mining, World War II, and other aspects of Arizona's diverse history. A large, outdoor replica of Roosevelt Dam describes how this structure was made and the importance it plays in Arizona life.

The permanent exhibits are exceptional. Start with the "people" who represent those groups who settled the state. Inside are historic rooms, films, and outstanding photographs. Be sure to go upstairs to enjoy the "Fair." The main agricultural exhibit is designed to teach children about the important contribution of agriculture. Kids can have a lot of fun answering the questions posed, and so can grown-ups! This museum will continue to add exhibits as fund-raising is complete, so it will always be worth repeat visits. Free. (480) 929-0292. www.tempe.gov/ahs.

Arizona Military Museum. 5636 East McDowell Road in the National Guard Complex. Enter through the main gate of Papago Park Military Reservation. This museum houses the weapons, uniforms, photographs, maps, etc., of Arizona's military history, dating from the sixteenth through twentieth centuries. The building served as a prisoner-of-war camp during World War II. Free. (602) 267-2676.

Desert Botanical Garden. 1201 North Galvin Parkway (next to the Phoenix Zoo in Papago Park). The Desert Botanical Garden presents a living museum of desert plant life and is one of the nation's only informal science centers dedicated to the desert, desert plants, ecology, and conservation. Here are more than 10,000 plants and 3,500 different species of cacti, succulents, trees and flowers, and attendant wildlife. Adults and children should experience the exhibit entitled "Plants and People of the Sonoran Desert." Gardeners will enjoy the Demonstration Garden and the new Desert House, which demonstrates how technology that is currently available can produce an environmentally pleasing home. There is also a shop that sells books and gifts on the grounds.

Be sure to visit the Desert Discovery Trail, the brick-paved path that leads to all trailheads and facilities. This will take you to the Cactus House and Succulent House. The Plants & People of the Sonoran Desert Trail is a ⅓-mile, hands-on trail that illustrates how Sonoran Desert plants have been used by people for centuries to provide food, fiber, and shelter. The Sonoran Desert Nature Trail is a ¼-mile trail that is somewhat steep. It affords panoramas of the distant mountains as well as close-up views of the desert butte, which is the backdrop for this special garden. The fourth trail, the Center for Desert Living, showcases desert landscaping displays, vegetable gardens, herb gardens, and the Desert House exhibits. Fee. (480) 941-1217 or (480) 941-1225. www.dbg.org.

Hall of Flame. 6101 East Van Buren. Turn south on Project Drive from Van Buren to see the world's largest display of fire-fighting equipment. More than one hundred pieces are in this private collection, including hand-to-hand, horse-drawn, and mechanized fire-fighting equipment that dates from 1725 to 1955. Fee. (602) 275-3473. www.hallofflame.com.

Papago Park. This 1,200-acre desert island gets its red color from iron oxide–hematite. Formed six to fifteen million years ago, this is a sedimentary formation and is among the oldest exposed rock found anywhere in the state. You can wander 13 miles of hiking and biking trails, fish the Urban Fishing Waters, climb to Hole-in-the-Rock, or play golf at the public course within the park. Full picnic facilities are available. Free. (602) 262–6111.

Papago Park, Tempe. Curry Road and College Avenue. This 296-acre park is contiguous with the Phoenix Papago Park. In addition to natural desert and picnic facilities, there is a softball field, an area to play Frisbee, a golf course, a lake/lagoon, a playground, and a nature trail. Free. (480) 350–5200. www.tempe.gov/pkrec.

The Phoenix Zoo. 455 North Galvin Parkway. Rated as one of the top ten zoos in the country, this 125-acre zoo presents more than 1,400 animals, including 200 endangered species. Special exhibits not to be missed are the African Savanna, Arizona Trail, Sumatran tigers, and Tropical Flights. Even grown-ups will be wowed by the Phoenix Zoo, where giraffes gambol freely in a natural grassy setting framed by the Papago Buttes.

The Children's Zoo is self-contained. There are complete food and beverage facilities, gift shop, and shaded picnic areas available. Strollers and wheelchairs may be rented, and the Zoo Train offers a convenient way to cover the vast grounds. Fee. Open daily. Summer hours, May 1 through Labor Day, 7:00 A.M. to 4:00 P.M. (602) 273–1341. www.phoenixzoo.org.

Pueblo Grande Museum and Cultural Park. 4619 East Washington. Art and architecture have ancient histories, as Pueblo Grande Museum and Cultural Park in East Phoenix reminds. This in-town Native American ruin is replete with platform mound and remnants of an ancient canal as well as a small but charming museum of artifacts and art. The discovery of the ruin and subsequent park development prompted Phoenix to hire an archaeologist on city staff, the first city in the country to do so.

Occupied from A.D. 500 through A.D. 1450, Pueblo Grande was an important village that sported a ball court, homes, ceremonial mound, and canals. The canals and platform mound can be visited on the grounds. Permanent and rotating exhibits inside the museum describe the art and culture of the Hohokam and other prehistoric Native Americans. Fee. (602) 495–0901. www.pueblogrande.com.

Red River Opry. 730 North Mill Avenue. Take Curry Road west to Mill Avenue and turn left. It's on the corner. The opry stages live variety shows that feature country music, comedy, and nostalgia. Fee. Call for show times. (480) 829-6779. www.redrivermusichall.com.

Salt River Project History Center. 1521 Project Drive. Off the main lobby of the Salt River Project Administration Building. A small but well-designed museum describes the history of irrigation and water in the Phoenix Valley. Artifacts are displayed, and video presentations explain the Hohokam civilization and Roosevelt Dam. www.srpnet.com.

WHERE TO EAT

Phoenix offers every type of cuisine—from Mongolian and Mexican to Thai and elegant continental. Ask anyone in Phoenix to name a favorite dining spot, and you'll get a different answer. In the last few years, Phoenix has nurtured and attracted a variety of fine young chefs, making this a new town for "foodies" to explore. Here are a few local favorites:

Biltmore Fashion Park. Twenty-fourth Street and Camelback. The upstairs of this outdoor shopping mall has some of Phoenix's best casual restaurants, including Roxsand. These trendy restaurants serve food that is moderately priced, well presented, and, most importantly, good!

Eddie Matney's. 2398 East Camelback Road. Eddie is one of the valley's most inventive chefs, who blends Southwest cooking with his own creative style. Eddie Matney's is a local favorite that attracts a loyal following of fans who can't get enough of Eddie and his exciting cuisine. Be sure to save room for dessert—Eddie's desserts are as inventive as his first and second courses. $$-$$$; ☐. (602) 957-3214.

Los Dos Molinos. 8646 South Central Avenue. Authentic Mexican fare—pronounce that *very hot*—served in a unique hacienda setting in South Phoenix. Very much worth the trip for those who love true Mexican food. Since there is usually a wait for seating, plan to visit the gallery on the grounds. See the other location in Mesa. $-$$; ☐. (602) 243-9113.

Roxsand. Twenty-fourth Street and Camelback in Biltmore Fashion Park. Southwest gourmet cuisine served in great style is

Roxsand's trademark. She also does outstanding vegetarian fare. $$-$$$; ☐. (602) 381-0444. www.roxsand.com.

Rustler's Rooste. 7777 South Pointe Parkway at South Mountain. (That silent *e* on *Rooste* tells you that this is one of The Pointe's resort centers.) There's a slide, for those who choose to use it, that deposits you into the restaurant. The specialty here is hearty western fare, especially barbecued items. It's all a mite corny, but it's a good place to see city lights twinkling over the desert. $$-$$$; ☐. (602) 431-6474.

Vincent Guerithault on Camelback. 3930 East Camelback Road. Vincent has joined the rare list of fine American chefs whose specialties feature native ingredients with superior and artistic presentation. One of Arizona's most outstanding restaurants, Vincent is open for lunch and dinner. Reservations are suggested. The atmosphere is elegant yet relaxing; the food is outstanding. $$$; ☐. (602) 224-0225.

Windows on the Green. The Phoenician Resort, 6000 East Camelback Road, Scottsdale. One of the finest restaurants in the city, the menu features unique dishes such as ostrich with blueberry sauce. The creative menu is superbly prepared and always outstanding, and the ambience, overlooking the green fairways of the Phoenician Resort, is one of the best in the valley. $$$; ☐. (480) 423-2451. www.thephoenician.com.

WHERE TO STAY

Metropolitan Phoenix enjoys one of the world's finest collections of hotels and resorts. For a complete listing contact the Greater Phoenix Convention & Visitors Bureau. But these are two outstanding historic properties should not be missed.

Arizona Biltmore Resort & Spa. Twenty-Fourth and Missouri Streets. The grand dame of Phoenix resorts, opened in 1929, the Arizona Biltmore should be on every visitor's list. If you can, spend a few days and nights on this magical property. At the very least, visit it and sip some refreshing liquid on the patio looking over the grassy lawn. Frank Lloyd Wright is not the architect of record for this historic property, but his flamboyant fingerprints are everywhere—from the cement block to the prairie-type lines of the massive original hotel. Over the years, the hotel has been added onto with more casitas, shops, and a conference center. But through the changes the structure has remained supremely elegant, a reminder of when gentlemen traveled with a dozen tuxedos and ladies with trunks-full of dinner gowns to spend "the season" at this grand hotel. The restaurants are all superb. The wine room is particularly special. $$$. (602) 955-6600.

Wigwam Resort. 300 Wigwam Boulevard, Litchfield Park. From downtown Phoenix, take I-10 west to Litchfield Road. Turn north to Indian School Road and follow to Wigwam Boulevard and the hotel. Like the Arizona Biltmore, the Wigwam Resort was built in 1929 to accommodate an era of leisure guests who took the train to Arizona and stayed for the season. The Wigwam presents a charming face of "Old Arizona" in an elegantly relaxed and updated environment. Always known for great golf at three championship courses, the resort has all amenities including horseback riding. Dining at all four restaurants is outstanding. $$$. (623) 935-3811 or (800) 327-0396.

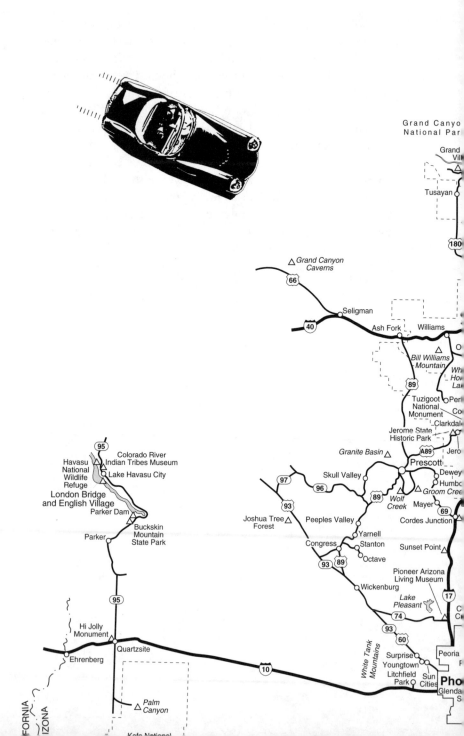

U
AR

Grand Canyon
National Par

Grand
Vill

Tusayan

180

△ Grand Canyon
Caverns

66

Seligman

40   Ash Fork   Williams

△
Bill Williams
Mountain   Wh
Ho
La

89

Tuzigoot   Per
National
Monument   Co
Clarkdal

Jerome State
Historic Park

97   Granite Basin △   A89   Jero

Havasu   95   Colorado River   Skull Valley   Prescott
National   Indian Tribes Museum   96   Dewey
Wildlife   Lake Havasu City   89   Humb
Refuge   Wolf   Groom Cree
London Bridge   Creek   Mayer   69
and English Village   Parker Dam   Cordes Junction
Buckskin   93   Joshua Tree △   Peeples Valley
Mountain   Forest
Parker   State Park   Yarnell   Sunset Point △
Congress   Stanton
93   89   Octave   Pioneer Arizona
Living Museum
95   Wickenburg   17
Lake
Pleasant
74

Hi Jolly   93
Monument   60
White Tank   Peoria
Quartzsite   Mountains   Surprise
Ehrenberg   Youngtown   F
10   Litchfield   Sun   Pho
Park   Cities
Glenda
S
FORNIA
IZONA   △ Palm
Canyon

Kofa National

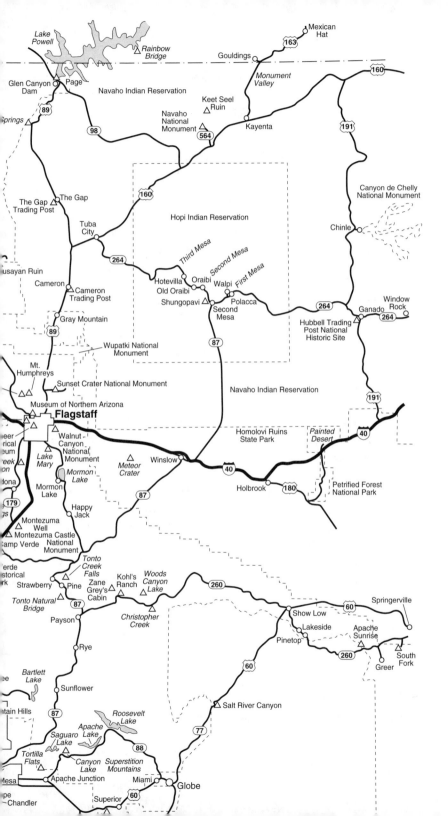

Flagstaff

With Flagstaff as your base (see Day Trip 4 North from Phoenix), the entire northern third of Arizona is open to you. You'll see wonders of the ancient world such as the Grand Canyon, the quiet beauty of lakes and forests, and remote Native American villages whose inhabitants live very much as their ancestors did hundreds of years ago.

As you plan your trips, remember that northern Arizona is different from the southern and central sections of the state. During the winter, snowstorms can rush in quickly, covering the highways and turning an easy drive into a snowy challenge. If you're planning a visit during the fall, winter, or early spring, phone ahead to check the weather.

In summer, temperatures around Flagstaff remain moderate, with warm days and cool evenings. But as you travel into the high desert areas of the northeastern section of the state or to the far western border near California, you're back in the sizzling heat. In these areas, don't forget to carry water in your car and be prepared for high temperatures.

The following trips are planned to include a maximum amount of sightseeing in a minimum of time. For northern Arizona, stretch your time limit for a day trip from two to four or even five driving hours one way. Many of these trips are better done in tandem—doing one trip one day and picking up the following trip the next day without heading back to Flagstaff. Combining trips cuts the driving distance and lets you maximize out-of-the-car time.

However, if you don't have a weekend or can't string a couple of days together, relax. You can make each of these a separate overnight experience as long as you're prepared to go the distance to get back to Flagstaff.

One last piece of advice: This vast area is sparsely inhabited. You are wise to carry some food in the car, as well as water, soft drinks, or juice. Clean, well-equipped rest stops are often few and far between, so when you see a decent-looking gas station, you should stop if your tank is below two-thirds full or somebody needs to use a rest room. Often you won't see another gas station for miles. Thus forewarned, you shouldn't get caught in the wilds.

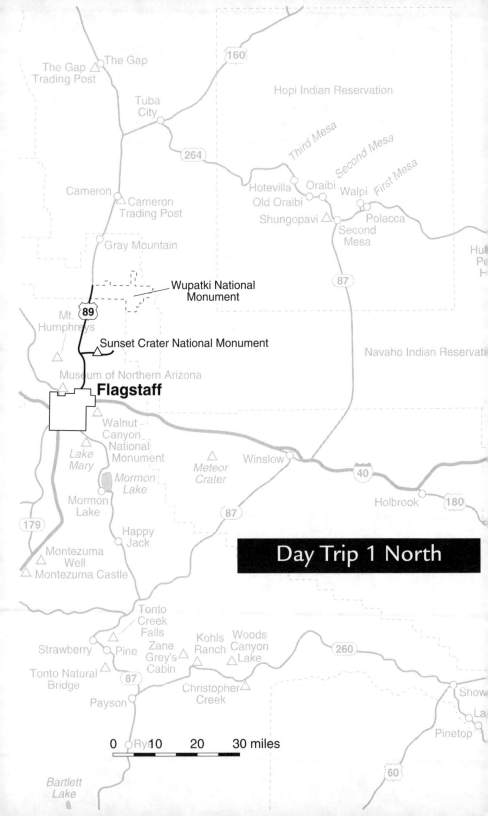

The Gap Trading Post
The Gap

160

Hopi Indian Reservation

Tuba City

264

Third Mesa

Second Mesa

First Mesa

Cameron

Hotevilla
Old Oraibi

Oraibi

Walpi

Cameron Trading Post

Shungopavi

Polacca

Second Mesa

Gray Mountain

Hu
Po
H

Wupatki National Monument

87

Mt. Humphreys

89

Sunset Crater National Monument

Navaho Indian Reservati

Museum of Northern Arizona

Flagstaff

Walnut Canyon National Monument

Lake Mary

Winslow

Meteor Crater

40

Mormon Lake

Mormon Lake

Holbrook

180

179

Happy Jack

87

Day Trip 1 North

Montezuma Well

Montezuma Castle

Tonto Creek Falls

Kohls Ranch

Woods Canyon Lake

Strawberry

Pine

Zane Grey's Cabin

260

Tonto Natural Bridge

87

Christopher Creek

Show

Payson

La

Pinetop

0   Ry 10   20   30 miles

Bartlett Lake

60

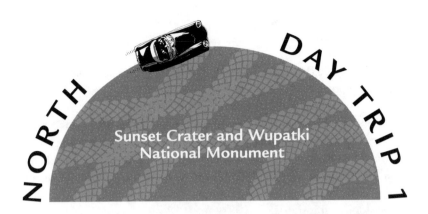

SUNSET CRATER AND WUPATKI NATIONAL MONUMENT

From Flagstaff, head north on this scenic drive to enjoy past treasures.

SCENIC DRIVE

Volcanoes and Ruins Loop. The complete tour will take two to three hours and cover 70 miles. Drive 12 miles northeast on US-89 to the Sunset Crater–Wupatki turnoff. Turn east (right). It's about 36 miles around this road back to US-89 and then 22 miles back to Flagstaff. The road passes through the most recently active portion of the San Francisco volcano fields that surround the city. The last eruption occurred around A.D.1250, but wounds heal slowly in an arid land, so much of the area looks as if it had been fuming and spurting just yesterday.

During this excursion, plan to stop at the visitors centers at both Sunset Crater and Wupatki.

Sunset Crater National Monument is a 1,000-foot-high historic cone. Here you will find strange rivers of lava that erupted 900 years ago that look as though they happened yesterday. There are many trails to hike along and explore; visitors, however, are asked to stay on the trails and not forge their own. The lava flow is brittle and can be damaged easily. John Wesley Powell, who was the first man to successfully run the Colorado River, named Sunset Crater for the red-orange hue that is found near its peak. This is a strange and eerie landscape, but one that is well worth a visit. Fee. (928) 526-0502. www.nps.gov/sucr.

Wupatki National Monument. These well-preserved Native American ruins are the remains of structures built by the Sinagua Indians. The Sinagua were prosperous traders and farmers who left behind 35,000 acres of prehistoric ruins containing apartment houses, ball courts, and artifacts. The ball court is considered very rare by archaeological standards.

There is a park service station and and interpretive center that explains the history and geology of the area. Self-guided trails make it easy to stroll among these structures and understand the significance of the sites. Fee. (928) 556-7040. www.nps.gov/wupa.

From Wupatki, return to Flagstaff on US–89.

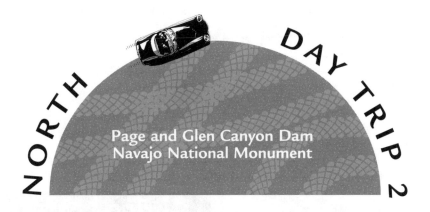

PAGE AND GLEN CANYON DAM

From Flagstaff, go north on US-89 to Page and Lake Powell. You may want to plan to spend the night at Lake Powell before going on to the Navajo National Monument. You can also pick up Day Trip 1 Northeast from Flagstaff at Kayenta, or you can stay overnight in Page, then go on to Navajo National Monument the next morning and pick up Day Trip 1 Northeast from Flagstaff at Kayenta. Taking two days to see Lake Powell and Navajo National Monument allows ample time to explore, visit Page and Lake Powell, and tour Navajo National Monument. If you have only one day to cover this, you'll drive through Page, see Lake Powell from the shore, and take a fast trip to the Navajo National Monument. But cramming all this into one day will leave you hungry for more.

As you proceed north on US-89 from Flagstaff, you'll pass the tiny hamlet of **Gray Mountain.** Here you enter the vast expanse of the Navajo Indian Reservation. Summer travelers need to move their watches ahead one hour: While Arizona doesn't observe daylight saving time, the Navajo Nation does. This time change can be confusing and even frustrating if you aren't forewarned. You don't want to plan to arrive somewhere by 5:00 P.M. only to find that it's 6:00 P.M. and you've missed what you want to see.

Eight miles north of Gray Mountain on US-89, you'll see the **Cameron Trading Post,** the first of a number of Native American trading posts in this region. Cameron is actually a complex of buildings made of lovely native stone and wood. Discover a treasure trove of items—some exquisite, others tourist trinkets. There's also food

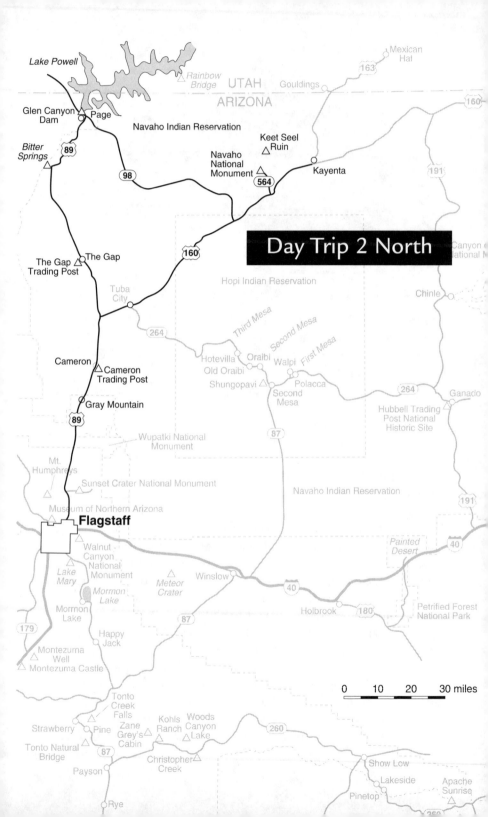

service in a lovely, spacious dining room as well as some very nice overnight accommodations. Don't miss the display of Navajo weavings inside the trading post.

After leaving Cameron, the highway crosses the Little Colorado River, one of the major tributaries of the Colorado River. Another 31 miles up the road you'll come to a second famous trading post, **The Gap.** Both Cameron and the Gap played important roles in opening the Arizona Territory. Trading posts helped to establish an economy that benefited both the white and Native American societies. To today's casual observer these places appear to be scenic tourist stops, but they aren't. Years ago, trading posts were lifelines for the Native Americans and traders who depended upon them. The Native Americans traded rugs, jewelry, and other handcrafted items for groceries and needed supplies. Occasionally, a Navajo man or woman would pawn a prized piece of jewelry for money, and the trader would keep the item until the owner could redeem it. Some owners never were able to get their heirlooms back, and "pawn jewelry," cherished by collectors, eventually was sold.

With a full day facing you, unless you need to stop, push on and explore these posts another day. Page and the wonders of Lake Powell await.

At Bitter Springs, US–89 bends east. Continue on US–89 to Page. Like all towns built to support generating plants, this community owes its life to power and glory—the power of Glen Canyon Dam and the glory of the Grand Canyon. The dam was built in the 1950s; the canyon has been under construction for millions and millions of years.

Glen Canyon Dam was constructed at a cost of $260 million, a hefty sum, especially when you consider that the cost to replace that plant today would be $800 million. It was October 15, 1956, when President Dwight D. Eisenhower pushed a button on his desk in the White House, 2,100 miles away, to set off the first blast. Four years later, June 17, 1960, the last of 4,901,000 cubic yards of concrete was poured. The resulting dam, a 583-foot-high wall, holds back the second-largest manufactured lake in North America. (Lake Mead, also formed by the Colorado River, is the largest.) Glen Canyon conserves water from a 246,000-square-mile watershed, provides electricity for the Pacific Southwest and the Rocky Mountain areas, and gives Page a reason for being.

A small, friendly community dedicated to tourism and electricity, Page was first staked out as a temporary government construction camp in 1957. It was named for the first commissioner of the Reclamation Service established under President Theodore Roosevelt. Since then, the town has thrived. There is a busy airport, visitors center, museum, library, and eleven churches side by side on just one street. (Two other churches are located elsewhere in town.)

Near Page, US–89 climbs, and you'll get your first view of Glen Canyon Dam below. Behind it, the magical blue world of Lake Powell spreads out, improbably set into a rocky abyss of this far-eastern section of the Grand Canyon. Lake Powell is renowned throughout the world for its astonishing beauty, and no tourist yet has been disappointed by the views.

Just outside of Page, visitors will often find Navajo artists selling their wares. It's fun to stop and browse and even shop. Often you can meet the artists, who are happy to describe their work to you. While it's fine to bargain with them, if you want to take a picture of the artists, always ask permission first. If you do take a photograph and don't purchase anything, it's good form to leave a "thank you" in the form of a tip.

WHERE TO GO

Glen Canyon Dam and Carl Hayden Visitor Center. On US–89. This is a highly recommended stop. In the visitors center, an illustrated history depicts the construction and use of the dam. If you have time, watch the audiovisual program. If not, at least browse through the easy-to-follow displays, which reveal fascinating details about the dam. You can easily spend thirty minutes in the Carl Hayden Visitor Center. If you have time, take the guided tour of the generating plant given almost every hour. Visitors can also tour the dam on their own. The tour takes you from the crest of the dam down one of three elevators into the power plant, where you can see the inner workings of the turbines and understand how this dam delivers power to much of the western United States. Nearly an hour in length, the tour is not strenuous; you'll walk about ⅓ mile. It's a cool fifty degrees Fahrenheit down under, so bring a wrap. Free. (928) 608-6404. www.pagelake powell.org; www.nps.gov/glca.

John Wesley Powell Memorial Museum. 6 North Lake Powell Boulevard. This is a small museum dedicated to Maj. John Wesley

Powell, who not only explored the Colorado River but also wrote passionately and lyrically about it. In addition to presenting exhibits on Powell and his expeditions, the museum documents the story of Page and presents artifacts from ancient Anasazi-Hisatsinom culture through modern Native American history. A fluorescent mineral and rock display is also exhibited. (928) 645–9496. www.powell museum.org.

The Page Visitor Center/Museum. 644 North Navajo, Suite C; museum: 6 North Lake Powell Boulevard. Continue north on US–89 until you see a sign for the business district of Page. Follow the signs. Drive over the bridge and take Lake Shore Boulevard to the Chamber of Commerce and Visitor Center and Museum, all located in one building. Check with the visitors center for additional information on the area, and then take a quick trip through the museum, which is filled with artifacts and memorabilia commemorating John Wesley Powell and his expeditions.

Major Powell is acknowledged as the first explorer of the Colorado River and the Grand Canyon. A Civil War veteran, he lost his right arm at Shiloh before setting out on this expedition. The thirty-five-year-old adventurer first conquered the Colorado in 1869, settling in at Green River, Wyoming. He went back in 1871 and did the trip again. Thanks to his meticulous personal journal, generations of "river rats" (people who run the rapids in the Grand Canyon) and canyon and river enthusiasts relive his experiences and can identify with his thought-provoking impressions. Free. (928) 645–4095. www.chamber@pagelakepowellchamber.org.

Wahweap Lodge and Marina. Four and a half miles from Glen Canyon Dam on US–89 northwest of Page. Turn right at the sign for the marina (the only way you can turn) onto a paved road that leads to Wahweap. One of four marinas on Lake Powell, Wahweap (pronounced Waa-weep) is the most accessible for tourists. Here you'll find overnight accommodations, fine dining, a gift shop, and a host of tours and adventures. Even if you don't plan to spend the night or eat at Wahweap, you'll want to stroll through the lodge to lose yourself in the views of the lake. Lake Powell is a complete recreational wonderland—the fishing is great, the views better, and the deep, cool, blue water and the out-of-the-way beaches are the best. Other lakes in Arizona may be closer to major cities or have more sandy beaches, but only Lake Powell, with its fjords and inlets, scallops and gulleys, wrapped in a golden desert sun, comes so close to perfection.

WHAT TO DO

There's so much to do in this area that you can spend a week or an entire season at Lake Powell. In addition to the following listed trips, you can rent a personal watercraft with a top speed of 35 miles per hour. The Tigershark is easy to ride with a jet drive. While it is not inexpensive to rent, the thrills are worth it. All of the trips depart from Wahweap. Even if you can only squeeze in a two-hour excursion, do so. You'll see the lake from the shore, but you can only *experience* its mystic setting when you're on it and surrounded by its sandy, sculpted mountains. To make reservations for boat tours or accommodations, or to inquire about adventures in the area, contact Del E. Webb Recreational Properties, Box 29040, Phoenix 85038, or call (800) 528-6154 toll free or (602) 278-8888 if calling from Phoenix. www.visitlakepowell.com

Here is a sampling of the cruises you can take on the lake:

The *Canyon King*. Make arrangements at Wahweap Lodge and Marina, where the boats depart. Treat yourself to a ride on the only genuine paddle wheeler operating west of the Rockies, or enhance this experience with a sunset/moonlight dinner cruise. The *Canyon King* ferries 150 guests at a time and is closed December through March for maintenance. You can also make special arrangements for large groups or parties through Del E. Webb Recreational Properties, Box 29040, Phoenix 85038. Fee. (928) 645-2433.

All-Day and Half-Day Rainbow Bridge Tour. Both tours leave from Wahweap Marina. The half-day involves a five-hour trip; the all-day allows for more side-channel cruising. You'll depart from Wahweap in the early morning and follow the main channel of Lake Powell to Rainbow Bridge. This natural wonder literally fills the sky as you approach the docking area. You can read the dimensions, but the size of the stone arch will still astound you. The dome of the U.S. Capitol building could fit underneath it. After your boat docks, there's a short hike to get to the base of the bridge. Be sure to read the inspiring commemorative plaque.

Glen Canyon Dam was built over strong environmental objections. People grieved over the flooding of Glen Canyon, which John

Wesley Powell considered one of the most beautiful areas in the Grand Canyon. They feared what traffic would do to fragile places like Rainbow Bridge. The dam did doom the canyon to a watery death, but the trade-off was Lake Powell, a shimmering body of water that dances between the intricate, spidery spires and rolling sandstone mountaintops. Neither the water nor the exposed desert canyon seem aware of the other's presence. You'll see the two worlds of lake and land meeting but not merging.

Since the dam was built and Lake Powell formed, more people see Rainbow Bridge each month than had ever seen it before the dam was built. But so far, visitors are considerate, and the area surrounding the bridge appears to be surviving well. Fee. For more information contact Del E. Webb Recreational Properties, Box 29040, Phoenix 85038. (928) 645-2433.

The Navajo Tapestry Cruise. This short excursion on Lake Powell (two and one-half hours) gives travelers a fast but true flavor of this wonderland. You leave from Wahweap Lodge, and the boat glides between the walls of Antelope Canyon, cruises through Navajo Canyon (from which the cruise takes its name), and then returns via Antelope Island, Warm Creek, and Castle Rock Strait. This is a brief but intensely satisfying way to see Lake Powell. Fee. Contact ARA Leisure Services, Box 56909, Phoenix 85079. (800) 528-6154 or (602) 278-8888.

Houseboating. Enjoy the water for a couple of days and nights or stay a week on a well-equipped, luxurious floating house. The best speeds for a houseboat are "slow" and "stopped," so wise houseboaters dock their boats at secluded coves early on and use a speedboat to water-ski and explore the thousands of skinny little canyons that lead from the main body of the lake. With 1,900 miles of shoreline to choose from, you can houseboat on Lake Powell repeatedly and never explore the same spot twice. Be prepared to get lost on Lake Powell. Most first-timers do, but keep reading your maps, and you'll come out fine. During the height of the summer season, you'll need to reserve a houseboat far in advance. This is an ideal family experience. For price information and availability, contact ARA Leisure Services, Box 56909, Phoenix 85079. Fee. (800) 528-6154 or (602) 278-8888.

Colorado River Float. Departs from the Page Museum, 6 Lake Powell Boulevard. For would-be river runners who don't like white-water craziness, a float trip provides the ideal alternative. You'll float for a day through the polished splendor of Marble Canyon, stop for lunch on the bank, and see ancient petroglyphs from the canyon floor. After the 15-mile float trip, you'll feel as if you've "done" the Colorado. This is great fun for families with young children and anyone who wants the see the Grand Canyon the most scenic way—from the bottom up. Fee. Inquire about float trips by calling (800) 528–6154, (602) 278–8888, or (928) 645–3279 at Wahweap.

Page Loop Trail. Mountain bikers can have a blast on this 10-mile loop that is partly single-track and rough four-wheel-drive road. Beginning riders can complete the loop in about two hours with an occasional dismount for the more difficult sections. Experienced riders can do it in about one hour. There's also a three-hour ride that incorporates a detour to enjoy the slickrock. This is recommended for experienced riders only. The trail begins at the nature trail at the north end of Page near Lake View School. Free.

WHERE TO EAT

The Dam Bar & Grille. 644 North Navajo. Trendy and fun by any standards, this restaurant is Page's most upscale spot. Find casual dining, a great bar, and wonderful historic photographs of when Glen Canyon Dam was constructed. Notice the etched glass "mural" that is dedicated to the water and power theme. This is a popular gathering spot for locals and visitors. $-$$. (928) 645–2161. www.damplaza.com.

Wahweap Lodge. Wahweap Marina, Lake Powell. The main dining room has a dazzling view of the lake. At night the room shimmers with elegance, and by day you can gaze out on the blue expanse. The specialty is prime rib, but the menu is varied and well prepared. Ask about the daily specials. $$; ☐. (928) 645–2433.

WHERE TO STAY

Wahweap Lodge. Wahweap Marina, Lake Powell. The rooms are large and spacious, but if you aren't on the ground floor, be prepared to tote your own luggage up the stairs. You can reserve rooms at the Lake Powell Motel, get a housekeeping unit, or rent space for a camper or RV through the central reservation service. While the views and locations are excellent, the rooms, while spacious, are basic "motel"—not exciting, but clean and comfortable. Contact ARA Leisure Services, Box 56909, Phoenix 85079, or call (800) 528-6154 or (602) 278-8888. www.visitlakepowell.com.

The Ramada Inn. 287 North Lake Powell Boulevard in Page. This is right up the street from the Page Chamber of Commerce/visitors center/museum building. Although not on the lake, the motel units are quite nice. Call (928) 645-8851.

Note: In the past few years, a number of excellent new hotels have been built that serve all price ranges.

NAVAJO NATIONAL MONUMENT

When you're ready to push on another 88 miles, leave Lake Powell and drive southeast on A-98 for 66 miles to US-160. At the junction, head northeast on US-160 toward Kayenta. Twelve miles farther, you'll see a sign for A-564. Turn left and follow it north for 9 miles.

This drive will take about two hours, during which time you'll cross the Navajo Indian Reservation, an often desolate landscape. Watch for the Navajo hogans—low, round houses that many Navajo families still use as homes. The hogan doorway will always face east, where the sun rises. When you reach A-564, you'll be on a paved road that leads to Navajo National Monument. This is a collection of three wonderfully preserved Native American ruins: all that is left of pre-Columbian communities known as Keet Seel, Betatakin (pronounced Be-tah-tah-kin), and Inscription House. Remote enough to be off the beaten tourist track and romantic, these ruins provide an unusually personal look into the past for travelers who have the stamina and time to go the distance.

As is recommended for all national parks and monuments, your first stop should be the visitors center. Here you'll get your bearings. Although this is called the Navajo National Monument, the name refers to its location on the Navajo Reservation. The remnants of dwellings are from the Anasazi civilization, a pre-Columbian people who inhabited this area around 1200 B.C. The exhibits and the slide program at the center describe the life and items of the Anasazi. You'll learn about their homes and crops and also get a quick lesson on the geology of this area. For more information on Navajo National Monument, write HC 71, Box 3, Tonalea 86044–9704. Free. (928) 672–2366. www.nps.gov/nava.

WHERE TO GO

Betatakin. Guided tours are available to this Anasazi cliff dwelling throughout the year. Take an easy walk along Sandal Trail, which leads to an overlook of Betatakin. As you peer into this ruin, you'll sense that these people have left only momentarily and are due to return soon. During the season, June 1 to mid-September, there are three daily tours. After September, there is just one tour a day scheduled.

Betatakin means "house on a ledge," and this cluster of dwellings is literally set into a massive cavern in the canyon wall. The most accessible of the ruins here, Betatakin was constructed and abandoned in two generations between 1250 B.C. and 1300 B.C. The 135 rooms constituted a total community. There's a kiva, or ceremonial chamber; granaries; and living quarters.

Discovered in 1909 by Byron Cummings, a pioneer archaeologist of the Southwest, and John Wetherill, a rancher and trader, Betatakin was made safe for exploration in 1917 by Neil M. Judd of the Smithsonian Institution. The 1-mile round-trip walk from the visitors center takes about an hour. Bring binoculars to see these dwellings from the vantage of the rim. Ranger-guided tours, which descend into the ruin, are limited to twenty people at a time because of the fragility of the area. These excursions take about three hours and involve some strenuous climbing. The canyon is 700 feet deep, equal to a seventy-story building, and the altitude is 7,200 feet, which can be tiring for anyone, even those who are physically fit. Anyone with a heart condition should not attempt this climb. Free.

Inscription House. As of this printing, tours are no longer available. The site is closed for stabilization to make it safe and to prevent erosion under the stress of future exploration and tours.

Keet Seel. Tucked away in a remote canyon 8 miles from the visitors center, Keet Seel is the largest cliff dwelling in the state and can only be reached on foot or on horseback. Either way, it's a strenuous trip, but the journey is well worth the trouble for people who have adventurous hearts, strong legs, and iron seats.

You must make arrangements for this trip with a ranger ahead of time, because visits to Keet Seel are limited to twenty tourists a day. A Navajo family leads tours on horseback to Keet Seel, and if you are up for this rugged trip, be ready for some rough riding. The horses have two speeds: walk and wild gallop. Sure, you'll take a ride on the wild side, but when you reach Keet Seel, you'll forget your soreness and marvel at this extraordinarily well-preserved Anasazi ruin. Make arrangements for this experience at the visitors center. Fee for renting the horse.

From Navajo National Monument you can head south on A-564 to US-160, then south on US-160 to US-89, and US-89 south back to Flagstaff. Or you can return to Page for the night.

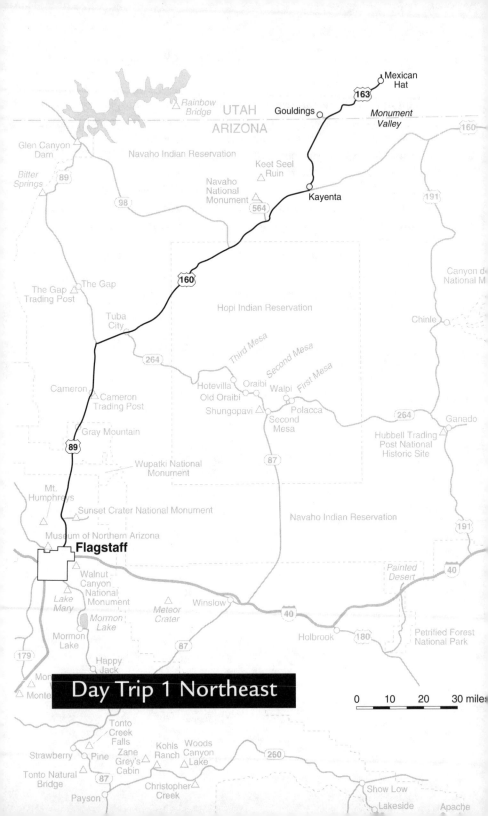

Day Trip 1 Northeast

KAYENTA

Kayenta is located 150 miles northeast of Flagstaff, and the trip takes about three hours. Go north on US–89 to its junction with US–160 and continue northeast on US–160 to Kayenta. This is a tiny town by American standards, but it is a major community on the Navajo reservation.

Be sure to visit the Navajo Nation Cultural Center, which is part museum, part gift shop. This is one of the new enterprises of the Navajo Nation Department of Tourism. The arts and crafts and other objects displayed here for sale are authentic, and prices are reasonable. The purpose of these centers is to help the Navajo Nation support its own craftspeople and artists, and they are a visual statement of an aggressive program to help the Navajo Nation expand its economy through tourism.

The center is located at the crossroads of US–160 and US–163, on the northwest corner. Kayenta is the jumping-off point for Monument Valley, your next destination. From Kayenta, turn north on US–163 to Monument Valley and Mexican Hat.

WHERE TO EAT

The Golden Sands Cafe. On US–163, 1 mile north of the Kayenta Holiday Inn. Feast on the Golden Sands Navajo taco, a delectable combination of chili and Navajo fry bread. You can choose from two sizes of tacos. The place is a favorite of locals and tourists, and there is usually a collection of pickup trucks in the parking lot. The portions are huge, the prices are reasonable, and the atmosphere is authentic Navajo Indian Reservation. $–$$. (928) 697-3684.

WHERE TO STAY

Hampton Inn of Kayenta. Highway 160. Approaching Monument Valley from Flagstaff, this new property greets you before you get to the Tribal Park. It's near the junction of US-160 and US-163. Navajo-owned, the inn is located in a new three-story adobe style building and contains seventy-three immaculate, charming rooms. The decor is contemporary Native American with a spacious and inviting lobby. The glowing fireplace invites guests to linger but the wonders of Monument Valley are just outside your door.

The hotel gift shop is called the **Kayenta Trading Company,** and it contains a fine collection of jewelry, baskets, Native American art and craft, clothing, books, and more. The Navajo Cultural Center adjoins the hotel where visitors can see the traditional ways of the Navajo people through exhibits and demonstrations. A great find and a wonderful place to spend the night. Continental breakfast is included. P.O. Box 1217, Kayenta 86033. $$; ☐. (928) 697-3170.

Holiday Inn, Kayenta. At the junction of US-160 and US-163. You'll find clean, adequate accommodations. Nothing fancy, but considering the remote location, this Holiday Inn offers a surprisingly nice option for travelers. There's even a swimming pool. $$; ☐. (928) 697-3221. E-mail: hi.monumentvalley@worldnet.com.

MONUMENT VALLEY, UTAH

From Kayenta, take US-163 north approximately 20 miles. At a crossroads just over the Utah state line, bear right to the Monument Valley Visitors Center. If Salvador Dali had sculpted a landscape, this would be it. Stark spires rise abruptly from the sandy floor, and the rock formations appear to have been dropped onto the flat earth, as if some ancient people flew in from the stars, deposited their rocky cargo, and disappeared.

Monument Valley is not a national park but, rather, a Navajo Tribal park consisting of 29,816 acres owned and managed by the

Navajo Tribal Council. The valley was made famous by John Wayne, who starred in many classic westerns that were filmed here.

At the visitors center, you'll see a sign pointing to a 17-mile unpaved scenic loop through the park. You can pick up a brochure inside, which describes a self-guided tour. Along the way there are eleven numbered scenic stops. Although the signs say you can drive your car on this road, think twice before you do so. The road is narrow, rutted, and banked by deep sands. In short, it isn't terrific. Most people prefer to take a guided jeep tour, especially since many of the more spectacular rock formations can be seen only from off the road.

During the summer season, expect high daytime temperatures and long lines to get into the visitors center or the park, but know that it's well worth any inconvenience. In the winter, Monument Valley is often closed because of snow. Fee. (435) 727-3287 or (435) 727-3353.

WHERE TO EAT AND STAY

Gouldings. Six miles west of the visitors center, just over the Utah state line off US-163. As you approach Monument Valley, you'll see a cluster of reddish-colored buildings built into the cliff to your left. Gouldings Trading Post complex is a wonderful blend of nostalgia and convenience.

Meals are no longer served family-style here, because a new, modern restaurant has been built. While it is efficient, it is less charming than the old, small dining room. The food is adequate, the atmosphere is modern and clean, and the native help is unfailingly pleasant and helpful.

Accommodations are clean and pleasant, and the views are spectacular. There is even a swimming pool—perfect for a dip after a trip out into the sands of Monument Valley.

Be sure to visit the small theater on the property. It shows a breathtakingly beautiful film. The museum is charming and informative and traces the history of Gouldings, which has long been a favorite place for western movie makers. The gift shop offers a nice collection of native-made artifacts.

Even if you are not an early-morning person, make a point of getting up to watch a sunrise in Monument Valley. Both day's beginning and end are spectacular sights in this ethereal land of vast spaces and otherworldly rock formations.

And do take a Gouldings open-vehicle tour of Monument Valley. Open vehicles are the most pleasant way to tour this impressive place. Guests can take either all-day or half-day trips. Goulding's guides are well versed in history and lore. If you're up for adventure, you can take a horseback day trip or overnight into Monument Valley with Native American guides. There are two stables in the park to choose from. These trips are not recommended for novice riders. $$; ☐. For reservations or information, write P.O. Box 1, Monument Valley, UT 84536. (435) 727-3231. www.gouldings.com.

From here you can retrace your steps to Flagstaff or pick up Day Trip 2 Northeast from Flagstaff. If you have the time, combining these trips can make a marvelous four- to seven-day vacation. *One word of caution:* Outside of Monument Valley, enterprising Native Americans have set up a "village" to display and sell crafts. Buy with caution. Not all of these items are authentic. This is a problem that the Navajo Nation is well aware of and is trying to fix. Examine items carefully, and if you are not certain that a piece is authentic, don't purchase it. Save your money for reputable outlets such as those sponsored by the Navajo Nation or galleries.

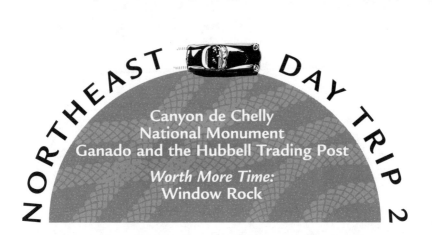

NORTHEAST DAY TRIP 2

Canyon de Chelly
National Monument
Ganado and the Hubbell Trading Post

Worth More Time:
Window Rock

CANYON DE CHELLY
NATIONAL MONUMENT

Canyon de Chelly Monument is approximately 135 miles southeast of Monument Valley on Indian Route 64. From Monument Valley, drive south on US–163 to Kayenta. At the junction of US–160 and 163, drive east on US–160 about 40 miles to where US–160 meets US–191. Go south on US–191 for 75 miles to Chinle and the entrance to Canyon de Chelly (pronounced de Shay). To see Canyon de Chelly properly requires at least one overnight if you are coming from Monument Valley and two if Flagstaff is your base.

Canyon de Chelly is quite unlike Monument Valley. Where Monument Valley is stark and golden desert, Canyon de Chelly is pink and warm. It is one of the most appealing of Arizona's canyons. As you enter the canyon on Indian Route 64, you will see the visitors center directly ahead of you.

This park boasts towering sculpted rock formations, sheer and colorful cliffs, and picture-postcard scenery. It is inhabited both by modern-day Native Americans and memories of ancient ones. The Pueblo Indians, who vanished from this area around A.D. 1350, abandoned their dwellings forever. Their spirit infuses the ruins within the canyon walls. Hundreds of ancient communities, many of them poised on sandstone ledges within colorful caverns, give witness to the earlier vitality of this place.

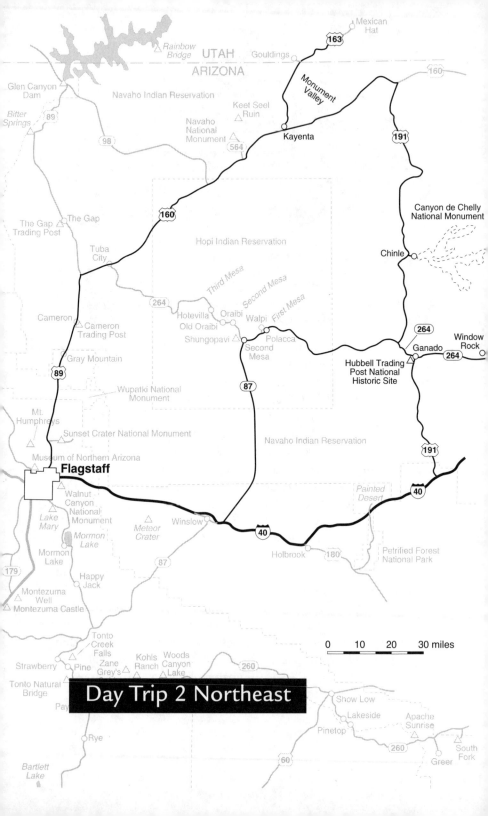

Day Trip 2 Northeast

The Navajos arrived in the area sometime before the eighteenth century. Even today, a small enclave of Navajo families live in modern dwellings on the canyon floor, tend sheep, and grow crops.

WHERE TO GO

Self-guided tours. Pick up brochures that describe these tours at the Canyon de Chelly Visitor Center (928-674-5500; www.nps.gov/cach.com). When walking or driving on the rim, be sure to obey all signs. In places, it's a dizzying 400-foot drop onto the canyon floor.

The walk to White House Ruins is a pleasant hike along a well-marked path. The walk down takes less than an hour, but remember to add extra time to hike back up again. Wear tennis shoes and carry some water.

At the bottom you will cross the sandy wash that, in the winter and spring, can be running, so be prepared to get wet. Once across, you can gaze at this well-preserved ruin and imagine what it was like for these prehistoric people to live and farm in this incredible canyon.

Usually a native jeweler is seen here, his blanket laden with rings, bracelets, and necklaces that he's made. The prices are good, so if you see something that catches your eye for a reasonable price, don't hesitate to buy it. It could be handmade.

As you drive around this canyon, remember that the best way to see Canyon de Chelly is outside of your car. Many trails beckon. Take advantage of them and enjoy the views. Pay attention to signs and respect the natural site.

Canyon de Chelly is a favorite spot for Native American entrepreneurs, who also sell their wares on the canyon rim. Again, buy with care, as not everything you'll see is authentic.

Guided jeep tours. To fully appreciate the geology, history, and anthropology of this exquisite canyon, take a guided half-day or full-day jeep tour. Make arrangements at the Thunderbird Lodge, P.O. Box 548, Chinle 86503. Unless you have an extensive interest in ancient Native American civilization, the half-day trip is your best bet; a full day could leave you exhausted. In summer, as you bounce along the canyon floor in an open jeep, you may need the protection of sunscreen and a hat. You may even want to take a canteen or thermos with water. Open daily. Fee. ☐. (928) 674-5841 or (928) 674-5842. E-mail: tbirdlodge@cybertrails.com.

WHERE TO EAT

Thunderbird Lodge Motel. On US-191. The food tends to be heavy and starchy, but it's prepared and served by a Navajo staff in a charming building, circa 1896, which was the original trading post. The only dining establishment in the immediate area of the canyon, this is your only choice. The staff knows this and is not very friendly or courteous. The best option is to bring food and eat in your cabin. Open daily during breakfast, lunch, and dinner hours. $-$$; ☐. (928) 674-5842 or (928) 674-5841.

WHERE TO STAY

Thunderbird Lodge Motel. On US-191. This historic lodge offers the most complete facilities in Navajoland. The rooms are clean and moderately priced, and the location, at the mouth of the canyon, is magnificent. The staff is not very hospitable, so don't expect a gracious welcome and you won't be disappointed. You'll find a gift shop to browse through, and you can make arrangements for tours right at the lodge. Make sure you bring a light jacket or sweater for summer evenings if you visit from April through November. In the winter, you'll need to bundle up. For information, write to Thunderbird Lodge Motel, P.O. Box 548, Chinle 86503. $$; ☐. (928) 674-5842 or (928) 674-5841.

Canyon de Chelly Motel. As you enter Chinle, south on US-191, turn left at the intersection—the only one in town. Don't depend upon the road signs in this area. Often, if the road is under repair, the signs come down. (Take solace in the fact that Chinle is tiny and you really cannot get lost.) $$$; ☐. (928) 674-5288. www.canyondechelly.com.

GANADO AND THE HUBBELL TRADING POST

Hubbell Trading Post National Historic Site. One mile west of Ganado. Before returning to Flagstaff from Canyon de Chelly, you can continue south 30 miles on US-191 to the intersection of A-264, then 5 miles east to Ganado and the Hubbell Trading Post National Historic Site. A national treasure, the trading post is worth a visit.

The rug room at the Hubbell Trading Post rivals any museum collection in the world. If you're in the market for a Navajo rug, this is an ideal place to shop. The knowledgeable salespeople will be happy to tell you about the patterns and weavers. The only modern-day touch is that, along with the name of the weaver, you'll also occasionally find a Polaroid photograph of the weaver attached to the ticket. You also can browse through exquisite jewelry, sandpaintings, books, and trinkets or even pick up food supplies if you plan to camp in the area. Groceries are sold in the front room.

John Lorenzo Hubbell was the dean of traders for the Navajos, and his trading post continues to act as a bridge between the Native American and Anglo worlds. In its heyday, the post offered a place for Navajos to socialize as well as to conduct business. VIPs of every culture who passed through northeastern Arizona during the late 1800s and early 1900s stopped here. The guest list includes presidents, generals, writers, scientists, and artists.

Today, business continues as usual in this elegant pocket of the state. The atmosphere hasn't changed; Navajos and tourists still come by to trade and talk.

Hubbell's career spanned critical years for the Navajos. When he came to the territory to open his trading post, the Native Americans were adjusting to life on a reservation and were attempting to cope with the restrictions placed on them by the U.S. government. Hubbell offered his friendship when great numbers of Navajo were struggling to free themselves from the confines of Fort Sumner in New Mexico. He sympathized with the Navajo and often spoke out on their behalf. When he died in 1930, one of Hubbell's native friends eulogized him at the memorial service saying:

> You wear out your shoes, you buy another pair;
> When the food is gone, you buy more;
> You gather melons, and more will grow on the vine;
> You grind your corn and make bread which you eat;
> And next year you have plenty more corn.
> But my friend Don Lorenzo is gone,
>   and none to take his place.

After browsing through the trading post, walk around the grounds to see the Hubbell home. Limited tours are available and are

restricted to four tours per day. Free. (928) 755-3254. www.navajo
rugs.spma.org.

From Ganado, there are several ways to return to Flagstaff. The
fastest route is US-191 south to I-40. Then head west on I-40 to
Flagstaff. Another alternative is to take A-264 west to A-87, turn
south on A-87, and then west on I-40 to Flagstaff. Get some sleep
at Canyon de Chelly if you plan to head west on A-264 to Polacca
for Day Trip 3 Northeast from Flagstaff after visiting Ganado.

WORTH MORE TIME: WINDOW ROCK

Window Rock. The capitol of the Navajo Nation, Window Rock is
worth a visit. The trip to Window Rock will take about two hours from
Ganado. It is located about 30 minutes from Gallup, New Mexico.
From Hubbell, take US-191 south to A-264 and continue east to
Window Rock. In Window Rock, visit the Navajo Nation Cultural
Center, which includes a museum and indoor and outdoor theater,
and of course, Window Rock—the rock that gives this town its name.

WHERE TO STAY

Navajo Nation Inn. A-264 and A-12. This well-equipped modern
inn has good amenities, including a dining room that features some
traditional Navajo dishes. The inn offers individual and family tours
of the area. The gift shop is surprisingly inadequate for an inn that
draws so much traffic. However, the Navajo Nation Cultural Center
is well within walking distance, and here you'll find a superb display
of Navajo arts and crafts. Prices are fair (don't expect bargains), but
both the quantity and quality are good. $$; □. (800) 662-6189 or
(928) 871-4108.

Navajoland Day's Inn. St. Michael's (located next to Window
Rock). This property in St. Michael's is an alternative to the Navajo
Nation Inn. It is just a mile or so up the hill from the Navajo Nation
Inn and is a bit newer and has an indoor swimming pool. The rooms
are clean and spacious. Breakfast is complimentary. $$; □.

First, Second,
and Third Mesas

INDIAN COUNTRY

This is a wonderful trip that shouldn't be rushed. Because of the great distances in this part of the state, visiting more remote areas means stretching your usual day-trip time limit.

As you plan, consider that the Hopi Reservation roads found in this sector are often narrow, two-lane byways. You won't make fast time, so add another hour to your excursion limit.

You can begin the trip in Flagstaff by heading east on I-40 to Winslow and picking up the turnoff for A-87 north 3 miles east of there. Follow A-87 north for 65 miles to Second Mesa on the Hopi Indian Reservation, then turn right (east) for 7 miles and actually start at Polacca on First Mesa.

A better option might be to combine this trip with Day Trip 2, previously described. Time permitting, you will enjoy this journey more if you can begin it refreshed after a good night's sleep at Canyon de Chelly. After driving 30 miles south to Ganado and stopping at the Hubbell Trading Post (see Day Trip 2 Northeast from Flagstaff), head west on A-264 to Polacca.

If you look at a map, you'll see that the Hopi (pronounced Ho-pee) nation is plunked down in the middle of the vast Navajo Reservation. Although they live in close proximity, the Hopi and the Navajo couldn't be more different. Historically, the Hopi, whose ancestors are the Anasazi, have been pueblo dwellers—homebodies content to build permanent villages and cement family ties. The Navajo, in contrast, are nomadic farmers and sheepherders. In fact, the word *hopi*

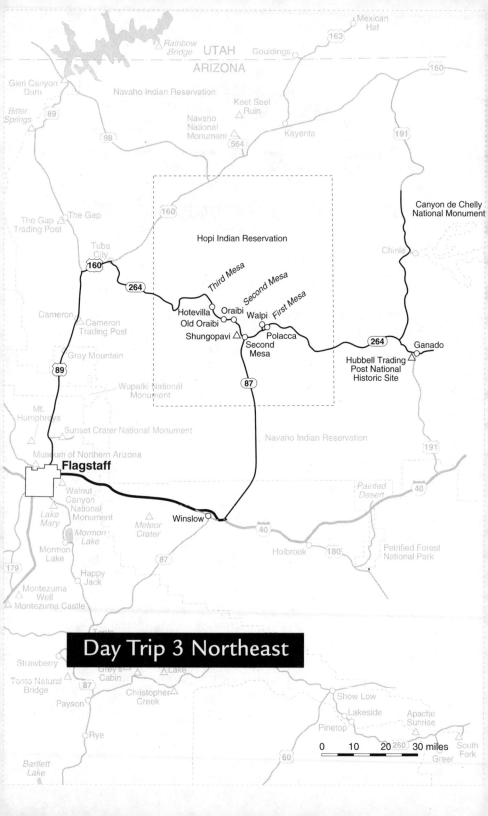

Day Trip 3 Northeast

means "the peaceful ones," and traditionally these people have led a peaceful, agrarian life.

The windswept mesas of the Hopi Reservation have long been a source of inspiration to the Hopi and non-Native Americans alike. As you drive through this reservation on A-264, you'll feel a subtle pull, the magic that makes life in the fast lane seem ridiculous. At first, the landscape seems barren, but look again. Everywhere you will see corn growing, even in the most improbable corners of backyards and in the rockiest soil. To the Hopi, corn represents life, and they cherish this food for its nutritional and spiritual values.

If this is your first trip to the Hopi Reservation, or Hopi, as it is more commonly called, you may wonder where the ancient villages are. Etched against the horizon, high on flattened mountaintops, the tiny pueblos jut against the sky like jack-o'-lantern teeth. Although the Hopi have lived here for hundreds of years, they do not intrude upon Mother Earth. They live gently and inconspicuously, coaxing life from this rocky soil they call their land.

All but one of the villages you may visit are located on or near the areas called First, Second, and Third Mesas. The names refer to the chronological shift of the Hopi population from A.D. 1500 to A.D. 1900. First the Hopi settled in Walpi (the area now known as First Mesa), and they gradually moved westward to Oraibi and Hotevilla.

Life goes on here, in many instances as it always has, with families living in ancient pueblo dwellings high on treeless cliffs. Some villagers have moved down from the mesa, spending most of the year in modern, government-built housing at the foot of the mountains. These Hopi go back to the old village only for festivals and holidays.

During the year, Hopi dances are frequently held on the mesas. These ceremonies are often open to the public. To inquire when public dances are scheduled, call the Hopi Cultural Center at (928) 734-2401. If you decide to plan a visit during a dance, understand that the Hopi do not share our Anglo clock fetish. Dances begin when they begin—no sooner, no later. They end when they are over. This can be one hour or six hours. Native Americans have a totally different concept of time. Bring patience, a chair, and a warm blanket or heavy jacket. Above all, *do not bring cameras*. Picture taking is not allowed during dances.

The Snake Dance. This dance is held in late August and currently is banned to anyone other than Hopi. It is, however, worth it to call the Hopi Reservation to check, since rules may change. Tribal dances are pageants full of color and drama, and if you are fortunate enough to be invited, don't hesitate. Go! The snake dance is famous because, for this ceremony, men dance with live snakes in their mouths to invoke the gods' mercy to send rain for their crops.

WHERE TO GO

Walpi, First Mesa. All the ancient villages are off the main roads, situated high atop the mesas. In the past, a mountaintop location protected the village from intruders.

As you drive through the reservation on A-264, you'll see signs pointing to Polacca, a Native American village. At Polacca, you'll spot a gravel road that leads north to Walpi. (There are no names on the few streets that lead to these ancient villages.) The narrow road climbs and makes several sharp turns. Although the pueblo buildings may appear to be closing in on you, don't worry. This road is fine for passenger car travel. Once on top of the mesa, park. Proceed immediately to the visitors center. There you will be assigned to a guide. You'll see the ancient plaza, still used for ceremonials, with its kiva (underground ceremonial chamber) near the center. While you may freely explore the plaza and old pueblo dwellings, the kiva is off-limits.

Walpi is an especially picturesque village that comes to life during important ceremonies. You will find that the Hopi who live here are extremely friendly, and you may be invited inside some homes to see handcrafted art items. If you are interested in native arts, by all means, accept the invitations.

However, *don't* take Hopi hospitality for granted. Observe all the signs posted in the ancient villages that ask you not to take any photographs, make sketches, or make any sound recordings. *Remember:* When you are in Hopi (or any other reservation), you are a guest in another country.

When you leave First Mesa, continue west on A-264, and you'll see signs that lead to Shipolovi (Shi-pah-lo-vee) and Shongopovi (Shun-gó-pa-ee), other well-known, old villages on **Second Mesa.** You may either visit or see them from a distance. Continue toward Oraibi. Soon you'll see the Hopi Cultural Center, a cluster of pseudo-pueblos, on your right. If you're hungry, thirsty, or tired of driving, this is a good place to stop. You'll find a restaurant, gift shop, small museum, and overnight accommodations here.

Oraibi, Third Mesa. From the cultural center, continue west on A-264 to Oraibi. You may want to take a quick trip to Old Oraibi. Like Walpi, this community hovers on a high, narrow, rocky ledge. The road to Old Oraibi heads off to your left (south) shortly after you pass Oraibi (sometimes called "New Oraibi"). Although parts of the settlement are in ruins, the village is very much a part of modern Hopi life. When you're finished visiting here, drive west on A-264 toward Hotevilla to see that village.

WHERE TO EAT AND STAY

The Hopi Cultural Center. On A-264, 5 miles west of the junction with A-87. The dining room is big and airy, and you'll be served by Hopi women in native dress. Order the Hopi specialties: Hopi stew made with chunks of lamb, and anything made with blue corn, a special type of corn grown and used here. $-$$; ☐.

If you plan to spend the night, call ahead for reservations and be prepared to rough it some. You will not find the same quality of service and accommodations on the reservation as you'll find in the cities, but unless you are pulling a camper or driving an RV, this is your only choice for an overnight stay. $$; ☐. (928) 734-2401.

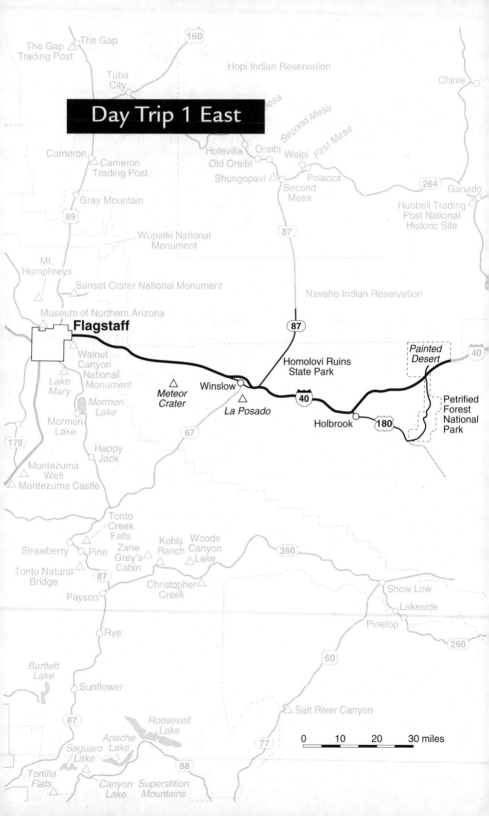

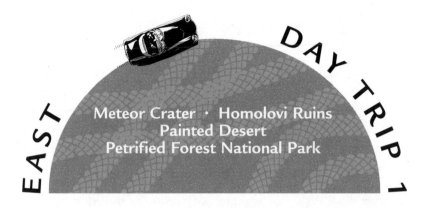

METEOR CRATER

Leaving Flagstaff, drive east on I-40 toward Winslow. Twenty miles before you reach Winslow, you'll see an exit for Meteor Crater. Head south on the well-marked, paved road to this fascinating natural site.

Meteor Crater was formed in 20,000 B.C. when a meteoric mass, traveling 33,000 miles per hour from interplanetary space, struck Earth. The impact, blasting nearly a half billion tons of rock from the surface, destroyed all plant and animal life within 100 miles. In contemporary times, this perfectly preserved, huge hole in the ground has tantalized scientists, who use it as a living laboratory. Meteor Crater hit the news when the Apollo astronauts used it as a practice surface to train for their lunar walk. Discovered in 1871, the crater has impressive statistics. It measures 4,150 feet from rim to rim, is more than 3 miles in circumference, and is 470 feet deep. In addition to staring at the crater, you can visit the Museum of Astrogeology, the Astronaut Hall of Fame, and well-appointed gift and lapidary shops. Open daily. Call for extended summer hours. Fee. (928) 289-2362. www.meteorcrater.com.

From Meteor Crater, continue to Winslow on I-40. The town is named for F. Edward Winslow, who was president of the St. Louis and San Francisco Railroad, and like its neighbor, Holbrook, is devoted to transportation. Situated 30 miles west of the Mogollon Rim, this community serves as a conduit for more remote and scenic areas of the state.

Known as "The Hub City" because of the transportation lines that intersect here, Holbrook also serves as the seat of Navajo County. It caters to tourists who are on their way to the Painted Desert and Petrified Forest National Park. It's a good place to stretch your legs, pick up a snack, or fill up the car with gas before going on.

WHERE TO STAY

La Posada. 303 East Second Street, Winslow. At the intersection of US-66 and A-87, ¼ mile from I-40. This historic hotel was designed by Mary Colter, who was one of the most important architects in the Southwest. She designed for the Fred Harvey Company in the early part of the twentieth century. When the Harvey Company decided to build a new hotel in Winslow, they hired Colter, who arrived in Winslow in 1929. She designed and built a seventy-room inn patterned after a Spanish hacienda. When the era of the Harvey hotels passed, the hotel was abandoned until 1996, when Allan Affeldt and his artist wife bought the property, moved in, and began to painstakingly renovate it. Today, the hotel has twenty rooms available for guests, each one decorated individually. Breakfast is included in the price. $$; ☐. (928) 289-4366. www.laposada.org.

From Winslow, continue east on I-40 for 33 miles to Holbrook.

HOMOLOVI RUINS

Homolovi Ruins State Park is located approximately 3 miles northeast of Winslow. Take I-40 to exit 257, then go 1³⁄₁₀ miles north on A-87. The park has more than 300 archaeological sites, including four major fourteenth-century pueblos you can roam through. There is also a campground and several hiking trails that wind through the ruins. Open daily. Fee. (928) 289-4106. www.pr.state.az.us.

PAINTED DESERT

From Holbrook, continue on I-40 approximately 19 miles to exit 311. As you approach the parks, the Painted Desert is the area due north of the highway; the Petrified Forest National Park lies south of it. Although the parks are referred to as separate entities, they are, in fact, contiguous. The Painted Desert offers a superb backdrop for travelers who enjoy the desert at its most delicately pastel, but the Petrified Forest is the better attraction.

Try to time your arrival during the early morning or late afternoon hours. At sunup or just before sunset, the fallen logs in the Petrified Forest seem most lifelike and the colors of the Painted Desert appear most vibrant.

WHERE TO GO

Painted Desert Inn. One mile north of I–40, at the entrance to the park. This is your first stop. Inside you will learn how both the Painted Desert and the Petrified Forest were formed. Exhibits illustrate the evolution of the Painted Desert, and a short film describes how natural forces turn the forest to stone.

Wander around the displays and pick up information for a self-guided tour of both parks. Check for summer and winter hours. Fee. (928) 524–9753.

PETRIFIED FOREST NATIONAL PARK

The Petrified Forest National Park is the greatest and most colorful concentration of petrified wood ever discovered on Earth. The park, which consists of 93,431 acres of brilliantly colored stone logs, preserves the glassy remains of an ancient coniferous forest. About 200 million years ago, the trees grew in the highlands to the west and southwest. The area of the present forest was swampland, and as streams carried the dead logs down to this flat, depressed area, they were buried in sediment rich with volcanic ash.

Over eons, the chemical process worked its magic. The logs were slowly impregnated with silica until they turned to solid stone. Iron oxide and other minerals then stained the silica, producing the stone rainbows we see today. In the process, the logs became stony jewel boxes for quartz and other gemstones that developed in the wood during petrification.

Today, each chip and rock is carefully protected. No one is allowed to pick up even the tiniest souvenir. But in ancient times, the people who lived here carved on the petrified wood, chiseled messages on the rocks, and fashioned tools and weapons from the rainbow forest.

You'll want to take a slow drive through the area. If you've stopped at the Painted Desert Visitor Center, you've picked up a pamphlet that describes a self-guided drive. This brochure explains all the places you'll want to see. If you don't have a brochure, don't worry, because you'll find, as you approach each site, a written description clearly posted. Be sure to stop and get out of your car to see these unusual rock formations. You should hike to **Agate Bridge** in the First Forest. Here a petrified tree fell across a canyon, forming a stony bridge for eternity. Plan to climb down the 120 steps to **Newspaper Rock,** a large boulder covered with ancient writing. No doubt this served as a kind of local bulletin board, announcing activities and goings-on to the Native Americans who lived in the area. If you follow all the side roads that are marked in this stony forest, you'll drive about 38 miles before you reach the south entrance, which is your exit point.

WHAT TO DO

Rainbow Forest Museum. Near the south entrance. This is your final stop before leaving the Petrified Forest. Inside you'll see geological exhibits. If you didn't stop at the north entrance, you can learn how the forests were formed here. Check for summer and winter hours. Fee. (928) 524-6822. www.nps.gov/pefo.

Return to Flagstaff by following US–180 northwest to Holbrook, where you'll pick up I–40 west to Flagstaff.

SOUTHEAST · DAY TRIP 1

Mormon Lake · Happy Jack
Worth More Time:
Payson

MORMON LAKE

Approximately 30 miles southeast of Flagstaff on Mormon Lake Road, Mormon Lake is an optimum destination for a quick, easy, scenic loop through some of Flagstaff's best outdoor country.

To get there from Flagstaff, follow I-17 south to the Lake Mary Road exit. Stay on Lake Mary Road until you reach the Mormon Lake area. As you drive, the road will wind through the Coconino National Forest and will take you near some great fishing lakes. Lake Mary is one of the favorites.

This area is long on scenery but short on facilities. Numerous campgrounds dot the countryside, but wise travelers will carry picnic hampers filled with lunch goodies. You won't find any fast food here, unless, of course, you are especially quick with hook and bait. What you will find, however, is serenity—ponderosa pines trimming lush meadows, backed up by a panorama of the San Francisco Peaks.

As you continue southeast, you'll see a dirt road off to your left (east), which leads to Ashurst Lake. Unless you have a four-wheel drive, avoid this. Dirt roads in this area can be hazardous to the health of your car. Unless you are driving a four-wheel-drive vehicle or a truck, it's advisable to stay on paved surfaces. During the rainy season you can get flooded out, and during the dry periods, these roads can be extremely rough.

Continuing on Lake Mary Road, you'll come to Mormon Lake Road, a dirt byway that leads off to your right (west). Take this un-

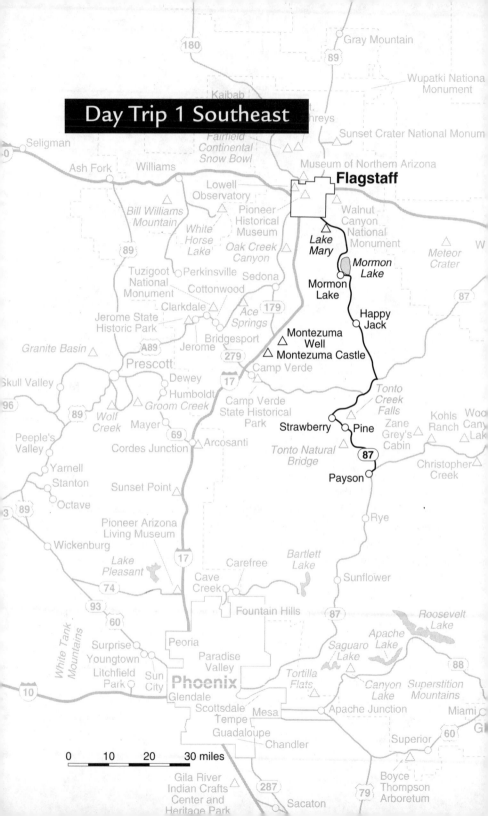

Day Trip 1 Southeast

Gray Mountain

180

89

Wupatki Nationa
Monument

Kaibab

Seligman

Fairfield
Continental
Snow Bowl

-hreys

Sunset Crater National Monum

Ash Fork   Williams

Museum of Northern Arizona

Flagstaff

Lowell
Observatory

Bill Williams
Mountain

White
Horse
Lake

89

Pioneer
Historical
Museum

Oak Creek
Canyon

Walnut
Canyon
National
Monument

Meteor
Crater

W

Lake
Mary

Mormon
Lake

Tuzigoot
National
Monument

Perkinsville

Cottonwood

Sedona

Ace
Springs

179

Mormon
Lake

87

Clarkdale

Jerome State
Historic Park

Granite Basin

A89

Jerome

Bridgesport

279

Montezuma
Well

Montezuma Castle

Happy
Jack

Camp Verde

Prescott

Dewey

17

Camp Verde
State Historical
Park

Tonto
Creek
Falls

Skull Valley

Humboldt
Groom Creek

96

89

Wolf
Creek

Mayer

69

Cordes Junction

Arcosanti

Strawberry   Pine

Zane
Grey's
Cabin

Kohls
Ranch

Woo
Can
Lak

Peeple's
Valley

Tonto Natural
Bridge

87

Christopher
Creek

Yarnell

Stanton

Sunset Point

Payson

3

89

Octave

Rye

Pioneer Arizona
Living Museum

Wickenburg

Bartlett
Lake

Lake
Pleasant

17

Carefree

Sunflower

74

Cave
Creek

Roosevelt
Lake

93

60

Fountain Hills

87

Apache
Lake

88

White Tank
Mountains

Surprise

Youngtown

Litchfield
Park

Peoria

Paradise
Valley

Saguaro
Lake

Tortilla
Flats

Canyon
Lake

Superstition
Mountains

Sun
City

Phoenix

10

Glendale

Scottsdale

Tempe

Guadaloupe

Mesa

Apache Junction

Miami

G

60

Chandler

Superior

0   10   20   30 miles

Gila River
Indian Crafts
Center and
Heritage Park

287

Sacaton

79

Boyce
Thompson
Arboretum

paved road, which will loop around Mormon Lake, the largest natural lake in Arizona. Cattle that roamed over the meadowland stamped down the earth, forming a natural dish that held the winter snowmelt. The Mormons, who remained in this vicinity for many years, ran a dairy and even built a cheese press here. It's not known why they left the area, but probably a drought forced them out.

Over the years, the snowmelt continually refilled the depressed area and formed a large natural lake surrounded by open range where cattle graze. The lake is also a haven for ducks and duck hunters.

Adjacent to the water is the village of Mormon Lake, which consists of Montezuma and Mormon Lake Lodges, a post office, a dance hall that seats 350 people, a steak house, and a general store. During big holiday weekends (including Fourth of July and Labor Day), the dance hall resounds with live entertainment.

WHAT TO DO

Cross-Country Skiing. During the winter you'll find some of the best cross-country skiing in the state. You can drive up and ski for the day or make overnight arrangements at either of two lodges in the area. (See Where to Stay.)

WHERE TO EAT

Mormon Lake Lodge. Mormon Lake. The menu features seven kinds of steak, all reasonably priced. The restaurant is one of the few operating open-pit steakhouses in the state. During the summer, the lodge is open for breakfast, lunch, and dinner. In winter, only dinner is served during the week, with all meals available on the weekends. $$–$$$; ☐. (928) 774-0462.

WHERE TO STAY

Montezuma Lodge. Mormon Lake. Follow the Mormon Lake dirt road 3 miles to the lodge. Guests can stay in twenty well-equipped kitchenette cabins nestled in the woods against the Mormon Mountains. This is a favorite "ride-in" stop for bicyclists, who come, packs on their backs, to rest and then ride in the area. Closed in winter. Meals by prior arrangement only. $–$$; ☐. (928) 354-2220.

Mormon Lake Lodge. Mormon Lake. From Lake Mary Road turn right onto Mormon Lake Road and continue 9 miles to the lodge. (You will pass Montezuma Lodge.) The property dates back to 1924 when it was built as Tumbler's Lodge. It was a place for men to bring their families and have a good meal. On July 4, 1924, the lodge burned to the ground while men were planning a big rodeo event. The local ranchers vowed to rebuild it on Labor Day weekend in time for the next rodeo. When they completed it, they burned their branding irons into the walls as a symbol of protection. The brands are still visible today.

The dining room of the Mormon Lake Lodge has seating for 400 and serves casual western-style dining. The 1880s-style saloon keeps its old-time charm.

The rustic resort features forty-six bunkhouses and cabins, all nestled in the forest. Some have fireplaces and kitchenettes. Rentals are daily and weekly. $$; ☐. (928) 774-0462. www.mormonlakelodge.com.

HAPPY JACK

Another 12 miles southwest on Lake Mary Road is Happy Jack, a logging community. You'll see campgrounds and some private cabins tucked away on this not-so-beaten path. From Happy Jack you have a few options. You can continue to the junction with A-87 and follow A-87 northeast to Winslow. From Winslow, follow US-180 back to Flagstaff.

Or you may follow Lake Mary Road to the junction of A-87 and take A-87 to Strawberry and Pine, and then follow General Crook Highway west to Camp Verde. There you can pick up I-17 north and continue to Flagstaff. Along the way, you can stop at Montezuma Castle and Montezuma Well. (See Day Trip 2 North from Phoenix.)

WORTH MORE TIME: PAYSON

A third option is to follow Lake Mary Road south to A-87 and continue on A-87 to Payson. See Day Trip 2 Northeast from Phoenix for more details on what to see and do around this community.

Oak Creek/Sedona

Worth More Time:
Montezuma Well
and Montezuma Castle

OAK CREEK/SEDONA

From Flagstaff, head due south on US–89A to A–179 and Oak Creek and Sedona. (Refer to Day Trip 4 North from Phoenix for all there is to do and see here.) From Flagstaff, the trip to Sedona takes less than an hour.

WORTH MORE TIME: MONTEZUMA WELL AND MONTEZUMA CASTLE

From Sedona, stay on A–179 south to its junction with I-17. To visit Montezuma Castle or Montezuma Well, drive south on I-17 to the exits marked for each. (See Day Trip 2 North from Phoenix for additional information on these historic sites.) Fee. (928) 567–3322. www.nps.gov.

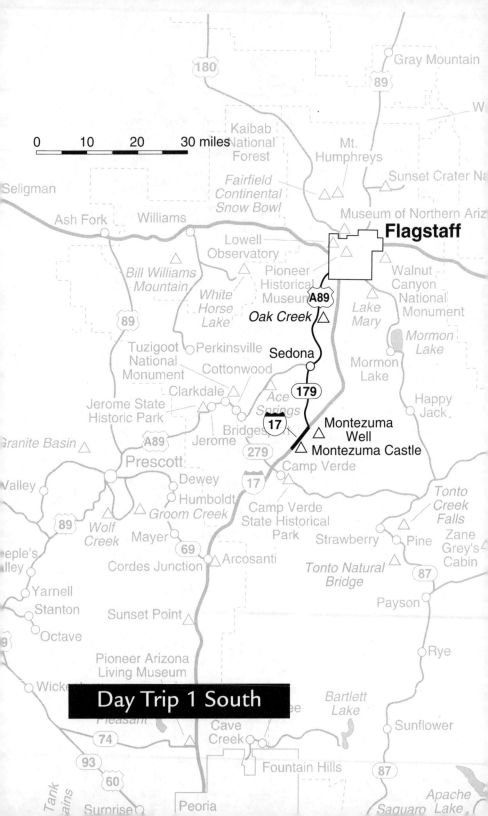

0   10   20   30 miles

180

89

Gray Mountain

W

Kaibab National Forest

Mt. Humphreys

Sunset Crater Na

Seligman

Fairfield Continental Snow Bowl

Museum of Northern Ariz

Ash Fork

Williams

Flagstaff

Lowell Observatory

Bill Williams Mountain

White Horse Lake

Pioneer Historical Museum

A89

Walnut Canyon National Monument

89

Oak Creek

Lake Mary

Mormon Lake

Tuzigoot National Monument

Perkinsville

Sedona

Mormon Lake

Cottonwood

Clarkdale

179

Happy Jack

Jerome State Historic Park

Ace Springs

Granite Basin

A89

Bridges

17

Montezuma Well

Jerome

279

Montezuma Castle

Prescott

Dewey

Camp Verde

Tonto Creek Falls

Valley

89

Humboldt

17

Groom Creek

Camp Verde State Historical Park

Zane Grey's Cabin

Wolf Creek

Mayer

69

Strawberry

Pine

87

eple's alley

Cordes Junction

Arcosanti

Tonto Natural Bridge

Payson

Yarnell

Stanton

Sunset Point

Octave

9

Rye

Pioneer Arizona Living Museum

Day Trip 1 South

Bartlett Lake

Sunflower

Wicke

Pleasant

Cave Creek

74

Fountain Hills

87

93

60

Apache Saguaro Lake

Surprise

Peoria

Jerome · Prescott

JEROME

Follow US-89A due south from Flagstaff. You'll drive about an hour to reach Jerome, a charming semi-ghost town. (Read about Jerome in Day Trip 2 North from Phoenix.)

PRESCOTT

From Jerome, continue 41 miles southwest on US-89A to Prescott, Arizona's picturesque community famous for its Victorian homes and historical significance. Here territorial Arizona springs to life. The first capital of the Arizona Territory, Prescott ultimately lost its bid to become the permanent state capital to Phoenix. Still, much Arizona history was made here and, fortunately for visitors, remains well preserved. For more information, see Day Trip 1 North from Phoenix.

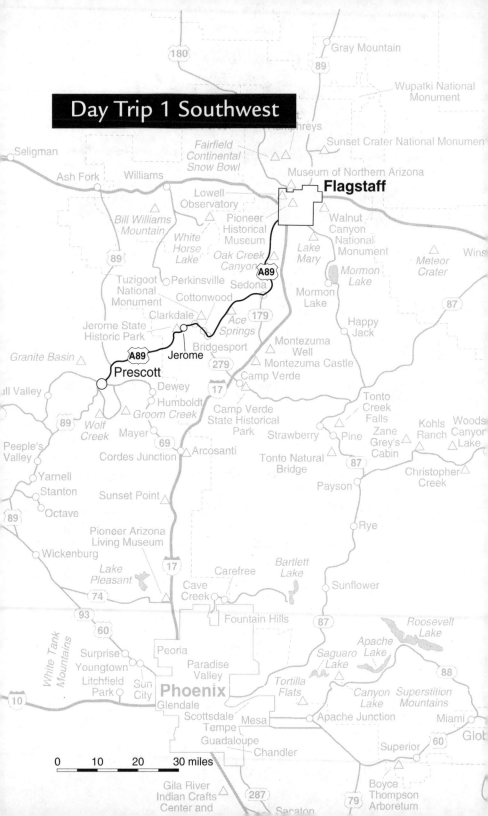

Day Trip 1 Southwest

Gray Mountain

180

89

Wupatki National
Monument

Seligman

Ash Fork

Williams

Fairfield
Continental
Snow Bowl

Sunset Crater National Monumen

Museum of Northern Arizona

Humphreys

Flagstaff

Bill Williams
Mountain

89

White
Horse
Lake

Lowell
Observatory

Pioneer
Historical
Museum

Walnut
Canyon
National
Monument

Meteor
Crater

Wins

Oak Creek
Canyon

A89

Lake
Mary

Tuzigoot
National
Monument

Perkinsville

Cottonwood

Sedona

Mormon
Lake

Mormon
Lake

87

Clarkdale

179

Happy
Jack

Jerome State
Historic Park

Ace
Springs

Bridgesport

Montezuma
Well

Tonto
Creek
Falls

Granite Basin

A89

Jerome

279

Montezuma Castle

Prescott

Camp Verde

Woods
Canyon
Lake

Kohls
Ranch

ll Valley

89

Dewey

Humboldt

17

Zane
Grey's
Cabin

Pine

Groom Creek

Camp Verde
State Historical
Park

Strawberry

Christopher
Creek

Wolf
Creek

Mayer

Peeple's
Valley

69

Arcosanti

Tonto Natural
Bridge

87

Yarnell

Cordes Junction

Payson

Stanton

89

Octave

Sunset Point

Rye

Pioneer Arizona
Living Museum

Wickenburg

17

Lake
Pleasant

Carefree

Bartlett
Lake

74

Cave
Creek

Sunflower

93

Fountain Hills

87

60

Roosevelt
Lake

White Tank
Mountains

Surprise

Peoria

Apache
Lake

Youngtown

Saguaro
Lake

88

Litchfield
Park

Sun
City

Paradise
Valley

10

Phoenix

Glendale

Scottsdale

Tortilla
Flats

Canyon
Lake

Superstition
Mountains

Tempe

Mesa

Miami

Guadalupe

Apache Junction

Chandler

Superior

60

Glob

0   10   20   30 miles

Gila River
Indian Crafts
Center and

287

79

Boyce
Thompson
Arboretum

Sacaton

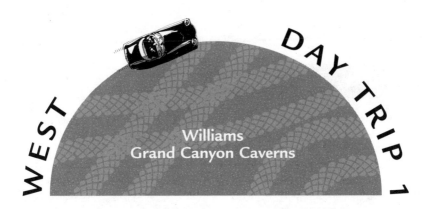

WEST DAY TRIP 1

Williams
Grand Canyon Caverns

WILLIAMS

From Flagstaff, drive west 32 miles on I-40 across the golden mead-owland known as Garland Prairie. During spring and summer, the meadow is a carpet of wildflowers. The fields shimmer with azure blues and dashing reds. As you continue toward Williams, you drive through the pine-scented, lush greenery of the **Kaibab National Forest.**

Called "The Gateway to the Grand Canyon," Williams is named for William S. (or "Old Bill") Williams, a master trapper and Native American scout who traveled on the Santa Fe Trail during the 1820s. A rugged eccentric, he was known to drink and gamble excessively. Called the "lone wolf" of trappers, like many of the mountain men of his day, Old Bill spent most of his time working and sleeping in the wilderness. He only emerged from the mountains long enough to lose his money fast. Then he'd retreat to the wilds to trap and re-stock his supply of furs. Soon he'd reappear in town, get cash, and start the cycle again.

Although mountain men like Old Bill Williams are remembered primarily as trappers, they played a key role in Arizona history. True, they were an environmental disaster, wiping out the entire popula-tions of grizzlies and beavers that once roamed through the forests and swam in the streams. But as explorers, mappers, and later guides for the military, these reclusive individuals provided invaluable ser-vices. Their knowledge of the wilderness made it possible to open the land for the settlers who followed.

283

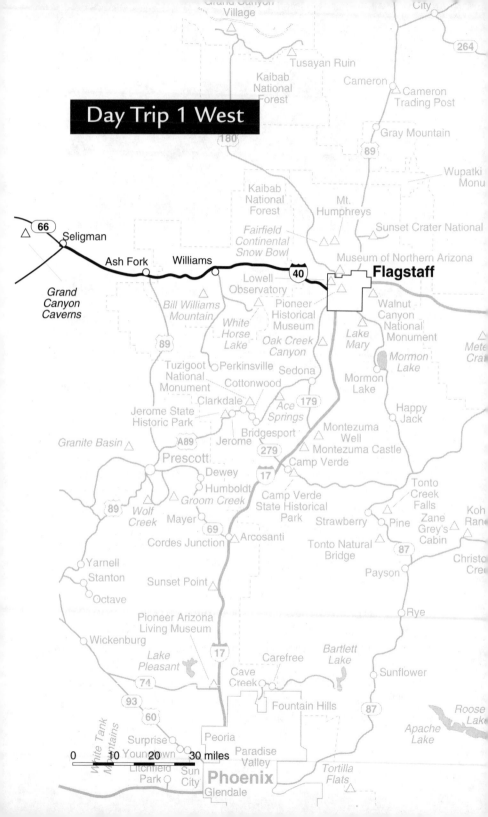

Day Trip 1 West

Grand Canyon Village

City

264

Tusayan Ruin

Kaibab National Forest

Cameron

Cameron Trading Post

180

Gray Mountain

89

Wupatki Monu

Kaibab National Forest

Mt. Humphreys

Sunset Crater National

66

Seligman

Fairfield Continental Snow Bowl

Museum of Northern Arizona

Flagstaff

Grand Canyon Caverns

Ash Fork

Williams

40

Lowell Observatory

Pioneer Historical Museum

Walnut Canyon National Monument

Mete Crat

Bill Williams Mountain

White Horse Lake

Oak Creek Canyon

Lake Mary

Mormon Lake

89

Tuzigoot National Monument

Perkinsville

Cottonwood

Sedona

Mormon Lake

Happy Jack

Clarkdale

Ace Springs

179

Jerome State Historic Park

A89

Bridgesport

Jerome

279

Montezuma Well

Montezuma Castle

Granite Basin

Prescott

Camp Verde

Tonto Creek Falls

Dewey

Humboldt

Groom Creek

17

Camp Verde State Historical Park

Strawberry

Pine

Zane Grey's Cabin

Koh Ran

89

Wolf Creek

Mayer

69

Arcosanti

Tonto Natural Bridge

87

Christo Cree

Cordes Junction

Payson

Yarnell

Stanton

Octave

Sunset Point

Rye

Pioneer Arizona Living Museum

Wickenburg

Lake Pleasant

17

Carefree

Bartlett Lake

Sunflower

74

Cave Creek

87

Roose Lake

93

60

Fountain Hills

Apache Lake

Surprise

Youngtown

Peoria

Paradise Valley

Tortilla Flats

0   10   20   30 miles

Litchfield Park

Sun City

Phoenix

Glendale

Today the spirit of Old Bill Williams is kept alive through the Bill Williams Mountain Men, who have their headquarters in Williams. If you are in town during any of the town's celebrations (see the Festivals and Celebrations section at the end of the book), you may have an opportunity to see them in full regalia, dressed in furs and leather. This group of Williams men meets regularly to celebrate the spirit of Old Bill and reenact the mountain men's unique period of frontier history. They ride in parades, take part in rodeos, and whoop it up in festivities in Williams and elsewhere throughout the state.

Like many northern Arizona communities, Williams is a sportsman's paradise. The town sits in the shadow of Bill Williams Mountain, a 9,286-foot-high peak just south of this small community. Good walking trails scale both sides of the mountain. Seven fishing lakes, many with cabins and boating facilities, surround the town. During the winter, there's a small (450-foot vertical drop) downhill ski run. In addition to skiing, **The Benham Snow Play Area,** just south of town on County Road 173, echoes with "snow tubers," kids and adults careening down snowy slopes in inner tubes. For complete information on camping, fishing, and hiking in the vicinity, visit or write the Williams Grand Canyon Chamber of Commerce, 200 West Railroad Avenue, Williams 86046 or call (928) 635-1418. www.the grandcanyon.com.

WHERE TO GO

DeBerge Gallery of Fine Art and Saddle Shop. 133 West Route 66. The owner not only makes saddles, he also is an artist. The store features a variety of leatherwork, including tack, belts, handbags, and boots. The gallery side includes prints, pottery, carvings, oils, watercolors, and bronzes. (928) 635-2960.

Grand Canyon Deer Farm. 6752 East Deer Farm Road. As you drive toward Williams from Flagstaff, you'll see this unusual petting zoo that faces I-40. It is 8 miles east of Williams and some 24 miles west of Flagstaff. This is a fun stop for families with children. Adults who enjoy observing eight varieties of these graceful animals will also like this farm. Some deer are common to Arizona and other areas of the United States, but there are more unusual types, such as Japanese Sika deer and a herd of Spotted Fallow, a type found in the

Mediterranean. Phone for specific hours. Fee. (928) 635-2357 or (800) 926-DEER. www.deerfarm.com.

The Little Grand Canyon (also called Sycamore Point). Twelve miles south of White Horse Lake on Forest Service Road 110. This is a side trip for adventurous explorers. Locals call this "The Little Grand Canyon," and when you see it, you'll understand why. Follow the paved CR-173 south of Williams (toward Perkinsville and Jerome) to the unpaved Forest Service Road 110, which leads to White Horse Lake. Drive 12 miles south on Forest Service Road 110, a rugged, bumpy road to Sycamore Point. When you arrive, feast your eyes on the steep limestone walls and pillars of sandstone that form this canyon.

Although Oak Creek Canyon offers a more dramatic vertical drop, and the Sedona area has more rocky sculptures, the Little Grand Canyon exudes a solitary beauty. With its rocky spires and stands of aspen, oak, and sycamore, it is largely undiscovered and appeals to those individuals who like the thrill of discovering a majestic, pristine jewel. Rugged adventurers can hike among the cliffs and rock formations. Since there are no established trails or facilities here, inexperienced hikers should not attempt to walk in this wilderness.

Planes of Fame. At Grand Canyon Valle Airport near the junction of A-64 and A-180. Aviation enthusiasts will find this museum to their liking. The original museum is in Claremont, California, and was founded in 1957 by Edward T. Maloney. The collection has grown remarkably since then. This branch of the California museum houses thirty aircraft, all of which are flyable. Among those on display is the aircraft that Gen. Douglas MacArthur used as his personal transport plane. Called the *Bataan*, it is a Lockheed Constellation, and tours of the plane are available for an additional charge. The entrance to the museum is through the airport's terminal at the gift shop. It is the only gift shop in northern Arizona that specializes in aviation artifacts, gifts, books, etc. Open 9:00 A.M. to 6:00 P.M. in summer and 9:00 A.M. to 5:00 P.M. in winter. Fee. (928) 635-1000. www.planesof fame.org.

Steam Train from Williams to the Grand Canyon. 233 Grand Canyon Boulevard. Take I-40 to exit 163, then follow Grand Canyon Boulevard for 1½ miles south to the depot. Steam engines opened the West, so what better way to see the territory than aboard one? The Grand Canyon Railway uses a 1923 Iron Horse to pull restored 1920s Harriman coach cars along original 1901 rails from April 1 through September 30, and a diesel engine October 1 through March 31. Passengers are delivered to the threshold of the Grand Canyon. The train travels at a top speed of 35 miles per hour, so the trip takes about two and one-half hours. Entertainment and refreshments add to the fun, and complimentary soft drinks and snacks are provided. Box lunches may be purchased.

Spend about three hours at the canyon and come back, or stay the night. Summertime is a popular time to ride the rails to the Grand Canyon, but winter snows bring a unique beauty to the area. Ride the new first-class glass-domed car, which gives a 360-degree view of the ever-changing landscape of northern Arizona.

The Grand Canyon RR offers numerous value packages that combine the vintage train travel with a stay at the Fray Marcos and other hotels in both Williams and the canyon. Round-trips operate daily year-round, leaving Williams at 9:30 A.M. $$; ☐. For information on fares, schedules, and special overnight packages at the canyon, call (800) THE-TRAIN (800-843-8724). www.thetrain.com.

WHERE TO EAT

Max and Thelma's. Located adjacent to the Historic Williams Depot. Max and Thelma's is named for the owners of the Grand Canyon RR. The restaurant features an all-you-can-eat buffet and menu entrees. $-$$; ☐. (928) 635-8970.

Rod's Steak House. 301 East Route 66. Established in 1946, Rod's bills itself as "world famous," and since it has survived for more than fifty years, who can argue with that? The menu includes steaks, seafood, prime rib, ribs, and chicken. Lunch and dinner are served in this "roadhouse" style restaurant. $$; ☐. (928) 635-2671.

WHERE TO STAY

The Fray Marcos Hotel. 235 North Grand Canyon Boulevard. From I-40, take Williams exit 163 to Grand Canyon Boulevard. Go ½ mile south to the Grand Canyon Railway complex. This new hotel offers eighty-nine rooms, all decorated in classic Southwest style. Spencer's Lounge features a beautifully carved wooden bar, which was bought in London and lovingly reassembled in Williams. It was originally carved in England by George O. Spencer, a London cabinetmaker. As part of his agreement, he had the privilege of drinking free at the bar. $$. Reservations: (928 635–4010. www.thetrain.com.

In recent years, Williams has started a new cottage industry—B&Bs. All are clean and comfortable. Here are a few favorites:

Red Garter Bed & Bakery. 137 Railroad Avenue. Stay upstairs in a restored 1897 saloon and bordello and enjoy the aroma of fresh-baked croissants and pastries being made in the bakery on the first floor. Timid souls need to know that there's a ghost reported to live on the premises. A cowboy was thrown down the steep flight of stairs (known in its day as the "Cowboy's Endurance Test"), and his spirit continues to float around the place. $$; ☐. (928) 635–1484. www.redgarter.com.

Sheridan House Inn. 460 East Sheridan. This private home-turned-inn offers eleven suites, each with private bath. The owners serve a full breakfast. Located among the pines in a residential neighborhood, this inn features a flagstone patio with a hot tub, a pool room, and entertainment centers for guests to enjoy. $$; ☐. (928) 635–9441 or (888) 635–1484. E-mail: egardner@primenet.com.

Terry Ranch Bed & Breakfast. 701 Quarterhorse Road. The owners have furnished their log home with antiques and offer four guest suites, each with private bath and king beds. Rooms have fireplaces and verandas. Full gourmet breakfast is served. $$; ☐. (928) 635–4171.

GRAND CANYON CAVERNS

Continue west approximately 44 miles on I-40 through Ash Fork, which calls itself the "Flagstone Capitol of the World," and go on to Seligman. Exit the interstate and pick up A-66, or "Old 66." Follow A-66 about 25 miles to the Grand Canyon Caverns.

Here is one of the world's largest completely dry cave systems. Meandering twenty-one stories beneath the earth, Grand Canyon Caverns are known to be closely related geologically to the Grand Canyon. Yet because of the off-the-beaten path location, tourists often ignore them. Professional cave explorers are well acquainted with the caverns, and excavation goes on continuously because experts are certain that more rocky rooms wait to be discovered.

You'll enter through a commercial center, which has a coffee shop, motel, gift shop, and airstrip for private planes. A forty-five-minute guided tour leads you through the expanse of vaulted rooms, filled with colorful rock formations. You'll wander through mysterious passageways and hear an intriguing commentary about the history of the caves. For all its wild beauty, this is a comfortable experience for explorers of all ages; the paths are paved, and the formations are well lit.

The caverns became well known in 1927 when a heavy rain widened the natural funnel-shaped opening to the upper level. However, the Hualapai (Wal-pee) Indians, a tribe that lived here centuries ago, were familiar with that level of the caverns. Even today, elders caution young people that the original entrance is a sacred place and should be observed as such.

From fossils embedded in the redwall limestone, scientists have determined that many prehistoric sea and land dwellers once lived in these caves. Fossils of a giant ground sloth, estimated to have lived here more than 20,000 years ago, were also discovered in the caverns. Call for hours. Fee. (928) 422-3223. www.gcc@seligmannet.com.

To return to Flagstaff, follow old A-66 east to Seligman. Pick up I-40 east through Williams to Flagstaff.

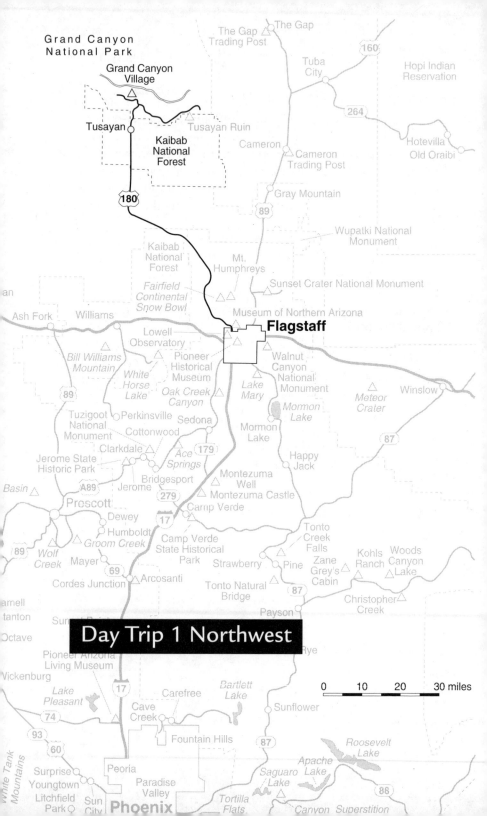

Grand Canyon
National Park

Grand Canyon
Village △

Tusayan ◯
Tusayan Ruin

Kaibab
National
Forest

The Gap
Trading Post   The Gap

160

Tuba
City

264

Hopi Indian
Reservation

Cameron

Hotevilla
Old Oraibi

Cameron
Trading Post

US 180

Gray Mountain

89

Wupatki National
Monument

Kaibab
National
Forest

Fairfield
Continental
Snow Bowl

Mt.
Humphreys △ △

Sunset Crater National Monument

Museum of Northern Arizona

Flagstaff

Ash Fork

Williams

an

Lowell
Observatory

Pioneer
Historical
Museum

Walnut
Canyon
National
Monument

Winslow

Meteor
Crater

Bill Williams
Mountain

White
Horse
Lake

Oak Creek
Canyon

Lake
Mary

Mormon
Lake

89

Tuzigoot
National
Monument

Perkinsville

Cottonwood

Sedona

179

Mormon
Lake

87

Clarkdale

Ace
Springs

Happy
Jack

Jerome State
Historic Park

Jerome

Bridgesport

Montezuma
Well

279

Montezuma Castle

Tonto
Creek
Falls

Zane
Grey's
Cabin

Kohls
Ranch

Woods
Canyon
Lake

Basin △

A89

Camp Verde

Prescott

Dewey

17

Humboldt

Groom Creek

Camp Verde
State Historical
Park

Strawberry

Pine

Christopher
Creek

89

Wolf
Creek

Mayer

69

Arcosanti

Tonto Natural
Bridge

87

arnell
tanton

Cordes Junction

Payson

Octave

Sun

Rye

Day Trip 1 Northwest

Pioneer Arizona
Living Museum

Vickenburg

17

Carefree

Bartlett
Lake

Sunflower

0   10   20   30 miles

Lake
Pleasant

74

Cave
Creek

Fountain Hills

87

Roosevelt
Lake

93

60

Apache
Lake

88

Surprise
Youngtown
Litchfield
Park

Peoria

Paradise
Valley

Saguaro
Lake

White Tank
Mountains

Sun
City

Phoenix

Tortilla
Flats

Canyon Superstition

The South Rim of
the Grand Canyon

THE SOUTH RIM OF THE GRAND CANYON

From Flagstaff, drive north on US–180 approximately 60 miles to Grand Canyon Village, headquarters for this most spectacular national park. All visitors to Arizona put the Grand Canyon at the top of their "must see" list, but few realize that the Grand Canyon is actually two parks: the North Rim and the South Rim. The South Rim is closer to Phoenix, located 223 miles north of that city, and is open to tourists all year. The more rugged and remote North Rim is a 230-mile drive from the southern park. Although it is possible to "do" the South Rim of the Grand Canyon in a long day's trip starting and ending in Phoenix, the experience is exhausting. It is far better to use Flagstaff as your headquarters if you plan to see the canyon in one day. Better yet, stay overnight in the Grand Canyon park area.

Should you decide to see both rims, you'll be in for two distinctly different experiences. The North Rim, more than 1,000 feet higher than the South Rim, is the more remote and rugged park. It is closed from late fall to mid-spring because the roads are snowed in from about late October through mid-May. Facilities at the North Rim exist on a smaller, more rustic scale. In contrast, although the facilities at the South Rim are superb, it's often crowded during the summer.

The fascination with the Grand Canyon spans every age, nationality, and experience. The view into the chasm appears to be pure illusion, for it seems that nothing can be that deep, that mysterious, that endless. While volumes have been written about its majesty, no words or pictures can do justice to the happy shock of coming upon it. One writer notes that people who stare across and into the magnificent abyss, no matter how many pictures they've seen of it, find themselves instinctively looking back to check that the earth they're standing on is solid.

Although you may suppose that it will be enough for you to just stand and gaze at this massive split in the heart of the earth, once you arrive you'll discover that you may want to participate more fully in the canyon experience. Then you must decide how to do it, for there are many ways to see the South Rim. You can travel on foot, on horseback, or cling to a mule. You can view the Grand Canyon from the top down: flying over it in a small plane or helicopter; or from the bottom up: riding the torrents of the Colorado River rapids. For more information on the South Rim, call the National Park Service at (928) 638-7888. During the busy tourist season (spring, summer, and early fall), you'll need reservations for either camping or lodging facilities. You must also make prior arrangements if you plan to journey into the canyon for an overnight hike or pack trip, because overnight hikers and campers must have permits. As with all national parks, there is an entrance fee. www.thecanyon.com/nps.

WHERE TO GO

Grand Canyon IMAX Theatre. Seven miles south of the South Rim on A-64/US-180 in Tusayan (Too-see-an). If you haven't experienced an IMAX film, you're in for a treat. An IMAX film puts you into the action. You sit surrounded by a six-track soundtrack, looking up at a 70-foot-high screen. Even if you've seen any of the other IMAX films (they cover many subjects, from time to outer space), see this one especially if this is your first trip to the Grand Canyon. The IMAX Theatre is a superb introduction to the history and geology of the Kaibab Plateau and the Grand Canyon and is a film that children and adults of all ages will greatly enjoy. *The Grand Canyon—The Hidden Secrets* is the most popular IMAX production shown in this country. In thirty-four minutes you get a crash course on the Grand Canyon and the Colorado River and their geography, geology, history, and anthropology.

Thanks to the wonders of photographic magic, you even experience a wild river ride down the rapids of the Colorado River. The film is shown daily. For schedule information telephone or write to The Grand Canyon IMAX Theatre, P.O. Box 1397, Grand Canyon 86023-1397. Fee. (928) 638-2203. www.imaxtheatre.com/grandcanyon.

Visitors Center. In the Grand Canyon National Park, 1 mile east of Grand Canyon Village on Village Loop Drive. This should be your first stop once you enter the park. No matter how you choose to experience the canyon, you'll get more out of it if you have an understanding of how grand it really is.

Spend some time studying the exhibits and dioramas that describe the formation of the canyon and the flora and fauna in the area. You'll find brochures and information on several self-guided walking tours that traverse the rim. Here you can also pick up trail maps for hiking into the canyon and get information on driving tours along the East Rim and West Rim drives.

East Rim Drive. A paved road leads from the visitors center past the **Yavapai Museum,** a delightful and informative geological facility, to Mather, Yaki, and Grand View points. The road continues to Desert View, a spectacular lookout 25 miles east of Grand Canyon Village. Along the way, you may stop at any of the turnoffs to experience the panorama of the Canyon. This is an especially impressive drive in the early morning hours or just before sunset, when the colors of the canyon are their richest.

West Rim Drive. This takes you past Powell Memorial and Hopi, Mohave, and Pima Points—equally outstanding places from which to observe the majesty of the canyon. This drive ends at Hermit's Rest. From April through September, the West Rim road is limited to tour buses to relieve traffic congestion and help preserve the ecological integrity of the canyon. For information about the bus tours, inquire at the visitors center.

Don't leave the visitors center without browsing through the selection of scientific and illustrated books for sale. The more you can learn about the canyon, the more you'll enjoy your visit. Even nonscientific types should know that this region encompasses five of the Northern Hemisphere's seven ecological zones, and that no other place in the world so clearly illustrates such a vast panorama of time. Free. (928) 638-7888.

El Tovar Hotel. On Village Loop Drive. From the visitors center follow Village Loop Drive west about ½ mile to the first right turn. This road takes you to the parking lot for El Tovar. Even if you do not intend to stay or eat at this hotel (see Where to Eat and Where to Stay sections), make it a point to visit this historic place. El Tovar is a rambling, wooden hotel that has long served as headquarters for activity at the South Rim. On any day, as you stand in the spacious, high-ceilinged lobby, you may hear a dozen different languages, see sunburned hikers who have just emerged from the canyon floor, listen to river rafters still riding high on their exhilaration, and see celebrities and dignitaries who have come to relax in the stately splendor afforded by this charming setting. (928) 638-2631.

Bright Angel Trail. As you leave El Tovar, turn left and follow the Rim Walk toward Bright Angel Lodge. There's a sign pointing to the Bright Angel Trail, a well-maintained hiking path that twists and turns $20\%_{10}$ miles into the canyon floor.

For the first ½ mile, Bright Angel is gentle enough for even non-hikers to negotiate without any special equipment other than good walking shoes. However, as you peer down the trail from the rim, you'll see a splash of deep green in the distance. The green glistens against the sun-bleached yellows, oranges, and peach tones of the Grand Canyon. This is **Indian Gardens,** a $4\%_{10}$-mile hike from the top. The trek to Indian Gardens takes you through manufactured tunnels and down a series of steep switchbacks. You can rest and picnic at this remarkable natural oasis, which is shaded by tall cottonwood trees. The hike to Indian Gardens is an excellent round-trip day experience that gives you a good workout and a sense of the serenity of the inner canyon.

The less ambitious may prefer a fifteen-minute walk down Bright Angel Trail. Go at least as far as the first tunnel or hole-in-the-rock. Remember, it will take you twice as long, or a half hour, to walk back up. Even this short excursion will give you a feeling for the grandeur of the canyon, an understanding that you can never get from standing at the rim and looking down into it.

WHERE TO EAT

El Tovar. In the park on Village Loop Drive. Count on hearty breakfasts and superb views from the dining room window. Pancakes are light and fluffy, and the syrup is hot. Lunches and dinners are more elegant. The food and the service rival those of any fine restaurant in the Phoenix or Tucson areas. During the spring, summer, and early fall, reservations are recommended for dinner. $$; ☐. (928) 638-2631.

WHERE TO STAY

El Tovar. In the park on Village Loop Drive. Fred Harvey Inc., P.O. Box 699, Grand Canyon 86023. Because this is a historic hotel, each room is different—some large and airy, others smaller—but the accommodations are uniformly charming. If you are looking for atmosphere and convenience, El Tovar is an outstanding choice. $$; ☐. (928) 638-2631.

The Grand Hotel. About a mile south of the entrance to the Grand Canyon National Park on US-180/A-64 in Tucson. This newer hotel enjoys architecture reminiscent of the historic, grand hotels of the Old West. In addition to 120 fine rooms, some with balconies, the property includes an indoor pool and spa, shopping, and dining in the Canyon Star restaurant. The most unique feature, however, is the emphasis on educating visitors about the Native Americans who lived in and around the Grand Canyon before Europeans "discovered" this area. Workshops are scheduled along with Native American dance groups, singers and drummers, storytellers, and art and craft demonstrations. $$; ☐. (928) 638-3333. E-mail: thegrand@gcanyon.com.

WHAT ELSE TO DO

Colorado River Trips. Motor-powered raft and rowing trips are regularly scheduled down the Colorado River during the summer months. Various kinds of boats and trips are geared to different types of travelers. You can choose anything from a rugged few weeks of boating and hiking to an exciting but still relaxing experience.

If you plan only one "outdoorsy" experience in your lifetime, this should be it. Nothing beats it. The Colorado River not only has the most rapids, but the most exciting rapids of any river, and there is only one Grand Canyon in the entire world to provide such a glorious backdrop for the thrills. If you're worried about roughing it, don't be. There are plenty of luxuries, including excellent food and even cakes baked fresh on the beach. For thrills in an incomparable setting, this trip cannot be equaled.

Would-be river rats (the local terminology for those who've run the river) should be in good physical condition. Each rafting company has its own list of requirements. Fee. For a complete listing of companies, write or telephone the National Park Service at the Grand Canyon. Address inquiries to the Superintendent, Grand Canyon National Park, Grand Canyon 86023, or call (928) 638-7888.

Hiking and Backpacking. Day hiking, whether for one hour or from sunrise to sunset, requires no permit. Day hikers are entirely on their own in the canyon—this means that if you plan to hike any of the trails, you are responsible for bringing your own water and allotting one-third of your time to hike down and two-thirds of your time to hike back up.

There are no loop trails for day hikers. Your hike will take you on the same trail in both directions. Great trails beckon. These include the West Rim and South Rim trails, which are moderate-to-easy hikes, and the hike down to Indian Gardens and back, which is more strenuous. The South Kaibab Trail and Grandview Trail are both quite difficult. The Grandview Trail is unmaintained, steep, and is recommended only for experienced hikers. The Hermit Trail, like the Grandview Trail, is very strenuous, steep, and not maintained. Casual hikers should avoid both of these.

If you plan to hike into the canyon, a day hike beyond Three-Mile Resthouse is *not* recommended, as hikers who continue beyond this point have a much greater probability of heat-related illness. Under no circumstances should hikers attempt to hike from the rim to the river and back in one day. It is important, when hiking into the canyon, never to hike in the heat of the day, especially in the warmer months, and to be equipped with good hiking shoes and a hat. The Grand Canyon is a vast and wonderful natural landscape, but you must respect it.

Permits and fees are required to camp below the rim; the current cost for a permit is $20. In addition, you are charged an impact fee of $4.00. To obtain an overnight camping permit, call or fax the Backcountry Office. Beginning with the first day of a month, permit requests are accepted for a proposed trip start date in that month and the following four months. For example, beginning on December 1, 2001, permit requests for any start date through April 30, 2002, are accepted. Permit requests must be sent to Backcountry Office, P.O. Box 129, Grand Canyon 86023. They can also be faxed to (520) 638-2125. Call (520) 638-7875 for more information.

Muleback Trips. Mules descend the Bright Angel Trail at the South Rim on full-day, half-day, and overnight trips. This is a strenuous trip—good physical condition is a must. A weight restriction for riders is enforced. Reservations are mandatory from May through October. Fee. For information about these excursions, contact Grand Canyon National Park Lodges, Reservations Department, P.O. Box 699, Grand Canyon 86023, or call (928) 638-2401.

DIRECTORY
Festivals and Celebrations

PHOENIX AREA

Fiesta Bowl Day, Tempe. This is becoming one of the major college bowls in the country and each year attracts top university football talent. (480) 350-0900.

Glendale's Glitter & Glow, Glendale. Held in Murphy Park, this festival features hot-air balloons and twinkling holiday lights, music, and artists. Free. (623) 930-2299.

Barrett-Jackson Desert Classic Road Rally, Scottsdale. Rare, historic car—worth $100,000 and more—rally. (480) 421-6694.

Phoenix Open Golf Tournament, Tournament Players Course, Scottsdale. One of the PGA Tour's top golf events, this draws the largest crowds on the tour. (602) 870-4431.

TUCSON AREA

Southern Arizona Square & Round Dance Festival, Tucson. Square dancing, clogging, and round dancing performances are judged in this annual event. (520) 885-6273 or (520) 795-8288.

American Hot Rod Association's Winter Nationals, Tucson. The biggest national drag race goes on for four days at Tucson Dragway. (520) 791-4873.

FEBRUARY

PHOENIX AREA

Lost Dutchman Days, Apache Junction. The Lost Dutchman lives again each year during the three-day rodeo, parade, arts-and-crafts exhibit, antique car show, and carnival. (480) 982-3141.

Parada del Sol, Scottsdale. Enjoy top professional rodeo, an elaborate horse-drawn parade, and Wild West fun. Scottsdale celebrates the entire week as the town dresses, thinks, and acts western. (480) 945-8481.

Yuma Crossing Day, Yuma. This festival celebrates the "Crossing of the Fathers," when the Spanish crossed the Colorado River into Arizona to settle the territory. Dance performances and exhibits are held at cultural and historical facilities throughout the area. Horse-drawn wagons shuttle visitors to and from each facility. (928) 783-0071.

Quartzsite Annual Gem and Mineral Show, Quartzsite. Thousands of rock hounds flock each year to this tiny desert community to buy and sell at one of the world's largest gem and mineral shows. See demonstrations of rock tumbling and learn about the world of gems. (928) 927-6325.

TUCSON AREA

La Fiesta de Los Vaqueros, Tucson. This is Tucson's big rodeo. Usually held in February, it is kicked off by the longest nonmechanized parade in the world. (520) 792-1212 or (520) 741-2233.

Tubac Arts Festival, Tubac. A nine-day outdoor festival featuring international craftspeople. Demonstrations, exhibits, and food booths make this a perennial favorite. (520) 398-2704.

FLAGSTAFF AREA

Winterfest, Flagstaff. Events include sled-dog races, llama games, cross-country and downhill skiing, sleigh and snowmobile races, and winter sports. Even fun in years when there's no snow. (928) 774-4505 or (800) 842-7293.

MARCH

PHOENIX AREA

Phoenix Rodeo of Rodeos, Phoenix. Professional cowboys converge on Phoenix to compete in a national indoor rodeo of top caliber. An impressive parade in downtown Phoenix highlights the week's festivities. (602) 254-6500.

Old Town Tempe Spring Festival of the Arts, Tempe. The center of Tempe becomes a shopper's paradise as artists and craftspeople from all over the country set up booths to show and sell their wares. You'll find everything from "junque" to true art—often at bargain prices. (602) 967-4877.

O'odham Day Celebration, Organ Pipe Cactus National Monument, near Ajo. Exhibits and demonstrations illustrate traditional arts, crafts, and farming at this beautiful national monument. Free. (520) 387-6849.

Scottsdale Center for the Arts Annual Arts Festival, Center for the Arts, Scottsdale. Rated among the top in the country, this juried fair brings 185 artists, performances, artist demonstrations, and presentations to eight stages. (480) 994-ARTS.

TUCSON AREA

Annual Civil War battle re-enactment at Picacho Peak State Park, halfway between Tucson and Phoenix. Picacho Peak was the only battle fought in Arizona during the Civil War. (520) 466-3183 or (602) 542-4174.

Tombstone Territorial Days, Tombstone. This tiny town celebrates its beginnings with a carnival of fun. Shoot-outs, the Arizona Firehose Cart Championship, and a pet parade make this fun. (520) 457-2211.

APRIL

PHOENIX AREA

Arid Land Plant Show, Superior. Held at the Boyce Thompson Southwestern Arboretum, this show features a wide variety of drought-resistant trees, shrubs, cacti, and succulents from as far away as Australia and Africa. Gardeners find this a great place to look, browse, and buy. Learn how nature equips these beautiful, unusual plants to survive in water-short lands. (520) 689–2811.

Heard Museum Indian Fair, Phoenix. Stroll around the museum grounds and see dances, arts, crafts, and exhibits from many Arizona Native American tribes. Munch on delicious Navajo fry bread, made hot on the grounds, and other native delicacies. Bring the entire family for this popular, authentic Native American fair. (602) 252–8848.

TUCSON AREA

San Xavier (Ha-veer) Pageant and Fiesta, San Xavier Mission. This dramatic event is held the Friday after Easter and begins in the late afternoon with more than one hundred Native American dancers celebrating the history of the mission. As night falls, one hundred bonfires are lit, and the coming of Father Garces, who built the present mission, and Father Kino, who opened the land for the Spanish, is commemorated through narration and drama. More than twenty costumed horsemen ride into the area lit by bonfires, and the evening ends with a spectacular procession of worshippers, the joyous pealing of bells, and fireworks. Throughout the weekend, the Tohono O'odham Indians host a food and crafts market. (520) 792–1212 or (520) 294–2624.

Fiesta de la Placita, Tucson. The Hispanic community of Tucson turns out for a bilingual, full-fledged Mexican fiesta full of slowly simmered Mexican food, piñata games, dancing, and music. Everyone, regardless of heritage, is invited to attend. (520) 792–1212 or (800) 638–8350.

MAY

PHOENIX AREA

George Phippen Memorial Invitational Western Art Show and Sale, Prescott. This show, held over Memorial Day weekend, attracts western artists from all over the country. Well-known names compete for medals, and unknowns have a chance to be discovered.

There's an art auction and reception so that the public can meet the show's painters and sculptors. (928) 445-2000 or (928) 778-1385.

Annual Square Dance Festival, Prescott. Pick up some new twists and dips and watch teams from around the country compete in this most American dance experience. This is a fun festival for dancers and toe-tappers. (928) 445-2000.

FLAGSTAFF AREA

Bill Williams Rendezvous Days, Williams. This festival is held on Memorial Day weekend. In addition to the in-town arts and crafts booths, cow-chip throwing contests, live music, and food booths, the Williams city park hosts an authentic Mountain Men Rendezvous. Here men and women from around the country camp (1840s-style) in tepees and compete in authentic mountain man black-powder events. The "Raw Egg Shoot" is a favorite. If a contestant misses the egg, he eats it. See mountain men compete in the "Seneca Run," which combines all wilderness skills into one marathon event. Men must shoot, throw a tomahawk, canoe, run, set a bear trap, and light a fire. (928) 635-0273.

JUNE

PHOENIX AREA

June Bug Blues Festival, Payson. All kinds of bands, including blue-grass, country, and buck-dancing, compete in this nationally recognized music festival. (928) 474-4515.

International Innertube Race, Parker. Hundreds of people, dressed in outlandish costumes, converge on the Colorado River to compete in a 7-mile race. (928) 669-2174.

JULY

PHOENIX AREA

Prescott Frontier Days and Rodeo, Prescott. The town turns out for the Fourth of July weekend in flag-waving frontier style, with a glittering parade, rugged professional rodeo (the oldest rodeo in the country), dancing, and general wild fun. In Arizona, Prescott's Whiskey Row is the place to be this weekend. (928) 445–2000 or (928) 455–3103.

AUGUST

PHOENIX AREA

Payson Annual Continuous Rodeo, Payson. See the world's oldest continuously held professional rodeo. Watch cowboys from around the world ride bucking broncos and rope steers while they compete for big money. The rodeo weekend includes all kinds of western festivities. (928) 474–4515.

FLAGSTAFF AREA

Arizona Cowpunchers' Reunion and Old Timers' Rodeo, Williams. If you want to see real, working cowboys, this is the place to come. Only working cowboys are allowed to compete. All events involve skills cowboys use in their profession. Spectators can watch three-man teams compete in a wild-horse race where men must catch, saddle, and ride a wild horse across a finish line. Another favorite is the wild-cow milking contest, where two-man teams rope and milk a cow, catching the milk in a Coke bottle. This is not as crazy as it sounds, because often a wild cow won't nurse her baby. Cowboys must catch and milk the cow, then put the milk into a Coke bottle so they can save the young calf. (928) 635–0273.

SEPTEMBER

PHOENIX AREA

Annual State Championship Old Time Fiddlers Contest, Payson. This is one of Payson's most famous festivals. You can hear fiddlers from all over the state compete with their fanciest fingerwork. This is a delightful art form for spectators as well as contestants. (928) 474–4515.

National Indian Day, Parker. This is celebrated in Manataba Park the last Friday of September and the following Saturday. The four tribes in the area, as well as others from throughout the Southwest, converge for traditional games, singing, dances, and other activities. Arts and crafts and traditional foods are sold. The celebration begins in midafternoon and picks up toward evening. (928) 669–2174.

FLAGSTAFF AREA

Annual Navajo Nation Fair, Window Rock. Window Rock is the headquarters for the Navajo Nation. Feast your eyes on fine Navajo arts and crafts and your tummies on hot Navajo fry bread dripping with honey. There's even a Navajo fry bread–making contest, as well as horse racing, rodeos, a parade, and an authentic Native American powwow. Other events include a 10,000-meter run and a traditional Navajo singing and dancing competition. (928) 871–6478.

OCTOBER

PHOENIX AREA

Arizona State Fair, Phoenix. Livestock shows, exhibits, big-name entertainment, and a carnival are just part of the action when the annual state fair comes to town. (602) 252–6771. www.azstatefair.com.

TUCSON AREA

Helldorado Days, Tombstone. This is the event that puts Tombstone on the map every year. If you ever wondered what the Old West was like, come to Helldorado Days and find out. Shoot-outs, a fast-draw contest, and a parade add to the general Wild West craziness. (520) 457–2211.

NOVEMBER

PHOENIX AREA

Fountain Festival of the Arts, Fountain Hills. More than 200 artists, artisans, and craftspeople move into Fountain Hills for a three-day show and sale. The juried competition attracts some of the finest artists in the country. The pottery and sculpture are always outstanding. (480) 837–1654. www.fhchamberofcommerce.org.

Annual Swiss Village Christmas Lighting, Payson. Set among Payson's pine forests, the Swiss village looks amazingly appropriate when dressed for Christmas. The celebration brings out the entire town. (928) 474–4515.

DECEMBER

Nearly every community has a Christmas tradition. Festivals abound. For a more complete listing, consult the Chamber of Commerce in each city or call the Arizona Office of Tourism at (602) 230–7733. The following is a sampling of what happens during the holiday season:

PHOENIX AREA

Old Town Tempe Fall Festival of the Arts, Tempe. If you miss the Spring Festival, come to this one. Mill Avenue, the main street of town, becomes a bazaar of arts, crafts, and unusual collectibles as artists set up booths to show their wares. The art on display is often terrific and always interesting. (480) 967–7891 or (480) 967–4877.

Pueblo Grande Indian Market, Phoenix. Held at South Mountain Park Activity Center, this market attracts more than 450 Native American artists who set up shop to sell their wares. Food and entertainment make this a fun market in which to browse and buy. (602) 495–0901.

Victorian Christmas at Heritage Square, Phoenix. Phoenix turns back the clock to the 1800s as Dickens comes to the desert. The dress at this celebration is heavy with velvet and lace. Christmas stories are read aloud, choirs sing, and the historical district glows with the spirit of Christmases past. (602) 262–5071.

Wickenburg Annual Cowboy Christmas Cowboy Poets Gathering, Wickenburg. Held at the Community Center and Desert Caballeros Western Museum. Poetry, ballads, and stories make this a special western celebration. (928) 684–5479.

Christmas Parade and Courthouse Lighting, Prescott. With its Victorian setting in place all year long, Christmas comes naturally to Prescott. The entire town turns out for the parade and comes to the square to see the courthouse blaze with colorful lights. (520) 445-2000.

TUCSON AREA

Annual Fourth Street Fair, Tucson. An arts-and-crafts and performance fair held downtown on Fourth Avenue. (520) 624-5004 or (800) 933-2477.

Luminaria Night, Tucson. The Tucson Botanical Garden is lit by hundreds of luminarias (lighted votive candles nestled in brown paper bags that are filled partway with sand). Mariachis, bands, Yaqui Indian dancers, and other musicians add to the festivities. (520) 624-1817.

Tumacacori Fiesta, Tumacacori. Folk dancing, music, food, and crafts from many of Santa Cruz County's cultural groups make this a special Southwestern holiday celebration. (520) 398-2341.

Christmas Boat Parade of Lights, Lake Havasu. Watch as gaily trimmed and lit houseboats glide across Lake Havasu in an unusual salute to the season. (520) 855-2178.

Holiday boat parades also are held on Lake Powell, Lake Mead, and Lake Mohave. Check with the local Chambers of Commerce at Page, (520) 645-2741; Bullhead City, (520) 754-4121; and Parker, (520) 669-2174, for dates and times.

FLAGSTAFF AREA

Sedona Annual Festival of Lights, Sedona. Entertainment and 6,000 luminarias light up Tlaquepaque. The town shines for the holidays. (520) 282-4838 or (877) 386-8687.

Annual Christmas Arts and Crafts Fair, Window Rock. Sponsored by the Navajo Nation Library. (928) 871-7303 or (928) 871-6376.

National Parks

Arizona is studded with a wonderland of national parks, monuments, and forests. Although the state is vast in its physical size, popular parks can fill up quickly. It's always wise to write or call ahead for information, instructions, camping permits, and other details when planning a visit to a national recreation site.

Apache-Sitgreaves National Forest
P.O. Box 640
Springerville, AZ 85938
(928) 333-4301
www.fs.fed.us/r3/asnf

Canyon de Chelly National Monument
P.O. Box 588
Chinle, AZ 86503
(928) 674-5500
www.nps.gov/cach

Coconino National Forest
2323 East Greenlaw Lane
Flagstaff, AZ 86004
(928) 527-3600
www.fs.fed.us/r3/coconino

Grand Canyon National Park
Back Country Reservation Office
P.O. Box 129
Grand Canyon, AZ 86023
(928) 638-7888
www.thecanyon.com/nps

Kaibab National Forest
200 West Railroad Avenue
Williams, AZ 86046
(928) 635-4707 or (800) 863-0546 (for the visitors center)
www.fs.fed.us/r3/kai

In addition to forests, monuments, and parks operated by the federal goverment, other public land in Arizona is under direction of the U.S. Bureau of Land Management (BLM). Information about hiking or camping on BLM lands is available from the following address:

Bureau of Land Management
Arizona State Office
222 North Central
Phoenix, AZ 85004
(602) 417-9200
www.az.blm.gov

Native American Reservations

Arizona is home to twenty-one Native American tribes that represent more than 160,000 people. A total of twenty reservations cover more than nineteen million acres. As you read this list, you will see many hyphenated tribal names. Over the years, the U.S. government has combined tribes, giving them new homes together on a single reservation. Nevertheless, each has managed to retain its own distinct heritage.

Visitors who wish to travel on Native American reservations may do so without prior permission. If, however, you want to know where to go to buy arts or crafts or observe dances, celebrations, or rodeos, you should call ahead or write to the tribal office for dates, times, and locations. Following is a brief description and location of each tribe:

Ak-Chin Reservation, 56 miles south of Phoenix in Pinal County. This tribe is noted for basketry. Ak-Chin Indian Community, 42507 West Peters and Nall Road, Maricopa, AZ 85239, (520) 568-2227.

Camp Verde Reservation, 94 miles north of Phoenix in Yavapai County. This reservation includes Montezuma Castle National Monument and Montezuma Well. Basketry is the major art form. Yavapai-Apache Indian Community, P.O. Box 1188, Camp Verde, AZ 86322, (928) 567-3649.

Cocopah East and West Reservation, 12 miles southwest of Yuma in Yuma County. This tribe is well known for its intricate beadwork. Cocopah Tribal Council, County 15, Bin "G," Somerton, AZ 85350, (928) 627-2102.

Colorado River Reservation, 189 miles west of Phoenix in Yuma County. Collectors may want to buy baskets, beadwork, and Native American–motif wall clocks made by these tribes. Colorado River Indian Tribes, Route 1, Box 23-B, Parker, AZ 85344, (928) 669-9211.

Fort Apache Reservation, 194 miles northeast of Phoenix in Apache, Gila, and Navajo Counties. The Apache Tribe owns and operates Apache Sunrise Resort, a ski lodge and resort facility. Skiing aside, the people create excellent beadwork and the highly prized "Burden Baskets," wonderfully woven baskets that are trimmed with leather thongs and silver metal "bells." White Mountain Apache Tribe, P.O. Box 700, Whiteriver, AZ 85941, (928) 338-4346. www.wmat.nsn.us.

Fort McDowell Reservation, 36 miles northeast of Phoenix in Maricopa County. The Fort McDowell Indians manufacture jojoba bean oil, which is a superb substitute for the environmentally scarce whale oil. Basketry is a specialty. Yavapai Nation Tribal Council, P.O. Box 17779, Fountain Hills, AZ 85268, (480) 837-5121.

Fort Mojave Reservation, 236 miles northwest of Phoenix in Mohave County. This reservation borders Arizona, Nevada, and California; tribal headquarters are located in California. The Fort Mojave Indians are noted for their beadwork. Fort Mojave Tribal Council, 500 Merriman Avenue, Needles, CA 92363, (760) 629-4591.

Gila (Hee-la) River Reservation, 40 miles south of Phoenix in Maricopa and Pinal Counties. Pima basketry and Maricopa pottery are prized native items. Gila River Indian Community, P.O. Box 97, Sacaton, AZ 85247, (480) 963-4323 or (520) 562-3311.

Havasupai (Have-a-sue-pie) Reservation, at the bottom of the Grand Canyon via an 8-mile trail from Hilltop to Supai. The people of the "Blue-Green Waters" are best known for their exquisite, remote reservation, reachable only by mule or foot. The Havasupais produce basketry and beadwork. Havasupai Tribal Council, P.O. Box 10, Supai, AZ 86435, (928) 448-2961 or (928) 448-2731.

Hopi (Hoe-pee) Reservation, 323 miles northeast of Phoenix in Coconino and Navajo Counties. The Hopi produce an assortment of art and collectibles. Basketry and plaques are exquisite, but Hopi are better known for hand-carved and painted kachina dolls, which are spirits of the gods worshipped by this tribe. The Hopi are also leaders in silver and gold jewelry, crafts, and pottery. Hopi Tribal Council, P.O. Box 123, Kyakotsmovi, AZ 86039, (928) 448-2731.

Hualapai (Wall-pie) Reservation, 252 miles northwest of Phoenix in Coconino, Yavapai, and Mohave Counties. Dolls and basketry are the primary art forms of this tribe. Hualapai Tribal Council, P.O. Box 179, Peach Springs, AZ 86434, (520) 769-2216.

Kaibab-Paiute (Kigh-bab–Pie-ute) Reservation, 398 miles north of Phoenix in Mohave County. This tribe specializes in coiled, shallow baskets known as "wedding baskets." Kaibab-Paiute Tribal Council, Tribal Affairs Building, 8C65, Box 2, Fredonia, AZ 86022, (928) 643-7245.

Navajo Reservation, 356 miles northeast of Phoenix in Apache, Coconino, and Navajo Counties. Best known for their museum-quality, hand-woven rugs and blankets, the Navajo also create magnificent silver crafts and some basketry. Cultural Resources Department Visitor Services, P.O. Drawer 9000, Window Rock, AZ 86515, (928) 871-4941 or (928) 871-6352. www.navajonation parks.org.

Tohono O'odham Reservation, 136 miles south of Phoenix (adjacent to the city of Tucson). This reservation stretches across Maricopa, Pinal, and Pima Counties. Best known for its distinctive and valuable basketry, the tribe also produces fine pottery. Tohono O'odham Tribal Council, P.O. Box 837, Sells, AZ 85634, (520) 383-2221.

Pascua-Yaqui Reservation, 135 miles southwest of Phoenix (adjacent to the city of Tucson) in Pima County. Collectors appreciate the "Deer Dance" statues and cultural paintings created by the children of the tribe. Pascua-Yaqui Tribal Council, 7474 South Camino de Oeste, Tucson, AZ 85746, (520) 883-5000. E-mail: pyit@liveline.com.

Quenchan Indian Tribe Fort Yuma, 185 miles southwest of Phoenix in Yuma County. This reservation borders Arizona and California. Information may be obtained by writing to an Arizona address or by calling the tribal headquarters in California. Collectors may buy beadwork and other artifacts from this tribe. Quechan Tribal Council, P.O. Box 1899, Yuma, AZ 85366, (760) 572-1242.

Salt River Pima-Maricopa Indian Community, 15 miles northeast of Phoenix adjacent to the city of Scottsdale. The Salt River Indians produce basketry and pottery. Salt River Pima-Maricopa Tribal Council, 10005 East Osborn Road, Scottsdale, AZ 85256, (480) 850-8000.

San Carlos Reservation, 115 miles northeast of Phoenix in Gila and Graham Counties. Along with basketry and pottery, the San Carlos Apaches create unusual jewelry set with peridots, pale green semiprecious gemstones found in that area. San Carlos Apache Tribal Council, P.O. Box O, San Carlos, AZ 85550, (928) 475-2331.

Tonto-Apache Reservation, 94 miles northeast of Phoenix in Gila County. Native crafts of basketry and beadwork are emphasized. Tonto-Apache Tribal Council, P.O. Box 30, Payson, AZ 85541, (928) 474-5000.

Yavapai-Prescott Reservation, 103 miles northwest of Phoenix in Yavapai County. Best bet for collecting native baskets. Yavapai-Prescott Tribal Council, 530 East Merritt, Prescott, AZ 86301, (928) 445-8790.

For more information about Arizona's Native American tribes, contact:

Arizona Commission of Indian Affairs
1400 West Washington, #300
Phoenix, AZ 85007
(602) 542-3123
www.indianaffairs.com

State Parks

Land of the great outdoors, Arizona has nineteen state parks with historical and recreational settings. Each offers strollers, hikers, boaters, backpackers, and climbers a variety of experiences. Twelve of the recreational parks have hiking trails, and six of those include equestrian trails. Campground facilities are available at eleven of the parks, and seven offer boating opportunities. There is a nominal per-vehicle fee charged at each park. For more information on any of the state parks, call or write to:

Arizona State Parks
1300 West Washington Street
Phoenix, AZ 85007
(602) 542-4174
www.pr.state.az.us

For specific information on Arizona trails and hiking, write for information to:

Arizona State Parks, Trails Coordinator
1300 West Washington Street
Phoenix, AZ 85007
(602) 542-4174

Regional Information

Arizona is divided into fifteen counties, and not all of them have recreation departments. For information concerning local trails and bike paths, contact the board of supervisors in the area that interests you. Following is a list of recreation departments for Arizona's three largest metropolitan areas:

PHOENIX

Maricopa County Parks and Recreation Department, 3475 West Durango Street, Phoenix, AZ 85009, (602) 506-2930. www.maricopa.gov.

Phoenix Parks, Recreation, and Library Department, 200 West Washington Street, Phoenix, AZ 85004, (602) 262-6861. www.ci.phoenix.az.us.

TUCSON

Pima County Parks and Recreation Department, 1204 West Silverlake Road, Tucson, AZ 85713, (520) 740-2690.

Tucson City Parks and Recreation Department, 900 South Randolph Way, Tucson, AZ 85716, (520) 791-4873. www.ci.tucson.az.us.

FLAGSTAFF

Coconino County Parks and Recreation Department, HCR 30, Box 3A, Flagstaff, AZ 86001, (928) 774-5139. www.co.coconino.az.us/information.cfm.

Flagstaff Parks and Recreation Department, 211 West Aspen, Flagstaff, AZ 86001, (928) 779-7690.

Tourist Safety Tips

FLASH FLOODS

When a violent thunderstorm breaks out over the mountains and deserts of the Southwest, runoff from the torrential rains cascades into the steep canyons in a matter of minutes. Walls of water, sometimes 10 to 30 feet high, swirl through the canyons and arroyos, picking up mud, boulders, trees, and other debris. Plants, animals, and sometimes humans are caught and swept along, for a flash flood stops for nothing that is unlucky enough to be in its path.

Flash floods can result from thunderstorms miles away and can occur in Arizona at any time of the year. Isolated thunderstorms are the main cause from late June through mid-September, while tropical storms or Pacific storms are the main culprit from August through October.

A thunderstorm cloud, called a cumulonimbus, is a large, towering formation that frequently spreads out at the top into the shape of an anvil. This cloud usually appears dark and threatening when viewed from below but very bright and white when seen from the side at some distance.

The National Weather Service issues a flash-flood watch when such a flood is a possibility. A flash-flood warning is issued when flash flooding has been reported or radar indicates heavy rain in a flood-prone area.

What to Do

- Stay tuned to a radio station that gives flood-watch warnings.
- Keep an eye on the sky and watch for thunderstorms.
- Avoid deep canyons and dry washes during stormy or threatening weather.
- Camp on high ground, but not on top of exposed peaks or ridges.

- Never cross a flooded dip in the roadway. The water may be deeper than you think or the roadway washed away.

- If your vehicle is stuck in a low-lying area, abandon it and move to higher ground.

- If local authorities want you to leave an area—leave. People die needlessly because they ignore warnings to seek safety.

- Inform someone of your destination and when you expect to return. Police should be notified immediately if you do not return on time.

DESERT SURVIVAL

Having great weather year-round means that Arizonans spend more time outdoors than most people in the country. With the elegant Sonoran Desert surrounding us, it's no wonder that the urge is to get out and enjoy it. Unfortunately, too many people go out into the desert unprepared. Here are some important desert survival tips:

THREE RULES OF DESERT SURVIVAL
NEVER BE ALONE · TELL SOMEONE · STAY PUT

- If you do get lost, make a large X—at least 14 feet long—where you are. This can be made by dragging your foot, breaking off bush branches, or any other means at your disposal.

- Start blowing a whistle at regular intervals using three short blasts. This is the international distress signal.

- Light three fires in the shape of a triangle near where you are. This is a good signal both day and night.

- Don't eat in the desert. Eating draws fluid out of your body and makes you dehydrate faster.

- Keep a water jug with a straw in the car. Remember that children dehydrate quicker than adults.

- Remember these three points about water in the desert: *TAKE IT, DRINK IT,* and *DON'T SAVE IT!*

- Always tell someone the make of your car, its color, where you are going, and when you'll be back. This will make it easier for searchers to find you.

THE CLIMATE OF ARIZONA

Arizona is a land of dramatic contrasts, as varied in its climate as in its beauty. Temperatures and rainfall vary tremendously throughout the three main topographical areas within the state, for extremes in elevation are matched by extremes in temperatures. These three topographical areas can roughly be divided as follows: The desert mountains and valleys, elevations of 1,500 to 2,500 feet; the high mountain plateau, with average elevations of 5,000 to 7,000 feet; and the mountains, with peaks from 9,000 to 12,000 feet.

Temperatures can range as much as sixty degrees in a single day due to the dry air, but generally average temperatures are governed by elevation. As a rule of thumb, figure on a three and one half degree Fahrenheit difference for every 1,000-foot change in altitude.

When it comes to extremes, there are usually worse days on record. The hottest daytime temperature ever recorded was 127 degrees Fahrenheit at Parker in 1905. The coldest day on record was -40 degrees Fahrenheit at Hawley Lake on January 7, 1971. Of course, new records are always being set. Both July 14, 1982, with 113 degrees Fahrenheit recorded, and September 6, 1982, with 110 degrees Fahrenheit, set new high maximum temperatures for those dates. From the beginning to the end of October, the greatest temperature changes are recorded in Phoenix—greater changes than any seen during the year in central Arizona. By November, the mild winter season is established in the Salt River Valley.

Sunshine in Phoenix averages 86 percent of the possible amount, ranging from a minimum monthly average of 77 percent in January and December to a maximum of 94 percent in June.

Elevation and season also affect the amount of rain and snow that Arizona receives. These amounts vary dramatically. On the average, some desert areas have only 3 to 4 inches of rain a year, while certain mountain areas receive up to 30 inches. Pacific storms cause most of the rainfall from November through March, with winter snowfall totals sometimes reaching 100 inches on the highest mountains. Summer rainfall begins in July and extends through mid-September, when moisture-bearing winds from the southeast and south cause the Arizona monsoon. The thunderstorms that result can cause strong winds, blinding dust storms, and heavy rainfall. Heavy thunderstorms can cause flash flooding, and while major flooding is rare, it can—and does—happen.

Dry spells can last for many months, but count on April through June to be the driest part of the year. However, when thunderstorms occur, they can be wild. The damaging winds accompanying these storms are usually straight-line winds that can move in at speeds upward of 75 miles per hour.

HEAT WAVE SAFETY RULES

If you are not used to the extreme heat that can occur in the desert, it's easy to overdo it and get sick. Below are some basic rules for living in—and enjoying—Arizona's high-temperature times.

- **Slow Down.** Your body cannot keep up with extremely high temperatures, especially when the humidity rises.
- **Dress for Summer.** Lightweight, light-colored clothing reflects the heat and sunlight and helps maintain normal body temperatures.
- **Put Less Fuel in Your Inner Fires.** High-protein foods increase metabolic heat production and also increase water loss.
- **Don't Dry Out.** Hot weather can wring the water out of you before you know it's happened. The first sign of dehydration is being cross. Recognize this symptom and drink lots of water when the weather is hot.
- **Don't Get Too Much Sun.** Sunburn makes the job of heat dissipation that much more difficult. Not only is sunburn uncomfortable, but too much sun invites skin cancer. Wear a good, protective sunscreen whenever you are in the sun.
- **Take Care of the Children and Pets.** Never leave the kids or animals in the car on a hot day—not even for that quick trip into the store.
- **Vary Your Thermal Environment.** Try to get out of the heat for at least a few hours each day.

INDEX

ABOUT THE AUTHOR

Pam Hait is a freelance writer and award-winning author of thirteen books. A member of the American Society of Journalists and Authors, she is a graduate of Northwestern University Medill School of Journalism. Pam is Southwest Editor of *Metropolitan Home,* has covered Arizona for *Sunset* and *Travel & Leisure,* and has written for many national publications. She is a longtime contributor to *Arizona Highways.* Pam and her partner own Strategies, a media relations and marketing firm that focuses on tourism and has special expertise in eco and heritage tourism.

THE COLONIAL MOMENT IN AFRICA

This book includes the first five, thematic, chapters from the *Cambridge History of Africa*, Volume 7. They deal with Africa south of the Sahara, during a period in which economic and cultural changes greatly enlarged the horizons of Africans, even though colonial rule seemed set to last for a very long time.

The contributors break much new ground in exploring a variety of topics which transcend colonial frontiers: the impact of Africa on the thought of the colonial powers; impulses to economic growth, and new frameworks directing the movement of people, goods and money; the rapid expansion of world religions and their interaction with indigenous beliefs and colonial regimes; the circulation of ideas among Africans, and the growth of new social identities, as reflected in the press, literature, art and music. Each chapter is accompanied by a bibliography updated for this edition.

THE COLONIAL
MOMENT IN
AFRICA

Essays on the movement of
minds and materials
1900–1940

edited by

A.D. ROBERTS

Professor of the History of Africa
School of Oriental and African Studies
University of London.

CAMBRIDGE
UNIVERSITY PRESS

Published by the Press Syndicate of the University of Cambridge
The Pitt Building, Trumpington Street, Cambridge CB2 1RP
40 West 20th Street, New York, NY 10011–4211, USA
10 Stamford Road, Oakleigh, Victoria 3166, Australia

The chapters in this Book were originally published in *The Cambridge History of Africa*, Volume 7, *1905–1940*

First published 1990
Reprinted 1992

Printed in Great Britain by The Bath Press, Avon

A catalogue record for this book is available from the British Library

Library of Congress cataloguing in publication data

The Colonial moment in Africa: essays on the movement of
minds and materials, 1900–1940.
1. Africa. Colonisation, 1900–1945
I. Roberts, Andrew *1937–*   II. The Cambridge history of Africa
960'.31

ISBN 0 521 390907 hard cover
ISBN 0 521 386748 paperback

UP

SE

CONTENTS

v

MAPS

FIGURES

TABLES

PREFACE

From the vantage-point of the late twentieth century, its first forty years constitute a 'colonial moment'. By 1900, most of Africa had been partitioned among seven European powers, and over the next few decades colonial regimes tightened their grip. By 1936, when Italian forces entered Addis Ababa, white rule prevailed throughout the continent except in Egypt and Liberia. At the outbreak of World War II, few doubted that, in Africa at least, colonial rule would endure for a long time yet. To be sure, there was mounting unrest in the 1930s, among African wage-earners as well as farmers, but this scarcely seemed to threaten white monopolies of power. For the foreseeable future, the white man expected to continue to bear his burden of responsibility for a continent in tutelage.

To some, then, this period may seem to be a mere interlude, in which Africa largely receded from the mainstream of history: a pause between the power-struggles of the 'Scramble' and the break-down of empires after 1945. But this is to take a Eurocentric view, and one, moreover, which ignores much of what matters most about the past. Colonial rule may have appeared to be firmly entrenched, but it facilitated economic and cultural changes which enlarged the horizons of Africans far more rapidly than their rulers cared to acknowledge. The years between 1900 and 1940 witnessed, on an unprecedented scale, transformations in social identities, cognitive systems and means of communication. These are of profound importance for the history of African thought and action in the twentieth century; they happen also to be crucial for any attempt to explain the timing and course of decolonisation. At the same time, it must be stressed that these transformations owed much of their impetus to sources outside Africa: to understand both the opportunities available to Africans and the constraints upon them, we must take due account of both whites and blacks in Europe and the New World.

I

This was the reasoning which led to the writing of the essays in this book. They first appeared in 1986, in the *Cambridge History of Africa*, vol. VII, 1905–1940 (hereafter *CHA*, vol. VII). Their purpose there was to complement ten chapters focused on specific regions, by discussing themes of more or less continent-wide significance. This provenance accounts for certain obvious limitations in scope. The emphasis throughout is on Africa south of the Sahara: relevant aspects of Mediterranean Africa are noted in chapter 4, on Islam, but are more fully discussed in a regional chapter on the Maghrib. Chapters 1 and 2 deal chiefly with Britain and British Africa, since they were intended to provide connections between four regional chapters on English-speaking Africa; for the same sort of reason, chapter 1 also considers Germany briefly. For France, Belgium and Portugal, on the other hand, the metropolitan background could be conveniently treated within the appropriate regional chapters, though it was unfortunately impossible to give proper attention to Italy. The five thematic chapters are preceded by the original introduction, duly adapted; this identifies salient features of the period.

The reader should bear in mind that the essays were completed in or before 1983. Apart from a few minor corrections, they have not been revised for this edition. It is hoped that they retain their value both as surveys of research and as explorations of previously neglected topics. The original bibliographies have been rearranged and updated, in order to direct attention to relevant new lines of research. On p. 194, and in several footnotes, there are cross-references to parts of the parent volume which are not included here.

September 1989   ANDREW ROBERTS

INTRODUCTION

By 1905 most of Africa had been shared out among half a dozen countries in Western Europe: Britain, France, Germany, Belgium (in the person of its king), Italy and Portugal; Spain had a few toe-holds. In 1908 Belgium acquired the Congo Independent State from Leopold II; in 1912 Morocco and Libya were taken over by France and Italy respectively. Nonetheless, Britain was clearly the most important imperial power in Africa, and not only in terms of land and population; in 1907 its territories accounted for four-fifths of African trade south of the Sahara. Two African countries had remained independent. The ancient empire of Ethiopia had preserved and indeed extended its sovereignty, while on the other side of Africa a different kind of black imperialism was exercised in Liberia by the descendants of freed slaves from the USA. In the far south, in 1910, former Boer republics and British colonies joined to form the Union of South Africa, a virtually autonomous Dominion of the British Empire. With these exceptions, final responsibility for governing Africa had been transferred to European capitals. South of the Sahara, major efforts of armed resistance had been suppressed in German South West Africa, German East Africa and Natal, between 1904 and 1907. In tropical Africa, there were signs of a shift away from the 'rip-off' economies so common in the later nineteenth century and towards more systematic and far-sighted methods of tapping the wealth of Africa. Its manpower, once exported for use overseas, was now being applied to production within Africa. The hunting and gathering of ivory or wild rubber yielded to the husbandry of pastures, fields and plantations. The search for quick profits by under-capitalised loggers or strip-miners was gradually being replaced by large-scale investment designed to yield assured returns over the long term. The infrastructures needed to attract such enterprise were taking shape. Railways reached Bamako in 1905 and Katanga in 1910, Kano in 1911, Tabora in 1912. Taxes were generally paid in cash, and the main clusters of population had almost all been brought under some sort of white administration.

However, the Scramble for Africa was by no means over. The two oldest empires on the continent, those of Ethiopia and

3

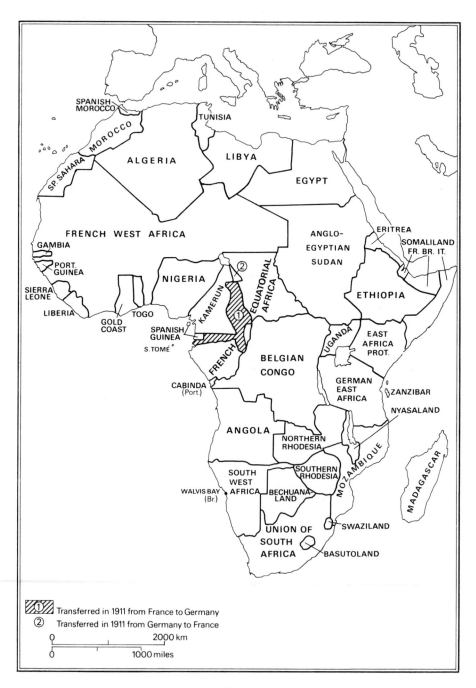

Transferred in 1911 from France to Germany
Transferred in 1911 from Germany to France

1   Africa in 1914

4

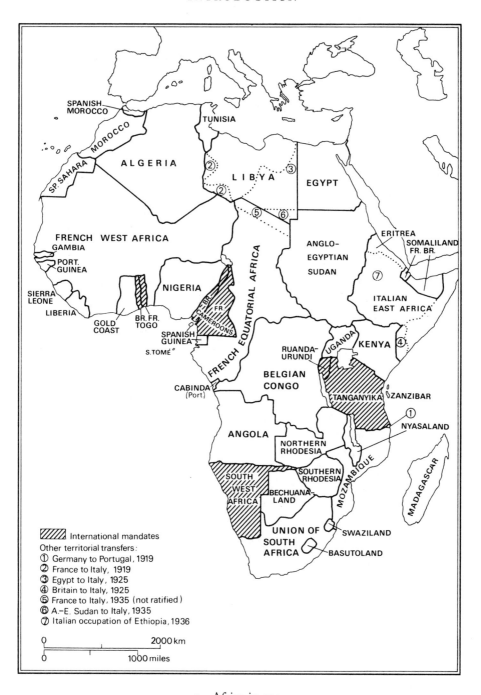

SPANISH MOROCCO
TUNISIA
MOROCCO
SP. SAHARA
ALGERIA
② ② ③
LIBYA
EGYPT
⑤ ⑥
FRENCH WEST AFRICA
GAMBIA
PORT. GUINEA
SIERRA LEONE
LIBERIA
GOLD COAST
BR. FR. TOGO
NIGERIA
BR. CAMEROONS
FR
SPANISH GUINEA
S. TOMÉ
FRENCH EQUATORIAL AFRICA
ANGLO-EGYPTIAN SUDAN
ERITREA
SOMALILAND FR. BR.
ITALIAN EAST AFRICA
⑦
CABINDA (Port.)
RUANDA-URUNDI
BELGIAN CONGO
UGANDA
KENYA
④
TANGANYIKA
ZANZIBAR
ANGOLA
NORTHERN RHODESIA
SOUTHERN RHODESIA
MOZAMBIQUE
①
NYASALAND
MADAGASCAR
SOUTH WEST AFRICA
BECHUANA-LAND
UNION OF SOUTH AFRICA
SWAZILAND
BASUTOLAND

▨ International mandates
Other territorial transfers:
① Germany to Portugal, 1919
② France to Italy, 1919
③ Egypt to Italy, 1925
④ Britain to Italy, 1925
⑤ France to Italy, 1935 (not ratified)
⑥ A.–E. Sudan to Italy, 1935
⑦ Italian occupation of Ethiopia, 1936

0   2000 km
0   1000 miles

2   Africa in 1939

Portugal, had indeed survived it, but greater powers doubted their durability and made plans to share them out if they should fall apart. Already, France controlled Ethiopia's rail access to the outside world, while the greater part of Portuguese East Africa was in the hands of chartered companies in which British interests were paramount. In the event, it was the German Empire which collapsed, following Germany's defeat by the Allied powers in the First World War. German Africa was redistributed between Britain, France, Belgium and South Africa, who ruled their new accretions on behalf of the League of Nations. South Africa, indeed, became an imperialist force in its own right. Its economic power came to be felt throughout a field of mining and labour migration which extended as far north as Tanganyika. In political terms, South African influence was due less to public policy than to the private vision of General Smuts, who had been prominent in the British imperial war cabinet. Early in 1919, Smuts argued that since the British Empire was 'specially poor in copper' it should acquire parts of Portuguese and Belgian Africa.[1] This idea came to nothing; instead, both Belgium and Portugal took steps over the next decade or so to strengthen their links with their African possessions and reduce the influence of alien capital and residents. Nonetheless, Smuts had important friends in Britain who, like him, hoped to see the whole of eastern Africa, from the Cape to the borders of Ethiopia, ruled by white colonists as a major bastion of the British Empire. This trend was countered by another 'sub-imperialism' in Africa: that of British India, to whose interests the British presence in eastern Africa had originally been dedicated. The Government of India defended Indian immigrants in East and South Africa against the wilder demands of white colonists; moreover, it supplied the British with expertise in the ruling of alien peoples which was found increasingly relevant to Africa in the 1930s.

While the Scramble continued, so too did opposition to white intrusion. The First World War not only set white against white in Africa; it also stiffened the determination of white rulers to subdue those parts of their territories which still remained free.

[1] Memorandum, 'The Mozambique Province', n.d., Smuts Papers (cited by W. R. Louis, *Great Britain and Germany's lost colonies, 1914–1919* (Oxford, 1967), 159; this document is omitted from W. K. Hancock and J. van der Poel (eds.), *Selections from the Smuts Papers*, IV [1918–1919] (Cambridge, 1966).

Wars of resistance were fought in eastern Angola; by the Barwe of Mozambique; the Luba in the Belgian Congo; the Somali; the Turkana in north-western Kenya; the Darfur sultanate in the Anglo-Egyptian Sudan; and the Tuareg of Niger. Even then, there were other areas which by 1920 had yet to pay colonial taxes. Most succumbed over the next few years without major violence: Moxico in Angola; the southern Kwango, Dekese and northern Kivu in the Belgian Congo; Buha in Tanganyika; Karamoja in Uganda; the territories of the Zande and Nuba in the Sudan. It was also about this time that Kaffa, in south-western Ethiopia, began paying taxes to the emperor's agents, if not to the imperial treasury. Elsewhere, the postwar decade witnessed further and often prolonged resistance to the colonial powers. In Egypt, a nationalist revolt in 1919 led to a sort of independence in 1922. In Morocco, there was rebellion in the Rif; the Sanūsi harried the Italians in Cyrenaica; and Italy first conquered north-eastern Somaliland. In French Equatorial Africa there was insurrection in eastern Gabon and among the Baya.

In the 1930s the Fascist regime in Italy introduced the last phase of the Scramble. From 1932 Mussolini began to make grandiose claims against France in Africa; in January 1935 he concluded an agreement with France to adjust frontiers in the Sahara which emboldened him to prepare for the invasion of Ethiopia. His conquest, in 1935–6, of this 'remote and unfamiliar' country[2] brought Africa briefly back into the mainstream of world politics, for it exposed the impotence of the League of Nations and in that sense marked the point when a second world war began to seem inevitable. British leaders wondered if Hitler could be bought off with the return of Germany's former colonies in West Africa, or by the surrender of Belgian or Portuguese Africa, but he was not to be thus deflected from his aims in Europe.

It is only recently that historians have begun to look analytically at the use of force by the colonial powers to extend and maintain their control in Africa. One obvious feature of our period is the introduction of air power, of special value in remote and difficult terrain. Aeroplanes were used for military operations in Libya in 1911 and Morocco in 1912. Egyptian planes were used against Darfur in 1916; planes of the RAF were used in 1920 against the

[2] Neville Chamberlain, *Hansard*, 19 December 1935, cited by F. Hardie, *The Abyssinian crisis* (London, 1974), 8.

7

Nuer, in the Sudan, and in the final defeat of Muhammad 'Abdallāh Ḥasan in Somaliland; and against the Nuer and Nuba in 1927–9. South Africa used planes against rebels in South West Africa in 1922 and 1925. The Fascists' bombing of Ethiopia in 1935–6 achieved instant notoriety, but it is also worth noting that in 1937 the RAF was the main instrument of Britain's last campaign of imperial conquest, in the Hadramaut of southern Arabia. The growing importance to the British of air power in Africa, especially as relations with Italy worsened, was demonstrated by the use of Nairobi as an RAF bomber base from 1936 and the appointment of an air vice-marshal as governor of Kenya in 1937. British strategy was also served by the annual cruise of RAF planes between Cape Town and Cairo which in 1935 enabled troops from Southern Rhodesia to be flown to the copper-mines in Northern Rhodesia to cope with African strikers. This incident demonstrated that imperial strength lay in mobility as well as firepower; the relatively very small size of colonial armies was a misleading index of the role of force in sustaining colonial power.

There was certainly a notable increase during our period in the power of the colonial state. To some extent this simply reflected the first stages of setting up government and fostering external trade. By 1914 most British administrations in Africa were paying their way: they no longer depended on grants from the British Treasury to balance their budgets. Moreover, private companies which during the Scramble had been entrusted with powers of government gradually yielded them up, as charters expired or were revoked in the Rhodesias in 1923–4, in Portuguese East Africa in 1929–30 and in parts of French Equatorial Africa. In the view of the colonial powers, the rule of law rapidly advanced within their territories, though how far Africans concurred is a matter for further research. The range of government activity was also deliberately extended, in response to African conditions as much as to changing practice in Europe. Where the cash nexus was still very patchy, government was liable to take a leading role not only in creating economic infrastructures, such as railways, but in regulating production through controls over labour and marketing. This trend was reinforced by policy, whether paternalist or openly segregationist. Africans were either prevented from competing with whites or, more deviously, protected from the cold winds of the free market. And in the virtual absence of

8

an indigenous middle class, as in much of tropical Africa, government was bound to take initiatives in education and medicine if their provision was not to be limited by the aims and resources of missionary societies. Furthermore, the flow of goods and currencies within and outside Africa was increasingly directed by colonial governments into channels intended to protect metropolitan interests. There was, in short, a general hardening of colonial frontiers: what had often been artificial borders came to define arenas of political, economic and cultural activity. This process was most evident in the Belgian Congo: as Belgium's only colony, it was the object of greater metropolitan interest than any other African territory, yet special efforts had to be made to secure Belgian economic and cultural hegemony.

In some senses, then, European power was on the increase in Africa throughout our period, and the constraints of armies and administrators were reinforced by those of the labour market as capitalist enterprise expanded. But there is another, perhaps more important, sense in which European power in Africa was already in decline. The extent of empire, in the sense of political overrule, was related in no simple way to metropolitan strength. This was especially true after the First World War, which had much inflated the empires of Britain and France, in the Middle East as well as Africa. The home bases of European empires were gravely enfeebled, first by the war itself and then by the world-wide economic depression of the 1930s. It has been reckoned that industrial development in Europe was set back eight years by the First World War, while it forged ahead in the USA. Warfare caused the deaths of over twenty million people in Europe (excluding Russia), a mortality rate of about 7 per cent.[3] The influenza pandemic of 1918–19 struck heavily in Europe, as in Africa and Asia, and like the war it took a specially heavy toll of young adults. Germany, by losing the war, not only lost its colonies but itself became, for a time, a kind of colony, deprived of its navy and airforce and precariously dependent for industrial growth in the late 1920s on short-term loans from US firms. France lost over two-thirds of its foreign investments as a result of the war, and at home it had suffered great physical damage as well as loss of life. The most impressive work of French

[3] Asa Briggs, 'The world economy', in C. L. Mowat (ed.), *New Cambridge modern history*, XII (Cambridge, 1968), 54.

colonisation in the 1920s was not overseas but in war-scarred north-eastern France. By 1925 some £700m had been spent on reconstruction there, and since French youth had been decimated much of the work was done by immigrants — mostly Poles, Italians and Kabyles from Algeria: indeed, with a total foreign population at this time of around three million, France supplanted the USA as the main host-country for immigrants.[4] The depression of the 1930s sharply checked France's recovery: from 1931 the annual value of its external trade was less, in real terms, than it had been in 1913. In Britain, war and depression compounded economic problems of long standing. Foreign competition continued to undermine industries on which British hegemony had rested in the mid-nineteenth century: textiles, coal, iron and steel, shipbuilding. Between 1919 and 1939 the volume of British exports was never more than two-thirds that of 1913; and throughout the 1930s Britain was a net importer of capital.[5] Real wages increased more slowly between the 1900s and 1930s than during any other such interval between the 1850s and 1960s.[6] In 1935, 62 per cent of British volunteers for military service were rejected as physically unfit, and the infant death-rate in Jarrow, a Tyneside town which no longer built ships, was nearly three times that in south-east England.[7]

It is true that despite such symptoms of national decline British preponderance in Africa remained very considerable. By 1935 the share of 'British Africa' (including South Africa) in the trade of sub-Saharan Africa was 84.7 per cent and in 1937 Britain accounted for 77 per cent of investments in this region. On the other hand, Britain's own share in African trade declined; whereas in 1920 it had still accounted for two-thirds of the trade of British Africa, by 1937 the proportion was well under half. In part, this was due to the economic revival of Germany: between 1935 and 1938 German trade with sub-Saharan Africa increased by a half (while Germany replaced France as Egypt's second-best trading partner). It was also due to the advances of US and Japanese

[4] D. W. Brogan, *The development of modern France* (second edition: London, 1967), 599, 609.
[5] D. H. Aldcroft, *The inter-war economy: Britain 1919–1939* (London, 1970), 246, 264; Briggs, *loc. cit.*, 79.
[6] S. Pollard, 'Labour in Great Britain', in P. Mathias and M. M. Postan (eds.), *The Cambridge economic history of Europe*, VII, part 1 (Cambridge, 1978), 171.
[7] Theo Barker (ed.), *The long march of Everyman* (London, 1975), 201–2.

industry into African markets between the wars. US products ranked second or third among the imports of British Africa in the 1930s. By 1929 Japan had replaced Britain as chief supplier of cotton goods to East Africa and by 1938 enjoyed 93 per cent of this market. In South Africa the Japanese were officially regarded as 'honorary whites' from 1930 and in the later 1930s Japan overtook France and Belgium to become South Africa's fourth-best trading partner; in 1936–7 only Germany bought more South African wool than Japan. Such shifts in trading patterns must of course be seen in a broader perspective; the trade of sub-Saharan Africa still played too small a part in the trade of the major imperial powers to affect their national economies very significantly.[8] These changing patterns were important for Africa not so much for their own sake as because they were symptoms of profounder shifts in power which would soon have far-reaching effects on the continent.[9]

Relations between the USA and Africa during our period are a neglected subject, despite the scale on which Africa has been studied by Americans in recent years. The USA did not see itself as a power in Africa. It had no colonies there, and nothing came of British suggestions in 1918 that it might take over German East Africa or the Belgian Congo and Angola.[10] In Liberia, however, the US did enjoy a decisive, if informal, hegemony. Through a series of loan agreements it controlled Liberian finance; it did not exert the crude compulsion evident in its own 'back-yard', the

[8] Percentage of metropolitan power's external trade with its territories south of the Sahara, 1935: Britain, 2.7 (trade with South Africa, 4.0); France, 5.0 (including Madagascar); Belgium, 3.3; Portugal, 9.4 (Angola and Mozambique only). In 1934–7 Japan derived 4.0 per cent of its export earnings from sub-Saharan Africa, and 3.6 from North Africa; 4.1 per cent of its imports came from Africa. In 1935 Germany derived 2.1 per cent of its external trade from sub-Saharan Africa (and 2.5 in 1938). In 1930–4 Italy derived 1 per cent of its imports from its colonies. (*Sources*: as cited in *CHA*, vol. VII, p. xix above; also *Japan year book 1938–9*, 397, 409; Royal Institute of International Affairs, *The colonial problem* (London, 1937), 411.)
[9] Percentage distribution of world exports of manufactured goods:

	UK	Germany	USA	Japan	France	Belgium
1913	29.9	26.4	12.6	2.4	12.9	4.9
1929	23.6	21.0	20.7	3.9	11.2	5.5
1937	22.4	22.4	19.6	7.2	6.4	5.9

Source: Aldcroft: *Inter-war economy*, 22.

[10] Louis, *Great Britain and Germany's lost colonies*, 110–13, 115, 125.

republics of Central America, but from 1927 it did protect a locally dominant economic interest: the holdings of Firestone Rubber. Elsewhere in Africa, US investment was less conspicuous but more important. American finance and technical expertise played a considerable role in mining. In 1906 Ryan and Guggenheim helped to initiate diamond-mining in Kasai; in 1917 J. P. Morgan and Newmont helped set up the Anglo American Corporation in South Africa. In 1927–8 Newmont, Kennecott and the American Metal Company acquired substantial interests in the development of large-scale copper-mining in Northern Rhodesia. When yet another US firm planned to join them early in 1929, it seemed likely that Northern Rhodesia's copper would pass into American hands at a time when the United States already controlled three-quarters of world copper production. Baldwin, the British prime minister, regarded this as strategically undesirable and would appear to have prompted the large injection of British and South African capital which checked this American threat. Nonetheless links with mining in the US were strengthened when in 1930 the American Metal Company took over the Copperbelt interests of Chester Beatty's Selection Trust.[11] American producers also dominated two sectors of the African market which rapidly expanded between the wars: films and automobiles. (Trucks and cars designed to meet the exacting demands of farmers and traders in middle America stood up far better than British vehicles to African soils and distances.) African goods were a tiny proportion of total US imports, but by 1934 the USA was the chief customer for African cocoa.

The USA also played a major part both in the cultural transformation of Africa and in the promotion of knowledge about the continent. One in ten US citizens were themselves of African descent, so the welfare of Africans, and especially their education, was a natural object of American philanthropy. In parts of Africa, notably the Witwatersrand, the Belgian Congo and Angola, Americans took a leading role in missionary work; such experience led in 1924 to a Wisconsin sociologist being commissioned to report on labour conditions in Portuguese Africa. Americans also funded most of the research into Africa's social problems between the wars, though little of this was done

[11] A. D. Roberts, 'Notes towards a financial history of copper mining in Northern Rhodesia', *Canadian Journal of African Studies*, 1982, **16**, 2, 348–9.

by Americans. A small but growing number of Africans found their way to American colleges and universities. Ethiopia exercised a particular hold on the imagination of black Americans, especially after Mussolini's invasion; the US government kept aloof from the dispute, but some of its nationals had been doing important work in the country. The Second World War gave the US government, for the first time, a direct interest in the fortunes of Africa. The American commitment to the defence and recovery of Western Europe involved a commitment to Africa insofar as the West increasingly depended on its African colonies. The decision-making of the imperial powers began to be influenced by American priorities, with consequences for both development and decolonisation.[12]

Within Africa, two further kinds of shift in power deserve consideration. One is so obvious that it is easy to overlook. It was during our period that tropical Africa began to constitute a significant economic counterweight to North and South Africa. In the latter regions, production had been stimulated in the course of the nineteenth century by white immigration and the investment of European capital. In 1907, North and South Africa each contributed twice as much as tropical Africa to the continent's total exports (including gold and diamonds). By 1928 the extension of colonial rule and capitalist networks had contrived to raise the share of tropical Africa almost to the South African level, while that of North Africa was scarcely affected. Ten years later, the picture had changed yet again: three-quarters of Africa's exports now came from the tropics and South Africa, in roughly equal proportions.[13] This was partly due to world demand, despite the

---

[12] W. R. Louis, *Imperialism at bay: the United States and the decolonisation of the British Empire, 1941–1945* (Oxford, 1977).

[13] Percentage of regional contributions to the value of African exports (including gold and diamonds):

	1907	1928	1938
North Africa	40	37.5	26.6
Tropical Africa	19	30.0	34.6
South Africa	41	32.5	38.8

Sources: S. H. Frankel, *Capital investment in Africa* (London, 1938), 198–9 (1907, 1928); M. J. Herskovits and M. Harwitz (eds.), *Economic transition in Africa* (London, 1964), 29–30 (1938); B. R. Mitchell, *International historical statistics: Africa and Asia* (London, 1982), 373–8 (North Africa). Ethiopia has been omitted from these calculations.

depression of the 1930s, for certain commodities which in parts of tropical Africa were first produced on a large scale in this decade: copper from Northern Rhodesia, tin and coffee from the Belgian Congo, coffee from Uganda, the Ivory Coast and Madagascar. (Up to 1935 almost half the tonnage of Africa's coffee came from Ethiopia and Angola; in 1936–9 the leading producer by weight was Madagascar.) But the main cause of rising export values in sub-Saharan Africa was the rising price of gold, which favoured not only the Union but the Belgian Congo and several territories in French as well as British tropical Africa. North Africa had no gold; besides, its trade was heavily dependent on the French economy, which suffered particularly during the depression. It is hard to make comparisons across space and time between different monetary zones during a period of fluctuating money values, but it would seem that the depression affected government revenues more severely in Algeria than anywhere else in Africa.

Economic power also shifted as between local and overseas capital, and white settlers and African cultivators. Before 1914, it was widely supposed in ruling circles that except in West Africa long-term economic growth in colonial Africa would depend on white settlement. In the 1920s this assumption was disproved by Africans in Uganda and Nyasaland, and came under strain in Tanganyika. In the 1930s the depression usually tilted the balance further in favour of Africans. In Algeria, Kenya and Madagascar, local white enterprise fought an uphill struggle against the larger resources of overseas capital and the lower costs of African peasant production. In South Africa, by contrast, the protection of white farmers and workers against African competition was not checked but intensified in the 1930s. The gold boom greatly improved the government's capacity to subsidise white business and labour, and thus to provide an economic underpinning both for industrialisation and for the legal structures of racial segregation. Prosperity also enabled white South Africans to advance towards another sort of mastery. No longer was the mining industry essentially an enclave of foreign capital; by the end of our period, one-third of its share capital may have been in South African hands.

Our period, then, was characterised by important changes in the distribution of power, both short-term and long-term.

Nonetheless, it remains true that, outside Egypt, there was little
change in the capacity of Africans under white rule to participate
in politics; insofar as they were involved in the structure of
colonial government, it was, with very few exceptions, at the level
of chiefdom or district. This has influenced the priorities of
scholarship. When academic interest in African history burgeoned
in the 1950s and 1960s, it was animated by a concern to
demonstrate the essential autonomy of pre-colonial Africa and to
examine the roots of African protest against colonial rule, which
by then was changing the political face of the continent. In this
perspective, much of African politics in the earlier twentieth
century was deficient in incident and of interest mainly as
'background'. The aftermath of decolonisation widened perspectives of colonial Africa. African wealth and poverty could no
longer be attributed simply to racial divisions; they had to be
explained as a consequence of enduring relations between African
countries and the developed world, and also of conflict within
African communities. The evident fragility of African nations cast
doubt on the value of explaining African political activity in terms
of nationalism. New solidarities based on regional or economic
divisions seemed at least as significant. These in turn provoked
questions about the terms on which colonial Africa traded with
the rest of the world.

Such questions had not indeed been altogether neglected; in
economic history, valuable work had been done which was
insufficiently recognised. But the new perspectives of Africanists
were reinforced both by the increasing accessibility of colonial
archives and by new ideas and priorities among historians at large.
These can be summarised as a preoccupation with 'social history'
transcending rather than merely supplementing the too-often
self-contained categories of political and economic history. Social
history in this sense has commonly been strongly materialist, if
not necessarily Marxist, in approach. It has given particular
stimulus to the study of southern Africa, where the processes of
industrialisation, capital accumulation and class formation have
gone further than elsewhere on the continent. More generally, it
has become possible to conceive of the history of Africa in the
twentieth century as social history in a particular geographical
setting rather than as belonging to a distinctive genre, 'colonial
history'. The historian who studies Africa, whether urban,

industrial or rural, finds much in common with the history of modern Europe or the USA.[14] The cultural differences stressed by white colonists and officials begin to seem less remarkable than the similarities. White sentiments about race do not seem far removed from the attitudes of ruling élites in Europe to the *Lumpenproletariat* of London's East End, or the mostly illiterate Polish and Russian workers controlled by pass-laws in eastern Germany before 1914.[15] An emphasis on Africa's essential distinctiveness was much more characteristic of the British than the French: it may be relevant that by 1939 less than 1 in 17 people in Britain worked on the land, whereas in France the proportion was 1 in 3. In terms of popular beliefs, rituals and diversions there were striking resemblances between Africa and parts of rural France in the 1930s.[16] And as historians of Africa begin to examine popular responses to colonial legal systems, it is important to recall that in France the rule of law was by no means universal at the end of the nineteenth century.[17]

For the historian of African population, our period was crowded with incident. Much remains, and indeed is bound to remain, obscure, but some trends are becoming reasonably clear. The initial impact of white intrusion in tropical Africa was often disastrous. Resistance in German territories provoked massive slaughter and destruction; less well known are the innumerable small-scale actions whereby white rule was extended. Working on mines, plantations and railways meant disease and high death-rates; in large part, this was due to neglect that had parallels in the industrial world, but the more men moved the faster they spread infection, of which the most lethal was sleeping-sickness in Uganda. The First World War prolonged such tribulations. In Europe, 65,000 men from French North and West Africa died on active service; in East Africa over 100,000 men died, and nearly all were carriers killed by disease rather than armaments. Conscription crippled agriculture, yet in places special efforts were made to increase production for military purposes. For non-white

[14] Cf. Paul Thompson (ed.), *Our common history: the transformation of Europe* (London, 1982).
[15] John Iliffe, *Tanganyika under German rule, 1905–1912* (Cambridge, 1969), 67.
[16] Theodore Zeldin, *France 1848–1945: ambition and love* (Oxford, 1979), 171; *idem, Taste and corruption* (Oxford, 1980), 52–8, 310–11, 350–1.
[17] Eugen Weber, *Peasants into Frenchmen: the modernisation of rural France, 1870–1914* (Stanford, 1977), 50-66.

wage-earners, wartime price inflation reduced already meagre real incomes by as much as one half. The damage done by the war rendered Africans highly vulnerable to the influenza pandemic of 1918–19: perhaps 2 per cent succumbed. Climatic change was probably yet another burden upon Africa; for there is reason to suppose that the present century has been unusually dry. This has mattered most in the semi-arid lands fringing the Sahara, but severe drought struck much of eastern and southern Africa in the early 1930s. In southern Africa, the ruthlessness with which labour continued to be mobilised damaged African health on a scale which far outweighed any local amelioration by western medicine. By the 1930s tuberculosis was rife in rural South Africa among returned mine-workers, while railway-building and work on sugar-plantations had spread malaria through Natal and Zululand. In tropical Africa, however, colonial regimes were by the end of our period on balance a positive rather than negative influence on population. For many people, the growth of trade meant somewhat better food and clothing, while the growth of government and motor transport made possible famine relief and rural medical services. The life-chances of Africans were not particularly good, but in many areas they were beginning to improve. In retrospect, one may discern in much of Africa a period of relative calm and rising hopes between the violence of the earlier twentieth century and the wars which have been either cause or consequence of decolonisation.

Movements of people were as much a feature of this period as of any earlier phase in Africa's past. Most moved to work for wages, in mines, plantations and towns. In 1910 about 2.5 million people in Africa were living in cities whose population exceeded 100,000; this number had roughly doubled by 1936, when 2.1m were in Egypt, 1.4m elsewhere in North Africa, and 1.3m in South Africa (where one in six Africans were living in towns). In tropical Africa, large towns were still exceptional: the biggest were Ibadan (318,000) and Lagos (167,000). But old seaports took on new life and new ports were developed, while in the far interior new towns grew from next to nothing. In 1936 there were populations of between 50,000 and 100,000 in Dakar, Luanda and Lourenço Marques (Maputo), and also in Nairobi, Salisbury (Harare) and Elisabethville (Lubumbashi). Many urban dwellers were short-stay migrants, like most workers on mines or plantations; it was not only in South Africa that urban authorities discouraged Africans from settling in towns. But many people came to town less because they could count on finding work there than because they had given up hope of making a living on the land. This was specially true of the poorer whites in South Africa, but during the depression in the 1930s it was also true of whites in Algeria and some Africans in French West Africa.

Other patterns of migration were also important. It was not only white employers who relied on hiring short-stay migrants; so too did African farmers in Uganda, the Sudan and West Africa (where there was widespread demand for seasonal labour at harvest time). Many African communities were uprooted to make room for whites — whether planters, as in the Ivory Coast, or farmers, as in the Rhodesias and Kenya (where the Masai were moved *en masse* before 1914). Campaigns against sleeping-sickness, as in Tanganyika, could involve forced resettlement in tsetse-free zones. Sometimes it was Africans who chose to move. Attempts by colonial governments to compel the cultivation of cash-crops (usually cotton) for very low returns induced families to escape across colonial frontiers: from Upper Volta to the Gold Coast; from Dahomey to Nigeria; from Mozambique to Nyasaland and Tanganyika; from Angola to Northern Rhodesia. Nor did the export of African slaves entirely cease; though it had now been driven underground, a sporadic traffic in slaves persisted across middle Africa, from the Niger bend to the Red Sea.

The growth of the cash economy had far-reaching effects on relations between men and women, between young and old, and between groups of kin. This is a subject which historians of Africa have only recently begun to explore, but some generalisations may be ventured. Wage-earning could expand the opportunities for young men to earn incomes; in accumulating bridewealth (payments by a husband to his wife's relations), a young man seeking a first wife might thus enjoy an advantage over older men seeking a second or third, especially when bridewealth began to take the form of cash rather than cattle. It is even possible that earlier marriage may in places have contributed to population growth. At the same time, the production of cash-crops increased the agricultural burdens of women. They had long planted and harvested food for their own households but were now liable to have to grow crops for sale as well; indeed, children too were under pressure to become farm-hands. Where men went off to work for wages, women were often left to support children and elderly relations. Separation strained marriages, and some women moved to town, not to join a husband but in search of economic independence. Inheritance in the female line (common in Central Africa and parts of the Gold and Ivory Coasts) tended to yield to patrilineal inheritance; not only was this often favoured by colonial officials but as property acquired cash value individual claims to it challenged those of lineage groups, and fathers favoured their own sons. In all these ways, colonial economies caused change in the structure and functions of African families, and thus in the closest personal relationships.[18]

The economic changes of the period greatly increased the scale and variety of social differentiation. Geographical contrasts were sharpened: outside the white-run sectors of mines and plantations there were areas of export-crop production, food supply or labour supply. (If nomadic pastoralists roamed on the fringes of the colonial economy, this was often due less to any sentimental attachment to livestock than to official quarantine regulations.) In practice, such functional specialisation was a good deal modified: households developed strategies for earning incomes from a variety of occupations. All the same, distinctions in terms of economic class became more evident in the course of the period. Most Africans still grew their own food, but dependence on wage-earning greatly increased. In the countryside, a small minority of African farmers (including some colonially approved chiefs) applied capital as well as labour to the land, which in turn began to constitute transferable capital: by the 1930s a kind of incipient African landlordism could be observed in parts of the Gold Coast, Kenya and Natal. In towns and mines, a minority of workers became proletarians, in that they developed a long-term commitment to wage-earning, raised children where they worked, and ceased to regard the countryside as a source of livelihood unless perhaps for retirement. Most African labour was still too mobile for trade unions to make much headway in our period, but there was a marked increase in strike action during the 1930s, especially in ports. Meanwhile, a new African élite had been called into existence by the needs of government, business and missions

[18] See *Journal of African History*, 1983, **24**, 2 (special issue on the history of the family in Africa).

for literate African assistants: clerks, interpreters, storekeepers, trading agents, teachers, clergymen. Along the West African coast and in South Africa, a middle class of this kind had been formed in the course of the nineteenth century and soon developed a strong sense of cultural superiority and corporate identity.

Ethnic identity was a further dimension of social differentiation. There is an important sense in which some African tribes, so far from being primordial units of social organisation, were first created during the period covered in this volume. Tribal affiliation is usually assumed to rest on an awareness of shared yet distinctive cultural habits, notably language: thus the strength and scope of tribal sentiment reflect changing perceptions of cultural difference. In the nineteenth century, the expanding scale of trade and warfare greatly extended African experience of African strangers, and increased the need for new names to signify new degrees of strangeness or solidarity. Under colonial rule, this process was intensified. Migrants far from home looked for material and moral support to those least unlike themselves. Colonial authorities used tribal labels in order to accommodate Africans within bureaucratic structures of control: such labels not only served to attach people to particular places or chiefs; they were taken to indicate temperaments and aptitudes. In local government, tribal distinctions were made to matter as never before: in the southern Sudan, vain efforts were made to sever ties between Nuer and Dinka. Meanwhile, the survival, or memory, of pre-colonial kingdoms gave an ethnic focus to political competition within the colonial system. In Uganda, tribal identities were sharpened by the desire to emulate the privileged kingdom of Buganda; in southern Rhodesia, attempts to resuscitate the defeated Ndebele kingdom put a new premium on distinctions between Ndebele and non-Ndebele or 'Shona'. The spread of literacy gave new significance to ethnic difference: the reduction of African languages to writing meant favouring some languages and dialects over others, thus redefining ethnic frontiers while moulding new channels of communication. Ibo and Tumbuka became articulate ethnicities, as well as Yoruba, Ngoni or Zulu. Moreover, sentiments of ethnic identity were explored and developed by African writers concerned to assert the strength and value of African cultures against alien encroachment. In all these ways, linguistic usage, educational advantage and political aspiration were shaping aggregations of a kind which in Europe had long been labelled 'nations'.[19]

Changing social horizons were both cause and effect of changes in religious affiliation (which were partly made possible by increased wealth). Whether helped or hindered by colonial regimes, Islam and Christianity made great advances in our period; by 1940 a majority of Africans adhered to one or other faith. Both offered universal perspectives on human existence which were more congruent with the enlarged scale of political and economic life under colonial rule than indigenous religions tied to specific groups and places: in this sense, both were modernising forces. Mediterranean Africa had long been very largely Muslim, but by the 1930s there were probably as many Muslims (around thirty million) in tropical Africa, mostly in the countries between Senegal and Somaliland. The expansion of Islam was promoted by proselytising Sufi brotherhoods, but it was greatly facilitated by urbanisation and the growth of trade and transport, and Muslim Africa was receptive to both fundamentalist and modernist trends in contemporary Islamic thought. South of the Sahara, there were probably as many Christians as Muslims by the end of our period; since it opened, the Christian population of Africa may have increased fivefold. European missionaries were in general far less hospitable than Muslim shaykhs to African social and cultural traditions, and contradictions between African and European (especially Protestant) interpretations of Christianity gave rise to a great many independent churches. But there were few areas in which there was a real choice between Christianity and Islam, and with few exceptions it was only the schools of Christian missions which could open doors to such opportunities as the colonial order offered literate Africans. In the short term, the paternalism of Christian missions frustrated African aspirations to leadership; in the longer term, the missions did much to determine where and when Africans south of the Sahara gained enough knowledge and experience to challenge white monopolies of power.

Throughout our period, the great majority of Africans remained illiterate, but those few who did learn to read and write, especially in European languages, wielded an influence out of all proportion

[19] Cf. John Flint in J. E. Flint (ed.), *Cambridge history of Africa*, V (Cambridge, 1976), 4.

to their numbers. Social horizons were widened by travel in pursuit of education, both within Africa and abroad, in Europe and the USA. By 1940 a few hundred black Africans, mostly in West and South Africa, had obtained university degrees; perhaps around 200 West Africans had qualified in London as barristers. Africans wrote for publication, chiefly in newspapers but also in books and pamphlets. African writers discussed what they had learned from the white man, what more they wanted from him, and what they wished to preserve from their own cultures. Men and women who had made great efforts to acquire what whites called civilisation found that so far from being welcomed as partners they were liable to be feared as threats to white vested interests. Contacts overseas with blacks of the diaspora, and with white critics of empire, encouraged some Africans to question not just the details but the moral justification of colonial rule. There was growing tension between literate, urban-based élites and the chiefs or other African agents of colonial rule in the countryside. In French-speaking Africa, both north and south of the Sahara, literate Africans began to lose patience with the official doctrine of political emancipation through assimilation into French culture. In the cities of Algeria and Tunisia there was agitation in the 1930s for independence, a goal which was beginning to be discussed on the coast of British West Africa. In these places at least, nationalism was coming to refer less to a sense of ethnic identity than to still embryonic nations united only by common experience of a particular colonial regime.

Thought of this kind was still quite exceptional. It was virtually unknown in the interior of tropical Africa, where the heirs of many pre-colonial rulers still exercised considerable authority, as in Uganda or northern Nigeria. In East and Central Africa, African political discussion was still framed largely in ethnic terms; in the Belgian Congo, white control was for the time being so complete that such discussion scarcely existed, and it was severely checked in Portuguese Africa. In South Africa, black opinion was highly articulate but almost wholly excluded from the country's formal political structures. All the same, the speed with which Africans had adopted European idioms and aspirations confounded prevailing white assumptions about the manipulation of social change among black peoples. Most colonial powers paid lip-service to the idea that in due course Africans should play a larger part in managing their own affairs, but they agreed that there was no question of Africans taking over the government of their own countries in the foreseeable future: those who called for this were given no official hearing. Yet while whites were educating Africans, some at least were being educated by them, even if African lessons often had to take the form of the strike or trade boycott. In Britain, the African Research Survey directed by Lord Hailey prompted efforts as our period ended both to invest in African welfare and to enlarge the political scope of the African intelligentsia. The Second World War was to strengthen the arguments for such strategies; it remained to be seen how far Britain, or any other colonial power, could retain control over the pace of reform as the rate of social change continued to increase.

CHAPTER 1

THE IMPERIAL MIND

For the period under review in this volume, explanations of much that happened in Africa must be sought in Europe. It is necessary to examine the impact of Africa upon the colonial powers if we are to understand the process by which these powers tried to mould Africa for imperial purposes.[1] The acquisition of African empire gave new point to questions about the aims and methods of white enterprise on the continent. How should Africa be governed, and to what end? How far should metropolitan governments intervene? Could the ambitions of governor, capitalist and missionary be reconciled? What steps should be taken to reduce African ignorance of the white man's techniques, and white ignorance of Africa? What use should be made of contemporary advances in knowledge? What part should Africans play in the colonial social order?

Even to list such questions, however, gives an exaggerated impression of the urgency with which they were usually regarded. The imperial mind, whatever its quality, was not in general much concerned with Africa during our period. The speed with which so much of Africa had formally been placed under European control should not be taken to be a measure of its importance to the invaders. Much of the Scramble had been motivated by the negative aim of excluding rival powers: it was not a defence of present interests so much as speculation in possible, but quite unproven, benefits. South Africa, certainly, was important to Britain: by 1911 (when it had just ceased to be a British responsibility), British investment there amounted to £351m; this was on much the same scale as British investment in India or Canada, or Australia and New Zealand combined; it was half the sum invested in the USA and a good deal more than that in

---

[1] For reasons explained in the Preface, this chapter give disproportionate attention to Britain, especially in discussing the 1930s.

Table 1. *Trade with parts of Africa as percentages of British external trade (excluding gold and diamonds).*

	1905	1913	1920	1930	1935	1938
Egypt	2.5	2.4	3.4	1.5	1.7	1.5
British possessions*	0.6	1.0	2.2	2.4	2.7	3.1
South Africa	2.5	2.6	2.1	2.9	4.0	3.9
Rest of Africa	1.0	1.0	1.1	0.8	0.9	0.8
Total	6.6	7.0	8.8	7.6	9.3	9.3

*Including Mandates, Southern Rhodesia and Anglo-Egyptian Sudan.
Note: For the sake of internal consistency, these calculations are based throughout on statistics for British domestic exports and for total British imports (including re-exports). For 1905 and 1913, the trade of the Anglo-Egyptian Sudan is credited to Egypt, and up to 1930 part of the trade of the Rhodesias is credited to Mozambique.
Source: Annual statements of the trade of the United Kingdom.

Argentina.[2] In 1913, Africa as a whole accounted for about 7 per cent and 10 per cent respectively of the external trade (excluding gold) of Britain and France. But this was mostly with Egypt, South Africa or Algeria. Tropical Africa contributed less than 2 per cent to Britain's trade, and less than 1 per cent to that of France (which owed much more to British India, Egypt and China). The Belgian Congo in 1912 contributed only 1 per cent of Belgian trade, and in 1910 Germany's African colonies had accounted for less than 1 per cent of German external trade, while returns on investment were meagre, except from diamonds in South West Africa.[3]

There is, then, an obvious sense in which colonial Africa was largely peripheral to Europe in the early twentieth century. Most politicians and businessmen who looked overseas at all were looking elsewhere, and this remained true throughout our period. All the same, trade with colonial Africa did become more important to its rulers, and substantial investments were made with long-term ends in view. Though few in Europe might think about Africa, those who did thought a good deal about the way

[2] L. H. Gann and P. Duignan, *The rulers of British Africa, 1870–1914* (Stanford, 1978), 371 (based on Paish).
[3] Cf. table 1; see also Marc Michel, *L'Appel à l'Afrique* (Paris, 1982), 139–40.

in which its resources, natural and human, might be turned to account, and about the moral responsibilities entailed in African empire. Much of the debate was conducted among those who had work in Africa — whether in government, business or the churches. In the course of our period, and especially in the 1930s, serious interest in Africa spread more widely into political and academic circles, and clusters of informal opinion began to exert pressure on those in a position to act. But it is with governments that we should begin.

1905–1914

By and large, the overriding concern of the colonial powers was to prevent their colonial possessions becoming financial burdens to the metropolis. Imperialism was not so popular in Europe that tax-payers, who were also voters, were ready to pay its bills. In much of Africa, invasion and administration had thus been left to chartered companies, but many failed. In some regions, notably the Rhodesias, most of Mozambique and parts of French Equatorial Africa, private companies continued to exercise powers of government well into the twentieth century, but in 1908 Belgium had to take over the Congo Independent State. By then, other metropolitan governments had more or less reluctantly committed themselves to governing Africa; they had at least created departments specifically concerned with this task and were beginning to regularise recruitment to their local administrations.

In France, a colonial ministry had been created in 1894, but its responsibilities in Africa were confined to West Africa, Equatorial Africa, French Somaliland and Madagascar. The French ministry of foreign affairs handled Tunisia and Morocco, while Algeria, formally a part of France, was watched over by the ministry of the interior. Italy created a separate colonial ministry in 1912, following the conquest of Libya. In Germany, as in Britain, it was the Foreign Office which had not only taken the lead in the Scramble for Africa but had supervised its 'effective occupation'. It was the reappraisal following expensive and extremely bloody wars of repression in German East and South West Africa which in 1907 led to the creation in Berlin of a separate Colonial Office.

Britain, of course, had long had a Colonial Office, but its historic function had been to supervise colonies of settlement, which in Africa meant the Cape, Natal and Sierra Leone; its original responsibilities in the Gambia, on the Gold Coast and at Lagos were mere afterthoughts. Once the Scramble had subsided, however, there was no reason for the Foreign Office to concern itself with African administration, and it began to transfer to the Colonial Office the care of its numerous African protectorates: in 1900, those which were now styled Southern and Northern Nigeria; in 1904, Nyasaland; in 1905, Uganda, the East Africa Protectorate (later Kenya) and Somaliland; in 1914, Zanzibar. In South Africa, the end of the Anglo-Boer War meant that in 1902–3 the Colonial Office also took charge of the Transvaal, the Orange Free State and Swaziland. This rapid expansion of scope transformed the Colonial Office: the administration of indigenous peoples began to loom larger than relations with progressively independent white settlers. In 1907 a special Dominions Department was created within the Colonial Office to look after relations with Canada, Australia and New Zealand; in 1910 the new Union of South Africa was added to these. The British High Commissioner in South Africa continued to be responsible for the protectorates of Basutoland, Bechuanaland and Swaziland, and for supervising the administration of the Rhodesias by the British South Africa Company. Elsewhere in British Africa, the Colonial Office exercised direct control over the local administrations, though the Foreign Office remained the ultimate authority for the Anglo-Egyptian Sudan since this was, at least in theory, an international condominium.

None of the colonial ministries exercised very much power. The ministers themselves did not rank highly in their own governments, and they presided over relatively small bureaucracies. Most officials in the British Colonial Office saw their role as being to supervise rather than to initiate policy. Winston Churchill, as parliamentary under-secretary, toured East Africa in 1907, with the one civil servant in the Colonial Office to visit tropical Africa before 1914. Officials in Paris and Berlin aspired to rather more direct intervention. French territories were periodically visited by members of a specialised inspectorate that was responsible only to the colonial minister himself. The German colonial secretary, Dernburg, visited East Africa in 1907; in 1908 he visited South West Africa, as did his successor, Solf, in 1912. But despite such tours, and the extension of telegraph cables, metropolis and colonial capital remained in practice far apart.

The main cause of friction between colonial governors and their masters in Europe was the cost of colonial rule. Governors might seek fame by increasing the quantity and quality of government, but their schemes seldom found favour in the metropolis, where many senior officials conceived of policy-making chiefly in terms of budgetary control. This was, after all, a period in which the states of western Europe were concentrating public investment in their own labour force: in Britain, the percentage of the budget devoted to social services rose from 18 in 1900 to 33 in 1913. But officials in metropolis and colony were also estranged by social distance. Metropolitan officials were career civil servants, and most had been recruited by competitive examination. In France and Germany, at least, they belonged to a bureaucratic élite in which financial expertise was highly regarded. In Britain, between 1904 and 1911, the two permanent under-secretaries of state for the colonies had previously served in the Crown Agents (a government procurement agency) and the Board of Trade. Such mandarins considered themselves far superior to the 'men on the spot'. The latter had mostly been recruited much more haphazardly, largely indeed for reasons of economy. In Britain, before 1914, the demand for officials to serve in the colonies 'was moderate in scale both in respect of the numbers and the qualifications required'.[4] Portugal created an Escola Colonial in 1906; Belgium created an École Coloniale in 1911, and France had had one since 1890, but by 1907 it had supplied only 70 of the nearly 500 senior officials in French Africa. As in British and German Africa, many of the rest were drawn from the armed forces: skill at arms and on the parade ground were often deemed qualification enough for the ruler of large numbers of people. Some recruits to German colonial administrations belonged to the home civil service and had received specialist training in Germany, but many were simply young men in search of adventure, and their terms of service were not standardised until 1910. It should moreover be noted that in both French and Belgian Africa Europeans were employed in a variety of subordinate jobs, both within and outside government, which in British West Africa or German Africa were likely to be performed by Africans, and in East Africa by Indians.

[4] R. Furse, *Aucuparius* (London, 1962), 18.

Final responsibility for colonial rule lay with the legislatures in the imperial capitals. In Britain the Liberal government formed in 1905 enjoyed an overwhelming majority in the House of Commons, though 53 Labour members had also been elected. The chief African causes of debate in the decade before 1914 were the Congo scandals and the South African constitution. Parliamentary approval was needed for grants-in-aid to balance colonial budgets, but the sums were small and usually shrinking. The 'left' in Liberal and Labour ranks began to move away from doctrinaire condemnation of empire *per se* towards discussion of how it should be managed, but it could not be said that African issues mattered much in British politics during these years. In France, parliamentary concern was concentrated on Algeria, which was represented by three senators and six deputies. Africa was of some consequence in German politics. Not only did Africa loom larger in the overseas empire of Germany than in those of Britain and France; the Reichstag (parliament) had full control over colonial budgets. Since in other respects its financial control was very limited, debate on colonial affairs became an important field for political manoeuvres which were really concerned with the government of Germany. Conflicts between those with direct interests in the colonies — soldiers, settlers, businessmen, missionaries — could be manipulated by liberal, Catholic or socialist politicians to improve their own bargaining positions. This was to have a considerable effect on colonial policy.[5]

Imperial bureaucrats might consider parsimony essential to the achievement of financial self-sufficiency in the colonies, but it was clearly not enough. The revenue base of colonial governments had to be increased, which meant expanding trade. Opinions differed as to how this could be done. William Ponty, governor-general of French West Africa from 1908 to 1915, valued close cooperation between commerce and administration but considered that agricultural production was best left to Africans. He remarked in 1908 that French West Africa 'was not established to facilitate the emigration of white workers. The blacks...make perfect settlers.'[6]

[5] A colonial advisory council, founded in 1891, had represented colonial interest groups, but it was abolished in 1908.
[6] Quoted by G. Wesley Johnson, 'William Ponty and republican paternalism in French West Africa', in L. H. Gann and P. Duignan (eds.), *African proconsuls* (New York, 1978), 141.

This view was confirmed by experience: Africans were clearly able to supply what were then expanding markets for tropical products, and Ponty could see no merit in entrusting production to concessionary companies. In French Equatorial Africa, however, government expense was reduced to a bare minimum by handing over huge areas to companies with concessions of monopoly rights to the purchase of local produce. Such empire often proved very profitable as well as cheap; it also gave rise to abuses such as had made Leopold's Congo infamous. In German Kamerun, concessionary companies were also prominent, while in German East and South West Africa white settlement had been encouraged.

In British West Africa this was never a serious proposition. True, the mines in the Gold Coast employed more whites than the government did up to 1914, but otherwise, as in Nigeria, whites were engaged in trade and business, and in 1910 African land rights in Nigeria were firmly protected by legislation directed against expatriates. In 1911 the Colonial Office resisted demands from mining companies in the Gold Coast and Nigeria for controls on labour which would have threatened African cocoa production. In the same year William Lever, the soap magnate, was thwarted by the Colonial Office's rooted objection to monopoly concessions. Harcourt, the British colonial secretary from 1910 to 1915, extolled in 1913 the expansion of exports grown by Africans; this pleased him both as an improving landowner himself and as the member for a Lancashire cotton-mill constituency.

Yet the Colonial Office could not easily override the vested interests of Europeans when these were backed by governors, as they were in 1914 by Lugard (over the Nigerian tin industry) and by Clifford (over land in the Gold Coast). And in other parts of British Africa the issues were still less clear-cut. The highlands of Kenya (then called British East Africa) had for some time been widely regarded in Britain as a natural field for white settlement, which was keenly promoted by Charles Eliot, commissioner from 1900 to 1904. Both Kenya and Northern Rhodesia attracted a modest flow of white immigrants, chiefly from South Africa, while Southern Rhodesia had from the 1890s been developed by the British South Africa Company as a colony of white settlement. In Uganda and Nyasaland, white settlers comprised only a few dozen planters, but their aspirations echoed those of their more influential neighbours.

In the eyes of metropolitan officials, white settlers were both an asset and a liability. In theory, they had the techniques and resources to initiate large-scale production; they were cheaper to employ in colonial administration than recruits from the metropolis; and they opened up the prospect of devolving both the responsibility and the cost of government, as in South Africa. But in practice settlers often needed special help from government if they were to compete successfully with African producers. Settlers were therefore liable to involve government in conflict with Africans which called for expensive military expeditions. In Kenya, the violence of 'pacification' in 1905–8 caused much concern in the Colonial Office, where one official advised that the settlers be repatriated.[7] The governor, Hayes Sadler, baulked at so radical a proposal, but in 1909 the Colonial Office replaced him by Girouard, whose Nigerian experience was thought a timely counterweight. In fact, Girouard promoted settler interests to the extent of initiating a mass removal of Masai herdsmen: this shocked the Colonial Office into requiring his resignation. In 1907 the Colonial Office interfered in Swaziland, where chiefs had alienated great tracts of land to settlers and speculators: one-third of this land now reverted to African ownership. In 1908 the colonial secretary, Lord Crewe, disallowed a Southern Rhodesian ordinance, already approved by the high commissioner, to restrict Indian immigration. Both here and elsewhere, however, there were practical limits to the effectiveness of metropolitan disapproval. Settler ambitions were sometimes thwarted, but not to the point of provoking disaffection: the Masai move in Kenya was not reversed.

There was comparable debate in Germany. The great African rebellions in 1904–5 in East and South West Africa had compelled reappraisal not only of administrative organisation but of economic strategy. More attention was now paid to those who argued that Africans were capable of 'rational' economic behaviour and could, given due incentives, produce certain crops more cheaply than whites. This view was shared by three new colonial governors: Zech (Togo, 1905–10), Seitz (Kamerun, 1907–10) and Rechenberg (East Africa, 1906–11). It was Rechenberg who

---

[7] Advice repeated in 1942 by Harold Macmillan, when he was briefly under-secretary of state for the colonies.

encountered most resistance from local whites. At first he seemed
to have the ear of the colonial secretary, Dernburg, but arguments
about African labour were soon woven into the shifting alignments of parties in the Reichstag. The settlers' friends proved to
have more political weight in Berlin, and when Rechenberg left
the settlers seemed more firmly entrenched than ever.

The most obvious measure of settler strength was their
membership of representative institutions in the colonies. In
French black Africa these were comparatively insignificant, since
outside Senegal they never acquired legislative powers. For
German settlers, as we have just seen, it was specially important
to be able to exert influence in Berlin, but they also made
constitutional advances in the colonies. In South West Africa,
where they were most numerous, they obtained control in 1909
of local government in their own areas, and they had as many votes
as officials did on the new territorial council, which was given
limited budgetary powers in 1913. In German East Africa, settlers
were granted a majority on the governor's advisory council in
1912, and in 1914 were able to elect councils in two coastal towns.
In the British Empire, there was a long tradition of sharing power
with local residents through legislative councils. As these created
a body of local law, so British statute law took on a mainly residual
importance. In the former colonies of white settlement — Canada,
Australia, New Zealand, the Cape and Natal — the councils had
originally comprised a majority of officials sitting alongside a
minority of government-nominated representatives of colonial
society; in the course of time, settlers gained the right to elect their
own representatives, who eventually became a self-governing
majority. In tropical Africa, settler populations were tiny, and it
was not at all clear how far this pattern could be developed.
Settlers were most numerous in Southern Rhodesia, which in any
case was run by a chartered company, and elected council
members were in a majority by 1907. In the same year, legislative
councils were created in Nyasaland and Kenya; they included a
few nominated non-officials. White settlers in Kenya were inclined
to regard this as opening the way towards white self-government,
but this ambition was challenged by the much larger number of
Indian immigrants. And in British West Africa the institution of
legislative councils at once raised the question of African political
status.

Superficially, the councils in West Africa resembled those in

British territories of white settlement. In Sierra Leone, the Gold Coast and Lagos the settlers happened to be black: there were substantial minorities of English-speaking, mostly literate and Christian blacks, some of whom were descended from repatriated slaves. These territories were termed 'colonies', which meant that all their inhabitants were British subjects, and thus enjoyed an innate right of appeal to the Privy Council, unlike the indigenous inhabitants of 'protectorates'. In each West African colony, the governor was advised by a legislative council, and by 1906 each council included one or more Africans among its nominated unofficial members. However, the scope of these councils varied. By the end of the nineteenth century the hinterland of each colony had come under British rule but was administered as a 'protectorate' distinct from the coast-based colony. In Sierra Leone, the power of the legislative council was extended over the protectorate. Elsewhere, the legislative councils were confined to the colony (except for an extension from Lagos to Southern Nigeria from 1906 to 1914 and again in 1922). Thus with the expansion of British power in the Gold Coast and Nigeria the relative importance of the legislative council declined.

This was part of a more general British trend to restrict African participation in central government. It was one thing to allow this to loyal 'black Englishmen' within the original colony. It was a very different matter to allow such men a share, however slight, in ruling the newly-subdued peoples of the protectorates: what might be allowed to white settlers in East Africa could not be allowed to blacks in the Gold Coast and Nigeria. So while educated West Africans lost ground at the centre of the political stage, they were also gradually excluded from the colonial administrative service. In the nineteenth century this had for a time made much use of anglicised blacks, but the recruitment of whites at their expense was encouraged both by medical advances[8] and by late-Victorian racial theory.[9] By 1900 Africans were debarred from the administrative (or 'political') branches of colonial government. They could at best hope to serve in the

---

[8] Among white officials in West Africa, the death-rate per thousand fell from 20.6 in 1903 to 11.8 in 1913. (Cmd. 920. *West Africa. Vital statistics of non-native officials. Returns for 1919*, 4.) By 1935 the rate had been reduced to 5.1, which for British colonial Africa was not exceptional.
[9] Cf. R. Symonds, *The British and their successors: a study in the development of the government services in the new states* (London, 1966), 119–26.

ancillary technical services, and even there, in 1914, a move by the Colonial Office to increase African recruitment to the medical services in West Africa was thwarted by local white opposition.

Thus as the British set about the task of governing not mere outposts but vast regions of tropical Africa, they began to think in terms of collaboration not with coastal élites but with indigenous rulers. Economy was certainly an important consideration in developing what later became known as 'indirect rule'. But both in London and Africa officials were keen to strengthen the powers of chiefs as a way of restricting the influence of educated Africans. Official nervousness, indeed, was such that in 1913 Lugard, in Nigeria, was allowed to discourage schools from teaching the Stuart period of English history, since this might foster 'disrespect for authority'.[10] African rulers by divine right were judiciously cultivated. In the sphere of civil law, African custom was upheld insofar as it was not 'repugnant' to British notions of justice and morality; to varying degrees, African authorities were also allowed to deal with minor criminal offences. Harcourt admired the 'civilised cohesion of Muslim Northern Nigeria'; so too did his German counterpart Solf, who actually paid it a visit in 1913 and congratulated Lugard on his work in preserving African institutions.

In southern Africa, imperial expansion had likewise undermined the position of middle-class blacks. The Act of Union put at risk the former Cape Colony's policy that 'civilisation', not race, should be the test of fitness for political rights. In support of this principle, the high commissioner, Selborne, disallowed a Southern Rhodesian bill in 1906 which would have excluded blacks from the common voting roll, but in 1912 Harcourt approved new franchise qualifications which had virtually the same effect. Rhodes's high-sounding principle of 'equal rights for all civilised men' was degraded to a Jim Crow tactic for ensuring racial hegemony.

In some ways French official attitudes were rather different, yet they can be seen to have traversed a somewhat similar course. The old communes of Senegal were actually a part of France, insofar as they elected a deputy to the National Assembly. This was the birthright of all men who were native to the communes. But it

[10] P. H. S. Hatton, 'British colonial policy in Africa, 1910–1914' (Ph.D. thesis, University of Cambridge, 1971), 181.

was wholly exceptional: no more than the Lagos colony did the four communes provide a precedent for the extension of colonial government. True, the elected council which helped run the communes was extended in 1920 to represent the whole of Senegal, but this served to boost chiefs at the expense of the communes and in any case the council's powers were reduced to insignificance: indeed, it closely resembled the superfluous Nigerian Council created by Lugard in 1913. The notion that black Africa might be part of France was not wholly abandoned: from 1912 French citizenship was made available to Africans throughout French West Africa. Yet the qualifications required were about as hard to obtain as those for Africans who wished to vote in Southern Rhodesia; outside the communes of Senegal there were only 94 black French citizens in West Africa by 1922 and about 2,000 in 1937. All other Africans were defined as French subjects, bound by local law and custom as approved by white officials and by a severe penal code introduced in 1907–9. A somewhat similar distinction obtained in Algeria, where a majority subject to Muslim law but also to a severe penal code contrasted with a minority consisting of French citizens subject to French law. It was possible for Muslims to apply for French citizenship, but this involved losing their status in Muslim law, and even by 1936 there were only 8,000 French citizens of Muslim origin in Algeria.

In German Africa, the question of citizenship or voting rights for Africans never arose. Among the literate élites of the coastal towns, German culture was by no means universal. Many such Africans, in both East and West Africa, had been educated by English-speaking missions. German colonial governments did much more than the British at this period to promote African education, if only because mission schools did not satisfy their needs for clerical staff. But in East Africa Swahili seemed the most useful language for government clerks. There was more consistent emphasis on teaching German to Africans in Togo and Kamerun, whence by 1914 two missionary societies had sent a number of Africans to Germany for training. But no amount of German culture could qualify an African for equal status with whites. From 1908 two Togolese could advise on the administration of Lomé, but an African petition for legal equality in 1913 was ignored, while black entrepreneurs were prevented from competing with white traders. In Kamerun, Seitz argued in vain for African representation on his advisory council, and after his departure the rights of African proprietors in Duala were set aside.

Ruling the new empires in Africa involved cultivating local allies, whether white settlers, the black bourgeoisie or black chiefs. It also involved learning about Africa and Africans. European knowledge of the continent's languages, cultures and natural resources was still fragmentary, and filling the gaps could benefit both government and trade. At this early stage, administrators in the field played a leading part in extending knowledge about Africans. In 1905 officials in French West Africa were urged to study traditional law, and in 1909 Maurice Delafosse initiated work on a code of civil law for use in 'native' courts. Knowledge of Islam in black Africa was furthered by a special department of Muslim affairs, in which Paul Marty made numerous regional studies. In German Africa, attempts were also made to collate customary law,[11] a particular interest of Zech in Togo, while in Italian Eritrea important work in this field was done by Conti Rossini.

Germans led the way in applying science to agriculture and forestry in Africa, at research stations in East Africa (Amani) and Kamerun (Victoria). The British obtained plants and expertise from the botanical gardens at Kew. Like the Germans, they soon established agricultural departments in their African territories, though that in the Gold Coast was for long concerned with quality control in the cocoa trade rather than with experimental production. Surveying advanced very unevenly. Private expeditions from Europe did valuable work in the Ruwenzori mountains, Ethiopia and southern Angola; French officers greatly improved maps of the Sahara. But outside South Africa little geodetic triangulation had been done before 1914, and not much more by 1940; even then it was concentrated on the frontiers dividing the colonial powers. Again, South Africa and Southern Rhodesia were the only countries with an official geological survey before 1914, though there was a mineral survey in Nigeria. Medical knowledge grew rather faster, due partly to the advent of doctors, even if they were still much preoccupied with the health of

[11] This belatedly bore fruit in E. Schultz-Ewerth and L. Adam, *Das Eingeborenenrecht*, 2 vols. (Stuttgart, 1929–30).

whites.[12] Indeed, the range of European professional expertise exposed to African problems had increased substantially. By 1914 the senior government staff in the seven African territories under the British Colonial Office included 258 medical officers and almost 600 other technical officers, as against only 540 administrators.

What was learned in the field was, at least in part, pooled and disseminated in the metropolis. In Britain, the Imperial Institute had been established in 1887 to promote the exchange of scientific knowledge within the Empire. In 1906 the Colonial Office took the initiative in enabling the Institute to extend its network to tropical Africa. In 1899 schools of tropical medicine had been founded in Liverpool and London; the foundation of the London school was instigated by the then colonial secretary, Joseph Chamberlain, and the Imperial Bureau of Entomology, created in 1913, grew from a suggestion by H. J. Read, then in charge of the East African department of the Colonial Office. Meanwhile, the Colonial Office kept in touch with outside knowledge and experience through newly-established advisory committees on medicine, entomology, sanitation and surveys. In Paris, the Pasteur Institute became a centre for teaching and research in tropical medicine; in Hamburg an institute for these purposes was founded in 1899 and in Brussels a school of tropical medicine was opened in 1910. The Colonial Economic Committee in Germany, set up in 1896, both initiated colonial research and circulated its results among interested businessmen. Germany pioneered the academic study of African languages, which had been taught in the Oriental Seminar at Berlin since 1887. In 1909 Delafosse

---

[12] Between 1905 and 1940 about 60 dissertations on African topics were accepted at British universities for the MD degree. Some doctors made notable contributions in other fields, e.g. Norman Leys, Meredith Sanderson and H. S. Stannus, all of whom worked in Nyasaland before 1914. Doctoral theses were presented to French universities (including that of Algiers) between 1905 and 1940 as follows:

Area studied	Medicine	Pharmacy	Veterinary medicine
French N. Africa	237[1]	38	57
Sub-Saharan Africa	23	4	13
Madagascar	16[2]	3	9

[1] including 22 by Arab authors
[2] including 11 by Malagasy authors

introduced African language teaching at the École Coloniale in Paris, along with a new emphasis on the study of African history and institutions (in contrast to the earlier, assimilationist, focus on Roman law).

Scholarly interest in the peoples of sub-Saharan Africa was very unevenly distributed in Europe. It was most evident before 1914 in the German-speaking world, where ethnology and its ancillary craft, ethnography, were well established, even if their practitioners were not always conspicuous for logical rigour. Between 1905 and 1914 ten ethnographic expeditions under German leadership visited most parts of tropical Africa; their sources of support included the government and universities as well as museums seeking to expand collections. Elsewhere, few such initiatives were taken. Belgium despatched Captain Hutereau to study the Zande, and Belgian sociologists devised a questionnaire to elicit a series of ethnographies from missionaries and others. Marty's work on Islam in French West Africa has been mentioned. The few professional ethnologists in Britain made a very limited contribution to knowledge of Africa at this period. This was not for want of interest on their part. In 1896 and again in 1908 they vainly urged the government to form an Imperial Bureau of Ethnology (following American example); they had also vainly appealed in 1900 for funds to record native custom in South Africa. Two academic enquiries were undertaken. The Sudan government commissioned ethnographic surveys in 1909–12 from C. G. Seligman, who in 1913 became professor of ethnology in London. The Colonial Office appointed Northcote Thomas to make a series of ethnographic studies in Southern Nigeria (1909–10) and Sierra Leone. In addition, the Hungarian Emil Torday's expedition to the Congo in 1907–9 was sponsored by the British Museum, whose ethnographic collections had been compared unfavourably to those of the Berlin Museum.[13]

By and large, the study of African peoples was left by the British to those already on the spot. Nevertheless, laymen as well as academics were influenced by ideas of mainly German origin: there was a widespread assumption that preliterate peoples could be classified in terms of 'races' and 'tribes'. Between 1905 and

[13] Cf. Thomas's complaint in his preface to Alice Werner, *The natives of British Central Africa* (London, 1906), a volume in a series edited by Thomas on 'The native races of the British Empire'.

1914 there were published in Europe about eighty books of African ethnography; most were devoted to particular African peoples and most were written by serving administrators. This kind of work became the dominant genre in serious European writing about Africa, supplanting the detailed travel journals characteristic of the nineteenth century.

The social problems of sub-Saharan Africa received no more academic attention than its ethnography. In Brussels lectures on colonial studies were given by Henri Rolin, a lawyer with socialist sympathies who served on the Colonial Council from 1910 to 1922. In 1911–12 Rolin visited Katanga and the Rhodesias, but as a detached and sceptical witness to early colonial enterprise and administration in Africa he was almost alone. British opinion on Africa was largely articulated through societies which, as in other imperial capitals, brought together those who had been employed in colonial territories. The few available works of reference were mostly written by officials or ex-officials. The Anti-Slavery and Aborigines' Protection Society ventilated concern about the appropriation of African land and labour, and the South African Native Races Committee, led by lawyers and clergymen, published careful reports in 1901 and 1908. Otherwise, almost the only extended critical comment in Britain on African conditions in South Africa came in 1906 from Sydney Olivier, who then worked in the West African department of the Colonial Office and was an active Fabian. From 1905 Oxford University had a chair in colonial history, bequeathed by Alfred Beit, the mining magnate, but its first incumbent, who came straight from the Colonial Office, had no special interest in Africa; its colonial history received much more attention from French and Belgian writers. In Britain, informed journalism on sub-Saharan Africa came only from H. W. Nevinson, who wrote a scathing report on his visit to Angola in 1904–5, and E. D. Morel (founder of the Congo Reform Association and friend of the Liverpool trader John Holt), who visited Nigeria in 1910. The most far-reaching critique of British colonial rule at this period, including a long discussion of Natal, was produced by T. E. S. Scholes, a black Jamaican-born freelance writer who had worked as a mission doctor in West Africa and viewed with alarm signs of growing white racial solidarity.

Popular images of Africa were still coloured by tales of small wars in desert or jungle against veiled fanatics or naked savages. Rider Haggard's romances of the 1880s were superior examples of a genre much favoured by boys' magazines, both in Britain and on the Continent. The Anglo-Boer War brought many British families hard up against South African reality, but that was a war between whites. Yet post-war reconstruction, and the rebellion in Natal in 1906, inspired a boys' adventure story with a difference. John Buchan had worked on Milner's staff in the Transvaal; in *Prester John* (1910) he portrayed an educated African king, John Laputa, whom whites must both admire and fear. By witnessing the relapse of this African leader from 'civilisation' to 'savagery', the young white narrator learns 'the meaning of the white man's duty' and also 'the difference between white and black, the gift of responsibility'. The tale nourished imperial self-righteousness; yet it also raised awkward questions which would be taken up by metropolitan policy-makers ten years later. The defeat of Laputa's rising was crowned by the creation of a 'great native college...no factory for making missionaries and black teachers, but an institution for giving the Kaffirs the kind of training which fits them to be good citizens of the state. There you will find every kind of technical workshop, and the finest experimental farms, where the blacks are taught modern agriculture.' Two very different exemplars of this ideal could be found in contemporary Nyasaland. The one was strictly run by the Scots missionaries of Livingstonia; its aims were already being subverted by labour migration. The other was led by an African, John Chilembwe; ironically, he was himself to play the part of a Laputa by leading a rising in 1915. It is also curious that Buchan observes of the stone walling at Great Zimbabwe, 'now it is believed that it was built by natives'. For this alludes to MacIver's work in Rhodesia in 1905, the first by a professional archaeologist, which proved to those open to reason that the stone buildings were the work, not of exotic intruders, but of people ancestral to the present inhabitants. 'A corner is lifted of that veil which has surrounded the forgotten but not irrecoverable past of the African negro.'[14] At the time, however, few if any of Buchan's readers can have recognised his reference to scholarship which challenged prevailing white notions of African abilities, and over the next half-century very few archaeologists would follow MacIver's lead.

[14] D. Randall MacIver, *Mediaeval Rhodesia* (London, 1906), 87.

1914–1930

The First World War caused important changes in the way in which Africa was regarded by its white rulers. War compelled them to take new account of the resources of Africa, human and material. France chose to use men. Her trade with black Africa (which was mostly with Senegal) was scarcely 1 per cent of all French trade in 1913, and even less by the end of the war, but this was largely because potential African producers were conscripted south as well as north of the Sahara to bear arms on the Western Front, thus easing demands on French manpower which would otherwise have crippled industrial production. In Britain, the Colonial Office strenuously resisted War Office pressure to use African fighting troops in Europe, but they played a major part in the East African campaign, while huge numbers of men served in it as carriers and suffered still higher death-rates. Britain also increased her dependence on African produce during the war: the proportion of total British imports (excluding gold and diamonds) derived from sub-Saharan Africa rose from 2.8 per cent in 1909–13 to 4.3 per cent in 1919–23. These figures reflect a rapid growth in the relative value of raw materials from British colonial Africa, even if their absolute value, in real terms, changed little. Besides, colonial governments helped in a small way to pay for the war: not only did they contribute to the costs of African campaigns; they also made 'war contributions' to the metropolis.

The war revealed the value of Africans as servants of empire, and the scale of their efforts quickened in at least some of their rulers a sense of obligation; more generally the appalling experience of trench warfare could strengthen commitment to the service of an ideal — and scepticism towards higher authority.[15] But if the war helped to bring some whites and Africans closer together, it also sowed new seeds of white doubt and fear. Little weight need be given to the view that war between whites had tarnished white prestige: this says more about white anxiety and vanity than African deference. But it did matter that the pressures of war much increased the burdens imposed by colonial regimes. Here and there, especially in West Africa, Africans offered

[15] Cf. F. H. Melland, *In witchbound Africa* (London, 1923), 26–7; R. E. Wraith, *Guggisberg* (London, 1967), 69–70; W. B. Cohen, 'Robert Delavignette', in Gann and Duignan, *African proconsuls*, 186.

resistance to these burdens, and this was increasingly organised, as through the trade boycott. In March 1919 Sir Harry Johnston, a veteran explorer and pioneer pro-consul, told the African Society that the war had seen the 'beginning of revolt against the white man's supremacy.'[16] Already this supremacy was beginning to give way. Between 1919 and 1922 nationalists in Egypt compelled Britain to concede internal self-government, even if Britain hoped thereby to strengthen her grip on Egypt's external relations. And in 1917 the British government committed itself to 'the progressive realization of responsible government in India as an integral part of the British Empire'.[17] This was bound to have implications, sooner or later, for Africa as well.

In Britain, converging thoughts about the opportunities, obligations and hazards of empire were crystallised in the word 'trusteeship'. The aftermath of war gave this a special significance. Germany had been defeated and her colonies occupied by the Allies, while Turkey had been shorn of the Ottoman empire. The future of these spoils of war was a major concern of the Peace Conference in Paris in 1919. The USA, traditionally mistrustful of European imperialism, wished these occupied empires to become an international responsibility, a goal that was shared by pressure groups in France and Britain. The conference agreed that they should be governed by the victorious Allied powers, but as mandates of the League of Nations. The final distribution of mandates was not complete until 1922, but meanwhile the League had to determine the responsibilities of those to whom mandates were assigned. The African mandates were adjudged to be territories whose peoples were 'not yet able to stand by themselves under the strenuous conditions of the modern world'; their well-being and development was 'a sacred trust of civilisation'. Thus the African mandates required the mandatory powers to suppress slavery and the slave trade, and the use of forced labour for private gain, and forbade them to use African manpower to strengthen their own armed forces. The mandatory powers were further enjoined to maintain an open door to Christian missions and (except in South West Africa) to the trade of other League members; they were forbidden to grant monopolistic concessions.

[16] H. H. Johnston, 'The Africa of the immediate future', *Journal of the African Society*, 1919, **18**, no. 71, 163.
[17] Kenneth Robinson, *The dilemmas of trusteeship* (London, 1965), 4.

Finally, the mandatory powers were urged to 'promote to the utmost the material and moral well-being and the social progress of the inhabitants'.[18]

These goals were left conveniently vague, and although a Permanent Mandates Commission was set up in 1921 to monitor the performance of the mandatory powers, it was never given the means to interfere. Nonetheless, the code of behaviour expressed in the mandates was an implicit critique of earlier phases in colonial history. It represented a reassertion of the international conscience which had animated the anti-slavery conference at Brussels in 1890 and the campaign against the Congo Independent State. True, the code did not oblige Britain to change its ways; Britain, after all, had taken a lead in framing it. Yet there lay its main significance: as a formal statement of what Britain's rulers expected of a colonial administration. Indeed, the junior minister for the colonies, Leo Amery, had in July 1919 declared that parliament was 'in the position of trustee' to the peoples of the colonial empire in general. And in 1922 Lord Lugard, who had retired from Nigeria in 1918, published *The dual mandate in British tropical Africa*. This developed Joseph Chamberlain's view that the welfare of Europe and that of Africa were essentially interdependent, but Lugard refined it in the light of twenty years' more experience of colonial rule and stressed the need to protect Africans by restricting the scope of alien economic enterprise. A similar doctrine of trusteeship was extended to the colonial world at large when in 1922 the League of Nations set up the International Labour Organisation.

This emphasis on the protective role of the imperial trustee was at odds with the dominant trend among the makers of British colonial policy. The war had given new scope to imperialists. Milner, the architect of reconstruction in South Africa after the Boer War, entered Lloyd George's War Cabinet in 1916. Smuts, who had led the British imperial forces in East Africa in 1916–17, and was also a member of the South African parliament, joined the War Cabinet in 1917; he also took a leading part in the Paris Peace Conference, where he pressed South Africa's own claims to empire. As the economic power of Britain and France declined in relation to that of the USA, their governments became more

[18] *Ibid.* 20–1.

attentive to those who argued the value of imperial links, whether with dependent territories or with autonomous partners such as South Africa and other British Dominions. When Milner became colonial secretary in 1919, he sought to make the colonial empire an engine of economic growth. Like his radical French counterpart, Sarraut, Milner called for investment in colonial infrastructures to boost production. But the times were unpropitious. Economic weakness at home might be a reason for strengthening empire, but it was also an obstacle. Besides, there were more pressing concerns: for Britain, trouble in Ireland, India and the Middle East;[19] for France the reconstruction of her war-ravaged north-east. The trade depression of 1920–1 stiffened the ingrained reluctance of the British Treasury to facilitate colonial ventures. It was ready enough to join Milner in encouraging private enterprise (which had received much favour from colonial governments during the war). But this was opposed by senior officials in the Colonial Office.

Nonetheless, it still seemed worthwhile to pursue imperial ambitions on a political plane. Union in South Africa had very largely fulfilled one British dream of imperial federation; at the same time, it was also the inspiration for other such dreams, expounded in the pages of the *Round Table*. This journal was founded in 1910 (the year of Union) by Philip Kerr, a former member of Milner's 'kindergarten' in South Africa. It sought to promote closer links between populations of British origin and culture around the world, and it lent intellectual weight to belief in the genius of the British for government, especially over other 'races'. The defeat of Germany — where some had cherished visions of a *Mittelafrika* straddling the continent — gave new hope to imperial dreamers in Britain. Before the war, Britain and Germany had made provisional plans to dismember Mozambique, of which Portugal herself controlled only the southern third. Milner now enabled Union Castle, a British shipping line, to acquire confiscated German shares in a subsidiary of the Niassa Company, which mis-ruled the far north. Milner also enabled the British-dominated Mozambique Company to finance a railway from Beira to Nyasaland, at the expense of the latter; this was

[19] In 1920 Milner sought, against the advice of his own officials, to help the War Office use African soldiers in Mesopotamia, but the rising there was quelled by the RAF and Indian troops.

explicitly meant to boost British influence in an area on which American firms were thought to have designs. Most important of all, when the League of Nations assigned the mandate over most of ex-German East Africa to Britain, the way seemed clear for building some sort of British Dominion that might encompass the continent from the Limpopo to the borders of Ethiopia. However, plans towards this end had to wait upon events in Kenya and the Rhodesias.

By the end of the war, the charter of the British South Africa Company was approaching expiry. The company had no wish to renew it, but argued over the terms of transfer. When Winston Churchill succeeded Milner as colonial secretary in 1921, he tried to persuade the settlers in Southern Rhodesia to join South Africa as a fifth province: like Smuts, he saw them as a potential counterweight to nationalist Afrikaners. The settlers voted instead for self-government, which they achieved in 1923, and meanwhile Churchill had taken the fateful decision to let them run their own defence force. In theory, Britain retained control over external relations, but in practice this was rapidly obscured by Southern Rhodesia's participation in imperial conferences. Britain also reserved the right to veto legislation affecting Africans, but this was never used; more important, in practice, was the informal agreement that such legislation should be discussed in draft with officials in London. In this way, Britain sometimes exercised a moderating influence, but in matters of detail rather than principle. As for Northern Rhodesia, this was problematic. Back in 1899, Milner had considered that it lay beyond the proper frontiers of British-dominated southern Africa. Twenty years later, there was reason to see Northern Rhodesia differently. True, it had attracted little white settlement, and the prospects for large-scale mining had scarcely been investigated. But even if its main use to capitalists was still as a labour reserve for mines elsewhere, it could serve imperial ends as a link in a chain of white settlement up the central spine of eastern Africa. It was clearly too soon to think of self-government, and the Colonial Office took it over from the company in 1924. But the first governor, Herbert Stanley, was an old South Africa hand who soon set about plans for encouraging white settlement, while confining Africans in reserves.

Over Kenya, the British government was at odds with itself. White aspirations to self-government were encouraged by Milner when he allowed British subjects of 'European' descent a large elected minority in the legislative council. The much more numerous Indians were championed by the India Office. Settlers, alarmed by new plans for Indian representation, plotted rebellion in 1922: no less significant, settler non-cooperation had obliged the government to withdraw a new income tax. A constitutional compromise was achieved in 1923 when the 'paramountcy' of African interests was upheld by the colonial secretary, now the Duke of Devonshire. This could perhaps be seen as a reassertion by the Colonial Office of control over Kenya at the expense of the India Office as well as the settlers. But the Colonial Office continued to exercise this control very cautiously: official attitudes to both Kenya and Northern Rhodesia were henceforward dominated by concern to avoid any further confrontation with settlers. White interests in Kenya were effectively, if discreetly, served by the appointment of men with South African experience to key tasks in agriculture, the railways, education and local government. Besides, Kenya was central to any wider plans for entrenching white hegemony in eastern Africa. The first steps were taken by a parliamentary commission which toured Northern Rhodesia, Nyasaland and East Africa in 1924. It was instructed by the short-lived first Labour government to examine prospects both for coordinating policy in the region and for improving the condition of Africans. But it was dominated by the Conservative chairman, Ormsby-Gore; its conclusions, reported in 1925, were congenial to the new Conservative colonial secretary, Leo Amery; and Ormsby-Gore became Amery's deputy.

Amery remained at the Colonial Office throughout Stanley Baldwin's government from 1924 to 1929; his tenure was the longest of any colonial secretary between Harcourt and Creech Jones (1946–50). True, this degree of stability (and that of Amery's senior civil servants) must be measured against the reign of Warren Fisher as permanent secretary to the Treasury from 1919 to 1939; this undoubtedly cramped the style of other departments. Still, Amery made the most of his time. He set up the Empire Marketing Board in 1926, through which modest sums were directed to agricultural research in the colonies. He toured the Dominions in 1927–8 and made a point of visiting the Rhodesias; he furthered the interests of white tobacco farmers in Southern Rhodesia and sought to boost white settlement there.

In 1926 he arranged a £10m loan for transport works and scientific research in East Africa; this was justified as a way of stimulating British exports, and thus employment. The same rationale was offered for moving towards the idea of outright grants for colonial development: a Conservative policy implemented by the second Labour government in the Colonial Development Act of 1929. But Amery's special concern was to further the emergence of a white Dominion in eastern Africa. In 1925 he appointed as governor of Kenya Edward Grigg, neither a civil servant nor a soldier but a politician sympathetic to *Round Table* ideals. In 1927 Amery sent out the Hilton Young Commission to East Africa to report on the possibilities for closer union — a term generally understood to mean the subordination of regional policies to settler minorities, especially those in Kenya. This time, however, the visitors were much more impressed by the force of Indian (as well as African) opposition: their report in 1929 held out no hope of reconciling the rival claims of settlers and Indians. The cause of closer union was not abandoned, but it was seriously retarded by the fall of the Conservatives in 1929, the greater weight of India in imperial counsels, and the onset of the 1930s depression.

The Milner–Amery vision of empire was shared by few, if any, civil servants. Fiddes, permanent under-secretary at the Colonial Office from 1916 to 1921, had worked for Milner in South Africa but was plainly irritated by settler pretensions in Kenya. Samuel Wilson, head of the Colonial Office from 1925 to 1933, though more soldier than mandarin, was despatched to East Africa by Amery in 1929 to tackle local opinion on closer union yet again, but his few crumbs of comfort were offset by the vehement objections of the governor of Tanganyika, Sir Donald Cameron. Senior officials in London regarded Grigg's 'South African' plans for Kenya as a direct challenge to their own authority. But it is easier to say what the Colonial Office opposed than to say what it approved. The question came more sharply into focus when in 1925 the Dominions Office took over responsibility for relations with the self-governing empire. This might seem to have opened the way for the Colonial Office to achieve a distinctive new identity, as the chief trustee for Britain's subject peoples outside India. But Amery remained head of both departments; the accretions of the Colonial Office in the Middle East complicated the picture; and in any case senior officials had been trained to guard rather than to guide. The Colonial Office was organised to deal with places rather than problems; despite the appointment in the 1920s of specialist advisers on trade, medicine and agriculture, it was ill-adapted to promote the economic initiatives wished upon it by Amery. Ormsby-Gore in 1926 found it 'out-of-date and creaking badly'.[20] The same charge was made by Sir George Schuster, who as a member of the Hilton Young commission dampened Amery's hopes of closer union. Schuster, fresh from reorganising the finances of the Sudan, wrote from Northern Rhodesia in 1928 that 'it is astounding to find each little Government in each of these detached countries working out, on its own, problems which are common to all, without any knowledge of what its neighbours are doing and without any direction on main lines of policy from the Colonial Office'.[21]

These narrow perspectives were perpetuated by the structure and management of the colonial service. From 1919 all recruitment to administrative posts in Africa was handled by Ralph Furse, who firmly believed they required not brainpower so much as force of character, as developed by the team sports and prefectorial discipline of the average English public school. Selection was based on personal impressions: a degree was desirable (and most recruits had been to Oxford or Cambridge) but its quality mattered less than for entry to the Sudan Political Service, let alone the Indian Civil Service. From 1926 most recruits to the administrative service spent several months at Oxford or Cambridge, taking courses that included anthropology and colonial history. But this was much less rigorous than the training provided by the Écoles Coloniales in France and Belgium, or the Colonial University set up at Antwerp in 1920, and until 1937 there were no formal arrangements for in-service training. In Nigeria, as late as 1940, out of 110 administrative officers empowered to act as magistrates only thirteen were professionally qualified.

Furse's methods of selection accorded well enough with the priorities of colonial administration, which could still be defined as keeping the peace cheaply. Furse himself later remarked that good district administration consisted of 'a reasonable hut tax, the

[20] W. G. Ormsby-Gore, minute, 15 December 1926, CO 967/2B.
[21] Sir George Schuster, *Private work and public causes* (Cowbridge, 1979), 78.

preservation of tribal customs, young men respectful to their elders, proper care of native agriculture'.[22] It was logical to employ men who had been brought up to regard themselves as natural rulers, because holding down Africa was largely a matter of bluff. Members of the colonial administrative service remained thin on the ground in Africa, even if they continued slowly to increase. In Nigeria, they rose by 30 per cent during the 1920s but numbered only 431 in 1930, when the population was around 20 million. By then the Nigerian police included some 4,000 Africans and 80 British officers, but the armed forces numbered only 3,500; as elsewhere in British colonial Africa, military establishments were much smaller, in relation to total population, than those of the French, Belgians or Portuguese.[23] For all branches of government, mobility was a key element of strength; the motor car, and the motorable road, became central to the preservation of colonial authority between the wars. Ironically, this could mean that district officers spent less time than before 1914 on trek, and more time in court or on paperwork; their contact with Africans tended to become increasingly formal. Besides, medical advances (and improved steamship services) encouraged the advent of white women: between 1921 and 1931 their proportion of the white population of Nigeria rose from about one-tenth to one-fifth. As elsewhere in the tropics, the presence of white families tended to contribute to the estrangement of rulers and ruled, and officials with black mistresses or concubines faced still greater hostility in white circles in British territories than they did elsewhere in tropical Africa.

British rule in Africa between the wars was predicated on the assumption that routine tasks of local government should be delegated to 'traditional' African authorities. This accorded with the pressures to economise, and also with the diminishing need for governments to innovate once the foundations of an export economy had been laid and the financial basis of British over-rule secured. But to these negative reasons for relying on local African leadership were added positive arguments. Belief in the British

[22] Furse, *Aucuparius*, 298.
[23] Permanent armed forces as percentages of estimated total population, *c*.1930: Nigeria, 0.18; Gold Coast, 0.43; Kenya, 0.47; French West Africa, 0.86; French Equatorial Africa, 1.5; Belgian Congo, 1.6; Angola, 2.6 (based on data kindly supplied by Dr David Killingray and on Lord Hailey, *An African survey. A study of problems arising in Africa south of the Sahara* (London, 1938), 108).

genius for ruling alien races was quite compatible with the belief that the customs of alien races also had merit, albeit of a lower order. This view became easier to sustain as the less acceptable aspects of African tradition yielded to superior force, and it gained weight as educated Africans began to challenge white monopolies of power. Mixing cultures made trouble; it was better to keep them apart. The crudities of a legalised colour bar might indeed be abhorrent, but more subtle forms of discrimination were not necessarily to be opposed. Obviously African societies could not be wholly isolated from the forces of change if they were to contribute to the world's wealth. But the basis for social and political change should be African, not British, institutions. It was better to build upon African notions of justice and order, however primitive, than to risk anarchy by replacing them with patterns which few, if any, could understand.

Such thinking, which had a long ancestry in India, underlay Lugard's influential exposition, in *The dual mandate*, of the virtues of indirect rule. This term, already given currency by Lugard's erstwhile subordinate, C. L. Temple, was widely adopted in the course of the 1920s, as African styles of government were more systematically adapted to imperial ends. In part, of course, this trend was encouraged by the accumulation of colonial experience; but it also derived from the belief, widespread among the British ruling classes, that country life was good while towns were bad. British policy in Africa was informed not only by contemporary ethnology but also by the latest version of an ancient rural idyll: the virtue and beauty of the English countryside had been spoiled by modern industry.[24] Social policy in late Victorian London had been dominated by fear of a rootless, lawless, disease-ridden *Lumpenproletariat*, and such fear spread to Africa. Racial segregation in South African towns was rationalised on grounds of hygiene, and when Milner became colonial secretary he espoused academic schemes for urban segregation on similar lines, until forced to retreat by governors in Nigeria and Uganda who could see the practical difficulties of enforcing commercial as well as residential segregation. Hygiene, indeed, was a potent imperial metaphor: when Sir John Maffey arrived from India to govern

[24] Cf. Martin J. Wiener, *English culture and the decline of the industrial spirit, 1850–1980* (Cambridge, 1981).

the Sudan he sought to develop 'native states' which, as in India, might be protection against the 'septic germs' of nationalism.

If towns were feared, so too was trade, which helped to make towns and enticed people away from traditional authority. Trade might be a source of revenue, but it was also a dangerous social solvent; besides, it was not an occupation for gentlemen. British officials were often better guardians than their critics allowed: in Kenya and even in Southern Rhodesia some attacked the use of African taxes to subsidise white farmers; but they were usually lukewarm and ill-informed in their attitudes to entrepreneurs, whether African or Asian. To be sure, colonial governments promoted the conservation of natural resources: indeed, this (together with transport) largely accounts for the rapid expansion of British staff in the technical services during the 1920s; but African initiative was regarded more often as a threat to these resources than as their indispensable complement. Such paternalist concern largely accounts for the general reluctance of British colonial governments to enable Africans to register freehold titles to land, and thus become eligible for bank loans.

The ideology of indirect rule obstructed thought about long-term political change. Britain's rulers agreed that in theory they should, as trustees, prepare their wards in tropical Africa for eventual self-government, on the analogy of the white Dominions and recent trends in India. But this was a far-distant prospect. Lugard believed that 'the era of complete independence is not as yet visible on the horizon of time',[25] and this view was often repeated. There seemed no reason to think much about the possible role of Africans in the central institutions of government; it was far more obviously important to develop African participation within frameworks with which Africans were already familiar. The question was how best to integrate those frameworks within the structures and requirements of the colonial state. The answer was usually conceived in terms of chiefs and tribes. Indirect rule was by no means a doctrine of *laissez-faire*; it often involved meddling with African societies to make them conform more nearly to British notions of the ideal 'traditional' society. People without chiefs were given them, while chiefly hierarchies served to delineate tribal frontiers of which Africans themselves

[25] F. D. Lugard, *The dual mandate in British tropical Africa* (London, 1922), 198.

might hitherto have been little aware. Citizenship within the colonial state was to be fostered by degrees, by instilling attachment to local authority and language group. There is, indeed, a sense in which colonial regimes actually invented tribes: contrasts based merely on dialect, or location, or livelihood, were hardened into legal and administrative constructions. In the process, 'customary' law might also be invented: colonial courts were inclined to emphasise bonds of kinship (especially in the male line) at the expense of other, less clearly traditional, principles of association. The ethnic kaleidoscope of Africa was being transformed, not into modern states, but into a jigsaw of discrete tribal blocks.

Much as the British might wish to protect Africans from the modern world, exceptions had to be made. Literate blacks on the West African littoral had long been part of that world and pressed for a greater share in its counsels. Milner, while allowing whites in Kenya to elect legislators, refused to concede the same right to West Africans. He did not prevail; between 1922 and 1925 (and following constitutional advances in the smaller West Indian islands), a limited franchise was introduced for the legislative councils of Nigeria, Sierra Leone and the Gold Coast. But it was contingent on property qualifications and restricted to certain coastal areas. It is instructive to compare these arrangements with those for the only other legislative council (besides that of Kenya) to which elections were made between the wars. The franchise in Northern Rhodesia was extended in 1926 to all British subjects: it was thus ostensibly based on legal status rather than racial category (as in Kenya) or wealth (as in West Africa). Since, however, almost all British subjects in Northern Rhodesia were white, this was a trifling distinction; the key point was that indigenous Africans were classed as protected persons, whose spokesmen, at the level of territorial politics, were to be their self-appointed trustees, the colonial administration. In urban local government, white power was also on the increase: from the start, whites were given elective majorities in the municipalities of Nairobi (1918), Ndola (1927) and Livingstone (1930). In Sierra Leone, by contrast, Freetown council was reconstituted in 1927 with an official instead of an African majority, while in other town councils on the West African coast the minority of African-elected seats excited little interest.

In the 1920s, however, it was not African political rights but African education which created most complications for the theory of indirect rule. After all, colonial governments needed African clerks and interpreters, while businessmen and Christian missions also sought literate auxiliaries. But West Africa — and still more India — showed what trouble could follow from education uncontrolled by imperial guardians. Much thought was therefore given to advancing African education in such a way that it would promote rather than frustrate the ends of indirect rule. Since education was still so largely in the hands of missionaries, their collaboration was crucial, and the Colonial Office looked for guidance to J. H. Oldham, secretary to the International Missionary Council.[26] He in turn had learned much from the experience of negro colleges in the USA, and took a leading part in the newly-formed Colonial Office advisory committee which reported in 1925 that:

Education should be adapted to the mentality, aptitudes, occupations and traditions of the various peoples...Its aim should be to render the individual more efficient in his or her condition of life..., to promote the advancement of the community as a whole through the improvement of agriculture...the training of the people in the management of their own affairs, and the inculcation of true ideals of citizenship and service.[27]

This approach informed the development of secondary education in both West and East Africa between the wars. It was not an ungenerous vision, but it was firmly paternalist. As a compromise between tradition and progress, it seemed far-sighted at the time, but whether Africans would consent to it remained to be seen.

If the motives for cherishing African culture were often very mixed, it was certainly studied more systematically than hitherto. In West Africa, three British officials, Rattray, Meek and Talbot, were appointed 'government anthropologists'. In the Sudan and Southern Rhodesia, journals were founded in which officials and others reported local researches; other such journals followed in the 1930s in other British territories. A comparable development in French West Africa was the formation at Dakar in 1917 of a committee for historical and scientific studies. Far more than in British Africa, however, ethnography was dominated by the few

[26] See chapter 3.
[27] Advisory Committee on Native Education in British Tropical African Dependencies: *Education in British tropical Africa* (Cmd. 2374, 1925), 4.

officials who specialised in such work: Marty, Tauxier, Delafosse and Labouret. The courses on Africa at the École Coloniale were too often wasted: few French officials stayed in the same territory more than five years; few knew the language of their subjects; and they were not encouraged to pursue research.

Meanwhile, academic interest in Africa had gathered pace. The study of its languages was carried forward from the compilation of dictionaries (in which missionaries continued to do much notable work) to the investigation of grammatical structure and phonetics. The age of the gifted amateur reached a climax with the publication in 1919–22 of Johnston's comparative study of Bantu languages. The new paths were signposted by the work of Meinhof and Westermann in Berlin, Lilias Homburger in Paris, and Alice Werner, who taught at the School of Oriental Studies in London from its foundation in 1917. Linguistic expertise contributed to the improved recording and appreciation of African oral literature. The phonograph was occasionally employed for the recording both of speech and of music, though at this early stage in its history its use in the field was problematic.

There was also a new approach to the study of African institutions, at any rate in much of the English-speaking world. Before 1914, the academic study of 'primitive' peoples had consisted either of ethnology, with its search for genetic links between cultures, or of anthropology, which then usually signified the measurement of physical characteristics. These modes of analysis and differentiation now began to yield to sociological theory, which had already been applied to ethnographic data by Durkheim, Mauss and van Gennep. In such theory, human society was conceived somewhat in terms of a living organism, whose various parts (institutions, customs, beliefs, modes of livelihood and so forth) should be regarded as functionally interdependent. This emphasis on function characterised the new discipline of social anthropology. A chair in the subject was founded at Cape Town in 1920; the first professor was A. R. Radcliffe-Brown, whose own research had been outside Africa but whose influence, direct and indirect, bore much fruit among South African scholars between the wars. However, he left in 1925 and had no more to do with Africa until appointed to an Oxford chair in 1937. More central, in this period, was Bronislaw Malinowski, who taught social anthropology at the London School of Economics from

1922 to 1937. It was his particular distinction to have studied a
'primitive' people (on a Pacific island) by living among them as
a friendly neighbour rather than as someone in authority; unlike
almost all other scholars in this field he had learned through
observation and casual conversation rather than through formal
interviews. Fieldwork of this kind became characteristic of the
new discipline. It was Malinowski's example, rather than that of
his colleague Seligman, which guided their student, E.E. Evans-
Pritchard, who between 1926 and 1930 lived among the Zande
of the south-western Sudan and sought to relate their beliefs in
witchcraft to their social and economic context, a project for
which the work of Lévy-Bruhl on 'primitive mentality' was also
a potent stimulus.

Functional anthropology, especially that of Radcliffe-Brown,
has latterly been charged with retaining, albeit in altered guise,
the nineteenth century's predilection for biological analogies and
taxonomy, thus entrenching the notion of primitive societies as
discrete units or tribes; it has also been criticised for exaggerating
the importance of kinship in social relations.[28] There is indeed a
marked congruence between aspects of social anthropology and
the ideology of indirect rule; an interest in integration, stability
and continuity consorted more easily with conservation than with
change. Nonetheless, the new discipline represented an important
break with established attitudes towards colonial subject-peoples.
It rejected explanations of human behaviour in terms either of
'conjectural' history, based on mere inference from the present,
or of innate racial difference — a concept which, as in Seligman's
own work, muddled up cultural and physiological criteria. And
it opened the way to a more humane understanding of African
value-systems; this was no small matter when the weight of
missionary disapproval was still so widely felt.

The art of Africa made an impact on the West which extended
well beyond the restricted circles of those who worked in Africa
or read about it. A Fang mask acquired by the painter Vlaminck
in 1905 caused great excitement among other artists in Paris,
including Picasso and Matisse; by 1914, art from Africa, Oceania
and pre-Columbian America had been studied by them and by the
sculptors Epstein and Gaudier-Brzeska. The extreme stylisation

[28] E. R. Leach, 'Social anthropology: a natural science of society?' *Proceedings of the
British Academy*, 1976, **62**, 3-26; *idem, Social anthropology* (London, 1982), chapter 1.

characteristic of much primitive art was clearly congenial to Western artists moving towards abstraction, though it was scarcely responsible for the trend. African art was displayed not only in museums but in exhibitions at Marseilles in 1906 and 1922 and at Paris in 1925; in the 1930s it was prominently featured in a dozen exhibitions in Europe, while several important sales were held. The subject began to be discussed in aesthetic terms,[29] while von Sydow, Kjersmeier and others refined the ethnographic analysis of museum collections. Such work, however, was seldom informed by any first-hand acquaintance with Africa. Growing familiarity with African art in this period may have bred respect for its creators but it also tended to reinforce popular notions of the 'otherness' of Africa, and in particular the misconception of the primitive artist as the anonymous vehicle of a communal, rather than individual, imagination.

There was one kind of African art which could not be removed and displayed overseas: the rock paintings of northern and southern Africa. By 1930 many of them had been copied by a number of scholars, of whom the most remarkable was the German Leo Frobenius. More keenly, perhaps, than any other scholar of his time, Frobenius appreciated the imaginative power of African cultures and their various forms of expression. On numerous expeditions, both before and after the First World War, he collected artefacts, conducted archaeological excavations and recorded oral traditions. Unfortunately his methods were far from scientific, and his materials were pressed into the service of theories typical of the cloudiest German idealism. Frobenius believed his discoveries could throw light on the African past, but like lesser Germanic ethnologists he conceived of cultural history as a mixture of unsystematic comparison and speculation. It was hardly surprising that his grandiose schemes should have tended to discredit the very notion that Africa had a recoverable past of its own. Another approach to cultural history was available, in the chronological techniques characteristic of British archaeologists, but these were seldom applied to Africa. Sites in the Sudan, in Nubia and around Meroe, attracted expeditions both before and after the war; and by 1930 the study of the Stone Age had been initiated by Goodwin and van Riet Lowe in South Africa and by

[29] C. Einstein, *Negerplastik* (Leipzig, 1915); Paul Guillaume and Thomas Munro, *Primitive negro sculpture* (New York and London, 1926).

Louis Leakey in Kenya. But until 1929, when Gertrude Caton-Thompson followed up MacIver's work at Great Zimbabwe, no further light was shed by archaeologists on the cultural history of contemporary black Africans.

The study of African history was by no means neglected. Between 1905 and 1930 at least forty books on the African past were produced by British authors. Most, however, including those few written by academics, were about whites rather than blacks. Only nine were chiefly concerned with the history of Africans, and none of these dealt with Africa south of the Equator. The main focus of interest was northern Nigeria, and the work of its foremost scholar-administrator, Richmond Palmer, was vitiated by a preoccupation with the search for alien influences and origins. This was typical of the times: Seligman was by no means alone in ascribing African cultural achievements to light-skinned, long-nosed 'Hamitic' intruders. The white community of South Africa generated its own voluminous historiography, to which Afrikaner authors made a rapidly growing contribution after the First World War. And there the history of at least some African peoples had long been so closely involved with that of whites that it did not entirely escape attention. Bryant, for example, attempted to synthesise Zulu oral traditions. In the course of the 1920s the relations between white governments and black South Africans began to be studied by professional historians, notably W. M. Macmillan. But the only general histories of Africa to be written in our period, those by A. Moulin (1920), Delafosse (1921) and G. Hardy (1923), were produced in France; and perhaps the most impressive editorial achievement came from Italy — Fr Beccari's publication (1902–17) of reports by early western visitors to Africa.

One remarkable feature of the expansion of knowledge about Africa between the wars was the crucial part played by the USA. This was part of a broader movement to promote racial harmony, and the extension of capitalism, through greater understanding between white and black, and the dissemination of technical skills among Africans. In 1911 the Phelps-Stokes Fund was set up to further the education of blacks in Africa as well as the USA; the fund despatched two commissions to tour sub-Saharan Africa in 1920–1 and 1924 and report on the educational scene. In South Africa, educational planning owed much to a continuing connection with Columbia University.[30] From 1925 the Carnegie Corporation (established in 1911 to advance 'knowledge and understanding' in Britain and her colonies as well as North America) provided support for a variety of educational projects and also for the South African Institute of Race Relations. Meanwhile, American scholars conducted field research in Morocco, Liberia and Angola. In 1931 the anthropologist Melville Herskovits visited Dahomey while Harry Rudin completed a thesis on German rule in the Cameroons: more than any others, these scholars introduced the study of Africa to universities in the USA. But even their achievements were overshadowed by R. L. Buell's *The native problem in Africa* (1928), a comprehensive and frequently critical survey of colonial regimes south of the Sahara which was sponsored by Harvard University and based on a fifteen-month tour of the continent in 1925–6.

It was the Rockefeller Foundation which made possible the establishment, in 1926, of the International African Institute (IAI). The diplomacy was conducted by J. H. Oldham, secretary of the International Missionary Council; the moving spirits were Edwin Smith, an outstanding missionary–anthropologist; the philologist Diedrich Westermann; and Hanns Vischer, a former director of education in Northern Nigeria and now secretary of the Colonial Office advisory committee on education. Lugard served as an active chairman from 1926 until just before his death in 1945. The object of the Institute was 'To promote an understanding of African languages and social institutions, with a view to their protection and use as instruments of education'. Within a few years, it had gone far towards standardising the spelling of African languages; it stimulated African vernacular writing; pressed for the reform of schoolbooks; and founded the quarterly journal *Africa*.

Britain, France and Germany were strongly represented in the IAI, and it rapidly advanced the international exchange of ideas and information among scholars, educationists and missionaries. Among colonial rulers there was no such co-operation. The one organisation concerned with the comparative study of empire was the International Colonial Institute. This had been created in

[30] During our period, at least nine South Africans wrote Ph.D. theses for Columbia University about education in South Africa; they included C. T. Loram (1915) and E. G. Malherbe (1926).

Brussels in 1894. It held meetings almost annually up to 1913 and several times between the wars; these generated a mass of documentation on colonial principles and practice. In the 1920s its members included Lugard, Ormsby-Gore, Oldham, Lyautey, Delafosse and Rolin; but until the 1930s serving colonial officials seldom took part. By and large, British imperial circles showed remarkably little interest in other colonial systems. The French and Germans were less parochial. Before 1914 and in the 1930s at least nine French books of substance were published on non-French colonial Africa, other than works of ethnography. In Germany, at least 18 such books on non-German colonial Africa were published during our period. Britain, by contrast, could point to little beyond official handbooks and polemics against Leopold, the Portuguese and the Germans.

Colonial Africa was still in any case of marginal interest to British intellectuals. Journalists in Britain paid it scant attention; they produced nothing in the 1920s that could stand comparison with the damning reports on the French Congo by Albert Londres or André Gide, or the critique of the Belgian Congo by the socialist Arthur Wauters, who foresaw the trouble his compatriots were storing up for themselves by seeking profits in Africa rather than black partners. In Britain such criticism was most knowledgeably pressed by Norman Leys, who had been a medical officer in Kenya and Nyasaland, and MacGregor Ross, former director of public works in Kenya. Both became key members of the Labour Party's advisory committee on imperial questions. This was formed in 1924 by Leonard Woolf, who during the war had argued strongly for international trusteeship as an alternative to imperialism. But the formulation of a distinctive Labour policy for Africa was fraught with difficulties. In some respects, especially in its opposition to white settlers, the committee was close to opinion in the Colonial Office, whence indeed came one of its first members, J. F. N. Green. On education, Leys and Woolf had much more ambitious ideas. Leys valued education as a defence against oppression; Woolf believed that it should prepare Africans for self-government. This breadth of vision was shared by few in the Labour Party, which was mostly sceptical of African abilities. Besides, such concern as was shown by Labour MPs was understandably focused on Kenya; they cared little for colonial development or news of West Africa. Moreover, British trade unionists were more attentive to their white brothers in South Africa than to the claims of black or brown workers, despite the eloquent advocacy of Olivier. Racial difference was a more palpable fact than class solidarity.

The sentiment of 'race' continued to exert a powerful hold upon white people, and at all intellectual levels. Press coverage of Africa may have been too slight to have made much impact, but the entertainment industry popularised the image of the black man as at best a simpleton and at worst a monster. This was the message of pulp fiction, hunters' tales and the Broadway theatre,[31] and it was reinforced by the cinema: Africa was an apt setting for escapist fantasy, but Africans appeared only as a form of wild life. The belief that black people were fundamentally, and perhaps immutably, different from whites informed some of the best-intentioned paternalists. Lugard simultaneously extolled equal opportunity, race purity and race pride. Oldham acknowledged that 'race' was a term without scientific validity for the study of human beings, but he did not discard it: he concluded a sceptical discussion of intelligence tests by observing, 'while races presumably do differ in native capacity, how they differ, and to what extent, we do not know'.[32] 'Race' survived even in the highest-minded discourse partly because it was not yet possible to replace the all-too-convenient cultural–physiological concepts of 'the black man', 'the African', 'the Bantu' or 'the Hamite' with classifications based solely on physiological criteria: the study of blood groups, for example, was still in its infancy.

All the same, if men of good will continued to write of 'the African race', they were increasingly inclined to attribute its apparently distinctive characteristics to environment and history rather than to heredity: colonial governors as well as missionaries could be quoted to this effect. One eccentric theory was propounded by the psychiatrist C. G. Jung, who was so impressed in 1925 by the tribal displays in the British Empire exhibition at Wembley that he went off to East Africa and found evidence of the 'collective unconscious'. The Elgonyi people, on the Kenya–

[31] E.g. the plays *The Emperor Jones* (Eugene O'Neill, 1922), and *At home abroad*, or the musical *Golden dawn* (1927). Broadway musicals by American blacks presented black Africans in a more sympathetic (and even romantic) light, but were less successful: cf. *In Dahomey* (1902), *Abyssinia* (1906) or *Africana* (1934). Late in 1914 Oscar Asches had brought a 'Zulu show', *Mameena*, to London, but it flopped: no doubt it was ill-timed.
[32] J. H. Oldham, *Christianity and the race problem* (London, 1925), 61, 75.

Uganda border, were 'still sound in their instincts', due to minimal contact with whites: evidently the savage who lurked at the back of the white man's mind was a noble savage. More prosaically, some writers tackled the problem of race prejudice and attributed it to the defence of privilege. This was Olivier's view; it was also that of the zoologist Julian Huxley, who toured East Africa in 1929 on behalf of the Colonial Office advisory committee on education. Huxley noted that even in the mandated territory of Tanganyika the full implications of trusteeship were obscured by

various current assumptions which are felt rather than thought out, and felt as so self-evident that they are hardly ever questioned. The chief such assumption is that black men are in their nature different from white men and inferior to them. The second is that since white men know how to do a great many things of which black men are ignorant, they therefore know what is best for black men and are entitled to lay down what they ought to do and how they ought to live. The third, continuing the second, is that natives should develop 'along their own lines' — their own lines being those on which there is the greatest possible taking on of European useful arts; the least possible taking on of European ways of dress or ways of general thought; the least danger of their claiming or obtaining political, social or intellectual equality with Europeans; the greatest chance of perpetuating the gulf between the races. The fourth is economic: it is that production for export is virtuous, while production merely for your own local consumption is not — and is, indeed, rather reprehensible.[33]

Malinowski, in the course of a denial in 1930 that anthropology should be merely a tool of colonial government, saw Africa as a field of conflict between a variety of interests that cut across the lines of 'race'. A. V. Murray, who taught British missionaries how to teach, toured Africa in 1927 and concluded, 'It would almost seem as if the race problem is simply one aspect of the class problem'; he likened arguments against educating Africans to those advanced in the nineteenth century against educating the British working classes.[34] Charlotte Leubuscher, who taught political economy in Berlin, visited South Africa in 1929 and made the first extended study of Africans as workers and townsmen, though as it was written in German it made little impression on

[33] Julian Huxley, *Africa view* (London, 1931), 376–7.
[34] A. V. Murray, *The school in the bush: a critical study of the theory and practice of native education in Africa* (London, 1929), preface and appendix I. Even by the 1930s only 20 per cent of the adolescent population in Britain was receiving secondary education, and of these more than half paid fees.

the English-speaking world.[35] And in 1931 Robert Delavignette published *Paysans noirs*, a novel in which he drew on his own experience as an official in French West Africa to portray Africans, not as ethnographic curiosities, but as people whose attitudes were not essentially different from those of the French countryman. It was still a romantic view, which glossed over the extent to which African rural life was already moulded by colonial constraints, but it was Delavignette who most succinctly summarised the problem facing British as well as French officials in Africa at this time: 'the natives are evolving faster than the administrators or the administration'.[36]

1930–1940

The economic depression of the 1930s was a new stimulus to reappraise imperial attitudes to Africa. The trend towards imperial protection in economic policy accelerated the growth of trade between Africa and the metropolitan powers. This was most marked in France: Africa's share of her external trade rose from about one-tenth in the 1920s to over one-fifth by 1935. Algeria then took 12.5 per cent and had become France's main trading partner; the share of black Africa and Madagascar had risen to 5 per cent. By the end of the decade North Africa accounted for 27 per cent of French foreign investment; tropical Africa, 6 per cent. That fraction of British trade directed to sub-Saharan Africa increased from 5.3 per cent in 1930 to 7 per cent in 1938.[37] This was chiefly due to the gold boom in southern Africa and to copper-mining in Northern Rhodesia; by 1938 Britain's trade with the Rhodesias was two-thirds of that with West Africa. As the world moved out of depression, Africa's value as a source of base metals was revealed: by 1937–8 the continent provided 16 per cent of the world's copper output and 12 per cent of its output of tin. The imperial estates were giving abundant proof of their utility to Britain and France as their own economic stature continued to decline, and as Nazis made irredentist claims on Germany's former colonies.

[35] C. Leubuscher, *Der südafrikanische Eingeborene als Industriearbeiter und als Stadtbewohner* (Jena, 1931). In 1933 she was dismissed by the Nazis and thereafter worked in England on economic studies of Africa.
[36] Quoted by W. B. Cohen, *Rulers of Empire* (Stanford, 1971), 128.
[37] These figures exclude African exports of gold and diamonds. See above, table 1, p. 25.

Meanwhile the depression and its local consequences had compelled some reconsideration of priorities. White settlers were more clearly exposed as high-cost producers by comparison with African farmers. Cut-backs in employment, and industrial unrest, drew attention to the problems posed by semi-proletarianised African wage-earners. Financial crises provoked enquiries into the operations of colonial governments. At the centres of empire, trade was likely to seem more important than tradition. There was decreasing faith in indirect rule and the omnipotence of the district officer. At least in some quarters, there was a new awareness that not only the doctrine of trusteeship but imperial self-interest called for social as well as economic investment in Africa: manpower was itself a resource to be husbanded and nurtured. Besides, the British Empire was increasingly on the defensive. The enemy circle extended from Soviet Russia and Nazi Germany to Japan and Italy. All seemed real or potential rivals for the allegiance of colonial peoples. British imperial trustees became more sensitive to the movement of African minds, if only for fear that, if they did not seek to direct this movement, others would. In a still spasmodic and unsystematic way, African opinions were sought out and made known in the higher reaches of imperial government.

The intellectual climate was congenial to this new assertiveness. In Britain, there were conservatives as well as socialists who believed that national economies required deliberate management, while the economist John Maynard Keynes had radically questioned the value of balanced budgets. Moreover, thanks to American funding, there was now a substantial body of academic knowledge about Africa, much of which was specifically focused on contemporary social problems. Reform was in the air, even if its implementation was obstructed by officials invoking indigence to excuse inaction, or deferred by the outbreak of war.

For the visionaries who still saw the future of eastern Africa in terms of a new white Dominion, the decade brought new grounds for hope but also new setbacks. Smuts himself had forcefully pleaded their cause in his Rhodes Memorial Lectures at Oxford in 1929. In a probably accidental echo of Ruskin's inaugural Slade Lecture at Oxford in 1870, Smuts urged the British to populate their empire and thereby diffuse a higher civilisation. For Smuts, 'No flash in the pan of tropical exploitation will really help the cause of African civilisation. It will be a slow, gradual schooling of peoples who have slumbered and stagnated since the dawn of time, and only an ever-present, settled, permanent European order can achieve that high end.'[38] However, Smuts's enthusiasm for British colonisation was shared by few of his fellow Afrikaners; besides, plans for closer union in East Africa were in effect shelved after a joint select parliamentary committee in 1931 had heard eloquent objections from African as well as Indian witnesses. The field of controversy was inadvertently shifted to central Africa by Sidney Webb, the veteran Fabian who as Lord Passfield was colonial secretary in the Labour government of 1929–31. In 1930 he affirmed publicly that African interests should prevail in any clash with those of immigrants. This was ironic, since in the same year, while still serving also as Dominions secretary, Passfield had failed to exercise Britain's right to veto Southern Rhodesia's Land Apportionment Act — a measure ignored by the colonial experts in the Labour Party. Thus Passfield had provided two good reasons for settlers in Northern Rhodesia to seek escape from Colonial Office rule by joining up with their southern neighbours, and the region's growing mineral wealth fortified their hopes. Eventually settler pressure prompted the visit of a Royal Commission to Central Africa in 1938, but once again African opinion proved a stumbling-block to regional unification which threatened to entrench white supremacy. Furthermore, Africans in the High Commission Territories who opposed incorporation in the Union now had able advocates in London, and the British government became increasingly sceptical of white South Africa's eagerness to offer them a slow, gradual schooling.

In this respect, then, the momentum of Amery's years at the Colonial Office was not sustained. In another respect, it undoubtedly was. From 1930 the secretary of state no longer had to look after the Dominions Office. Despite the comings and goings of politicians,[39] the Colonial Office improved its ability to specialise in problems as well as territories, and to interfere

[38] J. C. Smuts, *Africa and some world problems* (Oxford, 1930), 66.
[39] Secretaries of state: Lord Passfield (1929–31); J. H. Thomas (1931); Sir P. Cunliffe-Lister (1931–5); M. MacDonald (1935); J. H. Thomas (1935–6); W. Ormsby-Gore (1936–8); M. MacDonald (1938–40). Permanent under-secretaries: Sir Samuel Wilson (1926–33); Sir John Maffey (1933–7); Sir Cosmo Parkinson (1937–9); Sir George Gater (1939–40).

accordingly. In 1927 and 1930 it had summoned colonial governors and senior officials to conferences in London, but this was an unduly cumbersome procedure. More significant was the handling of business according to subject as well as region, a process already initiated by Samuel Wilson. Africa was central to this reorganisation, for in the 1930s it accounted for four-fifths of the area and population of Britain's colonial empire, albeit only one-fifth of its trade. Within the Colonial Office, new departments were created for economics (1934), social services (1938) and defence (1939). Between 1932 and 1938 the administrative and specialist staffs of colonial governments were brought into a series of unified services according to function; this facilitated the transfer of expertise between territories. There were also occasional secondments of staff between the Colonial Office and the colonial administrative service. And the seasoned expert from outside played a growing part in the formulation of policy; indeed, in most fields of action it is only from this period, if then, that one can point to anything so definite.

Thought about the means and ends of colonial rule in Africa was stimulated from several quarters during the 1930s. Commissions of enquiry appointed by the Colonial Office crystallised trends of thought which were to become dominant in the 1940s. In 1933, the legal adviser to the Colonial Office chaired a commission to investigate the administration of criminal justice in East Africa. Of the four other members, all of whom came from East Africa, two were not lawyers, but all agreed that this work should in principle be shifted from officials in the administrative service, acting as lay magistrates, to professional lawyers of the High Courts (whose scope had recently been extended in Nigeria). This advice was opposed by the local governors, but they postponed rather than prevented the separation of judicial and executive powers. The Colonial Office also instigated a series of financial investigations by Sir Alan Pim, late of the Indian Civil Service: he reported on Zanzibar and Swaziland (1932), Bechuanaland (1933), Basutoland (1935), Kenya (1936) and Northern Rhodesia (1938). Pim's far-reaching reports, which proposed a variety of social as well as economic reforms, challenged the *status quo* in these territories more powerfully than any unofficial critiques in Britain at the time; they provided a valuable rationale for colonial development as government resources began once more to expand. For West Africa, a philosophy of state intervention was argued by the commission set up in 1938 to investigate protests by cocoa farmers against the marketing system; it advocated large collective agencies which would eliminate supposedly wasteful intermediaries.

Meanwhile, a policy on higher education in Africa had begun to germinate in Whitehall. In 1932 there were talks in East Africa about the possible future development of Makerere, a college for higher education in Uganda. As a result, a Colonial Office sub-committee was prompted to consider the whole future of higher education in British tropical Africa. The chairman, Sir James Currie, had been director of Gordon College, Khartoum. He swept past the hesitations of those who thought western civilisation a dubious gift to Africa, for Africans were already helping themselves: 'What the native wants is knowledge of a kind that will enable him to take his place in the world's economic struggle on equal terms with the white man.'[40] His report was at once imaginative and pragmatic: it concluded that five existing colleges should be developed into universities, for if the thirst of Africans for higher education was not satisfied they would continue to go abroad or create their own institutions at home. In either case, British prestige would suffer, African opinion would be alienated, and the risk of political trouble increased. The Currie Report was then circulated to colonial governors: in West Africa it ran into the sand, but in East Africa it prompted a commission in 1936-7 on the future of Makerere which recommended the early establishment of a university college. This advice was approved in London, though the immediate results were disappointing.

Social tensions within the colonial empire, and international tensions outside it, heightened concern both with maintaining British prestige and with finding new ways to shore up white authority. Even in the usually unpromising circumstances of tropical Africa, buildings were sometimes conceived not simply as shelter but as symbols of power. Moreover, the mystique of royalty was believed to exercise a powerful hold upon African imaginations, and it was sedulously cultivated by colonial governments. Architecture and royalty might even be jointly enlisted in

[40] Sir James Currie, 'Present day difficulties of a young officer in the tropics', *Journal of the African Society*, 1933, **32**, no. 126, 32.

the attempt to mould minds. In 1935, the year of the Silver Jubilee of King George V, Lusaka became the new capital of Northern Rhodesia; it was planned around a large Government House, designed in classical style by a pupil of Sir Herbert Baker (who had himself left a considerable mark on Nairobi and much of South Africa as well as New Delhi). Those who might have criticised the project for needless extravagance at a time of general retrenchment were reminded that 'Northern Rhodesia is a Protectorate in which the Africans outnumber the Europeans by a hundred and twenty to one. To them, this House and its great occasions will be the outward and visible sign at all times of the dignity of the Crown.'[41]

Yet in that same year, 1935, strikes by African mine-workers on the Copperbelt, some two hundred miles away, called in question the adequacy of such techniques of social control. This at least was the conclusion of the colonial judge who chaired a locally appointed commission of enquiry into the disturbances arising from the strikes:

It is all very well putting a District Officer in the open in the middle of 100,000 natives and with half a dozen askari to keep order...But mining areas are a different matter...The whole position rests on bluff — the prestige of the white man — a good and effective bluff which must continue in this country — but not at the mines.[42]

However, the commission persuaded itself that the root of the trouble lay in the subversive influence of literature distributed by Jehovah's Witnesses. There was little else for Africans to read, and the provision of more suitable reading material became a matter of official concern. The government started a newspaper for Africans in order to pre-empt the emergence of an independent and less desirable press. Elsewhere, too, there was anxious discussion of what Africans ought to be reading. The IAI had already begun to help Africans to produce the right sort of books themselves. Reginald Coupland, professor of colonial history at Oxford from 1920 to 1948, became chairman of a committee formed in 1937 to advise authors intending to write history books

[41] *Lusaka* (London, 1935), 44.
[42] Sir Alison Russell to Sir John Maffey, August 1935, quoted by Ian Henderson, 'The origins of nationalism in East and Central Africa: the Zambian case', *Journal of African History*, 1970, **11**, 4, 598.

for African schools; at least six such books on the history of individual British territories were produced in the course of the decade.

This was worthy work, but most Africans were illiterate. Films and broadcasting could exert far more influence, for good or ill, than the written word, especially where Africans gathered in large numbers for work in proximity to white people. In 1926 King George V had told Amery of his concern that Hollywood was projecting a disreputable image of the white man. In practice, the censorship needed to put this right was largely exercised by South Africa, from which were distributed the American films seen in East and Central Africa. A few commercial films provided useful, if crude, propaganda for white rule in Africa,[43] and in 1939 a short film for this purpose, *Men of Africa*, was specially commissioned. Besides, the cinema could also be used to instruct: films were made in Kenya and Nigeria to inculcate principles of hygiene, and in Egypt to combat drug-trafficking. The International Missionary Council, backed by the Carnegie Corporation, obtained the co-operation of the Colonial Office for the Bantu Educational Kinema Experiment; in 1935–7 this made both instructional and entertainment films in East and Central Africa, though the desire of the Colonial Office for some follow-up was not shared by the East African governments. The first attempts to promote broadcasting for Africans followed a similar course. The king's Christmas broadcast to the Empire in 1932 demonstrated the key role that radio could play in cementing imperial ties. In British West Africa, from 1934–5, rediffusion by wire to subscribers extended the reach of the BBC's Empire Service.[44] In 1936 the colonial secretary set up a committee to consider colonial broadcasting. This stressed the educational as well as political advantages, and governors were asked to develop plans for local broadcasting to African audiences, though little had been done by 1939.[45]

Labour, however, was the issue which most severely tested the

[43] E.g. *Palaver* (1926), *Sanders of the river* (1935), *Rhodes of Africa* (1935).
[44] By 1937 there were 1,600 African subscribers in Accra. Sir Arnold Hodson, then governor of the Gold Coast, had developed a keen interest when governor of the Falkland Islands, 1926–31. Sidney W. Head, 'British colonial broadcasting policies: the case of the Gold Coast', *African Studies Review*, 1979, **22**, 2, 39–47.
[45] The South African Broadcasting Corporation was formed in 1936; it succeeded a commercial service begun in 1924 and by 1937 there were over 160,000 wireless licences in the Union.

capacity of imperial governments to interpret social change in Africa and influence what was done there. It was also an issue on which there was pressure for reform from an international body. In 1930 the International Labour Conference approved a convention on forced labour. This was largely the work of a committee which included four former colonial governors (Lugard among them) and the official adviser on African mine labour in the Transvaal. The convention required little more than the restriction of forced labour to a limited range of public works and a commitment to its progressive abolition. Over the next seven years it was ratified by all colonial powers in Africa with the exception of Portugal, though France and Belgium made some reservations. Three more conventions relevant to Africa were issued in the course of the decade. None, however, could be said to have made any practical difference to labour administration in British Africa: more significant were discussions in and around the Colonial Office.

Metropolitan intervention in local labour policy was steadily opposed by senior civil servants in London, and they were not immune from lobbying by commercial pressure groups.[46] With the advent of the second Labour government in 1929, other views were encouraged. Passfield's deputy, Drummond Shiels, soon called for a thorough overhaul of colonial labour legislation. Throughout British colonial Africa, breaches of contract between black workers and their employers were subject to penal sanctions; this was a legacy from early English labour law. Since the 1870s, industrial relations in Britain had largely been removed from the sphere of criminal law to that of civil law, and India had followed suit in 1926. Shiels believed Africa should do the same, but he succeeded only in West Africa; elsewhere, it was widely argued that civil damages could not be expected from migrant workers who lacked distrainable property. Thus penal sanctions continued in East and Central Africa to subject African employees to what was in practice very lopsided justice. Shiels was still less successful in persuading governors to introduce local legislation regarding the formation of trade unions, even though he recommended this as a means of countering subversion. By July 1931 he was out

[46] Since 1923 the Joint East Africa Board, a group of British businessmen, had been in regular contact with the Colonial Office and with governors; it was also represented in the imperial affairs committee of the Conservative Party.

of office, and his reforming momentum was not sustained. Senior officials were indifferent, and colonial labour problems receded into the background as Palestine made increasing demands upon ministers, while India absorbed parliamentary time. Nor was much pressure in these matters exerted by the Labour Party's colonial advisory committee: it had, in Arthur Creech Jones, a pertinacious spokesman in parliament, but it was chiefly pre-occupied with wider political questions.

It was not trouble in Africa but the general strike and ensuing riots in Trinidad in 1937 which forced the Colonial Office to think again about labour. The colonial secretary, Ormsby-Gore, advised governors to review their own labour legislation and set up specialist labour departments. In 1938 the Colonial Office appointed its own labour adviser, G. Orde Browne, who had reported on labour for the IAI and the Northern Rhodesian government. Between 1937 and 1939 — when there were at least a dozen strikes in East and West Africa — trade-union legislation was introduced in Kenya, Uganda, Nigeria and Sierra Leone. It was becoming steadily harder to maintain the pretence that African workers were merely tribesmen on short-term loan to the capitalist; an influential white minority began to argue that labour relations and urban administration were too important to be left to companies, chiefs and district officers. Some officials in London argued that Britain had much to learn from the Belgians in Katanga, who in the 1920s had begun to create semi-permanent urban communities of relatively skilled and well-paid African workers. Meanwhile, the British labour movement was beginning to take a more informed interest: in 1937 the TUC formed a colonial advisory committee which closely resembled that of the Labour Party.

The involvement of rural Africa in the operations of capitalist enterprise was a major theme of social research in the 1930s. In South Africa, pioneering work on rural poverty had been done by W. M. Macmillan; now a variety of local academic expertise was deployed in 1928–32 in a study of the 'poor white' problem. This was funded by Carnegie, as was the team which in 1932 studied social conditions on the Northern Rhodesian Copperbelt on behalf of the International Missionary Council. Meanwhile Monica Hunter was investigating social change among the Pondo, in the eastern Cape, and in Northern Rhodesia Audrey Richards, also a pupil of Malinowski, was studying the Bemba, a people particularly affected by labour migration to the mines. Between 1932 and 1939 the IAI provided from Rockefeller funds 17 fellowships for extended research in Africa. All but three were for work in British territories, and most were given to social anthropologists trained by Malinowski in the study of 'culture contact', of whom six were South African, four were German or Austrian and two were British.[47] Social research in south-eastern Nigeria, and by Evans-Pritchard in the Sudan, was funded by the Leverhulme Trust.

Governments also promoted research. In Britain, a government research committee helped in the later 1920s to extend to Africa the new science of nutrition. A League of Nations report on the subject in 1935 prompted the Colonial Office to collaborate with the Medical Research Council and the Economic Advisory Council in organising a survey in 1938 of nutrition in British colonies. In probing the causes of malnutrition, the ensuing report stressed ignorance rather than poverty, despite evidence from Richards and others that economic pressures could seriously impair African diets. Nonetheless, there were leading experts who found good sense in African farming practices, and in any case there was increasing official concern to improve subsistence agriculture. The Colonial Development Fund helped to finance, among other research, ecological surveys in Northern Rhodesia. In Tanganyika and southern Nigeria administrative officers conducted full-time enquiries into land-tenure. Two academic social anthropologists were employed by governments: Schapera in Bechuanaland and Nadel in the Sudan. In 1925 the former German agricultural research station at Amani in Tanganyika had been revived. Scientists in government employment gathered at imperial conferences and at others held in East and West Africa. Museums were enlarged or created in the Rhodesias and provided bases for archaeological research (for which the South African government had created a department in 1935). In Northern

[47] Two IAI fellowships were given to French ethnographers for work in Algeria. Social research by French academics in tropical Africa in the 1930s consisted only of a team study of the Dogon people, in Soudan, led by Marcel Griaule of the Institut d'Ethnologie (from which the Musée de l'Homme was formed in 1938). In 1929 the administrator–anthropologist Henri Labouret wanted to study labour migration from Upper Volta to the Gold Coast, but the federal government at Dakar took no interest. Matters improved after the foundation at Dakar in 1938 of the Institut Français de l'Afrique Noire.

Rhodesia, the initiative of a colonial governor led to the foundation in 1937 of the Rhodes–Livingstone Institute for Social Research; its first director, the social anthropologist Godfrey Wilson, embarrassed the government by tackling the contentious question of Africans in towns. This episode illustrated the distance which in practice separated colonial governments and professional anthropologists, despite assertions from both sides of belief in the value of 'applied anthropology'.

There was a modest growth of concern with Africa in British universities, and in subjects other than social anthropology. Rockefeller, which had financed the expansion of the London School of Tropical Medicine in the 1920s, now advanced the study of African languages at the School of Oriental Studies. At the London School of Economics the anthropologist Lucy Mair lectured on colonial administration. At Oxford, Coupland's historical research treated Africa chiefly as a field for British philanthropy and diplomacy, but his younger colleague Margery Perham travelled widely on the continent and wrote a major study of indirect rule in Nigeria. Another Oxford lecturer, John Maud, was commissioned by Johannesburg to study its administration; a third, Christopher Cox, became director of education in the Sudan. In 1937 Coupland and Perham started an annual summer school on colonial administration for officials on home leave. From Cambridge, the economist E. A. G. Robinson contributed to the IMC report on the Copperbelt, and scientific expeditions visited the East African lakes. As in France and the USA, numerous doctoral theses were written on African topics.[48]

[48] British and US doctoral theses on Africa (excluding ancient Egypt):

	Total	Accepted after 1930	Humanities and Social Sciences				Natural Sciences				London	Oxford or Cambridge
			Total	N.A.	Trop. A.	S.A.	Total	N.A.	Trop. A.	S.A.		
UK: 1920–40	96	70	64	20	23	19	32	1	23	8	51	22
USA: 1905–40	104	66	90	22	35	27	14	—	4	8		

Many of the theses on South Africa were by South Africans, and most of those on Egypt for British universities were by Egyptians.

Much of the research achieved during the 1930s was drawn upon for the African Research Survey. This project may be said to have originated in Smuts's proposal at Oxford in 1929 for a centre of African studies that would serve the interests of European governments, but especially that of South Africa. Funds for this were not forthcoming, but the idea was transplanted and transformed at the Royal Institute of International Affairs (Chatham House). This had been founded after the war at the instigation of Lionel Curtis, a member of the *Round Table* group, and it was he who in 1931 persuaded the Carnegie Corporation to finance an African research survey. The aim was to examine the impact on sub-Saharan Africa of European civilisation, including its 'economic revolution', in the hope that through better-informed government this impact would help and not harm Africans. The survey was directed by Sir Malcolm Hailey, until recently a provincial governor in India. Ironically, in view of the survey's origins, the appointment thus epitomised the growing tendency of British rule in Africa to depend on expertise from India rather than South Africa.[49] The survey resulted in the publication in 1938 of three volumes: S. H. Frankel's *Capital investment in Africa* and two collective compendia, E. B. Worthington's *Science in Africa* and Hailey's own *An African survey*, which collated information on an international basis from academics and officials. Meanwhile Chatham House had also sponsored the first of R. R. Kuczynski's studies of African population statistics and W. K. Hancock's *Survey of Commonwealth*

Doctoral theses in law, letters and science for French universities, 1905–40:

Area studied	Total	1931–40	Law or letters	Science
Maghrib	353[1]	109	323	30
Africa S. of Sahara	131[2]	50	110	21
Madagascar	46[3]	19	31	15

[1] 5 by Arab authors; 85 for University of Algiers
[2] 3 by African authors (incl. 2 from Anglo-Egyptian Sudan)
[3] 1 by Malagasy author
In addition, there were 132 such theses on Egypt (excluding ancient Egypt); at least 90 authors were Arab. M. Dinstel, *French doctoral dissertations on Africa* (Boston, 1966).

[49] Next to Hailey and Pim, the most influential colonial adviser with Indian experience was Arthur Mayhew, secretary of the Advisory Committee on Education in the Colonies, 1929–39.

affairs; this last included searching analyses of economic change in South and West Africa.

Hailey's *An African survey* presented an enlightened and cautiously reformist view of the continent. It was the first British work to give serious attention to the African empires of other European powers, which Hailey himself visited during a tour of Africa in 1935–6. The *Survey* gave no currency to prejudices such as still survived in officialdom about African indolence or brain capacity.[50] It confronted many of the implications of economic change and implicitly at least offered a critique of indirect rule. The prevailing tone was humane and by no means complacent. Yet the *Survey* exhibited the faults as well as the virtues of the mandarin, and it reflected a dominant trend in contemporary social thought insofar as it implied that Africa was a vast laboratory for experiments in scientifically controlled social adaptation. 'The African' appeared frequently in its pages; individual Africans, scarcely at all. The existence of African organisations was barely acknowledged, let alone the diversity of contemporary African culture. 'Nation-building' was seen as work for administrators, not agitators. It was inevitable that the *Survey* should have taken little account of the African past, for this had been neglected both by historians and by anthropologists, who mostly ignored unmatched opportunities to record oral historical testimony. But it was significant that neither Hailey nor Worthington could find room for any account of such work as had been done on the Iron Age archaeology of Africa — which now included excavations at Mapungubwe in the Transvaal and Schofield's studies of pottery in southern Africa. All in all, what passed for a survey of Africa was primarily a survey of Europe in Africa.

Hailey's team, for all their distinction, might well have echoed the recent remark of a former official in Northern Rhodesia: 'We ...complacently rejoice in our high-mindedness, forgetting that we are still as arrogantly dictating, still every whit as compelling...'[51] Indeed, one senior administrator had recently accused himself and

[50] Two doctors in Nyasaland argued that one cause of African insanity was excessive education, and as late as 1939 the naked and indolent negro still basked in the condescending sunshine of a history book published by the Colonial Empire Marketing Board, *The story of the British colonial empire.*
[51] Frank Melland, in F. H. Melland and Cullen Young, *African dilemma* (London, 1937), 35.

his colleagues of being 'too much obsessed with our thoughts, our teaching, our plans. It is high time we heard a little from the other side.'[52] One remarkable purge for spiritual pride was supplied by a German museum curator who, before fleeing from Hitler, had sought out representations of white people by African artists.[53] Besides, Nazi behaviour had itself done much to discredit beliefs in racial superiority. Colonial rule in Africa was criticised in books by Leonard Barnes and W. M. Macmillan, both in the Labour Party's circle of advisers, and in Geoffrey Gorer's account of travels in French West Africa. The voices of Africans were mediated through Perham's collection *Ten Africans* (1936) and less directly through the novels of Joyce Cary.[54] But closer contact was exceptional. Creech Jones (who from 1936 served on the advisory committee on colonial education) corresponded with political leaders in West Africa. Jomo Kenyatta and Z. K. Matthews participated in Malinowski's seminar; Malinowski himself warned that by ignoring African agitators 'we may drive them into the open arms of world-wide Bolshevism', and noted the catalytic effect upon African opinion of Italy's invasion of Ethiopia.[55] But between colonial governments and their African wards dialogue scarcely existed: dissent was commonly treated as sedition. Even in West Africa, constitutions had stagnated since the early 1920s, while little came of Governor Guggisberg's bold plans for Africanising posts in the Gold Coast civil service. To be sure, African voices had not been wholly impotent: in eastern and central Africa they had influenced decisions regarding closer union, while strikes and boycotts compelled some official re-thinking in Northern Rhodesia and West Africa. But to rely on the dialectic of neglect, explosion and commission of enquiry was poor trusteeship by any standard. Against those who claimed that good government was better than self-government, there were grounds for arguing that government could not be good unless it was self-government, or at any rate moving in that direction.

[52] C. C. Dundas (chief secretary, Northern Rhodesia) to the International Colonial Institute, 1936, quoted by Rosaleen Smyth, 'The development of government propaganda in Northern Rhodesia up to 1953' (Ph.D. thesis, University of London, 1983), 43.
[53] Julius Lips, *The savage hits back* (London and New Haven, 1937).
[54] *Aissa saved* (1932), *An American visitor* (1933), *The African witch* (1936), *Mr Johnson* (1939). Cary had been in the Nigerian political service from 1913 to 1920.
[55] Introduction to Jomo Kenyatta, *Facing Mount Kenya* (London, 1938), x.

All the same, *An African survey* did induce some forward thinking. It acknowledged that 'the political future which British policy has assigned to the African colonies must be understood to be that of self-government based on representative institutions'.[56] It prudently refrained from attaching any sort of time-scale to this future, but it drew attention to the difficulty of reconciling elected legislatures with the structures of indirect rule. In October 1939 this problem was discussed at a meeting convened by the colonial secretary, Malcolm MacDonald. This exposed sharp disagreement. The officials, supported by Coupland, pressed the claims of the African intelligentsia to a share of power at the centre; Perham and Lugard wished to confine their scope to local government. Hailey was despatched on another tour of Africa, to make a report on which to base a policy. Meanwhile, the *Survey* had given weighty backing to those who believed that British investment in colonial development under the act of 1929 should be increased and extended in range: a new bill was drafted in 1939.

In September the Second World War broke out. Colonial questions, so far from receding into the background, seemed more urgent than ever. Reform was needed, both to forestall subversion and to advertise to the world Britain's fitness to be a great power. The Colonial Development and Welfare Act was passed in July 1940. War, and the threat of war, also changed Britain's attitude to the French empire in Africa. An early sign of awakening interest had been an academic enquiry in 1935 into education in French West Africa. But the War Office continued to regard France as the major threat to British power in Africa. By 1937 this was patently absurd, for a real menace to Britain's position in Egypt, the Sudan and Kenya was now posed by the Italians in Libya and Ethiopia. In 1938–9 air services connected French and British colonial capitals between Dakar and Khartoum. In October 1939 MacDonald made history by visiting the French colonial minister. But the time for such exchanges was fast running out. Paris would soon cease to matter; what Britain now needed in Africa was the goodwill of the USA.

[56] Hailey, *An African survey*, 1,639.

CHAPTER 2

ASPECTS OF ECONOMIC HISTORY

The economic changes that took place in Africa in the period under review have been summarised in terms of varied implication, as the economic revolution, the second stage of Africa's involvement in the world economy, the intensification of dependent peripheral capitalism, the completion of the open economy, or simply as the cuffing of Africans into the modern world.[1] The concrete fact, however, from which these descriptions take off in different directions is not itself in much dispute. Between 1905–9 and 1935–9, exports from African countries between the Sahara and the Limpopo[2] increased by about five times in value and by nearly as much in volume; import values rose by some three-and-a-half times, import volumes between two-and-a-half and three times. Total trade thus grew in real terms at an annual average rate of a little over 3 per cent.[3] At first sight this is hardly a momentous expansion. For even though it was nearly double the rate of growth of world trade taken as a whole, it started from such low levels that the global impact was hardly perceptible, and was not of primary significance for the economies of the colonial powers themselves; before the Second World War, trade with

[1] This selection alludes to the work of Allan McPhee, *The economic revolution in British West Africa* (London, 1926) and S. H. Frankel, 'The economic revolution in South Africa', chapter 3 of his *Capital investment in Africa* (London, 1938); A. G. Hopkins, *An economic history of West Africa* (London, 1973), 168 and ch. 6; I. Wallerstein, 'The three stages of Africa's involvement in the world economy', in P. C. Gutkind and I. Wallerstein (eds.), *The political economy of contemporary Africa* (London, 1976), 30–57 (cf. Frankel, *Capital investment*, ch. 5, 'Africa joins the world economy'); Samir Amin, 'Underdevelopment and dependence in black Africa', *Journal of Modern African Studies*, 1972, **10**, 4, 503–24; R. E. Robinson and J. Gallagher, 'The partition of Africa', in F. H. Hinsley (ed.), *New Cambridge modern history*, XI (Cambridge 1962), 640.
[2] This chapter pays no heed to Mediterranean Africa, nor, regrettably, to the Horn. South Africa, where the decisive changes began earlier, is excluded from this sentence but not from the chapter.
[3] These figures, especially the volume ones, must be taken as very approximate.

sub-Saharan Africa (South Africa still excluded) never accounted for a twentieth part of the United Kingdom's exchanges.[4] So inconspicuous, indeed, were the short-term and even the medium-term commercial gains accruing from the European conquest of tropical Africa that many metropolitan observers, unaware that the investment was a long-term pre-emption, have concluded either that it was a mistake or that it must have been undertaken for reasons that were not commercial. For Africa, however, none of the innovations of the early and middle colonial periods, apart from the spread of literacy, compared in importance with the advance of overseas trade, to which most other economic changes were directly related either as condition or as consequence.

The most crucial of the conditions was the conquest itself, that is to say the incorporation of African societies into larger and solider systems of political order than had existed before. (The reference is to the colonial empires, not to the individual units of colonial administration, which were not always decisively larger than earlier African states.) The linkage is unmistakable but its nature may need to be clarified. It was not primarily that trade was no longer interrupted by warfare or banditry, for in fact long-distance commerce had often been conducted across disturbed African frontiers. It was rather that most Africans were now released from the posture of defence and enabled to concentrate on productive enterprise. That is not to say that they had formerly spent all or most or even any large part of their time fighting one another, but readiness to fight had been the first obligation of males in the most vigorous period of their lives and work had had to take a subordinate place. In economic terms, the conquest meant (and this change appeared to be permanent) that the function of protection was specialised, taken away from the general body of adult males and assigned to very small numbers of soldiers and policemen, whose organisation and weapons gave them an unchallengeable monopoly of force. For the others, there

---

[4] See above, p. 25. For relations with other metropolitan powers see *CHA*, vol. VII, chapters 6 and 7 (France), 9 (Belgium) and 10 (Portugal). The gold-mining boom in the 1930s greatly increased South Africa's share of the British export market; in 1935–8 it averaged 8.7 per cent, as against only 4.7 per cent for the rest of sub-Saharan Africa. In 1925–8 the respective figures had been 4.8 and 4.1. (Calculated from B. R. Mitchell and P. Deane, *Abstract of British historical statistics* (Cambridge, 1962), 284, 320; Mitchell, *International historical statistics: Africa and Asia*, 414.)

was a loss of autonomy, even of the sense of manhood, as well as unprecedented possibilities of oppression, but the economy of human energy was very great.

Above all, the new order made long-term investment possible. It is no accident that tree-crops such as coffee and cocoa were not planted on any scale on the mainland of Africa until there was no longer a risk that they would be cut down by raiders just as they were coming into bearing. But most important was the investment in transport which, as most colonial rulers knew, was what colonial rule was mainly for. As Adam Smith had remarked,[5] nature had so constructed the African continent that most places were a long way from sea or navigable river, and so from what in his and all earlier times had been by far the cheapest mode of transport. In addition, diseases of stock were so prevalent that between the camels of the desert and the horses and trek-oxen of the far south there were no load-moving animals except a few donkeys. Tropical Africa thus moved straight from head porterage to the railway and the motor lorry. To an extent which can hardly be overstated, it is today the creation of these devices, and especially the former. Railways are uniquely large, expensive and vulnerable pieces of fixed capital, which demand political security over very wide areas. They are necessarily at least partial monopolies; but even so, since they yield mainly external econo-mies, the profits from their construction are more likely to accrue to other enterprises than to the builders. For all these reasons, even in societies otherwise committed to pluralistic capitalism, they have always been closely regulated, usually at least partly financed and very often built and managed by the state. More than anything else, it was the exigencies of railway-building that had brought the European states into Africa, persuading their ruling classes that they must move from informal to formal empire in a continent that could not provide the political cover needed for the revolution in transport without which the exploitation of its resources could not proceed much further.

The converse is also true. Once colonial governments had been established they had to build railways in order to justify their existence, and sometimes in order to be able to govern. There was in consequence some construction which, as will appear, was

[5] *The wealth of nations* (1905 edition), 16.

premature or wrongly located and yielded too little trade to justify the heavy burden of debt charges imposed on the peoples it was supposed to serve. Most lines, however, easily vindicated themselves, in the sense that they gave access to resources which would otherwise have been unusable and brought the territories far more revenue than they took out.

Railway-building was in full swing well before 1905, and by 1914 the crucial thrusts into the interior had mostly been completed. As in all forms of development, South Africa was far ahead of the rest of the continent; and even at the end of the period it contained nearly half the total mileage south of the Sudan (13,600 miles out of 30,700). Construction had of course been undertaken mainly to connect Kimberley and the Rand with the outer world, and had been stimulated by competition between the business and political interests identified with the ports of Cape Town, Port Elizabeth, East London, Durban and Lourenço Marques. Already by 1914, however, there was a true network, with lateral and interlocking lines as well as those leading to the coast, promoting activities other than mineral export alone.

Elsewhere there were at that time only tentative and isolated ventures, undertaken at the lowest possible cost and with no overall planning, each administration probing from its coastal base towards real or imagined sources of future wealth in the interior. Typically the railway struggled to the nearest stretch of navigable water, where it thankfully handed over to steam-boats. Thus the famous 'Uganda' Railway, having opened up the Kenya Highlands on its way, reached the easternmost gulf of Lake Victoria in 1901, bringing much of the fertile lake basin within reach of world markets. The Germans, though they pushed a line past the Usambara mountains to the base of Kilimanjaro by 1911, were slower to traverse the unpromising central and western parts of their East African sector and did not reach Lake Tanganyika till the eve of war in 1914; and by the next year the lake was also linked to the Atlantic by four separate bits of railway and three smooth stretches of the Congo river. Meanwhile the Nyasa country had been reached by a line which started from the just-navigable lower Shire, and the South African system had sent out a long tentacle through the Rhodesias, reaching Bulawayo in 1897, Salisbury (Harare) in 1902 and the Broken Hill mine in 1906; Salisbury had also been provided with a much shorter link to the coast at Beira as early as 1899. In West Africa, after a quarter-century of war and doubt, the French opened their line from Dakar to the Niger in 1906. Rival French administrations were also trying to attract the supposed riches of the Western Sudan to their ports; but whereas the line from Conakry to Kankan was completed in 1914 the northward thrust from Abidjan was long delayed by African resistance and heavy mortality in a conscripted labour force. In British territory, much of the Sierra Leone hinterland was joined to Freetown by 1908, and a line from the Gold Coast port of Sekondi to Kumasi, completed in 1903, helped to develop both the goldfield and the cocoa country. The major effort, however, was the railway which, having set out from Lagos in 1896, finally arrived at Kano in 1912, making it probable that Nigeria would become a single state. There was already an alternative route using the Niger for most of the way, and later there would be an eastern route to the north which would help to give the future state its unstable triangular structure.

That line belongs to the second main epoch of railway-building, which began in the optimistic years just after the First World War and ended to all intents and purposes in 1931, in time for the world slump. This was mainly a programme of consolidation, when feeder lines were built in some favoured areas, and some of the more awkward transhipments were eliminated. The most extravagant projects of the immediate post-war euphoria, such as the trans-Saharan line long dreamt of by the French, gave way to economic realism in the 1920s, but there was some undoubted over-investment in this sphere; the most flagrant example was the line from Brazzaville to Pointe Noire which, roughly duplicating the existing Belgian outlet, was constructed through difficult country at a cost of 900 million francs and at least 15,000 lives. Less certainly misconceived but still controversial was the Benguela railway, which was completed in 1931 as the culmination (in our period) of the efforts made to link the Central African Copperbelt to the sea. The emergence of this potential major source of wealth in the heart of the sub-continent provoked a new Scramble, in which railway contracts took the place of flag-plantings and treaties. British, South African, Belgian and North American capital, partly in collaboration and partly in rivalry, manoeuvred for profitable position; the Portuguese state again exploited its historic rights to crucial stretches of the coastline;

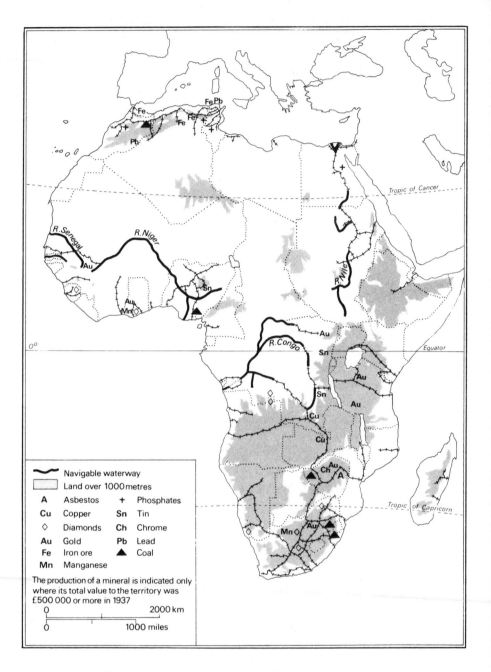

3   Africa: principal mining areas, railways and waterways, 1937

and a pertinacious Scots engineer, Sir Robert Williams, played the role of the partly independent empire-builder.[6] The upshot was that the copper deposits which straddled the border of Northern Rhodesia and the Belgian Congo were eventually supplied with rail or rail-and-river outlets in five different countries: South Africa, Mozambique, Tanganyika, Angola and the Congo.

Nearly all railways ran from the interior to the coastal ports, and the whole system was designed to facilitate the removal of bulk commodities from Africa and the introduction of mainly manufactured products from outside the continent, and for no other purpose, except sometimes a military one. Local traffic was welcome but incidental to the planners' intentions. It would be pointless to complain about this. Neither colonialists nor anyone else could have been expected at that time to construct lateral or purely internal communications which, joining territories with broadly similar resources, could not possibly have generated enough trade to justify the capital outlay. It is the high initial cost and the consequent rigidity of a railway system that is its outstanding disadvantage — and it is interesting, though futile, to speculate on the different course that the history of Africa might have taken if the internal combustion engine had been developed a generation earlier. As it was, colonial Africa came in at the tail-end of the great age of railway-building; and the lines lay across the land like a great steel clamp, determining which resources would be used or left unused, where people would live and work, even what shape the new nations would have and on whom they would be dependent. The railway, even more than the distribution of natural resources which only partly determined its location, was responsible for the uneven development that is so striking a feature of modern Africa. Anchorages which became railway termini grew into cities, while all others stagnated or fell into decay; and in the interior there was always a contrast, more or less pronounced, between the thronging 'line of rail' and the neglected hinterland.

However, as the railway system was being constructed, road transport was entering a new era, and road-building was the second great thrust of the colonial transport revolution. Some roads were in fact carved through the bush even before there were

[6] The story is told by S. E. Katzenellenbogen, *Railways and the copper mines of Katanga* (Oxford, 1973).

any railways, because of the illusory hope of using ox-drawn wagons or simply to make easier the passage of porters, donkeys and bicycles, which in Africa carried commodities as well as people. But the main stimulus was of course the advent of the motor-lorry. A few motor-vehicles made their appearance in the decade before 1914, but the main influx was in the 1920s, and it was then that the motor road began to penetrate deep into the countryside, widening the domain of the exchange economy well beyond the narrow confines of the unaided railway system. Except in the far south, there were hardly any tarred roads outside the towns until after the Second World War. In our period the term 'motor road', as well as the more cautious 'motorable road', connoted a track which a Dodge truck or tough Ford car could negotiate in the dry season without falling to pieces; but such highways were enough to produce economic stimulus second only to the first advent of the railway train. Road transport, moreover, involved Africans more deeply than the railways. It was not only that almost all African males had to turn out to make the roads, whereas the railway corvées were more localised. In West Africa, the vehicles themselves soon passed into African ownership, road haulage being for many the second step, after produce-buying, up the capitalist ladder, and everywhere it was mostly Africans who drove and maintained them. The internal combustion engine initiated many into modern technology, and the lorry-driver became the new type of African hero, the adventurer who, like the traders and porters of earlier times, travelled dangerously beyond the tribal horizons and even beyond the colonial ones.[7]

Africa, even sub-Saharan Africa, is far from being a single country, and the impact of the commercial revolution of the early colonial period varied widely according to the nature of the local resources, the policies of the different colonial powers and the previous history of the several regions. For example, between Lake Chad and the Nile valley, in the northern parts of French Equatorial Africa and the Belgian Congo, the southern Sudan and north-west Uganda, there was a wide expanse of sahel, savanna and forest margin in which the revolution can hardly be said to have occurred. Between Nguru in north-east Nigeria and El Obeid in the middle of the Sudan there was a gap of some 1,300

[7] This is one of the leading themes in Wole Soyinka's otherwise bleak vision of the colonial legacy, *The road* (London, 1965).

miles in which no railway ran during the colonial period, and some 800 miles separated El Obeid from the furthest station of the East African system in central Uganda. This region, which had suffered severely from slaving and local imperialisms in the nineteenth century, now enjoyed an interlude of peace, but its economic development remained negligible. South Africa, on the other hand, already possessed by 1905 a concentration of finance capital, an established professional class, a farming population of European descent which included prosperous entrepreneurs as well as simple pastoralists differing little, except for the amount of land at their disposal, from the subjugated tribes, and the nucleus of a skilled working class. Among the black population, moreover, a process was well advanced which in other parts of Africa was at most incipient: much of it had exchanged the tribal way of life for that of either wage-workers or peasants producing for an urban market. No change of similar scope took place in our period, which can in many ways be seen as an interlude allowing time for the consequences of the 'mineral revolution' to unfold. South Africa remained far ahead of the other African countries in the development of its international exchange sector; in the last years of our period it still supplied very nearly half the total value of exports from sub-Saharan Africa. But the rate of expansion was much less than the average, exports growing over the period by a factor of 2.3, compared with the factor of 5 for the remainder.

For West Africa too the factor of export expansion, 3.6, was below average. In this region, especially its seaward parts, the transition from the pre-colonial to the colonial scheme of things was less abrupt than elsewhere. Half a century or more of active 'legitimate' commerce, preceded by three centuries of the Atlantic slave trade and several more centuries of trans-Saharan commerce, had pre-adapted the peoples of West Africa in varying degrees to the twentieth-century type of exchange economy. Towns, markets, money (in the sense of conventional means of payment and standards of value), credit and writing were already familiar. Thanks to the ocean and several usable waterways, the new means of transport were valuable aids to import and export, not absolute prerequisites; and in fact not only the exploitation of the palm forests but also the cultivation of cocoa (in the Gold Coast and western Nigeria) and of groundnuts (in Senegambia) were well established by 1905. Here the changes of the next three decades, far-reaching though they were, could be seen as the amplification of two processes that had been going on for a long time: the growth of exchange, and the shift in the balance of economic activity from the desert-facing to the ocean-facing sector of the region.

In west-central Africa (Gabon, French Congo, the western Belgian Congo and Angola) there was a similarly long experience of European commerce, but here its effects had been more purely destructive, owing to the more direct intervention of European power. Indigenous organisation had been shattered, population (for whatever precise combination of reasons) was much sparser than in the Guinea region, and the very weakness of African society at the beginning of the twentieth century invited a colonialism of the most crudely exploitative kind.

It was in the eastern interior of Africa that the advent of government and railways was most truly revolutionary. Here 'production' for export had hitherto consisted almost entirely of the collection of elephants' teeth and the rounding up of human captives, and in many areas even these activities were recent developments. The possibility of agricultural and mineral exports introduced a new economic era, and it was in these countries that exports grew at the highest rates: nearly seven times in the Rhodesias and Nyasaland, eleven times in the Sudan, over fourteen times in the three East African territories.

The European peace and the new means of transport can be claimed as necessary conditions of the commercial expansion of the early twentieth century, but were they also sufficient conditions? To what extent was the expansion enforced, and not simply permitted, by the alien intervention? It is this question which has made the economic history of modern Africa an ideological battlefield. Some have seen the developments of the time as the welcome liberation of Africa from ancient impediments to economic growth, others as the imposition of the capitalist mode of production on societies that were not ready for it, in conditions that robbed it of its historically progressive role, so that it brought no material benefit to Africans, or none that could begin to compensate them for the loss of autonomy, security and cultural integrity. In this form, the alternative interpretations do not lend themselves to clear-cut decision — and the choice between them usually depends partly on the predilection of the observer and partly on which region of Africa he happens to know best. Some clarification of the issues may however be attempted. The optimistic liberal interpretation relies heavily on three propositions. First, Africa's natural endowment is distinctive enough to ensure that it would yield a large rent as soon as economic progress in other parts of the world had created an effective demand for its products, and as soon as the price that could be offered for them was no longer swallowed up by transport costs. Secondly, even though much of this surplus might be appropriated by foreign landowners and officials through the exercise of political power, by foreign traders through the exploitation of monopoly advantages and by foreign consumers through the mechanisms of unequal exchange, some part of it could hardly fail to accrue to the indigenous people in the form of additions to peasant income, wages that exceeded the product of subsistence farming, and services rendered by governments using the revenues they extracted from trade. Thirdly, the income derived from the commercial use of Africa's assets was in the main a true surplus, since the inputs needed to produce it were mostly not diverted from other employment, as the theory of comparative costs assumes, but were drawn from reserves of both land and labour which, for want of a market, had not hitherto been employed at all.[8]

PRODUCTION FOR EXPORT

The first of these assumptions is the least controversial, even though estimates of Africa's natural potential have fluctuated widely. Of the attractiveness of its subsoils, at least, there has never been much doubt. Most of its rocks are very old, and contain an abundance of metallic ores, especially of the rarer metals of complex atomic structure that were formed when the earth was young, as well as the highly metamorphosed form of carbon that we know as diamonds. Younger sediments, in which there were seams and lakes of fossil fuel, were not scarce. In fact there were few parts of the continent, apart from the volcanic

[8] The reference is to the 'vent-for-surplus' model originally formulated by Adam Smith and re-stated in modern terms by Hla Myint, 'The "classical" theory of international trade and the underdeveloped countries', *Economic Journal*, 1958, **68**, 317–37, *The economics of the developing countries* (London, 1964) and 'Adam Smith's theory of international trade in the perspective of economic development', *Economica*, 1977, **44**, 231–48.

highlands in the east, that did not contain exploitable minerals of one kind or another. However, the exploitation of many of them had to await the progress of technology and industrial demand or the depletion of reserves in more accessible continents; and in the early and middle colonial periods the only minerals that really counted south of the Sahara were diamonds, gold, copper and, to a lesser degree, tin.

The two first of these had been the dynamic behind the nineteenth-century transformation of South Africa, and demand for both continued to be buoyant. It is perhaps appropriate that the most distinctively African products in world trade should have owed their fortune in the first place to a symbolic mode of thought often deemed to be distinctively African. Engaged couples in Europe and America used the special qualities of the diamond to pledge the durability as well as the brilliance of their love; and as Europe grew richer more and more of them could conform to this convention. The role of this commodity in rituals of display gives it a peculiar place in economic theory, in that demand is actually a function of supply; the gemstones would have only a fraction of their market value if they were not believed to be scarce. Price can therefore be sustained only by strict regulation of supply, which, since diamonds are in fact strewn about the subsoils of Africa in great profusion, necessitates that rare form of economic organisation, absolute monopoly. The De Beers Company, created by Cecil Rhodes to control the entire South African output, came to regulate the sale of diamonds from all sources except the Soviet Union (which has been careful not to destroy the market). Independent producers in other parts of Africa quickly agreed to collaborate in a system without which they could have made only a very short-lived profit. The same system helped to sustain the value of what was really a separate commodity but a joint product with the gemstones: industrial diamonds, too small for display but finding more and more practical uses because of their unique cutting power. The result was that in 1937 the average value of diamonds (mainly gem) from South and South West Africa was not much less than twice as high as in 1913 and only fractionally less than in 1929, the year before the general collapse of commodity prices. This, however, was achieved at the cost of a steep decline, both relative and absolute, in the volume of South African output and sales, the latter falling from nearly six million carats in 1913 to three million in 1929 and under a million in 1937. Africa as a whole nevertheless continued to produce over 80 per cent of the world's output, for there was an overall rise in the production of industrial diamonds in the Belgian Congo, supplemented by the Gold Coast, Sierra Leone and Angola.

Diamonds had initiated the economic revolution in southern Africa but gold carried it much further. Early predictions of the rapid exhaustion of the great reef were repeated by cautious observers and interested parties with less and less conviction as time went on, and there was no question here of price being depressed by increased output. Gold production in South Africa represented over half of the world output in the 1920s, though it declined to about a third in the next decade. Its contribution to South Africa's exports fluctuated in our period between just under a half and as much as three-quarters, and South African gold was never less than a quarter and sometimes exceeded two-fifths of all exports from the whole of sub-Saharan Africa.[9] The peculiar social evolution of South Africa is of course the result of the chance or mischance that had placed the world's largest deposit of precious metal in a country where seaborne migrants, arriving for other reasons from the far side of the planet, had established military and economic supremacy but not numerical preponderance. The industry had special features with far-reaching consequences. In spite of the outcrops that had drawn attention to it, the main gold reef lay deep in the earth and could not be exploited without massive capital expenditure. After its earliest days, therefore, the industry belonged to large organisations having access to major sources of international finance. In fact most of it came to be controlled by six finance houses or 'groups', between which there were complex financial and personal connections, forming by far the greatest concentration of economic power in Africa and one of the greatest in the world. One of the groups, though not yet pre-eminent as it would later become, was the Anglo American Corporation. The name is misleading: though the firm was launched in 1917 with the help of copper-mining finance in the USA, it was created and controlled by Ernest Oppenheimer, a South African diamond broker who would later

---

[9] See Frankel, *Capital investment*, tables 12, 16 and 49.

secure control of De Beers; and this was one of a number of links between the two great extractive industries.

The South African gold ores are of immense extent but generally low grade, and this, combined with their depth, meant that other things being equal the costs of production would be high and there was a constant danger that the break-even point would exclude a large part of the potential output. Though the companies made the most of this argument in putting their case for low taxation and privileged access to labour, their problem was a real one. It was both alleviated and aggravated by peculiarities of the labour supply. The mines needed masses of hewers and carriers, and there were in southern Africa masses of men able to perform those tasks and having no other comparably lucrative occupation. But the mines also needed skills which at the beginning of the century were not to be found in any section of the South African population and so had to be imported at a heavy premium, largely from the decayed metal-mining districts of Britain. The huge differential for skill, originally determined by supply and demand, was perpetuated both by the exploitation of trade-union power and by the assertion of racial privilege. Finding it politically difficult to substitute cheaper black labour for expensive white labour, the companies exerted themselves to make maximum use of their greatest asset: the presence of numerous African workers for whom mine employment even at a low wage was the best economic option open. This initial advantage was in its turn perpetuated by widening the range of recruitment, restricting the freedom of the workers, and delaying the development of a stabilised labour force with all the external costs that that would entail. Permanently dear white labour, in other words, was offset by permanently cheap black labour, each having its allotted sphere. Even so, the inevitable decline in the crucial ratio of pennyweight of gold per ton of ore was becoming alarming to the industry in the 1920s. It was rescued by the disintegration of the world monetary system and the consequently much greater use of actual rather than notional gold. Britain left the gold standard in September 1931. South Africa did not follow until fifteen months later, and when it did the currency price of gold was at once almost doubled, remaining near the new level through the 1930s. Although the extraction rate continued to fall, this was offset by technical improvements and by the lower price

Table 2. *Gold output (metric tons).*

	1913	1916	1921	1930	1933	1938
South Africa	273.7	289.2	252.8	333.3	342.6	378.3
Southern Rhodesia	21.5	28.9	18.2	17.0	20.0	25.3
Gold Coast	11.9	11.8	6.3	7.5	9.5	21.0
Belgian Congo[1]	1.3	3.0	5.0[4]	5.9	9.5	13.5
Madagascar	2.0	—	0.5	—	—	—
French W. Africa[2]	—	—	0.5	0.3	1.6	4.0[5]
Tanganyika	0.4	—	—	0.4	1.0	2.5
Kenya	—	—	—	—	0.4	2.1
French Eq. Africa[3]	—	—	—	—	0.8	1.7
Sierra Leone	—	—	—	—	0.4	1.0
Nigeria	—	—	—	—	0.5	0.8
Uganda	—	—	—	—	—	0.7

[1] exports   [2] mostly from Guinée   [3] including Cameroun   [4] 1920
[5] exports in 1937.

of imported equipment, the money wages of African workers remaining constant. So profits soared, and the South African economy received its biggest stimulus since the initial discovery of gold.

It gradually became clear that the riches of the Transvaal are not repeated elsewhere in Africa — except in the Orange Free State. The Rhodesian goldfields, though they were easily the country's most valuable resource throughout the period, were a considerable disappointment to those who thought they had become the owners of King Solomon's mines. The small deposits in Tanganyika and Kenya could be worked at a profit only in the special conditions of the 1930s. In fact, the only significant supplements to the output from southern Africa were made in the Gold Coast and the Belgian Congo. In the former, modern technology had been applied to an ancient industry by 1905, and its output then was not equalled in the Belgian colony until 1930. By 1936 gold exports from the latter were worth £3.6m and those from the Gold Coast £3m, but this last was only 60 per cent of exports from Southern Rhodesia and a mere 4 per cent of those from South Africa.

Apart from gold, the most important mineral produced in West Africa before the Second World War was the tin of the Jos plateau in northern Nigeria. These alluvial deposits had been worked for centuries before the colonial era, contributing to the ornamental metalwork for which the region was celebrated; but, with the coming of settled government and the railway, output was greatly expanded to serve the needs of Western industry. Some African entrepreneurs survived as 'tributors' of the European firms who now organised the industry, but the excavation of the deeper deposits required the more direct application of foreign capital. The industry was not, however, highly capital-intensive and was composed of numerous small companies and individual enterprises, though in this sector as in others the hard times of the 1930s led to a marked increase in concentration. Among the production companies one had a special position: as part of the terms for the surrender of its charter in 1900 the Niger Company received half the royalties accruing from mineral output in Northern Nigeria. It should also be noted that the entire output of the field was consigned to a smelter in the United Kingdom. By 1929 Nigeria had become the world's fourth largest tin-producer. It lost ground slightly in the next decade, largely as a result of the international restriction scheme to which the British government subscribed on its behalf in 1931. It has been said of later commodity agreements that they 'tend to be an international conspiracy against Africa',[10] which is generally the 'new' producer and the one with the lowest costs. In this case, however, the deal probably saved the Nigerian industry from a more severe contraction, since its production costs, though lower than Bolivia's, were higher than those of its main competitors in South-East Asia. Besides, Nigeria now had an African competitor, for tin mines in the Belgian Congo had been developed in time to gain a share in the restriction scheme, and by the later 1930s their output approached that of Nigeria. Almost a quarter of the ore was smelted in the Congo; the rest was shipped to Belgium.

On the continental scale tin was less significant than copper, which by the late 1930s had achieved second place to gold —though a very poor second — among Africa's mineral exports. This output came overwhelmingly from the great metalliferous region around the Congo–Zambezi watershed, straddling the border between British and Belgian territory. The anciently worked deposits lay on the Belgian side of the line, and it was

[10] W. Arthur Lewis, *Aspects of tropical trade, 1883–1965* (Uppsala, 1969), 26.

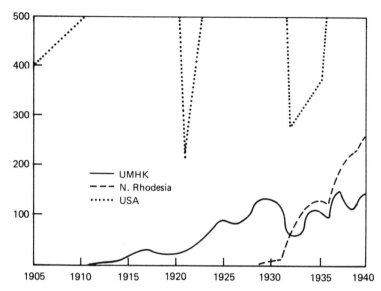

Fig. 1. Copper production, Belgian Congo, Northern Rhodesia and USA
(in thousand tons)

here that capitalist production started, the first exports beginning in 1911 as soon as there was a rail connection to the sea. The venture, however, owed much to the initiative of Sir Robert Williams, through whose organisation, Tanganyika Concessions, British capital secured a substantial stake in the monopoly concessionaire, the Union Minière du Haut Katanga.[11] Nor was the British sector as inferior as it seemed at first. New treatment processes made possible the exploitation of its sulphide ores, and when development was taken seriously in hand in 1923 it was found that Northern Rhodesia was endowed with a great deal of high-grade and low-cost copper to make up for its lack of other obvious resources. Financial control was here divided about evenly between Oppenheimer's Anglo American Corporation and the Rhodesian Selection Trust. RST was formed in 1928 as an offshoot of Chester Beatty's Selection Trust, whose chief African interests had hitherto been in Gold Coast diamonds; but from 1930 the majority shareholder in RST was the American Metal Company. Thus Northern Rhodesia became in effect the joint annexe of the South African gold and diamond mines and the

[11] See Robert Hutchinson and George Martelli, *Robert's people* (London, 1971), chs. 8, 9 and 11.

93

North American base metals industry. Growth was very rapid, being inspired by the development of the electrical industries of the West, which imparted a stimulus to demand so vigorous that it was only briefly checked by the general economic collapse of the early 1930s. By 1937–8, Northern Rhodesia supplied a quarter of Britain's copper imports, and one-fifth of Germany's.

Though not to any extent an export, coal was very important to the economy of South Africa and the Rhodesias, and also to that of Nigeria, where the state-owned colliery at Enugu provided cheap fuel for the railways almost from the time of their construction. Other minerals which were produced on a smaller scale for export included chrome, asbestos, wolfram, columbite, platinum, mica and uranium. This last metal was mined in the Belgian Congo from 1921 onwards, mainly as a joint product with radium though it had also a minor use as a colorant. In the 1920s the Shinkolobwe mine was almost the only source of either substance, and although Canadian deposits began to be worked in the next decade the Congo suddenly acquired a new global significance in 1939, when the possibilities of nuclear fission dawned on scientists. Alerted by French interest, the chairman of Union Minière, Edgard Sengier, farsightedly shipped 30 tons of uranium ore to New York in the summer of 1940, well in time to be used in the Manhattan Project.[12]

Africa's other great future mineral asset, petroleum, was held in reserve during this period. Northern Angola was explored intensively but vainly in the 1920s. Petroleum was found west of the Niger delta in 1908, but in 1913 Lugard refused to provide the government finance needed for deep-level drilling, and Britain continued to rely on Persian supplies that lay nearer the surface. In 1938 Shell and Anglo-Iranian (later British Petroleum) jointly acquired, for £50 a year, an exclusive licence to explore for petroleum in Nigeria,[13] thus ensuring that mainly British capital would have a first claim on the oilfield likely to be found among the sediments of the lower Niger basin, though it would be nearly two decades before the time was ripe for its discovery.

The full exploitation of Africa's mineral wealth lay in the future, yet even in our period important fractions of international capitalism had been attracted to mineral production, far more

[12] Margaret Gowing, *Independence and deterrence* (London, 1974), 350.
[13] L. H. Schätzl, *Petroleum in Nigeria* (Ibadan, 1969), 1, 78.

strongly than to any other sector of the African economy. One reason was the very easy terms on which access was generally granted to this natural wealth. Only in South Africa were there political forces strong enough to extract mineral rents from the exploiting companies on a substantial scale. In Northern Rhodesia government revenue from the mining industry amounted to £645,000 in 1938, a mere 12.5 per cent of the sums remitted abroad by the companies.[14] In the ten years from 1928 to 1937 the Nigerian government received about 4.5 per cent of the income generated by mining, or about 8 per cent of the share that accrued to capital.[15] So it is not surprising that, as S. H. Frankel remarked in 1938, 'mining has been the touchstone of economic development in most parts of Africa, and the areas most advanced economically are those whose main activities rest on mineral exploitation'.[16] He went on to show that 66 per cent of all the capital invested in Africa from outside, and 71 per cent of the private capital, had gone to what he called the 'special mineral territories' — the Union, South West Africa, the Rhodesias and the Belgian Congo. The predominance of minerals among Africa's exports, strongly established by the beginning of our period, weakened only slowly as other forms of extraction were developed; 64 per cent of all exports were minerals in 1907, 57 per cent in 1935.

In other respects nature has been less generous to Africa. With rare exceptions its soils are of low to moderate fertility, heavily leached, vulnerable to erosive forces whenever they are exposed for cultivation. Over the greater part of the continent — even when actual deserts are excluded — the rains, though they may be adequate in most years, are not reliable enough to give the farmer peace of mind; and in the forest zone, where rainfall is sure, the soils are especially deficient. Pests and diseases prey on both plants and animals with ceaseless tropical malignity. The adaptation of these environments to the needs of international commerce was not an easy process, and in the first years of

[14] See Phyllis Deane, *The measurement of colonial national incomes* (Cambridge, 1948), 53–4. The total tax paid was 25 per cent, which was quite high by contemporary standards, but this was paid to the government of the United Kingdom, where the companies were domiciled, and only half of it was remitted to the country of origin.
[15] See P. A. Bower, 'The mining industry', in Margery Perham (ed.), *The economics of a tropical dependency*, I. *Mining, commerce and finance in Nigeria* (London, 1948), 12.
[16] Frankel, *Capital investment*, 210.

colonial rule the main supplement to minerals in the export market was not provided by agricultural products proper but by animal and vegetable substances that lay more immediately to hand. Ivory, which had been the staple of 'legitimate commerce' in the nineteenth century in East and Central Africa, quickly dwindled into insignificance, as elephants had been all but exterminated except in the remotest regions and the new governments enforced a change from general slaughter to a strictly regulated culling. Another natural product, however, continued for a few years to enjoy the prominence it had suddenly acquired in the 1880s, when the surging industrial demand for rubber caused the forests of tropical Africa to be ransacked for the various species of latex-yielding trees and vines that were scattered through them. This was, however, a strictly temporary expedient, for it was far more profitable in the long run to procure rubber from deliberately planted trees of a single Brazilian species, which was better suited to other parts of the wet tropics than to Africa. After the second decade of the century, therefore, rubber ceased to be important to any African country except Liberia. While it lasted, the wild rubber boom gave rise to the most notorious episode of colonial exploitation, the brutal harassment which caused the hapless subjects of the Congo Independent State to deliver large quotas for little or no reward. This business was passing its peak when our period begins, partly because of humanitarian pressure but even more (so it has recently been argued)[17] because of diminishing returns. That there was no intrinsic connection between rubber-collecting and atrocity is shown by the experience of the Gold Coast and southern Nigeria, where many Africans welcomed this temporary addition to the range of gainful activities open to them.[18]

The forest of course also yielded valuable hardwood timbers, which became an increasingly valuable resource and were the principal export from otherwise undeveloped regions such as French Equatorial Africa and parts of the Ivory Coast. Other gifts of nature such as kapok, gum copal and gum arabic were of no

[17] Robert Harms, 'The end of red rubber; a reassessment', *Journal of African History*, 1975, **16**, 1, 73–88.
[18] Raymond E. Dumett, 'The rubber trade of the Gold Coast and Asante in the nineteenth century: African innovation and market responsiveness', *Journal of African History*, 1971, **12**, 79–102; E. D. Morel, *Affairs of West Africa* (London, 1902; new edn. 1968), 119ff.

general significance. But almost in the same category were hides and skins, the natural by-product of subsistence pastoralism, which were the leading exports from Kenya until after the First World War and were a useful bonus to the commerce of a number of other countries of the savanna belts. A similarly ambiguous position, midway between foraging and agriculture, was occupied by the exploitation of the oil-palm. Like the yam, this plant had been used for thousands of years and had greatly extended its habitat with the help of man. Unlike the yam, it did not come to be cultivated but was merely preserved when other trees were cut down or burned. The resultant palm forests of southern West Africa, and to a less extent those of the Congo basin, had been exploited for the purposes of overseas trade, as well as for consumption and for regional trade within Africa, since the early nineteenth century; and contrary to some expectations they went on being exploited through the colonial period and beyond it. Palm oil, which had replaced slaves as the main export from West Africa, supplying material for soap, lubricants and lighting fuel to distant markets, had suffered growing competition from both vegetable and mineral substitutes in the latter part of the nineteenth century; but against that, the chemists had found ways of making it edible in the form of margarine, and this demand gave economic value to the kernel as well as to the pericarp. So although palm products lost ground relatively to other export commodities — representing nearly 20 per cent of all exports from sub-Saharan Africa except the Union in 1913 but only 15 per cent in 1929 and 8.5 per cent in 1935 — they still remained the chief support of many regional economies.

The oil-palm is potentially a fully cultivated plant, and it became one in the Belgian Congo and to a small extent elsewhere. It is evidence that Africa did have some comparative advantages in the international market for agricultural commodities. Simply by virtue of being in the tropics, African plants have special properties: they envelop their seeds with oily substances; in the drier areas they develop strong fibres; for purposes of their own they use the sunlight to build up complex chemicals which are valued by man for their pungent flavour, their insecticidal potency or their effect on the nervous system. So Africa was in a good position to exploit the needs of industrial societies in the temperate zone for edible and inedible oils, for textile and rope materials and

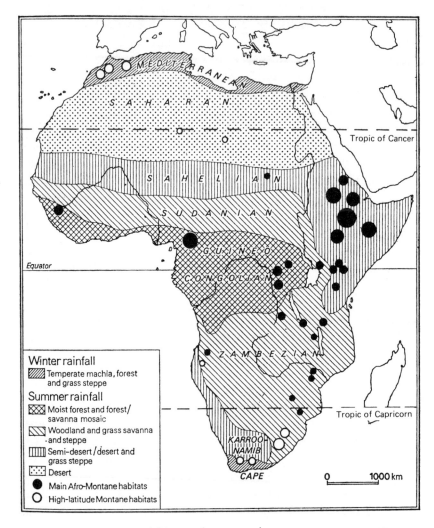

4   Africa: major vegetation zones

for those frequent small doses of nicotine, caffeine and theo-
bromine without which the stresses of industrial life would have
been harder to endure.

Apart from the West African oil-palm, oil-yielding plants
included the coconut palm, which continued to be exploited
commercially on the East African coast, and sesame (simsim,
benniseed), an indigenous food plant which now entered into the

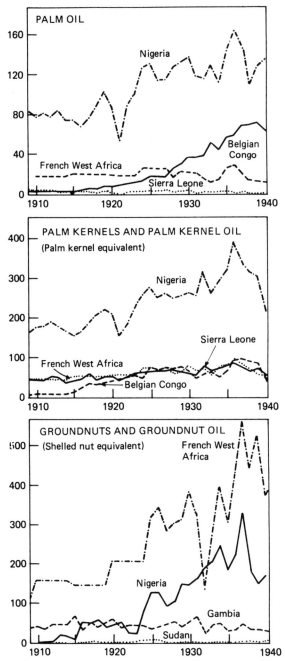

Fig. 2. Exports of palm-oil, palm kernels, groundnuts and groundnut oil
(thousand metric tons) from selected countries
Source: M. J. Herskovits and M. Harwitz, eds., *Economic transition in Africa*
(London, 1964), 158–9

export trade in a small way in both East and West Africa; but much the most important was the groundnut (or peanut), principal export from the Sudanic zone of West Africa. The groundnut had many attractions for peasant farmers in this region: it positively enjoyed dry conditions; being a legume, it put nitrogen into sandy soils instead of removing it; above all, if other crops failed, it could be eaten locally rather than being sold. (It also responds enthusiastically to phosphate fertilisers, but this fact did not become relevant until the 1950s.) Production for export was established in Senegambia during the nineteenth century, and it took off spectacularly in the densely populated Hausa country of Northern Nigeria in 1912, within weeks of the railway's arrival at Kano. This episode has been celebrated as a demonstration of African economic responsiveness;[19] and rightly so, although the complex society of Hausaland was to some extent a special case, having, unlike most other parts of sub-Saharan Africa, a true peasantry long accustomed to the provisioning of an urban market and a numerous class of professional or semi-professional merchants quick to recognise an opening for profit.

The leading commercial fibre in terms of export value throughout this period was actually not a tropical product at all, but wool, which came almost entirely from the backs of South African sheep. It is an index of South Africa's continuing economic dominance of sub-Saharan Africa that it supplied the chief non-mineral as well as the chief mineral export commodity. By the 1920s, however, wool was being run close by cotton. This had long been the mainstay of Egypt's foreign trade, and in the middle colonial period it achieved similar dominance in the Sudan and Uganda, was important to Nyasaland and Tanganyika and had some significance for Mozambique, the Belgian Congo and several West African countries. Cotton had traditionally a very special place among the raw materials imported by Great Britain, and at the beginning of the colonial era the Lancashire cotton interest had a sharp eye on tropical Africa not only as a promising market for cloth but also as a possible major source of lint. Likewise the alleged need to break the British–American monopoly of cotton supplies had figured largely in the propaganda of the colonial lobby in Germany. It is therefore natural to suspect

[19] Jan S. Hogendorn, *Nigerian groundnut exports: origins and early development* (Zaria and Ibadan, 1978).

that the rapid rise in production owed more to metropolitan pressures than to African self-interest. (This is separate from the more general question, which will be discussed later, of coercion to take part in the exchange economy as such.) It is certainly true that compulsory cotton-growing was the proximate cause of the great insurrection of 1905 in German East Africa and that in the British East African territories the element of compulsion, though rather more tactfully applied, was no less present in the early stages of cotton development. It is also true that the crop was enthusiastically promoted by the young Winston' Churchill, then under-secretary for the colonies and MP for Oldham; that the British Cotton-Growing Association, a body formed by Lancashire interests and enjoying a small government subvention, helped to initiate production in both East and West Africa; and that it was succeeded in 1919 by a fully state-financed organisation, the Empire Cotton-Growing Corporation, which imparted a bias towards cotton in agronomic research and extension work all over the British tropical colonies. The corporation's medallion, which showed Britannia sitting on her throne while straining black and brown figures laid bales of cotton at her feet, was a gift to critics of British colonial egotism. Yet neither the Colonial Office nor the colonial administrations were in any simple way instruments of metropolitan business interests; and the administrations had interests of their own which sometimes pointed in a contrary direction. For their own part, they would want their subjects to produce whatever paid them best, because that would make them more contented and so more easily governed, and also because the maximising of taxable incomes was conducive to the well-being of the government itself. Thus, though London wanted the peasants of Northern Nigeria to grow cotton, when most of them decided to grow groundnuts instead the Nigerian authorities did nothing to impede their choice. And the East African governments remained keen on cotton-production even when metropolitan pressures had died away; it is ironic that by the 1920s, when African cotton-growing really got going, the Lancashire industry had entered its terminal decline, and most of the new output went to feed the mills of India and Japan.

The other significant fibre crop was sisal hemp, among whose functions was to supply the vast amounts of twine that were needed at that time for the harvesting of temperate-zone cereals.

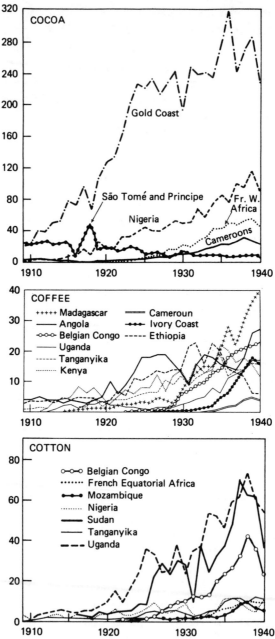

Fig. 3. Exports of cocoa, coffee and cotton (thousand metric tons) from selected countries

Source: (cocoa, cotton) M. J. Herskovits and M. Harwitz, eds., *Economic transition in Africa* (London, 1964), 157, 159; (coffee, and cocoa from S. Tomé) Mitchell, *International historical statistics: Africa and Asia*,

Introduced by German entrepreneurs to East Africa, it became the principal export of Tanganyika and a very important product of Kenya as well. It had the great advantage that, being adapted to semi-arid conditions, it could be grown in large areas of East Africa that were good for little else.

In the production of the crops so far mentioned Africa had no very special advantage over other regions of the tropics and sub-tropics; and insofar as African countries had an edge over competitors in Asia and South America, or even over southern Europe and the southern United States, it was because their labour was cheaper. The same holds for tobacco, the most valuable export crop of the Rhodesias. It was with certain tree products that parts of Africa had a more truly distinctive role, and it was these that provided the most obvious agricultural success stories. Cloves had been introduced to the hot, wet islands of Zanzibar and Pemba in the early nineteenth century. Despite the fears of many, the industry survived the abolition of slavery and continued to provide about 90 per cent of the world's supply until the expansion of clove-production in Madagascar in the late 1930s. By a reversal which might well have become proverbial, large quantities were shipped to Indonesia, the original homeland of the spice. Tea was found to grow very well in the wetter western parts of the Kenya Highlands as well as in the hills around Lake Nyasa (Malawi), and production was rising rapidly towards the end of the period. But the main commodities of this kind were coffee and cocoa. Forest species of coffee, native to equatorial Africa, were produced in large quantities, especially on the shores of Lake Victoria in Uganda and Tanganyika, in Angola and in the Ivory Coast. Mountain coffee, producing fine-flavoured beans for the European and American markets, was much more exacting in its requirements. The subtle combination of soil and climate needed for the production of the most lucrative kinds was found on the slopes of Mt Elgon in Uganda, the Aberdare mountains in Kenya and Kilimanjaro and Meru in Tanganyika, and these became districts of quite exceptional prosperity, though in highland Ethiopia the value of the crop was reduced by lack of quality control. Both kinds of coffee could be grown in the eastern part of the Belgian Congo, and in 1937–8 this territory produced more than any other in mainland Africa. Still better rents accrued to those Africans who had access to land that was favoured by the cocoa tree, a plant of the American tropical lowlands that does well in parts of the West African forest zone and in few other places in the world. By 1905 cocoa-growing had been developing in the Gold Coast for about three decades and it went on expanding rapidly for another two, by which time this one country was producing not far short of half the world's supply. Cocoa in fact did even more than gold to make the Gold Coast easily the richest of the 'black' African dependencies; and it also made south-west Nigeria a much more than averagely prosperous region, though here the crop was slower to establish itself and output barely reached a quarter of the Gold Coast total.

In the organisation of colonial agricultural extraction there was in principle a clear choice of method: primary production could be left to African smallholders working on their own lands in their own time, or the producers could be assembled in large enterprises under capitalist direction. The choice was not easy and the outcome of competition between the two systems was usually hard to predict. There was little difference at this time between alien planter and African cultivator in the equipment or the techniques of cultivation; insofar as higher output was obtained on the plantations it was because the work was better organised and disciplined, not because it received any large application of capital, and it was often doubtful whether the gain would be enough to offset the heavy costs of the foreign management by which it was secured. On the other hand, from the African point of view it was by no means always clear that a higher income could be gained from independent production than from wage-earning, and even the non-monetary advantages were not all on the side of the homestead, when account is taken of the boredom suffered by young men in rural communities where war had been abolished and politics had been reduced to triviality.

It was in the processing of the product that advantages of scale sometimes became significant. Certain specialised crops, namely tea, sugar, sisal and flue-cured tobacco, were strong candidates for the plantation mode, because harvesting and processing needed to be closely linked. (Tea must be treated within hours of plucking sugarcane and sisal leaves are too bulky to be carried to distant factories.) Sugar was chiefly grown in Natal, though it was also produced in Uganda, mostly for local consumption; tea, tobacco and sisal were mostly grown in East and Central Africa. Cotton on the other hand lent itself with special ease to cultivation on African smallholdings. It fitted well into many systems of subsistence farming, and the necessary labour, most of which was needed briefly for the picking of the ripe bolls, was most economically supplied by the farmer's family. Moreover there was no compulsory connection between cultivation and processing, as the raw cotton could be carried to small independent ginneries spaced around the countryside. The Gezira scheme in the Sudan, where cotton was grown on newly irrigated land, was a special and interesting variant; here the crop was produced by small-holding tenants of a private company, the Sudan Plantations Syndicate, which provided processing, marketing and technical services, and the proceeds were divided between the cultivators, the company and the government, which had carried out the major irrigation work. Elsewhere irrigation was neither necessary nor usually feasible. In its absence, and without either slave labour on the one hand or effective boll-picking machines on the other, there was no case for the large plantation. So the economics of cotton, the crop most coveted by the metropolis, helped to ensure that Uganda especially developed as a nation of sedentary peasants rather than of migrant wage-earners.

Similar considerations applied to groundnuts, which were never even thought of as a crop for large-scale cultivation before the ill-considered East African venture of 1947, and to cocoa, which fitted easily into the traditional forest-gardening systems of West Africa and needed only simple processing before export. The story of cocoa, however, serves to correct any notion of an absolute distinction between the 'plantation' and the 'peasant' (or 'petty-commodity') modes of commercially oriented production, or of the synonymy of 'capitalist' and 'non-African'; many of the Gold Coast growers, especially, hired labour and operated with a business style and objective that put them in much the same category as the smaller European planters in some other African countries,[20] as did some African coffee-growers, notably in Buganda.

With coffee the question of scale and organisation was more ambiguous. The indigenous *robusta* coffee already took a minor part in many African economies, and the sun-dried beans could

[20] Polly Hill, *Migrant cocoa farmers of southern Ghana: a study in rural capitalism* (Cambridge, 1963).

be taken without much difficulty to central curing works, so there was no need to bear the costs of foreign management or investment. The more valuable mountain coffee, on the other hand, needed processing of a kind which gave some advantage to units larger than a normal African holding. But the advantage was not decisive, and the striking success of African coffee-growers on the slopes of Mt Elgon (Masaba) and Kilimanjaro between the wars showed that there was no real impediment to 'native production' of this crop. The practically exclusive control of it by European planters in Kenya and Angola was a function of their political power much more than of superior economic efficiency.

The oil-palm presented problems of a rather different kind. Here organised plantations had distinct advantages over the traditional West African method of production. Harvesting of the fruit was easier because the palms grew less tall when they did not have to compete with forest trees; yields were higher, more efficient processing expressed more oil from a given quantity of fruit, and it was oil of a higher quality, with a lower percentage of free fatty acid. William Lever, anxious for larger and more secure supplies of his raw material, sought to overcome the last difficulty by setting up oil-mills at strategic centres in Nigeria in 1911. But to make these pay he would have needed monopoly purchasing rights in the catchment areas, and this the authorities refused to grant him. After the war he returned to the attack, now seeking land for plantations, and was again rebuffed. The episode shows that official favour did not always go to the most capitalistic of the available forms of production. On the first occasion the refusal reflected the Colonial Office's rooted dislike of monopoly concessions, reinforced by opposition from Lever's mercantile competitors; but the post-war controversy elicited ideological pronouncements about the superiority of 'native production'[21] and these would become settled doctrine in British dependencies during the inter-war period, except where European interests in land were already entrenched.

Meanwhile Lever had secured large grants of land from the more complaisant Belgian authorities, and his Huileries du Congo Belge became the second pillar, after the Union Minière, of the Congolese economy. Since palm plantations were being estab-

---

[21] See especially Sir Hugh Clifford, address to the Nigerian legislative council, 1921.

lished in Malaya and Indonesia as well, it was feared that West African export production must succumb to the competition of more progressive industries. And indeed it steadily lost ground in the world market. Yet in absolute terms the Nigerian export at least continued to grow for a long time, even though the producers were slow to move to more systematic cultivation. For in fact the old methods fitted in well with their other activities, and they had the great advantage over capitalist planters of being able to consume their produce or to trade it locally when the external market was adverse.

On the whole, then, the classical tropical plantation had only a modest role to play in colonial Africa. But there were divergent forms of European enterprise that call for special consideration. One was the concessionary system, whereby private companies were in effect granted control over whole populations as well as the land they lived on. This was of course an expedient by which metropolitan governments tried to avoid the capital expenses of colonial development, thereby renouncing its profits and tolerating the inevitable abuses of private monopoly. The British 'chartered companies' of the late nineteenth century were obvious examples, and in the Rhodesias a somewhat modified form of company government persisted until 1923–4. The Congo Independent State was a private empire of much the same kind, and spawned a number of sub-empires. King Leopold's role was much the same as that of Rhodes and Goldie in their respective spheres: to bring a tract of Africa to the point of development at which metropolitan finance capital would find it profitable to take over. In the high colonial period, however, concessionary regimes survived only under weak colonial governments and in unpromising regions where population was sparse and few exploitable resources were apparent. The chief examples were in French Equatorial Africa and in Mozambique. Most of the latter territory was misruled during the first three decades of this century by private firms, of which the two largest and most nearly sovereign, the Mozambique and Niassa Companies, came to be controlled by British and South African financiers. Between 1928 and 1930 the Niassa Company and the lesser concessions were replaced by the new Salazarist bureaucracy, but the Mozambique Company retained its prerogatives until 1941.

Then there was that special kind of entrepreneur, the white colonist. Whereas the most characteristic type of plantation is owned by a company domiciled in the metropolitan capital and operated by a salaried manager who will eventually return home, the 'true' colonist or settler is a working farmer who endeavours to replicate in a more spacious land the agricultural patterns of his European homeland, thinks of himself as belonging to a permanent community of emigrants and does not envisage return either for himself or for his descendants. In practice the distinction was not clear-cut, for many Europeans in Africa were planters by virtue of the kind of agriculture they practised (coffee-growing for example) but settlers by virtue of the scale of their operations and the source of their finance, and also by their political aspirations and their social role. It is however conceptually important, in that the economic decisions of settlers were less strictly determined by prospects of financial profit.

To describe the white settler as a 'special' type was perhaps misleading. It is true that liberal commentators have commonly looked on settler Africa, most of all of course South Africa, as a deviation from the norm of colonial development that was represented by West Africa and Uganda and had its archetype in the great Indian empire. But at the beginning of our period many Englishmen would have reversed the emphasis, seeing colonisation as the ideal and the West African mode as a last resort where malaria and dense native populations kept the door closed to settlers. The idea of creating an Indian type of empire in tropical Africa had appealed only to limited sections of the business and professional classes, but there was much wider enthusiasm for the dream of new Australias, where British workers could find a better life, become efficient suppliers of Britain's needs and high-income consumers of British goods, and send their strong-grown sons to help Britain in her wars. Likewise the need for colonies where land-hungry peasants could find living-space without being lost to the Fatherland had played a large part in the rhetoric and some part in the actual calculations of German imperialism. It is now widely believed that the prime object of colonialism was to extract surplus value from African labour, but at the turn of the century it seemed that for many colonialists the ideal Africa would have been one without Africans, or one where the aborigines played no greater part than they did in Australasia or North America, or Siberia or Chile. This was the condition which to all appearance the Germans were trying to create in South West Africa at the beginning of our period. Only later would they regret that so few Herero had survived to work the lands from which they had been driven; and only later would Britons begin to assure one another, in a cliché very popular between the wars, that the greatest asset of Africa was the African.

So it was more or less taken for granted in the first two decades of the century that the frontier of white settlement would advance far beyond its long-established strongholds in the far south and that European farmers would be encouraged to move into all areas where they could live and raise children in reasonable health. In practice this meant the irregular but nearly continuous tract of malaria-free upland that stretched through the eastern interior from the Drakensberg to Mt Kenya, inviting the intrusion of some thousands of hopeful settlers, some of whom moved up from the old Afrikaner and British colonies in the south while others were newly arrived from Britain, Germany and other parts of Europe. Here they attempted to rear crossbred sheep and cattle, to grow wheat or, failing that, maize, or to plant more specialised crops such as coffee and tobacco. But the vision of colonisation was not firmly based in economic reality. The white farmers were not occupying an untamed wilderness, as some of them supposed. They were inserting themselves into lands which were already being exploited, if not always very intensively, by a numerous and resilient native population. It was not simply that, short of genocide, there was no way of making room for a mass influx of colonists, but also that African labour-power, by its mere presence, drove down the market price of white labour, leaving no economic space for unskilled and semi-skilled emigrants, or for the independent homesteaders who were the nucleus of European colonies elsewhere. In East Africa, moreover, European artisans and small traders were confronted by unbeatable Asian competitors. Thus the people of European origin did not come to constitute whole communities as some had hoped, but formed an upper stratum of landowners, urban and rural capitalists and professional people, separated from the indigenous masses by increasingly rigid caste barriers. The new societies north of the Limpopo were formed on a caste basis from the outset; and the history of South Africa in this period is essentially the consolidation of a caste society, as nearly all white men were enabled to move out of the ranks of unskilled labour in town and country and to become either capitalists or a specially privileged stratum of the working class.

Further, in the production of meat, cereals and dairy produce the white farmers of Africa were at a serious disadvantage in comparison with the better-established, lower-cost suppliers in other continents. This did not seem to matter in our first decade, when world demand was rising fast, but the glut that developed between the wars created a serious crisis. Thus they depended on local urban markets, which were not yet sufficiently developed except in the far south. But here again there was the same problem: Africans were able to provision these markets at much lower cost. Technically there was no decisive gap at this time, certainly not a wide enough gap to justify the far higher returns that the farmer of European origin needed if he was to stay in business. (Ironically, it is in the last twenty years that effective mechanisation, together with fertilisers, insecticides and herbicides, has everywhere generated crucial advantages of scale in cereal farming, so that the professional, highly capitalised farmer has been acquiring an indispensable economic role at the time when his political privileges were disappearing.) Hence one of the main bones of racial contention in 'settler' Africa was the local market for foodstuffs. During the nineteenth century and the first years of the twentieth many South African tribesmen had gone a long way towards transforming themselves into peasants, producing systematically for the market and sometimes adopting radically new techniques such as the ox-drawn plough. At the time this trend was encouraged by the authorities, but after 1910 it was deliberately reversed by political action; from then on, the roles assigned to the African majority were to be those of subsistence cultivator and wage-earner, and no other.[22] Further north, where the entry of Africans into commercial production was slower, similar policies were adopted, though their application was less rigorous.

It is clear that there was a close link, almost a symbiosis, between white farming and the mining enterprise which alone could generate a sufficient demand for its product. In Kenya,

[22] See especially Colin Bundy, *The rise and fall of the South African peasantry* (London, 1979).

where minerals were lacking, the true working smallholder never managed to establish himself, and the smaller capitalist farmers, those who could not go in for coffee-growing or large-scale ranching, survived only because of their political influence, which won them a great variety of favours in the form of technical assistance, branch railways, differential freight rates, tariff protection and, from 1931, cheap finance from the state land bank. Even in southern Africa, urban capitalists complained bitterly that the farming sector was more parasitic than symbiotic, that the economy was massively distorted in support of an uneconomic agriculture whose real strength was that it was conducted by members of the dominant ethnic group.[23] In the last resort, however, they would tolerate its exactions for the sake of the political underpinning which it provided for their own position.

With hindsight the idea of the mass colonisation of Africa seems so improbable that it must be suspected of having been little more than the cover for what actually happened: the appropriation of large quantities of African land by the British, and for a time also the German, ruling class. Significant here was the 'Soldier Settlement Scheme' of 1919 in Kenya, which turned out to be a scheme for the allocation of virtually free estates to officers and gentlemen, with generals and ex-governors (or their wives) rather more prominent than the survivors of the trenches.[24] Here and in the Rhodesias much of the early alienation of land was the 'staking of claims' on the increment of value which transport and commercial developments would give it in the future. Would-be landed proprietors did not, however, have things all their own way, since colonial administrators held more or less strongly to the conviction that this increment belonged, not to 'speculators', but either to the indigenous communities whom they governed or to the state which they embodied. Yet officials were also constrained by the fear of discouraging the inflow of capital into their territories. The outcome of this often acrimonious dispute varied. The Southern Rhodesian referendum of 1923 was a

[23] A characteristic statement from the 1930s was that of C. S. Richards, 'Subsidies, quotas, tariffs and the excess cost of agriculture in South Africa', *South African Journal of Economics*, 1935, **3**, 365–403. Cf. the Rhodesian complaints cited by V. Machingaidze, 'The development of capitalist agriculture in Southern Rhodesia...1908–1939' (Ph.D. thesis, University of London, 1980), 308.
[24] The *East African Standard*, 22 August 1919, reporting the results of the ballot held in London.

victory for white proprietors over both kinds of government, that of the chartered company and that which was directed from Whitehall. In Kenya the Crown Lands Ordinance of 1915 did indeed declare the land of Kenya (then nominally a protectorate) to be the property of the British Crown, but it also provided that those parts of it not actually being used by Africans could and would be handed over to Europeans on 999-year leases, which amounted to outright property. In Tanganyika, on the other hand, the British administration declared all land to be 'public' unless already alienated, signifying that it was the property of the African communities, and in Uganda too official policy hardened in the 1920s against permitting alien rights in land. In British West Africa, as we have seen, alienation was practically excluded.

The white farm in Africa, as distinct from the highly capitalised plantation, was always a somewhat artificial construction. While some critics have seen it as the highest as well as the most offensive form of colonialism, others have dismissed it as a mere epiphenomenon, a colourful but not really important feature of the drama of capitalist exploitation, which took other and more serious forms. Certainly the support given to it by finance capital was lukewarm at best, as settlers complained between the wars and as would be implied by political events north of the Limpopo after 1950. Yet in our period it was too prominent in the scenery of East and southern Africa to be easily ignored; nor was it by any means entirely an obstacle to African freedom and progress, given the general context of colonial domination. Wherever a substantial European population established itself, the development of a modern infrastructure proceeded much faster than elsewhere, as the government felt obliged to provide it with roads and hospitals and technical services and urban amenity; and although these developments were in the short term irrelevant to the needs of the mass of the people, and took place partly at their expense, they would eventually be a valuable endowment for the emergent nations. By the same token, as we shall see, governments of these countries had to adopt less deflationary fiscal and monetary policies than in the pure African dependencies. Perhaps more important still, independent European proprietors were a countervailing force competing with governments and mine-owners and merchants for African labour and so enhancing its value. The Kikuyu who went to 'squat' on European estates were not only gaining access to land which had hitherto belonged to the Masai if anyone; they were also escaping from the oppressions of government-appointed headmen and the obligations of road corvées and the like. Conversely, the system of 'native production' adopted in British West Africa, in Uganda and for the most part in Tanganyika ensured that the increasing rental value of African land was not directly appropriated by foreigners, but did not necessarily prevent a large part of it from being diverted away from Africans through monopoly profits of merchants or through government taxation.

TRADE AND FINANCE

The peasant producer of export crops was a long way from the final markets for his product and from the manufacturing sources of the consumer goods that were a large part of his reward, and for the liberal model of the economy to have worked perfectly there would have had to be perfect competition at each of the intervening levels of exchange. Needless to say, this did not occur. At the lowest level there was usually a fair amount of competition to buy his produce and to relieve him of the resultant cash. In West Africa there was no lack of enterprising African produce-buyers and retailers,[25] and in East Africa, where indigenous commercial institutions were more weakly developed, the gap was largely filled by immigrants from the mercantile districts of western India. If competition weakened at this level in the 1930s, especially in East Africa, it was mainly because of the intervention of the state in favour of a few established and politically influential firms and organisations. There were, admittedly, exceptions: in French Equatorial Africa and the Belgian Congo firms enjoyed monopolies over the trade of very large areas. But in most of tropical Africa, competition, however imperfect, was the norm.

At the highest level, too, competition on the whole prevailed. The 'world market' was not the mystic expression of economic law, but neither was it a conspiracy to fix prices to the disadvantage of colonial producers. It consisted of complex institutions in London, New York and other centres which were sensitively adjusted to the shifting balance of supply and demand in the world

[25] P. T. Bauer, *West African trade: a study of competition, oligopoly and monopoly in a changing economy* (Cambridge, 1954), 22ff.

as a whole. (The long-term determinants of supply and demand for primary produce are another matter.)[26] Moreover, the rules of the Partition, implicit even when not written into formal agreements, provided that there was to be free communication between these markets and the African producers and consumers; import duties were to be for revenue only and neither import nor export taxes were to discriminate between different sources and destinations. For a while the rules were fairly well observed. In 1919 Britain reduced customs duties on various Empire products, which specifically benefited Rhodesian tobacco, but an attempt at about the same time to divert palm kernels to crushing mills in the United Kingdom by means of differential export duties was quickly abandoned as improper and on balance inimical to British interests.[27] But the crisis of the early 1930s put an end to the era of free-trade empire, and the economies of the African colonies became thereafter steadily less 'open'. In 1934, for example, the British West African dependencies all introduced customs duties that discriminated against Japanese textiles, which had just begun to invade markets hitherto dominated by British manufactures. (The East African territories could not follow suit because they were formally committed to free trade by the 'Congo Basin' treaties of the Partition era, to which Japan had acceded in 1919.) Understandable to anyone who saw the grey faces of unemployed weavers in the grey streets of Lancashire, this intervention was nevertheless an injustice to Britain's still poorer subjects, who were compelled to pay more than they need have done for what had become necessary imports. In some ways it was a more significant turning-point than the introduction, in the same year, of the imperial preference system, from which the African colonies benefited little. Britain was not of course alone in moving towards the closed imperial economy. Subjects of France and Portugal in particular were becoming more and more the captive customers of high-cost metropolitan industries.

Even without the help of fiscal or other overt discrimination, colonial rule had skewed the pattern of African trade in the direction of the metropolis. All the goods imported for the use of British colonial administrations were procured through the

See below, pp. 129–31.
[27] W. K. Hancock, *Survey of British Commonwealth affairs*, II, part i (London, 1941), 113–21.

Crown Agents, who placed almost all their orders with United Kingdom suppliers. Though French and German firms did business in British territories and British firms in French ones, merchants with a base in the homeland had linguistic and institutional advantages which tended to give them an increasing market share in their 'own' colonies; and even when there was no vertical integration they would have a bias towards metropolitan consumers and producers. In spite of this the United Kingdom's share of Africa's trade decreased slowly but continuously, apart from the lift given by the temporary elimination of German competition during the First World War. Of Nigeria's imports, for example, the British percentage was 77 in 1905, 71 in 1913, 82 in 1920, 68 in 1930 and 55 in 1938. The fall, however, was much less steep than the deterioration of Britain's position in the world economy as a whole; and so it could be argued that the colonial empire mitigated the effects of her slowing economic growth (and of the continuing stagnation of Portugal and France). It could also be held, however, that the possession of privileged colonial markets, by cushioning the metropolitan economies against the impact of inevitable change, was itself a major cause of their debility.

By its nature, a colonial economy cannot be an ideally open one, for however sincerely the government may think itself an impartial umpire of commercial exchanges it is in the last resort too closely linked to one set of players to perform that function properly. Nevertheless, until the 1930s at least, the trade-creating effects of peace and transport easily outweighed the trade-distorting consequences of imperial power; and even then none of the empires in Africa formed a fully closed system of state-imposed monopoly. Quite apart, however, from the direct action of colonial governments, there were forces at work which, especially in West Africa, tended to reduce the number of separate businesses competing in the import and export markets and so to strengthen the power of the survivors. The high overhead costs of long-distance trade in Africa, the advantages of scale in the procurement of standardised goods for the mass African market, the intensity of price fluctuations in the inter-war years favoured the largest concerns. Well before the end of the period the smaller independent European traders, as well as Africans, had been practically excluded from overseas operations and from the highest levels of internal commerce; and even in the middle levels African traders were increasingly becoming agents for particular European firms, or even their employees.

By the 1930s the general trade of British West Africa was dominated by the seven firms which belonged to the collusive organisation called the Association of West African Merchants, who were joined in the purchase of cocoa by agents of the British chocolate manufacturers.[28] These firms, moreover, were of very unequal size. One of them, the United Africa Company, is reckoned to have handled over 40 per cent of the entire overseas trade of Nigeria and a not much smaller proportion of the trade of the whole region.[29] This firm, itself merely one part of the great manufacturing and distributive organisation, Unilever, had a complicated genealogy. One of its ancestors was Sir George Goldie's Royal Niger Company which, after losing its title, its political functions and its presiding genius in 1900, maintained a rather unenterprising existence in Nigeria until 1920, when it was acquired by William Lever as one way of getting direct access to the raw materials of his soap. The purchase, made at the top of the market, nearly broke Lever Bros but left it firmly locked into the West African economy. The other parent was the African and Eastern Trade Corporation, the result of a series of mergers and take-overs which had united nearly all the old coastal trading concerns of the British sector. This group finally came to terms with the Niger Company in 1929 to form the United Africa Company. In the same year European competition for oils and fats was mostly eliminated by the merger between Lever Bros and the Dutch margarine combine of Van den Bergh and Jurgens. This concentration of commercial power had certain advantages for West Africa. Unilever's interest in keeping raw material prices at the lowest possible level was partly balanced by the opposite interest of its merchandising wing, which needed African peasants to be able to afford its goods.[30] To a certain extent UAC and the other big trading firms wielded countervailing power against another monopoly, the West African Shipping Conference, which

[28] For the organisation of external trade in French West Africa and the dominant role of SCOA and CFAO, see *CHA*, vol. VII, chapter 7.
[29] J. Mars, 'Extra-territorial enterprises', in Perham, *Economics of a tropical dependency*, II, 58–9. Bauer, *West African trade*, 71, 220, gives the market shares (for 'Firm A') in 1949 in tables 8 and 14.
[30] Charles Wilson, *The history of Unilever*, II (London, 1954), 318–23.

for most of the time consisted of Elder, Dempster & Co., with the Hamburg firm of Woermann as its junior partner.[31] And, although competition in West African commerce was very imperfect, it was not entirely suppressed. Approaches to actual monopoly or monopsony were checked by interlopers, often Greeks or Levantines or North Africans, such as the well-known Saul Raccah who broke UAC's control of the Kano groundnut market in the late 1930s, or by the concerted action of African producers and middlemen, as in the successful hold-up of cocoa in the Gold Coast in 1938.

All the same, it is unlikely that West Africans gained quite as much from the growth of external trade as they might have done if its structure had conformed more closely to the model of perfect competitiveness. In this respect they were worse off than the countries of eastern and southern Africa, where foreign merchants had to deal with more sophisticated consumers and more powerful producers, some of whom could sell directly on the world market through London brokers while others formed effective selling co-operatives such as the Kenya Farmers' Association. East Africa's external commerce was handled partly by Indian merchants and partly by London-based firms for which it was an annexe to a varied Indian and Australasian business.[32] None of these was in a position to dominate the market or had direct links with British domestic interests.

On the worst reckoning, excess profits of monopolistic merchants were not the most important of the deductions that were made from the income theoretically accruing to Africans from commercial expansion. That there were such deductions is evident from inspection of the trade balances. Countries in Africa's early stage of incorporation into the modern world economy would be expected to be substantial net importers of capital and therefore to show large deficits on visible trade; and the 'settler' countries did consistently run such deficits; but in the countries of 'native production' the picture was very different. In West Africa the trading accounts were approximately in balance before the First World War, and thereafter showed a very regular surplus, as they did also in Uganda. In the decade after 1945 such surpluses, which

[31] Charlotte Leubuscher, *The West African shipping trade, 1909–1959* (Leiden, 1963).
[32] Kathleen M. Stahl, *The metropolitan organisation of British colonial trade* (London, 1951), part 4.

were then associated with the operation of the State Marketing Boards, attracted a good deal of attention and criticism; but proportionately they had actually been slightly larger in the decade of the 1930s, when they amounted to 32 per cent of the value of the Gold Coast's exports, 27 per cent of Nigeria's and no less than 48 per cent of Uganda's.[33]

Among the mechanisms which generated such a large volume of unrequited exports there must be included the operations of colonial public finance. The peace and transport which made the new trade possible were not free gifts. The British Treasury reluctantly paid the military and administrative expenses of 'new' dependencies, but it insisted on self-reliance at the earliest possible moment, and the balancing of its budget had to be the first concern of every colonial government. Not just the balancing either: they were expected to achieve prudential surpluses, and generally did so except in the worst years of the 1930s. Except for the special case of the Uganda Railway, constructed at the expense of the British taxpayer, railways were financed by interest-bearing loans. In addition, since the work of colonial officials was deemed to be performed entirely for the benefit of Africa, it was Africa that had to pay them, not only while they were in service but also after they had retired to Britain. These fixed charges were made more onerous by the inter-war fall in the price level, and led to an outward flow of resources comparable to the 'drain' which had aroused passionate complaint in India in the late nineteenth century.

Taxation, it should be noted, took highly regressive forms. Africans usually paid a flat-rate hut- or poll-tax. The bulk of colonial revenue, however, came from import duties, which were calculated *ad valorem* and bore heavily on cloth and other items of common consumption. In British Africa north of the Zambezi, income tax was unusual before the 1940s, being introduced only in Northern Rhodesia and Nyasaland (from 1921 onwards), Kenya (briefly in 1920–2 and again from 1937) and Nigeria (from 1927 but not for companies until 1940). The larger trading and mining firms, however, were domiciled in the United Kingdom and paid tax there, though a half share of this was remitted to the colony in which the income was generated.

[33] A. Hazlewood, 'Trade balances and statutory marketing in primary export economies', *Economic Journal*, 1957, **67**, 74–82.

The impact of fiscal institutions and policies was strongly reinforced by colonial monetary arrangements, especially in the latter part of the period. At the beginning of the century trade was conducted in tropical Africa, not by barter, but partly by sterling coins issued at a substantial profit to the Royal Mint (or, in East Africa, by Indian rupees), partly by a variety of other European coins, and partly by 'traditional' currencies (cowries, brass manillas and the like) which had all the characteristics of money except that they were not subject to monopoly control of the supply. Under the new regime it was naturally thought essential to establish a more orderly system, and one which reflected the dominant role of exchanges with the capitalist world. So official currency boards were set up for British West Africa in 1912 and for British East Africa in 1920 (when the rupee was replaced by sterling) to regulate the money supply in their respective regions.[34] In order to assure traders and bankers of monetary stability, the boards (and therefore the colonial governments) were deliberately deprived of any powers of initiative, and the system is indeed one of the best illustrations of what 'dependency' actually means. They were instructed simply to issue local currency in exchange for sterling on a basis of parity. The money supply in the colonies was thus tied strictly to their export earnings. Fluctuations in world market prices were transmitted automatically to the domestic economies. Inflation-led growth was ruled out, and there was no opportunity for counter-cyclical action on the part of the local administrations. In addition, the boards were instructed to maintain a very high ratio of reserves to currency liabilities. The reserve funds, like the balances of the territorial governments, were of course invested in London, and most authorities believe that the interest earned did not compensate the dependencies for the deflationary effect of their absence. In this matter there was a very significant difference between the performance of the boards. The West African board achieved the target of 100 per cent reserve ratio in 1926 and exceeded that figure through the rest of the period.

[34] W. T. Newlyn and D. C. Rowan, *Money and banking in British colonial Africa* (Oxford, 1954), 25–71; A. G. Hopkins, 'The creation of a colonial monetary system: the origins of the West African Currency Board', *African Historical Studies*, 1970, **3**, 1, 101–32; J. Mars, 'The monetary and banking system and loan market of Nigeria', in Perham, *Economics of a tropical dependency*, II, 178ff.

In East Africa, where local interests carried more weight and the influence of the Treasury and the City of London relatively less, the ratio never reached 50 per cent before 1940 and in 1932 fell even below 10 per cent.[35]

The passivity of the monetary institutions would have had a less depressing effect if the banks had not shared similar traditions and objectives. Those operating in British colonial territories were few in number and homogeneous in character. In West Africa there was the Bank of British West Africa; in East and Central Africa (neatly reflecting the nature of this region as the zone of interaction of two sub-imperialisms) there were the Standard Bank of South Africa and the National Bank of India; and from 1926 Barclays (Dominion, Colonial and Overseas), an amalgamation of banks hitherto operating in South Africa, the Middle East and the West Indies, functioned in all territories. All these were based in London and had close links with one or more of the British joint-stock banks. Thus they were 'part of the British banking tradition and the London money market' and 'fundamentally their colonial operations resulted from the extension of British commercial banking into a colonial context'.[36] The main features of the tradition in question are well known. The historic function of banks in Britain has been to finance trade by providing a safe and modestly remunerative outlet for the liquid assets of the propertied classes. With the security of their depositors as the overriding consideration, risk has had to be eschewed. Productive enterprises might be supplied with working capital but not usually with long-term loans, still less with equity participation. Banks of this sort were very efficient and reliable lubricators of Africa's international exchanges but were not equipped to act as agents of its internal development. Moreover in the colonial context their behaviour was in certain ways more restrictive than in their home environment. The special talent of British bankers was the personal evaluation of the creditworthiness of borrowers. It might not be necessary to play golf with the branch manager in order to get a bank loan, but one had to be the kind of person with whom he might play golf. Needless to say, very few Africans were in this category; more seriously, very few Africans held land

[35] Newlyn and Rowan, *Money and banking*, 50, 59.   [36] *Ibid.*, 74.

on terms which rendered it a mortgageable asset to would-be borrowers.[37] Thus the banks found it hard to discern suitable opportunities for investment within Africa, and consequently the greater part of the funds entrusted to them by colonial governments and expatriate businesses was transferred to London.

So the repatriation of profits from territories dominated by mining enterprise was matched by the combined remittances of colonial treasuries, currency authorities and banks in the countries where production was in African hands. It was only where there were resident populations of European origin that the great bulk of the income generated by international trade was kept within the country. And this was the main reason why it was those parts of Africa that achieved the most rapid and diversified development. Elsewhere the funds retained were not sufficient to break the chain of underdevelopment: low productivity, low income, low demand and low investment.

LAND AND LABOUR

All this says little more than that Africa had to pay heavily for the capital and the capitalist organisation that were supplied to her in the colonial period. The other factors, land and labour, were, as was noted earlier (p. 87), assumed by the liberal model to be virtually free goods, which could be applied to export production at hardly any real cost; and that assumption now needs to be qualified. It is true that production for export was in this period almost entirely a net addition to total output, just as the compensating imports were in the main a net addition to consumption. Cash-crops were generally grown as well as subsistence food-crops, not in substitution for them; and where this was not so, as in parts of the West African cocoa belt, food was bought from neighbouring areas, thus widening the orbit of the exchange economy. Overall, Africa remained self-sufficient in basic foods. By the end of the period, as will be seen, there were more people in Africa than at the beginning and most of them

[37] There was a trend towards the establishment of individual land titles in parts of East Africa (see *CHA*, vol. VII, pp. 684, 696), and in West Africa the registration of freehold titles was discussed in the late 1920s and 1930s, but the legal complications were considerable and the registration of freehold was introduced only in Lagos, in 1935. The French in West Africa were less restrictive: see *CHA*, vol. VII, chapter 7, p. 382 and n.67.

were probably eating a little better, yet food imports were still small and consisted almost entirely of luxury and semi-luxury items consumed by the immigrant communities and a few of the most prosperous Africans. Nor would it be correct to say that Africa had been de-industrialised in order to make way for the export–import economy. The smelting of iron ores, formerly a widespread activity, had indeed practically ceased, and blacksmiths had been reduced to the reforging of scrap metal. On the other hand, where cotton textile-production was well-established (that is, mainly in West Africa) it had maintained its position, since the factory-made imports, though cheaper than the traditional product, were on the whole less desirable. And losses in some of the old crafts were at least offset by the rise of new ones, such as vehicle maintenance, bicycle repair and tailoring (with the now ubiquitous treadle sewing-machine), as well as the various 'modern' building trades.

At the same time, the application of land and labour to export production was far from being a cost-free process. It is true that land continued to seem abundant except in a few special areas, notably in south-east Nigeria, parts of Kenya, Basutoland and the native reserve areas of South Africa. But in a good many other areas the extension of cultivation, brought about by the combination of the export demand and the growth of population, began to disturb the often precarious ecological balance. Bush fallows were shortened and the depleted soils became more vulnerable to erosion. The removal of forest and woodland cover also promoted both erosion and leaching of the soil, and may have altered local climates for the worse. The alarms raised by ecologists in the inter-war period, which led to the appearance of books with titles like 'Africa, the dying land', seem with hindsight to have been excessive or at any rate premature;[38] but it cannot be doubted that agricultural activity was already causing some loss of natural capital. By comparison the effects of mining were less serious, for although minerals are more obviously a non-renewable resource than surface soils the operations in our period had hardly even begun to exhaust the reserves of any of the principal ores.

The salient feature of the colonial era for Africans was

[38] J.-P. Harroy, *L'Afrique, terre qui meurt* (Paris, 1944). A soil scientist, quoted by W. Allan, *The African husbandman* (Edinburgh, 1965), 385, warned in 1941 that erosion could put an end to organised life in the United States by the end of the century and in Africa almost certainly before that.

undoubtedly a great increase in the total amount of work done by men, and probably also (though this matter needs more investigation) by the already heavily burdened women. In conventional analysis the cost of this addition would be identified as the sacrifice of leisure. But 'leisure' was a concept alien to Africa, and it would be more pertinent to note that many of the new forms of labour required arduous journeying and long separation from home and family and that nearly all of them, whether in mines, on plantations or on peasant smallholdings, were repetitive and exhausting activities, such as no sensible person would undertake except by necessity or for large reward. And here was the crux of African development, quickly perceived by governments and other employers. Necessity did not drive, since the workers possessed the means of subsistence, and high rewards could not be offered, because in most cases they would eliminate profit and exhaust the revenues of states. African societies in the early twentieth century were not disintegrating, overcrowded peasant communities for whose members any sort of wage employment was an improvement. They were still functioning, essentially self-sufficient tribal societies, and 'subsistence' in this context did not mean bare physical survival but the material basis for a satisfying human life, however straitened it might appear to outsiders. When the rains failed, of course, this basis collapsed, and in the first years of the colonial system famine was sometimes an effective recruiter of wage labour; but such an occasional, and steadily less frequent, stimulus hardly provided an adequate foundation for a new economic system. Wage goods were usually not essentials, but were either sources of ephemeral pleasure (cigarettes, beer, purchased sex) or commodities such as cloth and ornaments that were acquired at least as much for status as for utility.

Thus the model of development with unlimited supplies of labour,[39] applicable to some other parts of the Third World, had little validity in early colonial Africa. The logical alternative would have been development with high wages, as in Australia or North America. Consumers of labour, however, argued that, given the limited need of the workers for money, high wages would actually reduce the amount of labour offered. The concept

[39] W. A. Lewis, 'Economic development with unlimited supplies of labour', *Manchester School of Economic and Social Studies*, 1954, **22**, 139–91.

of a 'backward-sloping supply curve for labour' has latterly come under heavy fire, because it was used as an excuse for paying abysmally low wages and because it is thought to imply that Africans were idle or irrational. In some circumstances, however, it implies entirely rational behaviour, and there is good reason to suppose that those circumstances obtained in early colonial Africa. It is true that the argument holds good only over a limited range of possible wages. A really large increase in the income obtainable from work, such as to make a decisive change in the African economic environment and to open up the prospect of continuous improvement, would certainly have produced a response of the kind considered 'normal' in capitalist economies. But the relatively primitive varieties of capitalist enterprise operating in Africa at this time could hardly have borne such high labour costs. So most employers, public and private, chose instead to try to alter the supply conditions, so as to make labour abundant even at a low price. And to some extent at least they had the power to bring about this change.

In the first place, imperfections in the market for export crops in regions of peasant production were matched in regions of mines and European farms by imperfection in the market for labour. In South Africa the market had long been rigged against the sellers by the notorious pass laws, which were now copied in the newer lands of European occupation. The Witwatersrand Native Labour Association (WNLA; 'Wenela'), set up by the South African Chamber of Mines, went a long way towards putting the gold industry into a position of monopoly control. Elsewhere there was enough informal solidarity between employers to establish a 'standard wage' that was difficult to raise. Counter-action was made extremely difficult by official discouragement of trade unions and by the fragmented and amorphous character of the labour force.

The most obvious solution to the problem, however, was to deprive Africans of the means of subsistence, and in South Africa this was done. From 1913 (except in urban areas and in the Cape) none of the 'Bantu' were allowed to acquire land rights outside reserved areas which were even then inadequate to support the population. The solution, however, was only partially applied, even in South Africa. For it was realised that if the workers became full proletarians the mines, municipalities or governments would have to bear the cost of feeding their families and of providing them with permanent housing and the other facilities that make regular urban life supportable. It was thought more expedient therefore to let the subsistence sector continue to carry part of the cost of development. The areas set aside for Africans were small enough to force most of the males to seek at least temporary wage employment but not so small that they would all have to bring their wives and families with them and find other means of providing for their retirement.

Outside South Africa structural change was less drastic. Initially at any rate, even in settler-dominated territories, Africans were left with enough land for their subsistence. Certain other features of the South African scene, however, were widely copied, especially the use of direct, flat-rate taxation as a means of compelling men to enter the money economy. But tax, which was usually calculated as the equivalent of a month's wages, was not by itself a complete solution, and most colonial authorities resorted to simpler forms of coercion, especially in the early stages of their rule. Conscription for public purposes, such as road-building and the carrying of officers' loads, was taken for granted before and during the First World War, and was often justified as an extension of traditionally sanctioned communal service, the colonial states being deemed to have inherited the right of the tribal authorities. It was condemned in principle by the international conventions of the post-war period, but loopholes were left for cases of special need and were often used. The early practice of 'supplying' forced labour to private employers was forbidden by the British government in 1908. Administrators, however, were still allowed and expected to 'encourage' Africans to seek wage employment, and the distinction was lost on most of the chiefs and headmen who actually did the encouraging. 'Forced labour', moreover, was a term that meant what it said. Pain and humiliation are of course matters for economic history even though there is no way of quantifying them; and it has to be recorded that the flogging of recalcitrant labourers, by private employers as well as by public officials, was a common feature of life wherever settlers and planters were present, at any rate in the first two decades of the century, and did not entirely cease until after the end of our period.

Nor was coercion confined to the recruitment of wage labour.

As we have seen, the forced cultivation of cotton by peasant farmers in German East Africa was the trigger for the great Maji Maji revolt at the beginning of the period; and though British methods were less heavy-handed, the production of export crops in Uganda and other territories of East and Central Africa was not initiated without an element of compulsion. In French Equatorial Africa and the Belgian Congo, peasant farmers were required throughout the inter-war years to produce certain quantities of cash-crops for sale at fixed prices to monopoly trading companies under pain of prosecution which could lead to flogging or imprisonment. However, as Lord Hailey later drily observed, 'It must not...be assumed that compulsion for the growth of marketable or "economic" crops had in fact been confined to the Belgian or French territories. The difference between their practice and that of the British Administrations lay in the fact that the latter did not have legal powers to stimulate the production of marketable crops.'[40]

To the extent that the exchange of African labour for the goods and services of the West was made under duress, the liberal model of colonial economic development is of course invalid; and in East, central and southern Africa the role played by coercion was undoubtedly a large one. But perhaps in retrospect the real cause for surprise is that so much labour was voluntarily supplied, both to the capitalist and to the 'petty-commodity' sectors of production. The most effective stimulus, as the more far-sighted capitalists had always recognised, was the development of new wants: the incorporation of imported consumer goods, obtainable only for money, into the catalogue of conventional necessities or of common aspiration. This development proceeded steadily through the colonial era and allowed the progressive withdrawal of the harsher kinds of constraint. As time went on the possible rewards for additional work came to include minor pieces of capital equipment such as bicycles, sewing-machines and permanent roofing materials, whereby genuine improvements in the standard of living could be secured, and the ideal of indefinite accumulation made its appearance. This process was perhaps assisted by an emphasis which, it can be suggested, was especially characteristic of African cultures: the supreme valuation of

[40] Lord Hailey, *An African survey (Revised 1956)* (London, 1957), 1370–1.

political goods — authority, recognition, power — and the use of material possessions primarily as counters by which those goods could be acquired.[41] It is in the nature of status symbols that they are subject to incessant depreciation, so that when new goods are introduced into a society addicted to such symbols it finds itself committed to ever-increasing expenditure of acquisitive effort. This may have been one reason why wages and peasant income could be held low enough to allow an elementary kind of capitalist development to proceed. Be that as it may, the distribution of political goods was radically altered by the new economy. One of the chief consequences of colonial trade was to speed up the rate at which power and status, and women, were transferred from one male generation to the next.

Another consequence was the massive geographical mobility of labour. It is true that the combination of European capital and African labour now took place on African soil, and not in the New World as it had done in earlier centuries. But the application of capital, as we have seen, was spatially very selective, so that very large numbers of Africans could enter the exchange economy only by leaving home for varying periods of time. The most spectacular migration was caused by the insatiable appetite of the mines of southern and central Africa for human muscle-power, so that the whole of the region has been quite aptly designated as 'the Africa of the labour reserves'.[42] But elsewhere too there was a steady drift of clerks, domestic servants and general labourers, and in West Africa also of petty traders and mechanics, into the growing seaports and centres of government. In addition, the expansion of commercial agricultural production, whether under European or African control, was made possible only by large-scale emigration from the regions less favoured by nature or transport investment or both. Every year thousands of people trekked from Upper Volta and the Northern Territories of the Gold Coast to the cocoa groves of the south, from outlying areas of Uganda and from the densely populated territories of Ruanda and Urundi to

[41] In a little-noticed essay, Lloyd A. Fallers suggested that in Africa production and exchange have typically been undertaken 'as an adjunct – a means – to the organisation of power, the field in which, it appears, the African genius has really concentrated its efforts...[There is] a tendency for economic structures and processes to be overshadowed by – perhaps better, *contained within* – political structures and processes.' ('Social stratification and economic processes', in M. J. Herskovits and M. Harwitz (eds.), *Economic transition in Africa* (London, 1964), 115, 119).
[42] Amin, 'Underdevelopment and dependency in black Africa'.

the rich cotton and coffee farms of Buganda, as well as from western and southern Tanganyika to the sisal estates of the north and east. By far the greater part of this movement was at least formally voluntary; and indeed the function of the cruder kinds of coercion was not, on the whole, to force Africans into the labour market but to prevent them from making optimal use of it: not to drive them to the City of Gold but to stop them getting there, so that they might work for lower wages in weaker enterprises of Rhodesia, Angola and Mozambique or the rural parts of white South Africa.

The migrations were also for the most part circular, not final. The African worker left his homestead for a season, for a year, for a few years, occasionally for a working lifetime. Hardly ever did he set off for the city, the mine or the foreign farm without the intention of returning, and rarely did he fail to return in fact. There were exceptions. An increasing number of originally migrant labourers managed to secure permanent farming tenancies in Buganda. The government of the Belgian Congo set out to establish a small but significant proportion of the African population in the *centres extra-coutumiers*, the enclaves of European economy and culture; and its principal private firm, Union Minière, had decided by the 1930s that its long-term interests required the creation of a labour force that was fully committed to wage employment and urban life. Other capitalists, however, baulked, as we have noted before, at the short-term and medium-term costs of 'stabilisation'; and British administrations regarded what they called detribalisation as a threat to everything that they valued. At this time, nearly all Africans undoubtedly concurred. Nothing in the 'modern' sector of the colonial society could offer any substitute for the material and psychological security provided by membership of the rural community and the land rights that went with this membership. At the same time, outside the most favoured regions of cash-crop production, the natal village could supply men with no inducement to permanent residence. The results were in many ways unhappy. Men lived a good part of their lives in encampments of urban scale that lacked the rudiments of urban civility, while women struggled to raise their children without the material and moral support of their husbands. However, it would probably be sentimental illusion to suppose that, other things being equal, African men would choose to spend all their time at home being husbands and fathers; and the material loss from their absence was serious only in those agricultural systems, a minority of the whole, in which the main input had previously been male labour. Moreover the coming and going of workers contributed to that widening of intellectual horizons that was the main intangible benefit of the new order.

THE COURSE OF CHANGE

The changes outlined in this chapter followed an erratic course, with several marked alterations of pace and character even within the limited time-span that is here held in view. The principal regulator was the fluctuating price of Africa's exports, together with the closely related terms of its trade with the outer world. For individual colonial governments and foreign entrepreneurs as well as for African communities, these were facts of life over which they had little or no control, and so they have to be taken as given by Africa's historians too. It need only be said that the demand for primary products, African and other, rose and fell in approximate harmony with the irregular rate of industrial expansion in the capitalist countries, while the supply side of the price equation was mainly determined at any given time by the size of recent capital investment, not in Africa alone but throughout the tropical, sub-tropical and mineral-bearing regions of the world. World prices were indeed controlled by diamond-producers in South Africa, and briefly influenced by producers of copper, chrome and asbestos in Central Africa (through inter-national restriction agreements in the early 1930s). But apart from chrome (in 1929), cloves and cocoa were the only commodities of which tropical Africa contributed more than half the world's supply at any point in our period, and controlling buyers' prices for these was impracticable. At the same time, almost every country in tropical Africa was highly vulnerable to price movements for one or two commodities. Such dependency varied considerably: indeed, in contrast to most other parts of the British colonial empire, most British territories in Africa widened their export base between the two world wars. It was widest, in the later 1930s, in Nigeria, followed by Kenya and Southern Rhodesia; Nyasaland, the Gold Coast and Somaliland (like Malaya) owed around half their export earnings to a single commodity; while in Northern Rhodesia and the Gambia the proportions were 87 and 98 per cent.

The figures for external trade were among the less inaccurate of colonial statistics, but there are serious difficulties in the construction of price indices where exports are composed of a very few commodities, the relative prices and volumes of which are subject to large and frequent changes. Moreover, if Africa is aggregated the picture is dominated by the price of gold, which was constant for most of the period and then moved in the opposite direction to all other prices. For those African countries that were not primarily gold-producers the fluctuations are clear in outline, though their amplitude is often open to doubt.

At the beginning of the period export prices were on a rising trend which continued until 1920, becoming very steep towards the end, thanks to the monetary inflation and the world-wide commodity famine induced by four years of war. The prices of imported manufactures were rising too, but until 1913 their increase was slower, and so Africa on the whole enjoyed a decade or so of markedly improving terms of trade,[43] following a long period of stasis or decline. This therefore was a time of spiralling activity and change. Though Africa, apart from the far south, was still too raw to attract more than a small proportion of the capital that was pouring out of Europe to the primary-producing regions of the world at this time, there was a mood of optimism and enterprise, a sense of widening opportunity — for foreigners certainly but also for many African individuals and groups. 'Favourable' terms of trade, however, were not an unmixed blessing to Africans. They stood to benefit as peasant producers,

[43] The reference is to the 'net barter' or 'commodity' terms of trade, which measure changes over time in the quantity of imports that can be paid for by a given quantity of exports. In principle, a better indication of changes in the *relative* positions of Africa and its industrialised trading partners would be the 'double factoral' terms, which take account of differences in the rate of growth of productivity as well as of fluctuations in the price ratios. These are even harder to calculate but would certainly show a marked deterioration for Africa over the whole period. (Since it is much easier to improve productivity in secondary industries than in primary ones, there is a sense in which the commodity terms ought, in compensation, to move continuously in favour of primary producers, and this of course they have not done.) On the other hand, the 'income' terms, which include changes in export volume as well as in export and import prices, and are therefore the best measure of the *absolute* gain from external trade, were on a rising trend throughout, except in the early 1930s.

as wage labourers and as consumers of state services, but they also came under especially heavy pressure to *be* peasants or wage earners, to reshape their lives to the often oppressive demands of the market economy. From 1914 to 1920 a rising price level was unusually combined with deteriorating terms of trade, so that the pressures intensified while the benefits were less. The commodity boom broke in the summer of 1920 and was followed by a brief but very sharp recession. By the middle 1920s there had been a partial recovery, but the terms of trade were not restored to the 1913 level in our period, perhaps not at any time since.[44] By now vast new supplies of food and raw materials were pouring into the industrial countries from the farming and mineral regions opened up by the heavy capital outlays of the pre-war decade. Lord Lugard's 'dual mandate', one side of which proclaimed the duty of the colonial powers to make Africa's resources available to 'the world', was partly obsolete when it was publicly formulated in 1922, by which time the world's appetite for Africa's wealth had markedly abated.

This temporary decline in Africa's commercial fortunes has to be related to the characteristic colonial ideology of the 1920s: the complex of ideas summed up in the term 'indirect rule', the insistence that Africans should 'develop along their own lines', even if this meant that in most accepted senses of the word they would hardly develop at all. The relationship was of course permissive, not determinant. Officials who at heart preferred social stability to economic growth were more likely to have their way when external conditions made rapid growth in any case unattainable. For example, the contrast which has often been seen between the aggressive developmentalism of the German rulers of Tanganyika and the paternalist inertia of their British successors is a contrast of economic epochs at least as much as of colonial cultures; few capitalists would have rushed to invest in the wastes of Tanganyika in the inter-war years even if its government had been more eager to receive them; and, conversely, it was British

---

[44] This is the result of G. K. Helleiner's calculations for Nigeria, presented in his *Peasant agriculture, government and economic growth in Nigeria* (Homewood, Ill., 1966), appendix A, table IVA.6. There is no systematic index of the terms of trade for any other African country before the Second World War, but preliminary calculations for East Africa suggest that, while the general pattern was similar, the 1913 peak was not quite so dominant.

Tanganyikans whose initiative, in the very different conditions created by the Second World War, led to that *reductio ad absurdum* of developmentalism, the Groundnut Scheme of 1947.

So long as the 1920s lasted, commodity prices were good enough to attract a modest flow of capital to the more favoured regions of Africa and to make more Africans willing partners in the international exchange economy. But between 1929 and 1933 nearly all prices, except that of gold, fell to unprecedented depths, some export commodities losing more than half their average value in that period. Partial recovery in the mid-1930s was followed by a renewed collapse in 1938, and the outbreak of war, with restrictions on shipping and loss of European markets initially made matters worse still. Moreover, primary producers suffered even more heavily than industrial workers from the economic sickness of the time, and Africa's terms of trade worsened still further, reaching their lowest point ever about the middle of the Second World War. And so our period ended in deepening gloom.

The gloom was not caused only by the periodic ebb tide of the world capitalist economy. There were more fundamental reasons why the first two or three decades of colonial rule should have been an 'age of improvement' but the next two decades a time of doubt and discontent. The colonial stimulus worked, we have suggested, by creating the conditions for the fuller employment of both land and labour. Once the slack of the pre-colonial economy had been taken up, progress slowed towards a halt.[45] Production for export did increase during the 1930s, because governments brought greater pressure to bear on the people in order to sustain their revenues, because the people themselves sought to sustain what had become a customary level of consumption, and because in the case of tree-crops and mines the greater part of the production costs had already been incurred. But expansion was achieved with a growing sense of strain and the limits of the process were in sight. The limits were both structural and technological. Wage labour and production for distant markets had been superimposed upon, but had not

[45] The most ambitious econometric study, Robert Szereszewski's *Structural changes in the economy of Ghana, 1891–1911* (London, 1965) suggests that the decisive period was the quarter-century before 1914 and that thereafter (p.92) the pace of structural change was 'rather slow' until the mid-1950s.

superseded, older systems of local and domestic economy. Extension of the market had greatly enhanced the value of the marginal product of Africa's land and labour, but physical productivity had hardly altered. The ox-drawn plough had been widely adopted by African farmers in South Africa, but elsewhere they had rarely found it feasible or profitable. Mechanisation was not very far advanced even on white-settler farms and was unknown on African holdings. Secondary industry made some headway in South Africa, where the foundations even of heavy industry were being laid in the prosperous 1930s. But elsewhere manufacturing did not go beyond the elementary processing of agricultural products, with here and there a plant for the production of lager beer, soft drinks or cigarettes, though the necessary repair workshops run by the railways, the posts and telegraphs and the public works departments should be mentioned as important nurseries of the basic engineering skills. The fundamental reason for the failure to move out of the extractive phase of development was not technical or political but economic: outside South Africa purchasing power was too small to warrant the local establishment of forms of production whose virtue lies in the economies of scale. Advanced technology could have been hired or bought, skills could have been imparted if it had been worth while to impart them, and political considerations were relevant only in that the economic impediments could not have been overcome except by tariff protection or other forms of state assistance, to offer which would have been inconsistent with the basic objectives and philosophies of the colonial regimes.

The admission that African societies, even towards the end of our period, were still too poor to provide an adequate base for local industrial development concedes that the gains accruing to the mass of the people from the systems of exchange described in this chapter were not remarkable. The gains, however, did not consist solely of an increased supply of consumer goods but also of the extension of public services, especially in the fields of education and health. These services were provided mainly through the agency of the missionary societies, the resources being provided partly by the contributions of the people themselves, partly by the Christian congregations of Europe and America (easily the most important donors of 'aid' in this period)[46] and partly by subventions from the colonial state, which of course was in the main merely returning part of the money levied in direct and indirect taxation. (The Colonial Development Act of 1929 may be a landmark in the history of British colonial policy, but its impact was barely perceptible, and in any case the scope of the term 'development' was still narrowly economic; it was only in 1940 that the words 'and welfare' were added to legislation of this kind.[47])

Education was regarded instrumentally by most of those concerned: by governments as a way of meeting their own and the commercial organisations' need for employees who were literate, numerate, disciplined and not prohibitively expensive; by teachers for similar reasons and often also to help in propagating the message of salvation; by pupils and their parents as a means of personal and group advancement. Yet the extension of knowledge must surely be seen as one of the most valuable fruits of economic progress, and not just as one of its most crucial preconditions. Better health was even more obviously an intrinsic good, and hospitals and rural dispensaries, inadequate though they were, received the most unambiguous welcome of all the twentieth-century innovations.

Hardly any African would doubt that, other things being equal, an increase in the quantity of life is to be desired above all other ends. Demography is therefore the most important measure of the success of any economic system. Unfortunately, however, there is the usual lack of hard figures. Though most of the administrations conducted periodic 'censuses' they did not have the means to make genuine and comprehensive counts of a suspicious population, and registration of births and deaths, if attempted at all, was hopelessly incomplete. Each census usually showed a large increase on the previous one, but improved recording certainly accounted for part of the increase and it is difficult to know how large a part. After 1945, in some though by no means all territories, census-taking became thorough and sophisticated

[46] This assertion is made confidently, although the financial aspect of the missionary effort has received little scholarly attention, and there appears to be no systematic estimate of the cash investment.
[47] Between 1929 and 1938 British colonial Africa received from the Colonial Development Fund some £2.4m as grants and £1.6m as loans (of which most were remitted under the 1940 Act). These moneys were chiefly devoted to the improvement of water supplies, the prevention of soil erosion and the expansion of transport facilities.

enough for the general trend of African population to become clear; by the time of independence it was growing fast, often at more than 2 per cent per annum, in a few areas at as much as 3 per cent; in other words Africa was by then experiencing the population explosion that was convulsing the rest of the Third World. But exactly when the upsurge began is still uncertain. Some trust can probably be reposed in the figures from South Africa, which show that African population almost doubled in the first thirty years of this century; but the South African experience was certainly atypical, and for the rest we have to rely mainly on circumstantial reasoning.

The general pattern of pre-colonial African demography was that which would be expected in rural societies with simple technologies and no knowledge of scientific medicine. Mortality and fertility rates were both very high, and some 'normal' excess of births was offset by periodic disasters. There was probably a long-term upward trend but it was very slow. And whatever growth there may have been was checked in many areas, especially in East and Central Africa, by the unheard-of disasters that immediately preceded the colonial conquest. The conquest itself, though for the conquerors it consisted only of minor campaigns and punitive expeditions, was for many African communities the most violent event in their historical experience, and the revolts that followed, notably those against the Germans in East and South West Africa at the beginning of our period, led to very heavy loss of life. Then, when things seemed at last to be settling down, there began the great conflict which from Africa's point of view was the last act of the Scramble. In Cameroun, in South West Africa and most of all in East Africa the conquerors fought with one another on African soil, with African auxiliaries and with calamitous results. In East Africa the British alone recruited nearly a million troops and 'carriers', of whom, according to conservative official figures, not less than a hundred thousand died, nearly all from disease and malnutrition.

This war service was in fact only the heaviest of many lethal burdens laid on the African peoples in the first decades of colonial rule. Those who died in battle, whether fighting against the colonialists or against one another at their behest, were few in comparison to those who succumbed or were permanently enfeebled while engaged in arduous labour in unaccustomed climates, sustained by inadequate quantities of unfamiliar food, and exposed to a new range of diseases. Most notorious, because of the accompanying brutalities, was the fate of those who had to ransack the forests for wild rubber in King Leopold's Congo. That scandal was passing its peak as our period opened, but the tribulations of the concession-ridden French section of the Congo basin, as of Angola, would get worse for some time to come. On a smaller scale, there were many deaths among the highland Kikuyu recruited for unsuccessful plantations on the Kenya coast, and many more among railway-building gangs in Moyen-Congo and the Ivory Coast. And worse than any of the direct consequences of the conquest were the results of the sudden increase in human and animal movements that preceded and accompanied it; for these opened the way for the agencies of disease to spread among populations not inured to them. Smallpox and bubonic plague were not new to Africa, but there is every reason to believe that their incidence greatly increased in the latter part of the nineteenth century and the early years of the twentieth, as did measles, tuberculosis and in some savanna countries sandfly fever and cerebrospinal meningitis. Venereal diseases likewise multiplied, becoming almost pandemic in the regions of most extreme social disruption; they are held responsible for the belt of unusually low fertility that extended, during and even beyond the colonial period, over the northern part of the Congo basin. The worst single demographic disaster occurred when the tsetse flies native to the northern shores of Lake Victoria became infected with a virulent strain of human trypanosomiasis, and before the outbreak died away, mainly through the forced evacuation of the affected islands and coastlands, very large numbers of people — 300,000 is the usually accepted figure for Uganda — had died the miserable death of sleeping-sickness victims during the first decade of the century. More widespread and long-lasting were the effects of animal trypanosomiasis, which also took advantage of ecological disarray to establish itself in vast tracts of former grazing land, denying them to cattle and their human partners. By 1905 the herds were just beginning to recover from the great rinderpest epidemic which swept through eastern Africa from Ethiopia to Natal in the 1890s, reducing pastoralists to starvation and rendering mixed husbandmen far more vulnerable to the effects of crop failure; but recovery was made slow by the attacks of other cattle plagues: foot-and-mouth, redwater, east-coast fever, pleuropneumonia. And then came the culminating human disaster, the influenza pandemic that was the last and worst consequence of the conflict which the greed and stupidity of Europe's rulers had wished upon the world. It may well be that 2 per cent or more of Africa's population perished in 1918–19 from this cause alone.

Africa's peoples have great resilience, however, and there were countervailing forces which gathered strength throughout the colonial period. Even before 1914 the security of life had been improved in some parts of Africa, and by no means all of it was lethally affected (except through the influenza) by the European war. Thereafter there were two decades of almost total peace. In addition, the intruders were able to do something to combat the diseases which their coming had helped to spread, and eventually to produce a net gain in health. The scale and timing of the improvement are hard to assess. Outside the towns — which were actually healthier places than the countryside — skilled medical help was very thinly spread; and in any case, apart from quinine, certain remedies for dysentery and a very successful treatment for yaws, medical science had few specific remedies for Africa's ills until after the Second World War. On the other hand the administration did to some extent manage to curb the most lethal epidemic diseases, vaccination playing some part in this, but quarantines and destruction of plague-infected dwellings a greater one. Though epidemics of various sorts were reported year by year by almost every territory throughout the period, mass mortalities of the kind common in the previous half-century do not seem to have occurred after 1920.

However, medicine and public health measures probably had a less significant positive effect than a general improvement in the standard of living that can be noticed in the more favoured territories from the beginning of the period and in nearly all of them by its half-way mark. Here again it is difficult to be very specific. There was no general or radical change in housing or other features of the economic environment. The rapid and widespread increase in the use of washable cloth doubtless had some effect on health; but the main improvement is likely to have been in diet. After the early scandals and disasters, most labourers in European employment were adequately and regularly, though monotonously, fed. For those who stayed in the villages there were some additions to the agricultural repertoire, notably the New World plants, maize and cassava, which had been spreading slowly into the interior since the sixteenth century but made rapid headway in the twentieth. This was not an unequivocal improvement, either agronomically or nutritionally — if it had been, it would have been effected much sooner — but on balance it made people's diet more secure. Temperate-zone crops such as wheat and potatoes, together with woollen blankets, helped to make habitable the well-watered and malaria-free mountain countries, where population grew especially fast. More generally, the money incomes derived from the sale of crops or labour enabled people to eat more meat and dried fish and so to correct the protein deficiency that was the main drawback to life in the moister lowlands. In the cattle countries, wherever the tsetse fly permitted, there was marked expansion in the latter part of the period. Veterinary science had rather more to offer than human medicine, and of course livestock breed faster than people, so that in many areas the number of beasts per person was greater by the 1920s than it had ever been before; indeed, overgrazing was becoming the most serious threat to ecological equilibrium.

So people on the whole were eating a little better, and there were no longer years in which they did not eat at all. Thanks to the new means of transport, food could be moved into drought-stricken areas, if necessary from outside Africa, and most people had or could acquire enough money to buy it. Deaths from hunger did not cease with the arrival of colonial government. In East Africa, for instance, the administrations were unable to prevent many thousands from perishing in 1919, when a severe drought was added to the afflictions of that terrible time. But this was the last disaster of its kind. In the early 1930s there were three successive years of low rainfall and massive locust invasions as well, but the result was hardship and malnutrition, not the large-scale mortality that must have ensued at any earlier time.

For East and Central Africa, then, the outline story is that between 1880 and 1920 there was almost certainly an overall loss of population, but that this was rather more than made good by unprecedented growth, probably averaging already between 1 and 1.5 per cent per annum, in the next two decades. In West Africa, which had been exposed to the outer world for centuries, the most difficult phase of biological adjustment was already over; the colonial experience seems to have been a fairly steady acceleration of an upward tendency which can be detected from the early nineteenth century onwards and may have brought the annual increase to 2 per cent by the end of our period. In the healthy south too there was continuous expansion. So population was nearly everywhere denser in 1940 than it had been in 1905, or in 1880.[48] But, apart from areas where alienations to white land-owners had created artificial scarcity, it was only in a few special districts — in south-east Nigeria, in some of the hill countries of East Africa — that there was yet any real pressure on the land, or any serious threat to the ancient assumption that everyone had a right to enough land for his subsistence. That crucial change, probably the most drastic of all the long-term consequences of the colonial intervention, still lay in the future.

What is true in the demographic domain is true in other spheres as well; the consequences of the major innovations made at and just before the beginning of our period were only just beginning to work themselves out by its end. Moreover, many of the underlying long-term trends were masked by the effects of international recession and of war. Histories have to stop somewhere, but an economic history which stops in the middle of the colonial epoch is perhaps especially incomplete.

[48] The total population of Africa in the 1930s is likely to have been between 130 and 160 million. Over 33 million lived in the countries of Mediterranean Africa, and almost half of these were in Egypt. South of the Sahara, there were about 10 million in South Africa, perhaps rather more in the Belgian Congo, and twice as many in Nigeria, as also in French black Africa.

CHAPTER 3

CHRISTIANITY

Apart from the Coptic Church in Ethiopia and Egypt and the established settlements of Christian whites in North and South Africa and of Christian Creoles in Freetown, Monrovia and Cape Palmas, Christian influence in Africa at the beginning of the twentieth century was still largely restricted to a thin scatter of missionary outposts. Already, however, there were some dramatic exceptions to the overall lack of positive response, and already these cases had illustrated an ironic and prophetic fact. Some of the most notable Christian advances had been made in the absence of foreign missionaries, and the future development and maturity of the indigenous churches would largely depend on the elimination of missionary control and paternalism. It was while the missionaries had been excluded from Madagascar in the reign of Ranavalona I (1828–61) that Malagasy Christians had laid the foundations for a conversion of the Merina kingdom so intensive that by 1913 visitors could report that 'probably in no country in the world are the Christian Churches better attended'.[1] Similarly in Buganda, when the White Fathers temporarily withdrew in 1882, the young Catholic converts immediately displayed that zeal and conviction which in less than a decade was to carry them and their Anglican counterparts through persecution to a position of power and dominance. In coastal West Africa, where disease and mortality reduced the number of European missionaries, the expansion of Christianity among the Fante, Yoruba and Niger Delta peoples had been largely directed and accomplished by African clerics and laity. Other Africans were also beginning to find in Christianity fresh answers, often forgotten or belittled by Western missionaries, to traditional spiritual

[1] Anon., *Madagascar for Christ*, Being a joint report of simultaneous deputations from the London Missionary Society, the Friends' Foreign Mission Association and the Paris Missionary Society, to Madagascar, July to October, 1913 (London, 1913), 22.

concerns and opportunities. The momentum of African response[2] effectively restricted missionary surveillance and control. Independent churches, originating almost exclusively from the Protestant tradition, provided some of the clearest illustrations of the ways in which Christianity was becoming at home in Africa. Even in the Catholic Church distinctively African forms of ministry and spirituality were · gradually emerging. Already Christianity in Africa was by no means identical with the missionaries' understanding of the Faith; already it had a vitality independent of its contacts with the West.

For most missionaries, however, developments at the turn of the century appeared as divine interventions enabling them to intensify their rapid occupation of Africa. Steamers, railways and bicycles were removing problems of access; advances in tropical medicine enhanced the chances of survival; the constraints imposed by tribal warfare or by recalcitrant African rulers were being removed, and although the colonial regimes sometimes expelled missionaries of foreign nationality, this merely constituted a temporary setback which realignments with other missionary societies soon overcame. It seemed an era of unparalleled opportunity and the divided sections of Western Christendom were prepared to respond.

PROTESTANT PIONEERS

The pioneer pace-setters throughout the nineteenth century had been the great Protestant missionary societies, many of them originating from the evangelical revival at the end of the eighteenth century. Most influential in tropical Africa was the

[2] Even the best of statistics are an uncertain guide to religious movements. In Africa, the figures themselves are highly questionable. The following set conveys a broad idea, however, of the dimensions of the African response to Christianity, the difference between church and government statistics representing 'a nominal fringe around the churches but unrecognised by them':

	1900	1910	1930	1950	1970
Church statistics	4m	7m	16m	34m	97m
Government statistics	5m	9m	21m	44m	126m

(D. B. Barrett, 'A.D. 2000: 350 million Christians in Africa', *International review of missions*, 1970, **59**, table 3).

Church Missionary Society, which from Freetown had followed the Saros (returned ex-slaves) back into southern Nigeria, while in East Africa its early labours on the coast had been crowned with triumph in Buganda. The strange conjunction of David Livingstone's appeal at Cambridge in December 1857 and the impulse from the Anglo-Catholic Oxford Movement had brought into eastern Africa another Anglican mission, the Universities' Mission to Central Africa, while the much older Society for the Propagation of the Gospel had assisted in the establishment of the Anglican hierarchy at the Cape and in Natal and in missions in their hinterland. In southern Africa and Madagascar the prominent pioneer had been the London Missionary Society, which had also assisted the Paris Evangelical Missionary Society and the American Board of Commissioners for Foreign Missions to start their work among the Sotho and Zulu. Meanwhile the Dutch Reformed Church at the Cape gradually assumed a missionary role which took it north of the Limpopo and the Zambezi and even as far as the Tiv in Nigeria. Methodists and Scottish Presbyterians started influential missions throughout English-speaking sub-Saharan Africa, and from Basel a stream of south Germans and Swiss established a mission of fundamental importance at Accra, at Akropong and among the eastern Akan. German and Scandinavian Lutherans began work in South Africa and Madagascar and subsequently moved into areas which became German colonies. Finally, Baptists and other British missionaries forestalled Leopold by starting work in the Congo basin, and in the 1880s North American Methodists and Congregationalists opened missions in the interior of Angola.

Representatives from these Protestant pioneers met at Edinburgh in June 1910 to plan, for the first time, a strategy embracing the world. Compared with Asia, and particularly with China which was recognised as 'the chief storm centre of urgent opportunity',[3] African missions received a relatively low priority. Not until much later was Africa to emerge as the central focus of the modern missionary movement. For the first half of the twentieth century, as during the nineteenth, the greatest challenge was seen to be in Asia. One aspect of the African situation was, however, felt at Edinburgh to be of crucial significance. Reports from across the continent, from Nigeria to German East Africa,

[3] W. H. T. Gairdner, *Edinburgh 1910* (Edinburgh, 1910), 77.

emphasised the rapid and impending advance of another world religion: Islam. Delegates were urged 'to throw a strong missionary force right across the centre of Africa to bar the advance of the Moslem and to carry the Gospel northwards'.[4] Gustav Warneck, the veteran founder of Protestant missiology, explicitly repudiated the slogan championed by John R. Mott, the American chairman of the meeting at Edinburgh, which aimed at 'the Evangelisation of the World in this Generation'. If workers were scattered and pushed into countries not yet ripe for missions, wrote Warneck, 'we may lose hundreds of thousands to Mohammedanism, whilst perhaps winning some few Christians in a country like Tibet'.[5]

This clash over strategy was only one aspect of the differences which, at least at the level of missionary theory, divided continental Protestants, especially Germans, from the English-speaking missionaries. Led by Warneck, German Lutherans saw themselves accommodating 'foreign peculiarities' and fostering national churches tolerant of indigenous customs. In contrast, most British and North American missionaries, from their early alliance with the humanitarian anti-slavery movement, saw Christianity intimately linked with legitimate commerce and the introduction of African societies to Western ways of life. The convert, asserted one American missionary, must 'live in a permanent upright house, with a chimney in it'; he must no longer be befuddled by his hut's smoky atmosphere or degraded by creeping into it; he must be 'decently' clothed, an individual 'independent of everybody else'.[6] At such extremes, this difference in theory was of fundamental and enduring significance: much later on, after political independence, the churches founded by the missions would become increasingly aware of the dangers of being identified with westernised educated individuals cut off from great numbers of the underprivileged. But in practice, during these early decades of colonial rule, African realities forced most missionaries to adopt remarkably similar policies. Confronted

[4] G. Robson in *World Missionary Conference, 1910: report of commission I* (Edinburgh, n.d.), 406.
[5] Letter from G. Warneck in appendix to *World Missionary Conference, 1910, Report of Commission I*, 435.
[6] G. A. Wilder, quoted in J. K. Rennie, 'Christianity, colonialism and the origins of nationalism among the Ndau of Southern Rhodesia 1890–1935' (Ph.D. thesis, Northwestern University), 1973, 305–7.

with acculturation and African demands for modernisation, even the German missionaries in East Africa soon found that their theories required to be modified in practice. Ensconced among the Chaga in Kilimanjaro, Bruno Gutmann and the Leipzig mission held out for a tribal church, a communal morality with a Christianised kinship and ritual system, but already at the 1911 Evangelical Missionary Conference at Dar es Salaam other missionaries saw clearly that the detribalised were the key to the future. Karl Axenfeld, the influential inspector of the Berlin Mission, gave priority to educating a Christian, Swahili-speaking national élite, and Bishop Hennig, director of the Moravians, while still thinking in terms of a tribal church, wholeheartedly endorsed the educational strategy pioneered by the Scots at Livingstonia in northern Nyasaland. Most missions fostered some rudimentary form of school. Whether this developed early into a full-scale educational strategy in part depended on the theories of different missionary societies; but mission schools were also quickly and profoundly shaped by African responses. The social mobility of the Lakeside Tonga in Nyasaland and their demand for education were fundamental elements in Livingstonia's success.[7] Yet even where the response was far less spectacular, the pioneer bush-school proved generally to be the revolutionary spearhead of the Christian movement. Often imparting to many of its participants little more than a smattering of literacy, it was nevertheless summoning the youth, and sometimes the adults, of Africa towards a positive encounter with modernisation.

Another point of divergence among Protestant missionaries was their attitude towards non-Christian religions. One note of protest was recorded at Edinburgh against those who dismissed the values in African traditional moral and religious systems. It came from the Swiss missionary Henri Junod who asserted that 'among Bantu tribes there is a rich folklore...which illustrates the voice of conscience in a wonderful way'.[8] At the subsequent meetings of Protestant and Anglican missionaries at Jerusalem (1928) and Tambaram (1938), this basic theological issue had become dominant. The conservatives and continentals, led by H. Kraemer, denounced the dangers of syncretism and emphasised the radical discontinuity between Christianity and other faiths.

[7] See *CHA*, vol. VII, chapter 12.
[8] *World Missionary Conference, 1910: Report of Commission IV*, 13.

This debate was primarily focused throughout this period, however, on Christian relations with the religions of Asia. Among missionaries in Africa, the comparable divide was between those who, like Junod and E. W. Smith, had obtained a specific understanding of African cosmologies and social systems and those who continued to operate with second-hand stereotypes. For Africa the major debates among missionaries concerned questions of discipline, and at Tambaram it was the Gold Coast churches and a young African theologian, Christian Baëta, who raised the question which from the first had haunted the Christian mission in sub-Saharan Africa: 'whether monogamy is essential to Christianity'.[9]

At Tambaram this question still elicited a rigid monolithic response from the missions. Indeed it is significant that the issue itself was raised in the context of the progress of missionary co-operation and of unity in the life of the church. For much the most important result of Edinburgh 1910 had been the creation of a Continuation Committee which duly became in 1921 the International Missionary Council. The Council's secretary was the Scottish layman, J. H. Oldham, who more than any other person had been the moving spirit behind the Edinburgh conference. The impetus thus given by the missions to the development of the ecumenical movement as a whole was of universal consequence. Able to mobilise support throughout Christendom, the Council also substantially strengthened missions in their negotiations with the colonial regimes and, as will be seen, Oldham himself became a formative influence on British colonial policy in Africa during the inter-war period. The Council thus complemented and embodied that relative independence of action enjoyed by the modern missionary movement. This independence from the national state had its roots in the far-flung character and organisation of its home bases, which gave both Protestant and Catholic missions a financial and organisational freedom unknown before the nineteenth century. Missionary co-operation could, however, dangerously circumscribe the scope for African response and initiative. Comity arrangements, the agreement to respect each other's spheres of action, which were the practical fruit of many missionary consultations, could prevent a wasteful use of scarce

[9] International Missionary Council, *The life of the Church*, Tambaram Madras Series, IV (London, 1939), 405.

resources. They could also bestow on missionaries a monopoly of power leading to a dictatorship in matters of discipline. And when the mission school provided the main means of economic and social advance, such powers threatened not merely African converts but the local community as a whole. This threat to the customs and the cultural heritage of African societies might have been far more serious had not Catholics and some other Christian bodies continued to operate outside such comity agreements. For these differences among Europeans gave Africans, both Christian and non-Christian, the opportunity to contain and transform the missionary impact.

Africa also provided a spectacular demonstration of the difficulties on the road to church unity. Only three years after Edinburgh, the Protestant missionaries in Kenya met at Kikuyu, the principal station of the Church of Scotland mission, to consider a scheme of federation as a step towards a local African Church. The proposals for collaboration were tentative, but the fact that in this remote corner of Africa the delegates had participated in a service of Holy Communion celebrated by the bishop of Mombasa seriously threatened the cohesion of the whole Anglican Church. Frank Weston, the Anglo-Catholic bishop of Zanzibar, arraigned his evangelical neighbour before the Archbishop of Canterbury, and the controversy was still at its height on the outbreak of the First World War. That disaster made the furore soon appear incredibly parochial and irrelevant, yet in that eventful summer Anglicanism was still the religion of those who ruled much of the world, its fortunes were the concern of statesmen, and the young Ronald Knox's witty review of the Kikuyu crisis was read aloud to the prime minister, 'as he basked on the river bank at Sutton Courtenay'.[10]

In future decades the established Protestant missionary societies were to concentrate in Africa on modes of practical co-operation. Henceforth they formed missionary councils in the various territories, and the initiative in church union passed to south India. The presence at Kikuyu of delegates from the Seventh Day Adventists and the Africa Inland Mission (AIM) indicated, however, the extent to which the colonial era had opened Africa to new missionary initiatives. Interdenominational in recruitment but rigidly fundamentalist in theology, the AIM was typical of

[10] E. A. St J. Waugh, *Ronald Knox* (London, 1959), 117.

the 'Faith' missions first popularised by Hudson Taylor of the China Inland Mission and concerned to assert their absolute dependence on God. At a practical level this involved no soliciting of funds, no regular budget, no promise of permanent support. Consequently they were free to respond to new openings with extreme rapidity, uninhibited by any ongoing commitments; from one missionary in 1889 the AIM had increased to 158 by 1919 and their field had expanded from Kenya into the eastern Congo. This organisational flexibility coincided with a distinctive theory of missions, in which the preaching of the Gospel was seen as hastening Christ's second coming. Other established missions had already benefited from similar convictions — the wealthy eccentric Robert Arthington, guided by this motive, had decisively assisted the missionary occupation of Equatorial Africa. For the AIM in East Africa and other 'Faith' missions, such as the Sudan Interior Mission, however, the early emphasis was wholly on a mobile, rapid evangelism. They had no need of the planning and paraphernalia involved in bringing a Christian civilisation to Africa: they would achieve their mission through preaching, or the Lord's will would be indicated by a lack of response, and in either case they would move on to untouched fields. Like other missionaries untrammelled by a hierarchy or by institutional control, they exulted in their autonomy. 'Each of us is practically independent. We can work as in fact the Lord leads. We do not have a wrangling church board at home jealously watching us and asking us to do things of which they have a poor understanding.'[11] Yet by the 1920s most AIM missionaries had settled down to become supervisors of African Christian communities, involved in education and questions of discipline and church order, and in these situations their independence merely tended to accentuate their paternalist autocracy. They continued however to mobilise fresh recruits and resources on a scale which offset the economic depression of the 1930s and other factors later affecting Protestant recruitment in general, and, together with other missions such as the Salvation Army, these conservative fundamentalists continued to represent a vigorous individual strand of Christianity in Africa.

[11] J. Stauffacher to his fiancée, 23 October 1903, quoted in Kevin Ward, 'The development of Protestant Christianity in Kenya, 1910–40 (Ph.D. thesis, University of Cambridge, 1976), 22.

'ETHIOPIANS', ENTHUSIASTS AND PROPHETS

Some new Protestant arrivals, however, brought a much more distinctive and disruptive influence; they soon found a common cause in the social and political protests, and in the religious adaptations, of African Christians. Already in 1883 the first independent church in southern Africa had been founded by Nehemiah Tile among the Thembu, partly in protest against white political and ecclesiastical control, and in the 1890s several 'Ethiopian' churches were started in South Africa. By their use of this term, they asserted an independent, black appropriation of an ancient Biblical and Christian inheritance. They echoed the words of the Psalmist (Ps. 68.31) and recalled the apostle Philip's baptism of the Ethiopian eunuch. Some of them also looked northwards to Abyssinia, with hopes stirred by Menelik's victory at Adowa in 1896. One of the leaders, James Dwane, tried to collect funds for Menelik from Negroes in America, and later, during the Italo-Ethiopian war in 1936, thousands of new followers joined these churches in South Africa as a result of the nightly prayer-meetings held on behalf of Ethiopia's cause.

None of these independents, however, established links with the Ethiopian Orthodox Church, which remained almost as isolated from the rest of Africa during the whole of this period as it had been throughout the centuries, apart from its historic link with the Coptic Church of Egypt, whence it continued to import its *abuna* (metropolitan). With its Ark of the Covenant, its holy Zion at Aksum, its fasting, and its rich, distinctive liturgy, Ethiopia displayed a Christianity which was markedly indigenous. Its resistance to Italian aggression strengthened its symbolic potency for Africa, but the absence of actual contacts with Christians elsewhere in sub-Saharan Africa was one of the great impediments to the development of Christianity in Africa during this period.

With their Pan-African vision, the South African Ethiopians quickly established contact with black churches in the United States, one of which, the African Methodist Episcopal Church, immediately sent assistance. Bishop H. M. Turner arrived in 1898 to ordain some sixty ministers, and the AMEC entered on a missionary enterprise which in the following decades was to lead it along the routes of migrant labour as far north as the

Copperbelt. In West Africa the issue of white control, epitomised in the bitter controversy over Samuel Crowther, the Yoruba freed-slave who was an Anglican bishop from 1864 until his death in 1891, led to several independent African churches among Baptists, Anglicans and Methodists. Here also, with the mission of the African Methodist Episcopal Zion Church and other black churches, Christian Negroes from the New World were no longer mere auxiliaries to the Western mission societies but were now helping to proclaim among Africans a new and independent road to self-improvement and freedom.

It was not only black Christians who brought revolutionary influences to Africa. Radically independent, constantly ready to seize on new doctrines and Scriptural texts, Joseph Booth, who arrived in Nyasaland in 1892 to found on his own an industrial mission, had experienced in his own career something of the turbulent, self-instructed, enquiring background of the young African converts whom he introduced to a world of new opportunities and ideas. Booth also made contacts in North America, and he helped a few of the hundred or more Africans from South Africa who, joining others from West and Central Africa, set off in these years for study in America. Among them in July 1898 was Kwegyir Aggrey, 22 years old and already headmaster of the leading Wesleyan school in the Gold Coast, whose craving for higher education was later to inspire Africans throughout the continent and whose personality was to challenge men of all races. Aggrey was to become an apostle of racial cooperation, but a year before he left for the States, John Chilembwe, baptised by Booth in 1893, arrived in America with his radical mentor to lecture their audiences on 'Africa for the Africans'. In the States Chilembwe broke away from Booth and returned to Central Africa in 1900 with powerful Negro Baptist support and finance to found his Providence Industrial Mission at Chiradzulu, soon to be joined at this 'hornets' nest'[12] by other American Negro helpers. In his successful creation and leadership of a respected, educated Christian community, Chilembwe demonstrated an independent achievement of status and progress; almost inevitably he also became a spokesman for those who

[12] *Central African Times*, 20 April 1901, quoted in G. Shepperson and T. Price, *Independent African: John Chilembwe and the origins, setting and significance of the Nyasaland native rising of 1915* (Edinburgh, 1958), 136.

suffered from colonial rule and the settler economy and society of the Shire Highlands. Resentments deepened until, finally exasperated by the recruitment of Africans to fight a European war, he led a violent apocalyptic rising from 23 January until his death on 3 February 1915.

Chilembwe's life and death vividly illustrated the intellectual speculation and liberation which Christianity and the Bible brought to a wide range of Africans. It was not merely that some Africans had found within the independent churches a means of expressing revolutionary social and political aspirations and of creating new modes of association which could form a model for the future. More fundamentally, these men and women had glimpsed, along with many others who stayed within the mission churches, a new teleological, eschatological view of history. Like Chilembwe, they were to claim for themselves, and for Africa, prophetic texts which embodied a Biblical concept of history as progress. 'Have you forgotten,' wrote Booth to Chilembwe in 1911, 'the marvellous and unthinkable greatness of the promise of God to you in Isaiah 60 v.22 which you rushed to show me, in your canoe, as I came up river ... long ago?'[13] And among some of those who followed Chilembwe into revolt, millenarian expectations were running high.

Christian teaching concerning life after death presented a major, unexpected challenge to the cosmologies of most African peoples, particularly those who were relatively unaffected by Islam. It was proclaimed in sermon, catechism and confessional, and was supported by the calm, persuasive witness from the death-beds of many pioneer missionaries and African converts. No longer was the hereafter merely a faint reflection of this world, slipping imperceptibly into the forgotten past. Suddenly the future assumed a novel, almost overwhelming significance, and it was a future primarily determined by the individual's response to prophetic demands. Sometimes Christian eschatological symbolism was proclaimed and interpreted so literally that it powerfully strengthened traditional beliefs in the possibilities of restoring a utopian natural order, free of evil and suffering. But even where these expectations were not aroused, Christian eschatology

---

[13] J. Booth to J. Chilembwe, 10 December 1911, quoted in G. Shepperson, 'The place of John Chilembwe in Malawi historiography', in B. Pachai (ed.), *The early history of Malawi* (London, 1972), 420.

brought with it novel, disturbing and even revolutionary implications. The millenarian convictions which proliferated before the
First World War were thus but one aspect of a much wider
conceptual development that was taking place in these decades as
a direct result of the impact of Christianity. The particular form
of these millenarian beliefs owed much to another chance contact
with North America, mediated again by Booth; but the widespread
interest they aroused illustrated the extent to which the world-view
of an increasing number of African individuals and societies was
being challenged and changed.

The most dramatic African response to a Christian millenarian
message occurred among the Tonga in northern Nyasaland. In
1908 a young Tonga migrant worker, Elliott Kamwana, returned
to his people after an absence of some seven years, during which
he had first been baptised at Booth's mission in southern
Nyasaland, gone on to work at a mine near Johannesburg and
then had spent six months at Cape Town with Booth. By this time,
Booth had been converted to the millennial teaching of Charles
Taze Russell, the Pennsylvanian founder of the Watch Tower
Bible and Tract Society, later to be known as Jehovah's Witnesses.
It was therefore as a Watch Tower emissary that Kamwana
returned to the Tonga. Within a few months, before he was
deported, he had baptised more than 9,000 adherents. Here was
a faith which embraced not primarily an emerging élite but the
masses; its literature denounced in general terms the existing
structures of church and state and proclaimed exciting alternatives.
Such millennial hopes inspired some of Chilembwe's followers in
1915, but Kamwana dissociated himself from political revolt and
his main impact appears to have been religious rather than
political. Already among the Tonga and neighbouring peoples a
general response to the Gospel proclaimed by the Scottish
missionaries was developing, with enthusiastic audiences of
several thousands attending evangelistic services and impatiently
demanding baptism. Fearful that such enthusiasm might be
superficial, the missionaries insisted on an increasingly strict
probation and greater educational qualifications, and Kamwana
himself, when he had been a student at Livingstonia, had not been
granted baptism. In this situation Watch Tower offered an
immediate alternative to the mission and one which was open to
all, for Kamwana criticised the 'bad effect' of college education

and emphasised the importance of using 'knowledge properly for general interest'.[14]

As Watch Tower reached out to the multitudes, it became at times increasingly involved in traditional spiritual concerns, bringing new rites and concepts to the solution of long-standing problems. Mass baptisms could be experienced as a cleansing analogous to witchcraft eradication, and one of the converts to Watch Tower, Tomo Nyirenda, was to become not merely a finder but also a killer of witches among the Lala in Northern Rhodesia in 1925. But besides its wide and sometimes transient appeal in remote rural areas, Watch Tower spread among migrant workers on settlers' farms and in the urban areas of Central Africa, and it also developed some relatively prosperous agricultural settlements. Its links with the international society remained tenuous, but its adherents became so firmly established during the colonial period that later they were even seen by some politicians as threats to national mobilisation.

The fiercely independent Watch Tower groups had thus appropriated a specific eschatological emphasis in Christianity and around this message had formed significant and enduring movements in a crucible of rapid and disruptive social change. It would be wrong, however, to overemphasise the peculiar character of this experience or to see African Christian initiatives as uniquely exemplified by these independents. The *balokole* revival, which developed among evangelical Anglicans, both black and white, in Ruanda and East Africa in the 1930s, produced similar close-knit fellowships. It provided, like Watch Tower, a new 'lineage', in which dreams were taken seriously as in indigenous traditions, public confession was used to eliminate jealousy and mistrust, women found new roles and respect, and ecstatic phenomena were accepted as normal. In northern Nyasaland, only a year after Kamwana's preaching among the Tonga, a missionary evangelist drew even larger crowds to his revival services, and the thousands at Loudon who burst into public confession of sin may well have experienced a catharsis similar to that found in Watch Tower services. The initiatives could also look towards the future. As early as 1904 a well-known example of Tonga evangelistic initiative, David Kaunda's ministry

[14] Quoted in J. McCracken, *Politics and Christianity in Malawi 1875–1940* (Cambridge, 1977), 211.

among the Bemba, had been launched from his Livingstonia base. Labour migrants educated by him and by the Scots were to play a major part, especially in the inter-war period, in creating unaided the church in the Copperbelt and in founding the associations in Northern Rhodesia and Nyasaland which were to be forerunners of national political parties. 'We were reading our Bible,' recalled Donald Siwale, 'and knew that every human being was the same. Our idea of equality came from the Bible.'[15] Far more significant than the specific messages relayed by Booth or the particular emphases brought by the Scots was the fact that, in certain nuclear areas in Africa, Christian insights had been widely accepted as being deeply relevant to an increasing range of African experiences.

Ethiopianism and eschatology were but two of the novel aspects of Christianity which at the turn of the century were gaining acceptance among Africans. Of even greater significance, since it quickly fused with one of the most powerful elements in African religious traditions, was the Pentecostal emphasis on spiritual healing. Like Russell's millenarianism, this emphasis had its origins in the revival and 'Holiness' movements which had so deeply influenced Western Protestantism in the later nineteenth century, and it reached Africa in many diverse ways. In 1897 Petrus Louis Le Roux, a young Afrikaner Dutch Reformed Church missionary at Wakkerstroom in the eastern Transvaal, began reading *Leaves of Healing*, a periodical published by John Alexander Dowie, who had recently announced in Chicago his plans for Zion City. Refusing to hide the 'glad tiding' of divine healing from his Zulu congregation, Le Roux resigned from the DRC, and in May 1904 an emissary sent by Dowie held the first Zionist baptism in South Africa, immersing Le Roux and his Zulu followers in the river outside Wakkerstroom. Two years later 'the fire came down', marked by the charismatic speaking with tongues, at a Negro Holiness Church belonging to Azusa Street Mission in Los Angeles. 'Faith gives quaint sect new languages to convert Africa,' announced the press,[16] and in May 1908 a former member of Dowie's Zion went to South Africa, there to

[15] Quoted in D. J. Cook, 'The influence of Livingstonia Mission upon the formation of welfare associations in Zambia, 1912–31', in T. O. Ranger and J. Weller (eds.), *Themes in the Christian history of Central Africa* (London, 1975), 108.

[16] *New York American*, 3 December 1906, quoted in W. J. Hollenweger, *The Pentecostals* (London, 1972), 23.

be joined by Le Roux, to establish the Apostolic Faith Mission, the first of several Pentecostal missions in South Africa. Even before this new development, some of the Zulu Zionists at Wakkerstroom had split off from Le Roux to create their own symbols and practices. Soon the Zionist churches multiplied in South Africa and spread north across the Limpopo. They brought a fresh urgency in their challenge to divination and ancestor veneration: accepting the reality of the evils which the traditional religions confronted, they proclaimed that possession by the Holy Spirit was made manifest in faith-healing and rain-making. They encountered the message of God in dreams and visions, and almost all of them practised the purification ritual of baptism by immersion. In some cases they developed a far from orthodox theology. In 1911 Isaiah Shembe, the greatest of the Zulu prophets, founded the Church of the Nazaretha at Ekuphakameni near Durban, Natal. He seemed to his disciples to have the characteristics not of a pastor but of the Lord, 'the mask of the Black Christ'.[17] He called his people to worship 'the God of Adam' in indigenous songs and dances of great dignity and beauty. They responded in their thousands and continued to do so, led by his son after Isaiah's death in 1935. Shembe and many Zion leaders in southern Africa owed little or nothing directly to Pentecostal and North American leaders, but the career of Le Roux and other white enthusiasts indicates that the origins and affinities of these churches in southern and Central Africa lie not so much with 'tribal psychology' or a recrudescence of 'paganism' but rather with a world-wide, charismatic wave.

In southern Nigeria, the other principal area which witnessed the early emergence of African churches with a healing ministry, the initial contacts with overseas Pentecostalism were even slighter. The first African churches in Lagos differed but little in belief and emphasis from the mission churches out of which they had developed. Their dispute primarily concerned questions of organisation, leadership and discipline: the acceptance of polygamy by some of these African churches and its partial toleration by others was perhaps the aspect which most clearly distinguished their practice from that of the missions. The first major shift in emphasis appeared with Garrick Braide and the thousands who

[17] The phrase used by B. Sundkler, *Zulu Zion and some Swazi Zionists* (Uppsala, 1976), 193.

followed his teaching and example, first in the Niger Delta and then throughout southern Nigeria. In one respect Braide's break in 1915 with the Niger Delta pastorate, that branch of the Anglican Church led by Crowther's son and staffed entirely by Yoruba and other clergy of African descent, seemed yet another dispute over leadership, with Braide recruiting support from people at Bonny and elsewhere who resented being ruled by an alien clergy. But from the first, Braide's charismatic challenge had also a radical spiritual dimension, which led to an enthusiastic destruction of charms, mass baptisms and an acceptance of Braide as a prophet whose prayers — and, it was alleged, his bath-water — possessed the power of healing. Braide himself, imprisoned by the colonial administration, died in November 1918 and after his death his Christ Army Church divided into various sections, but the 1921 census reported 43,000 adherents and the emphasis on healing soon developed momentum.

During the influenza pandemic of 1918, a prayer-group of Yoruba Anglicans was formed in Ijebu-Ode. Renouncing all forms of medicine, they relied solely on prayer and divine healing. Their beliefs spread to the Ijebu in Lagos, one of whom, David Odubanjo, found a similar emphasis on prayer and healing in tracts published by the Faith Tabernacle of Philadelphia. Adopting the name of this American body, prayer-groups were established in other Yoruba cities: one was started at Ibadan in 1925 by Isaac B. Akinyele, who thirty years later became the *olubadan* or ruler of the city while his brother was its Anglican bishop. Other separate groups were also formed, the most notable of which, led by Captain Abiodun, daughter of a cleric, developed into the Cherubim and Seraphim. At first these *Aladura*, or prayer-groups, sought to remain within the mission-connected churches, holding that their beliefs and activities merely satisfied a need previously neglected by the missions. Many of their leaders were drawn from the relatively well-educated ranks of established Christian families and their theology was exclusively Biblical. Their desire for a Pentecostal awakening was intense and in July 1930, at a conference at Ilesha, the prayers of a young charismatic convert, Joseph Babalola, were followed by several dramatic healings. The wave of enthusiasm spread to Ibadan and other Yoruba towns and several prophetic figures emerged, including Josiah Olunowo Oshitelu of Ogere in Ijebu, who as a young Anglican teacher had already received visions. Great crowds attended open-air meetings in the markets. Many patients were cured, while others were cleansed from witchcraft. Baptism services continued all night. Soon the *Aladura* were no longer merely a small band of Christian deviants who had been separated from the main churches; suddenly with Babalola and the prophets they had become a dynamic evangelising force, which presented for the first time a Christian challenge to many illiterate farming communities.

The rapid expansion brought persecution: at different periods both Babalola and Oshitelu were briefly imprisoned on charges of making accusations of witchcraft. It also brought divisions and fierce theological debate. At Akinyele's house in Ibadan throughout the night of 23 January 1931 the leaders questioned Oshitelu and condemned on scriptural grounds some of his practices, particularly his use of 'Holy Names'. At the close, Oshitelu, firm in his own convictions but also in the ecumenical belief that, as he expressed it, 'there is but one tree and there are many branches',[18] withdrew to found the Church of the Lord (Aladura). For a period the Faith Tabernacle leaders developed contacts with the Apostolic Church, a British Pentecostal church, which as a result sent missions to southern Nigeria and the Gold Coast. The principal consequence, however, of the *Aladura* revival of 1930 was that Christianity was established in many previously unevangelised areas of Yorubaland where Muslim influences were penetrating quickly: in the crusade against the expansion of Islam, which had so concerned the 1910 Edinburgh conference, Western missionaries had received, albeit if they failed to recognise it as such, a powerful, independent reinforcement from a most unexpected quarter.

It seems an extraordinary coincidence that the Pentecostal emphasis on faith healing should have developed in Western Christendom precisely at the moment when large numbers of Africans were seeking in Christianity a solution to the problem of suffering and evil broadly consonant with their previous concepts of healing. The links, albeit tenuous, in Zululand and southern Nigeria with Western Pentecostalists helped to emphasise the universal significance of this local African response. Yet the careers and impact of two other prophetic figures — William Wade Harris and Simon Kimbangu — illustrate the fact

[18] Quoted by H. W. Turner, *History of an African independent church* (Oxford, 1967), 25.

that as Christianity reached a wider circle of Africans, as the immediate entourage of the mission station ceased to be the focal point of evangelism, the call to purification and healing almost inevitably emerged as a dominant emphasis of the Gospel to Africa irrespective of the presence or absence of Pentecostalist teaching.

A Grebo from Cape Palmas in Liberia, brought up under the influence of Episcopalian missionaries, Harris received his prophetic calling while in prison for having challenged the Liberian authorities. In a trance Harris heard the Archangel Gabriel proclaim that God was coming to anoint him and he felt the Spirit descend upon him. When released from prison, probably early in 1912, Harris discarded all European clothing and set out, with Bible, cross, calabash and a bowl of water, on a preaching mission along the coastal areas of the Ivory Coast to the western Gold Coast. 'Possessed by a holy horror of fetishism',[19] he proclaimed repentance and summoned his hearers to renounce the old gods, while acknowledging the reality of traditional spiritual anxieties. He offered them immediate baptism and healed them, casting out evil spirits by beating his patients on the head with his Bible. It has been estimated that about 200,000 people responded by burning their charms. Fearing political disturbances, the French expelled Harris from the Ivory Coast at the end of 1914, but he left behind him thousands of convinced converts. Some followed a variety of prophets and formed independent churches; others joined one of the mission-connected churches. Ten years later the first Methodist missionary to visit Harris's followers in the Ivory Coast found about 150 congregations with a total of some 30,000 members, many of whom, on the condition that they accepted monogamy, became the nucleus there of the Église Protestante Méthodiste.

In July 1915, Simon Kimbangu, aged about 25, was baptised at Ngombe Lutete, a station of the Baptist Missionary Society in the Lower Congo. Three years later, during the influenza pandemic, Kimbangu received his first summons to a prophetic mission, but, restrained by a sense of inadequate training, it was only in March 1921 that he responded by effecting a spectacular cure. News of the miracle spread rapidly, the mission hospitals

---

[19] The phrase is that of a Roman Catholic eye-witness, the Rev. P. Harrington SMA, quoted by G. M. Haliburton, *The Prophet Harris* (London, 1971), 38.

were suddenly deserted and for the next three months the prophet was at the centre of a tumultuous movement, which attracted thousands of adherents and produced an unprecedented demand for Bibles and hymn-books. Like Harris, he commanded his followers to destroy images and charms and, like Harris and the *Aladura*, Kimbangu appears to have seen his message not primarily as a challenge to the missions but as an extension of their activities, a translation of the Gospel to African spiritual realities. In June the Belgian administration, alarmed at the impact of his teaching, attempted unsuccessfully to arrest him, but in September he was arrested, condemned to death and then imprisoned for life, dying in prison in 1951. Many of his closest disciples were also arrested and exiled to other parts of the Congo, but the movement continued clandestinely. A large number of his adherents, led by his sons, remained faithful to his message, re-emerging as a well-organised, extensive church which in 1969 became a member of the World Council of Churches. Both Harris and Kimbangu were prophets proclaiming the New Testament. Both were shunned and persecuted by missionaries and administrators, and they had merely a fleeting contact with their followers during their brief public ministries, but both left a legacy at once profoundly indigenous, Christian and ecumenical.

CATHOLIC STRATEGY AND PRACTICE

Besides the established and the newly arrived Protestant missions, and the wide-ranging spectrum of independent Christian radicals and enthusiasts, Africans at the beginning of the twentieth century were also becoming increasingly exposed to a massive momentum of the Catholic missionary movement. The rapid Catholic expansion into tropical Africa which marked the closing decades of the nineteenth century was a direct consequence of the major reorganisation achieved earlier in the century. New missionary societies, closely linked to the Congregation of Propaganda Fide in Rome and based, like their Protestant counterparts, on a widespread mobilisation of recruits and finance, had replaced the earlier initiatives which had been heavily dependent on Catholic monarchs. The Congregation of the Holy Ghost, or Spiritans, reorganised in 1848 and with headquarters in Paris, had started work on the coast of Senegal and Gabon and later expanded into Angola and the East African coast. They had been joined in West Africa by the Society of African Missions (SMA) from Lyons, while in the Turco-Egyptian Sudan Bishop Comboni and priests from Verona attempted to make a reality of the vicariate of Central Africa established in 1848. In South Africa, where the hierarchy had been established largely to meet the needs of Catholic settlers, significant missionary initiatives were gradually developed by the Reformed Cistercians (Trappists) at Mariannhill, near Durban, by the Oblates of Mary Immaculate in Basutoland, and by the Jesuits north of the Limpopo.

None of these missions had, however, made an appreciable impact in the interior of tropical Africa before 1878, when Charles Lavigerie, Archbishop of Algiers, persuaded Propaganda Fide to entrust four enormous vicariates in Equatorial Africa to the Society of Missionaries of Africa, founded by him ten years earlier and known as the White Fathers from their adoption of the Algerian tunic. This extraordinary coup gave his society responsibility for the immense area from the Lower Congo to the great lakes, and the first caravans set off immediately for the kingdom of Buganda and Lake Tanganyika. Soon Cardinal Lavigerie's vicariates were drastically reduced, particularly in the Congo Independent State where Leopold insisted on preference for Belgian missionaries, especially the Belgian Jesuits and Scheutist Fathers, but in the east the White Fathers were still left with a vast, densely populated, undivided area which embraced all the interlacustrine kingdoms. Elsewhere the newly established colonial powers often preferred missionaries of their own nationality: German Benedictines and Pallotin Fathers were sent to German East Africa and Kamerun respectively; Mill Hill Fathers from Britain were introduced into Uganda, and Irish Spiritans moved into eastern Nigeria, speaking the same language as the colonial administrators but hardly sharing all their imperial attitudes. In French Equatorial Africa the French Spiritans, under the local leadership of Prosper Augouard, set their active assistance in the extension of French colonial rule as a counter against the demands of French anti-clericals, and in Madagascar French Jesuits were able to exploit their nationality first against British and Malagasy Protestants and then against anti-clerical attacks. In subsequent years many other Catholic orders and societies were allocated missionary responsibilities in Africa, but throughout the colonial period the scene was largely to be dominated by a few societies — the Spiritans, White Fathers, SMA, Verona Fathers, Scheutists and Belgian Jesuits — who, unlike most of their Protestant counterparts, were free to concentrate virtually all their energy and resources upon Africa.

This rapid occupation of sub-Saharan Africa by virtually independent, and sometimes rival, Catholic missionary societies created problems of co-ordination and control for the Vatican, even though the missionaries were among its most trusted supporters. Threatened and beleaguered after the Italian capture of Rome in 1870, the papacy found faithful and useful allies in the new missionary societies who owed their powers, and often their existence, to the encouragement and support of Propaganda Fide. Leo XIII had been able to use Lavigerie to launch a policy of reconciliation with the Third Republic, and missionaries were enthusiastic supporters of Pius X both in his condemnation of Modernism and in his confrontation with French anti-clericalism in the events leading to, and following from, the *Loi de la Séparation*, the law by which the government of Émile Combes separated church and state in 1905. As with the earlier case of Lavigerie and Gambetta, missionaries were able to exploit their positions of relative strength in the colonies. Their weapons were various. Sometimes a delicate, diplomatic tact was employed, as with the emissary, Princess Anne Bibesco, prioress of a Carmelite convent in Algiers, who helped persuade Combes to include the White Fathers among the orders which were to be reprieved. More often the defence was far more direct, as with Augouard's blunt assertion to Savorgnan de Brazza in May 1905 that it would cost the state 500,000 francs per annum to laicise the schools in the French Congo and that if there was to be 'a religious war' he would not hesitate to appeal to the powers who had signed the Berlin Act. In this conflict with European anti-clericalism, in which it sometimes seemed their very survival was at stake, both papacy and missions were firmly united.

Yet the Vatican could not allow the missionary societies to establish themselves as the undisputed, virtually autonomous rulers of enormous ecclesiastical jurisdictions. Rome's authority over the mission fields was enshrined in Propaganda's right to appoint the prefects and vicars apostolic, but since these dignitaries were in practice selected from the missionary society operating in the relevant area, the Vatican needed additional means of control and influence. Finance provided an important weapon and in 1922 Propaganda succeeded in centralising its control over the major fund-raising organisations; the negotiations provided Angelo Roncalli (later John XXIII) with his first assignment in Vatican diplomacy. In so far as the missions were dependent on grants from these organisations, this control provided an important set of sanctions, but for many of the established missions the grants supplied only a part of their total receipts. The societies could rely on private benefactors, relatives and friends of the missionaries and on a range of local resources — plantations, the profits derived from providing a variety of skilled services, and government grants for education. Thus besides these possibilities of remote control, Propaganda needed to exert some measure of continuous supervision over the activities of the societies in the mission field itself. In 1922 Pius XI created the post of apostolic delegate to southern Africa, considered by Catholics at that time to be the hardest and perhaps the most sterile mission field in the world, and this was followed in 1930 with the appointment of Mgr A. Hinsley and Mgr G. Dellepiane as apostolic delegates to British tropical Africa and to the Belgian Congo respectively. Hinsley's most urgent task was to coordinate the Catholic response to British educational policy, while Dellepiane operated within the favoured context provided by the Congo colonial regime. But in addition to the political dimension, the appointments carried a far wider ecclesiastical significance. The delegates were responsible not to the Secretariate of State but to Propaganda Fide, and were charged with exercising a direct surveillance of religious activity in their areas. As such they could furnish Propaganda with information of the highest value and in their turn act as channels of direct communication.

The ultimate check on the powers of the missionary societies depended, however, on the emergence of an African priesthood from which eventually could be recruited African hierarchies in direct relation with Rome. From its creation in the seventeenth century, Propaganda had insisted on the paramount need for an indigenous clergy which, following the Council of Trent, had to conform to universal standards of training and discipline. This charge was solemnly given absolute priority in Benedict XV's *Maximum Illud* (30 November 1919). It was reiterated in a circular letter dated 20 May 1923 sent from the prefect of Propaganda, Cardinal van Rossum, to every Catholic missionary institute, and in Pius XI's *Rerum Ecclesiae gestarum* (28 February 1926). At the same time Catholic missiology, as professed by Pierre Charles at Louvain, was turning from J. Schmidlin's earlier emphasis at Munster on the saving of souls or the evangelisation of individuals. As the overriding purpose of missionary activity, Charles stressed the *plantatio ecclesiae*, the establishment of the visible, hierarchical church in areas where it did not previously exist. The theological and cultural implications of this shift were far-reaching, for while the earlier emphasis had naturally favoured a policy of assimilation, the second opened the door to adaptation and eventually to a far more generous assessment of the potential contribution of Africa to a universal Christianity. Yet in the minds of most supporters of foreign missions and of most missionaries trained in the earlier tradition, the practical emphasis continued to be focused on an evangelism which sought to wrest individuals from the clutch of heathens or heretics.

In large part this was doubtless the result of inertia, ethnocentric ignorance and even racial arrogance. But in part it was also due to the often apparently insuperable difficulties which beset the task of creating an African priesthood. If the sacrifices demanded of the seminarians in those days were severe, so also were the consequences of concentrating scarce missionary resources on the seminaries. Cut off for almost ten years from their families, forbidden to speak their vernacular languages, provided with Cicero as recreational reading, regularly required to pass the standard examinations, few among the seminarians survived to take up their career of life-long celibacy. Similarly the cost for the missions was considerable: able and active missionaries absorbed for years on end in an experiment notable at first for its massive failures and with its rare triumphs still to be obtained. The 'failures' by no means implied a total waste of effort. It was while he was at the Libermann seminary at Dakar in the early 1920s that Léopold Senghor acquired the love of Thomistic synthesis which, when in 1931 he returned to the Faith, attracted him to the French philosopher Maritain and later to Teilhard de Chardin. But it was difficult for missionaries to appreciate these possibilities at that time, and it is little wonder that many missions, faced with the advance of Protestant or Muslim rivals into areas still unoccupied, decided to renounce or postpone the experiment. As late as 1920, Augouard could excuse the lack of progress by asserting to Propaganda that 'Africans place much more trust in the European priest than in those of their own race'.[20]

A few missions persisted, however, notably the White Fathers in their Nyanza dioceses. Here the resolution of their leaders, Bishops Hirth and Streicher, was steeled by Propaganda's admonition that 'a mission that can produce martyrs can produce priests'.[21] In 1913 the first Ganda priests were ordained. By the 1920s the experiment was obviously succeeding, and Cardinal van Rossum at Propaganda could insist that other societies followed this example. By the 1930s the apostolic delegates could begin to regulate the relations between indigenous and missionary clergy, and in 1934 an official at Propaganda, commenting on the fact that parts of Uganda and Ruanda-Urundi were witnessing the greatest mass conversion movements in the world, confidently predicted that 'in no great time African bishops would be chosen to rule these churches',[22] a promise first realised with the consecration of Mgr Kiwanuka as Bishop of Masaka in 1939. At the same time in Rome itself, Propaganda incurred considerable debts, underwritten in 1927 by the Archbishop of Chicago, in providing lavish new buildings for the Collegio Urbano, which from the seventeenth century had served to train priests from the mission territories. In the late nineteenth century these had come mainly from northern Europe and North America, but in the twentieth century it was first China and India and then Africa which were to benefit most. At the opening of the new buildings in 1931 a cardinal who was present is reported to have remarked to Cardinal Pacelli, then secretary of state, that it was too large and luxurious for these 'sous-développés', eliciting from the future pope the reply 'Eminence, these sous-développés will save the Church'.[23]

Gradually, then, it was becoming apparent that the Vatican was attempting to indigenise a universal institution, but to an extraordinary extent Catholic missions had been left to evolve

---

[20] Quinquennial report to Propaganda Fide, 1 January 1920, in Jehan de Witte, *Monseigneur Augouard: sa vie* (Paris, 1924), 348.
[21] Quoted by A. Hastings, *Mission and ministry* (London, 1971), 161.
[22] G. G. Considine in G. Monticone *et al.* (eds.), *Guida delle Missioni Cattoliche, redatta sotto gli auspici della saeva congregazione di Propaganda Fide* (Rome, 1934), 81.
[23] J. Metzler (ed.), *Sacrae Congregationis de Propaganda Fide memoria rerum 1622–1972*, III, no. 1. *1815–1972* (Rome, 1975), 102.

their tactics independently one from another. The degree of this isolation was felt, for instance, in 1905 by Mgr F. X. Geyer, whose priests in the missions recently re-established by the Verona Fathers in the southern Sudan had adopted radically different approaches to their task: among the Shilluk, the missionaries restricted themselves to learning the language, establishing a presence but avoiding any active proselytism, whereas in the Bahr al-Ghazal Antonio Vignato was intent on a vigorous evangelism. Geyer appealed to Propaganda for guidance, but it was not until 1914 that Vignato, by then Superior of the mission in northern Uganda, found in the White Fathers' methods both a revelation and in some respects a confirmation of his earlier practice. Both Benedict XV and Pius XI sought to counter this unpreparedness and lack of coordination by insisting on the need for 'missiology' and the better training of missionaries, yet there was a more fundamental cause of missionary confusion.

In the nineteenth century most Catholic missions in Africa had sought to create Christian villages, where ransomed slaves and a few other converts could be gathered under the rule of a missionary. This approach had come to be accepted as orthodox missionary practice, and the finance for missions was often specifically tied to the ransoming of slaves. African response and African initiative combined, however, to undermine this strategy and to pioneer fresh methods of evangelism. As Africans began to respond *en masse* to new religious challenges and to demand on an ever-increasing scale educational and other modernising facilities, the system of separate Christian villages became totally inadequate and even irrelevant.

Among the Ibo, where the response in the first decade of the twentieth century seemed to the Irish Spiritans to emulate that of the era of St Patrick, Bishop Shanahan was soon forced to realise that the village or bush school had become the crucial institution of Christian expansion. Adept at exploiting denominational rivalries, the Ibo made it clear that their allegiance would be given to the mission that provided the best educational facilities. Shanahan readily appreciated the opportunity this offered for evangelism, yet as late as 1912, in his annual report to Propaganda, he had to defend his emphasis on education by describing the school as 'the only breakwater' against 'the traffic in human flesh'. He had to plead desperately that the substantial subsidy for ransoming slaves should not be withdrawn if it was diverted to this broader purpose.[24]

Among the Ganda, the mass response had come more than a decade earlier and there it had completely transformed missionary tactics. Lavigerie, with his vision of Christian kingdoms, had indeed been more concerned with changing African society than with constructing isolated Christian villages. By reviving the catechumenate system of the early church, with adult proselytes being admitted as postulants for one year and then placed as catechumens under regular instruction for three years, he had opened the possibility of deeply influencing a large number of Africans. But the early stations of the White Fathers in East Africa around Lake Tanganyika had in fact been forced to become isolated, fortified havens. In Buganda the missionaries were at first confined to the capital, and it was only after the move to Buddu following the civil wars which started in 1888 that the White Fathers recognised the crucial role that could be played by African catechists. As he heard how in these troubled times many Africans, themselves under instruction, had taught others, how an old, blind flute-player, for instance, had 'prayed for five years' and had brought with him, to support his request for baptism, a group of 32 men whom he had instructed, Streicher decided to start employing full-time catechists, noting in the station diary that 'the first efficient plan of evangelisation of Africans by fellow Africans came to us from the Africans themselves'.[25]

It was not only male Ganda who forced the mission to recognise African initiative and leadership. There had been women among the early martyrs and converts, but at first the White Fathers had regarded them merely as future Christian mothers. Before long, however, the mission came to regard them as potential members of a religious order. This was mainly due to the determination of Maria Matilda Munaku, sister of one of the martyrs, who at her baptism in 1886 had told Father Lourdel that she had promised 'never to marry anyone but Christ'. Maria gathered together an association of unmarried women dedicated to support without payment the seminarists, 'our children', and

[24] Quoted in John Jordan, *Bishop Shanahan of Southern Nigeria* (Dublin, 1949), 89–93.
[25] Villa Maria diary, May 1891, quoted by J. M. Waliggo, 'The Catholic Church in the Buddu Province of Buganda, 1879–1925' (Ph.D. thesis, University of Cambridge, 1976), 97.

when the first White Sisters arrived in 1899 they found a large nucleus of aspirants already in existence. In 1910 some of these became the first Ganda to 'eat religious life' as members of the *bannabikira*, a congregation which finally received full recognition and self-rule in 1925. Indeed it has been convincingly argued that the success of the Buddu seminary, itself a key, as we have seen, to the Vatican's strategy in Africa, owed at least as much to the enthusiasm and support of these women and of the whole community of Buddu Catholics as it did to the determination of Propaganda and of Hirth and Streicher.[26]

The response in Buganda was startling and exceptional, yet the ministry of the catechist gradually developed and became widely accepted among other Catholic missions. Sometimes this ministry assumed unusual forms. In the Lower Congo, Belgian Jesuits started a system of chapel-farms to increase supplies of meat and to create small Christian nuclei. Three catechists, recruited from freed slaves, lived on each of these farms, visited the surrounding villages each morning, worked on the farm in the afternoons, and returned to the mission station each Saturday to report their progress and to attend Mass on Sunday, before returning to the farms in the evening. By 1902 there were 250 chapel-farms with more than 5,000 children located on them, many of these 'orphans' supplied by agents of the state. In part their success derived from the very wide initiative left in the hands of the catechists, but the system, particularly the recruitment of 'orphans', was open to abuse and the Jesuits were accused in 1911 in the Belgian parliament of creating 'a new Paraguay'. Some of the missionaries also felt that the system isolated the children too much from their environment, so in 1912 the decision was taken not to create any more farms. Henceforth catechists were placed in Christian villages, the agricultural aspect of their work becoming eclipsed by the scholastic.

Among the White Fathers, the Buganda example was from the first closely followed. By 1909 the two Nyanza vicariates were employing about 3,000 catechists, and through much of this area the pioneers of this method of evangelism were those Ganda who had gone out from Buddu. In some places they appeared to the local populace, at least at first, as military auxiliaries. At the first

[26] Waliggo, 'Catholic Church in Buddu', 169–82; see also pp.205–22 for Munaku and the *bannabikira*.

station to be established in Rwanda in 1900, the Ganda catechists mounted guard each night, firing into the air to frighten off intruders. During the day they rounded up Hutu children for training, and as late as 1903 Bishop Hirth stigmatised their activities at one station as those of an 'armée roulante'.[27] Even in this tense situation, however, there were gentle and friendly Ganda catechists, and most catechists came to be respected not for their force but as trusted intermediaries.

The majority of catechists were given little or no training and lived in their villages, passing on some rudiments of literacy and imparting to both children and adults a knowledge of the catechism often painstakingly acquired by rote. In contrast to these were the relatively few catechists who received formal education. They became the itinerant, professional supervisors of bush schools or lived at the central station assisting the missionaries full-time. Some of the latter became widely known, like Andréas Mbangue, who, after three years' training in Germany, returned to Kamerun to help the Pallotins in their translations; he may become one day 'the patron saint of Camerounian catechists'.[28] In their different spheres, both groups of catechists enjoyed in these early decades considerable prestige. In part this was derived from their successful acquisition — however slight — of some of the missionaries' skills, but it also reflected their position in a spiritual universe which combined both new and traditional elements. In the local communities the catechist, although ultimately depending on new and alien sanctions and gaining much of his conscious motivation from the eager response of a first-generation convert, nevertheless also assumed many of the functions of the traditional diviner and ritual expert. It was the catechist who, often with the help of a group of Christian elders, had to solve problems and reconcile disputes, lead prayers for those in sickness or troubled by the power of evil, prepare the perplexed for confession, and finally comfort and baptise the dying. And in homesteads and communities which lacked a formally recognised catechist, some of the more important of these functions were performed by unpaid prayer-leaders and baptisers, often even unknown to the mission. In the inter-war period much of the secular prestige of the catechists was to pass

[27] Quoted in Ian Linden, *Church and revolution in Rwanda* (Manchester, 1977), 41.
[28] E. Mveng, *Histoire du Cameroun* (Paris, 1963), 460–1.

eventually to the trained schoolteachers, but the development of this distinctive spiritual ministry was to remain one of the most notable aspects of the Africanisation of the Catholic Church.

The extent to which the day-to-day interpretation of the Faith was left to the understanding and initiative of these relatively untutored elders and leaders also assisted the process by which Catholic spirituality acquired an African flavour. Some features of missionary practice, such as Shanahan's lavish use of holy water as a precaution against injury at the hands of Satan, were easily accepted. Holy water was readily drunk to cure disease and was used to protect crops from evil charms. Other features had to be transposed. Catholic missionaries, in reaction to the rationalism and secularisation of their homelands, took with them to Africa a Marian devotion which had been intensified by the dogma of the Immaculate Conception and the development of Lourdes and, later, Fatima. In some areas of Africa the traditional respect for a queen-mother was used as an analogy to explain the powers of Mary. Traditional African titles were applied to the Blessed Virgin, and rosaries and Marian medals became accepted as protective religious charms. In rivalry with Protestants, this Marian devotion provided a useful, distinctive symbol; but it also moulded and bound together Catholic communities in a more positive and fundamental fashion. Whereas the shortage of priests and the rigidities of church discipline, especially on marriage, often prevented all but a few from regularly receiving Holy Communion, all adherents could participate equally in the devotion to Mary, recitals of the rosary, communal prayers and visits to her chapels. These rituals were therefore extremely popular and may well have helped to mitigate the traumatic division between the new religious discipline and the old.

Thus in some areas of Africa Catholicism gradually became accepted as a popular or folk religion, and great processions involving thousands of worshippers on the major feast-days became a recognised feature of the African scene. One other aspect of Catholic spirituality also gained significance. At the turn of the twentieth century missionaries, particularly those from France, took out to Africa the cult of St Thérèse of Lisieux, who in those decades became the focus of a world-wide veneration. The journals which reported her miracles carried a special section for the mission countries. Seminaries for African priests were placed under her protection. She was appointed 'regent' of at least one African country, and in 1927 she joined Francis Xavier as the patroness of all missions and missionaries. Her influence was not of course restricted to the miracles. Shanahan saw the example by which she became a great missionary without ever setting foot in foreign lands as a challenge to the whole Irish nation to adopt her weapons of prayer and sacrifice. This vision in part inspired his Maynooth appeal in 1920 and thus, eventually, the foundation of the Kiltegan Fathers. But the stress on the miraculous may well have been seen by many Africans as a most significant aspect of Catholicism, and St Thérèse was but one of the foci for this emphasis. Sometimes the impetus carried its adherents outside the Catholic fold. In the 1920s a devotion to the Holy Face developed in Calabar province, possibly brought there from Cashel in Ireland. Against mission orders, a prayer-house dedicated to the Holy Face was established and soon became a popular centre for healing. One of its main protagonists, a night-watchman from Benin, enthusiastically declared, 'this thing can cure; it will take the place of sacrifice at the juju house',[29] and eventually the mission felt compelled to excommunicate all who attended the prayer-house. Generally, however, as the veneration of St Thérèse illustrates, belief in miraculous cures could easily be accommodated within mission orthodoxy and it provided a Catholic counterpart to the spiritual healing of the Pentecostals and other enthusiasts. Inevitably in the period of missionary predominance and at a time when the beleaguered ultramontanism of the First Vatican Council still set rigid boundaries, the differences between Protestants, Independents and Catholics in Africa were emphasised and exaggerated by missionaries; but as the leadership and structures of the churches became increasingly African, and as theological perspectives gradually changed, the similarities of the common spiritual needs and experiences of many African Christians, already apparent in this early period, were to become ever more obvious.

[29] Quoted in C. M. Cooke, 'The Roman Catholic Mission in Calabar, 1903–1960' (Ph.D. thesis, University of London, 1977), 198.

MISSIONS AND SECULAR RULERS:
INDIGENOUS AND COLONIAL

Yet even if the new beliefs and practices were gradually becoming an integral part of African religious life, Christians in Africa, both missionaries and Africans, were primarily concerned with creating new, distinctive communities. This pursuit unavoidably involved the groups of Christians in a variety of relationships with the secular powers both indigenous and colonial. Few African rulers had entered into a wholehearted alliance with the pioneer missionaries. Even Khama of the Ngwato (1838–1923), often presented as the perfect model of a Christian chief, set firm limits to his co-operation with the mission, and elsewhere African Christian rulers were the rare products of far-reaching social and political changes. The young Christians, who divided between themselves the principal political offices in Buganda in 1890 and who supported the British against Mwanga's revolt in 1896, established a process of conversion promoted from above. This had been common enough in early Anglo-Saxon England but was almost unique in tropical Africa, where the Christian kingdom or theocratic state was to be a very rare response to missionary activity. At the other extreme, some African peoples consistently excluded Christian agents: missions were seldom welcome in Muslim areas, and some rulers, or fiercely independent groups of warriors, had prevented all access. Many powerful rulers, including those of the Asante, the Ndebele and the Zulu, successfully imposed rigid limits on missionary activities and a virtual veto on all conversions. Even where, for a variety of diplomatic, political and economic motives, missionaries were accepted or welcomed, most African societies sought to confine their influence within customary structures. The missions and their few adherents could thus be assimilated into the society, and they would constitute merely a new group of immigrant 'strangers' together with their dependants.

The frustrations inherent in these relationships were largely responsible for the fact that most missions, with a few notable exceptions, welcomed the extension of colonial rule. The establishment of the colonial regimes did not, however, immediately transform the relations between Christians and African rulers. At the local level, the missions and their adherents often remained dependent on the goodwill of chiefs and elders, if only to exclude a rival Christian denomination. On the other hand, in the years when the colonial governments were still seeking to establish their authority, generally with minimal resources, the missions often disposed of far greater immediate strength and could seek to improve and entrench their positions in the three-cornered negotiations with traditional rulers and the advancing adminis-trators. Throughout this period of adjustment, the relationships of missions and African authorities continued, therefore, to range from close cooperation to open hostility. Among Buganda's neighbours, the process of conversion from above spread rapidly. The rulers of Toro and Ankole became supporters of the Protestant ascendancy, and in Busoga the Church Missionary Society (CMS) was known as the *ekirya obwami*, the denomination out of which the chiefs were appointed. In Ruanda the White Fathers at first gained adherents among the Hutu and were regarded by the Tutsi court somewhat as rebellious nobles who were extending a potentially disruptive protection over the royal vassals. By the end of the First World War, the mission, strengthened by the Belgian take-over from the Germans, was a focus of influence rivalling that of the royal court. Already, however, the basis of an understanding with the Tutsi was also being laid. In 1931 a Christian *mwami*, Mutare IV, was eventually installed, thousands were swept into the church and by the mid-1930s 90 per cent of the chiefs and sub-chiefs were Catholic. As in Buganda, Christianity had in part assumed the role of a legitimating ideology, but despite this close alliance with the dominant élite the alternative, radical implications of the Gospel remained open to the Hutu majority.

Generally the tensions between missions and African rulers endured. As the missions insisted that their adherents should be freed from obligations which upheld traditional religious allegi-ances, the occasions for rivalry proliferated. A chapel, remarked the Bemba paramount in Northern Rhodesia, as late as 1915, could 'kill the chief',[30] and even among peoples predominantly Christian, such as the northern Ngoni in Nyasaland or the eastern Akan in the Gold Coast, accession to royal office was regarded as automatically debarring the holder from access to Christian

[30] Quoted in B. Garvey, 'Bemba chiefs and Catholic missions, 1898–1935', *Journal of African History*, 1977, **18**, 3, 424.

sacraments. One energetic ruler, Njoya at Foumban in Kamerun, faced with the competing claims of Hausa Muslims and the Basel missionaries, founded his own schools from 1910, invented his own script and sought to propagate a religion which combined Christian and Muslim elements with Bamum rituals and beliefs. Such deliberate and conscious syncretism was however extremely rare; more often the conflicts were left to run through a course first of resistance and sometimes persecution of Christian converts, and then to the stage where, as among the Bemba by the 1930s, the rulers' powers had been reduced to the confines of their villages. The chief's compound became a refuge for lapsed Christians, just as the pioneer mission stations had earlier given protection to the marginal fugitives from tribal society.

Increasingly the local relations of missions and African rulers merged into the wider relationships of missions and colonial regimes. The position of chiefs became merely one of several relatively minor issues — such as the importation of alcoholic spirits, the continuance of domestic slavery, or the legal recognition of Christian marriages — which were the subject of debate between missions and colonial administrators. Few missionaries welcomed the implementation of indirect rule, fearing that it would resuscitate forms of 'paganism' which were being forgotten; instead they generally supported the emergence of voluntary political associations, such as the Kikuyu Association founded in 1920, which strengthened mission-sponsored chiefs while seeking to neutralise the influence of hostile chiefs and of customary laws repugnant to missionaries. Kenya indeed became the arena for one of the most notorious conflicts between missionaries and African custom, with the Church of Scotland and other Protestant missions leading a determined attack in the late 1920s on the Kikuyu practice of female circumcision. The conflict helped to focus Kikuyu resentment against the whole range of European encroachments and, for the missions, it left a bitter legacy of separatism or schism in church and school.

These differences between missionaries and colonial administrators were, however, relatively unimportant compared with the furore and consequences of missionary participation in the campaign against King Leopold's Congo. No other single issue illustrated so vividly the far-ranging significance, but also the limits, of the political independence of the modern missionary movement. On no other occasion did missionaries influence so decisively the development of colonial Africa. In the fight against the abuses, and then against the concessionaire system itself, in the Congo Independent State, the missionaries were by no means the sole combatants. The strategy was devised by others and much of the impetus was to be derived from sources in no way identical with the missionary, or even the humanitarian, lobby; but it was the missions who provided the first startling denunciations, the initial mobilisation of international opinion, and the crucial, continuing supply of first-hand information and eye-witness evidence throughout the campaign. Yet it was those missionaries who were most independent of Leopold's system who took the major part. The first missionary criticism in the press was voiced in *L'Univers* in October 1894 by Augouard, who at Brazzaville was safely beyond the reach of Leopold and, as a Frenchman, was never reluctant to make a patriotic point. Whatever protests Belgian Catholic missionaries may have made in private, the brunt of the rest of the campaign until 1906 was borne by Protestant missions. In particular, it was American and Scandinavian missionaries who led the protests, not at first those British missionaries who had so notably joined forces with Leopold in 1884–5. In this situation, the strength of the American Baptists and Presbyterians was derived in part from the fact that their work in the Congo was relatively unimportant for them compared with their commitments elsewhere in the world; the international variety of the modern missionary movement gave the missions great local flexibility, while its breadth and the number of its supporters ensured that their protests reverberated throughout the home bases.

The Congo Independent State provided the test case for the humanitarian tradition in the early colonial period in Africa. The threatened condemnation by the signatories of the Berlin Act of this total disregard for so many human rights established, perhaps at a critical juncture in African history, a notable precedent for international concern and involvement in colonial policy. Elsewhere, however, the missions during this early colonial period were far less effective in challenging abuses. In Southern Rhodesia, in German South West Africa and in Natal only a few voices were raised to protest against the conditions which led large numbers of Africans into desperate rebellions. Although Harriet

Colenso, James White and Arthur Shirley Cripps kept alive a prophetic critique, most churches were too deeply involved with white congregations, segregation and land alienation to expose the system to an intensive scrutiny. Like the Belgian Catholics, these missions had lost a vital element of their independence, while the process of dispossession in southern Africa was, as a whole, both more gradual, and supported by far greater resources, than in Leopold's Congo. White supremacy, at least for the foreseeable future, seemed to many missionaries working there almost to be part of God's established order.

AFRICAN INITIATIVES DURING THE FIRST WORLD WAR AND IN THE TOWNS

It was the First World War, more than flagrant colonial abuses, which first shook to its foundations the complacency of Christian Europe. The spectacle, witnessed at first-hand in many areas of tropical Africa, of the whites murdering each other, struck at the whole ethical authority of the missions as at least one missionary, Albert Schweitzer, immediately realised. 'I make no attempt to explain or extenuate, but say that we are in 'front' of something terrible and incomprehensible.'[31] During the Second World War, increasing numbers of Africans were, like the young Ndabaningi Sithole, to see 'through European pretensions that only Africans were savages',[32] but in 1914–18 only a few, like John Chilembwe, directly challenged white demands and refused to enlist in a war which was none of their making. In Africa the conflict did not destroy white ascendancy; but in Europe the churches and the concept of a Christian civilisation were widely discredited. The few radical, rationalist critics of Christian missions were now joined by a far greater number whose previous certainties had been irrevocably shaken. Yet the immediate impact on the missions in Africa was much less damaging than has sometimes been supposed. In the doubts and questionings of the post-war period, the missions were able to challenge settler assumptions and to help consolidate the policies of trusteeship. Despite the disillusionment with Christian teaching in Europe and North

[31] A. Schweitzer, *On the edge of the primeval forest* (London, 1922), 138.
[32] N. Sithole, *African nationalism* (Cape Town, 1959), 19.

America, the numbers of recruits for the missions in Africa steadily increased, so that by 1938 there were twice as many Western missionaries in Africa as there had been in 1910. The more sensitive missionaries became far less certain of the superiority of Western values, but on the whole the war if anything strengthened the missions' voice in colonial policy-making in Africa.

Indeed the most serious setback for Christianity in Africa during this period was the fact that the experience of the war years did not result in a diminution of the missionary presence, and did not lead to a major reappraisal of mission policy, particularly on the central issue of Africanisation. For here the war had presented a great challenge and opportunity. The military operations, particularly in East Africa, and the fear, often exaggerated, that German missionaries represented a security danger, seriously disrupted missionary activity. Many German missionaries were interned and then repatriated; many Frenchmen were recalled for military service; and for the rest there was an almost total break for five years in recruitment and replacements. Most missionaries assumed this disruption would threaten the life of the African churches, especially in areas recently evangelised. Desperately they sought to extend their responsibilities and fill the gaps, but in many cases there were insufficient missionaries. Yet far from disintegrating, African congregations seized the initiative and revealed what to the missionaries were quite unexpected signs of mature vigour. In Buddu, in southern Uganda, the number of seminarians rose to 95 and some of the teaching was taken over by senior seminarians. Around Masasi, African priests of the Universities' Mission to Central Africa (UMCA) led their communities through famine and military oppression. In the Lutheran Bethel mission in Tanga province, where no Africans had been ordained, African teachers assumed leadership, maintained the coffee estates and banana plantations, and looked after lapsed Christians. Their congregations seem to have played a central role in the community at large, exercising the communal rituals and spiritual healing initiatives expected of them. 'During that time,' some of them nostalgically remembered long afterwards, 'there was a true manifestation of love. At funerals many came from far and sang hymns and played trumpets...They helped the sick even though some of them were pagans.'[33] Similar developments occurred in Kamerun, where in the Bamenda grasslands German Catholic missionaries had settled at Shisong only two years before the outbreak of war. A small band of catechumens spread the faith, and about 900 of the converts crossed to Fernando Po to be baptised by the expelled Pallotins before returning home to sustain the nascent Christian communities in the face of vigorous opposition from the traditionalists.

The challenge and disruption of the war had thus illustrated yet again the central, ironical paradox of African church history that, if the churches were to grow to maturity, the missionaries had either to transfer their responsibilities or be removed. To the original sacrifice involved in leaving family, home and country, the missionaries were now required to lay down their power and privileges in the lands of their adoption. With their vision clouded by the current paternalistic assumptions, the missions, however, failed to perceive and apply the lesson of this experience. Entrenched in their alliance with the colonial regimes, they settled down to what many of them assumed would be generations, if not centuries, of white control. African spontaneity was stifled and members of the Bethel Church in Tanga, for instance, looked back more than forty years afterwards to the brief period of African leadership as a golden age. 'When the missionaries came back, there were signs that the Holy Spirit had left, for the desire to co-operate to work for the Lord was no more seen. Trouble started when they started grading workers. Hatred started.'[34]

Only in the Gold Coast were African pastors able to insist successfully that the leadership, which had passed to them on the expulsion of the Basel missionaries, should remain in their hands. Here, as a result of Basel mission policy and of the wealth derived by the Akwapim congregations from the cocoa boom, substantial progress had already been made towards a financially-independent African church. In 1912 the Twi district was self-supporting and the local church sessions and district meetings were in the hands of African ministers and presbyters or elders. When in 1917 the Basel missionaries were somewhat ruthlessly expelled by the British colonial authorities, Scottish Presbyterians from Calabar were asked to take over their work. They could spare, however,

[33] Quoted in M. L. Pirouet, 'East African Christians and World War I', *Journal of African History*, 1978, **19**, 1, 127–8.   [34] *Ibid.*, 128.

only a handful of missionaries, and in August 1918 effective control of the church passed to the synod, where the missionaries were heavily outnumbered by 28 African ministers and 24 African presbyters. The executive committee of the synod consisted of eight Africans and three missionaries, and Africans were appointed to the key posts of moderator and synod clerk. In 1926 when the Basel missionaries returned, they found that they had to accept this situation and work under the authority of the synod and its committee with their African majorities. Power had been transferred irrevocably, though it would be several years before the Basel missionaries fully recognised the hand of Providence in this.

With this significant exception, the missions elsewhere re-established after the war their control and discipline over the churches. African catechists, prayer-leaders, baptisers and church elders still exercised a crucial influence at local, grass-roots level, softening the rigidities of demands inspired by an alien culture. Here much of the effective indigenisation of Christianity was in practice still located, but the activities of these African Christians remained, in the rural areas, under the ultimate supervision of the missionaries. In the inter-war period it was the towns which provided Africans with their greatest challenges and widest opportunities. In much of Africa the missions were anchored institutionally to the rural areas: even Blantyre mission, for example, was mainly a centre for rural out-stations; but the towns were the new frontier. Full of privation, danger, insecurity and poverty, they also opened new material, social and intellectual horizons. This was particularly the case in the vast industrial complexes of South Africa and Katanga, and then the Rhodesian Copperbelt, or in major commercial cities and capitals such as Leopoldville, Dakar, Lagos and Accra; but it was also true of the multitude of much smaller market and administrative centres which on a minor scale still presented the same opportunities for Africans. Fort Rosebery (Mansa) in the Luapula area of Northern Rhodesia was a typical example. Here a Bemba catechist, Romano Lupambo, was sent in 1915 to assist in the transport of provisions. He decided to remain in the town and for the next seventeen years, virtually unassisted by any missionaries, he built up there a flourishing Catholic community, helped by other voluntary catechists chosen from among them. And outside the mission churches, members of the Watch Tower were to find in such centres a major developing field for their somewhat similar, if less orthodox, initiatives.

Such local leadership was often left unrecorded, but the best-known case of urban Christian initiatives came from the early years on the Rhodesian Copperbelt. In 1925, only two years after the initial discoveries of the deep copper ores, African Christians working at Ndola decided to elect their own board of elders in order to organise, discipline and recruit an urban church. They opened their own school, built their own church, conducted services in the compounds and evangelised the surrounding Lamba villages. They created a community which transcended ethnic and denominational diversities. It was ten years before the Protestant missions set up an organisation to work specifically in the Copperbelt, and when in 1936 the 'United Missions in the Copper Belt' was formed it followed this ecumenical African example. The first steps had been taken by educated Nyasalanders — clerks, store-assistants and others — but the appeal of Christianity in the urban area was by no means restricted to a select élite. One of the first missionaries to work on the Copperbelt reported how 'passing through a compound after dark on almost any night you could find little groups of people gathered around the light of an underground worker's acetylene lamp, singing Christian hymns'.[35] These groups served significant material and social purposes, they provided nuclei of security and friendship in what could otherwise prove a terrifyingly anonymous new environment, and the faith of their members had also been enlarged and deepened in the challenges of urban life. Yet these congregations were mere islands in a shifting, anxious sea of people, and for many young men and women the towns were also places of neutrality or freedom where they could escape from the constraints and conflict imposed by both primal and Christian religions. It was all the more regrettable that the missions, burdened with their institutional rural cares and their increasing responsibilities in the sphere of formal, professional education, turned so little of their attention to this formative frontier in the inter-war period.

[35] R. J. B. Moore, *Man's act and God's in Africa* (London, 1940), quoted in P. Bolink, *Towards church union in Zambia* (Franeker, 1967), 178.

CATHOLIC HIERARCHIES AND COLONIAL POWERS

In the towns, in the independent, separatist churches and throughout the whole enterprise at the expanding periphery and at the local, homestead level, Africans were creating and shaping an indigenous Christianity. But at the top, at the level of policy-making, it was generally the missions who spoke for Christianity in Africa during the inter-war period. The missions' varied influence on colonial policy in Africa directly reflected, however, not so much African realities but the very different situations governing church–state relations in Europe. Although the French missionary orders had escaped the brunt of the 1905 *Loi de la Séparation*, the state, in the colonies as in the metropole, remained for French missionaries primarily a hostile antagonist. In Senegal and French West Africa as a whole, missionary education was discouraged and at times forbidden, and until the Second World War mission schools played an almost negligible role compared with the state system. In Madagascar a convinced anti-clerical, Victor Augagneur, was governor-general from 1905 to 1910. Immediately on arrival he took steps which resulted in the closure of about four-fifths of the mission schools. Open-air religious meetings were prohibited, and in 1913 the separation of church and state in Madagascar was formally decreed. Only in French Equatorial Africa did the missions succeed in retaining a substantial role in education. In France itself, the war and Pius XI's condemnation in 1926 of Action Française helped to modify anti-clerical sentiment, but French missions remained on the defensive, and in the Third Republic the tension between church and state seems to have inhibited any intimate missionary influence on official colonial policy or even their participation in an effective humanitarian lobby.

In the Belgian Congo the impact of the metropolitan situation was equally direct, though its result was the exact opposite. In Belgium, the Catholic party (the Parti Social Chrétien) participated in every government throughout the inter-war period and Catholics were particularly influential in the colonial ministry. In the Congo, therefore, the colonial state welcomed Belgian missionaries, virtually all of whom were Catholic, as allies against the forces of European anti-clericalism. When confronted by Maurice Lippens, a Liberal, anti-clerical governor-general, Catholics in the Congo and in Belgium played a large part in causing his resignation in 1923; all official and subsidised education in the Congo was entrusted to Belgian missions and they received other substantial financial assistance from the state and from the major corporations. The Catholic missions' wholehearted participation in the policies of Belgian colonial paternalism rested not merely on these financial advantages secured for their evangelistic activities at the expense of their foreign, Protestant rivals, but also, perhaps even more fundamentally, on the ideological alignments which directly reflected the political conflicts in their homeland.[36]

In Portuguese territories, the relations of missionaries with the metropolitan state had a far longer history. By 1900 the *padroado*, or patronal rights granted by the papacy to the Portuguese crown, which in the sixteenth century covered most of Africa and Asia, survived only in those areas ruled from Lisbon. There Catholic missionaries were still regarded by the state as agents of Portuguese 'civilization and national influence', a position thus defined and strongly reaffirmed by Salazar in his 1930 Colonial Act. Other missions, some of which, like the UMCA in northern Mozambique, had been pioneers before Portuguese rule was extended over the interior, had to operate within a framework of increasingly severe restrictions. Among the Catholics, few non-Portuguese were permitted to enter the African territories, but the number of Portuguese missionaries also remained very limited. Ecclesiastically, as well as economically, Portuguese Africa fell far behind the rest of the continent. Faced with this situation, the Vatican signed a Concordat and Missionary Agreement with Portugal on 7 May 1940, which, in return for an increased right of entry of foreign missionaries, recognised extensive powers of control by the state over church activity. The government retained a right of veto over the appointment of church leaders, mission schools had to use the Portuguese language and detailed reports on church work were required annually by the authorities. The agreement opened the door for an influx of Catholic missions, but the church was placed in colonial bondage. Not for another generation would some of these new arrivals move from their position of subservience to an open criticism of the colonial regime.

For the Vatican, it was Italian colonial ambitions that posed in

[36] See *CHA*, vol. VII, chapter 9.

the inter-war period the greatest political challenge in Africa. As Italy threatened and then invaded Ethiopia, Protestant missionaries, especially those who, like the Swedish Lutherans, had for long worked in the area and who had already been severely harassed in Eritrea by Mussolini, raised their voices in vigorous and concerted protests. The Catholic response was, however, much more ambiguous. A group of distinguished French Catholic intellectuals led by Maritain did not hesitate to denounce the unprovoked aggression and its racist justification, but the position of the hierarchies, and particularly that of the Vatican, was far more complex. 'Indignation has no bounds,' proclaimed Hinsley, now Archbishop of Westminster, in a sermon preached at the Church of St Edward the Confessor, Golders Green, on 13 October 1935, 'when we see that Africa, that ill-used Continent of practically unarmed people, is made the focus and playground of scientific slaughter.' Hinsley then tried to explain why the pope was unable to intervene and he referred to Pius XI, in a phrase that won instant international notoriety, as 'a helpless old man with a small police force... to protect his diminutive State'.[37] It was an unfortunate attempt to condense for an English audience a relationship of peculiar difficulty.

At the beginning of his pontificate, Pius XI and Cardinal Gasparri, his promoter and secretary of state, had skilfully and resolutely begun the negotiations which in 1929, with the Lateran Treaty and a concordat with the Italian state, finally created the Vatican state and, in a small measure, compensated the papacy for the losses incurred in 1870. Two years later, in a trial of strength with the Fascist regime, Pius succeeded in maintaining some of the independence of his favoured arm, Catholic Action, but, during this crisis, the publication of his crucial encyclical *Non abbiamo bisogno* was only ensured by sending several hundred copies to Paris in an aeroplane piloted by the young American, Mgr F. Spellman. If the concordat was to be preserved, the limits of resistance in Fascist Italy were narrow, and in the Ethiopian war the Vatican had no *locus standi*. The Vatican had been denied membership of the League of Nations, and the Lateran Treaty stipulated that it should not intervene in temporal disputes involving Italy unless asked to arbitrate by the contending parties. Within these limitations, the Curia attempted to urge restraint and

[37] Quoted in J. C. Heenan, *Cardinal Hinsley* (London, 1944), 56.

on 28 July 1935 Mussolini was warned of his opponent's right to self-defence. There was, however, no public condemnation of extravagantly patriotic statements by Italian clergy, from Cardinal Schuster, Archbishop of Milan, downwards. Immediately after the war, Pius himself seems to have been caught up in similar emotions when on 12 May 1936 he referred to 'the triumphant joy of an entire great and good people', while Italian missionaries hastened to seize their apparent advantages in Ethiopia. With the publication of *Mit brennende Sorge*, Pius was soon to return to a much clearer denunciation of racialism, and in two addresses to the students of the Collegio Urbano in August 1938 he publicly ridiculed the Fascist imitation of German racist policies and denounced the 'curse of exaggerated nationalism',[38] but in the Ethiopian crisis, Italian patriotism, concern with concordat diplomacy and what seems to have been a measure of European ethnocentricity had seriously transmuted the voice of the Vatican.

TRUSTEESHIP AND EDUCATION

The most significant contribution of the churches to colonial policy in this inter-war period did not come from those who, beset by the conflict with anti-clericalism in Europe, somewhat inevitably saw the African mission field as an extension of this arena. British and American missionaries were free of this incubus. Coming from what, by the twentieth century, was a far more pragmatic tradition of church–state relations, they could approach colonial policy in Africa unhindered by these pre-occupations. In the International Missionary Council they had an instrument well fashioned to mobilise the principal Protestant missions on issues of common political concern, and J. H. Oldham, its secretary, was a man well equipped to translate the humanitarian tradition into the colonial politics of the 1920s. In the two areas of policy most crucial to this tradition — the development of the concept of trusteeship and the missions' role in African education — American experience and ideology made notable contributions; but in both cases it was Oldham's industry, tact and expertise which converted principles into practice.

The principle of trusteeship, of colonial rule as a trust to be

---

[38] Quoted in D. A. Binchy, *Church and state in Fascist Italy* (London, 1941), 621.

exercised in the interests of the subject peoples, was developed and applied in East Africa in the 1920s as a counter-balance to the older, and locally stronger, imperial tradition of colonial settlement. South of the Zambezi, the settlers were firmly entrenched and missionaries exerted little direct influence on the main lines of policy. Smuts and other imperial strategists saw a similar pattern of European settlement as the steel framework for development north of the Zambezi. Kenya with its 'white highlands' provided the strongest core of settlers, and here the missions and Oldham played a major part in challenging their demands and ambitions. First the Anglican bishops of Uganda and Mombasa together with Dr Arthur, leader of the Church of Scotland mission, denounced official instructions in 1919 designed to compel Africans to work for white settlers. Oldham took up their protests, and in successive memoranda presented to Milner and Churchill at the Colonial Office by the Archbishop of Canterbury in December 1920 and July 1921, he set out the range of issues which a policy of trusteeship, as enunciated by the Covenant of the League of Nations, would involve. As an alternative to settler economic enterprise, Oldham pointed to the potentials of African production. Politically he helped to check settler pretensions, first in the negotiations which resulted in the Devonshire Declaration of 1923 on the paramountcy of African interests in Kenya, and secondly as a member of the Hilton Young Commission which in 1928 frustrated the plans to give European settlers a predominant place in the development of East and Central Africa.

In the main these were negative, defensive achievements. Of far greater significance for the missions was the co-operation between missions and the Colonial Office in the field of African education, decisively fostered by Oldham. In British territories in both West and South Africa, the colonial governments had already assumed limited direct responsibility for education by the establishment and maintenance of a few government schools. They also provided some modest financial assistance for some of the larger mission schools, and they had begun to link this aid with an incipient system of official inspection and controls. By 1920 the most famous institutions for African education were situated in the eastern Cape, culminating in the Scottish

Presbyterian educational complex at Lovedale with its neighbouring Fort Hare College. This was soon to be affiliated with
the University of South Africa, and had been opened in 1916 as
a result of African, government and missionary initiative. But
government intervention in African education in South Africa
had developed furthest in Natal. There a separate, specialised
inspectorate for African education had been established, and close
co-operation with the missions was achieved through their
participation on an advisory board and on government school
committees. This system was seen as a possible model for the rest
of Africa, but here, as in the Transvaal and Orange Free State,
government provision for African education was severely restricted by white opposition, while earlier the attitude of Milner's
young administrators in the Transvaal had been firmly secular,
depriving denominational schools of any subsidy.

In West Africa, despite the early pre-eminence of Freetown,
with its Fourah Bay College, owned by the CMS and affiliated with
the University of Durham since 1876, and with its concentration
of secondary schools, the lead was being taken by the Gold Coast,
enriched by its cocoa exports which in 1919 provided more than
half the world's supply. A system of inspecting those mission-
schools which qualified for financial assistance was well established
there, and the governor, Sir Gordon Guggisberg, placed education
in the forefront of colonial policy. Yet even in the Gold Coast
less than 10 per cent of children were enrolled in government-
assisted schools, and in the whole of the northern territories,
which contained about a third of the total population, four small
government schools were the only recognised provision for
education. In the far larger territory of Nigeria, government
expenditure on education was less than half that of the Gold Coast,
and a fifth of the total number of government and assisted schools
were concentrated in the city of Lagos. The governor of Nigeria,
Sir Hugh Clifford, asserted in 1920 that the northern provinces
had not yet produced a single person 'sufficiently educated to
enable him to fill the most minor clerical post in the office of any
government department', while education in the southern
provinces was, he thought, 'in even worse case' with 'an
abundance of schools but very little genuine education'. Faced in
the south with a rapidly growing demand and 'the extraordinary
irruption of "hedge-schools"', Clifford anxiously wished to

extend government control in this field but was seriously hampered by lack of resources.[39]

This issue of government participation in education was also acutely posed in East Africa. In Kenya, settlers demanded that Africans should merely be educated to serve white economic interests, and the government's director of education, like Milner's officials in the Transvaal in the early 1900s, was opposed to mission dominance, claiming in 1923 that 'no African should be compelled to receive doses of Catholicism or Calvinism in his endeavour to learn'.[40] The missions feared that the British colonial governments might decide to direct all government resources towards establishing a rival school system, and it was to meet this threat that Oldham, exploiting his earlier contacts, arranged a meeting with the Colonial Office in June 1923. It was decided to establish an Advisory Committee on Native Education in Tropical Africa to facilitate and implement a permanent system of co-operation with the missions. Basically this alliance merely recognised the realities of the situation in Africa, and it underlined yet again the immense significance of the early, independent base of the modern missionary movement. In many cases mission schools, however rudimentary, had long preceded the onset of colonial rule; virtually everywhere it was the missions and the first African converts who had begun to overcome African reluctance to expose their youth to this new form of initiation; and having aroused an irreversible demand for education, it was the missions, drawing upon their independent sources of finance and recruitment, who were able to commit men and money in the schools on a scale far beyond that of any colonial government in the crucial early decades. So when in the 1920s Clifford and others sought to curb and control this 'extraordinary irruption', they found themselves confronted with a momentum they could not confine, and they recognised that they could merely seek to influence education by closer inspection and syllabus planning, purchased with larger financial grants. At the same time, the missions, faced with the rising demands on their often declining financial resources, welcomed the opportunity of continuing to

[39] Quoted in *Education in Africa: a study of West, South and Equatorial Africa* (Report of the Phelps-Stokes Commission prepared by T. Jesse Jones, chairman. New York and London, 1922), 175.
[40] J. R. Orr quoted by K. J. King, *Pan-Africanism and education* (Oxford, 1971), 111.

play a leading role in this field, even if they sacrificed to some degree their earlier independence.

Acceptance of this compromise was facilitated by influential promptings from North America. During the preparations for the Edinburgh conference of 1910, Oldham had been brought into contact with Dr T. Jesse Jones, who advocated that the approach to Negro education, pioneered in the Southern States by Booker T. Washington and other individuals at Hampton and Tuskegee, should be applied elsewhere. Following a visit to these institutions in 1912, Oldham became convinced that their emphasis on moderation, racial co-operation and rural community development could prove crucially relevant in Africa. It would not merely correct an alien and literary bias in education. More strategically, it might counteract the growth of an embittered African nationalism similar to that of the Congress Party in India. After the First World War, with interest in African education aroused by the mandates system of the League of Nations, some American missions approached Jesse Jones, by then educational director of the Phelps-Stokes Fund, which had been established in New York in 1911 to assist 'the education of Negroes both in Africa and the United States'. As a result, the Fund appointed commissions under his chairmanship to visit Africa in 1920–1 and 1924. The commissions worked closely with Oldham. Their reports emphasised the importance of adapting education in Africa to the needs of local, rural development and stressed the potential contributions of both missions and governments. These ideas provided an acceptable theoretical consensus for the co-operation of missions with the Colonial Office, but the actual implementation and maintenance of this alliance depended to a very large degree on Oldham's personal links in London with politicians, government officials and church leaders.

The consequences of this co-operation for the missions in Africa were considerable. The attempt to provide staff and facilities for schools which would meet the standards set by government inspectorates involved many missions in a major diversion of their resources. The Scots and some of the other older Protestant missions experienced the least difficulties, as they had already developed a commitment to education far beyond the narrow confines demanded by evangelisation, literacy and the need to train African agents. The CMS indeed found that government grants covering the salaries of missionary educationalists in tropical Africa made an important contribution to the society's funds, especially in the 1930s when other sources were diminished by the depression. As its official historian has commented: 'these grants not only made it possible to maintain a total missionary force comparable in numbers with the pre-war period; they were a chief factor in a massive redistribution of missionary forces between Asia and Africa'.[41] Yet if some missions, well placed to recruit teachers with recognised qualifications, benefited financially, others made considerable sacrifices and missions generally made a major contribution to African education in purely material terms. In 1936 it was officially estimated that about 60 per cent of the cost of schools in Nyasaland was provided by the missions from their overseas resources, and in the far wealthier Southern Rhodesia the financial contribution of nine of the largest missions almost matched that of the government.

Most Catholic missions were ill-prepared to meet this challenge and opportunity. After his initial experience with the foundation of Christian orphanages in Algeria, Lavigerie had become determined that the White Fathers should avoid introducing an alien educational system into tropical Africa. Apart from the rigid professional training of the seminaries in the Nyanza diocese, the educative role of the White Fathers was often virtually restricted to catechetical teaching. Sometimes this did not even involve the acquisition of literacy, for among the Bemba the catechism was learnt by rote. Even in Buganda, 41 Catholic chiefs had been driven by the inadequate educational provisions for Catholic children to complain directly in 1901 to Livinhac, who had succeeded Lavigerie as superior-general. Rubaga High School was founded only in 1906 and right into the late 1920s Bishop Streicher's priority remained a purely religious education.

It was the Vatican, in the person of Hinsley, when Apostolic Visitor, that persuaded most Catholic missions in British Africa to accept the conditions of educational cooperation with the colonial authorities. By January 1929 Streicher had obediently reversed his priorities, accepting the school as henceforth 'the heart' of the missionary organisation in each vicariate, and it was Hinsley's visit to southern Africa in February 1928 that gave

<hr />

[41] G. Hewitt, *The problems of success. A history of the Church Missionary Society 1910–1942*, I (London, 1971), 432.

Catholic missions there the impetus to acquire government grants for their schools. In eastern Nigeria, as a result of Shanahan's early response to the Ibo demand for education, the Spiritans already in 1926 had more than 1,000 primary schools with 60,000 children enrolled. But they had nothing else: no secondary schools, and their teacher-training college had been closed after the war. Here Hinsley had to persuade the mission to accept the Nigerian Education Ordinance of 1926 with its emphasis on quality rather than quantity. This coincided with the Ibo's fierce desire for higher qualifications and Hinsley had no difficulty in carrying the Irish missionaries with him, but the French Spiritans remained deeply antagonistic to any state interference in their work, fearing that it would distort their mission and restrict their religious activities.

It was not only French Catholic missionaries, with their experience of anti-clericalism in Europe, who opposed the alliance with colonial education. A similar response came from a quite different ecclesiastical tradition. Evangelical Fundamentalists shared with conservative Catholics the conviction that educational responsibilities should not be allowed to divert resources from direct evangelism and expansion. After a brief initial acceptance of government grants in 1924, the Africa Inland Mission in Kenya reverted for the rest of the inter-war period to the position that its status as a Faith mission prevented it from entering into ongoing commitments with the state. In Ruanda, the most evangelical of the CMS missions in Africa regarded education purely as a means of evangelisation. Only after the Second World War did they accept Belgian financial assistance and then only because 'to refuse would have meant handing over the whole youth of the country to the Roman Catholics'. Ironically, in 1912 it had been the entry of German Lutherans into Ruanda that had caused the White Fathers to intensify their educational efforts there in the conviction that 'error will soon establish its schools everywhere'.[42] The logic of missionary rivalry eventually overcame the reluctance to cooperate with the state, and, as in other spheres, it also forced them to meet African needs and demands.

Yet while most missions were compelled to strengthen their commitment to education and in many cases to redeploy their

[42] Mgr L. Classe quoted in Linden, *Church and revolution*, 111; P. St John, *Breath of life* (London, 1971), 169.

resources, the increasing government intervention affected the content of African education far less than had been anticipated. The emphasis of the Phelps-Stokes reports on the importance of adapting the syllabus ignored the revolutionary impact already exerted by the denigrated and inefficient bush schools and it ran directly counter to emergent African demands. Theorists and government inspectors sought to rationalise the educational structure and syllabus, but villagers insisted on the multiplication of schools, district councils diverted funds into educational expansion and in 1929 Johnstone Kenyatta, on behalf of the Kikuyu Central Association, demanded facilities for secondary and further education and for the teaching of *ngirigaca* (agriculture), the acquisition of science and skills needed to produce cash crops, rather than mere digging. Dr Aggrey as a central figure in the Phelps-Stokes commission might advocate rural adaptation and racial moderation, but, quoting Latin tags at Fourah Bay, fêted by Guggisberg, welcomed as an equal by missionaries and liberals throughout the continent, he symbolised for his countrymen in the Gold Coast and for the thousands of Africans who saw and heard him elsewhere, the successful seizure from the whites of the advantages of their classical education. Only much later would more Africans begin to demand syllabus revision and an emphasis on communal development. Government intervention from the 1920s led to a much greater emphasis on the training of teachers and to a rationalisation of standards; but it failed to eliminate much wasteful proliferation and the schools remained a narrow and precarious ladder up which a few persistent and fortunate individuals managed to climb towards a position from which they could challenge the whites' claim to superiority.

The missions preserved a major role in a field where they had already rendered a great service to Africa, and any church, in Africa or elsewhere, has inevitably a keen interest in the development and nature of education. But this increasingly secular commitment proved a major liability to the missions. In the villages, the earlier prestige of the evangelist and catechist was supplanted by that of the schoolteacher; in the churches, the missionary tended to become a bureaucrat, remote, linked with the colonial state, concerned with the pressures of administering a system. As a consequence, the missionary was often unaware of the spiritual problems facing African Christians and of the challenges confronting the churches in the urban areas, where most of those whom he had come to convert were receiving their sharpest initiation into the modern world. For many Africans, the mission churches as institutions became synonymous with education, identified with white leadership and with an African educated élite, who were preoccupied with an essentially alien mode of living, organisation, standards, discipline and thought. Yet the missionaries and the educated élite did not constitute the major component of Christianity in Africa; already their preoccupations presented a stark contrast to the desperately eager and anxious search on the part of their fellow men and women for new forms of community and for an integrated cosmology, confronting traditional concerns with fresh spiritual insights, which might together provide a measure of social and intellectual security in a rapidly changing environment.

CHAPTER 4

ISLAM

Islam was still a new faith when it was carried across North Africa and down the East African coast. Within six hundred years of the Prophet's death it had penetrated the Sahara to the Sudanic belt stretching from the Atlantic to the Red Sea. By the late nineteenth century the range of Islamic institutions in Africa's Muslim communities resembled the complexity of those in the heartlands of Islam; indeed, the northern third of Africa was firmly integrated into the Islamic world, both through the faith itself and through its overlapping economic networks. The region that was to provide a testing ground for Islam during our period was the middle third of the continent. There the combined forces of Christian missions and colonial governments generally sought to mitigate or at least control the advance of Islam, and Muslim communities were thereby spurred on to answer this challenge, occasionally under the aegis of the Europeans but also in contradiction to the Western values associated with the colonial order.

The particular adaptations of Islam in sub-Saharan Africa were typical of the variety of Muslim communities on other frontiers of the Islamic world. There were a few Shi'ite communities in North Africa and along the East African coast, but nearly all African Muslims were 'orthodox' Sunni. Islamic law (*sharī'a*) and the scholars (*'ulamā'*) and jurists (*qāḍis*) who interpreted it served as the foundation for each community, whether a cluster of nomads' tents or a polity of several million souls. Among the four schools of Islamic law, two were widely represented in Africa: the Mālikī rite predominated in North Africa and West Africa, and the Shāfi'i school in East Africa. Treatises from the other schools were found in libraries and were noted in legal decisions of the day, and adherence to differing schools of law rarely led to political confrontation as did controversies over legal inter- pretation, or compromise between the *sharī'a* and pre-Islamic practices.

More important still in providing group identity were the mystic Sufi orders or brotherhoods (*ṭuruq*, sing. *ṭarīqa*). These were generally known by the founder's name, taken on by adherents who observed a litany and teachings of the saint and his disciples or holy men (shaykhs) who served brotherhood members as intercessors between this world and the next. Important orders in Africa included some of the oldest, such as the Qādiriyya (named after the twelfth-century Baghdad mystic ʿAbd al-Qādir) and the Shādhiliyya (after the thirteenth-century Maghribi saint al-Shādhilī); and one of the most recent, the Tijāniyya (founded by the Algerian mystic Aḥmad al-Tijānī who died in 1815). The Muslim brotherhoods have traditionally been in the vanguard of Islam, and this was no less true in Africa where shaykhs on the frontiers of the Muslim world imaginatively adapted the teachings of the Prophet and of their own orders to incorporate local religious sensibilities. The inherent tension between a highly personalised Sufism and an often rigid *sharīʿa*, and between the advocates for each, was also found in Africa's Islamic communities. The most important and sensitive arena of cultural influences across Muslim Africa was the educational system. Religious education began (and for most ended) in Koranic schools where youths memorised the holy book of Islam; students seeking advanced training in the Islamic sciences sought out *'ulamā'* and libraries at a centre of scholarship (*madrasa*). Such training developed informal regional and transcontinental networks amongst the *'ulamā'*, as did the pilgrimage (*ḥajj*) to the holy city of Mecca, though relatively few believers from distant lands found this obligation practicable before the mid-twentieth century.

The significance of the thirteenth century after the Prophet's *hijra* or flight from Mecca in AD 622 (from which time the Islamic calendar begins) deserves special mention, for Islamic literature had widely announced the arrival then of an 'awaited deliverer' (*mahdī*) who would prepare the world for the end of time. The end of the thirteenth century AH marked the appearance of a mahdi in the Sudan, Muḥammad Aḥmad b. ʿAbdallāh, in AH 1299/AD 1881, but during the nineteenth century numerous other mahdist predictions, expectations, self-declarations and denials had affected Muslim communities throughout the Sudanic belt. Muḥammad Aḥmad died in 1885, but there was speculation that the Mahdi might in fact appear soon after the thirteenth century AH, and amid the political uncertainties following the partition of Africa mahdism retained a populist appeal which lasted into the late 1920s.

The European conquest of Algeria (1830), of Tunisia (1881) and of Egypt (1882) led to change in many Islamic institutions. In Algeria, even the Arabic language was replaced by French for official use. In Tunisia and Egypt, the westernisation of state institutions was under way well before the French and British, respectively, began their rule, and leading Muslim intellectuals debated the issue of modernisation. Neighbouring Libya, at the same time, remained under vestigial Ottoman control, although for the last quarter of the nineteenth century the province of Cyrenaica was largely administered by the Sanūsiyya, a Muslim brotherhood founded by a mid-century Algerian holy man. Morocco was governed by a centuries-old Muslim dynasty where the office of sultan was one of the few institutions holding together disparate economic and ethnic groups.

Across the southern Sahara and Sudanic belt European intruders in the late nineteenth century encountered a number of Islamic states that had mostly been founded earlier in the century. Some overlaid centuries of Islamic culture. Some, such as Futa Toro in the Senegal river basin and the Sokoto caliphate in what became Northern Nigeria, traced their origins to eighteenth- and nineteenth-century Islamic reform movements that predated European colonial interests in the region. Others, such as al-Ḥājj 'Umar's state at Segu and the Mahdist state in the eastern Sudan, were stimulated by the challenge of infidel incursions as well as by their leaders' call for a purified Islam.

Islam had also spread along trade routes into the West African rain forest, as in Asante, and in south-western Nigeria it was well established by 1905 in several Yoruba towns. On the eastern fringes of Ethiopia, Islam had long been dominant, and there was another string of Islamic communities along the East African coast, from the Horn to the Portuguese colony of Mozambique. In the later nineteenth century Muslim influence reached inland from the east coast to Lake Nyasa (Malawi) and the Congo basin. Further south, in Natal, some Indian immigrants followed Islam, while the small Muslim community in the western Cape originally derived from Malay slaves and political prisoners. Between and beyond all these centres of Muslim settlement moved Muslim traders; they were often accompanied by teachers associated with the Sufi brotherhoods who implanted Islamic institutions where previously there had been only cursory knowledge of the Prophet's message.

By the end of our period, Muslims may have constituted nearly half the population of Africa and were bound together by their common colonial experience. They had witnessed movements of resistance to infidel rule; they had evolved mechanisms to reject that rule where it intruded upon fundamental aspects of Islam; and they were experiencing a regeneration and expansion of Islam within their regions. The form and content of this resurgence varied according to the interplay of several factors: the nature of contacts between Muslim communities and European colonisers early in the century, the policies of colonial administrations, and the communications between particular communities and other parts of the Muslim world. By the early 1940s there were broadly parallel developments within Islamic communities on a regional basis throughout the continent and a linking of those communities and regions across Islamic Africa. Our survey of these changes will consider first the hostility of Muslim communities towards European invaders during the first quarter of the century; it will then examine the attitudes of colonial administrators towards Islamic communities; and it will conclude by reviewing the signs of expansion and regeneration of Islam in Africa between the wars. The focus will mainly be upon sub-Saharan Africa. Islamic institutions and trends in North Africa are surveyed in *CHA*, vol. VII, chapter 6, and other regional chapters provide further information regarding topics treated here.

RESISTANCE

Appeal to jihad (holy war) against backsliders and infidels was frequently synonymous with reform and expansion in Islamic polities during the nineteenth century in Africa. During the first quarter of the twentieth century in the Maghrib and across the Sudanic belt, jihad continued to provide powerful motivation for diverse Muslim communities, although its focus was not so much internal reform as a defence of Muslim lands against the encroachments of European infidels. Most of these militant

Islamic movements sought to maintain or re-establish an Islamic state that was either under attack or had been recently occupied by the European powers. They tended to be led by officers or descendants of notables in the former regimes, although some drew inspiration from religious visionaries who stepped into the void of Muslim leadership in conquered territories. Their resilience was due as much to their inaccessibility and the lack of resolve by colonial powers during the early years of the century as to their ideological cohesion and belief in a divine ordination. They shared a belief that the occupation of Muslim lands by Europe might be stemmed by a frontal attack and that military action constituted the only correct response for the Muslim whose country was being invaded by infidels. In view of the modest number of European troops seen in many parts of the continent during the opening years of the century, the success of jihads in the recent past, and the number of such movements affecting the continent, it is understandable that holy war held a widespread appeal for Muslim communities confronted with European occupation.

The four regions in which militant Muslim resistance to colonial rule proved to be the most determined — the Sudan, Somaliland, Libya and Morocco — were also among those territories in which Islamic states flourished at the time of European conquest. In Libya and the Sudan those states were recent, late nineteenth-century creations, and colonial forces faced opponents who were among the vigorous first- and second-generation leaders in those polities. In Morocco, it was the compromises forced upon the venerated office of sultan, first by the French and then by the Spanish administration in the north of the kingdom, that precipitated two calls to jihad.

The Sudanese resistance took its inspiration from the Mahdist state founded by Muḥammad Aḥmad in 1882, which fell with the British victory at Karari (Omdurman) in 1898. For the next eighteen years the western sultanate of Darfur remained an autonomous regime under 'Alī Dinār who maintained his independent slave army, and an administration modelled on that of the Mahdist state. 'Alī Dinār successfully retained control over Darfur until 1916, despite French advances in Wadai and along the western marches of Darfur. From his capital at El Fasher he entered into correspondence with young Turkish leaders and remonstrated over the British deposition of Khedive Abbas II. The final British action against El Fasher, complete with air support, came after the British concluded that 'Alī Dīnār was about to launch an invasion of the Sudan. Of lesser significance were the 'Kaffiyya Rising' in 1908 led by the Mahdist 'Abd al-Qādir in the Gezira and the jihad announced in southern Darfur in 1921 in response to British taxation schemes.

During the first two decades of the century the British were also preoccupied with a movement in the Horn of Africa which owed its inspiration in part to the Sudanese Mahdiyya. This was the jihad launched by Muḥammad 'Abdallāh Ḥasan, called by the British the 'Mad Mullah', who preached holy war against all infidels, including Somalis who did not recognise his claims or who had not joined his branch of the Ṣāliḥiyya brotherhood. His strict discipline, and his efforts to create a Pan-Somali allegiance transcending clan loyalties, gave particular force to his anti-European sentiments. The British sent four expeditions against him between 1900 and 1904, and in 1909 he was denounced by the leader of the Ṣāliḥiyya, but his reign over northern Somaliland continued until 1920.

In Libya and the central Sahara it was the Sanūsiyya brotherhood that served as a focal point for Muslim resistance to alien intrusion. Between 1879 and the Italian invasion of Libya in 1911, the Cyrenaica province of that territory had been administered jointly by Ottoman officials and Sanūsi shaykhs. Their common combat against the infidel forces of France, Italy and later Britain was an extension of this collaboration, despite the uneasy tolerance each party maintained toward the other. Sanūsi forces held out against Italian advances into the interior from the departure of Ottoman troops in 1912 until 1916. Sayyid al-Mahdī (d. 1902), the successor to the brotherhood's founder, had expanded the Sanūsiyya into the central Sahara where another theatre of Sanūsi warfare developed in the first two decades of the century. Sayyid al-Mahdī's successor, Sayyid Aḥmad al-Sharīf, tried unsuccessfully to defend the order's settlements against French incursions in 1906 at al-Kawar and Bilma and in 1909 in Wadai. During the First World War the Sanūsis were able to recapture French and Italian posts in the region, only to lose them again during the French reconquest between 1917 and 1920. The second Italian-Sanūsi war (1923–32) was a popular uprising fought in the name of Islam for an independent Cyrenaica.

Militant confrontations with European infidels in Morocco came first from the Sahara where by the turn of the century Shaykh Mā' al-'Aynayn had collected some ten thousand followers at Samara in territory to the south of Morocco that was soon to be claimed by Spain. His status as the most revered figure in the northern Sahara, a region famous for its holy men, persuaded the Moroccan sultan, 'Abd al-'Azīz, to despatch to him a deputy and arms for the defence of the Sahara in 1905 as the French began their advance northwards from the Senegal valley. Two years later the shaykh helped to precipitate the sultan's deposition in favour of 'Abd al-Hafīz who would, he believed, offer sterner resistance to French inroads in the kingdom and seek closer ties with the Ottomans. In 1908 Mā' al-'Aynayn declared a jihad against the French; when French advisers obliged the sultan to sever relations with the shaykh in 1910, Mā' al-'Aynayn declared himself sultan and advanced through Marrakesh towards Fez. Here he was decisively defeated by the French and in September of that year he retired to his retreat at Tiznit where he died the following month. His son and successor, al-Hayba, continued the struggle against the Christian infidels and for a unified Morocco and Sahara. In 1912 he declared himself both mahdi and sultan and temporarily regained Marrakesh, but he was forced to retreat to the desert. His guerrilla warfare continued during the First World War with the help of arms obtained through traders in the Rio de Oro. At his death in 1917 one of his brothers took up leadership of the struggle until 1926, and in 1929 another of his relatives, Muḥammad al-Mamūn, revived the shaykh's cause by preaching jihad and taking the offensive against French outposts. Not until 1934 could the French claim that their 'pacification' campaigns had successfully crushed the last of this Islamic resistance in their Saharan territories. In the north of Morocco yet another genre of militant resistance to European occupation emerged in 1922 with the creation of the Rif Republic under the leadership of 'Abd al-Karim (1882–1963). He had been educated both in Islamic and in Spanish Catholic schools, after which he worked until 1919 in the Spanish colonial administration. Thus 'Abd al-Karīm was able to bring some knowledge of Western methods of government and warfare to the task of creating an Islamic republic which might defend its own against the infidel. He leased mineral concessions to European firms in return for arms and military technicians, and launched devastating military offensives against the Spanish forces before being defeated by French and Spanish troops in 1926. This warfare, reinforced by news of Islamic militancy from elsewhere in the Maghrib and the Sudanic belt, served to identify Islam with an anti-colonial stance amongst those Africans who sought such an ideology.

This last point can be illustrated from several other parts of Africa in the first quarter of the century. Conversions followed in the train of French campaigns against Samory Toure's state in the West African Sudan during the last two decades of the nineteenth century, strengthening Islam among the Mandinka despite the casual adherence of Samory himself. In German East Africa, the savage repression of the Maji Maji revolt in 1905–7 induced the Ngindo and other peoples in the south-east to espouse Islam as a modern belief-system which owed nothing to Europeans. In 1908 an Arab trader in Zanzibar, Rumaliza, whose business had been ruined by the Germans, caused the distribution on the mainland of a letter, supposedly written in Mecca, which promised an early anti-colonial millennium. During the First World War the Central Powers further promoted the image of a militant, anti-colonial Islam, allied through the Ottomans to Germany and against the British and French occupation of Muslim lands. This accounts in part for the alliance in 1915 between Muḥammad 'Abdallāh Ḥasan and the Ethiopian emperor Iyasu, whose own flirtation with Islam contributed to his deposition in 1916.

The feature that distinguishes the militant Islamic movements of the early twentieth century from preceding jihads, and the feature that most alarmed the colonial powers, was the Pan-Islamic links between them. For example, regular communication between the Sudanese Mahdi's camps and potential religious reformers in Bornu at the end of the nineteenth century promoted a number of declarations of mahdis which the British in Northern Nigeria regarded as among the chief threats to their early administration. In 1906, British officers reported mahdis in Bauchi and Gombe as well as Kontagora; German intelligence uncovered a likely mahdi in Adamawa. Another mahdi was said in the northern Gold Coast and Ivory Coast to have come from Bornu in 1904–5. But the major challenge to British rule in Nigeria was the offensive taken in Satiru, a village near Sokoto, in 1906, when a mahdist force successfully attacked a British column and acquired considerable weaponry as well as open pledges of assistance from the emir of Gwandu. Within a month punitive expeditions had dispersed the Satiru threat and razed the village. But subsequent investigations by French officers pointed to possible links between the Satiru affair and a wider conspiracy against French forces in nearby Zinder, and possible collaboration in such an offensive by the emir of Kano. During the First World War, the youngest son of the Sudanese Mahdi was recognised by the British as a religious leader, since they saw him as a natural ally against the Ottoman Empire.[1] The ensuing revival of Mahdist organisation in the Sudan gave a new impetus to mahdist activity in northern Nigeria, and Fulani from Bornu and Gombe rallied in 1923 around Malam Sa'id, son of Muhammad Bello's descendant, Hayātu, who had acted as the Mahdi's agent in Sokoto at the close of the nineteenth century. Malam Sa'id was deported, but as late as 1927 British officers detected mahdist activities in Katsina.

The Pan-Islamic network within Africa also linked the Sudanese Mahdi's legacy with Sanūsī leaders and, during the second decade of the century, both briefly with Northern Nigeria. One of the most effective Sanūsī chiefs in the central and southern Sahara was Kawsen ag Muhammad, a Tuareg who in 1904–5 left his exile in Kanem to fight against French incursions in the southern desert. He affiliated with the Sanūsī in 1909 and two years later travelled to Darfur where he contemplated joining 'Alī Dīnār's forces before returning to the Fezzan with his troops to join a Turkish garrison. By 1916 his forces were laying siege to Agades and could claim control over the main commercial entrepôt of the central Sahara, having rallied Tuareg compatriots against the French throughout the Fezzan, Ahaggar and Aïr. In a rare display of co-operation, British administrators in Kano were prompted by the Kawsen threat to provide military supplies to French troops as they took the offensive against him in 1916; three years later Kawsen was caught and put to death at Murzuk.

During the first two decades of the century the most pervasive Pan-Islamic influence associated with militant Islam in Africa was that of the Ottoman Turks. Sultan Abdülhamid II, who reigned from 1876 to 1908, attracted an allegiance from many African Muslims who acknowledged Turkey as the only remaining Islamic power of consequence in a world of aggressive Christian

---

[1] See *CHA*, vol. VII, chapter 15, pp. 760–1

states. Thus the sultan had been addressed by and replied to the Muslim community of Lagos in 1894 on the importance of Western education; from the 1870s there were links between Istanbul and Cape Town Muslims. The sultan of Zanzibar, Sayyid 'Alī b. Hamūd (1905–11) was entertained by Abdülhamid; and as late as 1910 Friday prayers in Dar es Salaam were still being said in the name of the Ottoman sultan. During the period of the Young Turks (1908–18) there emerged a Turkish intelligence service with African ties that provided substance to previous vague notions of fealty. At the outbreak of the First World War, the Ottomans issued a call to jihad against the Allied powers which was widely distributed in North Africa. It surfaced also in East and Central Africa, where in 1915 the British arrest in Nyasaland of a Muslim from Mozambique uncovered Swahili tracts bearing Istanbul's call for holy war against the English. During the war Ottoman and German arms and technicians were provided for the Sanūsī movement after Turkey formally withdrew from Libya, and an attempt was made by Germany to smuggle arms to Mā' al-'Aynayn's successor; 'Alī Dīnār had representatives in Istanbul, and Ottoman recognition was extended in 1916 to Muḥammad 'Abdallāh Ḥasan, who also received a Turkish adviser at his headquarters in northern Somaliland.

If the extent of these Pan-Islamic ties and sentiments set these militant movements apart from the jihads of earlier times, their avowed aim of maintaining Muslim authority in the face of threats to a rightly guided practice of Islam united them with a centuries-old tradition which was at once their main strength and their chief liability. Popular support for calls to jihad against the Christian infidels is evident from the tens of thousands of believers who joined these movements. But in the end their success in opposing European armament depended upon their own access to such armament. By the mid-1920s, apart from the continuing Sanūsī war and minor skirmishes in the Sahara, jihad had been rejected as an anachronism in Muslim Africa. Islamic leaders and communities who sought to distance themselves from their Christian rulers joined others who, from the advent of colonial rule, had simply withdrawn from the political realities of infidel occupation.

The most dramatic form of withdrawal was emigration from European-occupied lands. The little information that is available suggests that this option was taken up by individuals and communities throughout the continent. Families and clans from Shinqit, in northern Mauritania, migrated to Syria and the Hijaz during the first decade of the century. Several hundred descendants and associates of the nineteenth-century Segu reformer, al-Ḥājj 'Umar, passed through the central Sudan fleeing French columns as they approached the Niger in 1890; the refugees settled in the Sokoto emirate of Missau, but continued eastwards in 1905 when the British conquered Sokoto's domains. The most famous of this group, Alfa Hashim, finally settled in the Hijaz where he and his son, as shaykhs of the Tijāniyya brotherhood, were to wield considerable influence over West African pilgrims to the holy lands of Islam. Indeed, the belt of villages and clans of West African origin that stretches from Lake Chad to the Red Sea owes its origin both to permanently settled pilgrims *en route* to or from the holy lands and to migrants seeking escape from infidel rule. Among the thousands who did so were the Hausa saint, 'Umar Janbo (who lived in Darfur under 'Alī Dīnār before fleeing to Mecca where he died in 1918) and Sultan Mai Wurnu (son of a former Sokoto notable who settled in the Sudan in 1906). There was also emigration from North Africa; in 1911, heeding a call from the *mufti* of Tlemcen, some 800 Algerians departed for Syria.

More frequent than physical withdrawal from European rule was the response of numerous holy men who, in keeping with an Islamic tradition advocating non-involvement in temporal affairs, sought to ignore the European presence. Examples of the recluse could be found in nearly every major Muslim community across the continent: three from West Africa must suffice here. Shaykh Bay al-Kunti (1865–1929) inherited the leadership of the famous Kunta holy family of the Timbuktu region on the Niger bend in 1896. Shaykh Bay was something of a recluse prior to French occupation of his land in 1904; thereafter he refused to present himself to French authorities who took him to be hostile to their presence in the early years, although it may have been his counsel that discouraged some from joining Muḥammad Kawsen's attack on Agades. Shaykh Bay was chiefly responsible for the Tuareg Islamic revival in the years after the First World War, and his library functioned as a legal centre for the central-southern Sahara during the first quarter of the century. He maintained a refuge and redistributed the wealth disbursed to him. His hermitage and his erudition effectively linked Tuareg and Moorish traditions of Islamic scholarship in the central Sahara. A comparable figure in Guinea was Fanta Mady (d. 1955) who resided in Kankan, an Islamic centre dating from the sixteenth century which had long disseminated teachings fostered by the Kunta family from the Niger bend. Fanta Mady's father had been a spiritual adviser to Samory Toure, and the shaykh himself studied with a son of Samory. He thus enjoyed a link with one of West Africa's major resistance movements while observing strict neutrality in political matters and, by the early 1940s, the 'Grand Cherif Fanta Mady' was recognised as one of the most erudite and influential figures residing in the West African savanna. In the Gold Coast another such savant was al-Ḥājj 'Umar Kratche, a Hausa scholar who settled at Salaga during the 1870s. Between his return from pilgrimage around 1913 and his death in 1934 he was widely regarded as the spiritual head of the Gold Coast Muslim community. Other holy men distinguished themselves as shaykhs in the Sufi brotherhoods, and still others developed working relationships with the colonial authorities in order to promote Muslim education or applications of the *shari'a*. Indeed, the most characteristic holy men were those, discussed below, who responded positively to the new opportunities offered by colonial rule to them and their communities. They were the main agents of the expansion of Islam in Africa during our period, and their moderating influence, both within and beyond areas of open confrontation, confirmed the wisdom of colonial policies aimed at the incorporation and appeasement of Muslim authority.

COLONIAL POLICIES

Colonial attitudes towards Islam were influenced both by early Muslim responses to colonial intrusion and by past experience in dealing with Muslim populations. British administrators in the Sudan and in Northern Nigeria drew upon experience in India, especially in matters of Islamic law. French containment of Muslim resistance in mid-nineteenth century Algeria contributed to the preoccupation of French officials with the potential dangers elsewhere of the Sufi brotherhoods; North African experience also demonstrated the efficacy of French policies of appeasement toward Muslim authority. No less important were the personalities of certain administrators whose policies not only affected their own Muslim subjects but served as examples for other parts of Islamic Africa.

One of the most imaginative of early colonial administrators was Louis-Hubert Lyautey. As resident-general in Morocco from 1912 to 1925, Lyautey developed a system of indirect rule through the office of sultan and a restructured Muslim state. Although the sultan's administration was greatly circumscribed by the resident-general, the Moroccan protectorate dramatically contrasted with French government in Algeria. Lyautey's philosophy of respectful paternalism in Morocco had parallels in sub-Saharan Africa. Maurice Delafosse acquired an extensive experience of, and respect for, West African societies which led him to introduce African language teaching to the École Coloniale in 1909. Paul Marty published numerous studies of Islamic societies in French West Africa while chief of its department of Muslim affairs during the second decade of the century; they formed the basis for future French Islamic policy. An analogous influence upon Islamic societies and the preservation of Islamic authority in Northern Nigeria was the high commissioner there from the British conquest to 1906, Frederick Lugard. 'Lugardisme' was to have considerable popularity amongst French administrators also; its effect upon Islam in Nigeria lay in the creation of emirates where no Muslim authority had effectively ruled before, and in the extension and expansion of Islamic law.

The practical effect of such systems of indirect rule upon Muslim communities lay mainly in the colonial sanction of Islamic offices. The power of a sultan, emir, pasha, $q\bar{a}\,^\cdot id$, khalifa, or $q\bar{a}\d{d}\bar{\imath}$ might now be severely circumscribed, but it might also be enlarged and in any case was backed by the authority of the colonial administration. Between the two world wars such offices and their incumbents were sometimes attacked as props to colonial authority by conservative Islamic leaders and also by modernisers. But for those regions on the frontiers of Islam, the colonial powers' approval of Islamic titles, like their sanction of Arabic and their acknowledgement of the $shari\,^\cdot a$, served to confirm and reinforce the importance of Islamic institutions. The favoured position of Muslims as agents in the colonial administration in German East Africa, and the recruitment of Muslims into most colonial military and police forces, similarly gave prestige to their communities. So too did the spectre of Pan-Islam which so alarmed colonial authorities, even though as a cultural and even political reality it rarely measured up to European fears. This had come to be understood by colonial administrations in the aftermath of the First World War, as was the potential danger of policies that acknowledged Muslim authority over any large territories. In Senegal an officer charged with Muslim administration reasoned that 'reduced to the role of ethnic-group religion, Islam loses all character of a religion of opposition [to our interests]'.[2] By the 1920s most colonial administrations had established networks of Muslim holy men, many recruited from the ranks of the Sufi shaykhs, who could be counted on to dispense mediation and moderate counsel to their communities.

At the beginning of the colonial era, Muslim Africa was served by tens of thousands of Koranic schools whose students subsidised as many teachers and holy men. The added prestige accorded to Islam by colonial powers and the association of Islam with a rival, non-European ideology further enhanced the importance of Koranic education. Colonial attitudes toward Islamic education were initially supportive, although the Koranic schools were generally regarded as irrelevant and their pedagogical technique arcane. Some administrations envisaged the development of a civil servant cadre in Muslim territories through fostering advanced training in Arabic and Islamic law, along with such subjects as geometry, mathematics and surveying. By the end of the first decade of the century Gordon Memorial College, opened in Khartoum in 1902, had become a model for British education officers; staffed by Egyptians, it comprised a training college for teachers and *qāḍis*, an industrial workshop, and primary and upper schools. Hanns Vischer, the first education officer for Northern Nigeria, drew on Sudanese experience for the school he opened in Kano in 1911 and the following year schools at Sokoto and Katsina were incorporated under government supervision. Such integration of Western and Islamic advanced education in Northern Nigeria led to the establishment in 1923 of Katsina Teachers' Training College and, by the mid-1920s, some 69 government schools in the region. A government law school was opened in Kano in 1934 staffed by Sudanese jurists. But the

[2] Robert Arnaud, 'L'Islam et la politique musulmane française en Afrique', *Bulletin du Comité de l'Afrique française, Renseignements coloniaux*, April 1912, 152.

numbers served by these schools were modest when compared to student attendance in Koranic schools.

In Sierra Leone and the hinterland of Lagos, early Muslim education owed much to Dr E. W. Blyden who, while not himself a Muslim, served as an Agent of Native Affairs from 1895 in Lagos and as Director of Mohammedan Education in Sierra Leone in 1902 until his retirement in 1906. Blyden brought a Sierra Leonean Arabic tutor from Fourah Bay College to Lagos in the 1890s, and by the turn of the century three government Muslim schools were functioning at Lagos, Badagry, and Epe; these continued with government subsidy until 1926, drawing heavily upon Muslim teachers from Sierra Leone. In Sierra Leone, Blyden supervised five such government schools and in 1906 Arabic and Islamic legal studies were incorporated into the curriculum for the School for the Sons of Chiefs at Bo. In French West Africa the School for the Sons of Chiefs at St Louis was converted in 1906 into a *madrasa* modelled on the Algerian government *madrasas*; another was opened in 1907 at Jenne, in the Soudan, a centuries-old centre for Islamic studies. Other government *madrasas* were opened at Timbuktu and at Boutilimit, in southern Mauritania, with staff from Algeria. These schools resembled government-sponsored Muslim schools in southern Nigeria and Sierra Leone inasmuch as Western pedagogy tended to displace the Islamic sciences. In East Africa the government-sponsored school in Mombasa, belatedly opened in 1912, offered a curriculum comparable to the government Muslim schools in Zanzibar and Tanga in which neither Arabic nor Koranic studies had a place. Low enrolment at Mombasa and at a similar school at Malindi nearly doubled once the Kenya government agreed to the inclusion of Koranic studies in 1924, but the great majority of Muslim youths remained outside this westernised education system.

Colonial administrations exercised their most subtle effect upon Muslim Africa through the codification and administration of Islamic law. A new degree of uniformity and consistency was introduced in applications of the *shari'a* throughout individual colonies or protectorates, as was the concept of a division between state authority and religious sanction. While this undermined the adaptability of the *shari'a* to local customary law which characterised its applications in pre-colonial days, it also extended the *sharī'a* into legal matters and to some communities where Islamic law had previously had little impact. Indeed, Governor-general William Ponty in French West Africa felt obliged in 1910 to prohibit indigenous tribunals from applying what he called 'Koranic law' in cases where it contradicted local custom (and in 1911 he ordered that tribunal judgements and administrative correspondence be issued in French rather than Arabic). But where Islamic law did not interfere with 'native law and custom' (as the British formula read), its application was tolerated, even encouraged in Muslim areas, mainly in matters of family and personal law. In fact, legal administration in Muslim communities in the British possessions made little distinction between Islamic law and 'native law'; in northern Nigeria, where only 'native law' was recognised, the extent and enforcement of Islamic law was surpassed in the Muslim world only by legal practice in Saudi Arabia. In the Gambia the *sharī'a* was applied in civil cases involving Muslims (most of the population) through a system of *qāḍis'* courts created by statute in 1905. Elsewhere in British colonial Africa, the *sharī'a* was applicable to Muslim contestants, just as 'native law' was applicable to non-Muslim Africans. In French black Africa, customary law was until 1946 applied to all non-citizens, which in Muslim areas meant in effect the application of the *sharī'a* (first formally recognised as a legal code for Senegalese Muslims in 1857). In the Sudan, legislation in 1902 and 1916 established a court structure and system of legal administration closely paralleling that of Egypt.

Islamic legal administration under colonial rule has not been well studied, but several tendencies deserve mention. In most areas there developed, formally or informally, parallel legal and court systems, the one being informed by Islamic law, the other by European law or by administrators' perceptions of customary law. All colonial-sanctioned court systems specified an appeals process which ultimately terminated in the local or regional administrative officer, who was generally ill-equipped to handle the intricacies of Islamic law. In northern Nigeria the standard reference on Mālikī law was F. H. Ruxton's summary translation (1916) of a French translation of the *Mukhtaṣar* of Khalīl. It followed from the dual court system and the appeals process that government-recognised *qāḍis* held highly political positions in colonial administrative systems. Predictably the administration of the *shari'a* by *'ulamā'* in Muslim communities thus continued, outside colonial systems of justice, and may well have increased in importance since pre-colonial days, even while the European sanction of the *shari'a* and the incorporation of *qāḍis* into the administration contributed to the status of these Muslim authorities.

In North Africa it was the modernisation of the *shari'a*, encouraged by colonial authorities, that preoccupied Muslim jurists. An example had been provided by the Young Turks who developed Ottoman law on family rights in 1917, the first major modernist influence to affect the *shari'a*. From the 1920s Egypt took the lead in writing new legislation in matters of family law and in the establishment of tribunals. Similar moves followed in the Sudan and Libya which paralleled earlier developments in the Algerian *Code Morand* (1916) and a *Code Santillana* in Tunisia enacted in 1906. Only in Morocco did the pre-colonial structure of the *shari'a* remain essentially untouched by these modernising influences. French attempts in 1930 to remove the Berber population from the jurisdiction of the *shari'a* resulted in an alliance between the Berber tribes and Moroccan nationalist leaders.

From the late nineteenth century, Christian missionary societies regularly criticised colonial government policies and attitudes towards Islam. Mission strategists correctly believed that many colonial administrators were indifferent if not hostile toward their own evangelical objectives, even if they approved their educational enterprise. British officials invoked the Indian precedent of non-intervention in religious matters; in Nyasaland, government directives in 1894 specified that missions should gain the approval for their work in Muslim districts from the Muslim chiefs. Hostilities between missionaries and Muslim authorities in Northern Nigeria in 1900 caused the government to restrict Christian mission activity to non-Muslim areas. Such policies, the utilisation of Muslim authorities in systems of indirect rule, the colonial sanction of Islamic education and law, and the concomitant expansion of Islam throughout sub-Saharan Africa were viewed with great anxiety by Christian missions. In 1910 the World Missionary Conference declared its 'protest also against anything which serves to identify British State policy with the predominance of Islam, considering it to be a danger not only to the cause of Christian Missions, but ultimately to the very government which practises it'.[3]

Confrontations occurred between Muslim communities and Christian evangelists and their followers, despite the efforts of colonial administrators to avert them, and frequently the two groups of believers were thrown into political or economic competition. Under such circumstances each ideology took on something of an ethnic, linguistic, or occupational mark by which competitors and their clients might identify themselves. Thus the Ngindo and the chiefdoms of Ifakara and Kiberege in southern Tanganyika, like the speakers of Manding or of Hausa in West Africa, are associated with Islam, as too are butchers in much of West Africa, and tailors and long-distance transport drivers in certain areas. The explanations for these associations of Islam with specific groups cannot be generalised, although 'stranger' communities whose home areas were dominantly Muslim or Christian tended to carry their belief-systems with them and, indeed, to emphasise them with special zeal. In areas where large Muslim and Christian communities lived alongside each other, such as western Nigeria, southern Tanganyika, or Sierra Leone, competition between Muslim and Christian educational establishments was common. But the level of financing, the number of schools, and opportunities for Western-trained students of the mission schools increasingly put Muslim schools at a disadvantage. At the beginning of the century both types of education may have been accepted as options for modernising societies, but by the end of the 1920s it was clear that students from Muslim schools could rarely compete in the colonial economy with school-leavers from the mission station.

EXPANSION

By 1940 perhaps almost half the population of Africa adhered to Islam, and the impressions of colonial administrators and missionaries suggest that there had been a rapid expansion of Islam since the opening years of the century. Two-thirds of Africa's Muslims were in Egypt, Nigeria, Algeria, Morocco and the Sudan; by 1950 nearly 40 per cent were in Egypt and Nigeria alone. By 1940 over half the population was Muslim in French

[3] *World Missionary Conference 1910: report of Commission VII* (Edinburgh, n.d.), 60.

North Africa, Libya, Mauritania, Senegal, Guinea, Soudan, Niger, Chad, the Gambia, Nigeria, the Sudan, Somaliland and Zanzibar. Moreover, both in these countries and elsewhere there were districts in which the Muslim population increased two- or three-fold. In central Cameroun nearly one-third of the 80,000 Bamum were converted following their ruler's acceptance of Islam in 1918.

The most pervasive single group of agents in this process of Islamisation were the Sufi brotherhoods. Superficially, the brotherhoods represented simply a set litany and disciplined prayer-response which, if fulfilled with other prescriptions of the order, generally assured the believer a place in the world to come. In practice, the brotherhoods frequently linked ethnic groups and intellectual traditions, and provided tangible evidence of Pan-Islamic ties for members. In the face of rapid social change during the colonial era, they became increasingly important in urban centres, and they also provided a migrant or traveller with credentials that might link him to fellows in a stranger community.

The oldest of the Sufi orders in West Africa was the Qādiriyya, which gained widespread adherence during the late eighteenth and early nineteenth centuries from propagation by the Kunta holy men in the Timbuktu region. In the course of the nineteenth century it became associated with the '*ulamā*' class in many centres of learning such as Boutilimit in Mauritania and Kankan and Touba in Guinea, while it was associated with the ruling class in the Islamic states of Futa Toro, Masina and Sokoto. Among the best-documented of the Sufi orders in West Africa is a populist offshoot, the Murīdiyya, named after the followers (*murīds*) of the Senegalese Shaykh Ahmadu Bamba (*c.* 1850–1927), whose early career and large following brought him under suspicion among the French administration in St Louis. He was exiled to Gabon in 1895, and within a few months of his return to Senegal in 1902 his rapidly growing number of Murids led the French to exile him again, to the custody of the Mauritanian shaykh, Sidiyya Baba, where he remained until 1907. Ten years after his return from exile he was estimated to have had 68,000 disciples; by 1940 over a quarter-million members of the Murīdiyya were to be found in Senegal. Their economic colonisation of the Senegalese hinterland was inspired by Ahmadu Bamba's injunction, 'Work as if you would never die and pray as if you would die tomorrow.' It was the Murids' commitment to labour that placed vast stretches of the Senegalese Ferlo under groundnut cultivation, and it was groundnuts that provided the economic base both of the order and of the colony of Senegal. The success of the Murīdiyya can partially be attributed to the anti-French posture with which the brotherhood was associated in the popular mind at the turn of the century. Much of its early recruitment came from the lower classes of Wolof society, although nobles in the old social order soon saw the advantage of joining forces with the Murid shaykhs. The order came to represent an alternative to French notions of assimilation, a development reinforced by the increasing co-operation between Ahmadu Bamba and French authorities during the years following his exile.

One of the Murids' chief competitors in Senegal, the Tijāniyya, illustrates a more common phenomenon: a brotherhood appealing to a clientele across ethnic or linguistic lines, albeit lacking in highly centralised control. There developed in Senegal two major Tijāni branches, one located at Tivaouane and another at Kaolack under the direction, respectively, of al-Ḥājj Mālik Si (d. 1922) and al-Ḥājj 'Abdullahi Niass (d. 1922). Both traced their inspiration to the mid-nineteenth-century reformer, al-Ḥājj 'Umar. Both presided over a religious centre (ẕāwiya) and mosques that attracted adherents from throughout Senegal and beyond (totalling nearly half the Senegalese population by the 1950s); both maintained links with fellow Tijānis in North Africa and across West Africa. There were other branches of the Tijāniyya inspired by al-Ḥājj 'Umar in the former empire of Sokoto where the reformer lived during the 1830s on his return from Mecca. Disciples were initiated in Bornu and throughout the Sokoto emirates, and a Tijāni ẕāwiya was founded in Zaria, but individual Tijāni groups had little influence during the nineteenth century, when the emirate authorities emulated Shehu 'Uthmān dan Fodio's patronage of the Qādiriyya brotherhood. When the emirs of Kano and Katsina accepted the Tijāni litany from a Mauritanian holy man during the second decade of the twentieth century, it symbolised a break from Sokoto's hegemony just as it gave a prestige to the brotherhood in Northern Nigeria that steadily increased during our period. This process was accelerated in 1937 by a meeting in Mecca between Ibrahim Niass, successor to the founder of the Kaolack Tijāni *zawiya*, and the emir of Kano. On his way out, Ibrahim Niass had visited Fez to renew his father's links with Tijāni authorities; on his way home, he visited Kano, and thereafter he was widely regarded as spiritual head of the Tijāniyya in West Africa, in succession to Alfa Hashim in the Hijaz, who had died in 1931. Tijāni shaykhs can be found across the Sahel of Africa and throughout North Africa, but it is in West Africa that the brotherhood has had its widest following. The reasons for its popularity varied from place to place. It was an exclusivist order, prohibiting members from joining other brotherhoods; at the same time, in line with al-Ḥajj 'Umar's own preaching, it appealed to the unlettered folk, thus setting the order apart from the older Qādiriyya, commonly associated with the jurists and learned men in the nineteenth century.

The loose association of Tijāni leaders, the rapid expansion of the brotherhood and its popular appeal made it susceptible to a splintering effect typical of the growth and multiplication of Sufi orders throughout Islamic history. Besides the two main branches of the brotherhood in Senegal, there was another Tijāni tradition in the Senegal valley led by a grandson of al-Ḥajj 'Umar whom the French appointed as the 'Grand Marabout' of the colony. Yet another source of Tijāni teaching from the mid-nineteenth century onwards was that of the holy men of the Mauritanian Idaw 'Ali tribe. All these branches were on good terms with the French authorities, in contrast to the Hamalliyya. Shaykh Hamallah (c. 1886–1943) was initiated into the Tijāniyya by a Tlemcen shaykh and settled in Nioro, east of Kayes, at the turn of the century. His followers expressed hostility to non-Muslims and Muslim collaborators with the French, a doctrine no more acceptable to orthodox Tijāni than to the French administration. Shaykh Hamallah was arrested in 1925 and exiled for ten years in Mauritania and the Ivory Coast, which exacerbated the anti-colonial sentiments of his followers. In 1940 a Hamallist band near Nioro killed many of its rivals; the shaykh was exiled to Algeria and then France, where he died in 1943. Shaykh Hamallah's militancy appealed to Muslims who associated the privileged position of certain shaykhs with the largesse provided them by the French administration. The Hamalliyya itself gave rise to a further offshoot, founded by a Hamallah disciple Ya'qūb Sylla, who began preaching to his Sarakolle countrymen in Kaedi in

1929. His was a message with millenarian overtones, advocating absolute equality between followers, irrespective of sex, age or former social status; although the Ya'qūbiyya broke with its Hamallah origins, it joined that movement in its antipathy towards the orthodox Tijāniyya.

It would be impractical to trace in further detail this process of fission and expansion among the Sufi orders in West Africa; every major Muslim community in West Africa had its shaykhs or brotherhoods that were offshoots from the Tijāni or Qādiri orders. In the Sahara alone, a list of the major brotherhoods would include the Qādiriyya, Mukhtāriyya, 'Aynayniyya, Fādiliyya, Sanūsiyya and Tijāniyya, each with an estimated following of tens of thousands. In the Maghrib the brotherhoods were also widespread. Their importance there lay less in proselytisation than in the social and political networks which they represented, but there too their organisational structures ranged from the highly centralised to loose associations, they appealed both to learned men and to the unlettered, and their influence was as much a function of the status of their leading shaykh as it was of their numbers. Conservative estimates from Morocco in 1939 set brotherhood membership at a quarter-million; in Fez some 13 per cent of the total population was affiliated to the orders. Membership tended to be highest in rural areas and on the Algerian frontier, and nearly three-quarters of the Sufis were to be found in seven brotherhoods, the largest being the Tijāniyya. In Algeria the Rahmāniyya, Qādiriyya and Tijāniyya accounted for one-fifth of the adult male population in 1956; comparable figures from Senegal would be close to two-thirds. This contrast can be explained by the absence of alternative Islamic associations in sub-Saharan Africa; besides, the brotherhoods came under attack in the Maghrib in the twentieth century from advocates of reform and modernisation who viewed them as an anachronism and denounced them as agents of the colonial administration, with which their leaders usually enjoyed mutually beneficial relations.

The brotherhoods had come under attack in the Sudan at the time of the Mahdiyya when the orders were outlawed and their leaders sought exile in Egypt and the Hijaz. They were re-established after the British occupation of the Sudan, which was actively supported by some of the seven principal orders, such as the Mirghaniyya and its offshoot, the Ismā'īliyya. Although the Mahdiyya was not a *tariqa*, its political significance in the Sudan as a rallying point for descendants of the Mahdi's followers, and its popular appeal during the twentieth century, bears comparison with the social and religious function of the *ṭuruq*, with which it successfully competed.

On the East African coast the major brotherhoods at the close of the nineteenth century were the Qādiriyya and the Shādhiliyya. Three branches of the Qādiriyya expanded rapidly in the early twentieth century not only in Zanzibar, Dar es Salaam and Bagamoyo, but also far into the interior, where Muslim communities were already established at commercial centres. Shaykh Uways b. Muḥammad (d. 1909), from Brava in southern Somalia, was the main inspiration to the spread of Qādiri practice in Zanzibar and Dar es Salaam as well as southern Somalia; his disciples settled in Tabora, Bagamoyo and, during the 1930s, in Ujiji. A second strand of Qādiri propagation had great success in the Rufiji area, whence disciples of Shaykh 'Alib. 'Umar al-Shirazi (d. 1925/6) spread it to Lindi, Nyasaland and Mozambique. The third and perhaps the largest Qādiri branch had its origins in Bagamoyo in 1905; disciples of Shaykh Ramiya (d. 1931) carried it to Tanga, Ujiji, the Manyema region and Ruanda. The Shādhiliyya came to the coast from their base in the Comoro Islands at the end of the nineteenth century, but it was mainly through a school at Kilwa, directed by the Shādhili shaykh Husain b. Maḥmūd, that the brotherhood spread to students from Mozambique; other shaykhs in the order were to be found in Tabora and Dar es Salaam, Ujiji and Kampala. Other, smaller brotherhoods developed in the 1930s — the 'Askariyya in Dar es Salaam and the Aḥmadiyya–Dandarawiyya in Bagamoyo — but the region was dominated by the Qādiriyya and Shādhiliyya during the first half of the century. The spread of these brotherhoods took place at the same time as many communities in the interior were adopting Islam, and their role in this may be likened to the contemporary activity of West African brotherhoods. In central and north-western Tanganyika Islam was spread by Muslim traders, and just as it had spread in the aftermath of the Maji Maji rebellion, so too it spread during and after the First World War, which had caused widespread upheavals and forced Christian missions to retreat. For the recently converted, the brotherhood represented a progressive movement offering links to the wider Muslim world.

Criticism of the brotherhoods came from the *'ulamā'* and from advocates of modern reform, and centred on their supposed compromise of Islamic ideals. While some Sufi shaykhs studied and preached a highly esoteric mysticism founded on the classics of the eleventh-century savant al-Ghazālī, others also sought lucrative return in this world through their thaumaturgical services. The close association of medicine (*ṭibb*) and mysticism in traditional Islamic scholarship found expression in the Sufi shaykhs who ministered to diverse needs of their communities by writing amulets, interceding between God and their followers, or administering holy water. Such practices, like the veneration of holy men's tombs and the search for holy essence (*baraka*) and miracles (*karāmāt*) from revered authorities, were by no means new, yet the efficacy of amulets, as of *baraka* and *karāmāt*, was in no way impaired by the changed economic and political circumstances of colonial rule. Indeed, modern improvements in transport contributed to the popularity of visiting particular holy men, and such shrines as the tombs of Abdullah Abdu-Salam at Cape Town; Muhammad al-Fāḍil (father of Saʿad Bū and Māʾ al-ʿAynayn and founder of the Fāḍiliyya) in the southern Sahara near Walata; or Ahmad al-Tijāni at Fez.

The colonial peace and the advent of mechanical transport also contributed to the growing importance of pilgrimage (*ḥajj*) to Mecca and Medina which every Muslim is enjoined to perform once in his lifetime. During the nineteenth century, caravans linked West and North African communities with the Hijaz, providing opportunities for the wealthy and pious to make the sometimes hazardous journey which could take two to ten years to complete, and these continued into the twentieth century. One representative account from Chad in 1905 reported a caravan of 700 pilgrims that had been collecting travellers since its departure from Timbuktu the previous year; in 1909 five caravans passed through Fort Archambault. Records from the Ottoman health authorities in 1905–6 show 2,300 pilgrims from Morocco, Algeria and Tunisia and indicate that of the total number of 70,000 pilgrims over one-third entered Arabia from Africa. In 1925 an administrator in the Sudan estimated that there might be some 25,000 West African pilgrims in transit. Colonial authorities tried to limit the number of pilgrims, warning them of the dangers of the journey and of the presence of Africans in servitude in the Hijaz. Nevertheless, when the *ḥajj* was prohibited in 1940 as a result of the war, it was commonplace to find *ḥajjis* in most of the large Islamic communities of the continent. By the 1930s the British had begun to subsidise the *ḥajj* for select local dignitaries, a practice that dated from the nineteenth century in francophone Africa.

The importance of *ḥajj* extended far beyond the status which it offered to select, usually already wealthy men and women upon their return home, and the Pan-Islamic contacts it fostered, not only in the Hijaz but in Khartoum and Tunis, Cairo, Fez and Zanzibar. As the number of pilgrims increased from West Africa, so too did the number of West Africans settled along the pilgrimage route, particularly from Maiduguri, west of Lake Chad, to Port Sudan. These settlements, in turn, facilitated and benefited from the overland pilgrimage, as did the community of several thousand permanently settled Africans in the Hijaz. As the *ḥajj* thus became increasingly accessible to African Muslims, so too the Hijaz took the place of Istanbul as a spiritual focal point, and from the establishment of the Saudis as rulers of the Hijaz in 1925 the exponents of Wahhābī reform demonstrated the viability of an orthodox Islamic state in the modern world.

Asian Muslims settled in Africa afforded another, albeit limited, contact between the continent's Islamic communities and the Muslim world beyond. In the West African commercial centres the small numbers of Lebanese merchants (including Sunnī and Shiʿite as well as Christian families) kept apart from African Muslims. In East Africa, on the coast and at major commercial centres, Indian immigrants, who first arrived in significant numbers during Sayyid Saʿid's reign at Zanzibar (1840–56), included Muslim communities who mostly kept apart from their African and Arab neighbours. The fragmented nature of the Indian Muslim communities restricted their influence upon Arab and African Muslims. The major Shiʿa groups included both Ithnā'-ʿashariyya ('Twelvers') and Ismāʿiliyya communities, and a still smaller number of Sunnīs; further divisions in the Ismāʿili community separated the Mustaʿli (Bohora) from the Nizārī (Khoja). This last group, also known as the Eastern Nizārī, was the most highly structured of the Indian communities; their *imām* was the Aga Khan. The third Aga Khan (b. 1877) lived throughout our period and was firmly committed to the British Empire. In South Africa, a minority of Indian immigrants in Natal were Muslims and are unlikely to have proselytised. But at the Cape, Muslims of Malay descent had made converts among other non-whites in the nineteenth century and this process evidently continued. By 1915 it was reckoned that one-third of the Cape Province's Muslim population was Coloured (as distinct from 'Asiatic'), and there were more mosques than churches in Cape Town. By 1936 there were 35,000 Coloured and 42,000 'Asiatic' Muslims in the Union. Missionaries viewed with alarm the steady communication between Cape Town and Zanzibar, Mecca and Istanbul, and in 1925 they reported the appearance of Islamic literature in Afrikaans and in Arabic script.

Indian Muslim missionaries from the Aḥmadiyya, founded by the Punjab saint Ghulām Aḥmad (d. 1908), were active from the 1920s. Fante Muslims in the Gold Coast sought help from the Aḥmadiyya, who in 1921 sent out from London an Indian missionary, 'Abd-ur-Raḥim Nayyar, who visited Accra, Lagos, Zaria and Kano. In 1933 a permanent Aḥmadi missionary settled in West Africa. The Aḥmadis in Lagos were estimated at 500 in the early 1940s; the largest community was that of the Fante Aḥmadis at Saltpond where the West African headquarters of the Aḥmadiyya was established. In the northern Gold Coast, an Aḥmadi mosque was built at Wa in 1936 and was soon followed by others. In Sierra Leone a permanent Aḥmadi missionary settled in 1939 at Baomahun, near Bo. In East Africa, Aḥmadi mission enterprise appeared only in 1934, at the request of local Indians; the first Aḥmadi mosque was erected in Tabora in 1942. The significance of the Aḥmadiyya lay in part in the violent reaction commonly aroused by the espousal of Ghulām Aḥmad's claims to be a peaceful mahdi, the Messiah and a prophet after Muḥammad. In addition to their theological heresies, Aḥmadi missionaries advocated teaching the Koran through use of an English translation, which threatened the status and livelihood of 'ulamā' trained in Arabic. Their main impact lay in their educational facilities, which competed favourably with Christian mission schools.

The Aḥmadi missions, like the expansion of Sufi brotherhoods and the increased ease of pilgrimage, contributed to a regeneration of Islam during the period between the wars which also found expression in the growing political consciousness of many Muslim communities. This was largely independent of colonial government encouragement and it evolved with little direct influence from the wider Islamic world. This development generally took the form of new urban, regional, or colony-wide associations or societies of Muslims; some were overtly political forums representing special interests within Islamic communities. On the East African coast, Muslim associations reflected the ethnic and economic divisions of Arabs, Indians and Africans. In Zanzibar four separate groups were formed: the Arab Association (established at the turn of the century), the Indian National Association (formed before 1914), the African Association (1934) and the Shirazi Association (1939), each professing Islamic ideals of unity while promoting their own economic interests. Analogous cleavages appeared in Kenya. The legislative council there included from 1920 one seat for a nominated Arab member, and in 1921 the Coast Arab Association was formed to seek elective representation. This was obtained in 1923, but elections polarised rivalries which in 1927–8 produced the Afro-Asian Association and the Arab Association. In Tanganyika tensions within the East African Muslim Association led, in 1934, to the formation of a Muslim Association of Tanganyika in reaction to Indian exclusiveness. In Senegal, Sufi brotherhoods rather than ethnicity were determining political allegiance by the mid-1930s. The return of Ahmadu Bamba from exile was gained through the intervention of the Senegalese deputy to the French National Assembly, François Carpot (1902–14), who had received support from the Murīdiyya. Both Tijānī and Murid leaders developed relations with Senegal's rival politicians; in the 1934 elections Tijānī support helped Galandou Diouf to defeat the Murid candidate, the socialist Lamine Guèye. In the Gambia, the Muslim community of Bathurst was represented on the local branch of the National Congress of British West Africa and thus formed a counter-weight to Christian Creole domination. In British West Africa the possibility of Muslim trade unions was discussed by colonial officials in 1941. Each of these examples points to an involvement by Muslim communities in colonial affairs that was a dramatic departure from earlier resistance and collaboration, even when their participation tended to be circumscribed by ethnic, economic or sectarian interests.

Another new type of association was devoted to cultural affairs. The Brigade de la Fraternité du Bon Musulman was founded in

Senegal in 1934 and sponsored by Tijāni groups who sought to promote religious and historical studies for Muslims. Of the same genre was the short-lived Mohammedan Reform League which pressed the Mombasa Municipal Council in 1934 to ban spirit-possession cults and other organisations that the League feared would corrupt the young. More typical, however, were associations to promote Islamic education, generally reflecting a new generation of Muslim leaders who sought to modernise their education along the lines of Western schools. Western Nigeria's four major Muslim communities in Lagos, Ibadan, Abeokuta and Ijebu-Ode illustrate this well. Two of the five factions in the Lagos community in the early 1920s were led by modernisers; the Lemomu group at the Central Mosque which founded the Young Ansar Ud-Deen Society in 1923, and the Aḥmadi group from which the Zumratul Islāmiyya originated in 1924. Both associations declared their non-sectarian educational aims and their desire to obviate the necessity for Muslim youth to attend Christian schools. Founders of the Ansar Ud-Deen declared their objective of 'education on Western lines; by this means alone can Islam be better studied and understood; as lack of proper knowledge of the essence of Islam and failure to grasp its spirit and correct teaching have been the greatest cause of the backwardness of the Muslim'.[4]

During the 1930s in Abeokuta a comparable society, the Young Nawair Ud-Deen, was formed to carry on the work of the Abeokuta Muslim community which opened its first school in 1920; the Ijebu Muslim Friendly Society, formed in 1927, opened its first school at Ijebu-Ode in 1930. Divisions in the Lagos Aḥmadi community in 1940 led to the break-away of a group calling itself the Aḥmadiyya Movement-In-Islam which was not officially accepted by the Aḥmadis but which focused almost exclusively on education. Some of these local societies were formed in response to the British decision to withdraw education subsidies for Muslim schools in Yorubaland in 1925; in their turn, the societies provoked conservative reform groups to organise against them. In East Africa, the movement for modern Islamic education centred on Shaykh al-Amin, son of one of Mombasa's

[4] *A review of the Society's work, 1923–1943* (Lagos, 1943), 4; cited in G. O. Gbadamosi, 'The establishment of Western education among Muslims in Nigeria, 1896–1926', *Journal of the Historical Society of Nigeria*, 1967, **4**, 1, 114.

most illustrious scholars, who began a career in journalism on the Kenya coast in 1930. It was Shaykh al-Amin's influence which led to the first co-educational *madrasa* in Mombasa, and the first government school for Muslim girls in 1938. But divisions in Mombasa's Muslim communities precluded large-scale educational associations.

Shaykh al-Amin's inspiration, and that of the Lagos Ansar Ud-Deen, was *salafiyya* doctrine, which owes its origins to the Egyptian writer Muḥammad 'Abduh (1849–1905), who was himself a student of the Pan-Islamist al-Afghānī (d. 1898). Al-Afghānī sought a reformed, revitalised Islam that would not be beholden to Western, modern trends any more than it would be weighed down by age-old traditional accretions. 'Abduh, his master's most famous disciple, taught, held influential positions in the Egyptian press, went into exile in Paris, and returned to serve in the judiciary; he concluded his career as the chief legal officer of Egypt. He argued that a reformed Islam could co-exist with Western ideas, accept their challenges and replace the slavish imitation either of Europe or of antiquated tradition with a dynamic and innovative culture such as distinguished Islam at the time of the first generation or *salaf*. Thus the *salafiyya* doctrine came to be associated with attacks on mysticism, saint-veneration, and specifically the Sufi orders, just as it was embedded in programmes for modern education that emphasised reason and rational sciences.

The impact of *salafi* doctrine was keenly felt across the Maghrib. By the early 1920s it inspired a social and religious reform group in Fez that was opening 'free schools' for Muslims and in the mid-1920s taking the offensive in Rabat and Fez against collaboration by Sufi brotherhoods with the French administration. Similar developments in Algeria led to the foundation of the Association of the 'Ulamā' in 1931 under the guidance of Ibn Badis, which campaigned against Sufi brotherhoods and for the adoption of Arabic as the official language; it devoted itself mainly to educational efforts. In Tunisia, *salafi* doctrine was disseminated in the early 1920s through the Destour party of Shaykh 'Abd al-'Azīz Taalbi. In each of these countries the *salafi* advocates had an ambiguous relationship to the emerging nationalist movements. Anti-colonial conservatives approved their counsel to return to the fundamentals of Islam but their attacks on Sufi orders and traditional education offended many; to anti-colonial radicals their advocacy of cultural revival provided common ground, yet their moderation in political affairs was a handicap to movements that were increasingly militant. In Morocco, by the late 1930s, *salafi* doctrine and leaders had largely been incorporated into the nationalist cause; in Tunisia Taalbi had been eclipsed by the formation of the Neo Destour party in 1934. The Islamic Congress of Algiers that was called in 1934 marked both the height and collapse of alliance between the '*ulamā*' and Western-educated advocates of Islamic reform; thereafter leadership in the nationalist cause passed to more radical spokesmen.

Reformers in West Africa who voiced *salafi* ideas appeared in Kano and Bamako at the close of our period, but their numbers were small and their influence slight. In Kano it was Sa'ad Zungur (1915–58) who advocated Egyptian notions of Islamic reform as well as the Ahmadiyya in the late 1930s. In the French Soudan, students who had studied at al-Azhar in Cairo, where they had come under the influence of such organisations as the Society of Young Muslims, returned to Bamako in 1943 and began to adapt *salafi* doctrine.

Other symptoms of the Islamic cultural revival between the two world wars ranged from the dissemination of printed Arabic and Swahili texts to the adoption of Muslim dress. Printed Arabic reading matter had regularly reached sub-Saharan Muslim communities from Egypt and North Africa from the mid-nineteenth century. In the early twentieth century, government presses published occasional administrative circulars in Arabic with moderate counsel by favoured Muslim holy men. It was in this spirit that the French administration saw to the publication in Tunisia, in 1914–15, of 22 tracts by the Senegalese Tijāni shaykh, al-Ḥājj Mālik Si, who was among the first Muslim West African authors to appear in print. One work by Mā' al-'Aynayn had been published in Fez at the end of the nineteenth century, and during the 1920s some of his other religious tracts appeared in Cairo, as well as the major work of the nineteenth-century reformer al-Ḥājj 'Umar. In the 1930s the Senegalese Tijāni Ibrahim Niass and Abubakr Atiku from Kano had works printed in Cairo, while presses in Khartoum and Abeokuta, Kano, Zanzibar and Damascus published works by and about Africa's Muslim notables. From 1930 to 1932 Shaykh al-Amin produced a Swahili newspaper in Mombasa.

Among the vast majority of newly-converted Muslims, not touched by the printed word, the Islamic cultural revival was identified with the adoption of the long flowing *jallabiyya* or dress commonly associated with traditional Middle Eastern wear. In areas as far removed as Nyasaland and Sierra Leone, visitors commented on the growing popularity of Muslim dress, equated with conversion to Islam; this trend stimulated cloth imports, tailoring and embroidery (which was popularised by Middle Eastern imports). There were local variations in the style or colours of customary dress, the use and styles of hats or turbans or the types of rosaries, but it is the dramatic expansion of the general style of dress during our period that attests to a popular confirmation of the Islamic cultural revival.

During the first forty years of the twentieth century, Africa's Islamic communities exhibited the full range of contemporaneous forces and contradictions at work in the Muslim world: resistance, adaptation to infidel overrule, receptivity to proselytising by Sufi orders, and a new political consciousness encouraged by both fundamentalist and modernising Pan-Islamic influences. For the two centuries prior to 1900 and independent of European contact, the Muslim world had generated numerous reform movements which sought a social and moral reconstitution of Islamic society, attacked economic and social injustices and called for political action. The eighteenth- and nineteenth-century jihads in West Africa, the Sanūsiyya in Libya and Mahdism in the Sudan were thus part of a phenomenon that included Wahhabism in eighteenth-century Arabia, the *Padri* movement in nineteenth-century Indonesia and diverse reform movements in India. It was this momentum, however highly fragmented and dispersed, that was channelled into confrontation with the West during the nineteenth century. This confrontation elicited two broad patterns of response which were illustrated with a certain irony in the fortunes of the two spiritual centres of Islam during our period: Istanbul and the sultanate under the modernising pressures of the Young Turks, and Mecca, representing the traditional values of Wahhabism. The contradictions are profound, for Sa'udi control over the holy lands and their rise in influence as champions of Wahhābi norms for tens of thousands of annual pilgrims was contemporaneous with the flowering of the modern press, nationalism, and educational ideas that were forcing secular,

Western liberal notions, first embraced on a national scale by the Turks, upon the world of Islam. During our period the common anti-colonial struggle largely overrode these divergent forces in the Muslim world.

The most remarkable feature of Islam in twentieth-century Africa has been the rapidity with which diverse communities embraced the Faith. Muslim Africa not only mirrored and shared the contradictions and vitality of Islam in the Middle East and Asia; it proved to be one of the most rapidly expanding regions in the Islamic world. The agents of this Islamisation, mainly the Sufi brotherhoods, and the catalysts that promoted it, such as better communications and rapid urbanisation, may explain how and where Islam expanded. To understand why this process moved with such vigour in such widely varying social and political settings requires, in part, an assessment of the impact of the European presence in colonial Africa. Islam was widely perceived as a modernising influence which, at least until the late 1930s, could compete with Western and missionary education systems; it was an ideology that offered believers a wider world that was not exclusively tied to the colonial order. This served to link sub-Saharan Africa to Pan-Arab issues just as it created a bridge that brought North Africa and Egypt into Pan-African causes, especially from the late 1940s onward. But Islam was also highly compatible with notions of corporate responsibility stressed in many African societies and religions, and the faith was well served by able and imaginative interpreters whose energies brought about religious change in diverse communities.

CHAPTER 5

AFRICAN CROSS-CURRENTS

This chapter is concerned with the circulation of ideas among Africans south of the Sahara, and in particular those ideas which travelled across the frontiers by which the succeeding regional chapters are circumscribed. Growing awareness of belonging to a particular colonial territory was one very important feature of our period, but the units of colonial government were by no means the only new frames for social action. They overlapped with spheres of economic pressure and religious affiliation which also created new routes for travel and new occasions for the exchange of ideas. These routes led Africans from one part of the continent to another, and for a tiny but most important group they also led overseas, to Europe and the USA. As their social horizons expanded, Africans refined their comprehension of the colonial condition and reflected on their multiplying social identities: as blacks, as Africans, as colonial subjects; as workers, soldiers, students or professional men; as Christians or Muslims; as members of tribes and as potential citizens of future nation–states.

This process had of course begun well before 1900. The great expansion of trade in much of sub-Saharan Africa during the nineteenth century had caused free Africans to move further from home than ever before. Caravan routes were extended or created. The old networks across the Sahara linked up with routes across the length and breadth of West Africa. South of the equator, traders pushed into the interior from both east and west coasts; the great lakes, and the rivers of the middle Zaïre basin, became important highways. This greatly accelerated the interchange of information, customs and beliefs between African peoples. Languages were learned, and some, such as Hausa, Swahili or Lingala, became lingua francas. Religious cults acquired new followings; wars of conquest extended fields of political allegiance; and as people became more aware of cultural difference they acquired a sharper sense of their own ethnic identity: many of the tribal names current in Africa today were invented by Africans in the last century. Meanwhile, religions of alien origin were developing their own networks in Africa: those of the Muslim brotherhoods and the already bewildering variety of Christian missions. These enabled a very few Africans not only to leave Africa (which all too many had had to do) but to come back again and share with their fellows their experience of the outside world.

Thus, even outside the 'westernised' enclaves in the Cape and along the West African coast, the social experience of many Africans was more rich and varied than European intruders commonly appreciated. All the same, the changes of the earlier twentieth century enormously extended the range of social contacts. As the colonial presence was extended and intensified, so more and more Africans were drawn into a variety of large-scale structures and developed appropriate forms of solidarity. It seems helpful here to consider four types of structure which could transcend territorial or regional frontiers: those of capitalism, those of the imperial powers, those of Christian missions, and those of higher education.

THE MOVEMENT OF PEOPLE

Networks of empire

By the early twentieth century, the pressures of capitalist enterprise had begun to draw Africans along new routes to congregate in new centres of production. Southern and Central Africa, from the Cape to Lake Victoria, comprised in effect one vast market for black labour. This was dominated by the gold mines on the Rand, though countervailing force was exerted by mines, plantations and farms throughout the region. The search for higher wages and better working conditions moved men to cover great distances, on foot as well as by train or truck, with small regard for political frontiers, despite the efforts of governments to regulate the flow. Workplaces, towns and wayside labour camps became forums for the exchange of news and ideas. A colonial labour official remarked in 1933: 'The degree to which the African is not only travelling, but also observing, is probably not generally recognised; it is, however, easy to hear a camp-fire conversation in the Congo during which conditions in the Union,

Rhodesia, Tanganyika and Angola are all discussed and commented upon...'[1] Within this great region, the incidence of labour migration was on average far higher than anywhere else in Africa. Nonetheless, other patterns of movement were also important. Cotton and coffee farmers in Buganda employed migrant workers from north-western Uganda, Ruanda and Burundi. In the Sudan, cotton-growers in the Gezira made use of workers from the impoverished hinterlands of West Africa, whence others migrated to cocoa farms in the Gold Coast or the Ivory Coast, or groundnut farms in Senegal and the Gambia. And throughout Africa the growth of exports caused harbour towns to become magnets for workers on the move. Seamen saw strange countries, and some settled abroad: between the two world wars, there was probably an annual average of well over a thousand West Africans and Somalis living in British ports. For literate Africans there were special opportunities for travel in the service of trading firms: in the late nineteenth century a few from British West Africa had worked as agents in French territory, and by 1914 one Nigerian had twice visited London on behalf of his employers in Lagos.

For most purposes, colonial government was organised in territorial or at most regional compartments. In British Africa, there was little movement between territories among white civil servants, except at the highest level. To be sure, movement from one civil service post to another within the same territory could be an important experience for Africans, and like other forms of employment requiring literacy the civil service provided opportunities for Africans to work outside their native territories. Nyasaland was especially productive of such migrants. But the colonial powers had various ways of making Africans feel that they belonged to empires wider even than the shores of Africa. The British Crown was one such instrument: the main occasions for its use were the coronations in 1911 and 1937 and the Prince of Wales's African tour in 1925.[2] Africans were occasionally rewarded by Britain with imperial and royal honours. Empire Day (24 May) was marked in schools by sports competitions, parades and concerts. Loyalty to a distant sovereign, and pride in belonging to so great an empire, were characteristic of those blacks in West or South Africa who aspired to British culture.

[1] G. Orde Browne, *The African labourer* (London, 1933), 120.
[2] The Belgian king and queen toured the Congo in 1928; the crown prince in 1933.

However, mounting racial discrimination in the early twentieth century strained it severely, and the more precise attribute of imperial citizenship was restricted to a narrow circle. Indeed, it was only France which conferred, however sparingly, formal citizenship in the sense of civil rights equal to those of natives in the metropolitan country; to be 'British subjects', as were Indians and a handful of Africans in colonial Africa, brought no comparable advantage. Blacks in British Africa perhaps came closest to imperial citizenship when in 1931 ten were summoned from East Africa to testify before a parliamentary committee.

War, however, compelled many thousands of Africans to travel in the service of empire. Before and after the First World War, Senegalese soldiers served in Morocco. In the Allied struggle against the Germans, men from British West Africa fought in East Africa; men from French North and West Africa fought on the Western Front, and black men from South Africa served in non-combatant roles. For some, at least, these experiences profoundly altered their perspectives of white rule. And for a small but crucial minority soldiering became a way of life. For them, social life was principally defined by membership of a regiment, an organisation no less totalitarian than the average mine compound but probably a good deal more satisfying. Indeed, army or police service was likely to offer the best hope of social advancement to members of the 'martial tribes' favoured by colonial recruiting officers, for in the last analysis their supposed martial qualities consisted in the lack of sophistication consequent upon lack of access to economic and educational opportunities. Recruitment ignored imperial frontiers: many Hausa and Mossi from French West Africa served in British units. One minor offshoot of war deserves passing mention here. Baden-Powell's Boy Scout movement, influenced by his experience of African campaigns, was explicitly dedicated to imperial ideals. In the 1920s it was established among Africans in West and South Africa, though in the latter country blacks could only become 'pathfinders' or 'wayfarers' and the founder himself was unable in 1937 to blaze a trail for them into the company of white Scout troops.[3]

[3] In 1938, when there were nearly 15,000 Pathfinders in South Africa, the Chief Pathfinder there was Senator J. D. Rheinallt Jones, a leading member of the Institute of Race Relations. In the Gold Coast, where the governor was Chief Scout, there were 3,500 Scouts in 1934.

Christian missionaries formed yet another new series of networks criss-crossing Africa. Some had established spheres of influence in the nineteenth century which were overlaid, but not abolished, by later economic and political developments. By 1910 the Universities' Mission to Central Africa had a base in Zanzibar, two centres in German East Africa and outposts in Nyasaland, Mozambique and Northern Rhodesia. The Free Church of Scotland had one base in the eastern Cape and another on the shores of Lake Nyasa (Malawi); the Paris Missionary Society had one in Basutoland and another on the upper Zambezi. The Catholic White Fathers were pre-eminent over a huge region centred on Lake Tanganyika. In West Africa, the Church Missionary Society maintained links between Sierra Leone and south-western Nigeria. As in colonial government, it was European management which was most conscious of wide-ranging institutional affiliation, but as Africans too became teachers and even priests they also tended to move from one post to another within the sphere of their mission. Moreover, certain missions had been much involved in the liberation of African slaves: the networks of employment organised by the CMS in West Africa or by the UMCA served to redistribute African freedmen who had been gathered by slavers from still larger catchment areas.

Links were also made in Africa with the descendants of Africans once shipped to the New World. American blacks worked as Protestant missionaries in the Belgian Congo and Angola. Elsewhere, two black American churches were especially influential: the African Methodist Episcopal Church in southern Africa and the AME Zion Church in West Africa. Between 1902 and 1910 graduates of Tuskegee, the black college in Alabama, assisted cotton-growing schemes in Togo, Nigeria, the Sudan and the Belgian Congo.

Education

For the widening of African perspectives, institutions for secondary and higher education were of fundamental importance. In our period, these were still very thin on the ground. Few schools for Africans provided classes beyond the eighth or ninth annual grade. In 1938 there were some 5,500 Africans receiving secondary education in this sense in South Africa; there were probably no more than this in tropical Africa.[4] Only in the Union, the Gold Coast and Sierra Leone did they even approach one-tenth of one per cent of the total population, and in these countries, as elsewhere, access to all kinds of education was heavily biased towards certain areas. Any school which offered post-primary instruction was likely to attract Africans from far and wide, perhaps more indeed than those who lived nearby:

Every boarding school is a cosmopolitan place, and there is no guarantee in setting up a school 'for a territory' that it will really serve that territory. Thus, too, when the little cathedral schools of the twelfth century branched out into higher studies, men in England travelled to Paris and students from Bohemia found themselves in Oxford. There is something almost sacramental in all this coming and going. It is as if a new world of thought required for its due appreciation a change of circumstances.[5]

In southern Africa, the most significant schools of this sort had been founded by the Free Church of Scotland, at Lovedale in the eastern Cape and at Livingstonia in northern Nyasaland. In 1936 there were about fifty Africans from Southern Rhodesia studying in South Africa for want of secondary education at home. In French West Africa, the most able, determined and fortunate found their way to the government's William Ponty School in Dakar: between 1918 and 1939 only 1,500 completed courses there. By 1930 British colonial governments had added Achimota, near Accra, in the Gold Coast, Yaba in Lagos, southern Nigeria, and Makerere in Kampala, Uganda. Makerere had to cater for students from all over East Africa, but Lovedale's catchment area was even larger. From Northern Rhodesia, for example, came sons of the Lozi king in 1908; some years later, a young man from near the Tanganyika border paid his way through Lovedale with what he had saved from working as a foreman in the Belgian Congo.

To begin with, the emphasis at such schools was on vocational training, but by the 1930s Lovedale, Makerere and Achimota were teaching up to university entrance standard. Lovedale, indeed, enlarged its pupils' sense of community in terms of time as well as space: a visitor in 1927, struck by its far from utilitarian library,

[4] Figures for children in secondary schools in tropical Africa would be a good deal higher, since such schools often included classes at primary levels.
[5] A. V. Murray, *The school in the bush* (London, 1929; 2nd edn. 1938), 98.

remarked that 'what Lovedale really does, whether it teaches carpentry or Latin, is to put its students into a historical succession and to give them a sense of belonging to a distinguished company'.[6] There was a 'university feeling about the place', and this was scarcely surprising, for out of Lovedale had grown the nearby Fort Hare, a university college where between 1923 and 1936 some fifty BA degrees were obtained from the University of South Africa; the first woman graduated in 1928. In 1938 the Fort Hare graduates included one from Kenya; in 1939, the first from Southern Rhodesia. Outside the Union, university education was available south of the Sahara only at Achimota, where in 1938 there were 37 students working for London degrees, and at Fourah Bay College, in Sierra Leone. This had been founded in the nineteenth century and attracted students from all parts of British West Africa; two or three each year obtained degrees awarded by the University of Durham.

The development of higher education for Africans both in South Africa and in British colonial Africa was intended to reduce the flow of African students overseas. This subject is still too little known. In 1913 about forty Africans attended a conference for African students in London. West Africans had for some time gone to London to read law. By the late 1920s there were some sixty African lawyers in the Gold Coast and about as many in Nigeria; in both countries there were several lawyers from Sierra Leone. Smaller numbers of West Africans studied medicine in Britain, usually at Edinburgh; in 1913 there were seven African doctors in Nigeria.[7] In 1920 there were hardly any West Africans who had obtained British degrees in arts or sciences, but between 1930 and 1937 there was an annual average of 53 West Africans, other than law students, at British universities; and in 1938–40 the average had risen to 71,[8] reflecting Nigeria's provision from 1937 of scholarships for study in Britain. By 1939 there were also a dozen students from East Africa in Britain, though few were black.

[6] *Ibid.*, 117.

[7] The composer Samuel Coleridge-Taylor (1875–1912) was the son of a Sierra Leonean doctor; the band-leader Reginald Foresythe (1907–58) was the son of a West African barrister. Both musicians were born and educated in England, and made their careers there; both also worked in the USA.

[8] A. T. Carey, *Colonial students* (London, 1956), 28. There were about twice as many West Indian university students in Britain in the 1930s.

Black South Africans seldom went to Britain as students; the first black barrister in South Africa qualified in London in 1909. But by 1906 at least 150 were said to have gone to study in the USA; most would have been following up contacts established through American missionary networks. One was Charlotte Maxeke, the first black woman graduate from South Africa; she went to the USA in a touring choir and in 1905 graduated from the AME church's Wilberforce Institute, Ohio. The First World War interrupted the diaspora, but in 1919 fifty African students attended a conference in Chicago at which the African Student Union of America was formed. The first Kenyan (a Masai) went to the USA in 1908; in the 1920s the Phelps-Stokes Fund helped some Africans, including three from Uganda, to study in the USA; a few obtained postgraduate teaching diplomas at Columbia University. In 1931 the white South African educationist C. T. Loram moved to Yale University, and this led to three black South Africans, including Z. K. Matthews, pursuing graduate studies there. Between 1920 and 1937 twenty students went to the USA from Nigeria; most had been sent by missionary societies to pursue religious studies. Twelve more came in 1938; most had private African sponsorship and all but one went to Lincoln, Pennsylvania, a black university whose graduates included Nnamdi Azikiwe (1931) and Kwame Nkrumah (1939). Several Africans remained in the USA after qualifying as teachers, doctors or lawyers: perhaps sixty by 1940. One who did not stay was Hastings Banda, from Nyasaland, who in 1925 had come to Wilberforce with the help of AME contacts made in Johannesburg; he studied at Indiana and Chicago, and finally obtained a medical degree in Nashville; in 1938 he moved on to Edinburgh in order to obtain British qualifications.

Most African students in France during our period came from North Africa. In the early 1920s the government of French West Africa sent 23 Ponty graduates to France for further teacher-training. It later sent nine Africans to French universities, mostly for veterinary studies; Léopold Sédar Senghor, from Senegal, was the only one to take a degree in arts or letters. Perhaps no more than a dozen black students from French West Africa obtained university degrees in our period, while in the late 1920s there were only two African lawyers in the region. It offered even less scope for African professional men than did British West Africa, and several of those who did get to France for study stayed on after obtaining qualifications. M. K. Tovalou-Houénou, from Dahomey, practised at the Paris bar after 1911, while Senghor taught at *lycées* in Tours and Paris in 1936–40. Of the many Africans who served in France during the First World War, a few either contrived to stay there, as did the self-taught writer Bakary Diallo, or else went back soon after their return to Africa, as did Lamine Senghor. In his case, as with Tovalou-Houénou and others, political activity in Europe made him unwelcome to the rulers of his own country. The same was probably true of Panda Farnana, who, like a very few other Congolese, had been taken in youth as a servant to Belgium and was there given a secular education. Farnana spent the war as a prisoner in Germany and then settled in Brussels; he eventually obtained a Belgian passport.

Language and literacy

Colonial conditions generated new routes for the circulation of people and ideas; they also fostered new channels of expression. Inside and outside school, African languages already established as lingua francas became still more important. Those languages learned by officials or missionaries acquired a special utility. Government policy in much of East Africa (including part of the Belgian Congo) favoured Swahili; missionaries in Sierra Leone favoured Mende. In Southern Rhodesia, the Ndebele were taught in Zulu, which is related to but distinct from their own language. Labour migrants might have to learn some crude language of command used by white supervisors; they would certainly have to understand one or other of the main languages represented in their compound or location. In Northern Rhodesia, Bemba and Nyanja became dominant in different areas along the railway line, hundreds of miles from their country of origin. For a rapidly growing minority, the languages of the colonial powers afforded the means to transcend African language barriers.

As the scope of the spoken word expanded, so also did that of the written word. Far more Africans read and wrote than ever before. Postal services enabled migrants to keep in touch with those they had left at home. Statistics of mail use reflect much besides African literacy, but they help to indicate its extent and growth. In 1934 the mails were most used in South Africa, followed well behind by Southern Rhodesia, Tunisia and Egypt. Between the Zambezi and the Sahara, the mails were most used in Senegal and Northern Rhodesia; they were least used in the Belgian Congo and Ethiopia.[9] Between 1920 and 1938 the volume of mail roughly tripled in the Belgian Congo, Kenya, Nigeria, Tanganyika and Uganda; it doubled in the Sudan, Southern Rhodesia and South Africa (which in 1938 accounted for 42 per cent of all mail on the continent); and increased by a half or less in Egypt, the Gold Coast, Nyasaland and Sierra Leone. A more precise, if very localised, measure of the use of literacy is provided by the bookshops of the Church Missionary Society; in 1935 two in eastern Nigeria sold 11,800 copies of Bibles, prayer- and hymn-books in Ibo or English, and 21,000 copies of other books in Ibo.[10] But missionaries not only distributed books; they also published them. In South Africa, the Lovedale mission press produced most of the 238 titles in Xhosa which had appeared by 1939, a higher number than in any other African language except Swahili.

The press

Newspapers played a large part in the growth of Africans' understanding of the contemporary world. They were likely to learn most from those published by whites for whites, but those published in vernacular languages circulated much more widely among Africans. Some newspapers were designed by missionaries,

[9] Posted letters and postcards per inhabitant, 1934 (statistics compiled by Universal Postal Union, Berne):

Europe		Africa				
France	41.5	S. Africa	24.3	Senegal	1.7	Kenya, Uganda 0.7
Belgium	38.8	S. Rhodesia	9.0	N. Rhodesia	1.7	& Tanganyika
Italy	20.1	Tunisia	8.9	Madagascar	1.0	Togo 0.6
Portugal	11.1	Egypt	5.2	Gold Coast	0.9	Mozambique 0.6
				Sierra Leone	0.7	Nyasaland 0.5

For Angola, Nigeria and all territories of French black Africa not listed above, the figure was 0.3 or less; for the Belgian Congo it was 0.14.

[10] Mary Nicholls, 'History of CMS Nigeria bookshops, 1869–1969', Ms. in archives of Church Missionary Society, University of Birmingham.

big business or colonial governments to influence African thought, but Africans too founded and edited newspapers. Moreover, most papers, of whatever kind, were platforms on which African correspondents could address whites or Africans. And the printed word, whether in newspaper, pamphlet or book, sometimes reached far beyond those who could actually read it: in Tanganyika in the 1930s, vernacular reading circles were attended by a hundred or more listeners.

Although the first English-language newspaper in Africa appeared in Cape Town in 1800, the modern newspaper era in South Africa dates from the appearance of *The Cape Argus* (1857) and *The Cape Times* (1876). The former became the flagship of the Argus Printing and Publishing Company (1889), whose shares were held by the leading South African commercial and mining interests. During the next forty years the Argus group became the most powerful publishing enterprise in South Africa and acquired every English-language newspaper in Southern Rhodesia and Nyasaland. In 1903 it acquired a substantial interest in the Central News Agency, which was eventually to establish a virtual monopoly over newspaper distribution in southern Africa.

The black press in South Africa, as in most regions, had its origins in Christian missionary efforts. Although certain African-language publications had begun to appear as early as the 1830s, it was the establishment of the Lovedale Mission Press (1861) and the Morija Printing Works in Basutoland (1874) that created a solid base for the promotion of African-language publications and for the training of African journalists and printers. The Lovedale-sponsored *Isigidimi Sama Xosa* (1876) was the first South African newspaper edited by Africans. The missions continued to expand the range and the interests of their publications, but African journalists began to strike out on their own. In 1884 John Tengo Jabavu (formerly editor of *Isigidimi*) established *Imvo Zabantsundu*, the first newspaper in South Africa owned and controlled by Africans; this was published in English and Xhosa and became the most influential vehicle of African opinion in the Cape Colony. Other African newspapers followed from 1894. In 1905 the Native Affairs Commission advised that the African press did a useful job and required no special controls; this was not wholly surprising, since three papers at least depended on white financial support. By 1912 there were six weeklies in the Union owned by Africans, and two in Basutoland; all were published in English and one or more African languages. There were also two fortnightly papers in Coloured hands.

Between the two world wars, white influence over the black press greatly increased. Since the foundation of the African National Congress in 1912, its main organ had been the weekly *Abantu Batho*, published in Johannesburg, and from 1918 this reflected the most radical opinion in Congress. When African mineworkers struck early in 1920, the Chamber of Mines tried to kill off *Abantu Batho* by founding its own weekly, *Umteteli wa Bantu*. This was edited by Africans and at once became an important organ of middle-class African opinion, but it remained firmly under white control. *Abantu Batho* survived, but its finances became ever more precarious and it was eventually forced to close in 1931. Yet, despite the onset of economic depression, white businessmen began to take an interest in African readers as a potential market: in 1921 it had been reckoned that one in ten black South Africans was literate. In 1932 a white liberal, B. G. Paver, founded the Bantu Press, a company which with financial backing from Africans launched the *Bantu World*. The editor, R. V. S. Thema, was himself a Congress member and made the paper a major forum for African writers; it was printed in several languages and in 1934 had a circulation of 6,000, which in the African market was a very large figure. However, the Bantu Press had by then been taken over by the Argus group, and the last African (Thema) on the board of directors was ousted in 1936. The Bantu Press itself took over *Ilanga lase Natal* (founded in 1903) in 1934 and in 1936 it took over a paper in Southern Rhodesia; the successor, *Bantu Mirror*, catered for readers throughout British Central Africa. Soon afterwards, *Imvo* also fell to the Bantu Press. By 1941 there were eight newspapers in the Union (excluding missionary publications) which were edited by Africans, but only three were not exclusively white-owned; two of these were published by the multiracial Communist Party of South Africa and the third was *Inkundla ya Bantu*, an English–Zulu monthly founded in 1938 (and then called the *Territorial Magazine*). The Coloured press, which had virtually disappeared between 1923 and 1932, consisted of two weeklies, the *Sun* and the *Cape Standard*. The two main Indian newspapers during our period, both weekly, were *Indian Opinion*, which Gandhi helped to found in 1903, and *Indian Views*, which was primarily addressed to Indian Muslims.

In East Africa, the English-language press was dominated by the Standard group. The Mombasa *African Standard* was founded in 1902 by A. M. Jeevanjee, one of the richest Indian merchants in East Africa. In 1905 it was sold to European owners and came to represent the interests of European settlers and commercial interests in Kenya. As the *East African Standard*, the newspaper was moved to Nairobi in 1910. With the *Mombasa Times* (1910), the *Tanganyika Standard* (1930) and the *Uganda Argus* (1953), the Standard group eventually excluded all other European newspaper interests in East Africa. But as the genesis of the Standard group indicates, there was also a strong Asian journalistic tradition in East Africa, most vociferously represented by the *East African Chronicle* (1919) in Nairobi.

An independent African press in East Africa made its début in the 1920s and 1930s. Its most striking characteristic was the use of vernacular languages, particularly Luganda, Kikuyu and Swahili. (This contrasts with the bilingual format of southern African newspapers and the English or French mostly used by the West African press.) The first newspaper in East Africa owned and edited by Africans was *Sekanyolya* (1920), a Luganda monthly catering for Ganda at home and in Kenya. Other Luganda papers followed soon after, many of them critical of Ganda chiefs and — eventually — the colonial administration in Uganda. The first African-controlled newspapers in Kenya and Tanganyika were *Muigwithania* (1928) and *Kwetu* (1937) respectively. Such African newspapers usually appeared on an irregular monthly basis and seldom had a printed circulation of more than 2,000 copies. The different languages used did restrict wider regional circulation, but editors were aware of what was happening in neighbouring territories. *Sekanyolya* was actually published in Nairobi rather than Buganda, and the editor of the Swahili-language *Kwetu*, Erica Fiah, was himself a Muganda in touch with East African events and Pan-African issues. Even the Kikuyu-language *Muigwithania* claimed it was read in the Kilimanjaro area across the border in Tanganyika. By the early 1930s black newspapers from South Africa were being read in East Africa.[11]

The English-language press in West Africa is as old as that of South Africa, with the crucial difference that it has mostly been in African hands, beginning with the black American immigrants

[11] For the press in Portuguese Africa, see *CHA*, vol. VII, chapter 10; for that in Ethiopia, see *ibid.*, chapter 14.

in Liberia and the freed slave populations of Sierra Leone. They and their descendants established newspapers all along the West African coast during the nineteenth century — in Monrovia, Freetown, Cape Coast, Accra and Lagos. These newspapers were aimed at a very small educated élite and for long were printed only in English. Several lasted only a few years, but three Lagos weeklies founded in the nineteenth century survived to 1920 or later, while the *Gold Coast Independent* continued from 1918 throughout our period. Newspaper circulation in Lagos increased rapidly between 1918 and 1923, when that of a dozen weeklies may have totalled around 8,000. Daily papers first appeared in Lagos in 1925, Accra in 1927 and Freetown in 1933. The *Nigerian Daily Times*, founded in 1926, was published by a company in which expatriate trading firms predominated; it not only made use of Reuters news agency and British broadcasts but had enough capital to modernise its format and organise distribution throughout Nigeria; it also attracted the bulk of expatriate advertisers. Two other Lagos dailies were fully under African control, but for ten years there was no serious challenge to the *Daily Times*. Then in 1937 the *West African Pilot* was founded by Nnamdi Azikiwe, who as a student and teacher in the USA had learned from radical black journalism there and in 1934 had launched a successful daily in the Gold Coast. By the end of 1937 the *Pilot*'s populist style and nationalist policies had gained it a circulation of 9,000, thereby doubling the total sales of Lagos dailies. Meanwhile there had been a remarkable expansion elsewhere in southern Nigeria;[12] by 1937 six provincial weeklies had a combined circulation of about 15,000, of which 3,000 belonged to a Yoruba-language paper (others had been published in Lagos since 1923).

By comparison with British West Africa, the press in French black Africa was a tender growth. This was due partly to the very low levels of African literacy and partly to customs regulations which favoured the import of French newspapers rather than the production of local papers. The white-owned press consisted chiefly of a paper founded in Cameroun in 1919 and papers founded in Dakar (1933) and the Ivory Coast (1938) by a firm which already had papers in Tangier and Morocco. The first African-owned paper of any consequence was the *Voix du*

[12] This is inferred from the government statistics given in Fred I. A. Omu, *Press and politics in Nigeria, 1880–1937* (London, 1978), 263–4.

Dahomey (1927).[13] In the course of the 1930s a number of papers came and went in Senegal and the Ivory Coast; most were critical of government.

Literature

Apart from the press, much of the literature available to Africans consisted of translations. Christian scriptures occupied much of the energies of missionary and African translators, and the most frequently translated secular book was Bunyan's *Pilgrim's progress*: there were at least ten African versions by 1905 and another seven by 1940. Much translation was made for the classroom and probably derived from European schooltexts. *Robinson Crusoe* was translated into Kongo (1928) and Yoruba (1933); extracts from Aesop, *Arabian nights*, Swift, R. L. Stevenson, Rider Haggard and Kipling appeared in Swahili. In the late 1930s an African literature committee in Northern Rhodesia promoted moral uplift by arranging translations of suitable black life-stories, such as those of Booker T. Washington or J. E. K. Aggrey. The first plays by Shakespeare to be published in African translations, both into Tswana and both by Sol Plaatje, were *The comedy of errors* (1930) and *Julius Caesar* (1937).

Translation commonly prepared the way for Africans to write for publication in their own languages. But these themselves were problematical. It was in the interests of missions, governments and indeed African authors to promote the standardisation of both spelling and usage. 'Standard' Yoruba was based on the Bible translation (1900) initiated by Bishop Crowther. In Nyasaland, a syncretic form of Nyanja was used in translating the Bible, and this became an accepted literary medium. Lack of agreement on Tswana orthography was a major obstacle to Plaatje's efforts to publish in that language. In 1932 a prolific Ganda writer, J. T. Ggomotoka, called a conference to standardise Luganda orthography, on which Catholic and Protestant missions had conflicting views. In northern Nigeria, in the 1930s, the government sought to propagate the writing of Hausa in Roman rather than Arabic script. In Southern Rhodesia, in 1929, C. M. Doke investigated the possibilities for unifying Shona dialects, and in 1930 a committee was formed in East Africa to advance the use of the

---

[13] See *CHA*, vol. VII, chapter 7, pp. 389–90.

Zanzibar dialect of Swahili, though neither venture bore any early literary fruit.

African writing in the earlier twentieth century included work in the established literary languages of Africa, literary adaptations of oral performances, and ventures into genres derived from Europe. In parts of West Africa, and in Somalia, poetry continued to be written in Arabic and sometimes achieved, through printing, a wider circulation than hitherto. Verse chronicles, in an Islamic didactic tradition but about recent events rather than legends or holy men, were written in Swahili early in the century and in Hausa in the 1920s. Little Swahili verse was written outside Lamu between the world wars, though singer-poets flourished in popular musical clubs along the coast. Imaginative writing in languages other than those with a Muslim literary tradition was comparatively slow to develop. The first generations of literate African Christians in both West and South Africa tended to regard English as the proper medium for writing, while their mission education had seldom introduced them to much fiction or poetry in English. It was thus very significant that the Paris Missionary Society in Basutoland should from the end of the nineteenth century have published literary versions by African teachers of Sotho stories, praise poems and proverbs. A Sotho translation of *Pilgrim's progress* had appeared in 1872, and this provided a model for more ambitious ventures, notably the first novel, written in 1906, by Thomas Mofolo. Mofolo went on to write a historical novel, about Shaka, and this was emulated by other black South African writers.[14] Imaginative writing in Xhosa, which was mostly published by the Lovedale Press, flourished especially in the 1920s; in Zulu and Tswana, such writing first began to appear in the 1930s. Elsewhere in non-Muslim Africa, imaginative writing in the vernacular was essentially a development of the 1930s, apart from some stories in Amharic and Twi, and poems in Yoruba. A major stimulus was provided by the International African Institute, which from 1930 held competitions to encourage vernacular writing. In East and Central Africa, this had little result in terms of publications: one novel in Swahili and another in Nyanja, but nothing at all in Shona. The West African coast

[14] Thomas Mofolo, *Moeti oa bochabela* (1912; written 1906); tr. as *The traveller of* [sic] *the east* (London, 1934); *Chaka: an historical romance* (1925; written 1906); tr. F. H. Dutton (London, 1931); tr. Paris, 1939.

yielded one novel in Ibo and another in Efik; some verse in Efik and Twi; two novels and a collection of stories in Yoruba; most was achieved in Fante. Meanwhile, in Muslim northern Nigeria, an official literature bureau encouraged and published several Hausa writers of prose fiction and in 1939 founded the first Hausa newspaper.

Writing in prose, for instruction rather than recreation, had a long ancestry in Muslim Africa; in our period it flourished chiefly in Senegal, especially among members of the Tijānī brotherhood. The historical work of one convert, Sultan Njoya of Bamum, in Cameroun, is of particular interest in that it was first composed in an ideographic script invented by his councillors and then translated into a secret language fabricated from the vernacular, German and French. By the late nineteenth century, Christian Africans were pioneering the recording of oral historical traditions. Yoruba historians published in both Yoruba and English; great influence was exerted by Samuel Johnson's *The history of the Yorubas* (1921). History was often mingled with autobiography and pressed into the service of local politics: in Buganda, much controversy was provoked by the work of Sir Apolo Kagwa. Few Africans, however, concerned themselves with the history of ethnic groups quite different from their own; special interest therefore attaches to the work of E. F. Tamakloe, a government clerk from the coast of Togoland who carefully recorded traditions of the Dagomba state.

Most work of this kind, like the parallel efforts of missionaries, owed more to its oral sources, and to Christian scripture, than to any acquaintance with European secular literature. This after all was confined to a very small readership. (Even this had little opportunity in Africa to extend such acquaintance: in the Transvaal a Carnegie Non-European Library was established in 1931, but elsewhere public libraries open to Africans were first developed some years later.) Extended works of non-fiction other than history were usually written in European languages and, with few exceptions, were produced in our period only on the west coast and in South Africa. More will be said of these later, but it may be noted here that in French black Africa at least a dozen Africans published dictionaries, grammars and ethnographic studies during our period, while in the Gold Coast grammars were compiled by Tamakloe and Akrofi. By 1940 three students from tropical Africa had obtained doctorates from British universities.[15] One Senegalese, Lamine Guèye, obtained a doctorate in law. Two eminent Africans were prevented by public service from completing doctoral theses. J. E. K. Aggrey (1875–1927) qualified in 1923 to submit a thesis on education to Columbia University but then resumed his work for the Phelps-Stokes Commission before joining the teaching staff at Achimota. Z. K. Matthews received a grant from the IAI in 1935 for research in social anthropology in Bechuanaland, but while teaching at Fort Hare he was appointed to the De la Warr commission on higher education in East Africa.

In English-speaking Africa, English was little used for imaginative writing. Casely Hayford's *Ethiopia unbound* (1911) is less a novel than a series of ruminations tied by a loose narrative thread. Black South Africans published some English poetry in magazines. The only real works of fiction in English by Africans during our period came also from South Africa: Sol Plaatje's historical novel *Mhudi* (written around 1920, though not published until 1930), a story by Rolfes Dhlomo (1928) and a play by Herbert Dhlomo (1936).[16] Outside English-speaking Africa, writing by Africans was almost wholly in European languages. By and large, French and Portuguese authorities did not favour the literary use of the vernacular, and they exercised much control over education. In the French territories, Africans wrote either in languages such as Wolof, with a Muslim literary tradition, or else in French. Apart from a Bambara dictionary, and versions of folk tales, the first book in French by an African writer since the 1850s was Bakary Diallo's autobiographical novel (1926); this was probably ghosted. A teacher in Dahomey, Félix Couchoro, published a novel in 1929; Ousmane Diop, a Senegalese university graduate, published a novel of town life in 1935 and a collection of folk tales in 1938, when Paul Hazoumé produced a historical novel based on his academic researches into pre-colonial Dahomey. In the mid-1930s, students at William Ponty were encouraged to make dramatic versions in French of folklore and dances from their home areas; some of these were produced and published in Paris. By 1939

[15] J. B. Danquah (London, 1927); A. K. Nyabongo (Oxford, 1939); N. A. Fadipe (London, 1940).

[16] Robert Grendon (*c.* 1867–1949), a Coloured teacher, is known to have written much in English that may yet be discovered.

African writers in the Ivory Coast had formed a touring company to perform their own plays. In Equatorial Africa, a black official from Martinique, René Maran, expressed his disgust with economic exploitation in a novel, *Batouala*, which in 1921 won the Prix Goncourt. Nothing of consequence by Africans in the Belgian Congo was published in our period, but in 1934 a *mestiço* in Angola, Assis Junior, published a novel and meanwhile, among the *mestiço*s in the Cape Verde Islands, there was a literary revival, expressed chiefly in poetry; the merits of the local Creole language were reasserted.

Music and dance

Whereas the written word, even in the vernacular, could seldom reach far beyond an educated minority, the performing arts had a much wider appeal. Poetry for oral declamation continued not only to be composed but to exert influence on belief and action: Muḥammad ʿAbdallāh Ḥasan, in Somalia, and Isaiah Shembe, in Zululand, were poets as well as prophets.[17] The prestige of Hausa emirs continued to be reinforced by court musicians. Elsewhere, African priests and rulers often found it hard to maintain traditions of sacred and ceremonial music in face of economic and missionary pressures. But Africans also made music for recreation which, free from ties to specific institutions, could more easily adapt and survive in colonial conditions. The history of popular African music clearly shows how the cross-fertilisation of indigenous traditions with alien influences could attract new audiences. This process was not new: styles in music and dance had long been exchanged and diffused along trade routes. But it was only in this century that exotic music, from Europe and the Americas, made a widespread impact on black Africa. Foreigners imported music; Africans travelled ever further afield; and as towns expanded so did the opportunities for the travelling entertainer.

By the end of the nineteenth century the church choir and the military band were familiar features of many coastal towns. Missionaries and bandmasters introduced diatonic harmony, musical notation and new instruments; black American missionaries introduced the spiritual. Africans not only performed but

[17] Shembe wrote down his hymns, and a collection was published in 1940. For the poetry of Muḥammad ʿAbdallāh Hasan, see *CHA*, vol. VII, chapter 14, p. 719.

began to compose in exotic idioms. The hymn which became an anthem for blacks in South Africa was written at Lovedale in 1897. Hymns were also composed by a Fante church organist at Cape Coast who offered postal tuition in music and in 1916 boldly but vainly established a training college 'of music and commerce'.[18] A more lasting impact was made in the Gold Coast by another music teacher, Ephraim Amu, who in the 1920s began to study indigenous music and in 1932 published songs of his own composition, prefaced by exercises in the reading of African rhythms. White missionaries were slow to acknowledge the incompatibility of European church music with African tonal languages, but imported hymnody was freely adapted in the singing of independent churches, and in many of them dancing continued to be an important form of African religious expression. Further scope for turning local tradition to account was provided by the morality plays or 'cantatas' mounted by missions and independent churches in West Africa; by using a stage, these introduced a novel distinction between performer and audience. Meanwhile, overseas influences were altering secular music. Europeanised black élites developed a taste for European and American dance music. In Freetown, one enterprising African businessman, bent on what might be called 'horizontal integration', advertised himself as an importer of music, musical instruments and fireworks, and a manufacturer of aerated water. Along the coast, from Freetown to Durban, black American sailors, and Kru sailors and stevedores from Liberia, taught Africans their songs and introduced them to the guitar, concertina and mouthorgan; these instruments were cheap, portable and adaptable to African idioms. From early in the century gramophone records began to make available samples of ragtime, jazz, 'cowboy ballads' and vaudeville songs; when the cinema acquired sound, it further extended the range.

Ghanaian 'highlife' is one well-known example of the fusion of African and exotic music. Highlife derived from syncretic popular music current on the Gold Coast early in the century. This was gradually adopted by musicians playing for the concerts and dances of the élite; they elaborated the orchestration for their popular tunes and called the results 'highlife' by way of ironic compliment to their patrons. One early highlife has been analysed

[18] M. J. Sampson, *Gold Coast men of affairs past and present* (London, 1937; repr. 1969), 149.

as a synthesis of West African gong rhythms, a local two-fingered style of guitar playing, and hymn music. By the 1920s, highlife was being played in the Gold Coast by dance orchestras, brass bands and guitar bands. The growth of highlife intersected with innovations in theatrical entertainment. It was usual for schools to celebrate Empire Day with a 'concert party', and much more than imperial sentiment was propagated on these occasions. One celebrated comedian in Ghana, Bob Johnson, has recalled that in the early 1920s 'Our teachers used to say, "Empire Day is coming. Let's learn songs"'; one was 'Minnie the moocher'.[19] Highlifes were often played at concert parties, and another popular feature was the story-teller, familiar to the Akan peoples, who impersonates different characters. Johnson studied one such performer, a schoolteacher whose sketches were supported by ragtime and ballroom music from a trap drum and harmonium; Johnson also learned from a visiting black American vaudeville team, from silent films (including Chaplin's) and from the first 'talkie', *The jazz singer*; ironically, the white Al Jolson's disguise as a 'black minstrel' became a favourite mask for Johnson. In 1930 he formed a group which performed in a mixture of Fante and English; in 1935 he toured Nigeria with a number of Gold Coast musicians. They made some records and on their return some of them toured their own northern territories. By 1940 there were several travelling groups of musicians in the Gold Coast and Nigeria.

There were comparable developments in South Africa. In Johannesburg, associations of the black middle class enlivened social functions with performances by choirs, dance orchestras or variety artistes. At shebeens (illegal drinking houses), workers held *amatimitin*, musical parties modelled on those of missionary 'tea meetings'; the women who brewed liquor for the shebeens spent their earnings on pianos and gramophones as well as silk dresses. Workers also formed clubs for music parties, and it was in these that the syncretic style called *marabi* flourished between the wars. By 1914 players with mission or military training had begun to form their own bands. In 1917 the choir of Ohlange, an all-African training college in Natal, toured several towns; its director, R. T. Caluza, 'made ragtime respectable and élite choral music popular'.[20] As gramophones became cheaper in the 1920s,

---

[19] Efua Sutherland, *The story of Bob Johnson, Ghana's ace comedian* (Accra, 1970), 6.
[20] D. Coplan, 'The African musician and the development of the Johannesburg entertainment industry, 1900–1960', *Journal of Southern African Studies*, 1979, **5**, 2, 139.

record sales increased, and gained large followings for Louis Armstrong, Duke Ellington and the black vaudeville duo Layton and Johnstone. Numerous professional singing groups and dance bands in Johannesburg performed in a variety of styles and brought together Africans of different social classes and age groups. Music, especially that of black America, reinforced the solidarity of urban Africans, in spite of ethnic and social distinctions. Whites were slow to notice the new urban music, but in 1938 one music-theatre group, the Lucky Stars, was taken to perform in London while the South African recording industry engaged an African talent scout.

In eastern Africa, the most important musical innovation of the early twentieth century was the *beni* style of dancing. *Beni* is a Swahili word derived from 'band'. Brass bands were formed in the late nineteenth century by freed slaves on the east coast. But *beni* itself originated in the competitive dance societies of Swahili towns. By about 1900 one society in Mombasa had a brass band inspired by that of the Sultan of Zanzibar and instructed by Mgandi, a deserter from a German African band. Competition bred imitation along the coast. In Mombasa, *beni* societies were élitist; members had to be sufficiently prosperous to afford the uniforms which became obligatory. But in the coastal towns of German East Africa *beni* became the focus of competition between élite and popular societies. Clerks and labour migrants both spread *beni* to towns up-country along the lines of Swahili penetration in the previous century. Local societies paid travelling musicians to teach them the latest tunes, some composed by Mgandi. In this way, *beni* generated a network of communication which not only ignored tribal distinctions but spanned one very large colonial territory. Moreover, since *beni* societies drew together Africans in towns it was natural that they should concern themselves not only with entertainment but also with welfare: dance teams gave rise to friendly societies. Mass conscription in the First World War disrupted the organisation of *beni*, but also diffused it into rural Tanganyika, to Nairobi, the eastern Congo, Nyasaland and the Rhodesias. As *beni* spread, it moved far from its origins in brass bands: the characteristic features were rhythms and dance routines which evoked (by way of both parody and emulation) the white man's language of gesture. Multiple cross-rhythms contrived to suggest 'European-sounding rhythm... Each drum and the song are in strict relation to each other, and yet, as it were, mutually independent, going on their own ways and preserving an individual freedom.'[21] By the 1930s *beni* was yielding in parts of Central Africa to other, though similar, dance modes, such as *kalela* or *mganda*. In Tanganyika, the coastal élite discarded it in favour of *dansi*, a style modelled on ballroom dancing which made use of accordion and guitar and which had been derived in the 1920s from Christian freedmen in Mombasa. By the end of our period, a jazz band had been formed in Dar es Salaam, and the first records of black music made in South Africa were on sale there.

Art

Our knowledge of the history of plastic art in black Africa before the 1950s is still more patchy than that of musical history. Art, as well as music, had long been associated with kingship, and in parts of West Africa at least royal patronage persisted. The doors and pillars of Yoruba palaces were elaborately carved by several artists, some of whom belonged to an *atelier* of master and apprentices. The Benin brassworkers' guild survived and in 1926 admitted the first member not to belong to one of the traditional guild families. Much carved furniture was made between the wars for royalty in Abomey. In Bamum, the philosopher-king Njoya appointed an artist to his school in 1908, and in 1918 commissioned him to build a new palace. Nor were royals the only African patrons. Wealthy Yoruba commoners built stately houses, adorned with cement sculpture, in a style introduced by former slaves repatriated from Brazil. In eastern Nigeria, Christian Ibibio began in the 1920s to build elaborate funerary monuments in cement.

But in several ways colonial rule had done much damage. Most pervasive were the economic pressures. Imports of tools, domestic utensils and fabrics undermined local crafts, even if these were in places more resilient than is sometimes supposed. The need to work for the convenience of white people deprived men and women of the time and opportunity to learn and practise arts and

---

[21] A. M. Jones, 'African music: the *mganda* dance', *African Studies*, 1945, **4**, 4, quoted by T. O. Ranger, *Dance and society in Eastern Africa, 1890–1970: the Beni 'ngoma'* (London, 1975), 73. See also *CHA*, vol. VII, chapter 13, p. 670.

crafts. Besides, some areas had lost much of their artistic heritage to museum collectors: Frobenius was criticised for this in 1914 by van Gennep. (In Belgium, in 1925, the Congolese Panda Farnana attacked the white theft of African art and called for local museums in Africa.) Cults and societies which had patronised artists were liable to fall foul of suspicious governments and missionaries. Controls on the ivory trade struck at the use of an important medium for carving. In the Belgian Congo, want of ivory ended a major artistic tradition among the Lega and caused two artists elsewhere to take up watercolours; in this new medium they gained a *succès d'estime* among Europeans but by 1936 one of them, Lubaki, was too poor to buy his imported materials.

Here and there, white tourists and local residents began to provide a new sort of market, not indeed for art but for stereotyped souvenirs. Woodcarving among the Kamba of Kenya seems to have begun during the First World War with Mutisya Munge, who learned his craft while a conscript in Dar es Salaam. Back at home, he began selling his work on the streets of Nairobi and founded a family business. In Gabon, in the 1920s, an official encouraged his African neighbours to make souvenirs from the local steatite. In Northern Rhodesia the peoples of the upper Zambezi were selling 'curios' near the Victoria Falls in the 1930s.

By this time, there were forces making for a revival of traditional artistic skills. The apostolic delegate to the Belgian Congo, Mgr Dellepiane, promoted the use of African art in churches. Some colonial authorities tried to repair artistic traditions by engaging Africans to teach arts and crafts in schools: one was Makerere and another was Achimota. Finally, Europeans began to give publicity not only to African are but to living African artists: watercolours from the Belgian Congo were exhibited in Europe from 1929 and in 1938 the work of the young Nigerian painter and sculptor Ben Enwonwu was seen in England for the first time. Colonial models and networks were beginning to affect African art, as they had for some time affected African music and literature, though the results by 1940 were still too slight and scattered to admit of useful generalisation.

THE CRITIQUE OF COLONIALISM

The scale on which Africans exchanged ideas and the means by which they did so clearly changed greatly during our period. It remains to be seen what sort of messages were conveyed. Africans underwent a wide variety of new experiences, for which they sought explanations; they encountered new problems for which they sought solutions. At every point, social change presented challenges to African ideas of justice and propriety. Colonial rule and capitalism created opportunities for some, but for many they disrupted accustomed ways of earning a livelihood; they spread disease and aggravated jealousy and greed. Christianity claimed to offer salvation to all, but in practice could easily seem indifferent to African worries, contemptuous of African custom, and pre-occupied with perpetuating white domination. The white man's schools and hospitals displayed new kinds of knowledge which clearly commanded respect, but whether Africans could take what they wanted was not at all obvious. Few disputed that in colonial conditions the new kind of education was essential to political maturity, but the painstaking efforts of Africans to 'improve' themselves seemed more often to lower than to raise them in the white man's esteem.

It was nothing new for African artists to be social critics, but colonial rule gave their comments a new edge. African kings and chiefs were especially vulnerable; they were the most easily identified agents of alien regimes whose protection they too often exploited for personal advantage. In Nigeria, in the 1920s, the king of Oyo banned a travelling theatre troupe because its performances at religious festivals satirised the royal household. In 1934 the Yoruba poet Ajisafe criticised the late king of Abeokuta in a verse biography. In southern Africa the 'praise poem' was a medium for much more than mere encomium. When the Prince of Wales visited South Africa in 1925, the Xhosa poet Mqhayi sarcastically apostrophised 'Great Britain of the endless sunshine...You sent us the light, we sit in the dark...'[22] Among the Chopi of southern Mozambique most large villages had their own xylophone bands, and these performed with singers who voiced topical concerns. Comments on local intrigue and scandal

[22] Quoted in A. C. Jordan, 'Towards an African literature: II. Traditional poetry', *Africa South*, 1957, **2**, 1, 104–5.

were overshadowed by the all-pervasive theme of Chopi life: labour migration to the Rand. Songs recorded in the early 1940s told of women lamenting their absent menfolk, of men fearing the labour recruiter, of venal mine policemen and mineworkers crippled for life. Chopi continued to play and sing on the mines (one in ten there was a performer), though the mingling of different village traditions created tuning problems. In central Mozambique, music expressed the suffering of plantation workers on the lower Zambezi. One song which originated in the 1890s spread widely in different versions, and came to involve dancing and drumming. The song denounced and satirised the brutal regime of a monopolist sugar company; more than that, it preserved for singers, who in most respects were creatures of the company, 'one small region of the mind which refuses to capitulate completely'.[23]

Ideas about health and healing were central to African thinking about white rule. Some insight into popular attitudes may be gained from a play by the Zulu writer Herbert Dhlomo which he wrote in the 1930s and called simply 'Malaria'. He blamed white penetration for the spread of diseases into the African countryside and significantly made the central character at once a dispenser of western medicine and a traditional healer who has the qualities of a saint.[24] This epitomised the eclectic approach of Africans to western medicine. It was commonly seen as a useful adjunct to customary techniques but inadequate insofar as it predicated a separation between body and mind. Christian missionaries might pay lip-service to the integration of spiritual and physical healing, but to achieve this in practice Africans were often obliged to form churches of their own.[25] A concept of wholeness which encompassed not only human nature but the entire natural world lay at the root of beliefs in witchcraft, and much discontent with colonial conditions was expressed in the idiom of witchcraft fears. In Central Africa, these came to a head in the 1930s and in part reflected the impact of the depression. In earlier years, villages had been drained of young men; now they were thrown

[23] Leroy Vail and Landeg White, 'Plantation protest: the history of a Mozambican song', *Journal of Southern African Studies*, 1978, **5**, 1, 25.
[24] Shula Marks, 'Approaches to the history of health and health care in Africa', unpublished seminar paper, SOAS, 23 February 1983. For the actual spread of malaria in Zululand at this time, see above, p. 17.
[25] Cf. chapter 3.

out of work and began to come home, but their values were no longer those of the village. Witch-finders roamed far and wide, offering to rid the land of witchcraft once and for all. Nor was this the only millennial prospect to seize the imaginations of migrant workers and their families. Well before 1914, the doctrines of the Watch Tower Bible and Tract Society had begun to spread northwards from the Cape along the migrant labour routes. Its literature, imported from New York, was eagerly studied by clerks and other literate Africans on the mines in the Rhodesias; applying it to their own situation, they looked forward to an imminent last judgement in which blacks, not whites, would be saved. Between the wars, these beliefs, sometimes mingled with action against witches, gave rise to several movements of popular protest in Central Africa.[26]

Much African social thought crystallised around town and tribe. The moral threat posed by town life, especially in the conditions of acute deprivation that were usual for Africans, was an obvious theme for early African writers of fiction. Tales of the triumph of rustic simplicity and virtue won the approval of missionary patrons, while they provided an excuse to describe dangers endured and delights forsworn. One such story by a Xhosa writer was thought so edifying that it was translated into Swahili and English.[27] The Senegalese writer O. S. Diop produced a sophisticated variant of this theme; in his novel *Karim* (1935) the values of the new capital, Dakar, are contrasted with those of the old town of St Louis, by then something of a backwater. Most adult Africans, however, had been raised in the countryside. It was rural tradition which they contrasted with their urban experience and indeed with all the white man's innovations. Inevitably, those who were most articulate were also the least representative of 'traditional' Africa: it was mission-educated writers who in South Africa in the 1930s used the play or the novel to debate ethical conflicts between the community and the individual, or the competing imperatives of polygamy and Christian marriage. But such debate did not necessarily involve any simple equation between 'traditional' communities and backwardness. The all-too-evident failings of the colonial town as a form of

[26] *Ibid.*; and cf. *CHA*, vol. VII, chapter 12, pp. 618, 622–3, 645–7.
[27] E. S. Guma, *U-Nomalizo* (Lovedale, 1918); tr. S. J. Wallis, *Nomalizo, or The things of this life are sheer vanity* (London, 1928).

community were themselves one reason for a growing sense of attachment to tribe: for migrant workers, fellow-tribesmen were a source of help while away from home and of social security back at home when no longer employed. Missionaries and colonial officials might have reservations about some 'tribal' customs but, in English-speaking Africa at least, there was a widespread consensus among whites that African progress should be rooted in the countryside. To a large extent, literate Africans were willing to accept this. It is an educated chief who is the protagonist of *Ingqumbo yeminyanya* ('The wrath of the ancestors') (1940), a novel in Xhosa by A. C. Jordan. The tribe, indeed, could be seen as at once the repository of ancient wisdom and a vehicle for social improvement and uplift in the best modern way.

This belief informed much African writing between the wars. It inspired the first Kikuyu newspaper, *Muigwithania*, whose first editor, Johnstone Kenyatta, visited London in 1929–30 in an attempt to defend Kikuyu interests in discussions about East Africa's future. He made a second such visit in 1931 (sailing on a ship named *Mazzini*) and remained in Europe for the rest of the decade. In 1936–7 he took part in Malinowski's seminar for social anthropologists and wrote a study of Kikuyu customs, *Facing Mount Kenya* (1938), under a new first name, Jomo. This book offered a deeply romantic and partisan vision of pre-colonial society which concluded by accusing Europeans of robbing Africans of the material foundations of their culture. Much the same point was made by a very different writer, Martin Kayamba, the most senior African civil servant in Tanganyika and a loyal Anglican. No less than the footloose Kenyatta, Kayamba thought that Africans should be allowed to decide for themselves what to take from Europe. In his book *African problems*, written in 1937, Kayamba perceived three kinds of threat to the good society in Africa: ill-considered meddling by missionaries, migrant labour, and landlessness caused both by white settlers and by the growth of African commercial farming. He called for 'the development of tribal industries and agriculture in their own home areas so that Africans can possess an economic status of their very own'.[28] The cure might seem naively utopian but the diagnosis was clear-sighted and forthright. It is not surprising that Kayamba should idealise village life, for he had no first-hand acquaintance with it:

[28] Martin Kayamba, *African problems* (London, 1948), 93.

his father had been a mission teacher (and had even been to school in England). But the idealisation of pre-colonial Africa was characteristic of many African writers who, like Kayamba or Kenyatta resented the cultural arrogance of the white man. History could restore a people's dignity, whether it was presented in the guise of fiction (as by Sol Plaatje or Rolfes Dhlomo in South Africa), through records of proverbs or traditional narratives, or through studies of law and custom (as by J. Mensah Sarbah and J. B. Danquah in the Gold Coast, or J. H. Soga among the Xhosa).

In cultivating the sentiment of tribe, Africans were liable to be no more disinterested than were colonial officials. The promotion of tribal unity could usefully obscure or deflect emergent feelings of class conflict. The educated defenders of Kikuyu culture were in fact less truly radical than Martin Kayamba, insofar as they were allied to chiefs and others bent on accumulating land for commercial gain. Similar alliances between old and new wealth and leadership could be cited from the Gold Coast or Zululand between the wars. But in the larger towns Africans with wealth or education above the average were keenly aware of belonging to a distinctive social class with few precedents in pre-colonial Africa. This was most obvious on the West African seaboard and in South Africa. It found expression in the biographical entries to Macmillan's *Red book of West Africa* (1920), M. J. Sampson's *Gold Coast men of affairs* (1937), Mweli Skota's *African yearly register* (*c.* 1931) and Mancoe's *Bloemfontein Bantu and Coloured people's directory* (1934). These books, indeed, provide black Africa's most revealing 'self-image' of a middle class between the wars: Egypt was as yet the only part of the continent where the novel performed this function.[29] But the aspirations to 'respectability' which are so eloquently and indeed poignantly concentrated in these works of reference were voiced in many places. In 1920 literate Africans on the Rand argued in defence of wage claims that they needed 'all the things practically required by the European'.[30] In 1925 African civil servants in Tanganyika told their new governor, 'Civilisation means one to have enough money to meet his ends...just to keep him up to date in the class

[29] Cf. M. H. Haykal, *Zaynab* (Cairo, 1913), and Roger Allen, *The Arabic novel* (Manchester, 1982).
[30] Quoted by P. Bonner, 'The Transvaal Native Congress, 1917–1920', in S. Marks and R. Rathbone (eds.), *Industrialisation and social change in South Africa* (Harlow, 1982), 277.

and company he belongs to...'[31] In many parts of Africa teachers, clerks and traders formed local 'welfare associations', 'progress unions' or youth clubs. Urban black élites developed distinctive tastes, not only in dance and music but in drink, in dress and in styles of house-building. Their members often intermarried, and they set great store by education: some of the richest West Africans sent their children to school in England. By 1920 more than two hundred Africans in the Gold Coast owned motor-cars. Pride in social achievement was recorded in photographs for newspapers and family albums; in West Africa, several Africans became professional photographers.

Within the ranks of a very broadly defined 'middle class', a commitment to particular occupations was beginning to emerge. Civil servants were among the first Africans to form professional associations, since relatively large numbers shared a common employer. Teachers were mostly divided by affiliations to different missions, but associations of African teachers were formed in all four provinces of South Africa, and by 1934 three produced their own magazines. Inevitably, the growth of professional solidarities was handicapped by the reluctance of governments — in tropical as in southern Africa — to allow blacks to threaten white jobs: even in West Africa, few Africans became doctors or engineers. It was these obstacles, as much as hope of private gain, which caused ambitious West Africans to enter the legal profession: its practice did not depend upon government employment (which in any case was seldom offered to black lawyers). Even so, the scope of lawyers in colonial courts was severely restricted, and in Nigeria this became the object of a campaign for legal reform which gave rise in the 1920s not only to professional associations but to a law journal. Meanwhile, West African businessmen also combined to advance their interests. Cocoa farmers tried to raise cocoa prices by forming associations, while efforts were made to unite farmers and African traders in challenging the hegemony of European trading firms, though these foundered on the inherent conflict of interest between producer and trader.[32]

There were also signs of conflict between the African middle class and African workers. Little is known of African employers, since most were in the countryside and escaped the attention of

[31] Quoted by John Iliffe, *A modern history of Tanganyika* (Cambridge, 1979), 268.
[32] See *CHA*, vol. VII, chapter 7, p. 389; chapter 8, pp. 433, 441, 443-4.

officials concerned with labour. In Nyasaland, in 1912, nearly fifty Africans signed a petition asking to be allowed to compete for labour on equal terms with white employers. In South Africa, by 1918, there was sharp disagreement within the African National Congress as to the propriety of industrial action: many members of Congress believed that workers should allow their grievances to be handled by middle-class blacks in concert with middle-class whites. In 1920 and 1934 strikes in Lagos were condemned by African newspaper editors.

However, there was little real working-class consciousness among black Africans during our period. This was due above all to the prevalence of migrant labour: long-term commitment to wage labour, and to particular industries, was still exceptional. A generalised sense of class distinction was common enough in towns. Music and dancing could express this, as we have seen; so too could sport. In Tanganyika, football clubs polarised around contrasts between the educated and uneducated as well as between different tribes. At work and along the labour routes, Africans compared their experiences and developed informal critiques of employers. Sometimes such talk led to strikes, but there was little continuity of effort. Railway unions were formed in Nigeria and Sierra Leone in 1919, but before the Second World War industrial organisation was ephemeral. In 1922, 1930 and 1931–2 unsuccessful attempts were made in Lagos to create worker solidarity across a broad front. More success attended a venture of this kind in South Africa. In 1919 Clements Kadalie, a migrant from Nyasaland who had been educated at Livingstonia, founded the Industrial and Commercial Workers' Union (ICU). This soon established itself among African workers in harbour towns, but in 1926–7 overreached itself in seeking mass support in the countryside. It gained some support in Southern Rhodesia, but there too problems of organisation proved insuperable and meanwhile, in 1928, the ICU in South Africa had split up. It is only from this period that one can trace the history of trade unions proper in black South Africa, which begins, as one might expect, with the growth of small-scale associations among groups of relatively skilled and settled urban workers, and they owed much to advice and assistance from white Communists.

Within and across the emergent borders of social class, African women created bonds of solidarity. In Lagos, early in the twentieth century, women of the élite made concerted efforts to escape the economic dependence associated with Christian, monogamous marriage. In 1907 they opened a girls' school which offered 'a sound moral, literary and industrial education'.[33] The building was donated by Mrs Sisi Obasa, who in 1913 established the city's first motor transport company. She was also a moving spirit in the Lagos Women's League, which between the wars pressed the government on a variety of issues, including women's education, public health and prostitution. In eastern Nigeria, in 1929, Ibo women protested against the failure of the colonial government to acknowledge the extent to which they had long shared power with men. In Mombasa there were dance societies for Muslim women, similar to those formed by men. In southern Africa, new bases were created for female cooperation. Well before 1914 women were active in political protest; they had to contend with male chauvinism in Congress but formed a Bantu Women's League. Women in Johannesburg, many of whom were self-supporting, were a particular concern of white social workers. Women's prayer-unions on the Rand, in Natal and in Southern Rhodesia engaged in the struggle against polygamy. But all too few African women could write; while some composed songs and hymns, perhaps the only books by black women to be published in our period were stories and short novels by Lilith Kakaza (Xhosa, 1913–14), Victoria Swaartbooi (Xhosa, 1935) and Violet Dube (Zulu, 1935). Realistically, black schoolgirls in the Transvaal aspired to be teachers or nurses, according to an enquiry in 1935;[34] in the same year the first black woman barrister in West Africa was called to the bar in Nigeria, while in 1934 another Nigerian woman had graduated from Oxford.

IDEOLOGIES OF LIBERATION

As literate Africans developed deeper and wider-ranging solidarities, they pushed further their criticisms of the social order and began to question the whole basis of white domination. In doing so, they adopted a variety of ideological approaches. Four will be

[33] Kristin Mann, 'The dangers of dependence: Christian marriage among elite women in Lagos Colony, 1880–1915', *Journal of African History*, 1983, **24**, 1, 54.
[34] Deborah Gaitskell, 'Women, religion and medicine in Johannesburg between the wars', unpublished seminar paper, SOAS, 18 May 1983.

considered here: the appeal to what may be called the 'imperial conscience'; Pan-Africanism; socialism; and nationalism. In parts of Africa, Islam was also of great importance, and its political significance is discussed elsewhere in this volume.

In challenging white domination, Africans often invoked the values of their white teachers. Christian doctrine could not easily be reconciled with racial discrimination. Democracy, which some colonial powers professed at home in Europe, was scarcely compatible with the exclusion from power of educated men who happened to be black. And insofar as whites believed in free trade and the virtues of the market, they contradicted themselves by thwarting the aspirations of Africans to own land and accumulate capital. Black lawyers, teachers, clergymen, businessmen, civil servants and journalists justifiably regarded themselves as civilised according to the standards introduced by whites and thus felt entitled to participate in representative institutions. In British West Africa, spokesmen for the black middle class pressed for the right to elect representatives to the legislative councils in each territory. This was a principal aim of delegations which visited London in 1912 and 1920, in vain appeals to the seat of imperial power over the heads of colonial governors. The second delegation was sent by the newly-formed National Congress of British West Africa and persuaded Labour MPs to ask questions on its behalf in the House of Commons. It was characteristic that when the Congress met in Freetown in 1923 a local Methodist pastor spoke on the text, 'I am a citizen of no mean city' and exhorted his listeners to appeal for their citizens' rights to the king-emperor. In fact, limited franchises were conceded to West Africans in 1923–5; ironically, they undermined the reform movement by increasing the occasions for conflict between chiefs and educated commoners in the struggle for government favours. Elsewhere in colonial Africa, Africans continued to be represented, if at all, by white legislators. In Tanganyika, in 1929, coffee-growers on Kilimanjaro were asking for a seat in the legislative council. Kayamba wanted at least an African council, a demand that was revived in the late 1930s. In Angola, in 1938, an association of literate non-whites requested representation in the governor's advisory council. In Northern Rhodesia, a government clerk began a long letter to the *Bantu Mirror* in 1939 by blaming white settlers for African difficulties in obtaining education; he concluded by wondering

whether we shall come to the time when the African will be able to represent his own interests in the high courts of parliaments and enjoy the franchise; open up farms and businesses, and be employer instead of employee; be able to tackle his own problems...He is sick of being ever a hewer of wood and drawer of water! He desires something real and decent out of life...[35]

In South Africa, black prospects of power-sharing were steadily reduced: the Act of Union prevented the extension to Africans in other provinces of the common-roll vote which some still enjoyed in the Cape, and in 1936 even this was abolished. From 1910 to 1914 a black clergyman, Walter Rubusana, sat in the Cape Provincial Council, but he had no black successor. Thus the South African Native National Congress had still more reason than its counterpart in West Africa to appeal to imperial headquarters in Britain, even though the Union was virtually autonomous. In 1914 the Congress sent a deputation to London to ask the British government to veto the Natives Land Act of 1913. When war broke out, one member of the delegation, Solomon Plaatje, stayed on in London to keep up the pressure. For the next two-and-a-half years Plaatje spoke on average twice a week about Africa to meetings arranged by church groups and other sympathisers. Meanwhile, he wrote and published a book, *Native life in South Africa* (1916), which was much the most substantial study of contemporary African conditions to be written by an African in our period. It was primarily an attack on the Land Act and embodied Plaatje's own detailed observations during journeys around South Africa in 1913–14. In various ways Plaatje set out deliberately to woo the British reader. He invoked shared Christian beliefs and shared ideas of natural justice. He emphasised that he spoke, not for the 'naked hordes of cannibals' which peopled white fantasies of Africa, but for five million British subjects who (unlike some Afrikaners) had been unswervingly loyal to king and empire in the First World War. And in describing the destruction under the Land Act of a black South African peasantry, Plaatje evoked English literary classics: Defoe's *Journal of the plague year*, Goldsmith's *Deserted village* and Cobbett's *Rural rides*.

[35] Ackson Mwale, *Bantu Mirror*, 11 and 18 February 1939; quoted by Rosaleen Smyth, 'The development of government propaganda in Northern Rhodesia up to 1953' (Ph.D. thesis, University of London, 1983), 58–9.

Black South African appeals to British consciences proved vain, even though a further Congress deputation in 1919 made a strong impression on the prime minister, Lloyd George. But meanwhile Africans had found another source of moral support: the black people of the USA. They too had suffered from the rising tide of racism in the later nineteenth century. Emancipation from slavery, and the extension of civil rights, had soon been followed by disfranchisement and segregation. Blacks became ever more conscious of blackness as a handicap; in self-defence, they sought to make it also a source of pride and strength. But over the means to this end there was sharp disagreement. One approach was pioneered by Booker T. Washington, the principal of Tuskegee Institute in Alabama, who argued that black people should move gradually forward together, making the most of what whites could offer by improving their own capacity to contribute to modern industry and agriculture. This approach naturally commended itself to white educationists in the USA and Africa, but it also had African admirers. Ohlange College, in Natal, was founded by John Dube in emulation of Tuskegee. And in James Kwegyir Aggrey the gradualist approach found an African advocate whose influence spanned the continent. Aggrey left the Gold Coast to study at Livingstone College in North Carolina, which was run by the African Methodist Episcopal Zion Church. He graduated in 1902 and married a black American: in his courtship, as in Plaatje's, reading Shakespeare played an important part. Aggrey settled down to teaching and further studies in the US, and in due course was sought out by white American philanthropists concerned to foster the education they thought appropriate for blacks in the US and Africa. In 1920 Aggrey joined the Phelps-Stokes Commission on African education and in this capacity spent much of the next four years touring Africa. His firm belief in the value of co-operation between black and white made a particular impression in South Africa, where he helped white liberals and members of the black élite to discover a common interest in piecemeal reform. Yet for many more Africans, Aggrey's counsels of moderation and patient self-improvement counted for less than his own personal stature as a black man to whom whites listened as to an equal. When he died in New York in 1927 there were memorial services for him in the Gold Coast, Lagos and London.

Early in the century, the gradualist strategy for black progress had been challenged by W. E. B. DuBois, a sociology professor who had studied in Germany as well as at Harvard. In company with other black scholars in the US, DuBois asserted the right of the most able and educated blacks to full citizenship, while also stressing the importance of solidarity between black people throughout the world in face of white domination. In 1900 DuBois attended in London a Pan-African Conference (which consisted largely of blacks from the US and the West Indies), but his most important work for black unity was done after the First World War. DuBois was sent to Europe by the National Association for the Advancement of Colored People to try to represent African interests at the Peace Conference in 1919. The attempt failed; instead, DuBois hurriedly improvised a 'Pan-African Congress' in Paris. Most of the members were blacks from the New World: there were none from South Africa or British West Africa. White observers approved the Congress's moderate demands for progressive African participation in government. The creation of the League of Nations held out hopes that blacks might fruitfully appeal to an international conscience. DuBois took a leading part in organising further Pan-African congresses in 1921 (London, Brussels and Paris), 1923 (London and possibly Lisbon) and 1927 (New York). These were hardly more successful than the first in involving Africans. In 1921 DuBois read a paper on South Africa by Plaatje (who was then in the USA) and in 1923 some British socialists attended, but meanwhile DuBois lost the support of French-speaking blacks. The congresses were intended not only to register the discontent of black people but to advance their political education; little, however, was done to spread knowledge about Africa and DuBois was criticised on this score by West Africans.

All the same, Africans abroad were greatly stimulated by encounters with blacks of the diaspora. The latter promoted the concept of black nationhood, even if the connection between this and any particular people or territory remained uncertain. They encouraged Africans to recover their own history and cultivated the myth that the civilisation of ancient Egypt was the work of Negroes — a myth to which even the normally matter-of-fact Aggrey succumbed.[36] They demonstrated to Africans what could

[36] It is, of course, no more accurate to claim that ancient Egyptian civilisation was the work of 'whites'.

be achieved, despite white opposition, in education and business. John Chilembwe, from Nyasaland, attended a Baptist seminary in Virginia in 1898–1900 and returned with two black missionaries to found the industrial mission from which he launched his tragic rebellion in 1915. Chilembwe's death seems to have been little remarked by blacks outside Nyasaland; its history was written by his fellow-countryman G. S. Mwase around 1930, but this was not published until much later. However, widespread African interest was aroused by Marcus Garvey, a Jamaican, who in 1914 founded the Universal Negro Improvement and Conservation Association. Garvey's unusual eloquence soon won him a large black following in New York, where he declared himself Provisional President of Africa. Garvey had a more practical side: taking up an idea floated by West Africans, he founded the Black Star shipping line, wholly owned by blacks on both sides of the Atlantic. To DuBois and the NAACP, Garvey was an impudent demagogue. Aggrey denounced him; and in 1924 a young Sotho student in the USA referred to him sarcastically as 'the self-styled saviour of the African people'.[37] In the early 1920s Garvey tried to settle US blacks in Liberia; this project collapsed, and so did his shipping line. But Garvey was by no means eccentric in his concern to strengthen economic links between blacks in the US and Africa. This had long been a preoccupation of his associate Duse Mohamed Ali, a 'Sudanese Egyptian' who between 1912 and 1919 had run a magazine in London which voiced the grievances of colonial peoples and promoted their commercial interests. Up to the late 1920s, West African traders made several attempts, though none very successful, to escape the hegemony of British import–export firms by selling direct to the USA with the help of black American businessmen. And while Garvey excited both traders and workers in West Africa, the writings of black Americans made a great impact on the more educated Africans. The 'Harlem Renaissance' of the late 1920s was a reassertion of the cultural autonomy of black people: its leading authors, Langston Hughes, Claude McKay, Countée Cullen and Alain Locke, made a particular appeal to black intellectuals in South Africa, where the disjunction was sharpest between white repression and black aspirations to share in the best that has been thought and said in the world.

[37] I. Geiss (tr. Ann Keep), *The Pan-African movement* (London, 1974), 489.

Black solidarity in the French-speaking world developed on rather different lines. Its African base was very narrow. In Senegal, Africans in the four oldest colonial towns could elect a deputy to the French parliament; from 1914 to 1934 this was a black Senegalese, Blaise Diagne. The black lawyer Lamine Guèye was mayor of St Louis in 1925–7. In theory, after 1912, it was possible for Africans throughout French West Africa to qualify for French citizenship. In practice, such 'assimilation' was achieved by very few, and without it there was no scope for Africans to participate in colonial politics. In any case, Paris became their main field of action. Here, after 1918, a number of West Africans met Algerians and other French colonial subjects. Tovalou-Houénou, a lawyer from Dahomey who had fought in Europe, wrote a book in 1921 which claimed that Africa, no less than other parts of the world, could contribute to civilisation; besides, he had already discovered that 'civilisation is a colossal farce which ends in mud and blood, as in 1914'.[38] Houénou, like other black expatriates in Paris, despised Diagne as a colonial stooge; he invoked France's own revolutionary and republican traditions to demand for Africans either full integration with France or else autonomy. In 1924 he visited the USA and shared a platform with Garvey; he seems to have tried in 1925 to liberate Dahomey, but was arrested in Togo. Other Africans in Paris founded a journal, *La Race nègre*, which criticised Western civilisation and industrialisation. This vein of argument echoed the ideas of black Americans with whom Houénou had already made contact. During the 1930s Paulette Nardal, a black from Martinique, ran a *salon* in Paris for black intellectuals; she also edited a journal which brought together work by Langston Hughes, McKay and Locke, the Haitian writer Jean Price-Mars, and several white students of black culture, including Delafosse, Frobenius, Herskovits and Westermann.

By the late 1930s the leading African intellectual in France was the schoolteacher Léopold Senghor. More completely than any other African, he experienced a conflict of loyalties between Europe and Africa. Such conflict surfaced among French-speaking Africans later than in English-speaking Africa: it was felt well before 1914 by Blyden, Casely Hayford and Plaatje. But for French-speaking Africans the struggle was peculiarly intense, due

[38] K. Tovalou-Houénou, *L'Involution des métamorphoses et des métempsychoses de l'univers*, I (Paris, n.d. [1921]), 59.

to the opportunities and pressures on the literate minority to become 'black Frenchmen'. As a student in Paris, Senghor did so well that he could write a master's thesis on exoticism in Baudelaire. And it was as a Frenchman rather than an African that he discovered his own roots. In 1929 he was introduced by his fellow-student Georges Pompidou to a novel about cultural renaissance in the French provinces, Maurice Barrès's *Déracinés* (1897). This made a profound impression on Senghor. Within a year or so he underwent a reaction against the cultural demands of Paris which amounted to a conversion. Just as DuBois had gained inspiration from hearing Franz Boas lecture on the kingdoms of the Western Sudan, so Senghor now began to read the work of white Africanists; he attended lectures by the anthropologist Marcel Griaule and studied Lévy-Bruhl's work on 'primitive mentality'. Senghor even took a passing interest in European racist theory, though this subsided when Hitler came to power in 1933. Like other black intellectuals in Paris from Africa or the West Indies, Senghor came to regard official French notions of 'assimilation' as a personal affront. France might make room for black Frenchmen; it would not admit that they could still be African. Senghor and his friends refused to make the cultural surrender which seemed required of them; instead, they asserted the distinctive value of black culture, for which they coined the term *négritude*. It is hard to say what impact these Parisian Africans had in Africa at this period, but the concept of assimilation was increasingly criticised in the African press in Dahomey, and perhaps too in unpublished plays performed in Madagascar.

Socialist theory was an important element in the mixture of ideas to which blacks in Paris were exposed between the wars. In Senegal, something may have been learned from the newspaper which the French Socialist Party introduced in 1907; it is more certain that during and after the First World War soldiers returning from France to West Africa brought back ideas which helped to inspire strikes at this time. Then in 1917 the Bolshevik revolution established the Soviet Union as a great power explicitly opposed to colonialism and imperialism. This was to give Communist parties considerable potential prestige in the colonial world. The French party, formed in 1920-1, soon took an interest in expatriate blacks, and by 1924 it had recruited two students, the war-veteran Lamine Senghor from Senegal and T. Garan Kouyaté from Soudan; both took part later in organising black workers in French ports. Senghor founded the Committee for the Defence of the Negro Race, which elected Lenin posthumously as honorary president. In 1927 Senghor attended the inaugural conference in Brussels of the Berlin-based League against Imperialism. This gathering included delegates from North Africa and other parts of the colonial world (Nehru came from India), South Africa and Latin America. When Senghor died later that year an obituary in the monthly paper he had founded likened him to the hero of a classic French tragedy: 'to the work of the emancipation of his race he brought the mystical stubbornness of Polyeucte'.[39] Under Kouyaté's leadership the Committee (renamed League) used black seamen to distribute its paper in West Africa, sought financial help from DuBois in the USA, and developed close links with French Communists and trade unionists. However, there was soon fierce argument over the extent of Communist interference; government harassment was intensified; and the movement lost momentum in the 1930s.

In South Africa, socialist thought had influenced sections of the white working class since early in the century. The First World War provoked a split in the Labour Party: in 1916 pacifist dissidents formed the International Socialist League, which called for class solidarity across the colour line and sought African support. One Congress member, L. T. Mvabasa, attended meetings of the ISL in 1917; a year later he told the Transvaal Congress, 'The capitalists and workers are at war everywhere in every country.' 'The white people teach you about heaven...they don't teach you about this earth on which we live...The God of our Chiefs...gave us this part of the world we possess.'[40] By 1921 the ISL and other socialist groups had merged to form the Communist Party of South Africa, which both disavowed racialism and eschewed participation in electoral politics. At first the CPSA included no Africans, who were mostly suspicious of its white leadership; Clements Kadalie decided to keep his distance. However, other members of the ICU took an interest; from 1925 the party held night-school classes for Africans in Johannesburg; and

[39] Quoted in J. A. Langley, *Pan-Africanism and nationalism in West Africa, 1900–1945* (Oxford, 1973), 305.
[40] Quoted by P. Bonner in Marks and Rathbone, *Industrialisation and social change*, 293–4.

it won some support within Congress. By 1928 the CPSA consisted largely of Africans, and James La Guma represented it in Moscow in 1927 after attending the anti-imperialism conference in Brussels. Unfortunately for the CPSA, the Comintern had belatedly begun to concern itself with South Africa, which it found hard to analyse in terms of revolutionary strategy. Policy changes in Moscow disrupted the local party. In an attempt to strengthen South African allegiance, Africans were brought to Moscow: J. B. Marks, E. Mofutsanyana and Moses Kotane attended the Lenin School in 1932–3. Meanwhile Albert Nzula was working at the Eastern Workers' Communist University, and not only as a pupil: in collaborating on a book about labour in black Africa he had much to teach the founders of African studies in Russia. Nzula, however, died in Moscow in 1934, and by then the party line had swung round towards co-operation with imperialist powers against Fascism — i.e. Hitler's Germany. For many black people, international Communism stood revealed as merely a tool of Russian foreign policy, though the CPSA remained important as South Africa's only non-racial political party.

British West African contacts with Soviet Communism originated in America. Bankole Awoonor-Renner, son of an eminent Gold Coast barrister, went to Tuskegee, became secretary of the African students' union in the USA, attended the first meeting, in 1925, of the Comintern-inspired American Negro Labor Congress and was despatched with four American blacks to study in Moscow, where he attended the Eastern Workers' University until 1928. He then returned to the Gold Coast and on Casely Hayford's death in 1930 became editor of the *Gold Coast Leader*. By then, Russian interest in the black world had expanded from the USA to Africa. In 1930 a Negro Workers' Conference was held in Hamburg and attended by Africans from each territory in British West Africa. Among them was I. T. A. Wallace-Johnson, who had as wide a knowledge of Africa as any African at the time: he had served during the war as an army clerk in Cameroun, East Africa and the Middle East, and probably made his first contacts with communists while working in the late 1920s as a seaman along the coast from West Africa to South Africa. Wallace-Johnson went on from Hamburg to study in Moscow, where he got to know the Trinidadian George Padmore, secretary of the International Trade Union Committee of Negro Workers and editor of its paper, the *Negro Worker*. Wallace-Johnson returned to West Africa in 1933 and threw himself into a variety of protest activities.[41] His efforts to realise Padmore's aim of making the *Negro Worker* a 'mass organ' in Africa were frustrated by colonial governments, and in any case Padmore himself broke with Moscow in 1934, following its rapprochement with Britain and France. All the same, a good deal had been done to acquaint Africans with Marxist–Leninist arguments and sharpen West African criticism of colonial economies in the depths of the depression.

African nationalism developed in response to the whole range of ideas generated by higher education and foreign travel: constitutional reform, Pan-Africanism, international working-class solidarity. 'Nation' was itself one such idea. In our period, it mattered most in West Africa. In the Gold Coast, national feeling was invoked early in the century by writers who chiefly had in mind the Fante people around Cape Coast, but these writers also belonged to another sort of nation: the Christian élite whose enclaves along the coast of British West Africa were linked by familial and professional ties. When members of this élite combined for political purposes in 1920, they called themselves a 'National Congress', since their own field of action was the whole littoral of this region rather than any one colonial territory. By 1930 the commitment of this Congress to a united British West Africa was under strain, and the impact of the depression intensified the shift towards a territorial focus. Economic grievance combined with the spread of education (and the growing numbers of those who had studied abroad) to create a more popular and widely diffused basis for anti-colonial protest. Coastal élites developed links with their hinterlands: by 1932 the West African Students' Union (WASU), based in London, had branches in Kumasi and towns in Northern Nigeria. There was indeed a conflict of generations: the younger men with political ambitions, such as Nnamdi Azikiwe, were more sensitive than their elders to popular discontent, less respectful of British culture and civilisation, and more inclined to see indirect rule through chiefs as an obstacle to the extension of African freedom.

African thought about nationalism and imperialism was not

[41] See *CHA*, vol. VII, chapter 8, pp. 450–3.

simply provoked by African experience; it also responded to major currents in world politics. Japan's victory over Russia in 1905 showed blacks in Africa and the Americas that economic and technological mastery need not be a white monopoly. It made a great impression on Casely Hayford, and also on the young Ethiopian Gebre Heywet Baykedagn, who returned to Africa in 1905 after being educated in Germany and Austria. He extolled the merits of bureaucratic government, but he was also a pioneer African economic nationalist. He pointed out that his country's political independence was undermined by its economic subservience to foreigners: until it could trade, as did Japan, on equal terms with Europe, it was no more truly free than other African countries. African awareness of economic imperialism was later extended, as we have seen, through contacts both with black American capitalists and with international socialism.

A further challenge was posed by the rise of fascist dictatorships in Europe. In 1933 WASU's journal attacked the degeneration of German nationalism into racism; in the Gold Coast, J. B. Danquah reprinted anti-Nazi articles by German writers. For a time it was easier to admire Mussolini, but in 1935 Italy invaded Ethiopia. The shock was felt in many parts of Africa. Ethiopia had for some time represented to Africans a potent symbol of black independence, and not simply because its deficiencies were less well publicised than those of Liberia or Haiti: it was after all a Christian state with as long a history as any in Europe. D. D. T. Jabavu, a lecturer at Fort Hare who had been the first black South African graduate of a British university, observed that the invasion had revealed the white savage beneath the European veneer. For many West Africans, the invasion called in question the superiority of Western civilisation, while Britain's failure to take a firm stand against it discredited her claims to rule in Africa as a trustee for its people's welfare. In London, a group of blacks, mostly from the West Indies, organised a welcome party for Haile Sellassie when he arrived as an exile in 1936. In 1937 this group became the International African Service Bureau, a Marxist but non-communist body which was led by Padmore and C. L. R. James (also from Trinidad), Wallace-Johnson, and Jomo Kenyatta (who had visited Moscow in 1931–2). Growing African awareness of links between colonial problems and the world crisis was ventilated in July 1939 at a conference in London that was mainly organised by the relatively conservative League of Coloured Peoples; its resolutions included demands for national self-determination. Moves towards the amalgamation of black pressure groups in London were cut short by the outbreak of war, but close ties had been formed with a variety of British sympathisers, especially in the Labour Party; these were to bear fruit when peace returned.

At the end of our period, anti-colonial nationalism was widespread among literate people in British West Africa and beginning to influence illiterate workers and farmers. Both in West Africa and in London collective action was addressed not simply to participation in the structures of colonial government but to its replacement. There was a growing tendency to regard individual colonial territories as capable of being turned into nation–states, even if the means to do this had scarcely been developed. In South Africa, the African National Congress maintained a territorial network but had been reduced to a marginal role in the country's constitutional politics, and its social base was still very narrow. In Southern Rhodesia, a Bantu Congress had been formed in 1936 but it barely contained tensions between Shona and Ndebele. Elsewhere in sub-Saharan Africa, the only territory-wide African organisation was in Tanganyika, and this was still primarily a clerical élite. Four of the men who were eventually to lead their countries to independence were still working overseas: Léopold Senghor, Jomo Kenyatta, Kwame Nkrumah and Hastings Banda. They did not return until 1945 or later, and meanwhile the Second World War had transformed the conditions for political development in Africa. Only after the war did opposition to colonial rule reach a point at which Africans were forced to be explicit about the character of the nation which they sought to liberate: was this to be a group with a shared indigenous culture (whether or not it called itself a 'tribe'), or was it to be the whole population of a colonial territory, owing such unity as it might possess to alien intervention?

BIBLIOGRAPHIES

These bibliographies have been adapted, and updated, from those in the *Cambridge History of Africa*, vol. VII. The reader is referred to this both for the associated analytical essays and for guidance concerning archives, bibliographies, general works of reference, studies of international relations involving Africa, and the literature on particular regions. The lists for chapters 3 and 4 provide comprehensive coverage of localised studies of Christianity and Islam; otherwise, local and regional studies are normally listed here only where they illuminate a topic given special prominence in the text.

1. THE IMPERIAL MIND

PRIMARY SOURCES

Rulers

Amery, L. S. *The German colonial claim*. London, 1939.
  My political life, vol. II. *War and peace, 1914–1929*. London, 1953.
Bertram, A. *The Colonial Service*. Cambridge, 1930.
Colonial Office List. London, annual.
Fiddes, G. V. *The Dominions and Colonial Offices*. London, 1926.
Furse, Ralph. *Aucuparius. Recollections of a recruiting officer*. London, 1962.
Hailey, Lord. 'Nationalism in Africa', *Journal of the Royal African Society*, 1936, **36**, no. 143, 134–47.
  An African survey. A study of problems arising in Africa south of the Sahara. London, 1938.
Institut Colonial International. *Comptes rendus des séances*. Brussels, 1894–1939 (irregular).
  Annuaire de documentation coloniale comparée. Brussels, 1928–1938.
  Recueil international de législation coloniale. Brussels, 1911–
  Bibliothèque coloniale internationale. Brussels, 1895– [series of compendia on various topics].
Jeffries, C. *The colonial empire and its civil service*. Cambridge, 1938.
  The Colonial Office. London, 1956.
Johnston, H. H. *The black man's part in the war*. London, 1917.
  'The importance of Africa', *Journal of the African Society*, 1918, **17**, no. 67, 177–198.

'The Africa of the immediate future', *Journal of the African Society*, 1919, **18**, no. 71, 161–82.

Lugard, F. D. *The dual mandate in British tropical Africa*. London, 1922.

Orde Browne, G. St J. 'British justice and the African', *Journal of the African Society*, 1933, **32**, nos. 127–8, 148–59, 280–93.

Parkinson, C. *The Colonial Office from within, 1909–1945*. London, 1947.

Pogge von Strandmann, H. ed. *Walther Rathenau. Industrialist, Banker, Intellectual and Politician. Notes and Diaries, 1907–1922*. Oxford, 1985. (With Dernburg in East and South West Africa, 1907–8.)

Royal Institute of International Affairs. *The colonial problem*. London, 1937.

Schuster, G. *Private work and public causes*. Cowbridge, Glamorgan, 1979.

Stigand, C. H. *Administration in tropical Africa*. London, 1914.

Stuemer, W. von and Duems, E. *Fünfzig Jahre deutsche Kolonialgesellschaft 1882–1932*. Berlin, 1932.

Educators

Dumbrell, H. ed. *Letters to African teachers*. London, 1935.

Hussey, E. R. J. *Tropical Africa, 1908–1944: memoirs of a period*. London, 1959.

Huxley, Julian. *Africa View*. London, 1931.

Mayhew, A. I. *Education in the colonial empire*. London, 1938.

Murray, A. V. *The school in the bush: a critical study of the theory and practice of native education in Africa*. London, 1929. 2nd ed. 1938.

Notcutt, L. A. and Latham, G. C. eds. *The African and the cinema*. London, 1937.

Oldham, J. H. and Gibson, B. D. *The remaking of man in Africa*. London, 1931.

Scanlon, D. G. ed. *Traditions of African education*. New York, 1964.

Schlunk, M. *Die Schulen für Eingeborene in den deutschen Schutzgebieten am 1 Juni 1911*. Hamburg, 1914.

Critics

Barnes, L. *The duty of empire*. London, 1935.

Empire or democracy? London, 1939.

Crocker, W. R. *Nigeria: a critique of British colonial administration*. London, 1936.

Cunard, Nancy. ed. *Negro*. London, 1934. Reprinted New York, 1969.

Farson, Negley. *Behind God's back*. London, 1940.

Gorer, Geoffrey. *Africa Dances*. London, 1935.

Leys, Norman. *Kenya*. London, 1924.

Londres, Albert. *Terre d'ébène: la traite des noirs*. Paris, 1929.

Melland, F. H. and Young, T. Cullen. *African dilemma*. London, 1937.

Morel, E. D. *The black man's burden*. Manchester and London, 1920.

Nevinson, H. W. *A modern slavery*. London, 1906.

Olivier, S. *White capital and coloured labour*. London, 1906. 2nd ed. 1929.

The anatomy of African misery. London, 1927.

Perham, M. *Colonial sequence, 1930–1949*. London, 1967.

Ross, W. MacGregor. *Kenya from within*. London, 1927.

Scholes, T. E. S. *Glimpses of the ages, or the 'superior' and 'inferior' races so-called, discussed in the light of science and history*. London, 1905, 1908. 2 vols.

South African Native Races Committee. *The South African natives: their progress and present conditions*. London, 1908.

Steer, G. L. *Judgement on German Africa*. London, 1939.

Thwaite, D. *The seething African pot: a study of black nationalism 1882–1935*. London, 1936.

Wauters, Arthur, *D'Anvers à Bruxelles via le lac Kivu: le Congo vu par un Socialiste*. Brussels, 1929.

Woolf, L. *Empire and commerce in Africa*. London, 1920.

Scholars

Buell, R. L. *The native problem in Africa*. New York, 1928. 2 vols.

Davis, J. Merle, ed. *Modern industry and the African*. London, 1933.

Delafosse, M. *Les Noirs de l'Afrique*. Paris, 1921. *Les civilisations négro-africaines*. Paris, 1925.
  Much of both tr. F. Fligelman in *The Negroes of Africa*, Washington, DC, 1931. (Reissued Port Washington, NY, 1968).

Evans-Pritchard, E. E. *Witchcraft, oracles and magic among the Azande*. Oxford, 1937.

Frobenius, L. *Kulturgeschichte Afrikas*. Frankfurt-am-Main, 1933, 2nd ed. Zurich, 1954. French tr. Paris, 1933.
  Leo Frobenius: an anthology. ed. E. Haberland. Wiesbaden, 1973.

Hunter, Monica. *Reaction to conquest*. London, 1936.

Jung, C. G. *Memories, dreams, reflections*. ed. A. Jaffé. London, 1963.

Macmillan, W. M. *Africa emergent: a study of social, political and economic trends in British Africa*. London, 1938.

Mair, L. *Native policies in Africa*. London, 1936.

Malinowski, B. 'The rationalization of anthropology and administration', *Africa*, 1930, **3**, 4, 405–29.

Richards, A. I. *Land, labour and diet in Northen Rhodesia*. London, 1939.

Rolin, Henri. *Les Lois et l'administration de la Rhodésie*. Brussels and Paris. 1913.
  tr. D. Kirkwood, *Rolin's Rhodesia*. Bulawayo, 1978.

Seligman, C. G. *The races of Africa*. London, 1930.

Smith, Edwin W. *The golden stool. Some aspects of the conflict of cultures in modern Africa*. London, 1926.
  'Africa: what do we know of it?' *Journal of the Royal Anthropological Institute*, 1935, **45**, 1–81.

Westermann, D. *The African today and tomorrow*. London, 1934.
  ed. *Beiträge zur deutschen Kolonialfrage*. Berlin, 1937.

Worthington, E. B. *Science in Africa. A review of scientific research relating to tropical and southern Africa*. London, 1938.

SECONDARY SOURCES

Germany and Africa

Bairu Tafla. *Ethiopia and Germany: cultural, political and economic relations, 1871–1936*. Wiesbaden, 1981.

Bley, H. *Kolonialherrschaft und Sozialstruktur in Deutsch-Südwestafrika*. Hamburg, 1968. tr. H. Ridley, *South-West Africa under German Rule, 1894–1914*. London, 1971.

Crozier, A. J. *Appeasement and Germany's last bid for colonies*. Basingstoke, 1988.

Gann, L. H. and Duignan, P. *The rulers of German Africa, 1884–1914*. Stanford, 1977.

Gifford, P. and Louis, W. R. eds. *Britain and Germany in Africa*. New Haven, 1967.

Hildebrand, Klaus. *Vom Reich zum Weltreich: Hitler, NSDAP und Koloniale Frage, 1919–45*. Munich, 1968.

Iliffe, J. *Tanganyika under German rule, 1905–1912*. Cambridge, 1969.

Knoll, A. J. and Gann, L. H. eds. *Germans in the tropics: essays in German colonial history*. Westport, Conn., 1987.

Kuma N'Dumbe, A. *Hitler voulait l'Afrique. Les plans secrets pour une afrique fasciste, 1933–1945*. Paris, 1980.

Schiefel, W. *Bernhard Dernburg 1865–1937*. Zurich, n.d. [?1974].

Schmokel, W. *Dream of empire: German colonialism, 1919–1945*. New Haven, 1964.

Smith, Woodruff D. *The German colonial empire*. Chapel Hill, 1978.

Stoecker, H. ed. *Drang nach Afrika*. Berlin, 1977. (tr.) *German imperialism in Africa*. London, 1985.

The British in Africa

Baldock, R. 'Colonial governors and the Colonial Office: a study of British policy in tropical Africa, 1918–1925', Ph.D. thesis, University of Bristol, 1978.

Callaway, Helen, *Gender, culture and empire: European women in colonial Nigeria*. Basingstoke, 1987.

Gann, L. H. and Duignan, P. *The rulers of British Africa, 1870–1914*. Stanford, 1978.

Heussler, R. *Yesterday's rulers. The making of the British colonial service*. Syracuse and London, 1963.

Hughes, C. and Nicolson, I. F. 'A provenance of proconsuls: British colonial governors, 1900–1960', *Journal of Imperial and Commonwealth History*, 1977, **4**, 1, 77–106.

Kirk-Greene, A. H. M. 'The progress of pro-consuls: advancement and migration among the colonial governors of British African territories, 1900–1965', *Journal of Imperial and Commonwealth History*, 1979, **7**, 2, 180–212.

  'The thin white line: the size of the British Colonial Service in Africa', *African Affairs*, 1980, **79**, no. 314, 25–44.

  A biographical dictionary of the British colonial governor, vol. 1. *Africa*. Brighton, 1980.

Mangan, J. A. *The games ethic and imperialism*. Harmondsworth and New York, 1986.

Masefield, G. B. *A history of the Colonial Agricultural Service*. Oxford, 1972.

The politics of empire

Gregory, R. G. *India and East Africa: a history of race relations within the British Empire, 1890–1939*. Oxford, 1971.

Gupta, P. S. *Imperialism and the British 'Labour movement, 1914–1964*. London, 1975.

Hatton, P. H. S. 'British colonial policy in Africa, 1910–1914'. Ph.D. thesis, University of Cambridge, 1971.

Hetherington, P. *British paternalism and Africa, 1920–1940*. London, 1978.

Hyam, R. *Elgin and Churchill at the Colonial Office*. London, 1968.

'The Colonial Office mind 1900–1914', *Journal of Imperial and Commonwealth History*, 1979, **8**, 1, 30–55.

Killingray, D. 'The idea of a British imperial African army', *Journal of African History*, 1979, **20**, 3, 421–36.

Low, D. A. *Lion rampant: essays in the study of British imperialism*. London, 1973.

Mackenzie, A. J. 'British Marxists and the Empire: anti-imperialist theory and practice, 1920–1945'. Ph.D. thesis, University of London, 1979.

Marlowe, J. *Milner: apostle of empire*. London, 1976.

Newbury, Gertrude and Colin. 'Labour charters and labour markets: the ILO and Africa in the inter-war period', *Journal of African Studies* (Los Angeles), 1976, **3**, 3, 211–27.

Pearce, R. D. *The turning point in Africa. British colonial policy 1938–48*. London, 1982.

Rich, Paul B. *Race and empire in British politics*. Cambridge, 1986.

Roberts, B. C. *Labour in the tropical territories of the Commonwealth*. London, 1964.

Robinson, Kenneth. *The dilemmas of trusteeship*. London, 1965.

Robinson, Ronald. 'The moral disarmament of African empire 1919–1947', *Journal of Imperial and Commonwealth History*, 1979, **8**, 1, 86–104.

Tarrant, G. D. 'The Colonial Office and the labour question in the dependencies in the inter-war years'. Ph.D. thesis, University of Manitoba, 1977.

Tinker, H. *Separate and unequal. India and the Indians in the British Commonwealth 1920–1950*. London, 1976.

Wight, Martin. *The development of the legislative council, 1606–1945*. London, 1945.

Willan, B. P. 'The Anti-Slavery and Aborgines' Protection Society and the South African Natives' Land Act of 1913', *Journal of African History*, 1979, **20**, 1, 83–102.

Law and order

Adewoye, O. *The judicial system in southern Nigeria, 1854–1954*. London, 1977.

Allott, A. N. *Essays in African law*. London, 1960.

Anderson, David and Killingray, David. eds. *Policing the empire*. Manchester, 1990. 2 vols.

Chanock, M. L. *Law, custom and social order: the colonial experience in Malawi and Zambia*. Cambridge, 1985.

Clayton, A. and Killingray, D. *Khaki and Blue: military and police in British colonial Africa*. Athens, Ohio, 1989.

Jearey, J. H. 'Trial by jury and trial with the aid of assessors in the superior courts of British African territories', *Journal of African Law*, 1960, **4**, 133–46; 1961, **5**, 36–47, 82–98.

Johnson, D. H. 'Judicial regulation and administrative control: customary law and the Nuer, 1898–1954', *Journal of African History*, 1986, **27**, 1, 59–78.

Killingray, David. '"A swift agent of government": air power in British colonial Africa, 1916–1939'. *Journal of African History*, 1984, **25**, 4, 429–44.

Morris, H. F. 'A history of the adoption of codes of criminal law and procedure in British colonial Africa, 1876–1935', *Journal of African Law*, 1974, **18**, 6–23.

'The development of statutory marriage law in twentieth-century British colonial Africa', *Journal of African Law*, 1979, **23**, 1, 37–64.

Morris, H. F. and Read, J. S. *Indirect rule and the search for justice. Essays in East African legal history*. Oxford, 1972.

Medicine

Curtin, Philip D. 'Medical knowledge and urban planning in tropical Africa', *American Historical Review*, 1985, **90**, 3, 594–613.

Maegraith, B. G. 'A history of the Liverpool School of Tropical Medicine', *Medical History*, 1972, **16**, 360–8

Manson-Bahr, P. *History of the School of Tropical Medicine in London (1899–1949)*. London, 1956.

Worboys, M. 'Science and British colonial imperialism, 1895–1940'. Ph.D. thesis, University of Sussex, 1980.

See also below, pp. 279–80.

Education

Ashby, E. *Universities: British, Indian, African*. London, 1966.

Ball, S. J. 'Imperialism, social control and colonial curriculum in Africa', *Journal of Curriculum Studies*, 1983, **15**, 3, 237–63.

Berman, E. H. 'Educational colonialism in Africa: the role of American foundations, 1910–1945', in Arnove, R. F. ed. *Philanthropy and cultural imperialism: the foundations at home and abroad*. pp. 179–201. Boston, Mass., 1980.

Goodenow, R. K. 'To build a new world: toward two case studies on transfer in the twentieth century', *Compare*, 1983, **13**, 1, 43–59.

King, Kenneth J. *Pan-africanism and education. A study of race philanthropy and education in the southern states of America and East Africa*. Oxford, 1971.

Lyons, C. H. *To wash an Aethiop white: British ideas about black educability, 1530–1960*. New York, 1975.

Mangan, J. A. ed. *'Benefits Bestowed'? Education and British imperialism*. Manchester, 1988.

Ideology, propaganda and the media

Briggs, A. *The history of broadcasting in the United Kingdom*, vol. ii. *The golden age of wireless*. London, 1965.

Convents, G. *A la recherche des images oubliées: préhistoire du cinéma en Afrique, 1897–1918*. Paris and Brussels, 1986.

Coombes, Annie E. 'The Franco-British Exhibition [London, 1908].' in J. Beckett and D. Cherry, eds. *The Edwardian Era*. Oxford, 1987. pp. 152–72.

Jadot, J.-M. 'Le Cinéma au Congo belge', *Bulletin des séances à l' IRCB*, 1949, 20, 2, 407–37.

Killingray, D. and Roberts, A. D. 'An outline history of photography in Africa to *c*. 1940', *History in Africa*, 1989, 16, 197–208.

Low, Rachael. *The history of the British film 1929–1939: films of comment and persuasion of the 1930s*. London, 1979.

MacKenzie, J. M. *Propaganda and empire*. Manchester, 1985.
    ed. *Imperialism and popular culture*. Manchester, 1986.

Ranger, T. O. 'The invention of tradition in colonial Africa', in Hobsbawm, E. and Ranger, T. O. eds. *The invention of tradition*, pp. 211–62. Cambridge, 1983.

Reese, T. R. *The history of the Royal Commonwealth Society, 1868–1968*. London, 1968.

Richards, Jeffrey, '"Patriotism with profit": British imperial cinema in the 1930s', in Curran, J. and Porter, V. eds. *British cinema history*, pp. 129–43, 344–8. London, 1983.

Roberts, A. D. 'Africa on film to *c*. 1940', *History in Africa*, 1987, 14, 189–227.
    ed. *Photographs as sources for African history*. London, 1988.

Smyth, Rosaleen. 'The development of British colonial film policy, 1927–1939, with special reference to East and Central Africa', *Journal of African History*, 1979, 20, 3, 437–50.

Colonial architecture and urban planning

Akinsemoyin, K. and Vaughan-Richards, A. *Building Lagos*. Jersey, 1976.

Betts, R. F. 'Imperial designs: French colonial architecture and urban planning in sub-Saharan Africa 'in G. Wesley Johnson, ed. *Double Impact: France and Africa in the age of imperialism*. Westport, Conn., 1985, pp. 191–207.

Côte d'Ivoire: Ministère des Affaires Culturelles. *Architecture coloniale en Côte d'Ivoire*. Abidjan, 1985.

Curtin, Philip D. 'Medical knowledge and urban planning in tropical Africa', *American Historical Review*, 1985, 90, 3, 594–613.

Herbert, G. *Martienssen and the international style. The modern movement in South African architecture*. Cape Town and Rotterdam, 1975.

Home, R. K. 'Town planning, segregation and indirect rule in colonial Nigeria', *Third World Planning Review* (Liverpool), 1983, 5, 2, 165–75.

Lima, A. Pereira de. *Edifícios históricos de Lourenço Marques*. Lourenço Marques, 1966.

Mohammed, H. E. 'Colonial urban planning policy and the disintegration of Kano's physical structure', *Kano studies*, 1980, n.s., **2**, 1, 174–84.

Picton-Seymour, D. *Victorian buildings in South Africa, including Edwardian and Transvaal republican styles, 1850–1910.* Cape Town and Rotterdam, 1977.

Prussin, Labelle. 'The image of African architecture in France,' in G. Wesley Johnson, ed. *Double Impact: France and Africa in the age of imperialism.* Westport, Conn., 1985, pp. 209–35.

African Studies

Asad, T. ed. *Anthropology and the colonial encounter.* London, 1973.

Cell, J. W. 'Lord Hailey and the making of the *African Survey*', *African Affairs*, 1989, **88**, no. 353, 481–505.

Cole, D. T. 'The history of African linguistics to 1945', *Current Trends in Linguistics*, 1971, **7**, 1–29.

Easterbrook, D. L. *Africana book reviews 1885–1945.* Boston, Mass., 1979.

Fage, J. D. 'The prehistory of African history', *Paideuma* (Frankfurt), 1973–74, **19–20**, 146–61. Reprinted in UNESCO *General history of Africa*, vol. 1, pp. 25–43. Paris, 1980.

Forde, Daryll. 'Anthropology and the development of African studies', *Africa*, 1967, **37**, 4, 389–405.

Harries, P. 'The anthropologist as historian and liberal: H.-A. Junod and the Thonga', *Journal of Southern African Studies*, 1981, **8**, 1, 37–50.

Hendrix, Melvin K. *An international bibliography of African lexicons.* Metuchen, NJ, 1982.

Ita, J. M. 'Frobenius, Senghor and the image of Africa', in Horton, R. and Finnegan, R. eds. *Modes of thought*, pp. 306–36. London, 1973.

Johnson, Douglas H. 'Evans-Pritchard, the Nuer, and the Sudan Political Service', *African Affairs*, 1982, **81**, no. 323, 231–46.

Kuper, Adam. *Anthropologists and anthropology: the British school 1922–1972.* London, 1973. Second edition, 1983.

McCaskie, T. C. 'R. S. Rattray and the construction of Asante history: an appraisal', *History in Africa*, 1983, **10**, 187–206.

Macmillan, Hugh and Marks, Shula. eds. *Africa and empire: W. M. Macmillan, historian and social critic.* London, 1989.

Roberts, A. D. 'The earlier historiography of colonial Africa', *History in Africa*, 1978, **5**, 153–67.

Robinson, Kenneth. 'Experts, colonialists and Africanists', in Stone, J. C. ed. *Experts in Africa*, pp. 55–74. Aberdeen, 1980.

Vansina, Jan. 'Bantu in the crystal ball, I.' *History in Africa*, 1979, **6**, 287–333.

Winter, J. C. *Bruno Gutmann, 1876–1966. A German approach to social anthropology.* Oxford, 1979.

Zwernemann, J. *Culture history and African anthropology: a century of research in Germany and Austria.* Uppsala, 1983.

European fiction

Astier Loutfi, M. *Littérature et colonialisme. L'expansion coloniale vue dans la littérature romanesque française, 1871–1914.* Paris, 1971.
Cairns, M. C. 'The African colonial society in French colonial novels', *Cahiers d' études africaines*, 1969, **9**, no. 34, 175–93.
Echeruo, M. J. C. *Joyce Cary and the novel of Africa* London, 1973.
Fanoudh-Sieffer, C. *Le Mythe du Nègre et de l'Afrique noire dans la littérature française (de 1800 à la 2e guerre mondiale).* Paris, 1968.
Killam, G. D. *Africa in English fiction, 1874–1939.* Ibadan, 1968.
Mahood, M. M. *Joyce Cary's Africa.* London, 1964.
Milbury-Steen, S. L. *European and African stereotypes in twentieth-century fiction.* London, 1980.
Moser, G. M. *A tentative Portuguese–African bibliography: Portugese literature in Africa and African literature in the Portuguese language.* University Park, Pa., 1970.
Nwezeh, E. C. *Africa in French and German fiction (1911–1933).* Ile-Ife, 1978.
Ridley, Hugh. *Images of imperial rule.* Beckenham, 1983.
Steins, M. *Das Bild des Schwarzen in der europäischen Kolonialliteratur 1870–1918.* Frankfurt-am-Main, 1972.

European art and Africa

Honour, Hugh. *The image of the black in western art.* vol IV. *From the American Revolution to World War I.* Cambridge, Mass., 1988.
Laude, J. *La Peinture française, 1905–14, et 'l'art nègre'.* Paris, 1968. 2 vols.
Paudrat, J.-L. 'From Africa', in W. Rubin, ed. *'Primitivism' in twentieth-century art: affinity of the tribal and the modern.* New York, 1984, I, pp. 125–75.

2. ASPECTS OF ECONOMIC HISTORY

Surveys, collections and reference works

Austen, Ralph. *African economic history.* London and Portsmouth, N. H., 1987.
Brown, Ian, ed. *The economies of Africa and Asia in the inter-war Depression.* London, 1989.
Duignan, P. and Gann, L. H. eds. *The economics of colonialism (Colonialism in Africa 1870–1960,* vol. IV). Cambridge, 1975.
Frankel, S. H. *Capital investment in Africa.* London, 1938.
Great Britain: Admiralty (Naval Intelligence Dept). *Handbook of railways in Africa.* London, 1919, declassified in 1942. CB 910.
Great Britain: Board of Trade. *Statistical abstract for the British Empire.* London.
Great Britain: Colonial Office. *An economic survey of the colonial territories/empire.* London, 1932, 1933, 1935, 1936, 1937.
Great Britain: Department of Overseas Trade. *Reports on the economic conditions of . . .* [by commercial secretaries of embassies or consulates]. 1921– Irregular; most African countries given at least one report in period,

except for: French Equatorial Africa, Madagascar, Sudan. Microform: Chadwyck-Healey Ltd.

Gregori, T. R. de. *Technology and the economic development of the tropical African frontier.* Cleveland, 1969.

Guyer, Jane L. (ed.) *Feeding African cities: studies in regional social history.* Manchester, 1987.

Hailey, Lord. *An African survey. A study of problems arising in Africa south of the Sahara.* London, 1938.

Hopkins, A. G. *An economic history of West Africa.* London, 1973.

Iliffe, J. *The emergence of African capitalism.* London, 1983.

The African poor: a history. Cambridge, 1988.

Johnson, Douglas H. and Anderson, David M., eds. *The ecology of survival: case studies from northeast African history.* London and Boulder Col., 1988.

League of Nations. *International statistical yearbooks.* 1926–27; 1929; 1930–44 (*Stat. yrbk. L of N*); 1931–8 (*International Trade Statistics*).

Liesegang, G. *et al.*, eds. *Figuring African trade . . . 1800–1913.* Berlin, 1986.

Miers, S. and Roberts, R. eds. *The end of slavery in Africa.* Madison, 1988.

Mitchell, B. R. *International historical statistics: Africa and Asia.* London, 1982.

Munro, J. Forbes. *Africa and the international economy, 1800–1960.* London, 1976.

Neumark, S. D. *Foreign trade and economic development in Africa.* Stanford, 1964.

Palmer, Robin and Parsons, Neil. eds. *The roots of rural poverty in central and southern Africa.* London, 1977.

Perham, M. ed. *The economics of a tropical dependency,* vol. I. *The native economies of Nigeria* (by C. D. Forde and R. Scott). London, 1946; vol. II *Mining, commerce and finance in Nigeria* (by P. A. Bower, A. J. Brown, C. Leubuscher, J. Mars and A. Pim). London, 1948.

General economic studies

Clark, Grover. *The balance sheets of imperialism: facts and figures on colonies.* New York, 1936.

Frankel, S. H. *The economic impact on underdeveloped societies.* Oxford, 1953.

Greaves, I. C. *Modern production among backward peoples.* London, 1935.

Hammond, R. J. 'Economic imperialism, sidelights on a stereotype', *Journal of Economic History,* 1961, **21**, 4, 582–98.

Hazlewood, A. 'Trade balances and statutory marketing in primary export economies', *Economic Journal,* 1957, **67**, 1, 74–82.

Hopkins, A. G. 'On importing André Gunder Frank into Africa', *African Economic History Review,* 1975, **2**, 13–21.

Kamarck, A. *The economics of African development.* New York, 1967.

Lewis, W. A. *Economic survey, 1919–1939.* London, 1949.

'Economic development with unlimited supplies of labour', *Manchester School of Economics and Social Studies,* 1954, **22**, 139–91.

ed. *Aspects of tropical trade, 1883–1965.* Uppsala, 1969.

Tropical development, 1880–1913. London, 1970.

Growth and fluctuations, 1880–1913. London, 1978.

Rowe, J. W. F. *Markets and men: a study of artificial control schemes in some primary industries.* Cambridge, 1936.

British economic relations with Africa

Abbott, George C. 'British colonial aid policy during the 1930s', *Canadian Journal of History*, 1970, **5**, 1, 73–89.
'A re-examination of the 1929 Colonial Development Act', *Economic History Review*, 1971, 2nd ser., **4**, 1, 68–81.
Bauer, P. T. *West African trade: a study of competition, oligopoly and monopoly in a changing economy.* Cambridge, 1954.
Constantine, S. *The making of British colonial development policy, 1914–1940.* London, 1984.
Drummond, Ian M. *British economic policy and the empire, 1919–1939.* London, 1972.
The floating pound and the sterling area, 1931–1939. Cambridge, 1981.
Ehrlich, C., 'Building and caretaking: economic policy in British tropical Africa, 1890–1960', *Economic History Review*, 1973, **26**, 4, 649–62.
Frankel, S. H. *The tyranny of economic paternalism in Africa: a study of frontier mentality, 1860–1960.* Johannesburg, 1960.
Hancock, W. K. *Survey of British Commonwealth affairs*, vol. II. *Problems of economic policy, 1918–1939* (2 parts). London, 1942.
Killingray, D. 'The Empire Resources Development Committee and West Africa 1916–20', *Journal of Imperial and Commonwealth History*, 1982, **10**, 2, 194–210.
Leubuscher, C. 'Marketing schemes for native-grown produce in African territories', *Africa*, 1939, **12**, 2, 163–87.
Meredith, D. 'The British Government and colonial economic policy, 1919–39', *Economic History Review*, 1975, **28**, 3, 484–99.
Meyer, F. V. *Britain's colonies in world trade.* London, 1948.
Morgan, D. J. *The official history of colonial development*, vol. I. *The origins of British aid policy, 1924–1945.* London, 1980.
Munro, J. Forbes. *Britain in tropical Africa, 1880–1960.* London, 1984.
Yates, P. L. *Commodity control.* London, 1943.

Banking and Currency

Arndt, E. H. D. *Banking and currency development in South Africa, 1652–1927.* Cape Town, 1928.
Crossley, J. and Blandford, J. *The DCO Story.* London, 1975.
Fry, R. H. *Bankers in West Africa.* London, 1976.
Henry, J. A. *The first hundred years of the Standard Bank.* ed. H. A. Siepmann. London, 1963.
Hogendorn, J. S. and Gemery, H. A. 'Cash cropping, currency acquisition and seigniorage in West Africa, 1923–1950', *African Economic History*, 1982, **11**, 15–27.

Hopkins, A. G. 'The creation of a colonial monetary system: the origins of the West African Currency Board', *African Historical Studies*, 1970, **3**, 1, 101–32.

Kock, G. de. *A history of the South African Reserve Bank: 1920–1952*. Pretoria, 1954.

McCarthy, D. M. P. 'Media as ends: money and the underdevelopment of Tanganyika to 1940', *Journal of Economic History*, 1976, **36**, 3, 645–62.

Newlyn, W. T. and Rowan, D. C. *Money and banking in British colonial Africa*. Oxford, 1954.

Ofonagoro, W. I. 'From traditional to British currency in southern Nigeria: analysis of a currency revolution, 1880–1948', *Journal of Economic History*, 1979, **39**, 3, 623–54.

Sayers, R. S. ed. *Banking in the British Commonwealth*. Oxford, 1952.

Business

Albion, R. G. *Seaports south of the Sahara: the achievements of an American steamship service*. New York, 1959.

Alford, B. W. E. and Harvey, C. E. 'Copperbelt merger: the formation of the Rhokana Corporation, 1930–1932', *Business History Review*, 1980, **54**, 3, 330–58.

Davies, P. N. *The trade-makers; Elder Dempster in West Africa, 1852–1972*. London, 1973.

Fieldhouse, D. K. *Unilever overseas: the anatomy of a multinational, 1895–1965*. London, 1978.

Greenhalgh, P. *An economic history of the West African diamond industry*. Manchester, 1985.

Gregory, T. *Ernest Oppenheimer and the economic development of southern Africa*. London, 1962.

Hopkins, A. G. 'Imperial business in Africa, part I. Sources; part II. Interpretations', *Journal of African History*, 1976, **17**, 1–2, 29–48 and 267–90.
'Big business in African studies', *Journal of African History*, 1987, **28**, 1, 119–40.

Leubuscher, C. *The West African shipping trade, 1909–1959*. Leiden, 1963.

Pedler, F. *The lion and the unicorn in Africa: a history of the origins of the United Africa Company, 1787–1931*. London, 1974.

Perrings, C. A. *Black mineworkers in Central Africa: industrial strategies and the evolution of an African proletariat in the Copperbelt, 1911–41*. London, 1979.

Stahl, K. M. *The metropolitan organisation of British colonial trade*. London, 1951.

Wardle, W. A. 'A history of the British Cotton Growing Association, with special reference to its activities in Africa'. Ph.D. thesis, University of Birmingham, 1980.

Wilson, C. *The history of Unilever*. London, 1954. 2 vols.

Labour

Arrighi, G. 'Labour supplies in historical perspective: a study of the proletarianisation of the African peasantry in Rhodesia', *Journal of Development Studies*, 1970, **6**, 3, 197–234.

Berg, E. J. 'Backward-sloping supply functions in dual economies – the Africa case', *Quarterly Journal of Economics*, 1961, **75**, 3, 468–92.

'The development of a labour force in sub-Saharan Africa', *Economic Development and Cultural Change*, 1965, **13**, 4, 394–412.

Elkan, W. *Migrants and proletarians: urban labour in the economic development of Uganda*. London, 1960.

Kilby, P. 'African labour productivity reconsidered', *Economic Journal*, 1961, **71**, 2, 273–91.

'Backward-bending African labour supply curves – a reply', *Economic Journal*, 1965, **75**, 3, 637–41.

Orde Browne, G. St J. *The African labourer*. London, 1933.

Read, M. 'Migrant labour in Africa and its effects on tribal life', *International Labour Review*, 1942, **45**, 6, 605–31.

Agriculture

Allan, W. *The African husbandman*. Edinburgh, 1965.

Biebuyck, D. ed. *African agrarian systems*. London, 1963.

Johnston, B. F. *The staple food economies of western tropical Africa*. Stanford, 1958.

Jones, W. O. *Manioc in Africa*. Stanford, 1959.

Meek, C. K. *Land law and custom in the colonies*. London, 1946.

Miracle, M. P. *Maize in tropical Africa*. Madison, 1966.

Pim, A. *Colonial agricultural production*. London, 1946.

Rotberg, R. I. ed. *Imperialism, colonialism and hunger: east and central Africa*. Lexington and Toronto, 1983.

Tosh, J. 'The cash-crop revolution in tropical Africa: an agricultural reappraisal', *African Affairs*, 1980, **79**, no. 314, 79–94.

Whitford, H. N. and Anthony, A. *Rubber production in Africa*. Washington, DC, 1926.

Wickizer, V. D. *Coffee, tea and cocoa: an economic and political analysis*. Stanford, 1951.

Disease and Medicine

Arnold, David, ed. *Imperial medicine and indigenous societies*. Manchester, 1988.

Feierman, S. *Health and society in Africa: a working bibliography*. Waltham, Mass., 1979.

Ford, John. *The role of the trypanosomiases in African ecology*. Oxford, 1971.

Hartwig, G. W. and Patterson, K. D. eds. *Disease in African history: an introductory survey and case studies*. Durham, NC, 1978.

Schistosomiasis in 20th century Africa: historical studies on West Africa and the Sudan. Los Angeles, 1984.

Janzen, J. M. and Feierman, S. eds. *The social history of disease and medicine in Africa.* Special issue of *Social Science and Medicine*, part B, 'Medical anthropology', 1979, 13B, 4.

Nkwam, Florence E. 'British medical and health policies in West Africa, c. 1920–1960', Ph.D. thesis, University of London, 1989.

Pan, Lynn. *Alcohol in colonial Africa.* Uppsala, 1975.

Patterson, K. D. 'Disease and medicine in African history: a bibliographical essay', *History in Africa*, 1974, 1, 141–8.

Infectious diseases in twentieth-century Africa, a bibliography of their distribution and consequences. Waltham, Mass., 1979.

Patterson, K. D. and Hartwig, G. W. *Cerebrospinal meningitis in West Africa and Sudan in the 20th century.* Los Angeles, 1984.

Patterson, K. D. and Pyle, G. F. 'The spread of influenza in sub-Saharan Africa 1918–19: a geographical analysis', *Social Science and Medicine*, 1983, 17, no. 17, 1299–1307.

Phillips, H. 'South Africa's worst demographic disaster: the Spanish influenza epidemic of 1918', *South African Historical Journal*, 1988, 20, 57–73.

Sabben-Clare, E. E., Bradley, D. J. and Kirkwood, K. eds. *Health in tropical Africa during the colonial period.* Oxford, 1980.

See also, p.272 above.

Demography

Caldwell, J. C. 'The social repercussions of colonial rule: demographic aspects', in A. Adu Boahen, ed. *Africa under colonial domination 1880–1935.* (UNESCO *General History of Africa*. vol VII). Paris. London and Berkeley, 1985, pp. 458–86.

Cordell, Dennis D. and Gregory, Joel W., eds. *African population and capitalism: historical perspectives.* Boulder, Col., 1987.

Edinburgh University. Centre of African Studies. *African historical demography*, vol. I, 1977; vol. II, 1981.

Gregory, J. W., Cordell, D. D. and Gervais, R. *African historical demography: a multidisciplinary bibliography.* Los Angeles, 1983.

Kuczynski, R. R. *A demographic survey of the British colonial empire.* vols. I and II. London, 1948–9.

Conservation

Anderson, David, and Grove, Richard, eds. *Conservation in Africa: people, policies and practice.* Cambridge, 1987.

Journal of Southern African Studies, 1989, 15, 2: special issue on the politics of conservation.

MacKenzie, John M. *The empire of nature: hunting, conservation and British imperialism.* Manchester, 1988.

3. CHRISTIANITY

General

Baëta, C. G. ed. *Christianity in tropical Africa*. London, 1968.

Barrett, D. B. 'A.D. 2000: 350 million Christians in Africa', *International Review of Missions*, 1970, **59**, 1, 39–54.

Beach, H. P. and Fahs, C. H. *World Missionary Atlas*. New York, 1925.

Bibliographia Missionaria. Rome, 1933– .

Bibliotheca Missionum. ed. R. Streit, J. Dindinger, J. Rommerskirchen, J. Metzler. **18–20**, Freiburg, 1913–14; **22–3**, Rome, Freiburg, Vienna, 1963–4.

Craig, C. S. *The archives of the Council for World Mission (incorporating the London Missionary Society): an outline guide*. London, 1973.

De Craemer, W. 'The Congo/Zaire archives of the northern (Flemish) Belgian Jesuit province in Brussels, Belgium', *History in Africa*, 1977, **4**, 287–90.

Delacroix, S. ed. *Histoire universelle des missions catholiques*, vols. III and IV. Paris, 1956, 1959.

Etherington, N. 'Missionaries and the intellectual history of Africa: a historical survey', *Itinerario*, 2, 1983.

Hastings, A. *African Catholicism*. London, 1989.

Hastings, A. *A history of African Christianity 1950–1975*. Cambridge, 1979.

Jenkins, P. 'The archival collection in the mission house in Basel, with special reference to Africa', *Mitteilungen der Basler Afrika Bibliographien*, 1973, no. 9, 9–24.

Keen, R. *A survey of the archives of selected missionary societies*. London, 1968.

Ranger, T. O. and Weller, J. eds. *Themes in the Christian history of Central Africa*. London, 1975.

Raskin, A. 'The archives of the Congregation of the Immaculate Heart of Mary (CICM)', *History in Africa*, 1977, **4**, 299–304.

Sanneh, L. *Translating the message*. New York, 1989.

Shorter, A. *Jesus and the witchdoctor*. London, 1985.

Strayer, R. W. 'Mission history in Africa: new perspectives on an encounter', *African Studies Review*, 1976, **19**, 1, 1–15.

Walls, A. F. ed. 'Bibliography of the Society for African Church History', Part 3. *Journal of Religion in Africa*, 1967, **1**, 46–94.

Missionary policy, organization and church-building

Anderson, G. H. ed. *The theology of the Christian mission*. Nashville, 1961.

Arén, G. *Evangelical pioneers in Ethiopia. Origins of the evangelical church Mekane Yesus*. Stockholm and Addis Ababa, 1978.

Berry, L. L. *A century of missions of the African Methodist Episcopal Church, 1840–1940*. New York, 1942.

Binchy, D. A. *Church and State in fascist Italy*. London, 1941.

Blanc, R., Blocher, J. and Kruger, E. *Histoire des missions protestantes françaises*. Flavion (Belgium), 1970.

Bolink, P. *Towards Church union in Zambia*. Franeker, 1967.

Bouchaud, J. *Monseigneur Pierre Bonneau, Evêque de Douala*. Douala, 1969.

Boudou, A. *Les Jésuites à Madagascar au xixe siècle*. Paris, 1942. 2 vols.

Braekman, E. M. *Histoire du protestantisme au Congo*. Brussels, 1961.

Brásio, A. *História e missiologia inéditos e esparos*. Luanda, 1973.

Brown, W. E. *The Catholic Church in South Africa*. London, 1960.

Cason, J. W. 'The growth of Christianity in the Liberian environment'. Ph.D. thesis, Columbia University, 1962.

Cooke, C. M. 'The Roman Catholic mission in Calabar 1903–1960'. Ph.D. thesis, University of London, 1977.

Crampton, E. P. T. *Christianity in Northern Nigeria*. Zaria, 1975.

Dachs, A. J. and Rea, W. F. *The Catholic Church and Zimbabwe 1879–1979*. Gwelo, 1979.

Dah, Jonas N. *Missionary motivations and methods: a critical examination of the Basel Mission in Cameroon 1886–1914*. Basel, 1983.

Debrunner, H. W. *A church between colonial powers: a study of the Church in Togo*. London, 1965.

A history of Christianity in Ghana. Accra, 1967.

Denis, L. ed. *Les Jésuites belges au Kwango, 1893–1943*. Brussels, 1945.

Ellenberger. V. *A century of mission work in Basutoland (1833–1933)*. tr. E. M. Ellenberger. Morija, 1938.

Fusero, C. *Antonio Vignato nell'Africa di ieri*. Bologna, 1970.

Gabriel, M. N. *Angola: cinco séculos de cristianismo*. Queluz, n.d. [*c*. 1983].

Gairdner, W. H. T. *Edinburgh 1910*. Edinburgh, 1910.

Gaitskell, D. 'Female mission initiatives: black and white women in the Witwatersrand churches'. Ph.D. thesis, University of London, 1981.

Gale, H. P. *Uganda and the Mill Hill Fathers*. London, 1959.

Garvey, B. 'The development of the White Fathers' mission among the Bemba-speaking peoples, 1891–1964'. Ph.D. thesis, University of London, 1974.

'Bemba Chiefs and Catholic missions, 1898–1935', *Journal of African History*, 1977, **18**, 3, 411–26.

Gow, B. A. *Madagascar and the Protestant impact*. London, 1979.

Gration, J. 'The relationship of the Africa Inland Mission and its national church in Kenya between 1895 and 1971'. Ph.D. thesis, New York University, 1974.

Groves, C. P. *The planting of Christianity in Africa*. vols. III, IV. London, 1955, 1958.

Hallden, E. *The culture policy of the Basel mission in the Cameroons, 1886–1905*. Uppsala, 1968.

Hardy, G. *Un apôtre d'aujourd'hui. Le R. P. Aupiais*, Paris, 1949.

Hellberg, C. J. *Missions on a colonial frontier west of Lake Victoria*. tr. E. Sharpe. Lund, 1965.

Hewat, E. G. K. *Vision and achievement, 1769–1956: a history of the foreign mission of the churches united in the Church of Scotland*. London, 1960.

Hewitt, Gordon. *The problems of success. A history of the Church Missionary Society 1910–1942*, vol. I. London, 1971.

Hogan, E. M. 'The Society of African Missions in Ireland (1877–1916)'. M. A. thesis, University of Cork, 1973.

Hogg, W. R. *Ecumenical foundations: a history of the International Missionary Council and its nineteenth-century background*. New York, 1952.

International Missionary Council. *Tambaram Madras Series*, vols. I–VII. London, 1939.

Jacobs, Sylvia M. ed. *Black Americans and the missionary movement in Africa*. Westport, Conn., and London, 1982.

Jenkins, P. 'The Anglican Church in Ghana, 1905–1924', *Transactions of the Historical Society of Ghana*, 1974, **15**, 1, 23–39; 2, 177–200.

Johnson, W. R. *Worship and freedom. A black American church in Zambia*. London, 1977.

Jordan, John P. *Bishop Shanahan of southern Nigeria*. Dublin, 1949.

Koren, H. J. *The Spiritans: a history of the Congregation of the Holy Ghost*. Pittsburgh, 1958.

Kratz, M. *La Mission des Rédemptoristes belges au Bas-Congo: la période des semailles, 1899–1920*. Brussels, 1970.

Lopes, F. F. *Missões franciscanas em Moçambique, 1898–1970*. Braga, 1972.

MacPherson, R. *The Presbyterian Church in Kenya*. Nairobi, 1970.

McIntosh, B. G. 'The Scottish Mission in Kenya, 1891–1923'. Ph.D. thesis, University of Edinburgh, 1969.

Metzler, J. ed. *Sacrae Congregationis de Propaganda Fide Memoria Rerum 1622–1972*, vol. III, *1815–1972*. Rome, 1975.

Mobley, H. W. *The Ghanaian's image of the missionary: an analysis of the published critiques of Christian missionaries by Ghanaians, 1897–1965*. Leiden, 1970.

Mondain, G. *Un siècle de mission protestante à Madagascar* Paris, 1948.

Monticone, Mgr. G. *et al.* eds. *Guida delle Missioni Cattoliche, Redatta sotto gli auspici della Sacra Congregazione di Propaganda Fide*. Rome, 1934.

Moreira, E. *Portuguese East Africa: a study of its religious needs*. London, 1936.

Müller, K. *Geschichte der katholischen Kirche in Togo*. Steyl, 1958.

Murray, J. 'The Church Missionary Society and the "female circumcision" issue in Kenya, 1929–1932', *Journal of Religion in Africa*, 1976, **8**, 92–104.

Nembro, M. da. *La Missione dei Minori Cappuccini in Eritrea (1894–1952)*. Rome, 1953.

Nemer, L. *Anglican and Roman Catholic attitudes on missions*. St Augustin, 1981.

Nolan, F. P. 'History of the catechist in eastern Africa', in Shorter, A. and Kataza, E. eds. *Missionaries to yourselves: African catechists today*, pp. 1–28. London, 1972.

'Christianity in Unyamwezi, 1878–1928', Ph.D. thesis, University of Cambridge, 1977.

O'Shea, M. *Missionaries and miners: a history of the beginnings of the Catholic Church in Zambia with particular reference to the Copperbelt*. Ndola, 1986.

Pirotte, J. *Périodiques missionaires belges d'expression française. Reflets de cinquante anneés d'evolution d'une mentalité, 1889–1940*. Louvain, 1973.

Roe, J. M. *A history of the British and Foreign Bible Society, 1905–1954*. London, 1965.

Schweitzer, A. *On the edge of the primeval forest*. London, 1922.

Sicard, S. von. *The Lutheran Church on the coast of Tanzania 1887–1914*. Lund, 1970.

Smith, H. M. *Frank, Bishop of Zanzibar*. London, 1926.
Smith, N. *The Presbyterian Church of Ghana, 1835–1960*. Accra, 1966.
Storme, M. *Het ontstaan van de Kasai-missie*. Brussels, 1961.
Pater Cambier en de Stichting van de Kasie-missie. Brussels, 1964.
Konflikt in de Kasai-missie. Brussels, 1965.
Strassberger, E. *Ecumenism in South Africa, 1936–1960*. Johannesburg, 1974.
Sundkler, B. *The Christian ministry in Africa*. Uppsala, 1960.
Bara-Bukoba: church and community in Tanzania. London, 1980.
Thompson, T. J. 'Fraser and the Ngoni: a study of the growth of Christianity among the Ngoni of northern Malawi, 1878–1933', Ph.D. thesis, University of Edinburgh, 1980.
Tragella, G. B. *Pio XI, Papa Missionaria*. Milan, 1930.
Tucker, J. T. *Angola: the land of the blacksmith prince*. London, 1933.
Van Slageren, J. *Les origines de l'Église évangelique du Cameroun*. Yaoundé, 1972.
Verbeek, L. *Ombres et clairières: histoire de l'implantation de l'église catholique dans le diocèse de Sakania, Zaïre (1910–1970)*. Rome, 1987.
Verstraelen-Gilhuis, G. *From Dutch Mission Church to Reformed Church in Zambia*. Franeker, 1982.
Vignato, A. 'Note storiche sulla Missione d'Uganda', *Bolletino della Congregazione dei figli del sacro cuore*. December, 1950.
Ward, Kevin. 'The development of Protestant Christianity in Kenya, 1910–1940',. Ph.D. thesis, University of Cambridge, 1976.
Welch, A. W. 'Colonial stepchildren: Catholic and Methodist missionaries in the Ivory Coast, 1895–1939'. Ph.D. thesis, University of Birmingham, 1979.
World Missionary Conference, 1910. *The Reports of Commissions* 1–. Edinburgh, n.d.
Wright, Marcia. *German missions in Tanganyika 1891–1941*. Oxford, 1971.

Missions and colonial powers

Alladaye, T. 'Les Missionaires catholiques au Dahomey, à l'époque coloniale, 1905–1957'. Thèse de 3e cycle, University of Paris-VII, 1978.
Anderson, J. *The struggle for the school: the interaction of missionary, colonial government and nationalist enterprise in the development of formal education in Kenya*. London, 1970.
Anon. *Madagascar for Christ*. Being a report of simultaneous deputations from the London Missionary Society, the Friends' Foreign Mission Association and the Paris Missionary Society to Madagascar, July to October, 1913. London and Paris, 1913.
Bée, M. 'La Christianisation de la Basse Côte d'Ivoire', *Revue française d'histoire d'outre-mer*, 1975, **62**, no. 229, 640–73.
Berger, Heinrich, *Mission und Kolonialpolitik. Die Katholische Mission in Kamerun während der deutschen Kolonialzeit*. Immensee, 1978.
Boer, J. H. *Missionary messengers of liberation in a colonial context: a case study of the Sudan United Mission*. Amsterdam, 1979.
Bouche, Denise. *Les Villages de liberté en Afrique noire française, 1887–1910*. Paris, 1968.

Cochrane, James, *Servants of Power: the role of English-speaking Churches* [in South Africa] *1903–1930*. Johannesburg, 1987.

Der, B. 'Church-state relations in northern Ghana, 1906–1940', *Transactions of the Historical Society of Ghana*, 1974, **15**, 1, 41–61.

Eggert, Johanna. *Missionsschule und Wandel in Ostafrika: der Beitrag der deutschen evangelischen Missionsgesellschaften zur Entwicklung des Schulwesens in Tanganyika, 1891–1939*. Bielefeld, 1970.

Ekechi, F. K. *Missionary enterprise and rivalry in Igboland, 1857–1914*. London, 1971.

Engel, L. *Kolonialismus und Nationalismus im deutschen Protestantismus in Namibia 1907 bis 1945*. Berne, 1976.

Fields, Karen E. *Revival and rebellion in colonial central Africa*. Princeton, 1985.

Graham, Sonia F. *Government and mission education in Northern Nigeria, 1900–1919*. Ibadan, 1966.

Greaves, L. B. *Carey Francis of Kenya*. London, 1969.

Hansen, H. B. *Mission, church and state in a colonial setting: Uganda, 1890–c. 1925*. London, 1984.

Heenan, J. C. *Cardinal Hinsley*. London, 1944.

Heremans, R. *L'Education dans les missions des Pères Blancs en Afrique Centrale (1879–1914)*. Brussels, 1983.

Jones, T. Jesse. *Education in Africa: a study of West, South and Equatorial Africa*. Report of the Phelps-Stokes Commission on African Education. New York and London, 1922.

Education in Africa: a study of East, Central and South Africa by the second African Education Commission under the auspices of the Phelps-Stokes Fund, in cooperation with the International Education Board. New York and London, n.d. (1924).

Lagergren, D. *Mission and state in the Congo*. Uppsala, 1970.

Langworthy, Harry W. 'Joseph Booth, prophet of radical change in central and South Africa, 1891–1915', *Journal of Religion in Africa*, 1986, **16**, 1, 22–43.

Linden, I. *Church and revolution in Rwanda*. Manchester, 1977.

Lonsdale, J. M. 'European attitudes and African pressures: missions and government in Kenya between the wars', *Race*, 1968–9, **10**, 141–51.

Loth, H. *Die christliche Mission in Südwestafrika*. East Berlin, 1963.

McCracken, J. *Politics and Christianity in Malawi 1875–1940: the impact of the Livingstonia Mission in the Northern Province*. Cambridge, 1977.

Markowitz, M. D. *Cross and sword. The political role of Christian missions in the Belgian Congo, 1908–1960*. Stanford, 1973.

Meeus, F. de and Steenberghen, D. R. *Les Missions religieuses au Congo Belge*. Antwerp, 1947.

Mikré-Selassie, Gabre Ammanuel. 'Church and missions in Ethiopia in relation to the Italian War and occupation and the Second World War'. Ph.D. thesis, University of Aberdeen, 1976.

Ngongo, L. *Histoire des forces religieuses au Cameroun de la Ie guerre mondiale à l'indépendance*. Paris, 1982.

Oldham, J. H. *Christianity and the race problem*. London, 1925.

Oliver, R. *The missionary factor in East Africa*. London, 1952.

Parsons, R. T. *The Churches and Ghana society, 1918–1955*. Leiden, 1963.

Raymaekers, P. and Desroche, H. *L'Administration et le sacré. Discours religieux et parcours politiques en Afrique centrale, 1921–1957*. Brussels, 1983.

Renaud, F. *Lavigerie, l'esclavage Africain et l'Europe, 1868–1892*. Paris, 1971. 2 vols.

Rhodes, A. *The Vatican in the age of the dictators*. London, 1973.

Rotbcrg, R. I. *Christian missionaries and the creation of Northern Rhodesia, 1880–1924*. Princeton, 1965.

Sanderson, L. M. and G. N. *Education, religion and politics in Southern Sudan, 1899–1964*. London, 1981.

Sartorius, J. *Staat und Kirchen im francophonen Schwarzafrika und auf Madagaskar*. Munich, 1973.

Scanlon, D. G. ed. *Church, state and education in Africa*. New York, 1966.

Shaloff, S. *Reform in Leopold's Congo*. Richmond, 1970.

Shenk, C. E. 'The development of the Ethiopian Orthodox Church and its relationship with the Ethiopian government from 1930 to 1970'. Ph.D. thesis, New York University, 1972.

Shepherd, R. H. W. *Lovedale, South Africa, 1824–1955*. Lovedale, 1971.

Slade, R. N. *English-speaking missions in the Congo Independent State (1878–1908)*. Brussels, 1959.

Soremekun, F. 'Religion and politics in Angola: the American Board missions and the Portuguese government, 1880–1922', *Cahiers d'études africaines*, 1971, **11**, no. 43, 341–77.

Vidal, H. *La Séparation des églises et l'état à Madagascar 1861–1968*. Paris, 1970.

Villemagne, E. M. de. 'La Congrégation du Saint Esprit et l'oeuvre des missions catholiques en AEF (1839–1939/40)'. Thesis, University of Paris, 1965.

Vries, J. L. de. *Mission and colonialism in Namibia*. Johannesburg, 1978.

Waugh, E. A. St. J. *Ronald Knox*. London, 1959.

Witte, Jehan de. *Monseigneur Augouard: sa vie*. Paris, 1924.

African initiatives

Ajayi, J. F. A. *Christian Missions in Nigeria 1841–1891: the making of a new elite*. London, 1965.

Andersson, E. *Churches at the grass-roots. A study in Congo-Brazzaville*. London, 1968.
Messianic popular movements in the Lower Congo. Uppsala, 1958.

Asch, Susan. *L'Église du Prophète Kimbangu de ses origines à son rôle actuel au Zaïre 1921–1981*. Paris, 1983.

Ayandele, E. A. *The missionary impact on modern Nigeria 1842–1914*. London, 1966.
'The ideological ferment in Ijebuland, 1892–1943', *African Notes* (Ibadan), 1970, **53**, 17–40.
Holy Johnson: pioneer of African nationalism, 1837–1917. London, 1970.

Baëta, C. G. *Prophetism in Ghana*. London, 1962.

Barrett, D. B. *Schism and renewal in Africa: an analysis of six thousand contemporary religious movements*. Nairobi, 1968.

Bartels, F. L. *The roots of Ghana Methodism*. Cambridge, 1965.

Berger, Iris. *Religion and Resistance. East African Kingdoms in the precolonial period*. Tervuren, 1981.

Bhebe, N. *Christianity and traditional religion in western Zimbabwe, 1859–1923.* London, 1979.

Bimwenyi-Kwesi, O. *Discours théologique Négro-Africain: Problème des fondements.* Présence Africaine, Paris, 1981.

Binsbergen, W. M. J. van and Schoffeleers, M. eds. *Theoretical Explorations in African Religion.* London, 1985.

Bontinck, F. 'Donzwau Nlemvo (c. 1871–1938) et la bible kikongo', *Revue africaine de théologie,* 1978, **2**, 3, 5–32.

Brandel-Syrier, M. *Black woman in search of God.* London, 1962.

Bureau, R. *Ethno-sociologie religieuse des Duala et apparentés.* Yaoundé, 1962.

Bureau, R. 'Le Prophète Harris et la religion Harriste en Côte d'Ivoire', *Annales de l'Université d'Abidjan,* 1971, **3**, 31–196.

Comaroff, J. *Body of power, spirit of resistance.* Chicago, 1985.

Cotterell, F. P. *Born at midnight.* Chicago, 1973.

Cross, S. 'The Watch Tower movement in South-Central Africa, 1908–1945'. D.Phil. thesis, University of Oxford, 1973.

Daneel, I. (M.L.) *Quest for Belonging.* Gweru, 1987.

Daneel, M. L. *Old and new in southern Shona independent churches.* The Hague, 1971, 1974. 2 vols.

Dillon-Malone, C. M. *The Korsten basketmakers.* Lusaka, 1978.

Dwane, S. 'Christianity in relation to Xhosa religion'. Ph.D. thesis, University of London, 1979.

Ellis, S. *The Rising of the Red Shawls. A revolt in Madagascar, 1895–1899.* Cambridge, 1985.

Fernandez, J. W. *Bwiti. An ethnography of the religious imagination in Africa.* Princeton, 1982.

Fisher, H. J. 'Conversion reconsidered: some historical aspects of religious conversion in Black Africa', *Africa,* 1973, **43**, 1, 27–40.

Geuns, A. 'Bibliographie commentée du prophétisme Kongo', *Cahiers du CEDAF,* 1973, **7**, 2–81.

Greschat, H. J. *Kitawala. Ursprung, Ausbreitung und Religion der Watch Tower-Bewegung in Zentralafrica.* Marburg, 1967.

Hackett, R. I. J. *Religion in Calabar.* Mouton, Berlin, 1989.

Haliburton, G. M. *The Prophet Harris.* London, 1971.

Hebga, M. ed. *Croyance et guérison.* Yaoundé, 1973.

Hinfelaar, H. F. 'Religious change among Bemba-speaking women of Zambia'. Ph.D. thesis, University of London, 1989.

Horton, R. 'African conversion', *Africa,* 1971, **41**, 2, 85–108.

Isichei, E. *Entirely for God: the life of Michael Iwene Tansi.* Ibadan and London, 1980.

Janzen, J. M. and MacGaffey, W. *An anthology of Kongo religion: primary texts from Lower Zaïre.* Lawrence, Kansas, 1974.

Jules-Rosette, B. *African Apostles. Ritual and conversion in the church of John Maranke.* Ithaca, 1975.

    ed. *The new religions of Africa.* Norwood, 1979.

Ki-Zerbo, J. *Alfred Diban: premier chrétien de Haute-Volta.* Paris, 1983.

Koerner, F. 'L'Échec de l'éthiopianisme dans les églises protestantes

Malgaches', *Revue française d'histoire d'outre-mer*, 1971, **58**, no. 211, 215–38.

Lantum, D. N. 'The advent of Christianity in Nso, 1900–1923', *Cameroun Historical Review*, 1971, **1**, 83–93.

Linden, I. *Catholics, peasants and Chewa resistance in Nyasaland 1889–1939*. London, 1974.

MacGaffey, W. *Modern Kongo Prophets*. Bloomington, 1983.

Mackay, D. J. 'Simon Kimbangu and the B.M.S. tradition', *Journal of Religion in Africa*, 1987, **17**, 2, 133–171.

Martin, M.-L. *Kimbangu*. Oxford, 1975.

Mbiti, J. S. *New Testament eschatology in an African background*. London, 1971.

Mills, W. G. 'The role of African clergy in the reorientation of Xhosa society to the plural society in the Cape Colony, 1850–1915'. Ph.D. thesis, University of California, Los Angeles, 1975.

Mitchell, R. C. and Turner, H. W. eds. *A comprehensive bibliography of modern African religious movements*. Evanston, 1966.

Mudimbe, V. Y. *The Invention of Africa*. Bloomington, 1988.

Mumbanza mwa Bawele. 'La Contribution des Zaïrois à l'oeuvre d'évangelisation et à la prospérité des établissements missionaires. La mission catholique de Libanda (1933–1960)', *Études d'histoire africaine*, 1974, **6**, 225–74.

Munanyi Muntu-Monji. 'Le Mouvement kimbanguiste dans le Haut-Kasai (1921–1950)'. Thèse de 3e cycle, University of Aix -en-Provence, 1974–5.

Murphree, M. *Christianity and the Shona*. London, 1969.

Parsons, R. T. ed. *Windows on Africa: a symposium*. Leiden, 1971.

Paulme, D. 'Une religion syncrétique en Côte d'Ivoire: le culte *déima*', *Cahiers d'études africaines*, 1962, **3**, no. 9, 5–90.

Pauw, B. A. *Christianity and Xhosa tradition*. Cape Town, 1975.

Peel, J. D. Y. *Aladura: a religious movement among the Yoruba*. London, 1968.
Ijeshas and Nigerians: the incorporation of a Yoruba kingdom. Cambridge, 1983.

Perrin-Jassy, M.-F. *La Communauté de base dans les églises africaines*. Bandundu, 1970. English tr. New York, 1973.

Peterson, J. *Province of freedom: a history of Sierra Leone, 1787–1870*. London, 1969.

Piault, C. ed. *Prophétisme et thérapeutique. Albert Atcho et la communauté de Boregbo*. Paris, 1975.

Pirouet, M. L. *Black evangelists. The spread of Christianity in Uganda 1891–1914*. London, 1978.
'East African Christians and World War I', *Journal of African History*, 1978, **19**, 1, 117–30.

Ranger, T. O. 'Religious movements and politics in Sub-Saharan Africa', *African Studies Review*, 1986, **29**, 2.
'Christian independency in Tanzania', in Barrett, D. B. ed., *African initiatives in religion*, pp. 122–45. Nairobi, 1971.
'Taking hold of the land: holy places and pilgrimages in twentieth-century Zimbabwe', *Past and Present*, 1987, no. 117, 158–94.

Ranger, T. O. and Kimambo, I. eds. *The historical study of African religion*. London, 1972.

Raymaekers, P. 'Histoire de Simon Kimbangu, prophète d'après les écrivains

Nfinangani et Nzungu, 1921', *Archives de Sociologie des Religions*, 1971, **31**, 7–49.

Rennie, J. K. 'Christianity, colonialism and the origins of nationalism among the Ndau of Southern Rhodesia 1890–1935'. Ph.D. thesis, Northwestern University, 1973.

Robins, C. '*Tukutendereza*: a study of social change and sectarian withdrawal in the *Balokole* revival of Uganda'. Ph.D. thesis, Columbia University, 1975.

Sangree, W. H. *Age, prayer and politics in Tiriki, Kenya*. London, 1966.

Schlosser, K. *Eingeborenenkirchen in Süd- und Süd-westafrika*. Kiel, 1958.

Setiloane, G. M. *The images of God among the Sotho-Tswana*. Rotterdam, 1976.

Shank, D. A. 'A prophet of modern times: the thought of William Wade Harris, West African precursor of the reign of Christ'. Ph.D. thesis, University of Aberdeen, 1980.

Shepperson, G. A. and Price, T. *Independent African: John Chilembwe and the origins, setting and significance of the Nyasaland native rising of 1915*. Edinburgh, 1958; 2nd. ed. 1987.

Sithole, N. *African nationalism*. Cape Town, 1959.

Strayer, R. W. *The making of mission communities in East Africa: Anglicans and Africans in colonial Kenya, 1875–1935*. London, 1978.

Stuart, R. G. 'Christianity and the Chewa: the Anglican case, 1885–1950'. Ph.D. thesis, University of London, 1974.

Sundkler, B. *Bantu prophets in South Africa*. London, 1948; 2nd. ed. 1961.
Zulu Zion and some Swazi Zionists. Uppsala, 1976.

Tasie, G. O. M. *Christian missionary enterprise in the Niger Delta 1864–1918*. Leiden, 1978.

Taylor, J. V. *The growth of the church in Buganda*. London, 1958.

Taylor, J. V. and Lehmann, D. *Christians of the Copperbelt*. London, 1961.

Thiel, J. F. *La Situation religieuse des Mbiem*. Bandundu, 1972.

Tuma, A.D.T. *Building a Ugandan church: African participation in church growth and expansion in Busoga, 1891–1940*. Nairobi, 1980.

Turner, H. W. *History of an African independent church*, vol. I. *The Church of the Lord (Aladura)*; vol. II. *The life and faith of the Lord (Aladura)*. Oxford, 1967.
Bibliography of new religious movements in primal societies, vol. I. *Black Africa*. Boston, 1977.

Ustorf, W. *Africanische Initiative. Das active Leiden des Propheten Simon Kimbangu*. Berne, 1975.

van Butselaar, Jan. *Africains, missionaires et colonialistes: les origines de l'Église Presbyterienne du Mozambique (Mission Suisse), 1880–1896*. Leiden, 1984.

Waliggo, J. M. 'The Catholic Church in the Buddu Province of Buganda, 1879–1925'. Ph.D. thesis, University of Cambridge, 1976.

Wanyoike, E. N. *An African pastor*. Nairobi, 1974.

Webster, J. B. *The African churches among the Yoruba, 1888–1922*. Oxford, 1964.

Welbourn, F. B. *East African rebels*. London, 1961.

Welbourn, F. B. and Ogot, B. A. *A place to feel at home: a study of two independent churches in western Kenya*. London, 1966.

Wilson, Monica. *Rituals of kinship among the Nyakyusa*. London, 1957.
Communal rituals of the Nyakyusa. London, 1959.

4. ISLAM
General

Abun-Nasr, J. M. *The Tijaniyya. A Sufi order in the modern world.* London, 1965.
Anderson, J. N. D. *Islamic Law in Africa.* London, 1955; reprinted 1970.
Birks, J. S. *Across the Savannas to Mecca. The overland pilgrimage route from West Africa.* London, 1978.
Bravmann, R. A. *African Islam.* Washington, D. C., 1984.
Coulon, C. *Les Musulmans et le pouvoir en Afrique noire.* Paris, 1983.
Cruise O' Brien, D. B. and Coulon, C. eds. *Charisma and brotherhood in African Islam.* Oxford, 1988.
Islam et sociétés au sud du Sahara. Paris, 1987: annual.
Lapidus, Ira M. *A History of Islamic societies.* Cambridge, 1988.
Lewis, I. M. ed. *Islam in tropical Africa.* London, 1966.
Pearson, J. D. *Index Islamicus, 1906–1955.* Cambridge, 1958; supplements for 1956–60, 1962; 1961–5, 1967; 1966–70, London, 1972; 1971–5, 1977; 1976–80, 1983.
Works, John, Jr. *Pilgrims in a strange land. Hausa communities in Chad.* New York, 1976.
Zoghby, S. M. *Islam in sub-Saharan Africa. A partially annotated guide.* Washington, DC, 1978.
Ziadeh, N. A. *Sanūsīyah: a study of a revivalist movement in Islam.* Leiden, 1958.

Northern Africa: some relevant studies

André, P. *Contribution à l'étude des confréries religieux.* Algiers, 1956.
Drague, G. *Esquisse d'histoire religieuse du Maroc: confréries et zaouias.* Paris, 1951.
Evans-Pritchard, E. E. *The Sanusi of Cyrenaica.* Oxford, 1954.
Holsinger, Donald C. 'Muslim responses to French imperialism: an Algerian Sahara case study', *International Journal of African Historical Studies*, 1986, **19**, 1, 1–15.
Hourani, A. *Arabic thought in the liberal age, 1798–1939.* London, 1962.
Kèrr, Malcolm H. *Islamic reform: the political and legal theories of Muhammad 'Abduh and Rashīd Ridā.* Berkeley and Los Angeles, 1966.
Warburg, G. 'Religious policy in the northern Sudan: 'Ulama and sufism, 1899–1919', *Asian and African Studies*, 1971, **7**, 89–119.
Willis, C. A. 'Religious confraternities of the Sudan', *Sudan Notes and Records*, 1921, **4**, 175–94.

West Africa: General

Bravmann, R. A. *Islam and tribal art in West Africa.* Cambridge, 1974.
Clarke, Peter B. 'Islamic millenarianism in West Africa: a revolutionary ideology?', *Religious Studies*, 1980, **16**, 317–39.
West Africa and Islam. London, 1982.

Hiskett, M. *The development of Islam in West Africa*. London, 1984.
Trimingham, J. S. *Islam in West Africa*. London, 1959.
History of Islam in West Africa. London, 1962.

French West Africa

Alexandre, P. 'A West African Islamic movement: Hamallism in French West Africa', in R. I. Rotberg and A. A. Mazrui, eds. *Protest and Power in Black Africa*. New York, 1970, pp. 497–512.
André, P. J. *L'Islam noir*. Paris, 1924.
Arnaud, R. 'L'Islam et la politique musulmane française en Afrique', *Bulletin du Comité de l'Afrique française, Renseignements Coloniaux*, 1912, **4**, 2–30, 115–27, 142–54.
Audouin, J. and Deniel, R. *L'Islam en Haute-Volta à l'époque coloniale*. Abidjan, 1975.
Bourgeois, J.-L. 'The history of the great mosques of Djenné', *African Arts*, 1987, **20**, 3, 54–63, 90–92.
Brenner, L. *West African Sufi: the religious heritage and spiritual search of Cerno Bokar Saalif Taal*. London, 1984.
Chailley, M. *et al. Notes et études sur l'Islam en Afrique noire*. Paris, 1962.
Copans, J. *Les Marabouts de l'Arachide*. Paris, 1980.
Cruise O'Brien, D. 'Towards an "Islamic policy" in French West Africa, 1854–1914', *Journal of African History*, 1967, **8**, 2, 303–16.
The Mourides of Senegal. Oxford, 1971.
Saints and politicians: essays in the organisation of a Senegalese peasant society. London, 1975.
Diallo, Thierno *et al. Catalogue des manuscrits de l'IFAN*. Dakar, 1966.
Diop, Momar Coumba. 'La Littérature mouride. Essai d'analyse thématique', *Bulletin de l'IFAN*, 1979, B, **41**, 398–439.
Dumont, Fernand. *La Pensée religieuse d'Amadou Bamba, fondateur du mouridisme sénégalais*. Dakar-Abidjan, 1975.
Gouilly, Alphonse. *L'Islam dans l'Afrique occidentale française*. Paris, 1952.
Harrison, Christopher. *France and Islam in West Africa, 1860–1960*. Cambridge, 1988.
Lasisi, R. O. 'Religious freedom under international mandate: the case of French Togo Muslims – 1922 to World War II', *Journal of the Institute of Muslim Minority Affairs*, 1987, **8**, 1, 144–55.
Massignon, L. 'Une Bibliothèque saharienne: la bibliothèque du Cheikh Sidia au Sahara', *Revue du monde musulman*, 1909, **8**, 7–8, 409–18.
Mohammed, Abdullahi and Hay, Richard, Jr. 'Analysis of a West African Islamic library: the Falke collection', in B. Mittman and L. Borman, eds. *Personalized data base systems*, pp. 75–94. Los Angeles, 1975.
Moreau, R. L. *Africains musulmans, des communautés en mouvement*. Paris, 1982.
Robinson, David. 'French "Islamic" policy and practice in late nineteenth-

century Senegal', *Journal of African History*, 1988, **29**, 3, 415–35.

Salifou, André. *Kaoussan ou la révolte senoussiste*. Niamey, 1973.

Samb, Amar. 'Influence de l'Islam sur la littérature "wolof"', *Bulletin d'IFAN*, 1968, B, **30**, 628–41.

Essai sur la contribution du Sénégal à la littérature d'expression arabe. Dakar, 1972.

Sanneh, Lamine O. *The Jahanke. The history of an Islamic clerical people of the Senegambia*. London, 1979.

'Tcherno Aliou, the Wali of Goumba: Islam, colonialism and the rural factor in Futa Jalon, 1867–1912', in N. Levtzion and H. J. Fisher, eds. *Rural and urban Islam in West Africa*. Boulder, 1987.

Sy, Cheikh Tidiane, *La Confrérie sénégalaise des Mourides*. Paris, 1969.

Traore, A. *Cheikh Hamahoullah, Homme de foi et résistant*. Paris, 1983.

Triaud, J.-L. 'Lignes de force de la pénétration islamique en Côte d'Ivoire', *Revue des études islamiques*, 1974, **42**, 1, 123–60.

'La Question musulmane en Côte d'Ivoire (1892–1939)', *Revue française d'histoire d'outre-mer*, 1974, **61**, no. 225, 542–71.

'Un cas de passage collectif à l'Islam en basse Côte d'Ivoire au début du siècle: le village d'Ahua', *Cahiers d'études africaines*, 1974, **14**, no. 54. 317–37.

Nigeria

Fisher, Humphrey J. 'Early Muslim–Western education in West Africa', *Muslim World*, 1961, **51**, 4, 288–98.

Ahmadiyya: a study in contemporary Islam on the West African coast. London, 1963.

Gbadamosi. T. G. O. 'The establishment of Western education among Muslims in Nigeria, 1896–1926', *Journal of the Historical Society of Nigeria*, 1967, **4**, 1, 89–115.

The growth of Islam among the Yoruba, 1841–1908. London, 1978.

Graham, Sonia F. *Government and mission education in Northern Nigeria, 1900–1919*. Ibadan, 1966.

Hiskett, M. *A history of Hausa Islamic verse*. London, 1975.

'The "community of grace" and its opponents, the "rejectors": a debate about theology and mysticism in Muslim West Africa with special reference to its Hausa expression', *African Language Studies*, 1980, **17**, 99–140.

Paden, John N. *Religion and political culture in Kano*. Los Angeles, 1973.

Ryan, P. J. *Imale: Yoruba participation in the Muslim tradition*. Missoula, 1978.

Saad, E. N. 'The Paden collection of Arabic materials from Kano', *History in Africa*, 1980, **7**, 369–72.

Schacht, Joseph. 'Islam in Northern Nigeria', *Studia Islamica*, 1957, **8**, 123–46.

Tahir, Ibrahim. 'Scholars, Sufis, saints and capitalists in Kano, 1904–74: pattern of a bourgeois revolution in an Islamic society'. Ph.D. thesis, University of Cambridge, 1975.

Tomlinson, T. J. F. *History of Islamic political propaganda in Nigeria*. London, 1927.

Ubah, C. N. 'Islamic legal system and the westernization process in the Nigerian emirates', *Journal of Legal Pluralism and Unofficial Law*, 1982, **20**, 1, 69–93.

Wintoki, E. E. 'Ahmadiyya movement in Islam: a bibliography (with special reference to the Nigerian situation)'. Ibadan, 1974.

Eastern, central and southern Africa

Allen, J. W. T. *The Swahili and Arabic manuscripts and tapes in the library of the University College, Dar-es-Salaam: a catalogue.* Leiden, 1970.

Alpers, E. A. 'Towards a history of the expansion of Islam in East Africa: the matrilineal peoples of the southern interior', in T. O. Ranger and I. N. Kimambo, eds. *The Historical Study of African Religion.* London, 1972, pp. 172–201.

Aziz, Esmail. 'Towards a history of Islam in East Africa', *Kenya Historical Review*, 1975, **3**, 1, 147–58.

Becker, C. H. 'Materials for the understanding of Islam in German East Africa', ed. and tr. B. G. Martin, *Tanzania Notes and Records*, 1968, **68**, 31–61. German original in *Der Islam*, 1911, **2**, 1–48.

Bone, D. 'Islam in Malawi', *Journal of Religion in Africa*, 1982, **12**, 2, 126–38.

Crummey, D. 'Shaikh Zäkaryas: an Ethiopian prophet', *Journal of Ethiopian Studies*, 1972, **10**, 1, 55–66.

Greenstein, R. 'The Nyasaland government's policy toward African Muslims, 1900–1925', in Macdonald, R. J. ed. *From Nyasaland to Malawi*, pp. 144–68. Nairobi, 1975.

Hampson, R. M. *Islam in South Africa. A bibliography.* Cape Town, 1964.

Lewis, I. M. 'Sufism in Somaliland: a study of tribal Islam', *Bulletin of the School of Oriental and African Studies*, 1955, **17**, 3, 581–602; 1956, **18**, 1, 145–60.

Martin, B. G. 'Muslim politics and resistance to colonial rule: Shaykh Uways bin Muhammad Al-Barawi and the Qadiriyya brotherhood in East Africa', *Journal of African History*, 1969, **10**, 3, 471–86.

Nimtz, A. H. 'Islam in Tanzania: a bibliography', *Tanzania Notes and Records*, 1973, **72**, 51–74.

Islam and politics in East Africa: the Sufi order in Tanzania. Minneapolis, 1980.

Pouwels, R. L. 'Sheikh Al-Amin b. Alí Mazrui and Islamic modernism in East Africa, 1875–1947.' *International Journal of African Historical Studies*, 1981, **13**, 3, 329–45.

Rossie, J. P. 'Bibliographie commentée de la communauté musulmane au Zaïre des origines à 1975', *Cahiers du CEDAF*, 1976, **6**, 2–38.

Salim, A. I. *Swahili-speaking peoples of Kenya's coast, 1895–1965.* Nairobi, 1973.

Schacht, J. 'Notes on Islam in East Africa', *Studia Islamica*, 1965, **23**, 91–136.

Trimingham, J. S. *Islam in Ethiopia.* Oxford, 1952.

Islam in East Africa. Oxford, 1964

Walji, S. R. 'A history of the Ismaili community in Tanzania'. Ph.D. thesis, University of Wisconsin, 1974.

el-Zein, Abdul Hamid M. *The sacred meadows: a structural analysis of religious symbolism in an East African town.* Evanston, 1974.

5. AFRICAN CROSS-CURRENTS

PRIMARY SOURCES

General Collections

Dathorne, O. R. and Feuser, W. eds, *Africa in prose*. Harmondsworth, 1969.
Langley, J. A. *Ideologies of liberation in black Africa, 1856–1970*. London, 1979.
Perham, M. ed. *Ten Africans*. London, 1936. Reprinted 1963.
Westermann, D. ed. *Afrikaner erzählen ihr Leben*. Essen, 1938. French tr. by
   L. Homburger. Paris, 1943.

Experience of the diaspora

Azikiwe, N. *My odyssey. An autobiography*. London, 1970.
Duse Mohammed, ed. *African Times and Orient Review*. London, 1912–14,
   1917–18; reprinted London, 1973.
Garvey, M. *Marcus Garvey and the vision of Africa*. ed. J. H. Clarke with Amy J.
   Garvey. New York, 1974.
Hill, R. A. ed. *The Marcus Garvey and Universal Negro Improvement Association
   papers* (to August 1921). Berkeley *et alibi*, 1983, 1985. 3 vols.
Makonnen, T. Ras. *Pan-Africanism from within*. ed. K. King. Nairobi, 1973.
Matthews, Z. K. *Freedom for my people: the autobiography of Z. K. Matthews.
   Southern Africa 1901 to 1968*. ed., with a memoir, by Monica Wilson. London
   and Cape Town, 1981.
Nkrumah, K. *Ghana: the autobiography of Kwame Nkrumah*. London, 1957.
Padmore, G. *The life and struggles of Negro toilers*. London, 1931.
   How Britain rules Africa. London, 1936.
   Africa and world peace. London, 1937.
Pankhurst, R. 'An early Somali autobiography', *Africa* (Rome), 1977, **32**, 2,
   159–76; **3**, 355–84.
Scholes, T. E. S. *Glimpses of the ages, or the 'superior' and 'inferior' races so-called,
   discussed in the light of science and history*. London, 1905, 1908. 2 vols.

French-speaking Africa

Couchoro, F. *L'Esclave*. Paris, 1929.
Diallo, Bakari. *Force bonté*. Paris, 1926.
Dim Delobsom, A. A. *L'Empire du Mogho-Naba. Coutumes des Mossi de la Haute-
   Volta*. Paris, 1932.
Diop, O. S. *Karim*. Paris, 1935.
Dugué-Clédor, A. *La Bataille de Guilé*. St Louis, 1931.
Éboué, F. *Les Peuples de l'Oubangui-Chari*. Paris, 1933.
Guèye, Lamine. 'De la situation politique des Sénégalais originaires des com-
   munes de plein exercice'. Thesis for Doctorat d'Etat, University of Paris,
   1921.
Hazoumé, P. *Le Pacte de sang au Dahomey*. Paris, 1937.
   Doguicimi. Paris, 1938.

Houénou, K. Tovalou. *L'Involution des métamorphoses et des métempsychoses de l'univers*, vol. 1. Paris, n.d. [1921].

Hunkanrin, Louis. *Un forfait colonial: l'esclavage en Mauritanie*. Paris, 1931; reprinted in *Etudes dahoméennes*, 1964, n.s. **3**, 31–50.

Mademba, Capt. Abd el Kader. *Au Sénégal et au Soudan français*. Paris, 1931.

Mamby Sidibé. 'La Famille chez les Foule du Birgo, du Fouladougou Arbala et du Fouladougou Saboula (Cercle de Kita, Soudan français)'. *Bulletin du comité d'études historiques et scientifiques de l'AOF*, 1935, **18**, 4, 462–539.

Maran, R. *Batouala*. Paris, 1921. English tr. New York and London, 1922. *Djouma, chien de brousse*. Paris, 1927.

M'Ba, L. 'Essai de droit coutumier pahouin', *Bulletin de la Société de Recherches Congolaises*, 1938, **25**, 1, 5–51.

Moumé-Etia, I. *Dictionnaire du langage franco-douala*. Clermont-Ferrand, 1928.

Moussa Travélé. *Petit dictionnaire français-bambara et bambara-français*. Paris, 1913.

Njoya, Sultan. *Histoire et coutumes des Bamun*. tr. H. Martin. Douala, 1952.

Norris, H. T. *Sahara myth and saga*. Oxford, 1972.

Quenum, M. *Au pays des Fons*. Paris, 1938.

Raponda-Walker, A. *Dictionnaire mpongwe-français*. Metz, 1934. *Essai de grammaire tsogo*. Brazzaville, 1937.

Senghor, Lamine. *La Violation d'un pays*. Paris, n.d.

Senghor, Léopold S. *Négritude et humanisme*. Paris, 1964.

British West Africa

Ajisafe, A. K. *The laws and customs of the Yoruba*. Lagos, 1924.

Amu, E. *Twenty-five African songs in the Twi language*. London, n.d. [1932].

Attoh-Ahuma, S. R. B. *Memoirs of West African celebrities. Europe &c. (1700–1850), with special reference to the Gold Coast*. Liverpool, 1905. *The Gold Coast nation and national consciousness*. Liverpool, 1911.

Awoonor-Renner, B. *This Africa*. London, 1943.

Azikiwe, N. *Liberia in world politics*. London, 1934. *Renascent Africa*. Lagos, 1937. Reprinted London, 1968.

Blyden, E. W. *African life and customs*. London, 1908.

Campbell, J. G. *Observations on some topics 1913–1917, during the administration of Sir Frederick Lugard*. Lagos, 1918.

Casely Hayford, J. E. *Ethiopia unbound: studies in race emancipation*. London, 1911. Reprinted New York, 1969. *The truth about the West African land question*. London, 1913. *United West Africa*. London, 1919. *West African leadership: public speeches [1913–1930] . . . delivered by the Hon. J. E. Casely Hayford*. ed. M. J. Sampson. Ilfracombe, n.d., reprinted 1969.

Danquah, J. B. *The Akim Abuakwa handbook, compiled at the request of the Hon. Nana Sir Ofori Atta, KBE, MLC*. London, 1928. *Cases in Akan law: decisions delivered by the Hon. Nana Sir Ofori Atta, KBE, Paramount Chief of Akim Abuakwa*. London, 1928.

Gold Coast: Akan laws and customs and the Akim Abuakwa constitution. London, 1928.

Liberty of the subject. A monograph on the Gold Coast cocoa hold-up and boycott of foreign goods, 1937–8. Kibi, Gold Coast, n.d. [1938].

Delano, I. *The soul of Nigeria.* London, 1937.

Deniga, Adeoye. *The Nigerian Who's Who.* Lagos, 1919, 1920, 1921, 1933.

Egharevba, J. V. *A short history of Benin.* Lagos, 1934. 3rd ed. Ibadan, 1960.

Fadipe, N. A. *The sociology of the Yoruba.* ed. F. O. and O. O. Okediji. Ibadan, 1970.

Graft Johnson, J. W. de. *Towards nationhood in West Africa.* London, 1928. 2nd ed. 1971.

Historical geography of the Gold Coast. London, n.d. [1929].

Hutchinson, C. F. *The pen pictures of modern Africans and African celebrities.* London, n.d. [c. 1930].

Johnson, Samuel. *The history of the Yorubas.* London, 1921.

Mensah Sarbah, J. *Fanti national constitution. A short treatise on the constitution and government of the Fanti, Asanti and other Akan tribes of West Africa.* London, 1906. 2nd ed. 1968.

Sampson, M. J. *Gold Coast men of affairs.* London, 1937. Reprinted 1969.

Solanke, L. *United West Africa (or Africa) at the bar of the family of nations.* London, 1927. Reprinted 1969.

Tamakloe, E. F. *A brief history of the Dagbamba people.* Accra, 1931.

Dagomba (Dagbane) dictionary and grammar. Accra, 1941.

Wilson, Henry S. ed. *Origins of West African nationalism.* London, 1969.

Southern Africa

Assis Junior, António de. *O Segredo da morta. Romance de costumes angolenses.* Luanda, 1934.

Couzens, T. and Patel, E. eds. *The return of the Amasi bird. Black South African poetry 1891–1981.* Johannesburg, 1982.

Dhlomo, H. I. E. *Collected works.* ed. T. Couzens and N. Visser. Johannesburg, 1985.

Dhlomo, R. R. R. *An African tragedy.* Lovedale, 1928.

Jabavu, D. D. T. *The black problem.* Lovedale, 1921. 2nd ed.

The life of John Tengo Jabavu. Lovedale, 1922.

The segregation fallacy and other papers. Lovedale, 1928.

Johns, Sheridan, ed. *Protest and Hope 1882–1934* (Vol. 1 of *From Protest to Challenge: a documentary history of African politics in South Africa,* eds. T. Karis and G. M. Carter) Stanford, 1972.

Mahabane. Z. R. *The good fight. Selected speeches.* Evanston, Illinois, n.d. [c. 1965].

Mancoe, John. *The Bloemfontein Bantu and Coloured people's directory.* Bloemfontein, 1934.

Mofolo, T. *Chaka: an historical romance.* tr. F. H. Dutton. London, 1931.

Molema, S. M. *The Bantu past and present: an ethnographical and historical study of the native races of South Africa.* Edinburgh, 1920.

Nzula, A., Potekhin, I. I. and Zusmanovich, A. Z. *Forced labour in colonial Africa.* ed. R. Cohen. London, 1979.
Plaatje, S. T. *Native life in South Africa.* London, 1916, 2nd ed. Johannesburg, 1982.
    Mhudi: an epic of native life a hundred years ago. Lovedale 1930. 2nd ed. with introduction by T. Couzens. Johannesburg, 1975, London, 1978.
Schapera, I. *Praise poems of Tswana chiefs.* Oxford, 1965.
Skota, T. D. Mweli. *The African yearly register, being an illustrated national biographical dictionary (Who's Who) of black folks in Africa.* Johannesburg, n.d. [1930]. 2nd ed. 1932.
Soga, J. H. *The south-eastern Bantu.* Johannesburg, 1930.
    Ama-Xosa life and customs. London, 1932.

East and Central Africa

Abdallah, Y. B. *The Yaos. Chiikala cha Wayao.* tr. and ed. M. Sanderson. Zomba, 1919. 2nd ed. London, 1973.
Abdul Karim bin Jamaliddini. *Utenzi wa vita vya Maji-Maji.* tr. W. H. Whiteley. Supplement to the *Journal of the East African Swahili Committee,* 1957, no. 27.
Chibambo, Y. M. *My Ngoni of Nyasaland.* tr. C. Stuart. London, 1942.
Kagwa, Sir Apolo. *The kings of Buganda.* tr. M. S. M. Kiwanuka. Nairobi, 1971, from *Basekabaka be Buganda,* 2nd ed. London and Kampala, 1912.
    The customs of the Baganda. tr. E. B. Kalibala, ed. M. Mandelbaum. New York, 1934, from *Mpisa za Baganda.* Kampala, 1907.
Kayamba, M. *African problems.* London, 1948.
Kenyatta, J. *Facing Mount Kenya.* London, 1938.
Low. D. A. *The mind of Buganda: documents of the modern history of an African kingdom.* London, 1971.
Mockerie, P. G. *An African speaks for his people.* London, 1934.
Mwase, G. S. *Strike a blow and die. A narrative of race relations in colonial Africa.* ed. R. I. Rotberg. Cambridge, Mass., 1967. London, 1975.
Ranger, T. O. *The African Voice in Southern Rhodesia, 1898–1930.* London, 1970.
Ntara, S. Y. *Man of Africa,* tr. T. Cullen Young. London, 1934.
Nyabongo, A. K. *Africa answers back.* London, 1936.
    'Religious practices and beliefs of Uganda'. D.Phil. thesis, University of Oxford, 1939.

North-East Africa

Afewerq Gebre Iyesus. *Ityopya: guide du voyageur en Abyssinie.* Rome, 1908.
Andrzejewski, B. W. and Lewis, I. M. eds. *Somali poetry: an introduction.* Oxford, 1964.
Asfa Yilma. *Haile Selassie Emperor of Ethiopia with a brief account of the history of Ethiopia including the origins of the present struggle, and a description of the country and its peoples.* London, n.d. [1936].

Duse Mohamed. *In the land of the pharaohs. A short history of Egypt from the fall of Ismail to the assassination of Boutros Pasha.* London, 1911.

Eadie, J. I. ed. and tr. *An Amharic reader.* Cambridge, 1924.

Fusella, L. tr. 'Menilek e l'Etiopia in un testo del Bāykadāñ', *Annali dell' Istituto Universitario Orientale di Napoli*, 1952, **4**, 119–43.

Guèbré Sellassié. *Chronique du règne de Ménélik II roi des rois d'Ethiopie.* tr. Tesfa Sellassie, ed. M. de Coppet. Paris, 1930–31, 2 vols.

Melaku Beyene, ed. *The march of black men – Ethiopia leads: official report of the present state of affairs and prospects. An authentic account of the determined fight of the Ethiopian people for their independence.* New York, 1939.

SECONDARY SOURCES

General

Adewoye, O. *The legal profession in Nigeria, 1865–1962.* Ibadan, 1977.

Boahen, A. Adu. ed. *Africa under colonial domination 1880–1935.* (UNESCO General History of Africa, vol. VII). Paris, London and Berkeley, 1985.

Bradford, Helen. *A Taste of Freedom: The ICU in rural South Africa 1924–1930.* New Haven and London, 1987.

Chilcote, R. H. ed. *Protest and resistance in Angola and Brazil.* Berkeley and Los Angeles, 1972.

Couzens, T. 'An introduction to the history of football in South Africa', in Bozzoli, B. ed. *Town and countryside in the Transvaal*, pp. 198–214. Johannesburg, 1983.

Fajana, A. 'The Nigerian Union of Teachers: a decade of growth 1931–1940', *Nigeria Magazine*, 1974, no. 111, 79–89.

Hay, M. J. and Wright, M. eds. *African women and the law: historical perspectives.* Boston, 1982.

Iliffe, John. *A modern history of Tanganyika.* Cambridge, 1979.

Jenkins, Ray. 'Gold Coasters overseas, 1880–1919, with special reference to their activities in Britain', *Immigrants and minorities*, 1985, **4**, 3, 5–52.

Johnson, G. Wesley. 'The Senegalese urban elite, 1900–1945', in P. D. Curtin, ed. *Africa and the West.* Madison, 1972, pp. 139–87.

July, R. W. *The origins of modern African thought: its development in West Africa during the nineteenth and twentieth centuries.* New York, 1967. London, 1968.

Kimble, D. *A political history of Ghana: the rise of Gold Coast nationalism, 1850–1928.* Oxford, 1963.

Little, K. *Negroes in Britain.* London, 1947. 2nd ed. 1972.

Lotz, R. and Pegg, I. eds. *Under the imperial carpet: essays in Black history 1780–1950.* Crawley, 1986.

Mann, Kristin. *Marrying well: marriage, status and social change among the educated elite in colonial Lagos.* Cambridge, 1985.

Marks, Shula. *The ambiguities of dependence in South Africa: class, nationalism and the state in twentieth-century Natal.* Baltimore, Md., and Johannesburg, 1986.

Marks, Shula and Rathbone, Richard, eds. *Industrialisation and social change in South Africa: essays on African class formation, culture and consciousness, 1870–1930.* London, 1982.

Martin, Jane. 'Krumen "down the coast": Liberian migrants on the West African coast in the 19th and early 20th centuries', *International Journal of African Historical Studies*, 1985, **18**, 3, 401–23.

Page, Melvin E. ed. *African and the First World War*. Houndmills, Basingstoke, 1987.

Ranger, T. O. 'African attempts to control education in East and Central Africa, 1900–1939', *Past and Present*, 1965, **32**, 57–85.

Spitzer, Leo. *The Creoles of Sierra Leone: response to colonialism, 1870–1945*. Madison, 1974.

Vail, H. Leroy, ed. *The creation of tribalism in Southern Africa*. London, 1989.

Biography

Bontinck, F. 'Mfumu Paul Panda Farnana, 1880–1930. Premier nationaliste congolais', in V. Y. Mudimbe, ed. *La Dépendance de l'Afrique et les moyens d'y remédier*. Paris, 1980, pp. 561–610.

Gerhart, G. M. and Karis, T. *Political profiles, 1882–1964*. (vol. IV of *From protest to challenge*. eds. T., Karis and G. M. Carter), Stanford, 1977.

Hymans, J. L. *Léopold Sédar Senghor: an intellectual biography*. Edinburgh, 1971.

Iliffe, J. ed. *Modern Tanzanians*. Nairobi, 1973.

Julien, C. A. *et al. Les Africains*. Paris, 1977–8. 12 vols.

This biographical series includes fourteen essays relevant to this book (volume numbers in parentheses): Amadou Bamba (2), Atangana (5), Chilembwe (6), Diagne (12), Gueye (3), Hamahoullah (9), Karnou (4), Mandume (8), Matswa (11), Njoya (9), Ravoahangry (1), Samba (12), Thomas (9), Wongo (11).

King, Kenneth J. and Salim, A. eds. *Kenya historical biographies*. Nairobi, 1971.

Macmillan, Allister. *The Red Book of West Africa*. London, 1920.

Murray-Brown, J. *Kenyatta*. London, 1972.

Okonkwo, Rina. *Heroes of West African nationalism*. Enugu, 1985.

Shepperson, G. A. and Price, T. *Independent African: John Chilembwe and the origins, setting and significance of the Nyasaland native rising of 1915*. Edinburgh, 1958; second ed. 1987.

Twumasi, Y. 'J. B. Danquah', *African Affairs*. 1978, **77**, no. 306, 73–88.

Willan, B. P. *Sol Plaatje: South African nationalist, 1876–1932*. London, 1984.

The search for education

Bond, H. M. *Education for freedom. A history of Lincoln University, Pennsylvania*. Lincoln, Pa., 1976.

Bouche, Denise. *L'Enseignement dans les territoires français de l'Afrique occidentale de 1817 à 1920*. Paris, 1975, 2 vols.

Carter, F. V. 'Education in Uganda, 1894–1945', Ph.D. thesis, University of London, 1967.

Goldthorpe, J. E. *An African elite: Makerere College students. 1922–1960*. Nairobi, 1965.

Kerr, A. *Fort Hare, 1915–1948*. London, 1968.
King, Kenneth J. 'James E. K. Aggrey: collaborator, nationalist, Pan-African', *Canadian Journal of African Studies*, 1969, **3**, 3, 511–30.
    Pan-Africanism and education. A study of race philanthropy and education in the southern states of America and East Africa. Oxford, 1971.
Omolewa, M. 'Distance learning and the development of higher education in West Africa 1887–1934', *Journal of the Historical Society of Nigeria*, 1981, **10**, 4, 1–20.
Ralston, R. D. 'American episodes in the making of an African leader: a case study of Aldred B. Xuma (1893–1962)', *International Journal of African Historical Studies*, 1973, **6**, 1, 72–93.
Roelker, J. R. *Mathu of Kenya. A political study*. Stanford, 1970.
Short, Philip. *Banda*. London, 1974.
Smith, E. W. *Aggrey of Africa*. London, 1929.
Sumner, D. L. *Education in Sierra Leone*. Freetown 1963.
    See also Ashby, Mayhew and Murray on pp. 268, 272 above.

Language policy and language use

Afigbo, A. 'The impact of colonialism on the Igbo language: the origins of a dilemma', ch. 9 (pp. 355–87) in his *Ropes of Sand: studies in Igbo history and culture*. Ibadan, 1981.
Brumfit, Ann. 'The rise and development of a language policy in German East Africa', *Sprache und Geschichte in Afrika*, 1980, **2**, 219–331.
Doke, C. M. *Report on the unification of the Shona dialects*. Salisbury, S. Rhodesia, 1931.
Fabian, J. *Language and colonial power: the appropriation of Swahili in the former Belgian Congo, 1880–1938*. Cambridge, 1986.
Harries, P. 'The roots of ethnicity: discourse on the politics of language construction in south-east Africa', *African Affairs*, 1988, **87**, no. 346, 25–52.
Samarin, W. J, 'Protestant missions and the history of Lingala', *Journal of Religion in Africa*, 1986, **16**, 2, 138–63.
Whiteley, W. H. *Swahili: the rise of a national language*. London, 1969.
Yates, B. A. 'The origins of language policy in Zaïre', *Journal of Modern African Studies*, 1980, **18**, 2, 257–79.

The press

Howell, J. B. 'Sources for African newspapers: a reference guide', *Génève-Afrique*, 1983, **21**, 1, 128–38.

English-speaking Africa

Cutten, T. E. G. *A history of the press in South Africa*. Cape Town, 1935.
Ekwelie, S. A. 'Ghana: legal control of the nationalist press, 1880–1950', *Transafrican Journal of History*, 1976, **5**, 2, 148–60.
Gale, W. D. *The Rhodesian press*. Salisbury, 1963.

Jones-Quartey, K. A. B. *A summary history of the Ghana press 1822–1960*. Accra, 1974.

Omu, F. I. A. *Press and politics in Nigeria, 1880–1937*. London, 1978.

Scotton, J. F. 'The first African press in East Africa: protest and nationalism in Uganda in the 1920s', *International Journal of African Historical Studies*, 1973, **6**, 2, 211–28

Shaloff, S. 'Press controls and sedition proceedings in the Gold Coast, 1933–1939', *African Affairs*, 1972, **71**, no. 284, 241–63.

Switzer, L. and D. *The black press in South Africa and Lesotho: a descriptive guide to African, Coloured and Indian newspapers, newsletters and magazines, 1836–1976*. Boston, Mass., 1979.

Switzer, L. '*Bantu World* and the origins of a captive African commercial press in South Africa', *Journal of Southern African Studies*, 1988, **14**, 3, 351–70.

Twumasi, Y. 'Press freedom and nationalism under colonial rule in the Gold Coast (Ghana)', *Journal of the Historical Society of Nigeria*, 1974, **7**, 3, 499–520.

Westcott, N. J. 'An East African radical: the life of Erica Fiah', *Journal of African History*, 1981, **22**, 1, 85–101.

French-speaking Africa

Berlage, J. *Répertoire de la presse du Congo Belge (1884–1958) et du Ruanda-Urundi (1920–1958)*. Brussels, 1959.

Boulègue, M. 'La presse au Sénégal avant 1939: bibliographie', *Bulletin de l'IFAN*, 1965, B, **27**, 3–4, 715–54.

Codo Coffi, B. 'La Presse dahoméenne face aux évolués: *La Voix du Dahomey*, 1927–1957'. Thèse de 3e cycle, University of Paris-VII, 1978.

Guillaneuf, R. 'La Presse au Togo, 1911–1966'. Thèse de 3e cycle, University of Paris-I, 1970.

Lokossou, C. 'La Presse au Dahomey, 1894–1960. Evolution et réaction face à l'administration coloniale'. Thèse de 3e cycle, Paris, EHESS, 1976.

Lusophone and German Africa

Dias, R. N. *A imprensa periódica em Moçambique, 1854–1954: coordenação e notas*. Lourenço Marques, 1956.

Friedland, E. A. 'Mozambican nationalist resistance, 1920–1949', *Afrika Zamani*, 1978, 8–9, 156–72.

Lopo, J. de Castro. *Jornalismo de Angola. Subsídios para a sua história*. Luanda, 1964.

Pipping-Van Hulten, I. *An episode of colonial history: the German press in Tanzania 1901–1914*. Uppsala, 1974.

Literature

Blair, Dorothy S. *African literature in French. A history of creative writing in French from West and Equatorial Africa*. Cambridge, 1976.

Cornevin, R. *Littératures d'Afrique noire de langue française*. Paris, 1976.

Couzens, T. J. 'The social ethos of black writing in South Africa, 1920–1950', in Heywood, C. ed. *Aspects of South African literature*, pp. 66–81. London, 1976.

The New African: a study of the life and work of H. I. E. Dhlomo. Johannesburg, 1985.

Gérard, A. S. *Four African literatures: Xhosa, Sotho, Zulu, Amharic*. Berkeley, Los Angeles and London, 1971.

African language literatures. Harlow, 1982.

Goody, J. 'Restricted literacy in northern Ghana', in Goody, J. and Watt, I. eds. *Literacy in Traditional Society*, pp. 199–264. Cambridge, 1968.

Hamilton, Russell G. *Voices from an empire. A history of Afro-Portuguese literature*. Minneapolis, 1975.

Herdeck, D. E. *African authors. A companion to black African writing 1300–1973*. Washington, DC, 1973.

Jadot, J.-M. *Les Écrivains africains du Congo belge et du Ruanda-Urundi*. Brussels, 1959.

Jahn, J. and Dressler, C. P. *Bibliography of creative African writing*. Nendeln, Liechtenstein, 1971.

Jenkins, Ray. 'Gold Coast historians and their pursuit of the Gold Coast pasts, 1882–1917', Ph.D. thesis, University of Birmingham, 1985.

Jordan, A. C. *Towards an African literature: the emergence of literary form in Xhosa*. Berkeley and Los Angeles, 1972.

Kane, T. L. *Ethiopian literature in Amharic*. Wiesbaden, 1975.

Kesteloot, L. *Les Écrivains noirs de langue française: naissance d'une littérature*. Brussels, 1963. English tr. Philadelphia, 1974.

Law, Robin, 'Early Yoruba historiography', *History in Africa*, 1976, **3**, 69–89.

'A pioneer of Yoruba studies: Moses Lijadu (1862–1926)', in Olusanya, G. O. ed. *Studies in Yoruba history and culture*, pp. 108–15. Ibadan, 1983.

MacGaffey, W. 'Ethnography and the closing of the frontier in Lower Congo, 1885–1921', *Africa*, 1986, **56**, 3, 263–79.

Molvaer, R. K. *Tradition and change in Ethiopia. Social and cultural life as reflected in Amharic fictional literature c. 1930–1974*. Leiden, 1980.

Moser, G. M. *A tentative Portuguese-African bibliography: Portuguese literature in Africa and African literature in the Portuguese language*. University Park, Pa., 1970.

Omenka, N. 'The role of the Catholic mission in the development of vernacular literature in Eastern Nigeria', *Journal of Religion in Africa*, 1986, **16**, 2, 121–37.

Peires, J. 'The Lovedale Press: literature for the Bantu revisited', *History in Africa*, 1979, **6**, 155–75.

Pike, C. 'History and imagination: Swahili literature and resistance to German language imperialism in Tanzania, 1885–1910', *International Journal of African Historical Studies*, 1986, **19**, 2, 201–33.

Rowe, J. 'Myth, memoir and moral admonition: Luganda historical writing 1893–1969', *Uganda Journal*, 1969, **33**, 1–2, 17–40, 217–19.

Stella, G. C. 'Un personnaggio amletico: Afework Ghevre Jesus (1868–1947)', *Africa* (Rome), 1986, **41**, 4, 581–602.

Twaddle, M. J. 'On Ganda historiography', *History in Africa*, 1974, **1**, 85–100.
'The nine lives of Semei Kakungulu', *History in Africa*, 1985, **12**, 325–333.
Yates, B. A. 'Knowledge brokers: books and publishers in early colonial Zaire',
  History in Africa, 1987, **14**, 311–40.
See also Amar Samb, Diop and Hiskett, pp.291–2 above.

Performing arts

Adedeji, J. A. 'The church and the emergence of the Nigerian theatre'
  [1866–1945], *Journal of the Historical Society of Nigeria*, 1971, **6**, 1, 25–45;
  1973, **6**, 4, 387–96.
Collins, E. J. 'Comic opera in Ghana', *African Arts* (Los Angeles), 1976, **9**, 2,
  50–7.
'Ghanaian high-life', *African Arts*, 1976, **10**, 1, 62–8, 100.
'Post-war popular band music in West Africa', *African Arts*, 1977, **10**, 3,
  53–60.
Coplan, D. *In Township Tonight! South Africa's black music and theatre*. London,
  1986.
Jans, P. 'Essai de musique religieuse pour indigènes dans le vicariat apostolique
  de Coquilhatville', *Aequatoria*, 1956, **19**, 1, 1–16.
Jones, A. M. 'African music: the *mganda* dance', *African Studies*, 1945, **4**, 4,
  180–8.
Kirby, P. R. 'The effect of western civilisation on Bantu music', in I.Schapera,
  ed., *Western Civilisation and the Natives of South Africa*, London, 1934, pp.
  131–30.
Malan, J. P. ed. *South African music encyclopaedia*. Cape Town, 1979–85, 4 vols.
Mwakasak, C. S. 'Trends and development in the oral poetry of the Banyakyusa
  in this century', *Umma* (Dar es Salaam and Nairobi), 1975, **5**, 1, 35–47.
Nketia, J. H. K. 'Modern trends in Ghana music', *African Music*, 1957, **1**, 4, 13–
  17.
Opland, J. *Xhosa oral poetry*. Cambridge, 1983.
Ranger, T. O. *Dance and Society in Eastern Africa, 1890–1970: the beni ngoma*.
  London, 1975.
Sadie, S. ed. *New Grove dictionary of music and musicians*. London, 1980, 20 vols.
Said Samatar. *Oral poetry and Somali nationalism: the case of Sayyid Maḥammad
  'Abdille Ḥasan*. Cambridge, 1982.
Sutherland, Efua. *The story of Bob Johnson, Ghana's ace comedian*. Accra, 1970.
Tracey, H. *Chopi musicians: their music, poetry and instruments*. London, 1948.
Vail, Leroy and White, Landeg. 'Plantation protest: the history of a
  Mozambican song', *Journal of Southern African Studies*, 1978, **5**, 1–25.
'Forms of resistance: songs of perceptions of power in colonial Mozambique',
  American Historical Review, 1983, **88**, 883–919.
Waterman, C. A. '*Asíkò, sákárà* and palmwine: popular music and social identity
  in inter-war Lagos, Nigeria', *Urban anthropology*, 1988, **17**, 2–3, 229–58.

Plastic arts

Biebuyck, D. 'Effects on Lega art of the outlawing of the Bwami Association' in Okpaku, J. ed. *New African literature and the arts*, vol. 1, pp. 340–52. New York, 1970.
Bravmann, R. *Islam and tribal art in West Africa.* Cambridge, 1974.
Carroll, K. C. *Yoruba religious carving.* London, 1967.
Elkan, W. 'The East African trade in woodcarvings', *Africa*, 1958, **27**, 4, 314–23.
Geary, Christraud M. 'Art and political process in the kingdoms of Bali-Nyonga and Bamum (Cameroon Grassfields)', *Canadian Journal of African Studies*, 1988, **22**, 1, 11–41.
Mount, M. W. *African art. The years since 1920.* Bloomington, 1973.
Oloidi, O. 'Growth and development of formal art education in Nigeria, 1900–1960', *Transafrican Journal of History*, 1986, **15**, 108–26.
Périer, G.-D. 'L'Art vivant des noirs du Congo belge', *Artes Africanae* (Brussels), 1936, nos. 2–3, 1–13.
'L'Evolution de l'art du Congo belge et du Ruanda-Urundi sous l'influence de la colonisation belge', in *Les Arts au Congo Belge et au Ruanda-Urundi*, pp. 55–62. Brussels, 1950.
Vansina, J. *Art history in Africa: an introduction to method.* Harlow, 1984.
Vlach, J. M. 'The Brazilian house in Nigeria: the emergence of a 20th century vernacular house type', *Journal of American folk-lore*, 1984, **97**, no. 383, 3–23.
Willett, F. *African art.* London, 1971.

Pan-Africanism

Asante, S. K. B. *Pan-African protest: West Africa and the Italo-Ethiopian crisis, 1934–1941.* London, 1977.
Cronon, E. D. *Black Moses: the story of Marcus Garvey and the Universal Negro Improvement Association.* Madison, 1955. 2nd ed. 1969.
De Witte, P. *Les mouvements nègres en France, 1919–1939.* Paris, 1985.
Duffield, I. 'The business activities of Duse Mohammad Ali: an example of the economic dimension of Pan-Africanism, 1912–1945', *Journal of the Historical Society of Nigeria*, 1969, **4**, 4, 571–600.
'Pan-Africanism, rational and irrational', *Journal of African History*, 1977, **18**, 4, 597–620.
Esedebe, P. O. *Pan-Africanism: the idea and movement, 1776–1963.* Washington, DC, 1982.
Filesi, T. 'Il Movimento Pan-Negro e la politica coloniale italiana nel 1920–1923', *Africa* (Rome), 1975, **30**, 2, 159–97.
Geiss, I. *The Pan-African movement.* tr. A. Keep. London, 1974.
Harlan, Louis R. *Booker T. Washington.* New York, 1972, 1983. 2 vols.
Hooker, J. R. *Black revolutionary: George Padmore's path from Communism to Pan-Africanism.* London, 1967.
Huggins, N. I. *Harlem renaissance.* New York, 1971.

Jacobs, Sylvia M. *The African nexus. Black American perspectives on the European partitioning of Africa 1880–1920.* Westport, Conn., 1981.
Langley, J. A. *Pan-Africanism and nationalism in West Africa, 1900–1945.* Oxford, 1973.
Okonkwo, R. L. 'The Garvey movement in British West Africa', *Journal of African History*, 1980, **21**, 1, 105–17.
Partington, P. G. *W. E. B. DuBois: a bibliography of his published writings.* Whittier, Calif., 1977.
Robinson, C. J. 'The African diaspora and the Italo-Ethiopian crisis', *Race and Class*, 1985, **27**, 2, 51–65.
Ross, R. A. 'Black Americans and Italo-Ethiopian relief 1935–1936', *Ethiopia Observer*, 1972, **15**, 2, 122–31.
   'Black Americans and Haiti, Liberia, the Virgin Islands, and Ethiopia, 1929–1936'. Ph.D. thesis, University of Chicago, 1975.
Savage, D. C. 'Jomo Kenyatta, Malcolm MacDonald and the Colonial Office, 1938–9. Some documents from the PRO', *Canadian Journal of African Studies*, 1970, **3**, 3, 615–32.
Scott, W. R. 'A study of Afro-American and Ethiopian relations: 1896–1941'. Ph.D. thesis, Princeton University, 1971.
   'Malaku E. Bayen: Ethiopian emissary to black America (1935–1936)', *Ethiopia Observer*, 1972, **15**, 2, 132–8.
   'Colonel John C. Robinson: the Brown Condor of Ethiopia', *Pan-African Journal*, 1972, **5**, 1, 59–69.
Shepperson, G. A. 'Notes on American Negro influences on the emergence of African nationalism', *Journal of African History*, 1960, **1**, 2, 299–312.
'The African abroad or the African diaspora', in Ranger, T. O. ed. *Emerging themes in African history*, pp. 152–76. Nairobi, 1968.
'The Afro-American contribution to African studies', *Journal of American Studies*, 1974, **8**, 3, 281–301.
Weisbord, R. G. *Ebony kinship: Africa, Africans and the Afro-American.* Westport, Conn., 1973.

Communism and black Africa

Bunting, Brian, *Moses Kotane: South African revolutionary.* London, 1975.
Cohen, R. 'Introduction', pp. 1–19 in A. Nzula, I. I. Potekhin and A. Z. Zusmanovich (ed. R. Cohen), *Forced labour in colonial Africa.* London, 1979.
Darch, C. and Littlejohn, G. 'Endre Sik and the development of African studies in the USSR: a study agenda from 1929', *History in Africa*, 1983, **10**, 79–108.
Johns, S. 'The Comintern, South Africa and the black diaspora', *Review of Politics*, 1975, **37**, 2, 200–34.
   'The birth of the Communist Party of South Africa', *International Journal of African Historical Studies*, 1976, **9**, 3, 371–400.
Wilson, E. T. *Russia and black Africa before World War II.* New York, 1974.

INDEX